CONTENTS

The SUTTON *Companion to*

CASTLES

STEPHEN FRIAR

SUTTON PUBLISHING

First published in the United Kingdom in 2003 by
Sutton Publishing Limited · Phoenix Mill
Thrupp · Stroud · Gloucestershire · GL5 2BU

British Library Cataloguing in Publication Data
A catalogue record for this book is available from the British Library.

ISBN 0-7509-2744-5

Title page: The hall-keep at Castle Rising.
Contents page: Putlog holes at Tretower Court, Powys.

For Tom and Richard: 'Not *another* castle!'

Other books by the author:
A New Dictionary of Heraldry (Alphabooks/A & C Black, 1987)
The Batsford Companion to Local History (B.T. Batsford, 1991)
Heraldry for the Local Historian and Genealogist (Sutton Publishing, 1992; paperback, with revisions, 1996)
Basic Heraldry with John Ferguson (Herbert Press, 1993; paperback, with revisions, 1996)
A Companion to the English Parish Church (Sutton Publishing, 1996; paperback, with revisions, 1998)
The Local History Companion (Sutton Publishing, 2001)

Typeset in 9/11pt Times.
Typesetting and origination by
Sutton Publishing Limited.
Printed and bound in England by
J.H. Haynes & Co. Ltd, Sparkford.

INTRODUCTION

I do love these ancient ruins:
· We never tread upon them, but we set
Our foot upon some reverend history.

John Webster, *The Duchess of Malfi* (1612)

Castles – fortified feudal residences – are unique to the Middle Ages. And, contrary to the popular perception, they were more often lived in than fought over. Very few castles remain unaltered from when they were first built and none fits neatly into any particular category. Many have succumbed to the ravages of siege warfare, abandonment and despoliation, especially in the aftermath of the English Civil War (1642–9), while others have been adapted for domestic purposes. Some have been entirely rebuilt and most have been remodelled many times, according to the current military, domestic and architectural fashion. For several there is evidence of continuous occupation from the twelfth century to the present day. However, this book deals only with the castle as it was in the medieval period.

Before visiting a castle, study its site on maps of various scales in relation to other castles, route-ways, river crossings and physical features. Is there evidence of former fortifications in street names (e.g. Barbican Street) or in the delineation of streets and house plots, perhaps within a town wall? Attempt to determine the function and type of the original fortification. When you arrive, always walk round the exterior first and study the defences (ignoring modern additions such as wooden catwalks, bridges and flights of steps which are almost invariably in the wrong place!). Note each line of defence as you cross the moat and pass through the gate passage of a barbican or gatehouse into the middle or upper ward and the final refuge. Not all defences are as obvious as the drawbridge or portcullises: observe the relative angles of surrounding walls and flanking towers and the 'killing grounds' between. Look for 'layers' of development: how various parts of the castle have been adapted and remodelled to match the political circumstances of a particular age, the development of siege technology and the domestic and adminis-trative needs of an increasingly complex household organisation. Only then should you buy the guide book.

Where possible, parish churches should also be visited. These often contain monuments and window glass that relate to the magnates who constructed or occupied a nearby castle. For this reason entries such as CHURCHES, CHANTRY CHAPELS and MONUMENTS have been included.

Introduction

The *Companion* is arranged alphabetically and consists of a number of primary entries (e.g. GATEHOUSES) from which cross-references lead on to a larger number of secondary entries (e.g. GATE PASSAGE, MURDER HOLES, PORTCULLIS). Many of the terms encountered when researching the history of a castle are also included, either as short individual entries or by cross-referencing. These include the terminology of associated subjects, such as architecture, arms and armour and heraldry, while entries such as WALES, CONQUEST OF and WARS OF THE ROSES are intended to assist in placing research in a wider historical context. Some post-medieval terms have been included because reference is made in several entries to later additions and alterations to fortifications. The *Companion* is *not* a gazetteer (we have many excellent books to guide us) though an Index of Places is included in APPENDIX III.

Cross-references are indicated by CAPITAL LETTERS and, where necessary, these are picked out in *italic letters* in the entries to which the reader is referred.

APPENDIX I contains suggestions for further reading while the addresses of related organisations will be found in APPENDIX II.

Stephen Friar
Folke, Dorset
July 2003

ACKNOWLEDGEMENTS

The author acknowledges with gratitude the invaluable assistance of John Campbell-Kease, Mary Critchley, Jane Entrican, Christopher Feeney, Kate Friar, Tom Friar, Bob Hanton, Clare Jackson, Kate Robinson, Stephen Slater, C.E.J. Smith, Catherine Watson and Geoffrey Wheeler in the preparation of this book.

The author and publisher would like to thank the following for their permission to reproduce illustrations: B.T. Batsford: 56 (Alan Sorrell), 62, 215 (Alan Sorrell); City of Bayeux: 49; John Bethell Photography: plate 22, 65; Bridgeman Art Library: plate 9; British Library: 199 (Cott. Nero D I 23v), 285 (Cott. Jul E IV ART B 15v); Cambridge University Collection: 23, 78, 105, 181, 210, 239, 246; Philip Craven: plates 3, 17; English Heritage Photographic Library: plate 2, 117, 139 (Jonathan Bailey), 164, 167; John Ferguson: 6, 19, 35, 43, 44, 194, 195, 250, 261, 282, 303 (3); Stephen Friar: plates 8, 19, 5, 84, 97, 99, 137, 140, 182, 184, 213, 268; Tom Friar: 116, 273; V.K. Guy: 307; Hampshire County Council: plate 6; Robert Harding Photography: plates 4, 14, 16, 20; Historic Royal Palaces: 64, 135, 233; HMSO: 287; Andrew Jamieson: 45, 107, 115, 120; A.F. Kersting: plates 1, 23; Mary Evans Picture Library: 266, 267; John Mennell: 225; National Trust Photographic Library: plate 15, 12 (Alasdair Ogilvie), 112 (Alasdair Ogilvie), 153; Skyscan Ballon Photography: plates 5, 7, 21; The Board of Trustees of the Armouries, Royal Armouries Museum, Leeds: 113, 283, 326; Welsh Historic Monuments (CADW Photographic Library): 27, 51, 123 (C. Jones Jenkins), 125, 137, 148, 168, 183 (C. Jones Jenkins), 211 (T. Ball), 240, 296 (Ivan Lapper), 311, 313 (Alan Sorrell); Geoffrey Wheeler: plate 18, i, iii, viii, 3, 20, 25, 39, 55, 58, 65, 68, 70, 72, 81, 83, 90, 126, 127, 141, 142, 164, 166, 188, 189, 209, 252, 258, 274, 286, 294, 330 (top & bottom), 331; Geoffrey Williams: 41, 136, 187, 269; Jean Williamson/Mick Sharp Photography: plates 10, 11, 12, 13; Doreen Yarwood: 133

Raglan Great or Yellow Tower, Gwent.

A

ABACUS The flat slab forming the upper section of a CAPITAL (*see* PIER).

ABANDONED SETTLEMENTS *see* DESERTED VILLAGES

À BOUCHE *see* SHIELDS

ABUTMENT A mass of MASONRY or brickwork against which an ARCH abuts or from which it springs. Structurally, an abutment resists the lateral thrust of an arch and may be a PIER, wall or BUTTRESS.
(*See also* VAULTING)

ACCOMMODATION, ARRANGEMENT OF *see* HOUSEHOLD

ACHIEVEMENT OF ARMS An arrangement of armorial devices (*see* ARMORY, FUNERARY HERALDRY *and* HATCHMENTS).

ADIT An opening or passage.

ADMINISTRATION *see* HOUSEHOLD

ADULTERINE A term applied to a castle which was erected without a royal licence or an existing building which was fortified without a licence to crenellate (*see* CRENELLATIONS). In the absence of royal authority, adulterine castles proliferated during the civil war of 1135–54 (*see* ANARCHY, THE). Many of these adulterine castles were of earth and timber construction and were later demolished by Henry II as he attempted to restore order. Even in later centuries castles were often unlicensed and there are several instances where licences were granted retrospectively, usually in the form of a pardon: Bolton Castle in North Yorkshire, Dunstanburgh in Northumberland and Farleigh Hungerford in Somerset are but three examples.

ADVANCED WORKS Additional fortifications beyond, but still commanded by, the principal stronghold.

ADVENAE Norman and English feudal lords who held lands in the Welsh Marches (often described as 'adventurers' in Welsh manuscripts) together with the retainers, officials, merchants and burgesses who accompanied them.
(*See also* MARCH)

AFFINITY That element of a magnate's RETINUE comprising men who served him because of his personal standing (his 'worship') in contradistinction to those who served as a consequence of land tenure. While the gentry would often compete with one another for a place in a retinue, lords would control entry very strictly. Nevertheless, those fairly numerous gentry who were thereby unattached might still enjoy membership of a broader 'affinity', for the influence of a lord reached far beyond the ranks of household retainers, annuitants, tenants and other dependants into the middle and lesser gentry of a shire.
(*See also* LIVERY AND MAINTENANCE *and* WORSHIP)

AFORERIDERS Mounted scouts.

AID Payment due to a lord on special occasions such as the knighting of an eldest son or the marriage of an eldest daughter.

AILETTES Rectangular plates of stiffened paper or thin wood fastened upright on the shoulder for heraldic display (*see* ARMOUR).

AISLED HALL *see* HALL

AKETON A quilted garment usually worn beneath mail armour or as an independent protective covering. Known as the *arming doublet* in the fifteenth century, its name derived from the Arabic word for cotton.
(*See also* ARMOUR)

ALABASTER Calcium sulphate, a form of gypsum, found in certain strata of rocks in the north Midlands, the Isle of Purbeck in Dorset and elsewhere, and used in medieval sculpture (particularly in monumental effigies) because of the ease and speed with which it could be carved. Dressed alabaster is exceptionally smooth to the touch and is white with occasional flecks of red,

though most monuments were originally coloured and gilded.
(*See also* MONUMENTS)

ALBACIO *see* PLASTER, WHITEWASH AND PAINT

ALCOVE A vaulted recess or large niche.

ALIEN In a medieval context, one who was unable to hold or inherit titles or land.

ALIENATION The transfer of property.

ALLEGIANCE An obligation to the king that takes priority over loyalty to a lesser lord.

ALLOD An estate held without feudal obligation.

ALMERY *see* AUMBRY

ALMONER The HOUSEHOLD officer responsible for dispensing charitable gifts. A lord's generosity, particularly to the poor, was one measure of his 'honour' or influence.

ALURE *or* **ALLURE** A walk or passageway, especially that behind a parapet (*see* WALL-WALK).

ALWITE Plate armour of the period *c.* 1410–60 which, although very plain, was extraordinarily beautiful. Contours were so perfectly crafted that reflected light rendered the armour almost white to the eye. A full harness of alwite armour was tailored for a particular client and was therefore enormously expensive. The finest harnesses were imported from Italy (notably from the Missaglia workshop in Milan), and it is hardly surprising that owners should wish to display such magnificence, not only in the field of battle and tournament, but also in their memorials. For the most part, therefore, armour in brasses and effigies of the period was unadorned, without the JUPON of earlier periods or the later TABARD.
(*See also* ARMOUR *and* ARMS MANUFACTURE)

AMERCEMENT Once convicted of a crime, a man was 'at the king's mercy' (*amerced*) and liable for a monetary payment.

ANARCHY, THE
'. . . they filled the land full of castles. They cruelly oppressed the wretched men of the land with castle works and when the castles

were made they filled them with devils and evil men . . .'
Anglo-Saxon Chronicle, 1137

The civil war during the reign of Stephen (1135–54) was known as 'The Anarchy'. After the death of his only legitimate son in 1120, Henry I had made the barons swear to accept his daughter Matilda, the wife of Geoffrey Plantagenet of Anjou, as his heir. Despite taking the oath, the barons feared an Angevin takeover and following Henry's death in 1135 they supported his nephew Stephen, the third son of Count Stephen of Blois and William the Conqueror's grandson, as a rival candidate.

Stephen, one of the richest landowners in England, enjoyed the almost universal support of the Anglo-Norman aristocracy. He was crowned on 22 December 1135 and immediately declared the Empress Matilda illegitimate, attempted to strengthen his position with the assistance of Flemish mercenaries and alienated many potential allies by favouring a select group of nobles. In 1138 King David I of Scotland invaded the north country on Matilda's behalf but was defeated near Northallerton. At this time the lords' principal grievance concerned the arrest of three courtier bishops: the justiciar Roger, bishop of Salisbury, and his nephews Nigel, bishop of Ely, and Alexander, bishop of Lincoln. It was on these men that Henry I had relied for the administration of his kingdom – and they were all very rich. Stephen, however, was rapidly running out of money: he had to fund the war in the north and was obliged to pay off malcontents among the nobility. The bishops were arrested and their assets seized – a move which immediately alienated the former servants of Henry I who now felt increasingly insecure. Robert, earl of Gloucester, an illegitimate son of Henry I, and various others turned to Matilda, so that by 1139 she commanded sufficient support to force a claim to the throne – but not enough to win it. The result was a protracted and incoherent struggle in which neither side held the advantage for long and was so anarchic that, according to the Anglo-Saxon chronicler, men said openly that 'Christ and his saints slept'.

At the beginning of 1141 Matilda captured Stephen at the battle of Lincoln, but before she could be crowned the Londoners demonstrated their hostility by driving her out of the capital. She fled to Winchester where her half-brother Robert of Gloucester was captured in battle. By November all that could be achieved was an exchange of prisoners: Stephen for Robert. The remaining years of the struggle saw no pitched battles of note; both sides were preoccupied with defending the numerous adulterine castles which had been erected as a consequence of the war. It had become a deadly game of chess. Stephen, for example, held an important castle at Malmesbury, Wiltshire, which was cut off from his main support in the south-east by a rival castle of Earl Robert's at Faringdon, Oxfordshire. So important was this castle to Stephen's lines of communication that when it finally fell in 1146 the entire war began to move in his favour. In the next year Earl Robert died, and at the beginning of 1148 Matilda finally returned to Normandy.

Many of the baronial families held lands on both sides of the Channel and by the 1140s, with Stephen holding England and Geoffrey and Matilda holding Normandy, these families were often faced with severely divided allegiances. It was generally accepted that the solution to this dilemma was the promotion of Matilda's son, Henry of Anjou. Henry landed in England in 1153 and in August the two armies met at Wallingford. The result was a stand-off and the barons, realising that it was not in their interests for either side to win, proposed a compromise: by the Treaty of Winchester Stephen was to reign for his lifetime and Henry was acknowledged as his successor. Within a year Stephen was dead.

ANCASTER STONE An easily carved, grey limestone from Wilsford Heath, Lincolnshire.

ANCIENT (i) Descriptive of the original coat of arms of a family who have subsequently been granted an additional or alternative coat.
(ii) A standard (flag) and the military officer responsible for its maintenance.
(*See also* BADGES AND LIVERY, FLAGS *and* LIEUTENANT)

ANCIENT DEEDS Documents at the Public Record Office, mostly drawn from monastic and private muniments, relating to conveyances of land, covenants, bonds, wills, etc. 'earlier in date than the end of Elizabeth I's reign' (1603).

ANCIENT USER *see* TIME IMMEMORIAL

ANELACE A short, two-edged tapering dagger often depicted in effigial figures and brasses.
(*See also* MISERICORDE *and* WEAPONS AND HARNESS)

ANGEL (COIN) *see* COINAGE

ANGLE TURRET Angle turrets are a characteristic feature of several Scottish and Borders tower-houses such as Belsay Castle, Northumberland.

ANGEL BEAM The projection of a HAMMER BEAM, carved at the end with a representation of an angel.

ANGLE TURRET A corbelled turret, usually supported on a SQUINCH ARCH and attached to the outside corner of a tower. Angle turrets are a characteristic feature of many Scottish and borders tower-houses such as Chipchase and Belsay Castles, those at Belsay being machicolated. They are also found on the bars of York's city walls. The term BARTISAN is often used to describe an angle turret, but such use is erroneous.

ANGLO-SAXON CHRONICLE One of the prime historical sources for the Anglo-Saxon period, the Chronicle purports to run from AD 494 to 1154, the year of Henry II's accession to the throne. Much of the earlier material is almost certainly folk-lore and hearsay, but from the tenth century onwards it is very reliable. There are several versions since various monasteries kept annual records of what seemed to them to be significant events. Later chronicles, such as those of Henry of Huntingdon, Gervase of Canterbury, Ralph of Coggeshall and Roger of Howden, continued the tradition into the later medieval period.

ANGLO-SCOTTISH WARS *see* SCOTLAND, ENGLISH WARS IN

ANGLO-WELSH WARS *see* WALES, CONQUEST OF

ANGON *see* WEAPONS AND HARNESS

ANJOU County in north-west France and the seat of the Angevin dynasty. Anjou was linked to the English crown when Geoffrey Plantagenet, count of Anjou (1129–51) became Henry II of England in 1154. Anjou was a constant focus for rivalry between the Capetian kings of France and the Plantagenets and was finally taken from Henry II's youngest son, John, by Philip II of France in 1203–4. By the Treaty of Paris (1259) Henry III of England finally relinquished his rights in the county. (*See also* AQUITAINE *and* PLANTAGENET)

ANNUITANT A retainer in receipt of an ANNUITY. Many annuitants were provided with lodgings within their lord's castle and these might be graded according to rank. At Bolton Castle (1380), for example, provision was made for eight separate households, each with its own hall and chamber, and for at least another dozen lodgings suitable for minor officials and lesser guests. These were in addition to Lord Scrope's private suite of apartments in the west range and chambers for his bailiffs near the gate. The Neville castle of Middleham and Lord Lovel's Wardour were provided with at least two dozen lodgings while John Holland's Dartington Castle had as many as fifty.

ANNUITY An annual payment from a lord to his retainer, usually for an unspecified service.

ANNULET A decorative ring and in heraldic cadency the mark of a fifth son (*see* CADENCY (HERALDIC)).

ANTE-CHAPEL The western end of a collegiate chapel, originally separated from the choir by a screen or pulpitum.

AP In the Welsh, 'son of', eg. Llywelyn ap Gruffydd.

APARTMENTS *see* SOLAR

APEX STONE *also* **SADDLE STONE** The uppermost stone in a gable.

APOPHYGE That part of a column where it springs from its base or joins its capital.

APPROACHES Siege works: trenches dug towards a fortress in order to protect attackers.

APPROVER Particularly in the Saxon and Norman periods, a criminal who obtained a pardon by becoming an informer was required to undergo *Trial by Battle*, a custom (based on the notion of divine intervention) which had largely disappeared by the fifteenth century and was finally abolished in 1819. The accuser was usually expected to fight the accused five times and was hanged if he lost. In civil cases a champion could be nominated as substitute.

APRON WALL An intermediate line of defence: a low outer wall, encircling a principal building or part of it (*see* MANTLET WALL).

APSE A semicircular projection, most often found forming the eastern termination of a chapel.

APSIDAL In the form of an APSE. Apsidal towers are U-shaped or round-fronted and were common in the thirteenth century, as in the keeps at Ewloe and Roch Castles in Wales.
See also CHAPELS

AQUITAINE An ancient duchy in south-western France at times comprising the entire country from the Loire to the Pyrenees, though a permanent delineation of its boundaries was never feasible. The duchy included the counties of Poitou, Périgord, La Marche, Limoges, Berry, Saintonge and Gascony, all of which were subsumed in the Angevin Empire by the marriage in 1152 of Henry Plantagenet (1133–89), count of Anjou and the future Henry II of England (1154), and Eleanor of Aquitaine (c. 1122–1204). In the thirteenth century the terms Aquitaine, Gascony and Guyenne were effectively synonymous. The term *Gascony* was usually used to designate territory in south-western France that was actually held by the English. By 1224 the English had lost most of the northern part of the old duchy of Aquitaine, though the title of duke was not relinquished. As duke of Aquitaine, the king of England had to recognise the king of France as his feudal overlord in Gascony.
(*See also* ANJOU *and* PLANTAGENET)

ARBALEST, ARBALIST *and* ARBLAST A crossbow (*see* ARCHERY).

ARBALESTER, ARBALISTER *and* ARBLASTER A crossbowman (*see* ARCHERY).

ARCADE A range of arches resting on piers or columns. A *blind arcade* is a decorative arcade attached to a wall.

ARCH A curved series of radiating wedge-shaped bricks or blocks of stone (*voussoirs*) so arranged above an opening that they support one another and are capable of carrying a considerable weight (*see also* LINTEL). The uppermost central block is the *keystone* and the pair of horizontal blocks from which the arch rises on either side of an opening are the *springers*. Between the springers is the notional *springing line* which determines the geometry of the different types of arch. The walling or support on or against which an arch rests is the *abutment* and the width between abutments is termed the *span*. The under-surface of an arch is the *soffit* and the height of the arch, measured between the soffit of the keystone and the centre of the springing line, is known as the *rise*.

Saxon arches were usually of the *triangular* or *mitre* type, formed by a pair of stone slabs joined in a mitre at the top. From the semicircular classical arch of ancient Rome derived the ROMANESQUE arch of the early medieval period (popularly known as the *Norman arch*) which was either semicircular (with its centre on the springing line), *segmental* (with its centre below the springing line) or *stilted* (with its centre above the springing line). The essence of Gothic architecture was the *pointed arch* (the French *arc brisé* or 'broken arch') which originated in the Middle East and reached western Europe by the twelfth century (*see* VAULTING). Its principal forms were the tall narrow *lancet arch* associated with the Early English style of Gothic architecture; the *equilateral arch*, the radii of which were equal to the span; the *obtuse arch* with a span greater than its radius; the *ogee arch*, characteristic of the fourteenth century; and the *four-centred arch* which is commonly found in buildings dating from the late medieval and Tudor periods. A *strainer* is an arch which spans an internal space to prevent walls from leaning (the finest examples are those above the crossing at Gloucester Cathedral); *interlacing* consists of semicircular arches which interlace and overlap, especially in Romanesque blind arcading (*see* ARCADE); the *Tudor arch* is an extreme form of the late fifteenth-century four-centre arch in

A shouldered arch at Conwy Castle.

which the upper curves are almost flat; and the *straight arch* is a rectangular opening the lintel of which is composed of radiating voussoirs. There are, of course, numerous other variations including the *rampant arch* in which the springing at either side of the opening is at different levels, and the *shouldered arch*, the best examples of which are to be found throughout Caernarfon Castle, Gwynedd – hence, the alternative *Caernarfon arch*.
(*See also* GOTHIC ARCHITECTURE, MASONRY *and* SQUINCH ARCH)

ARCH BRACE *see* ROOFS (TIMBER)

ARCHÈRE *see* LOOPHOLE

ARCHERY Long grooves (*polissoirs*) may sometimes be found in the stonework of medieval buildings, the result of sharpening arrowheads and swords during the routine maintenance of weaponry (*see* WEAPONS AND HARNESS). Practice with the longbow was a statutory requirement in every town and village during the Hundred Years War in the fourteenth and early fifteenth centuries and an

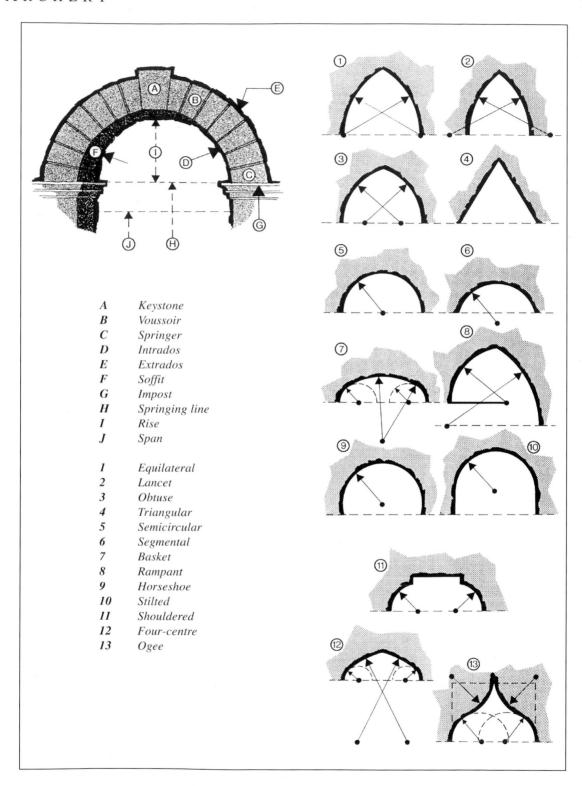

A	Keystone
B	Voussoir
C	Springer
D	Intrados
E	Extrados
F	Soffit
G	Impost
H	Springing line
I	Rise
J	Span

1	Equilateral
2	Lancet
3	Obtuse
4	Triangular
5	Semicircular
6	Segmental
7	Basket
8	Rampant
9	Horseshoe
10	Stilted
11	Shouldered
12	Four-centre
13	Ogee

enclosure, adjacent to the castle or parish church, was often used for weekly archery practice (*see* BUTT).

An English archer handled a bow differently from his European counterpart. Instead of keeping the left hand steady and drawing the bow string with the right, he kept his right in position and pressed the weight of his body into the horns of the bow. Thus, archers were taught 'not to draw with strength of arms, as divers other nations do, but with the strength of the body'.

The Longbow

The legendary longbow of Crécy and Agincourt could knock an armoured knight off his horse at a range of 300m (328yd). It was a longer form of the standard wooden bow, usually between 1.5m (5ft) and 1.8m (6ft) in length, shaped by a *bowyer* from a single stave of yew, which provided both strength and flexibility, and with a hempen string. Ordinary *arrows* were of light aspen wood, the heavier armour-piercing war arrows being of stronger ash, 85cm (34in) long, with a flight of feathers and a tip which was either hardened by burning or with a metal 'bodkin' head (*see also* QUIVER). An arrow had a flight of three goose feathers, the *cock feather* being that which faced outwards from the bowstring. If, in error, the arrow was placed in the wrong position in relation to the string, it was said to be a 'cock-up'. By the late thirteenth century these metal heads were often barbed, 7.5cm (3in) long and 5cm (2in) broad. Horn was sometimes used to protect the notch (*nock*) into which the bowstring was fitted. Examples from the Tudor warship *Mary Rose* were slightly shorter (75cm or 30in) and made of poplar wood. Longbows were used by the Vikings and, most probably, by the Normans at Senlac in 1066. While the longbow was used in France, Poland, Bohemia and the Low Countries, only in England was the longbowman considered to be a member of a military élite. But even here the longbow had traditionally been associated with poaching; indeed, its use had been banned in the royal forests until its military potential was recognised in the second half of the thirteenth century. Even in the fourteenth century military regulations specifically state that the crossbow was appropriate only to those living 'inside the forest', the longbow being the weapon of those who lived 'outside the forest' (*see* CHASE *and* FORESTS).

The fourteenth century was the great age of the English longbowman. The best archers were recruited into the great magnate retinues and fought in France where their shower-shooting technique caused havoc among the heavily armoured French cavalry. This technique required thousands of arrows to be loosed simultaneously, usually with a high trajectory, on to the heads of the enemy as they advanced through a 'killing field'. An English bowman could release up to fifteen arrows a minute and, although the technique probably resulted in relatively few casualties, it undoubtedly caused panic among the advancing men and horses. Another technique, used to considerable effect during the HUNDRED YEARS WAR, was the planting of pointed stakes in 'thickets' (*chevaux de frise*) as protection for infantry archers. Six or seven rows of stakes, each row a metre apart and angled towards the enemy, must have proved a formidable obstruction to a cavalry charge which could be diverted to face a heavily armoured line of men-at-arms by placing the thickets in pre-determined positions. It has also been suggested that archers may have deliberately encouraged an attack by standing in front of the stakes to conceal them, only retreating into the protective thicket at the last minute, thereby causing the front ranks of the attacking cavalry to impale themselves and their horses. It seems likely that the carnage suffered by the French knights at Crécy (1346) and Agincourt (1415) was inflicted by archers, emerging from their palisades with swords and daggers, during the ensuing confusion.

When compared with other types of bow, the longbow and arrow could be manufactured easily and cheaply. They were made in very large numbers during the Hundred Years War: records for the year 1359 list 20,000 bows, 850,000 arrows and 50,000 bowstrings delivered to the royal ordnance at the Tower of London (*see* ARMS MANUFACTURE). At this time there was a requirement that yew staves should be included in all consignments of imported goods as a form of taxation.

With rapid advances in the use of firearms the longbow ceased to be strategically effective after Flodden Field in 1513 and yet, with the threat of a French invasion, the statute was revived in 1543 and obligatory practice at the butts on Sundays and holidays continued well into the next century.

The Crossbow

Known as the *arbalest* or *arblast*, the crossbow was a bow-arm fitted to a wooden shaft with a mechanism to draw back the string and a lever to release it. The crossbow had survived in Europe as a hunting weapon since the fall of the Roman Empire but became popular for military purposes with the development of siege warfare in the tenth century.

By the twelfth century crossbowmen (*arbalesters*) were the most prestigious and highly paid infantry, notably Genoese mercenaries from northern Italy and Gascons from south-western France. The rapid development of protective armour in the twelfth and thirteenth centuries was probably a direct response to the increasing effectiveness of the crossbow which alone was capable of challenging the domination of the armoured knight in the battlefield. By the thirteenth century the élite of crossbowmen were mounted, though they still fought on foot and were, therefore, mounted infantry.

Crossbows were generally made of yew, Italian yew being particularly valued. By the late thirteenth century most bow arms were of a composite structure, incorporating yew wood, horn, sinew and sometimes bone which could be shaped after prolonged soaking in milk. A crossbow arm of steel is referred to in a document of 1314, but it seems likely that this was an experimental bow, steel bows appearing for the first time in any number in the fifteenth century.

The earliest surviving crossbow of the early medieval period dates from the eleventh century. In its simplest form the string was released by the upward movement of a wooden plug. Later crossbows incorporated a Roman device: a release nut which projected from the stock (or *tiller*) and over which the string was drawn back ('spanned') and retained while a missile (*bolt*) was put in place. The nut was retracted, and the string released, by means of a trigger. Initially, the centre of the bow arm was held beneath a foot while the string was spanned over the nut. A metal claw (*spanning hook*) attached to the archer's belt was sometimes used for this purpose. Crossbows of composite construction were first recorded in Europe in the second half of the twelfth century. The combination of wood, horn and sinew produced bows of considerable power, but greater strength was needed to span the bowstring and a metal stirrup was attached to the end of the stock into which the archer's foot could be placed while drawing the bow. By the beginning of the thirteenth century an average-size crossbow had a draw of about 85cm (33in), but as the weapons became stronger, the bow-arms shorter and the methods of spanning more efficient, the draw was reduced significantly. Spanning devices included the *windlass* and the *goat's-foot lever*, introduced in the mid-fourteenth century, which looked like a goat's cloven hoof. This mechanism comprised a stock with pins projecting along each side and a lever with claws at one end that could be fitted beneath the string. By pivoting the lever on the pins, the string

could be spanned with ease. The fifteenth-century *cranequin* was a sophisticated version of the windlass and consisted of a metal ratchet bar and geared handle which, when turned, drew back the crossbow string.

The crossbow missile was the *bolt* or *quarrel*. These were shorter than arrows, of somewhat greater diameter and aerodynamically superior, the earliest examples being 30cm (1ft) in length with a tapered and flattened butt and weighing less than 84g (3oz). The tempered steel head (*pile*) was usually a slender four-sided pyramid, similar in shape to the head of an arrow, and with a *flight* of goose wing feathers, also known as a *fletch*. A particularly sophisticated type of bolt, the *vireton*, had a spiral flight which would cause the bolt to rotate, thereby improving accuracy. Crossbow bolts were manufactured in large numbers throughout England and Wales in the thirteenth and fourteenth centuries, but the most notable centre of production was the Forest of Dean, Gloucestershire, where abundant supplies of iron, charcoal and wood charged the forest forges and kept the royal store-house of St Briavels Castle supplied with weaponry. Records show as many as 50,000 bolts delivered at one time, packed in barrels of 500.

By the thirteenth century a larger crossbow was used in the static defence of fortifications. This could be positioned on a parapet or wall, or on a cart in open battle, and would probably have been spanned by means of a windlass. The *great crossbow* was an even larger version made of yew wood and horn, up to 2m (6ft) long, frame-mounted on a bench and spanned by an integral screw-winch mechanism (*see also* SIEGES for the *espringal*, a siege machine operated on the crossbow principle). Despite the increasing use of cannon during the second half of the fourteenth century the great crossbow remained one of the most important anti-personnel weapons, particularly effective in the defence of fortifications (*see* SIEGES).

(*See also* ARMOUR, ARMS MANUFACTURE, FIREARMS AND CANNON, HELMETS, SHIELDS *and* WEAPONS AND HARNESS)

ARCHITECTS *see* MASTER MASONS AND ARCHITECTS

ARCHITECTURE *see* GOTHIC ARCHITECTURE *and* ROMANESQUE

ARCHITRAVE (i) A moulded frame round a window or door.
(ii) A horizontal beam resting on the tops of pillars.

ARDEN COUNTRYSIDE *see* COUNTRYSIDE

ARGENT The heraldic term for silver, usually depicted as white (*see* TINCTURES).

ARISTOCRACY A single class comprising the nobility and gentry, an élite based on the inheritance of substantial land-holdings.

ARMARIUM A recessed book cupboard or book store.

ARMATURE A metal structure used to reinforce tracery, canopies, slender columns or sculptural decoration.

ARMET A modern term (from the French) to describe a close helm with visor in which the BEVOR is formed of two cheek-pieces fastened together at the chin. (*See* ARMOUR *and* HELMETS)

ARMIGEROUS An *armiger* is one who is entitled to bear a COAT OF ARMS by lawful authority and is thereby armigerous. (*See* ARMORY)

ARMING DOUBLET *see* AKETON

ARMORY (i) A system of personal identification by means of hereditary devices placed on, or associated with, a shield. Armory is generally (and erroneously) referred to as HERALDRY.
(ii) Also a dictionary of coats of arms listed alphabetically by surname, notably Sir Bernard Burke's *General Armory of England, Ireland, Scotland and Wales*, published in 1842 and reprinted by Heraldry Today in 1984.

It is quite extraordinary that historians should so consistently undervalue a subject which was held in such esteem by the medieval and Tudor establishment. Coats of arms, badges and other armorial devices were ubiquitous in the architecture and decoration of castles and domestic and ecclesiastical buildings, in illuminated manuscripts and official documents, and on seals, monuments, tombs and memorials. Such devices provide not only an insight into the medieval mind but also a rich source of genealogical and historical information.

Unfortunately, so many medieval castles were slighted, abandoned and plundered, and the fabric exposed to the elements, that very little remains of the painted plaster walls, brilliantly glazed windows and coloured and gilded stonework, all of which would have included a considerable amount of armorial decoration. Neglect continued through the eighteenth and nineteenth centuries, when 'ivy-mantled towers' and decaying medieval ruins were perceived to be romantic and picturesque, and it is indeed surprising that so much decorative work has survived, albeit in isolated fragments. At Raglan Castle in Gwent, for example, a series of finely carved panels above the windows of the state apartments (*c*. 1469) provides evidence of the prominence given to armorial display at that time. Although they are no longer painted, the late fifteenth-century shields almost certainly bore the arms of Sir William Herbert (three silver lions rampant on a red and blue background) who was created earl of Pembroke by Edward IV in 1468 as a reward for his capture of Harlech Castle, Gwynedd – the last Lancastrian stronghold of the WARS OF THE ROSES. Alternate panels contain the Herbert badge of a *bascule* drawbridge, an unusual device which may also be seen above the entrance to one of the fifteenth-century porches at St Mary's church, Usk, and in a seventeenth-century copy of a seal to a

Herbert bascule *badge and shields, Raglan Castle, Monmouthshire.*

Raglan deed dated 1451 (*see* DRAWBRIDGE). In Northumberland a carved armorial façade (*c.* 1400) above the entrance to the great hall at Warkworth Castle declares the power and magnificence of the Percy dynasty, while at Wardour Castle, Wiltshire (*c.* 1393), the Arundell arms carved in an ornate classical panel above the entrance recall Sir Matthew Arundell and his son Thomas who reconstructed the castle in the second half of the sixteenth century.

The Origins of Armory

The origins of armory are obscure. The conventional theory is that the use of symbols on shield, surcoat and banner developed during the twelfth century in response to the need for identification in battle. However, the use of symbols, particularly on FLAGS, to denote dynastic and seigneurial allegiance and territorial authority pre-dates medieval European armory by several thousand years:

> Every man of the children of Israel shall pitch by his own standard, with the ensign of [his] father's house . . . And the children of Israel . . . pitched by their standards and so they set forward, every one after their families, according to the house of their fathers.
>
> The Book of Numbers 2:2 and 34

The Venerable Bede, writing in the early eighth century, describes the banners of King Edwin of East Anglia which 'were not only borne before him in battle, but even in time of peace, when he rode about his cities, towns or provinces . . . the standard bearer was wont to go before him'. Clearly, these banners bore the symbols of Edwin's dynastic and territorial authority, though Bede does not describe them in detail. There is evidence that flags bearing charges common to families or groups linked by blood or feudal tenure were in use in eleventh-century Europe, notably in Flanders. Whether the devices borne on the flags depicted in the BAYEUX TAPESTRY were of territorial or personal significance has long been a matter of dispute, but it is now generally accepted that the Normans had not, at that time, adopted the proto-armorial system evident in the lance pennons of their Flemish allies.

It is most likely, therefore, that the origins of British armory are to be found not in Normandy but in the system adopted by certain ruling families descended from the Emperor Charlemagne who ruled the Frankish Empire of northern Europe from 768 to 814. These families perpetuated much of the administrative organisation of the Carolingian Empire, including the use of dynastic and territorial emblems on seals, coinage, customs stamps and flags, indeed wherever officialdom needed to identify itself in both peace and war. There is evidence to suggest that these devices were common to families or groups linked by blood or feudal tenure, and were, of necessity, hereditary. With the redistribution of lands following the Norman Conquest (1066), the cadets in England of Flemish families (who were of Carolingian descent), and the devices used by them, became integrated into Anglo-Norman society.

The traditional theory that armory originated in the decoration of shield and surcoat in order that heavily armoured knights should be identified more easily in battle is of doubtful validity. Common sense suggests that the mud and debris of warfare would quickly obliterate the battered surfaces of shields, rendering them unrecognisable. Within the feudal system every man who held land subject to military service was 'known' or 'noted' (in Latin *nobilis*) and while these obligations were frequently commuted to other services or the payment of fines, the feudal *nobilis* retained its clearly defined superiority within a two-tier society in which there was an enormous gap between the upper and lower classes: the 'gentle' and the 'simple'. Armigerous status (in Latin *armiger* means 'arms-bearer') acknowledged the exclusive right of members of the twelfth-century military élite to possess emblems by which their feudal pre-eminence and authority might be recognised.

The extraordinarily rapid adoption of armory throughout western Europe in the early twelfth century was almost certainly a result of what is now known as the 'Twelfth-Century Renaissance'. The exuberance of spirit inspired by this movement expressed itself in a self-confident delight in adornment and visual decoration, of which the adoption of personal symbols and colours was an obvious manifestation. Promoted by the military households (the *familia Regis*) of the Angevin kings, popularised by the tournament and communicated throughout Europe by itinerant knights, minstrels and scholars, it was inevitable that the principles of armory should eventually be consolidated as an essential element of the law of arms.

Clearly, it was considered both convenient and desirable that an heir, on coming to his estate, should adopt the same armorial device as his father as a symbol of familial and feudal continuity. Although there is evidence to suggest that in northern Europe proto-armorial devices were often adopted by succeeding generations of the same family (on seals, for example), the emergence of a hereditary system based on the shield (in other words, armory as it is now defined) is said to date from 1127 when Henry I of England invested his son-in-law Geoffrey Plantagenet with a blue shield charged with gold lions. The same shield later appears on the tomb (at Salisbury Cathedral) of Geoffrey's bastard grandson William Longespee, earl of Salisbury (d. 1226), and the device would therefore seem to have acquired a hereditary significance.

Originally arms were largely self-assumed by members of the knightly class, though there are examples of arms being conferred as gifts of feudal superiors or in recognition of military leadership. Arms were (and remain) personal to the armiger and he alone displayed them on his shield and lance pennon and, from the early thirteenth century, on his banner and surcoat (hence 'a gentleman of coat armour' and the term 'coat of arms'). It became necessary, therefore, to ensure that each coat was sufficiently distinctive to avoid confusion with those of men related by blood, by seigneurialty or who had simply adopted similar devices from the comparatively small number of those available at the time. The 'differencing' of arms for this purpose and the MARSHALLING of two or more coats in one shield to signify marriage alliances, inheritance or the holding of an office to which arms appertained became essential (and increasingly complex) elements of armorial practice.

The Heralds

By the beginning of the thirteenth century admission to TOURNAMENTS was established as the prerogative of the knightly class. Not only was the pageantry of the tournament the perfect manifestation of the chivalric ethos (*see* CHIVALRY), it was also a flamboyant confirmation of the participants' social superiority. Heralds were attached to royal and magnate households as advisers and emissaries and it was they who were responsible for arranging and supervising tournaments which often lasted for several days and attracted knights from all the countries of western Europe. The heralds thereby acquired an expertise which was peculiarly their own – and because it was they who exercised this expertise it became known as 'heraldry'. Heraldry was concerned not only with the management of ceremonial and protocol but also with the ordering and recording of the personal devices used at tournaments, on seals and in warfare, an aspect of the heralds' work known as *armory*. Theirs was the motivating force which enabled armory to develop systematically; it was they who devised its conventions and terminology and it was

they who benefited most from the approbation of the medieval establishment (*see* COLLEGE OF ARMS *and* COURT OF CHIVALRY).

In the fourteenth and fifteenth centuries brilliantly emblazoned chantry chapels, memorials, tombs and window glass declared a medieval magnate's magnificence and lineage; his retainers mustered at his STANDARDS, fought in battle beneath his GUIDONS and, by their liveries and household badges, proclaimed his authority (*see* BADGES AND LIVERY *and* LIVERY AND MAINTENANCE).

However, by the fifteenth century 'the bearing of coat armor' was so widely abused that HERALDS' VISITATIONS were necessary in order to ascertain precisely who was entitled to use arms. Many claimed the right of ancient user (*see* TIME IMMEMORIAL) while others paid hefty fines to the officers of arms by whom their devices were confirmed. Visitations continued throughout the Tudor period which witnessed a proliferation of grants of arms and crests to the new establishment: gentlemen who were concerned more with the administration of the state and the development of commerce than with the tournament or battlefield. The ancient nobility, jealous of their status as *armigers*, established the practice of adding SUPPORTERS to their arms to distinguish them from the gentry. These were generally chimerical creatures many of which originated in seals and in the medieval period had been translated into badges and CRESTS.

During the late and post-Tudor period (sometimes described as *The Heraldry of the Decadence*) armorial practice degenerated. The practical application of armory in the battlefield and tournament was replaced by exaggerated ceremonial, and coats of arms became stylised and extravagant.

Armorial Practice in Wales

Welsh armory is fundamentally different in that its purpose is to proclaim ancestry. The majority of the Welsh nation consists of a pedigreed population, a distinct caste, descended from the native Welsh aristocracy, warrior farmers and ADVENAE. The ancient social system of the Welsh, in which so many rights and obligations were dependent on membership of a tribe, conditioned them to regard a pedigree as of the utmost importance. In Wales there was no such person as an 'armigerous gentleman' as there was in England, for a man was 'gentle' by virtue of his genealogy and 'gentility followed the blood'. Although the Welsh had been acquainted with medieval armory, it was not until the early

ARMOUR (BODY)

The unicorn crest of Sir Edward Dalyngrigge, builder of Bodiam Castle, together with the arms of Wardeaux, Dalyngrigge and Radynden, above the entrance to the gatehouse.

assert corporate identity in a form which could be equated with that of the feudal magnate, and by the fourteenth century many towns, guilds and corporations had adopted the devices of their seals as coats of arms, simply by depicting them in colour on a shield, and sometimes rearranging charges to conform with armorial conventions. In the sixteenth and seventeenth centuries several corporations took advantage of the heralds' visitations to record their previously unauthorised arms. Others retained their original emblems, many of which are still used today.

(*See also*: AILETTES, ATTRIBUTED ARMS, AUGMENTATION OF HONOUR, BASTARDY, BEASTS (HERALDIC), BLAZON, CADENCY, COLLEGE OF ARMS, COURT OF CHIVALRY, DONOR AND COMMEMORATIVE WINDOWS, FLAGS, FUNERARY HERALDRY, HATCHMENTS, ROLLS OF ARMS, ROYAL ARMS, SEALS, SHIELDS, STAINED GLASS *and* TINCTURES. For the Heraldry Society *see* Appendix II)

ARMOUR (BODY)

The following terms are most commonly used when describing body armour of the medieval period (* *see also* individual entries). *For* HELMETS *see* separate entry. *For* horse armour *see* HORSES AND HORSE-HARNESS.

Mail armour was the most common form of body armour during the early medieval period (*see* MAIL), though there was a clear distinction between the long and short forms of the mail shirt (*hauberk*) which was worn over a padded *gambeson* to prevent chafing. It is evident from the Bayeux Tapestry that Norman mounted troops also wore full-length leg mail, while that of the English, who for the most part fought on foot, was only knee-length. By the late eleventh century a separate mail *coif* had been introduced to protect the neck and head, together with a *ventail* laced across the lower part of the wearer's face and, from the twelfth century, integral mail *mufflers*. The mail hauberk remained the principal form of armour throughout the twelfth and thirteenth centuries and this was supplemented by separate leg armour which became increasingly popular from the mid-twelfth century, particularly with armoured cavalry, probably as a defence against the increasing efficiency of infantry. These mail *chausses* covered the entire leg from foot to thigh or were laced around the front of the leg and over the foot, supported by means of straps attached to a girdle beneath the hauberk. Separate gloves (*pons*) superseded mail mufflers in the late thirteenth

Tudor period that they produced a system. Those Welshmen who already bore arms were assumed to have inherited them from tribal ancestors while new arms were attributed to the ancestors of other, non-armigerous families. For example, the numerous descendants of Hywel Dda who lived in the tenth century, of Cadwaladr who lived in the seventh, of Cunedda who lived in the fifth and of Beli Mawr who probably never lived at all, all received retrospective coats of arms which they hurriedly registered with the English heralds of the new Tudor dynasty.

Civic Armory

Civic armory dates from the late twelfth century when officials of boroughs and other towns made use of seals bearing devices. Initially, these devices were rarely depicted on shields and were simply religious or other emblems of local significance, or seigneurial devices indicative of feudal allegiance or benefaction, contained within an inscribed border. With the gradual development of corporate authority in the Middle Ages came a corresponding desire to

AILETTES*	shoulder pieces for heraldic display
AKETON*	quilted garment worn beneath armour
ARMING CAP	padded cap worn beneath helmet
ARMING DOUBLET	alternative name for AKETON
AVENTAIL	a mail fringe attached to edge of helmet
BALDRIC*	sword belt
BARBOTE	alternative name for BEVOR
BESAGEWS	protection for the armpits
BEVOR*	plate armour to protect lower front of face
BRIGANDINE*	tight-fitting protective coat
CAMAIL*	mail protection for neck and shoulders
CHAIN MAIL	a pleonasm for MAIL
CHAUSSES	mail leggings
CINGULUM MILITARE*	broad hip-belt
COAT OF PLATES*	plates riveted inside a coat
COIF*	mail hood
COUDES	elbow protection
COUTER*	disc-shaped elbow protection
CUIRASS*	back- and breast-plate
CUIR BOUILLI*	hardened leather
CUISSES*	padding for thighs
CYCLAS*	over-garment
ENARMES*	straps on the inside of a shield
ESPALIER	padded shoulder protection
FAULD*	protective 'skirt'
GAMBESON*	quilted protective garment
GAUNTLET*	articulated plate gloves
GORGET*	plate armour form of CAMAIL
GREAVES*	protection for the lower leg
GUIGE	strap supporting a shield
HAKETON*	padded protective garment
HAUBERGEON*	a light form of hauberk
HAUBERK*	a mail shirt
JACK*	infantryman's body protection
JAZERENC	see HAUBERK
JUPON*	short sleeveless tunic
LAMBREQUIN	see MANTLING
LAMES*	thin metal plates
MAIL*	armour formed of circular links
MANTLING*	protective cloth affixed to helmet
MISERICORDE*	short thrusting dagger
MUFFLERS*	mail mittens
PAULDRON*	shoulder-guard
PLACKART*	lower part of breastplate
POLEYNS*	knee protectors
POMMEL*	rounded end of sword hilt
PONS	glove-like mail protection
POURPOINT	padded or quilted soft armour
REREBRACE	protection for upper arm
ROUNDEL*	protection for armpits
ROWEL*	star-shaped end of spur
SABATON	broad-toed mail foot armour
SOLLERETS*	pointed metal shoes
SPAULDER	plate shoulder protection
SURCOAT*	sleeveless cloth coat
TABARD*	heraldic coat with sleeves
TACES*	metal strips of 'skirt'
TARGET*	a circular shield
TASSETS*	metal plates to protect thighs
TIPPET*	neck and shoulder protection
VAMBRACE*	protection for forearm
VENTAIL	a mail flap to protect the lower face

century, while quilted or scale-lined thigh protection (*cuisses*) appeared at about the same time. Knee-caps (*poleyns*) of hardened leather were sometimes attached to the cuisses, while comparable small pieces of protection for the arms and armpits (*besagews*) were in evidence by the late thirteenth century.

In the fourteenth century body armour developed in response to the power of the steel-tipped, armour-piercing crossbow bolt (*see* ARCHERY) and later to small, hand-held guns. The élite heavily armoured cavalry wore increasingly sophisticated plate armour which covered not only the head and trunk but also the limbs. While limb protection of hardened leather (*cuir bouilli*), often decoratively tooled, remained in use throughout the late medieval period, fully plated steel arm defences were becoming increasingly popular by the mid-fourteenth century. These consisted of the *gauntlet* for the hand and wrist, the *vambrace* for the lower arm, a *couter* for the elbow, the *rerebrace* for the upper arm and the *spaulder* for the shoulder. By the end of the fourteenth century the front of the shoulder was protected by a large, plate *pouldron*, while the mail *camail* protection for the neck and shoulders was replaced by the steel *gorget* at the beginning of the fifteenth century. Initially, rigid pieces of leather leg armour for the thighs and shins may have been worn beneath cuisses and chausses. But, from the late thirteenth century, lower-leg protection (*greaves*) or 'shin-pads' (*demi-greaves*), metal plates to protect the thigh (*tassets*), poleyns and segmented foot protection (*sabatons*) were also made of metal plate and ultimately were incorporated into full suits of articulated plate armour, together with a skirt (*fauld*) of steel hoops over the lower stomach.

The finest fifteenth-century armour was imported from Italy and Germany (*see* ALWITE) and must have been incredibly expensive. Made of mild steel which was 'worked' or beaten at about 500 degrees Centigrade, armour was often *proofed* by shooting steel-tipped crossbow bolts at a test piece. But for the average knight – who in the 1370s enjoyed an annual income of at least £40 – a complete harness of bascinet, aventail, hauberk, breastplate, fauld and leg armour would have cost about £12, which does not seem excessive, bearing in mind that armour was usually passed on from father to son. Neither was he obliged to acquire a full harness: Henry II's Assize of Arms (1181) prescribed that the holder of a knight's fee should provide only a helmet, mail shirt, shield and lance.

The notion that late medieval men-at-arms were rendered immobile by the weight of plate armour, especially when unhorsed, is only partially true. A complete Italian harness of *c.* 1450, now at Glasgow, weighs just over 25kg (55lb) although specially reinforced jousting armour could weigh up to 38kg (83lb). But this was exceptional. Not only was a full suit of plate armour little heavier than the old forms of mail protection, but its weight was so skilfully dispersed and the joints so expertly articulated that a fully armoured man was perfectly capable of fighting on foot, running or mounting his horse unaided (unlike the French knights in Olivier's *Henry V* who had to be winched into the saddle by block and tackle!).

For the average infantryman a quilted jacket or garment of leather or rough canvas strengthened with plates of metal or horn (*brigandine* or *jack*) remained the principal form of body protection throughout the late medieval period, together with the distinctive *kettle hat* or *chapel de fer*, a wide-brimmed steel headpiece first introduced at the end of the twelfth century. The oft-repeated notion that plate armour was too expensive for any but the nobility ignores the fact that various items of low-grade plate armour (*ammunition armour*) were often ordered in large quantities to be worn by infantrymen and archers. These pieces could be obtained at a fraction of the cost of a noble's made-to-measure, decorated harness.
(*See also* ARCHERY, ARMS MANUFACTURE, CAMAIL PERIOD, CREST, FIREARMS AND CANNON, HELMETS, HORSES AND HORSE-HARNESS, SHIELDS *and* WEAPONS AND HARNESS)

ARMOURY A storeroom for weapons and armour.

ARMS, COLLEGE OF *see* COLLEGE OF ARMS

ARMS MANUFACTURE By the eleventh century a number of arms manufacturing centres had been established in western Europe and over the next four hundred years several of these became recognised centres of excellence, notably the German Rhineland, southern Germany and the Lombardy region of northern Italy (*see* ALWITE). Weapons smiths were highly specialised and skilled craftsmen and by the thirteenth century they had begun forming themselves into guilds. In Italy, for example, the Venetian smiths founded two guilds, one for specialised sword-makers and the other for makers of scabbards, belts and armour. Similarly the crossbow makers of early thirteenth-century Paris differentiated between those who made the weapons and those who manufactured the bolts. Skilled armourers and weapon-makers were highly paid: the Parisian helmet-makers reputedly earned more than an ordinary knight. Most were local craftsmen, though several established international reputations for the quality of their work – men like Peter the Saracen who was employed by King John in 1205. Women were often engaged to sew helmet linings, cloth armours and the fabric and soft leather elements of expensive suits of plate armour, while artists were engaged to provide the decoration on elaborate tournament armour and harness. Recent research suggests that high-quality weapon-making processes were extraordinarily time-consuming. A standard, early medieval sword blade may have been heated as many as 128 times and required 43 hours of work using the pattern-welded technique (*see* WEAPONS AND HARNESS), while a further 32 hours were needed to make the hilt, scabbard and belt. The finest decorated sword could take a month to produce: forging the blade alone required over 500kg of charcoal. It would have taken a similar length of time to make a hauberk (mail armour for the body and arms), while a batch of composite bows may have taken a year to make – each stage of manufacture requiring precise conditions of humidity and temperature.

Mass-produced weapons were usually made where the basic materials were all available in one place. By far the largest centre of production of crossbow bolts was St Briavels in the Forest of Dean where iron, charcoal, wood and water were readily available. Ropes for siege engines were manufactured at Bristol where a rope-making industry had developed to service one of England's major ports, while soft-armours of quilted cloth were made by the Guild of Tailors and Linen Armourers of London. Simple longbows (*see* ARCHERY) were fairly crude weapons that could be manufactured quickly and in very large numbers, especially during the Hundred Years War. Records show that 20,000 bows were made at thirty-five locations, together with 850,000 arrows and 50,000 bowstrings, in a single year (1359), while in the thirteenth century crossbow bolts were delivered for storage at the Tower of London in batches of 50,000.

ARMS, ROYAL *see* ROYAL ARMS, THE

ARRAS A large, richly decorated tapestry or WALL-HANGING. Wall-hangings of this type were intended to be both decorative and functional. They served to reduce draughts and condensation, to conserve heat within the room and to improve considerably the acoustics of a stone-built chamber. The term is generic but derived from the French town of Arras which, from the thirteenth to the sixteenth century, was famed for its tapestry weaving.

ARRIS In architecture, the sharp edge produced at the meeting of two flat or curved surfaces.

ARROWHEAD BASTION A post-medieval defensive projection in the shape of an arrowhead (*see* TUDOR COASTAL FORTS).

ARROW LOOPS *see* LOOPHOLES

ARROWS *see* ARCHERY

ARROW SLITS *see* LOOPHOLES

ARSENAL Originally a ship-building yard, subsequently a military storage depot.

ARTHURIAN BRITAIN When the legions of Rome withdrew from Britain at the beginning of the fifth century they left a Romanised, nominally Christian society of Celtic people to defend themselves against the Irish from the west and the Picts and Scots from the north. Vortigern, a dominant fifth-century British ruler, responded by inviting mercenaries – Angles, Saxons and Jutes – to assist in the defence of his kingdom, a practice which had been employed successfully by the Romans but which collapsed when Vortigern's resources were stretched to the limit and he could no longer pay his troops. The ensuing wave of carnage and devastation encouraged further Saxon invasion and resulted in the disintegration of Britain into a number of minor kingdoms. Gildas, writing in the sixth century, credits one Ambrosius Aurelianus, a Romano-British *imperator*, with a series of victories over the Saxons and the reunification of the south and west, and in contemporary chronicles a man called Artos, or Arthur, also begins to emerge as a significant soldier and leader, uniting the squabbling, petty kings of Britain against the common enemy. Artos was the Celtic form of the Roman name *Artorius* suggesting that Arthur was a noble Celt whose family had grown to prominence during the Roman occupation. Until the fifth century there is no recorded instance of the name, yet in the hundred years following his supposed death it became extraordinarily popular: indicative, perhaps, of the breadth of Arthur's fame.

The first reference to Arthur's military prowess is found in an elegy called the *Gododin*, written by the Welsh bard Aneurin in *c.* AD 600. Nennius, a monk at Bangor writing at the end of the eighth century, describes Arthur as the *dux bellorum* and enumerates twelve of his battles in the *Historia Britonum*. The *Annales Cambriae*, the ancient annals of Wales dating from the second half of the tenth century, tell of the 'Battle of Badon' in 518, in which Arthur carried the cross of Christ on his shoulders, and the 'Battle of Camlann' in 539 'in which Arthur and Medraut fell'. There are few references to Arthur in contemporary ecclesiastical records: the Celtic monks were generally antagonistic towards him, for his men are said to have plundered monasteries in their efforts to maintain supplies.

The rapidity with which Arthur and his guerrillas moved about the country suggests that they were organised in light cavalry units and enjoyed a mobility that could not be matched by the Saxons who rarely fought on horseback. Here, perhaps, is the foundation of the chivalric, knightly élite that flourished in Europe through the triumphs of the Norman and Flemish cavalry in the eleventh century, was manifest in the great orders of chivalry and the ceremonial tournaments of the high Middle Ages, and remains today in the glamour and tradition of the mounted regiments.

Arthur and several other characters may also be traced to figures in ancient Celtic mythology, but it was the 'Matter of Britain', the legend cycle that evolved from Geoffrey of Monmouth's highly imaginative twelfth-century chronicle *Historia Regium Britanniae* (*c.* 1138), through Robert Wace's *Geste des Bretons* (*c.* 1154) and the early medieval European verse and prose romances (notably those of Chrétien de Troyes), that succeeded in raising an obscure and shadowy *chieftain* to the patriot-king of the Arthurian legends, familiar in such works as the anonymous *Sir Gawain and the Green Knight* (1360–70) and Malory's *Morte d'Arthur* (1469).

The ideals of the Fellowship of the Round Table (first introduced by Wace) were precisely those of the medieval chivalric code and the Quest for the Holy Grail by Galahad, the perfect knight, its highest achievement. Although destroyed by infidelity, disloyalty and treachery, the Fellowship became the object of an international cult and the model for the medieval orders of CHIVALRY.

The Plantagenets clearly recognised the political advantages of association with such an illustrious British 'king'. 'Round Tables', festive pageants and tournaments were held throughout the reigns of Edward I and his successors. Edward III had a circular house built at Windsor Castle to accommodate a round table, and at the conclusion of a great tournament held there in 1344 he took a solemn oath that in time he would follow in the footsteps of King Arthur and create a round table for his knights. In 1348 the Order of the Garter was founded, comprising twenty-six knights companion, including the sovereign and his eldest son. The Welshman Henry Tudor, who became Henry VII in 1485, claimed he had restored the true 'British' royal line by his descent from Arthur through the Welsh princes. The Celtic legend, suppressed by the Plantagenets, that Arthur had not died but 'sleeps on until the day shall come for that Golden Age to be restored' was used as justification for his usurpation –

he was to be the instrument by which the Tudor dynasty was to create a new Golden Age. Henry ordained that his son (named Arthur) should be born at Winchester, the ancient capital of Wessex, where the legendary Round Table hung in the Great Hall of the castle, as it still does today. In Henry VIII's reign the table was repaired in 1516–17 and repainted in anticipation of the visit of the Holy Roman Emperor, Charles V, in 1522. The table, which is of oak and measures 5.5m (18ft) in diameter, was painted in twenty-four segments, alternately white and green (the Tudor livery colours), radiating from a central Tudor Rose, the figure of the sovereign himself occupying a further two. Each segment represents one *siege* or place for each of the twenty-six Garter knights. According to the chronicler John Hardynge the table was already in position on the wall of the Great Hall in *c.* 1463. Radio-carbon dating carried out in 1976 indicated that the felling date of the youngest tree used in its construction was *c.* 1255. A further test using tree-ring dating suggested that the table was made some time between 1250 and 1280 during the reigns of Henry III and Edward I, though there can be little doubt that it was later used by Edward III (*see above*).

There are numerous topographical references to Arthurian legend throughout Britain, particularly in the names of unusual physical features and megaliths, to which our ancestors ascribed mystical properties, such as Arthur's Chair, Arthur's Table, Arthur's Kitchen and Arthur's Finger. Many caves in Wales, Cumbria and Northumberland are said to contain the sleeping Arthur and his knights; two islets of the Scilly Isles are called Great and Little Arthur and in Scotland are Arthur's Seat at Edinburgh and Ben Arthur in the Highlands. Then there is the Arthurian landscape on which has been superimposed that of the archaeologist. Of the twelve battles listed by Nennius few have been identified, though the site of Mount Badon, the decisive battle of *c.* AD 518 that was to delay the Saxon advance for a quarter of a century, is thought to have been either Liddington Castle near Swindon in Wiltshire or Badbury Rings near Wimborne in Dorset. Most legends associate Arthur with the West Country to where the Celt Artos is said to have retired. Tintagel, now a Cornish tourist village, is reputed to be the place of Arthur's birth, and though the first Norman castle on the site dates from 1141 there is also evidence of an earlier fifth-century fortification. Geoffrey of Monmouth located Arthur's Camelot at Caerleon-on-Usk in Gwent, the Roman legionary fortress of *Isca*, but Cadbury Castle on the Somerset–Dorset border near Sherborne is a sixth-century stronghold of considerable military and administrative significance. While it was never the romantic, many-towered Camelot of legend, it was undoubtedly the headquarters of an important *dux bellorum* and has no archaeological equivalent in Britain. Twelve miles to the north of Cadbury, at Glastonbury – the *Isle of Avalon* – in the Somerset Levels, is the abbey where in 1190 the monks claimed to have exhumed a hollow log coffin containing the bones of Arthur and his queen, Guinevere. It is said that Arthur was buried here in the greatest secrecy so that the Saxons should not be encouraged by his death, and mystery has surrounded the place ever since. Recent research has shown that, although there was once a deep grave of the correct period and type at the location indicated by the monks, the 'discovery' was probably a hoax. It is certainly true that it greatly enhanced the abbey's prestige and the increased income from pilgrims enabled the monks to finance the rebuilding of the church and domestic buildings which had been destroyed by fire in 1184. Whatever the truth of the matter, the ground on which the present ruins stand is one of the most sacred, historic and mysterious sites in Britain.

ARTIFICIAL RUINS Most artificial ruins, castellated façades, towers and gateways date from the eighteenth century when they were constructed as Gothick *'eye-catchers'*: focal points in landscaped parklands. These ornamental ruins, with their chivalric overtones, correspond to the Gothic Revival of domestic architecture and the Romantic Movement in literature, in which 'the classical, intellectual attitude gave way to . . . claims of passion and emotion' (Sir Paul Harvey). Being integral to the geometry of a planned landscape, they should not be regarded as *follies* (man-made structures which have no apparent rationale other than to pronounce the eccentricity of the builder). 'When a wide heath, a dreary moor, or a continued plain is in prospect, objects which catch the eye supply the want of variety; none are so effectual for this purpose as buildings. The Mind must not be allowed to hesitate; it must be hurried away from examining into the reality by the exactness and the force of the resemblance' (*Observations on Modern Gardening*, Whately, 1770). The illusion was often enhanced by 'an intermixture of a vigorous vegetation' which 'intimates a settled despair of their restoration' (*ibid.*) and served as a reminder of man's mortality and the transience even of his most noble creations.

ARTILLER The member of a garrison responsible for maintaining military equipment.

'ARTILLERY' PLATFORMS These level grass platforms (similar in appearance to golf tees) are often post-medieval, having been erected to accommodate artillery. However, the term is also (erroneously) used to describe platforms, which were originally for medieval stone-throwing machines such as the trebuchet (*see* SIEGE PLATFORM).

ASHLAR Masonry made from smooth, finely cut blocks of stone that were tooled on one external face. Rare in most early functional castles, ashlar was used for several later keeps and gatehouses and for ornate domestic work. The magnificent late medieval castle of Raglan, Monmouthshire, is built throughout of ashlar.
(*See also* MASONRY)

ASSIZE OF ARMS *see* LAW AND ORDER

ASSIZE OF MORT D'ANCESTOR Established in 1176, a court concerned with determining a plaintiff's claim to an inheritance. An aggrieved claimant could obtain a writ requiring a sheriff to empanel a local jury, the members of which would be familiar with the circumstances of the case. Most common were instances of manorial lords who repossessed property following a tenant's death. The procedure was abolished in 1833.

ASSIZE OF NOVEL DISSEISEN ('recent dispossession') A procedure established in 1166 to decide whether a tenant had been wrongly removed from his holding. An aggrieved tenant could obtain a writ requiring a sheriff to empanel a jury to determine his case. Although the procedure was originally intended to effect a speedy resolution of such disputes, it came to be abused as a means of establishing a title through the filing of a fictional claim. It was abolished in 1833.

ATTACK AND DEFENCE *see* SIEGES

ATTAINDER Made after a judgment of death or outlawry on a capital charge, a declaration of attainder by act of parliament resulted in the absolute forfeiture of all civil rights and privileges. Acts of attainder were frequently applied during the Middle Ages in association with charges of treason, when a declaration of attainder implied also a 'corruption of the blood'. In these cases the goods, lands, titles and armorial bearings of an attainted person could not be inherited by his heirs until the attainder had been revoked, also by act of parliament. Lands, and any rights in them, reverted to a superior lord subject to the crown's rights of forfeiture. During the WARS OF THE ROSES, acts of attainder were regularly used by one side to liquidate the other. Even so, it is interesting to note that during the period 1453–1504, of 397 attainders no fewer than 256 were reversed. Henry IV, Henry VI and Edward IV had all been attainted and yet all three succeeded to the throne. Attainder was abolished as recently as 1870.

ATTRIBUTED ARMS The heralds of the medieval and post-medieval periods determined that, because all persons of consequence in their society were armigerous, so too were the characters of their religion and the heroes of legend and history. Armorial bearings were therefore devised and attributed not only to the saints and martyrs, the apostles and disciples and the Old Testament prophets and kings but also to concepts and abstractions. Banners of the Trinity, Christ's Passion and the Blessed Virgin Mary accompanied the medieval army into battle and many a warrior emblazoned the *inside* of his shield with religious emblems. To the Archangel Michael was attributed a red cross on a silver field and, not to be outdone, Satan himself bore arms (as a former seraph he was assumed to be armigerous) and to him was attributed a red shield charged with a gold *fess* (horizontal band) between three frogs, a reference from the Book of Revelation. The post-medieval heralds were particularly systematic, beginning with Adam (a plain red shield) and Eve (plain silver). To King David they attributed a gold harp on blue and to Joseph, not a multi-coloured coat as one might expect, but one of black and white chequers. Devices from the attributed arms of historical and legendary characters, and of ancient kingdoms, are much in evidence in the heraldry of civic and corporate bodies, the three *seaxes* (notched swords) of the kingdoms of the East and Middle Saxons and the gold *martlets* (swallows) of the South Saxons, for example.

AUDIENCE CHAMBER A room, usually in the vicinity of the PRIVY CHAMBER, in which guests and petitioners were received by the lord or senior members of his household.

AUDITOR A member of a HOUSEHOLD responsible for auditing the financial transactions of an estate. In a sixteenth-century survey of Middleham Castle, Yorkshire, a first-floor room next to the gatehouse is described as the 'Auditour Chambre' and a ground-floor room as the 'Auditour

Kechinge'. Although the survey describes rooms at a time (1538) when the castle had ceased to be a major residence, it is possible that from the early fifteenth century the north range was the administrative centre of the Middleham estate.

AUGMENTATION OF HONOUR Augmentations are 'additions' to coats of arms, usually awarded in recognition of signal service to the crown. They are of two kinds: the first being awarded 'by mere grace', the second being won by merit. In the first category are augmentations such as those granted by Richard II to his kinsmen Surrey, Exeter and Norfolk, who were permitted to add the attributed arms of Edward the Confessor to their own. In the second category there are many instances of augmentations granted as rewards for acts of valour or outstanding service. Such augmentations seem to have existed since the earliest days of ARMORY and may appear to 'break the rules' in order to draw attention to the distinction.

AUMBRY, AMBRY or ALMERY A secure chest or cupboard in which altar plate and other sacred items and relics were stored, usually within a rectangular recess in a north wall near a CHAPEL altar. The term is also used to describe cupboards with more mundane uses: those for storing towels, for example, or the 'civerys' in which eating utensils and table furnishings were kept.
(*See also* PISCINA)

AUNLAZ *see* WEAPONS AND HARNESS

AVENTAIL *see* CAMAIL

AZURE The heraldic term for blue (*see* TINCTURES).

B

BACHELOR *see* KNIGHT BACHELOR

BACKSTOOL A term used until the late eighteenth century, meaning a chair without arms. Inventories usually distinguish between the backstool and chair (which was either an *elbow chair* with arms or a *back chair* with sides) and the FALDSTOOL, lowstool and footstool.

BADGES AND LIVERY An armorial badge is a discrete emblematic device used to facilitate identification. It is not part of a coat of arms and is therefore not displayed in a shield. In England armorial badges came into general use during the second quarter of the fourteenth century, though the adoption of single (often allusive) devices on flags and in seals was a characteristic of the so-called Twelfth-Century Renaissance during which a European system of ARMORY began to evolve.

In the late medieval period there were four types of badge, all of which may occasionally be found in the decoration and fabric of castles: (i) personal devices used for the adornment of clothing, jewellery, fabrics, furnishings, artefacts and architectural features; (ii) insignia issued to members of bodies corporate, such as guilds and livery companies, and to members of the chivalric orders; (iii) badges of office associated with specific household or corporate offices, including those of the crown, government and judiciary; and (iv) *livery badges* (also known as *household badges*) which were issued to indentured retainers and armed retinues to be worn on uniforms (*see below*) and borne on mustering and battle flags (*see* LIVERY AND MAINTENANCE).

The use of *impressa* or personal emblems was widespread in the late medieval and renaissance courts of Europe, notably in pageants and TOURNAMENTS. Ashmole wrote of the fourteenth century: 'This age did exceedingly abound with impresses, mottoes and devices, and particularly King Edward III was so excessively given up to them that his apparel, plate, bed, household furniture, shields and even the harness of his horses and the like, were not without them.'

In England personal badges were often adopted for their hidden meaning: the enigmatic cranket device of the de Vere earls of Oxford, for example, which may have alluded to that family's strategy for increasing its power and influence; or the *falcon and fetterlock* of the house of York. Originally devised by Edmund of Langley when he was appointed Master of the Royal Mews and Falcons in 1399, the falcon (inherited from Edward III) was depicted within the fetterlock (manacle) which was closed to illustrate his frustrated political ambitions – 'locked up from all hope and possibility of the kingdom'. It was not until Edward, duke of York, became king of England in 1461 that the fetterlock was unclasped and the falcon no longer confined. Other badges often

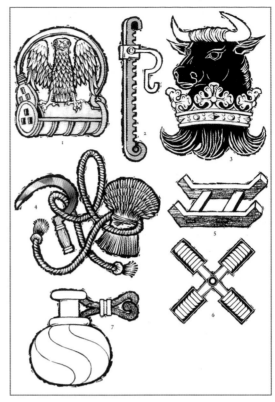

1. *Falcon and fetterlock badge of Richard Plantagenet, duke of York.*
2. *The de Vere cranket device.*
3. *The black bull's head of Hastings.*
4. *Sir Walter Hungerford's sickle and garb device.*
5. *Drag badge of the Lord Stourton.*
6. *Mill sail device of the Lords Willoughby.*
7. *De Vere's bottle with a blue cord.*

alluded to a name or title: a bottle with a blue cord was another de Vere badge, *de verre* being 'of glass'.

Muster rolls and writs of array provide many examples of livery badges which are roughly sketched in the margins alongside details of the troops pledged by a magnate to fight in a campaign. Many badges were simply charges taken from a shield of arms (the white lion of Mowbray, for example) while others were adopted for reasons that are no longer apparent. Typical are the mill-sail device of the lords Willoughby, the gold 'drag' (sledge) of the lords Stourton, the black bull's head of Hastings, the 'firy cresset' (fire-basket) of the Holland dukes of Exeter and various stylised *knots*, the most familiar being that of the lords Stafford. During the political crisis caused by Henry VI's insanity, Humphrey Stafford, 1st duke of

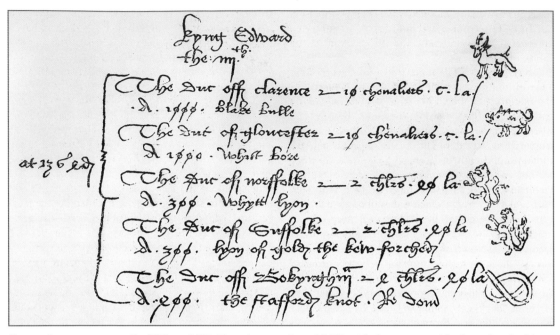

Extract from a muster roll of Edward IV's French campaign of 1475 with the magnates' badges sketched in the margin.

Buckingham, was rumoured in January 1454 to have ordered two thousand badges with the Stafford knot to be made for distribution among his followers.

So familiar were the livery badges of the medieval establishment that they sometimes become the source of ribaldry. The unpopular William de la Pole, duke of Suffolk, who was beheaded at sea in 1450 and whose livery badge was an 'ape clogge' (a leg restraint), was referred to contemptuously as 'Jack Napes' in contemporary broadsheets – hence 'jackanapes', a pert, vulgar, apish little fellow.

Perhaps the best known historical reference to livery badges is in the prophetic rhyme imprudently circulated by William Collingbourn, sometime sheriff of Wiltshire and Dorset, prior to 1483:

> The Cat, the Rat, and Lovel our Dog
> Doe rule all England, under the Hog.
> The crooke backt bore the way hath found
> To root our roses from the ground;
> Both flower and bud will he confound.
> Till king of beasts the same be crown'd:
> And then the dog, the cat, and rat,
> Shall in his trough feed and be fat.

The hog was Richard of Gloucester, later Richard III, whose badge was a white boar (Gloucester's pursuivant was called *Blanc Sanglier*); the cat was

Sir William Catesby, whose badge was a white cat spotted with black and wearing a gold collar; the rat was Sir Richard Ratcliff; and the dog was Francis Lord Lovel, whose device was a silver wolf-dog (*lupellus* – an allusion to his name). The roses were, of course, the members of the royal house whom Gloucester was alleged to have eliminated. Inevitably, Collingbourn was arrested and executed.

The military significance of livery badges is evident in the tradition which tells how the earl of Warwick, on the mist-shrouded field of Barnet (1471), mistook the earl of Oxford's badge, a silver star, for the Yorkist silver rose *en soleil*, and ordered his men to charge at Oxford's contingent, believing them to be royal troops:

> The envious mist so much deceived the sight,
> That where eight hundred men, which valiant
> Oxford brought,
> Wore comets on their coats, great Warwick's
> force, which thought
> They had King Edward's been, which so with
> suns were drest,
> First made their shot at them, who, by their
> friends distrest,
> Constrained were to fly, being scatter'd here
> and there.
> Michael Drayton, *The Polyalbion* (1613)

As a consequence Warwick was slain, Oxford fled the field 'and thereafter befell Tewkesbury, the murder of Henry VI, and the destruction of the House of Lancaster'.

Many badges were translated into CRESTS by those of 'tournament rank'. Sir Walter de Hungerford, for example, combined his livery badge of a sickle with the *garb* (wheatsheaf) badge of the Peverels when he married the co-heiress of Thomas Peverel. Hungerford's seal of 1432 shows both devices combined and borne as a crest: *A Garb between two Sickles*. The green wyvern crest of the Herbert earls of Pembroke (still in use today) derives from the medieval livery badge which is described as 'a dragon grene' in the records of the College of Arms.

From the fifteenth century badges also began to be introduced into coats of arms as SUPPORTERS, though their use was capricious and was not systemised until the sixteenth century. It is likely that the notion of armorial supporters, which at that time were invariably beasts, originated in the early practice of filling the interstices of SEALS with decorative creatures which appeared to 'support' the shield of arms. By the end of the fifteenth century many magnate families had accumulated a number of beast badges and, wishing to display them, placed them in coats of arms where they appear to be 'supporting' the shield (*see* BEASTS (HERALDIC)).

Liveries

Livery badges were worn on uniforms of the livery colours by domestic and military retainers: the men of Richard Nevill, earl of Warwick, wore (in 1458) 'Rede jakettys with whyte raggyd staves upon them', while those of John Mowbray, duke of Norfolk (d. 1476), wore their 'whytt lyon' badges on liveries of 'Blewe and tawny, blew on the leffte syde and both dark colors'. Retinues of the house of Lancaster wore liveries of white and blue and those of York blue and murrey (mulberry). It is interesting to note that the livery colours did not necessarily correspond with the tinctures of an armiger's shield of arms: the Mowbray arms were red and white (*Gules* [red] *a Lion rampant Argent* [white]), while the liveries were 'blewe and tawny'. Similarly, Lord Hastings' liveries were purple and blue, but his arms were white and black (*Argent a Maunch* [sleeve] *Sable*).

Different ranks of retainer were often distinguished by the quality and quantity of cloth they received as livery. The careful budgeting, bulk purchases and precise accounting needed to cater for numerous regular recipients did not leave stocks of spares for casual distribution. The number of liveried retainers could easily be extended in time of crisis to include those with few or no ties on a temporary basis, perhaps more commonly through the distribution of badges than the provision of uniforms. Thus in 1454 Humphrey Stafford, duke of Buckingham, was reported to have commissioned two thousand Stafford knots 'for what end your wit will construe'.

The widespread use of uniforms for domestic and military purposes is reflected in the accounts of the medieval textile industry. In 1409, for example, the Castle Combe estate in Wiltshire passed to the medieval entrepreneur Sir John Fastolf whose patronage helped to establish an impressive textile industry along the banks of the local stream. Fastolf succeeded in securing substantial orders for the local red and white cloth for, among others, 'the great livery of the lord beyond the sea' (the duke of Clarence), and these continued from the invasion of France in 1415 until his retirement from military service in 1440. 'For the space of 22 years or more,' William of Worcester records, 'Sir John bought every year to the value of more than £100 of red and white cloth of his tenants in Castle Combe. In this manner, he divided the rents and profits of his manors . . . among his tenants and clothiers of Castle Combe, and his doing so was one of the principal causes of the augmentation of the common wealth and store of the said town and of the new buildings raised in it.'

Of course, it is unreasonable to assume that all those who used livery badges for domestic or military purposes were able to provide every member of their retinues with uniforms of individual design and specially commissioned cloth. The provision of clothing (*livery*) was a contractual obligation for those whose households included indentured retainers, but for those of lesser degree a cloth or tin badge, affixed to a jack or sleeve, had to suffice.

Livery Flags

By the fifteenth century mustering and rallying functions were performed by *livery flags*: notably the *standard* and *guidon*. The standard bore, on a background of the livery colours, the various badges familiar to retinues from a magnate's estates, together with a motto and the national device: in England, the red cross of St George. The medieval English standard was usually 2.4m (8ft) long and about 0.6m (2ft) wide, though in the sixteenth century the Tudor heralds determined that flags of specific lengths should be prescribed to different ranks of the nobility. Also known as the *ancient*, maintenance of the standard was the responsibility of an officer of that name. The guidon was a small version of the standard, carried before a troop of retained men and essential as a rallying point in battle. It too was composed of the livery colours and bore one (or sometimes two) badges but no motto.

Royal Badges

Numerous badges have been adopted or inherited by British sovereigns and may be found in the glass and fabric of many royal palaces and castles, including those of magnates who once enjoyed (or anticipated) royal patronage.

Henry II used the broom plant (*Planta genista*), which is clearly a pun on the name Plantagenet, as did Richard I who also used the star and crescent device later adopted by King John. Both badges were used by Henry III and by Edward I who also inherited a golden rose device from Eleanor of Provence. Edward II adopted a golden castle (for Castile) and Edward III used many badges of which a sunburst, a tree stock (for Woodstock), a falcon and an ostrich feather were particularly favoured. Richard II used all of these, but his favourite badge was the ubiquitous white hart which he inherited from his mother, Joan of Kent.

The Lancastrian Henry IV used a monogram of esses (*see* COLLARS), a fire-basket (*cresset*), a red rose and the silver swan of Bohun, each on liveries of white and blue. Henry V used the silver ostrich feather, a chained heraldic antelope with the motto 'Dieu et Mon Droit' and a chained swan. Henry VI adopted the antelope and added a spotted heraldic panther to the royal bestiary.

Edward IV's Yorkist badges included the *falcon and fetterlock* (see above), the *sun in splendour*, the white rose and the white lion of March, with liveries of blue and murrey (mulberry). At various times he also used the black bull of Clarence and the black dragon of Ulster and, following his marriage with the Lancastrian Elizabeth Woodville, he adopted a red and white rose *en soleil* (surrounded by the rays of the sun). Richard III used the Yorkist badges to which he added his legendary white boar. (For further information on the white and red rose badges of York and Lancaster *see* WARS OF THE ROSES.)

The Tudors, with their white and green liveries, introduced the portcullis of the Beauforts, the red dragon, the silver greyhound and the TUDOR ROSE, a political combination of the Lancastrian and Yorkist roses. Henry VII also used a crowned hawthorn bush, with the cipher HR, to commemorate his exploits at Bosworth Field (1485).

(*See also* ARMORY, CYPHERS, REBUS *and* ROYAL ARMS)

BAILEY *or* WARD The defended outer enclosure of a castle. A bailey (or ward) is often described as a COURT or courtyard, though, strictly speaking, a court was an open space entirely surrounded by buildings, which many baileys are not. Most castles had at least one bailey for it was impossible to accommodate all the necessary ancillary offices within a single tower or KEEP. In the earliest motte and bailey castles (*see* MOTTE), the keep was occupied by the lord while barracks, stables, workshops and store-houses were located within a bailey. Almost invariably, a lord eventually built more comfortable quarters for his household in the bailey, while retaining the keep as a final refuge, and the garrison was removed to a second or outer bailey, also known as a *base court*. The majority of castles therefore have two baileys: a strongly fortified inner bailey containing the lord's chambers, great hall, chapel, lodgings and domestic offices, and an outer bailey in which the ancillary buildings were located and in which the day-to-day activity of a garrison took place. Both baileys would be accessible on horseback and were often separated by a ditch or moat with a drawbridge. The inner and outer baileys at Warkworth Castle were separated by a late fourteenth-century collegiate church, the connecting passage passing beneath the (unfinished) quire to provide a dramatic entrance to the inner bailey and its spectacular Great Keep.

While no two castles are the same, they are sometimes defined by the disposition of their baileys which may be classified as sequential, multiple or concentric. While this is a useful classification it is not entirely reliable. The type of bailey was often dictated by the topography of a particular site, as at Chepstow Castle where the lower, middle and upper baileys are confined within a narrow, cliff-top site, and at Carreg Cennen where an outer ward provided additional defence on those sides of the castle which were not protected by the vertical cliff-face to the south. Chepstow is an example of a castle with sequential baileys that were arranged so that each presented a further obstacle to attackers, as is Montgomery Castle though this is now in a ruinous condition. Several castles occupy earlier Roman sites and these may have determined the disposition of their baileys: at Carisbrooke Castle, for example, the Normans raised a massive rampart over the walls of the original Roman fort to form a bailey with a lofty MOTTE in one corner (the castle and its two Norman baileys are encircled by a stone-faced Elizabethan rampart).

Multiple baileys were added for convenience, or where additional protection was needed for functional buildings such as stabling and workshops (*see* Barnard Castle *below*). As the term suggests, concentric baileys were constructed one within the other, as at Harlech

Each building phase of Chepstow Castle was designed to take advantage of its position on a natural limestone ridge. Protected to the north by a vertical cliff rising from the River Wye, each of the castle's sequential baileys presented a further obstacle to attackers.

and Beaumaris Castles, where inner and outer wards were incorporated in the original designs, and Caerphilly, which has a concentric core of inner and middle wards with further wards located on an island reached by drawbridges and on a series of platforms formed behind a broad dam (*see* CONCENTRIC CASTLES). Middleham is effectively a concentric castle though it was not originally planned as such and, unlike true concentric castles, its core is not a courtyard but a massive twelfth-century keep. This is surrounded on four sides by an open courtyard and a rectangular thirteenth-century curtain wall with abutting fourteenth-century buildings. This inner ward was spanned by two footbridges that connected lodgings in the south and west ranges with the Great Hall in the keep. It is likely that there was an outer bailey at Middleham, though nothing of this remains other than the line of a ditch on the south side of the castle. Supporting evidence comes from a survey of the castle in 1538 which describes a wall 91m (100yd) long from the present gatehouse to 'the old drawe brige on the est side of the Castell' and, within it, 'stables with garners above, slaughter housys, housys for the powtre and the smithy with other housys of office'.

White Castle in south Wales was originally surrounded by an outer ward with earth and timber defences dating from the twelfth century. In the thirteenth century the northern quadrant of this area was reconstructed with stone walls, towers and a gatehouse to form a sequential bailey and the entire castle was effectively turned through 180 degrees so that it was approached through the bailey while the original (southern) entrance was relegated to the rear (*see* ENCEINTE). A geophysical survey of White Castle has established that there was once a very large rectangular building on the north-western side of the outer bailey, measuring 35 by 20m (115 by 66ft). This was almost certainly an aisled barn where the produce of the manor was processed and stored. Typically, there are also traces of several timber buildings, including a latrine, the slots for the wooden seat having survived in a recess in the curtain wall.

Single-bailey castles were either modest strongholds, such as Dolwyddelan and Dolbadarn, native Welsh castles comprising a walled courtyard and keep, or castles such as Grosmont and Skenfrith which were compact and moated and, with White Castle, formed a defensive combination guarding one of the major land routes from England into Wales (*see* THREE CASTLES, THE). However, a small number of single-bailey castles were of sufficient size to accommodate the ancillary activities that were otherwise found in an outer bailey. At Bodiam Castle, for example, one of the last medieval castles to be built (1388), the armoury, stables, huge storerooms and even accommodation for manorial labourers were all contained within the castle's elegant walls (*see* COURT AND COURTYARD).

Several TOWER-HOUSES appear not to have a bailey of any description though these may originally have been at some remove from the castle: at Nunney, for example, there is evidence of an embanked bailey for outbuildings beyond the moat to the north-west.

For the most part baileys tended to be of manageable proportions with perimeter walls that could be defended by modest numbers of men. Conwy Castle in north Wales was designed with an inner ward that was effectively an enclosed courtyard, surrounded by state chambers that could be isolated from the remainder of the castle and defended independently by a comparatively small garrison. At Kidwelly Castle a strongly fortified semicircular outer ward encloses an inner ward on three sides. There is no keep and, unusually, the inner ward is square with uniform corner towers. It is likely that there was a considerable interval between the construction of the inner ward, with its hall, solar and domestic offices, and the outer curtain walls and formidable KEEP-GATEHOUSE.

In several castles there is evidence that wards were enlarged periodically in order to accommodate increasing numbers of retainers and the activities associated with royal and magnate households. Corfe Castle had three baileys: the inner ward, in which were located the massive keep, great chamber, presence chamber, kitchens and other domestic offices and a small garden; the west bailey, which was essentially a self-contained prison block; and the outer (south-west) bailey of 1207 which was extended in 1235, when a defensive ditch (the Great Ditch) was excavated, and again in *c.* 1280 to form a large ward enclosing the steep hillside. On each occasion a stone cross-wall was built across the slope, while the last phase included the construction of mural towers, an outer gatehouse and bridge.

Barnard Castle provides an interesting example of a castle with multiple wards that outgrew their usefulness. The castle occupies a small plateau on a cliff-top high above the River Tees and in 1095 comprised a bailey with a timber gate-tower, hall and curtain wall. By 1154 plans for extending the castle and the laying-out of a town were already completed and by *c.* 1170 a series of outer wards, with walls, towers and gateways, had been constructed. These comprised the inner ward, now with a stone curtain wall, gatehouse, hall and keep; a middle ward, protected by a gatehouse and outer ditch; a 'town ward', with a number of service buildings and a gatehouse providing access from the adjacent town; and a large outer ward in which were the castle farm and St Margaret's chapel. When the castle changed hands in the fourteenth century the manorial farm and outer ward were abandoned (except for the chapel) while many of the activities that had been carried out in the town ward were transferred to a large building constructed in the middle ward. In this way the castle was reduced largely to the inner and middle wards where the defences were improved, a wet moat dug across the east face of the middle ward and a drawbridge provided across it. At the same time access to the inner ward was drastically altered and made more tortuous. From this it is clear that the disposition of the multiple wards at Barnard Castle did not meet the needs and aspirations of the new owner, Thomas Beauchamp, who required both domestic comfort and a considerable strengthening of the castle's defences.

For the most part large baileys were rarely provided with stone walls, though there are several notable exceptions: at Beeston and Dunstanburgh Castles, for example, the walls enclose vast outer baileys. Several of these castles have been described (somewhat spuriously) as castles of livery and maintenance because their large outer wards were built specifically to accommodate large numbers of retainers (*see* LIVERY AND MAINTENANCE, CASTLES OF). (*See also* COURT AND COURTYARD)

BAILEY WALL An inner wall within a curtain wall.

BAILIFF (i) A sheriff's officer appointed to execute writs and to distrain goods (*see also* SHERIFF). (ii) An estate manager, subordinate to a STEWARD (especially in the context of a manorial estate, *see* MANOR).

BAKEHOUSE *see* KITCHENS

BALDRIC Introduced in the mid-fourteenth century, a belt slung across the hips from which hung on one side the SWORD and on the other the MISERICORDE (*see* ARMOUR).

BALINGER A type of galley used for coastal patrols.

BALL-FLOWER ORNAMENTATION Architectural ornamentation in the form of a globular flower, partly opened to reveal a small sphere, and set repetitively in hollow mouldings. Ball-flower ornamentation is a particular characteristic of early fourteenth-century GOTHIC ARCHITECTURE.

BALLISTA Originally a Roman stone-throwing machine, in contradistinction to a *catapulta* which shot arrows or bolts. By the early medieval period the words had become interchangeable (*see* SIEGES). Confusingly, the Greek-derived word 'catapult' continued in use throughout the Middle Ages as a general term for siege artillery.

BALLOK DAGGER *see* WEAPONS AND HARNESS

BANNER *see* FLAGS

BANNERET The rank of nobility between knight bachelor and baron, and the highest degree of knighthood in the medieval period. Originally the term meant a chief feudal tenant (or lesser baron) as distinct from the knight bachelor. In the Middle Ages a knight banneret was permitted to lead troops in battle under his own banneret or small banner (*see* FLAGS). The degree of knight banneret appears to have been based on personal distinction, one kind being for a deed of valour done in the king's presence, the other being a request for promotion by the knight himself to the commander of the army. If the applicant was judged to be worthy of preferment, the heralds were called upon to cut the tails from his triangular or swallow-tailed pennon, thereby

transforming it into a small banner. Sir John Froissart, the great medieval chronicler, tells of just such an incident that took place before the battle of Najera in 1367. Sir John Chandos, a knight under the command of Edward, Prince of Wales (the Black Prince), was raised to the status of knight banneret by Pedro of Castile who removed the tails from his pennon. Sir John, on being handed his new 'banner', paraded it in front of his troops exhorting them to defend it well. The dignity of banneret gradually fell into disuse, the last occasion on which it was confirmed being at the battle of Pinkie in 1547 when Somerset, the Lord Protector, advanced Sir Francis Bryen and two of his comrades to the rank of banneret.
(*See also* KNIGHTHOOD AND CHIVALRY, ORIGINS OF)

BANQUETTE An infantry firing level.

BARBETTE Breastwork of a battery constructed so that guns may fire over it without the need for embrasures.

BARBICAN The term is used to describe both an outer extension to a GATEHOUSE and a defensive fore-work strategically placed in advance of a main gateway. Usually dating from the thirteenth and fourteenth centuries, both types of barbican were intended to increase the number of obstacles that a besieging force had to overcome when attacking a gatehouse (considered to be the weakest point in a castle's defences). They were designed to keep an enemy at a distance and, by dictating his approach, to expose him to attack from archers within the castle walls.

The most common type of barbican is a walled passage projecting from a gatehouse, often with corner turrets and unroofed so that attackers trapped inside the KILLING GROUND could be shot at from above. (This type of barbican should not be confused with a similar roofed structure or FOREBUILDING attached to a keep.) There are fine examples at Alnwick, Arundel and Warwick Castles, while Walmgate Bar at York is the only surviving example in England of a barbican protecting a city gate. One of the most impressive barbicans is that at Lewes Castle, which was added to an earlier rectangular gate-tower in the fourteenth century, with corbelled round towers at the corners, a machicolated parapet above the centre pointed arch and the whole faced with knapped flints.

The barbican at Newcastle-upon-Tyne, known as the Black Gate, was constructed by Henry III in 1247. It consists of two D-shaped towers set back to

back on each side of an entrance passage defended by a drawbridge over an outer ditch, a portcullis, folding gates and a murder hole in the vault. Set at right angles to the castle gatehouse, its position enabled archers to cover the entire length of the moat and provided a right-angled passage and open yard between the two gates to impede assailants should they succeed in taking the barbican gate.

The small, semicircular enclosure at Pembroke Castle is typical of the type of barbican platform which was strategically placed in front of a gatehouse so that attackers were required to make a right-angled turn from an outer gate in a confined space, thereby exposing their unprotected right flank to defending archers.

The second type of barbican is far more diverse, both in its form and in the ingenuity of its builders. The approach to the inner ward at Carreg Cennen Castle was dictated by the construction of an extraordinarily elaborate barbican consisting of a long, sloping ramp along the north side of the castle ditch. The first section of the barbican was set at right angles to the main axis so that an attacker approaching it from the outer gate would be forced to turn on to the ramp

One of the most impressive barbicans is that at Lewes Castle, Sussex, which was added to an earlier rectangular gate-tower in the fourteenth century, with corbelled round towers at the corners, a machicolated parapet above the centre pointed arch and the whole faced with knapped flints.

in full view of archers in the north-east tower. The next section of the ramp, over 30m (100ft) in length, was heavily defended by two pivoting drawbridges, the lower bridge protected by a small gate-tower and the upper by the formidable Middle Gate-Tower where the ramp turned again at right angles and crossed a third drawbridge before entering the gate passage of the castle's principal gatehouse.

Some barbicans were separated from the gatehouse by means of a drawbridge or defensive causeway traversing a moat, as at Goodrich and Bodiam Castles. The fourteenth-century barbican at Goodrich Castle retains only the lower section of wall, but its semicircular (or 'half-moon') ground plan and spur-moat illustrate clearly how an attacker would have been compelled to capture and pass over two drawbridges, set at right angles to each other above steep-sided dry moats, in addition to negotiating a confined gate passage containing a series of gates, portcullises and lateral loopholes, before reaching the gatehouse. The barbican drawbridge pit is set within the outer part of the gate passage and a small porter's lodge commands a view of the gate on the south side by means of a narrow, angled slit in the outer wall. From the barbican the gatehouse is reached by a sloping causeway over the moat, with a bridge of two spans separated by a deep drawbridge pit.

Farleigh Hungerford Castle provides a further example of a barbican that was added to an earlier castle. The fourteenth-century Inner Gate consists of two round-fronted towers with a paved passage (only 2.1m (6½ft) wide) between them. When an outer ward was constructed in c. 1420, a barbican was added to provide additional protection for the gate and the drawbridge which spanned the ditch between the inner and outer wards. The barbican had a semi-octagonal front and was connected with the original gate-towers by two walls, each 3m (10ft) thick, that crossed the ditch and were roughly bonded into the earlier work.

Bodiam, one of the last castles to be built in medieval England (1388), is now approached from the north by means of a wooden bridge that crosses the wide moat via an artificial octagonal island or 'platform'. Originally a wooden causeway linked this island with a drawbridge on the west bank so that an enemy would have been exposed on its right flank to archers on the castle's battlements. Turning through 90 degrees, a removable timber bridge (possibly a drawbridge) provided access from the island to a two-storey, crenellated barbican and a third bridge (also removable) that linked the barbican with the castle's gatehouse.

Chepstow Castle's barbican was added in the early thirteenth century in order to protect the potentially vulnerable west end of the castle. It was effectively a heavily defended outer ward, separated from the upper bailey by a rock-cut ditch and drawbridge which, prior to the construction of the barbican, were the outer defences of the castle. The barbican's curtain wall curves in an arc from the rectangular south-west tower of the upper bailey to the river cliff with a circular tower guarding the angle and a fine, three-storey upper gatehouse to the west. The battlements have survived and are provided with arrow loops, while a series of holes in the exterior wall suggest that there was also a wooden fighting gallery (see HOARDING). The D-shaped south-west tower, which appears to have been added as an afterthought, had three floors, each equipped with a battery of cruciform arrow loops. The absence of fireplace openings and other domestic offices indicates that the tower was intended purely for military purposes.

Undoubtedly the most spectacular barbican in Britain is at Caerphilly Castle where a series of revetted and buttressed earthworks, over 300m (330yd) in length, hold back the waters of an artificial lake surrounding the castle and collectively provide a formidable outer defence. Dating from the late thirteenth century, the south dam platform (1268–71) and the north dam platform (1277–90) incorporate three outer gatehouses, sluice-gates and a watermill, all protected by a moat, curtain walls and flanking towers. Before the north dam platform was built, there was a single outer gatehouse at the southern (town) end of the south platform. This meant that, were an attacking force to capture the gatehouse, it would have to fight its way along the south dam platform in full view of the castle's garrison before attempting to cross the inner moat to the east gatehouse of the castle itself (see MOATS AND WATER DEFENCES).

A number of castles have heavily defended enclosures instead of gatehouses and these are often described as barbicans: at Conwy Castle, for example, the western barbican is located between a fairly insubstantial outer gate and a gate passage through the curtain wall of the outer ward. Heavily defended by turrets and machicolated crenellations, the west barbican at Conwy was an integral element of the castle's original design, unlike that at Beaumaris (see above) which was added to the south gatehouse to compensate for the inadequacies of the gate passage which was never completed.

A detached barbican which is located at some remove from the main body of a castle should more

The west barbican at Conwy Castle.

accurately be described as an *outer gatehouse*: at White Castle, for example, a substantial outer gatehouse was the only means of access to the outer BAILEY. Clearly, its principal purpose was to defend the bailey rather than the castle gatehouse and this seems to confirm that the bailey was added (in 1256) as a defended enclosure where armies in the field could camp without fear of a surprise attack (*see* ENCEINTE).

BARBOTE An alternative name for BEVOR.
(*See also* ARMOUR *and* HELMETS)

BARBUTE Fifteenth-century Italian helmet with a T-shaped opening for the mouth and eyes, possibly developed from the BASCINET by extending the sides and back downwards to obviate the need for a CAMAIL.
(*See also* ARMOUR *and* HELMETS)

BARDING *or* BARD A general term to describe both the armour and the trappings of a horse. Early

barding consisted of a heavy covering of mail with four 'skirts' to protect the animal's legs. Later horse armour consisted of a series of plates protecting the head and neck to which, at a later date, were added the *peytral* (covering the chest), *flanchards* (protecting the sides) and the *crupper* (covering the hindquarters) of leather, wood or plate.
(*See also* CAPARISON *and* HORSES AND HORSE-HARNESS)

BARMKIN (i) A Scottish term, applied also to some English border strongholds, for a wall enclosing a courtyard.
(ii) The small courtyard of a PELE TOWER. Most pele towers had an outer enclosure of some sort, though stone curtain walls are rare.

BARON The word itself is of uncertain origin: it was introduced into England following the Anglo-Norman Conquest of 1066 to identify the 'man' (vassal) of a great lord, or of the Conqueror himself, though prior to the Conquest a *barony* was simply a chief's domain. In Ireland a *barony* was a medieval division of a county, corresponding to the English hundred. Following the Conquest, tenants-in-chief of the king below the rank of EARL were often referred to as barons. From the thirteenth century the title appears to have been reserved for those magnates summoned by writ to parliament, greater barons being those who were summoned by direct writ to the king's council and lesser barons those summoned through the county sheriffs. The style itself was introduced by Richard II in 1387. It is now the fifth and lowest rank of the British peerage and the Life Peerage Act of 1958 enabled the crown to create non-hereditary peerages with the rank and style of baron.

(*See also* PEERAGE, THE)

BARONET An hereditary rank of the British peerage created by James I in 1611 with the objective of raising money to support his troops in Ulster. The first recipients paid £1,095 for the style Sir and Lady (or Dame) and precedence above knights.

BARONS' WARS, THE (i) The conflict between King John and the barons (1215–17). The king's failure to honour the terms of MAGNA CARTA provoked the barons to offer the English crown to Louis, son of Philip Augustus of France (the future Louis VIII). In May 1216 Louis landed in Kent while John was campaigning in the north and Midlands. The king died in October of the same year and his son was crowned Henry III (1216–72). Henry immediately reaffirmed his commitment to Magna Carta and the tide turned in favour of the royalists. The barons were defeated at Lincoln (20 May 1217) and the capture of French supply ships off Sandwich forced Louis to acknowledge the treaty of Kingston-upon-Thames (1217) which granted a general amnesty to the rebels. Shortly afterwards Louis was paid 10,000 marks to leave England.

(ii) The civil war between Henry III and the barons (1264–7) led by Simon de Montfort, earl of Leicester (*c.* 1208–65). The barons' objective was a limitation of royal powers, a cause that was aided by the state of Henry's financial affairs in the 1250s. Not only had he committed himself to raising additional revenue for the papal crusade, but he desperately needed money for his campaigning in France and Wales. When Henry made further demands in support of his brother's claim to the Sicilian throne, the barons insisted on political reforms in return for their co-operation. They demanded that the king should consult them regularly on matters of state rather than his own counsellors and they secured the appointment of a joint committee, comprising twelve of their number and twelve royal nominees, which in 1258 issued the *Provisions of Oxford*. These sought to limit the king's power requiring, for example, that there should be a council of fifteen to supervise the government and that the council together with twelve elected nobles should meet as a parliament three times a year. Henry reluctantly accepted the Provisions but, finding them irksome, referred them to the French king who advised that they were not enforceable. In April 1261 Henry's financial problems eased and he persuaded the Pope to absolve him of his oath to support the Provisions of Oxford. He declared that the barons who opposed him were rebels and on 13 May 1264 Simon de Montfort repudiated his feudal oath. Although his forces were outnumbered, de Montfort defeated and captured the king at the battle of Lewes (14 May) and on the following day the *Mise of Lewis* was signed. This set out the terms for peace, including the reversion to rebel lords of all castles captured by the royalists and the release of rebel prisoners. Prince Edward (the future Edward I) and Henry of Almaine were held hostage as a guarantee for the royalists' good faith. De Montfort forced Henry to convene parliaments in June 1264 and early in 1265 but the barons quarrelled and Gilbert de Clare, earl of Gloucester (1243–95), and Roger Mortimer (*c.* 1231–82) joined the king. At the brief but bloody battle of Evesham (4 August 1265) the royal forces, led by Edward, defeated the barons and killed de Montfort. Peace was agreed on 16 September 1265 but baronial resistance continued, notably at the siege of Kenilworth (June–December 1266) and the Cinque Ports. It was not until 1267 that Edward finally overcame the last vestiges of resistance in the Isle of Ely. Despite their defeat, many of the demands made by the barons were granted by Edward I as a consequence of the *Dictum of Kenilworth* (31 October 1266). This was a declaration of terms agreed by Henry III and the barons by which the acts of Simon de Montfort were declared void and the king's powers restored. It also set out ways by which the lands that had been seized by the crown might legally be recovered by the dissident barons, who have since been known as the *disinherited*.

BARONY A feudal estate held in chief of the king or of another great lord.

BARREL HELM *see* GREAT HELM

BARREL ROOF *see* ROOFS (TIMBER)

BARREL VAULT *see* VAULTING

BARRIERS, THE *see* TOURNAMENTS

BARS The gatehouses in York's city walls (*see* TOWN WALLS).

BARTISAN *also* **BARTIZAN** A projecting gallery on a wall face or (erroneously) an overhanging, crenellated turret projecting from an angle at the top of a tower. The term does not appear in any dictionary before 1800 and was first used by Sir Walter Scott to describe a corbelled turret (*see* ANGLE TURRET). Thereafter, it was adopted by Victorian antiquaries and remains in common currency even though its use depends on a mis-reading by Scott of *bertisene* which is more correctly associated with the etymology of *bratticing*, a temporary wooden HOARDING.

BASCINET, BACINET *or* **BASINET** Characteristic head armour worn in the second half of the fourteenth century and the early fifteenth century. It probably developed from the plate armour reinforcement to the mail COIF which was worn beneath the GREAT HELM in the early fourteenth century. By the 1340s it was worn without the great helm and with a visor which was either hinged at the temples or attached to a single pivot at the forehead, forming a long point or 'snout' which gave rise to the terms *hounskull* and *pig-faced* bascinet.
(*See also* ARMOUR *and* HELMETS).

BASCULE *see* DRAWBRIDGE

BASE COURT An outer BAILEY.

BASELARD *see* WEAPONS AND HARNESS

BAS-RELIEF Sculpture or carving in low relief.

BASTARD FEUDALISM The term given by historians to the relationship between medieval retainers and their lords, a relationship which allowed those lords to wield political power in their localities appropriate to their rank. Increasingly, from the mid-twelfth century, service was no longer obtained through the granting of land: but through money payments (*see* FEUDAL SYSTEM).

In England the successful governance of the kingdom came to depend on the system. Parliament met only occasionally, and when not in session the sovereign needed to secure the cooperation of the medieval establishment through which he ruled. This was achieved through the appointment of the lords and gentry to public office and through an informal system which relied on indentured service and a sense of obligation to a superior. The sovereign's principal subjects thereby enjoyed considerable political autonomy. Their power rested not on lineage but on the acquisition of wealth and influence, and was reflected in the number and quality of men at their command. They created retinues of indentured servants, and others whose support was based on patronage (*see* AFFINITY), who were employed to manage a lord's estates, to hold public office on his behalf and to settle his legal and financial affairs. In time of war, or in defence of their superior, these men were summoned to array. Indeed, many of the more senior members of magnate households were themselves gentlemen of substance, capable of raising significant numbers of indentured retainers in their own right. Provincial political life revolved around these affinities and a magnate was expected to satisfy the aspirations of his followers. When he succeeded, his reputation (his 'worship') was enhanced and he thereby attracted more and better men to his service. Royal favour, and the ability to bestow offices, pensions and promotions on his followers, was therefore essential to the expansion of a lord's influence.
(*See also* LIVERY AND MAINTENANCE)

BASTARDY Care should be exercised regarding the historical concept of bastardy and the use of special devices to denote illegitimacy in coats of arms (*see* DISTINCTION, MARKS OF). Such devices were often intended to indicate not that an armiger was personally illegitimate but that he was not in the legitimate line of succession.

Strictly speaking, a bastard was the base child of gentle or noble blood but the term is applied more generally to an illegitimate child. Bastardy was a fairly public fact of life in medieval England. It is not unusual, therefore, to find references in documents and monuments to a noble illegitimate half-brother who was equally as distinguished as any of the legitimate line. A bastard was a child born out of wedlock or of a couple whose marriage was later found to be invalid. Under the law a bastard was not of inferior status but, since he was 'the son of no one' (*filius nullius*), he could not be heir to his parents, neither could he inherit property, even if he were acknowledged as their child. (One strange consequence of this principle was that the illegitimate son of a villein was legally incapable of inheriting his father's status and therefore became a free man on his father's death.) There was also a presumption at Common Law that children borne by a wife were fathered by her husband and were therefore legitimate. Because marriage was a sacrament, the validity or otherwise of a marriage was determined by Canon Law while questions of inheritance were brought before the secular courts to be determined according to the Common Law. Inevitably, the two systems sometimes contradicted one another. The Common Law, for example, held that children born out of wedlock could not be legitimated by the subsequent marriage of their parents, while Canon Law decreed that this could be so. Similarly, Canon Law held that, where a marriage was entered into 'in good faith' but was later found to be invalid, any children born prior to the nullification of the marriage were deemed to be legitimate. In such cases the Courts of Common Law would seek to establish only whether a child was born in or out of wedlock. The question of legitimacy was determined by the Church courts, even though the verdict may have been contrary to the principles of the Common Law.

BASTEL HOUSE *see* BASTLE

BASTIDE The Edwardian castles of Conwy (1282) and Caernarfon (1283–92) were CITADELS integrated within the defensive walls of the towns they protected (*see* TOWNS). This arrangement of castle and fortified town is often referred to as a *bastide*. Edward I's strategy of colonisation through the creation of Welsh PLANTATION TOWNS was clearly influenced by his experience in Gascony where, as duke of Aquitaine, he established more than fifty new towns (*bastides*) in the late thirteenth century. However, these were essentially administrative and commercial centres on strategic routes or near sensitive frontiers and were not necessarily fortified.

BASTION (i) A mural tower erected for purely defensive purposes, often semicircular or D-shaped with an open back and no interior accommodation. Strictly speaking, a semicircular bastion is termed a *demi-bastion* though in practice the terms appear to be interchangeable.
(ii) A triangular projection of masonry and rubble at the foot of a tower, constructed both as a buttress and to deter mining beneath the walls. The DRUM TOWERS of some medieval castles appear to be protected by bastions but are actually constructed on a square base, the triangular 'spurs' of which have a similar appearance (*see also* BATTER).
(iii) An angled projection of a post-medieval fortification from which defenders may observe the otherwise concealed area at the foot of the ramparts (*see* BULWARK *and* HORNWORK).

BASTIONED TRACE *see* TUDOR COASTAL FORTS

BASTIONETTES Small bastions which provide localised flanking cover.

BASTLE (*also* **BASTEL-HOUSE**) Warfare and an absence of central authority were endemic on the Scottish borders until the end of the seventeenth century. Many sixteenth- and seventeenth-century border farmsteads, especially those in north Northumberland, adopted a unique *bastle* design which afforded rapid protection to both stock and the inhabitants. Black Middens Bastle at Tarset in Northumberland is constructed of stone on two storeys. Cattle entered the ground floor through a door in the east gable while the upper room, which had a wooden floor and a fireplace at the west end, was illuminated by two small windows and was reached by means of an outside stair on the south wall.
(*See also* PELE TOWERS)

BATAILE *see* BATTLEFIELDS *and* WARFARE: CONDUCT OF

BATARDEAU A dam retaining water in a ditch.

BATHS *see* PLUMBING, WATER SUPPLY AND SANITATION

BATH STONE Oolitic limestone quarried in northern Wiltshire where it occurs in beds of up to 10m (11yd) depth. When quarried it is damp (with 'quarry-sap') and is easily cut and carved before being seasoned.

BATH, THE MOST HONOURABLE ORDER OF THE The premier meritorious Order of the Crown, established by George I on 18 May 1725, and modelled on 'a degree of knighthood which hath been denominated the Knighthood of the Bath' by Henry IV following his coronation in 1399. In the fifteenth century there was no 'Order of the Bath' in the same way as there was an Order of the Garter (*see* GARTER, THE MOST NOBLE ORDER OF THE). The medieval Knights of the Bath were not a defined and limited brotherhood but rather all those dubbed to knighthood using a particular ceremony. The designation 'of the Bath' acknowledged the ritual of purification undertaken by the knight-elect prior to receiving the accolade.

BATON SINISTER *see* DISTINCTION, MARKS OF

BATTER (i) A sloping masonry 'skirt' at the base of a tower to provide greater stability and to frustrate undermining.
(ii) The inward inclination from the perpendicular of a wall or REVETMENT. All eight flanking towers at Conwy Castle are gently, almost imperceptibly, battered towards the base in highly sophisticated masonry. As at Edwin Lutyens's wonderful Castle Drogo in Devon, some six centuries later, the battered walls of Conwy create an extraordinary sense of exaggerated perspective and increased height.

BATTERING RAM *see* RAM (BATTERING)

BATTERY A gun emplacement.

BATTLE (BATAILE) A division of a medieval army, usually one of three.

BATTLE AXE *see* WEAPONS AND HARNESS

BATTLEFIELDS Before the Norman Conquest battles were generally fought on high ground, often near well-established route-ways and fortified hill-top settlements. Much of our understanding of these early battles is derived from ninth-century chronicles which can be tantalisingly ambiguous so that many Anglo-Saxon sites have yet to be identified accurately. Most major battles of the Barons' Wars, the Wars of the Roses and the Civil War of the seventeenth century took place on the lowland plains to the west of the oolitic escarpment that runs from the Devon coast to Humberside. Documentary sources are usually confused and there is often conflicting evidence of what actually took place, much of it clouded by a variety of political perceptions.

With few exceptions medieval battles were fought during the campaigning season between May and October because of the logistical problems created by mud-churned tracks and swollen rivers. Generally, the advantage lay with a commander who was able to choose his site. Ideally this would present a variety of hazards to the oncoming enemy, who would be forced into a restricted space within which there would be little opportunity for manoeuvre, and an easily defended position, secure to the rear but providing a means of retreat if required. Senior commanders, magnates whose retinues were led by bannerets in their service, took up elevated positions from which they could direct the course of the battle. Each would have responsibility for a particular battalion, usually the *avant-guard*, the *bataile* or the *arriere-guard*. Baggage trains, consisting of supply wagons with

equipment and stores, were kept in the rear. Troops of hobelars, pikemen, archers and crossbowmen mustered beneath their lord's standard (the *ancient*) and followed his guidons into battle (*see* FLAGS). Field commanders, the bannerets who actually led these contingents into battle, were accompanied by a lieutenant whose responsibility it was to carry and maintain his master's personal banner. This flag (also called the *lieutenant*) represented the physical presence of a knight in the field and could never be relinquished without shame: 'The Lieutenant is to be saved before the Ancient . . .' (Shakespeare's *Othello*). Cavalry comprised mounted knights who were considered to be the élite corps of a medieval army. In the early Middle Ages, especially in France, archers and foot-soldiers simply prepared the way for the cavalry to participate in a knightly engagement not far removed from the ritual of the *tourné*. In the fourteenth century the efficiency of the longbow against the French cavalry was to have a lasting effect on military strategy (*see* ARCHERY). Nevertheless the medieval chivalric tradition of a mounted élite lasted into the present century and even now survives in the ceremonial pageantry of the Household Cavalry.

Medieval military campaigns were primarily concerned with attrition: destructive marches (*chevauchées*), raids and SIEGES. Full-scale battles were the exception and rarely proved decisive. It has been calculated that during the WARS OF THE ROSES, the thirty-two years of dynastic turbulence from the St Alban's incident in 1455 to the battle of Stoke in 1487, actual conflict occupied no more than thirteen weeks, the longest campaign (that of 1471 from Edward IV's landing to the battle of Tewkesbury) lasting only seven-and-a-half weeks. In Britain there have been comparatively few battles but innumerable skirmishes. The sites of these minor engagements are often overlooked and yet there exists a wealth of documentary evidence, particularly from the Civil Wars of 1642–51, which would enable the researcher not only to identify these lesser battlefields in the context of his own studies, but also to add further to the accumulated evidence of major campaigns.

The last true battle took place not on British soil but in the skies above southern England. Victory in the Battle of Britain (1940) secured command of the English Channel and the abandonment of Hitler's invasion plans. To the historian, the accurate recording of a pill-box is as significant as a thesis on Bosworth Field.

Any study of a battlefield must begin with the purchase of a large-scale map of the area and a visit.

Many battlefields remain evocative of the distant past, especially when visited in the same month and at the same time of day as that of the battle. Ancient churches in the vicinity of the battlefield should also be visited for it was there that the vanquished nobility were often laid to rest. Some battlefields, such as Bosworth Field (1485) near Market Bosworth in Leicestershire and Battle Abbey (1066) near Hastings in East Sussex, have official 'battle trails' with information boards and visitors' centres. Nearly all battlefields are located on private land but remain accessible through the network of footpaths and bridleways which may be identified from the Ordnance Survey 1:25000 'Explorer' maps, as may contours and other natural features which may otherwise be obscured by subsequent development.

BATTLE HAMMER *see* WAR HAMMER *and* WEAPONS AND HARNESS

BATTLEMENTS In medieval castles defence was conducted primarily from the wall-head and consequently WALL-WALKS (*alures*) with crenellated parapets are found in the earliest timber palisades of motte and bailey castles (*see* MOTTE) as well as in the defensive walls and TOWERS of later, stone-built fortifications. Curtain wall defence had three objectives: to harass the enemy and deter a direct assault on the wall; to make it as difficult as possible for the enemy to approach the base of a wall, especially with ladders or siege machines (*see* SIEGES); and to defend the BAILEY, should the enemy succeed in entering the castle.

CRENELS are the narrow gaps in a crenellated parapet through which defenders could shoot at an enemy, while MERLONS are the raised sections which shielded the defenders. Crenels were sometimes provided with hinged shutters for greater protection and the pivot holes in the adjacent merlons may still be in evidence. At Caernarfon Castle there is evidence that crenel shutters were held in vertical slots cut into the merlons. Merlons were of sufficient height to protect a man's head and considerably wider than the crenels. They were sometimes provided with LOOPHOLES and shallow EMBRASURES, while both crenels and merlons were finished with a coping. Inevitably a castle's crenellations are vulnerable to despoliation and natural erosion so that they may no longer have the appearance or proportions of the originals and the copings are almost invariably missing. They may also have been replaced with crenels which do not conform to the dimensions of the originals, while from the fifteenth century crenellations are found as decorative features on the walls of domestic buildings and churches. These are easily identified, being very much smaller than defensive crenellations and usually having crenels and merlons of equal size. In England there was a legal obligation to obtain a *licence to crenellate* before a castle could be built or a residence fortified (*see* CRENELLATIONS).

Rows of sockets (*see* PUTLOG HOLES) in the masonry immediately below the wall-walk or parapet were provided for the fitting of HOARDINGS, projecting timber galleries supported on joists and with sloping roofs; more substantial PENTISES, projecting wooden turrets or large, conical structures on towers; and *bretaches*, defensive wooden or stone structures protruding from a window part-way up a wall.

Hoardings enabled the 'blind' areas at the base of a wall to be defended by means of openings or trapdoors in the floor of the projecting gallery, similar in function to the very much more sophisticated (and permanent) stone-built MACHICOLATIONS of later castles. Most often found above gateways and on towers, machicolations were effectively embattled parapets which projected from the face of a wall on corbels, the gap between each corbel allowing defenders to observe, and defend, the vulnerable base of a wall. As with crenellations, machicolations may be found in several late medieval houses where their function is purely decorative. Timber hoardings and pentises were vulnerable to fire and to the ravages of the climate and none has survived, those which are now in evidence being modern replacements.

The stone walls of major castles were of considerable thickness with intra-mural passageways (*galleries*) reached by NEWEL STAIRS and providing access to a series of recesses (*see* EMBRASURES), the outer walls of which were pierced with LOOPHOLES and OILLETS for archers and crossbowmen and (from the fourteenth century) GUN PORTS for gunners (*see* FIREARMS and CANNON). The south curtain of Caernarfon Castle, Gwynedd, has two shooting galleries, one above the other, in the thickness of the walls; combined with the crenellated wall-walks and flanking towers, these must have provided one of the most formidable concentrations of 'fire-power' of any medieval castle. The Avranches Tower at Dover Castle in Kent, built in *c.* 1190, is sited at a vulnerable salient angle of the curtain wall which it covers with two intra-mural tiers of loopholes and a crenellated parapet. Each tier has sets of triple radiating embrasures sharing single loopholes, one embrasure at 90 degrees to the wall and two at

45 degrees on either side. There is a similar arrangement in the north-east curtain and King's gate at Caernarfon where, although only six openings are apparent from outside the castle, double that number of archers could discharge their bolts simultaneously. Not all arrangements appear to be so effective: at Caerphilly, the most innovative castle of its age, some lengths of wall had merlons that were too close together to allow for the lateral movement of a crossbow while the crenellations were so high that a longbow could only be used when standing back from the parapet. Perhaps, with its broad water defences, it was expected that the walls of Caerphilly would never be subjected to a close assault and so the battlements were designed specifically to accommodate archers shooting with raised trajectories over long distances.
(*See also* ARCHERY, GUN PORTS *and* SIEGES)

BAULK A strip of earth or turf separating areas of cultivation or retained between different parts of an archaeological excavation to facilitate the study of vertical sections.

BAWN A walled enclosure containing stables, storerooms, workshops, etc.

BAY (i) A section of wall between columns or buttresses or a division of a vaulted or timber roof.
(ii) A recess in a room, especially one formed by a projecting window (*see* WINDOWS).

BAYEUX TAPESTRY This is not a true tapestry but an enormously long piece of needlework comprising eight unequal sections of bleached linen embroidered with coloured wool. It is 69m (75yd) long and 50cm (20in) wide, and is apparently incomplete, though no part of the narrative is actually missing. The eight colours in which the wool is dyed are terracotta, buff, blue-green, sage green, dark green, yellow, blue and dark blue. Several sections were repaired in the nineteenth century and some scenes (the death of Harold, for example) are therefore largely restorations. The tapestry is part historical and part allegorical. The seventy consecutive scenes relate the events of the period 1064–6, including, of course, the battle of Hastings (14 October 1066). However, it is also intended as a clear warning of justice and retribution for those who, like Harold, choose to ignore a solemn oath.

It is likely that the tapestry was commissioned by Bishop Odo of Bayeux and that it was completed before 1082. Bishop Odo was rewarded for his part in the invasion of England with the earldom of Kent. He was a half-brother to Duke William and features prominently in the tapestry. It is likely that it was made in Canterbury and was probably the work of a single designer and a team of embroiderers. Certainly there are influences in the design reminiscent of early Anglo-Saxon manuscript illumination and the designer may have been English, even though the theme is chauvinistically Norman. Bishop Odo fell from favour in 1082 and returned to Bayeux, apparently taking the tapestry with him.

The tapestry contains, among other things, 626 human figures, 190 horses, 541 other animals, 37 ships, 33 buildings (including a splendid motte and bailey castle which was constructed shortly after landing at Pevensey), 243 shields and 27 flags. The shields are either kite-shaped (234) or round (9), the latter being exclusively of the English variety with strengthening bars, rims and a central boss (*see* SHIELDS). The designs painted on the kite-shaped shields continue to be a source of controversy among armorists: 41 are studded, 20 have 'windmill sail' crosses, 7 are charged with some form of beast, 2 have plain crosses and 1 has a wavy bar across the top. Eighty are plain or of a single colour with a different coloured rim. Whether these designs are examples of proto-heraldry has long been a matter of debate, as are the devices depicted on the pennons attached to 25 of the cavalry lances (*see* ARMORY).

BEACONS Before the technological revolution of the recent centuries the most efficient system of rapid communication was by means of beacons located on prominent hill-top sites at intervals of 8–16km (5–10 miles). There is biblical evidence for the early use of beacons (e.g. *Isaiah* 30 v. 17) and it must surely be assumed that local systems of beacon fires were used by prehistoric tribes to warn of approaching danger. The Romans developed a sophisticated system of signal stations and lighthouses and in the Anglo-Saxon period the activities of Viking raiders were communicated by means of beacons at lookout posts where observers 'toted' for danger (from Old English *tōtærn*). Many hill names retain this 'Tot', 'Tout' or 'Toot' element: Tothill, Lincolnshire; Tottenhill, Norfolk; Nettlecombe Tout and Worbarrow Tout, Dorset; and the Toot Hills of Essex, Hampshire, Staffordshire and Yorkshire, for example. A network of beacons is believed to have developed in the twelfth century and during the fourteenth century two major systems were established to combat French raids off the south coast and to warn of impending incursions from Scotland.

The primary function of a beacon was to warn of enemy landings or incursions, to identify the location and to raise a defending force as quickly as possible. By the fourteenth century beacons also indicated muster points for local defence forces (*see* MILITIA). In most counties a command beacon was maintained at the most widely visible point and this would be the 'hub' of other chains. Beacons were not simply large bonfires: the earliest fourteenth-century beacons appear to have been circular stone structures, measuring about a metre in height and with an internal diameter of just over 2m (2yd), each containing a stack of wood. Flues in the walls provided an up-draught and pitch was used to ensure that the stack was readily ignited. Other beacons were carried in metal baskets or fire-boxes (*cressets*) on tall poles, reached by ladders, and (in level landscapes) in braziers on castle and church towers, as at Blakeney in Norfolk (*see* CHURCH TOWERS). The construction and maintenance of a beacon was the responsibility of local sheriff or constable. Faggots of brushwood or furze were maintained at a beacon site and at various times a tax (*beaconage*) was collected for the maintenance of the local beacon. Each beacon was guarded, and if necessary ignited, by two teams of six men, the teams alternating day and night watches. These men also carried horns, bells and other signalling devices for use in inclement weather.

In the sixteenth century a complex network of beacons along the south coast and the Severn estuary formed part of the Tudor coastal defences, a chain of artillery forts guarding against invasion from the English Channel (*see* TUDOR COASTAL FORTS). Complex signal systems were devised to indicate, for example, the first sighting of the enemy and its disembarkation. There were also special signals for the mustering of troops. The beacons were fired in 1588 when the Spanish Armada was sighted, though it seems that the signal codes were not entirely successful and a simplified system was used to summon the trained bands to their parish churches.

BEADLE A parish officer whose responsibilities varied from one area to another. His original function was probably to supervise attendance at a manorial court and to serve writs (*see* MANOR) though in some areas his office was synonymous with that of CONSTABLE while in others he was a constable's assistant.

BEAKHEAD ORNAMENTATION *see* ROMANESQUE

BEAM A long piece of timber forming one of the main structural members of a building (*see* ROOFS (TIMBER)).

BEAM-HOLES Square or rectangular holes cut into the fabric of a wall to support the timber beams of a roof structure or the supporting members of a wooden floor. Former buildings may be traced through rows of beam-holes and ROOF CREASING in curtain walls, as at Rhuddlan Castle where the position of the former King's Hall and Chamber, Queen's Hall and Chamber, kitchens and chapel are evident in beam-holes and roof creasing in the north-east curtain wall of the inner ward. Beam-holes should not be confused with PUTLOG HOLES which are of a similar appearance but smaller and perform an entirely different function.

BEASTS (HERALDIC) *See* illustration opposite of the chimerical beasts most often found in coats of arms and armorial decoration.

BEAUFORTS, LEGITIMACY OF *see* WARS OF THE ROSES

BELFRY (i) *See* CHURCH TOWERS
(ii) A mobile siege tower (*see* SIEGES). Belfries had a dual purpose: to conceal the activities of besiegers at the foot of a defensive wall, and to serve as an elevated platform on which the smaller siege machines could be positioned and from which a wall-walk could be attacked, usually by means of a bridge. Belfries were constructed with a number of fighting platforms at different levels, each connected by ladders, and were usually higher than the walls against which they were placed so that missiles could be directed down on the defenders. The wooden framework of a belfry was covered with hides to protect it from fire and to shield the men inside.

BELL-COTE Many castles were provided with a bell-cote, usually an open-sided turret or an upward projection of a gable-end, in which a bell was hung beneath a pitched roof of slate or tiles. A bell-cote often housed the sanctus bell of a chapel which was rung at the saying of the *Sanctus* at the beginning of the Mass, and may also have been used to signal daily events or as an alarm bell. In the south-west tower of Bolton Castle there are two belfries: one for the chapel bell, which was rung from a small chamber inside the chapel doorway, and one for the main castle bell.

BELL FLÈCHE A slender spire (usually of wood) rising from a tower or stair turret and containing a bell or bells.

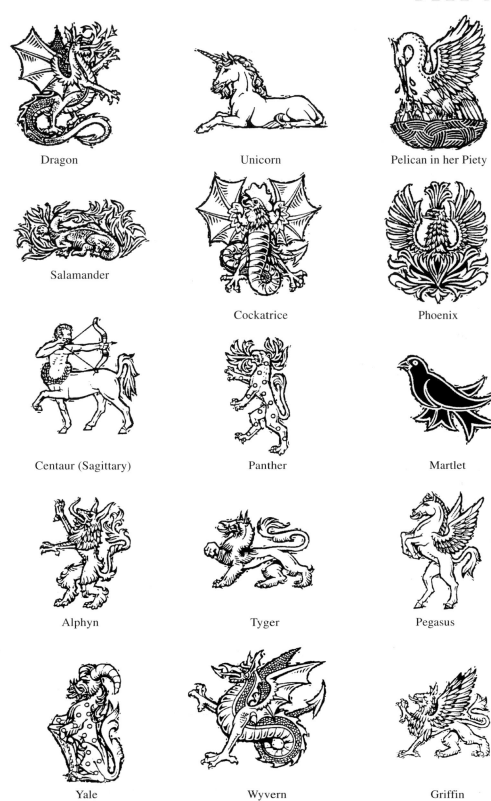

Dragon

Unicorn

Pelican in her Piety

Salamander

Cockatrice

Phoenix

Centaur (Sagittary)

Panther

Martlet

Alphyn

Tyger

Pegasus

Yale

Wyvern

Griffin

Heraldic beasts.

BELL METAL An alloy of copper and tin.

BELT FROG An ornamental button and loop attachment for a sword belt.
(*See also* WEAPONS AND HARNESS)

BELVEDERE A raised turret or pavilion.

BEND SINISTER *see* DISTINCTION, MARKS OF

BEREWICKE A dependent village or hamlet within a manor.

BERGFRIED A free-standing fighting-tower. Eynsford Castle, Kent, is of a type comparatively rare in England though reminiscent of early German castles where a fighting-tower (*bergfried*) was the central element in the design. In most British motte and bailey castles (*see* MOTTE) the essential element of the structure (and the first to be constructed) was the mound itself, to which the tower on its summit was secondary. At Eynsford, however, a free-standing tower (originally of timber) was erected first at ground level and the mound then piled up round it, apparently as an afterthought. Similarly, Geoffrey de Mandeville's timber donjon at South Mimms was constructed at ground level and a substantial motte built around it.

BERM The ledge formed between the foot of a curtain wall or rampart and the edge of a moat or ditch. In the event of the berm being occupied during a siege, defenders could counter-attack by emerging from a SALLY-PORT.

BERSERK Literally a 'bare-chested' or fanatical Anglo-Saxon warrior.

BESAGEWS Protection for the armpits (*see* ARMOUR).

BESTIARY A medieval treatise on beasts, both real and imagined. Many of the creatures were imbued with medicinal and spiritual powers or endowed with allegorical significance. The reader was often exhorted to emulate the qualities of certain beasts and to shun others.

BEVOR A section of plate armour to protect the lower face, usually worn in conjunction with a helmet such as the SALLET and KETTLE HAT, or incorporated into the helmet itself, as with the ARMET.
(*See also* ARMOUR *and* HELMETS)

BILL *see* WEAPONS AND HARNESS

BILLET (i) One of a row of short cylindrical blocks incorporated as an ornament in ROMANESQUE architecture.
(ii) A written order requiring the provision of accommodation for an armed retinue.
(iii) Requisitioned accommodation for troops.

BISHOPS' PALACES *see* ECCLESIASTICAL STRONGHOLDS

BIVALLATE *see* MULTIVALLATE

BLACK BOOK OF THE EXCHEQUER *see* PIPE ROLLS

BLACK DEATH, THE *see* PLAGUE

BLAZON To describe a coat of arms using the conventions and terminology of armory. Such a description is itself termed a *blazon*. Familiarity with blazon facilitates the rapid and accurate recording of heraldic devices, enables the historian to make effective use of reference works such as ordinaries, armories, peerages, etc., and to communicate with armorists, of whom there is a growing number. An accurate blazon is concise and unambiguous and from it heraldic devices may be painted (*emblazoned*) or researched. The conventions of blazon are well-established and logical. Relatively few terms are met with regularly and are learned best through practice. Blazons of arms may be obtained from works such as *The General Armory of England, Scotland, Ireland and Wales* by Sir Bernard Burke, published in 1842 and reprinted by Heraldry Today in 1984. This is essentially a list of armorial references, arranged alphabetically by surname, with blazons of arms for each, together with crests, supporters and mottoes where known.

BLIND A term used to describe raised architectural features, such as arcading and vaulting ribs, between which the intervening spaces are closed.

BLIND ARCADE *see* ARCADE

BLIND HOUSE *see* LOCK-UP

BLOCK CAPITAL *also* **CUSHION CAPITAL** A ROMANESQUE capital formed from a cube of stone, the lower edges of which have been rounded off to meet the circular shaft below.

BLOCKHOUSE A small detached fort located at a strategic point, or an artillery fortification such as the minor coastal forts of Henry VIII.
(*See also* BOOM, BULWARK *and* TUDOR COASTAL FORTS)

BOHORDE *see* TOURNAMENTS

BOLT *see* ARCHERY

BOMBARD An early medieval cannon (*see* FIREARMS AND CANNON). Short and with a large bore, the bombard could be raised to a considerable elevation but was capable of firing its stone balls only within a very limited range. Bombards were very heavy and difficult to manoeuvre and consequently their use was usually restricted to SIEGES. The Crécy Bombard, discovered in the moat of Bodiam Castle, has a cast-iron core, bound with shrunken iron hoops. Its chamber was charged with 1.36kg (3lb) of powder and it could fire a shot 37.5cm (15in) in diameter.

BONNET A small triangular defensive outwork.

BOOK OF FEES *see* FEUDAL AIDS *and* LORD OF THE MANOR

BOOM A chain across a river which could be raised to prevent enemy vessels from entering. The raising and lowering of a chain was often controlled from *boom towers* located on either bank, as at Portsmouth and Fowey. In 1420 the Round Tower at Portsmouth was built at the entrance to the harbour and another on the Gosport side of the river to protect the ends of a chain boom. By the sixteenth century the Round Tower had acquired three gun ports and a gun platform and was later incorporated into an eighteenth-century gun battery. In 1457 blockhouses were erected at Fowey and Polruan to protect a chain boom across the estuary. This was intended to counter Breton raids on the town – reprisals for constant raiding and piracy by the notorious 'Fowey Gallants' during the Hundred Years War.
(*See also* DECLINE OF THE CASTLE)

BORDERS (OF SCOTLAND) *see* MARCH

BORE A heavy pole with an iron head used for attacking the base of a wall during a siege (*see* SIEGES).

BOROUGH A town administered by a corporation and having privileges confirmed by royal charter or defined by statute. Ancient boroughs often enjoyed rights conferred by charters emanating from the medieval nobility. The Town Council of Sherborne in Dorset, for example, enjoys its mayoral and armigerous status on the strength of a charter from Bishop Le Poore of Salisbury, granted in 1228 to the former borough of Newland, now a suburb of the town. Anglo-Saxon boroughs had a military and defensive function as well as a mercantile one and by the tenth century were independent of the HUNDREDS, some having their own courts (*see* BURHS). A feature of the Norman invasion which began in 1066 was the creation of boroughs in association with motte and bailey castles at strategic locations (*see* MOTTE). Grants of exclusive rights to milling, brewing and holding markets made boroughs an important tool of conquest ensuring that surrounding districts became dependent upon them as their sole commercial focus. The importance of the 'planted' borough was recognised by Edward I in his Welsh campaigns, establishing settlements in association with a network of formidable fortifications, notably the castles and town walls of Caernarfon, Conwy and Denbigh. Many of the characteristics of a medieval borough may still be traced in these towns: the geometric street pattern and broad market streets, for example. Before 1835 many boroughs had the right to levy tolls at the town market, to hear certain civil and criminal cases, and to return a member to the House of Commons. Public elections were rarely held and borough administration was effectively self-perpetuating. By the 1835 Municipal Corporations Act councillors in the 178 boroughs were required to stand for re-election after three years and aldermen after six and franchise was extended to rate-payers with a residential qualification of three years or more.
(*See also* MARKETS)

BOSSES Decorative terminations in wood or stone where the cross-members of a roof or ceiling intersect. In a stone vault a boss is a projecting keystone at the intersection of ribs and is both functional and ornamental (*see* VAULTING). In castles the majority of bosses are late medieval, foliated decoration and simple quatrefoil and shield motifs, badges and rebuses being especially common.

BOTTLE DUNGEON *see* OUBLIETTE *and* PRISONS

BOWYER One who makes bows and crossbows (*see* ARCHERY *and* FLETCHER).

BOX-MACHICOLATION *see* MACHICOLATIONS

BRACE Diagonal subsidiary timbers added to a structure (such as a door or the frame of a roof) to increase its rigidity.

BRACED COLLAR *see* ROOFS (TIMBER)

BRACKET A flat-topped, right-angled projection of stone, wood or metal used to support a shelf, statue, candles, etc. Not to be confused with a CORBEL, an architectural feature of similar appearance which carries the distributed downward thrust of a larger structure. Both may be elaborately carved and were originally painted and gilded.

BRASSES (MONUMENTAL) *see* MONUMENTS

BRATTICE *see* HOARDING

BRATTISHING *also* **BRATTICING** The furnishing of the ramparts of a castle or fortified town with temporary wooden HOARDINGS.

BRAYS Water-filled defences.

BREASTWORK (i) A low, temporary defensive structure.
(ii) A timber HOARDING on a parapet.
(iii) The brick or stonework forming the breast of a fireplace.

BRESSUMER *also* **BREASTSUMMER** A horizontal beam, often carved ornamentally, which carries the superstructure in TIMBER-FRAME BUILDINGS and into wh ich the first-floor joists are tenoned. The term is also used to describe a heavy beam spanning a fireplace or other opening.

BRETACHE, BRETESCHE *or* **BRETÈCHE** A defensive wooden or stone structure protruding from a window part-way up a wall (*see* HOARDING).

BREWHOUSE *see* KITCHENS

BRICK BUILDINGS Although brick-built castles are comparatively rare (*see below*), brick was widely used in architectural details such as the linings of ovens and fireplaces (*see also* REREDOS), in ARCHES, WINDOWS, LOOPHOLES and GUN PORTS and as paving bricks and wall tiles (*see* TILES, ENCAUSTIC). In the Middle Ages bricks were often referred to as *flaunderstiles* or *walteghells*, though the latter more often implied

bricks or tiles used as a wall covering (*see* CHIMNEYS). One of the first references in England to brick by that name is the purchase of two thousand *breke pro chemeneys faciendis* at Langley in 1427.

Brick-making

Brick-making in medieval England had hardly changed since the Roman period. After excavation, clay was 'puddled' to remove unwanted material and to provide an even consistency; it was then moulded to the required form, using a wooden mould, and dried to reduce shrinkage. Final burning was carried out in a clamp in which the bricks were stacked together with faggots of brushwood as fuel. Clamp firing produced unevenness in size and colour (evident in the attractive variety of medieval and Tudor brickwork) and the system was eventually replaced by burning in kilns in which the bricks were stacked to allow the passage of hot air between them. Firing took about 48 hours, coal replacing wood as the principal fuel from *c.* 1700.

Roman bricks, used for bonding courses in walling and as facing to a concrete core, had the appearance of tiles: square or oblong, the latter between 30 and 45cm (12 to 18in) long, 15 to 30cm (6 to 12in) wide and about 2½ to 4cm (1 to 1½in) thick. Roman bricks are to be found in the excavated remains of villas and fortifications, but most were 'quarried' from the ruins and reused in Saxon and medieval buildings, being both durable and freely available. Roman bricks from Caerleon were used in the construction of the eleventh-century hall-keep at Chepstow Castle and misled eighteenth-century antiquaries into thinking it a Roman building.

There is little evidence of brick-making following the Roman withdrawal and the earliest known English bricks appeared in the eastern counties in the mid-twelfth century. It is surprising that the English for so long failed to recognise the obvious advantages of brick for domestic buildings: baking bricks on site or using local kilns was considerably quicker and cheaper than quarrying, dressing and transporting stone. Eventually, it was the inexorable depredation of the forests for building timber, combined with the immigration of Flemish weavers into East Anglia during the fourteenth century, that encouraged a quickening appreciation of the brick architecture of the Low Countries and the development of a brick-making industry along the east coast in the fifteenth century. The dimensions of bricks were first standardised in 1477 to conform to the grasp of the brick-layer's fingers and thumb.

Built by Ralph Lord Cromwell between 1430 and 1450, the keep of Tattershall Castle has been described with justification as the finest piece of medieval brick-work in England.

Brick Castles

Some of the finest late medieval brick buildings date from this transitional period, notably Tattershall (1430–50), Herstmonceux (1440) and Caister (1432–46) Castles, Kirby Muxloe (1480) and the gatehouse of Oxburgh Hall (*c.* 1482).

The accounts for Tattershall Castle, built by Ralph, Lord Cromwell between 1430 and 1450, record the vast number of bricks required for the magnificent tower-house, described with justification as the finest piece of medieval brickwork in England. In 1445–6, 384,000 large bricks and 84,000 smaller bricks were made locally, at Edlington Moor a few miles north of Tattershall, and to these were added a further 274,000 bricks already on site. The accounts suggest that a certain Baldwin Dutchman (probably a German), the highest paid and most prominent 'brickmason' among the (mostly foreign) craftsmen, was also the site master and architect. Lord Cromwell's new tower was intended to be an unambiguous declaration of his status (he was Lord High Treasurer of England) and

the choice of brick was clearly dictated by fashion rather than necessity. There was no shortage of local stone, indeed stone was used for Cromwell's fine collegiate church which stands nearby and for the door and window surrounds, newel stairs and the splendid machicolations of his tower.

Contrary to popular belief, the use of brick rather than stone does not necessarily weaken a castle's defences. But, as at Tattershall, many fifteenth-century magnates built in brick because it was fashionable and served to emphasise their status. Sir Roger Fiennes, Treasurer of the Royal Household and a veteran of the French wars, built Herstmonceux (1440) entirely of brick, stone being used only for doorways, windows and corbels. It is an immense quadrangular castle and, although licensed to defend the Channel coast, it was clearly intended primarily as a residence, capable of accommodating a large household. While retaining all the defensive characteristics of a medieval stronghold, its curtain is thinner, its flanking towers more slender and its walls weakened by the large size of several original windows.

Caister Castle was built (1432–46) for his retirement by Sir John Fastolf, though on his death in 1459 it passed to the Paston family whose interminable and sometimes bloody dispute with the duke of Norfolk is described in the *Paston Letters*. Having been frustrated in the courts, the duke attempted to force his claim to Caister. In 1469 he laid siege to the castle which held out for several weeks before surrendering to the duke's cannon: a creditable testimony to the strength of its brick-built defences. Regrettably, little of Caister's former magnificence remains, other than its splendid tower-house. The base court (of inferior brickwork) is fragmentary and of the main quadrangle only the north and west walls still stand, including a small section of the machicolated parapet which once ran the full length of the curtain. The elegant cylindrical tower-house, over 27m (90ft) high, with its machicolations, hexagonal stair turret, gun ports and five storeys of private apartments, appears to have been a copy of the *Wasserburg* or moated castle of the Rhineland, suggesting (as at Tattershall) that the architect was not English.

Kirby Muxloe, 4 miles west of Leicester, was built by William, Lord Hastings in the 1480s for £1,008 – though his execution in 1483 prevented its completion. Only the gatehouse and west corner tower remain: the former is a ruin but the tower, with its 3m (10ft) thick walls, is almost intact, demonstrating the formidable strength of brickwork. Oxburgh Hall, built entirely in brick by Sir Edmund

Bedingfeld in the 1480s, is a fine example of a late medieval fortified house: its wide water-filled moat and splendid gatehouse are the only concessions to defence, though even in the gatehouse several of the windows are too large to be effective.

During the reign of Henry VIII both the manufacture of bricks and their architectural use became more skilful and imaginative. Chimney-stacks and other architectural features were constructed of ornate brickwork, as at Compton Wynyates, Warwickshire, sometimes under the direction of Italian craftsmen.
(*See also* SLATES AND TILES *and* TILES (ROOFING))

BRICK CASTLES *see* BRICK BUILDINGS

BRICK NOGGING Patterned brickwork placed between the vertical timbers (*studs*) of a TIMBER-FRAME BUILDING to replace earlier lath and plaster or wattle and daub.

BRIDEWELL By the mid-sixteenth century every county possessed a *house of correction*, a place in which beggars and vagrants (and unmarried mothers) 'who threatened the peace of the community' were housed and set to hard labour. Modelled on (and named after) the Bridewell at Blackfriars in London, they were administered by the local justices. Several bridewells were located in the dank gatehouses and towers of redundant castles (*see* PRISONS).

BRIDGE-PIT The pit into which the lower edge of a DRAWBRIDGE is lowered when the bridge itself is raised.

BRIDGES *see* DRAWBRIDGE

BRIDGES AND BRIDGE GATES The medieval attitude towards the provision of bridges was ambivalent: while many local notables and parochial authorities were reluctant to bear the considerable costs of bridge-building and maintenance, elsewhere construction was on an impressive scale and reflected not only the demands of trade and commerce for improved communications but also an awareness by many of the benefits of philanthropy. Numerous individuals and corporations, such as guilds and fraternities, subscribed to the construction and maintenance of bridges at difficult fords and ferry passages, particularly in the hinterland of market towns and ports. Many bridges were associated with religious foundations or chantries,

and chapels dedicated to the observance of masses for the soul of a benefactor or patron saint may sometimes be found near by. A small number of bridges were provided with a bridge chapel: that at Bradford-on-Avon in Wiltshire, for example, was later used as a lock-up where drunks and trouble-makers were detained overnight.

In many instances tolls were collected and used both to finance the maintenance of the bridge and to swell the coffers of the patron, often a monastic or collegiate foundation or trade guild. Early medieval bridges were narrow stone structures, with low parapets to accommodate packhorses with their loads. Some replaced earlier (sometimes Roman) bridges or fords while others had fords alongside them for use by wagons. Later medieval bridges usually have a roadway width of about 3.8m (12½ft) and are supported by piers with arches, the undersides vaulted or ribbed and in-filled with rubble for economy. Cutwaters were often built into the bases of piers, sometimes only on the upstream side of the bridge. These triangular wedges of masonry were intended to reduce erosion and protect the piers from flotsam by dividing the current. On later medieval and Tudor bridges the parapets are often continued over the cutwaters to provide V-shaped jetties (*abutments*) in the refuges of which travellers could seek protection from passing vehicles. Recent repairs to the fourteenth-century White Mill Bridge at Sturminster Marshall, Dorset, revealed foundations consisting of oak piles driven into the river bed, each supporting a flat 'raft' of oak beams. This bridge, the original foundation of which may date from *c.* 1175, spans 61m (200ft) of the River Stour, carrying a 3.6m (12ft) wide roadway on eight ribbed arches of superb masonry. The engineering skill and financial resources required for its construction suggest that the route was once of major importance and yet today the bridge carries only a minor road. Many medieval bridges have subsequently been widened and there are several examples where one side of the bridge is medieval and the other side is of a later date. In 1285 the Statute of Westminster established that it was the responsibility of the manors to maintain the king's highway outside the towns, but it was not until 1530 that a county rate was permitted to finance the repair of those bridges for which there was no acknowledged responsibility.

Many medieval walled towns were strategically located on the banks of rivers and their defences often included a fortified bridge (*see* TOWN WALLS). Inevitably, the relentless demands of traffic have resulted in the destruction of nearly all

At Monmouth, the three-arched Monnow bridge is surmounted on one of its piers by a lofty bridge gate, the only surviving town gate of its type in Britain. The bridge was built in 1272 but the gate tower appears to be somewhat later and the tiled roof is Victorian.

these *bridge gates*, those at Warkworth, Northumberland, and Monmouth on the Welsh border being notable exceptions.

The splendid frontier castle of Warkworth guards the neck of a bold loop in the River Coquet, its massive keep dominating the market town which stretches down a hill behind it to the north. Anxious to encourage trade, the townspeople erected a bridge across the Coquet in 1379. But, conscious of their vulnerable position as a 'buffer' between the castle and the marauding Scots, they wisely included a gate-tower at the southern end of the bridge. This had a guard chamber on its west side, opposite which a door probably gave access to a wall-walk which ran east and west of the bridge. This is the only surviving bridge gate in England, though it is now in a ruinous condition.

Far more impressive is the Monnow Gate at the Welsh border town of Monmouth. The town itself occupies high ground between the River Monnow to the west and the Wye to the east. Together with nearby Chepstow, its castle was a key stronghold from which William Fitz Osbern launched his invasion of Gwent in 1067. The castle occupies a large ringwork on a bluff overlooking the Monnow on the west side of the old town. A town wall, linking the castle with the Wye, was constructed in

the early fourteenth century, though only a turret of the Dixton Gate remains. To the south, the town was protected by an embankment with a palisade, and beyond that by a bend of the Monnow which enclosed the lower town. The three-arched Monnow bridge is surmounted on one of its piers by a lofty bridge gate, the only surviving town gate of its type in Britain. The bridge was built in 1272 but the gate-tower appears to be somewhat later and the tiled roof is Victorian. The narrow gate passage once contained a portcullis, operated from a chamber above, while machicolations on the western façade have survived. The gateway has been widened to accommodate traffic and pedestrian passages inserted on either side. Before this, the building would have been narrower and the projecting garderobe in the portcullis chamber would have discharged directly into the river.

BRIGANDINE Small overlapping plates or bands of iron, steel or leather riveted inside a tight-fitting leather or canvas coat which sometimes had an outer covering of a finer material. More flexible and lighter than mail or plate armour, brigandines were worn by foot-soldiers from the thirteenth to the fifteenth century.
(*See also* ARMOUR)

BRISURE see CADENCY

BUCKLER A small, flat, circular shield made of wood, reinforced with a substantial wooden cross-bar which also forms a hand-grip inside a metal boss. It was designed to be used with an outstretched arm. A number of examples from the thirteenth and fourteenth centuries are made of willow or poplar and are further reinforced by a circular metal strip. (*See also* SHIELDS)

BUILDING CASTLES see CASTLES, CONSTRUCTION OF

BUILDING MATERIALS The earliest motte and bailey castles (*see* MOTTE) were earthworks with timber mottes and palisades. In many instances these were replaced with stone defences and by the twelfth century most castles of substance were constructed of stone. Inevitably, geology dictated which type of stone was most suitable for the purpose and how far it had to be transported. High quality ASHLAR masonry is indicative either of a reliable local source of stone or of the affluence of the builder who was required to obtain his materials from a distant quarry (sometimes even from France) at considerable expense. Even so, ashlar is no more than a veneer covering a rubble core. In the absence of suitable local stone, many builders resorted to the use of FLINT, while brick-built castles became fashionable in the fifteenth century when the transition from medieval fortification to magnate residence was gathering pace. Contrary to the popular view, brick masonry is no less strong than stone (*see* BRICK BUILDINGS) and was ideally suited to the construction of complex defensive features such as MACHICOLATIONS. (*See also* MASONRY)

BULLA *and* **PAPAL BULL** see SEALS

BULL-NOSED MOULDING A moulding with a rounded end.

BULWARK An early term for BASTION and BLOCK-HOUSE. A forward defensive position, a projection from the general outline of a fortification, from which the ground in front of the principal walls was defended by flanking cover. From the mid-sixteenth century bulwarks were generally four-sided projections.

BURGAGE Tenure in an ancient borough held of the crown, or of the lords of the borough, and subject to customary rents or services. In the Saxon period burgage rents were called *landgable* or *hawgable*.

BURGANET *or* **BURGONET** see HELMETS

BURGESS The inhabitant of a borough, entitled to burghal privileges.

BURGH (i) Used by some historians as an alternative spelling of BURH.
(ii) The Scottish equivalent of the English BOROUGH.

BURGHWORK The pre-Conquest royal right to demand labour for erecting fortifications (*see* CASTLES, CONSTRUCTION OF).

BURHS An Old English term for a fortified town or dwelling. The Anglo-Saxons themselves used the word *burh* when referring to prehistoric or Roman fortifications and applied it to their own fortified towns: refuges constructed in response to the Danish incursions of the ninth and tenth centuries and the first major settlements to be created since the Roman occupation. The *Burghal Hidage*, a remarkable Anglo-Saxon document, lists thirty *burhs* established in Wessex as an integrated defensive system by Alfred before his death in 899. Several were former Roman towns where the original defences were utilised (*ceasters*), at Winchester (Hampshire), Dorchester (Dorset) and Bath (Avon), for example, while others were newly created. Saxon burhs were strategically important settlements, located to take advantage of natural defensive features such as rivers, constructed or redeveloped to a regular street-plan, and surrounded by earthwork defences, apparently requiring four men to defend 5m (17ft) of rampart. A network of roads and trackways also developed, linking *burhs* with one another and with the scattered settlements between.

Perhaps the best example of a newly created *burh* is Wareham in Dorset. Located at the edge of Poole Harbour between the rivers Frome and Piddle, it is defended on three sides by earthworks dating from the late ninth century and on the fourth by the River Frome and its marshes. It was captured in 876 by the Vikings, who overwintered there, and thereafter developed as a port until the fourteenth century. The defences were strengthened in the early twelfth century and again during the Second World War. Other good examples of Saxon burhs at which some evidence remains of their original fortification and street-plan are Wallingford in Oxfordshire, Cricklade in Wiltshire and Lydford in Devon. The subsequent success of a *burh* depended on whether it was able to sustain its function as a trade centre and market: some prospered and became important route-centres, others declined. Former strongholds can often be identified in place-name elements such as '-burgh' or 'bury', though these usually relate to fortified buildings rather than settlements.

BUTLER *see* HOUSEHOLD

BUTT The place-name is commonly associated with what are believed to have been the sites of medieval archery butts dating from the time of the Hundred Years War in the fourteenth and early fifteenth centuries, when practice with the longbow was a statutory requirement in every town and village (*see* ARCHERY). Archery butts usually comprised low mounds against which the targets were placed and although similar mounds may still be found in fields or closes on the periphery of many villages the only surviving earthworks of certain provenance are those at Wold Newton in Yorkshire where they seem to have provided protection from stray arrows rather than serving as targets. The proposition that butts were provided for archery practice in the outer wards of castles is more tenable, indeed the name survives at a number of castles including Kenilworth and Corfe where the grooves caused by the sharpening of arrows may still be seen in the stonework.

BUTTERY From the French *bouteille* meaning 'bottle', the buttery was the division of a medieval household responsible for the provision and storage of wines and beers. The word was also used for a room in which wine and beer were stored, often located off the SCREENS PASSAGE between the kitchen and the hall (*see* HOUSEHOLD *and* KITCHENS).

BUTTRESS A projecting support constructed against a wall to counteract the weight of roofs and towers and to compensate for the structurally weakening effects of window openings. The walls of Saxon and Norman stone buildings were invariably of considerable thickness with small windows and comparatively light timber roofs supported by tie and collar beams. Consequently they required little reinforcement and buttresses of this period are generally wide but of low projection. The thinner walls, larger windows and heavy stone vaults of late medieval buildings required substantial buttressing with projections of greater depth at the base, reducing in upward stages to the roof level. During the thirteenth century *angle buttresses* were used at the corners of buildings where they met at 90 degrees (*see illustration below*). *Setback buttresses* are similar but are set back slightly to expose the corner of the

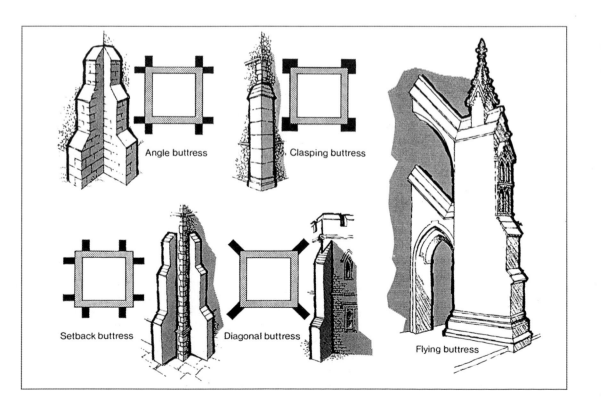

Angle buttress

Clasping buttress

Setback buttress

Diagonal buttress

Flying buttress

building. Less common are the large, square *clasping buttresses* which enclose the corners of a tower or porch. In the fourteenth century *diagonal buttresses* were widely used. These are set diagonally at right angles to the corners of a tower or building. The *flying buttress* (or *arch buttress*) is one by which the thrust of a vault is carried from a wall to an outer buttress by means of an arch or series of arches. The lofty stone vaults, vast windows and slender walls (often little more than cages of stone ribs) that characterise the Perpendicular style of Gothic architecture of the late fourteenth and fifteenth centuries demanded extraordinary ingenuity in order that the downward and outward thrust of roof, tower and (sometimes) spire should be evenly distributed and counteracted. Mainly through trial and error, the abutment system developed by which arches, placed at the point of greatest thrust (found to be immediately below the springing line of a vault on an internal wall), transferred the pressure through buttresses to ground level and, by means of heavy pinnacles on the buttresses themselves, successfully offset the effect of the thrust.
(*See also* PILASTER BUTTRESS *and* SPUR BUTTRESS)

BUTTRESS OFF-SET *see* OFF-SET

BYRNIE *see* HAUBERK

Brisures used by the eldest son (label, top), fifth son (annulet, centre) and third son (mullet, bottom). A crescent was used by a second son, a martlet by a fourth and a fleur-de-lis by a sixth.

C

CABLE MOULDING *also* **ROPE MOULDING** Decorative moulding imitating a twisted rope.

CADENCY (MARKS OF DIFFERENCE) The medieval tenet 'one man one coat' often necessitated the 'differencing' of coats of arms in order that each male member of a family, and of its cadet branches, should possess distinctive arms, a practice known as cadency. Originally this was achieved by making minor alterations to the design: by varying the colours (*tinctures*) or charges, for example. Since the Middle Ages the three-pointed *label* has been borne by an eldest son during the lifetime of his father. This was incorporated into a system of symbols

(*brisures*) devised by the Tudor heralds, each appropriate to a particular male member of a family. In practice (and with the exception of the label) this system has been found to be unsatisfactory and has generally been more honoured in the breach than in the observance. During the Middle Ages marks of difference were also used to signify feudal tenure and even political allegiance, elements of one coat being transferred to another for this purpose.
(*See also* DISTINCTION, MARKS OF *and* MARSHALLING)

CADET A younger son who is the progenitor of a subsidiary branch of a family.

CAER- *see* CAIR-

CAERLAVEROCK, THE SIEGE OF A famous siege of the castle of Caerlaverock, near Dumfries in Scotland, by the forces of Edward I in July 1300, noteworthy especially for the epic poem of that name in which details of the banners and shields of more than one hundred nobles and knights are given. C.W. Scott-Giles's translation (somewhat condensed) into English verse is available from the Heraldry Society (*see* APPENDIX II).

CAERNARFON ARCH *see* ARCH

CAIR-, CAER- *or* **CAR-** A place-name element meaning 'fortified place' commonly found in Wales and the Marches, Cornwall and the north-west of England. Caernarfon, for example, may be translated as 'the fort near Môn' (Anglesey). Such references are usually to Iron Age or Roman fortifications but may have retained their significance by subsequent medieval building on the same site. In Ireland it appears as *Caher-*.

CALAIS Captured by Edward III in 1347 after an eleven-month siege, Calais and its hinterland (the *English Pale*) was the only part of France to remain in English possession at the end of the HUNDRED YEARS WAR (1453). Strategically, Calais and its castle of Guisnes were of immense importance throughout the late medieval period. By controlling both sides of the Channel, the English established a bridgehead from which to undertake future campaigns against France and through which trade with continental Europe could be controlled. Furthermore, Calais had its own permanent garrison that could be used by its commander to exert considerable political and military influence on affairs at home (*see* WARS OF THE ROSES). Command of the Calais garrison was the responsibility of its governor or Captain, an office described by Commines as 'Christendom's finest captaincy' and the most important military command in the king's gift. By far the best known of the Captains of Calais was 'the Kingmaker' Richard Neville, earl of Warwick (1428–71) who was appointed by Henry VI in 1456 – a grave error of judgement on the king's part, for it provided the Yorkists with a foreign base, control of the Channel and a substantial garrison whose loyalty to Warwick was never in doubt.

The *Calais Staple* was a monopoly of some two hundred merchants established in 1363 for the exporting of English wool to the continent. Its creation resolved a number of problems for the English crown, not least the financing of the Calais garrison (which was dependent on annual exchequer subsidies of £1,500 in peacetime and between £3,000 and £4,000 when at war). Once the Staple was established, income could be assured by contracting loans with the Staplers and the garrison could be supplied and paid. The creation of the Calais Staple also brought to an end the long and often acrimonious argument regarding the exporting of wool and the taxes to be levied on it. On the one hand the king needed to restrict export rights to a clearly defined group of merchants whose profits could provide loans for the crown on the security of the subsidies levied on wool, while on the other the wool merchants needed to act corporately in order to bargain for the best possible prices for their exports. Initially, collection of the customs and wool subsidy remained a function of the exchequer, but by the Act of Retainer (1466) the Staple was given authority to carry out these responsibilities and for meeting the costs of the garrison out of the proceeds.

CALTRAP, CALTROP *or* **CHEVAL-TRAP** Intended to maim horses in a cavalry charge, when strewn on the ground metal caltraps would always land with one of their four points upright. Occasionally found as a charge in armory. (*See also* TRIBOLI)

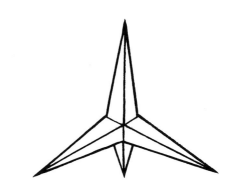

Caltrap.

CAMAIL *or* **AVENTAIL** A skirt of mail to protect the neck and shoulders, characteristic of body armour of the fourteenth and early fifteenth centuries. The camail was attached to the lower edge of the BASCINET by means of a leather band, pierced at intervals by brass or iron lugs (*vervelles*) through which a cord was passed and secured. (*See also* ARMOUR *and* HELMETS)

CAMAIL PERIOD A term applied to military brasses and effigies in which the figures are depicted wearing a CAMAIL which was introduced into English armour during the second half of the fourteenth century. (*See also* MONUMENTS)

CAMBER A slight upward curve in an otherwise horizontal structure.

CAMPANILE A bell tower, usually detached from other buildings.

CANALS *see* QUAYS

CANNON *see* FIREARMS AND CANNON

CANTILEVER A horizontal projection with no visible support.

CANTREF or CANTRED Derived from the Welsh *cant* ('hundred') and *tref* ('township'), an ancient land area of one hundred townships (*trefi*). Larger than a COMMOTE, a cantref was an administrative, judicial and fiscal unit and the basis for military recruitment. In medieval Wales the land lying between the rivers Conwy and Dee comprised the Four Cantrefi, or hundreds, of Rhos, Rhufoniog, Dyffryn Clwyd and Tegeingl.
(*See also* ROYAL PALACES)

CAP-À-PIE Fully armed – 'from head to foot'.

CAPARISON A favourite means of armorial display in the medieval and Tudor periods, particularly at tournaments and for ceremonial processions. The body of a horse was covered in cloths richly embroidered or painted with armorial bearings. The rider's personal arms were often emblazoned on his shield, other quarterings decorating the caparison, often without any pretence at marshalling. Fringes, rein-trappings and other appendages were usually charged with ciphers and badges. In battle the abbreviated (and more practical) *trapper* was used.
(*See also* BARDING *and* HORSES AND HORSE-HARNESS)

CAP HOUSE A small chamber at the top of a stair or wing.

CAPITAL A capital is the head of a column, PIER or PILASTER. Most capitals comprise a flat upper stone (*abacus*) and a tapering lower section (*necking*) which is usually separated from the shaft of the pier by a narrow moulding. The function of a capital is to provide an area, larger than the supporting pier, from which an ARCH springs.

The decoration of a capital is often a useful guide to the period of style of architecture (*see* GOTHIC ARCHITECTURE *and* ROMANESQUE). Roman-esque piers and capitals were of massive construction: clearly contemporary builders felt that new notions of structure were no substitute for mass. In the earliest examples both neck and abacus were combined in a single square or round block of stone. Early carved decoration was crude (though interesting) and

included interlacing. Typical of the Norman period is the *cushion* capital which is a cube of masonry, the lower parts of which were rounded off to conform with the circular shaft of the pier, leaving a flat face (*lunette*) on each of the four sides. From this evolved the *scalloped* capital in which each of the lunettes is divided into cone shapes, beneath a square abacus. Later Romanesque capitals are deeply carved with foliated motifs, animals, birds and (more rarely in England) figures. In Gothic architecture the capitals of the Early English period were generally moulded or splendidly foliated with a round or moulded abacus. Specific types of foliated capital include the *crocket* capital which has stylised leaves forming scrolls (*volutes*) beneath the abacus, the *stiff-leaf* capital (with long stalks) which developed from it and the *water-leaf* capital which has plain, broad leaves turned over beneath the angles of the abacus. Characteristic of the decorated period is the removal of the undercut hollow beneath the abacus to form a more unified capital, usually decorated with rolls of scroll moulding or foliage. By the fourteenth century foliated capitals of oak, ivy, maple and vine leaves were carved in a more naturalistic manner and with a profusion of fruit and flowers (*natural leaf ornament*). In the Perpendicular period of the fifteenth century octagonal capitals, often chamfered at the upper edge, were set on circular piers or groups of shafts and were, for the most part, moulded though foliated forms may be found.

CAPONIER A covered communication passage leading to outworks across a dry ditch and provided with loopholes for flanking fire.

CAPTAIN A middle-ranking military commander, though in the medieval period the term was often applied to senior 'captains of the field' who took command of an entire 'battle' or division. Command of the Calais garrison was the responsibility of its Captain, an office described by Commines as 'Christendom's finest captaincy'. The Captain, or governor, of the Calais garrison was the most important military command in the king's gift and brought with it considerable influence, both political and military (*see* CALAIS).

CAPUT The chief place in a lordship where the court was held.

CARBON-14 DATING also RADIO-CARBON-14 DATING A method of dating organic matter. There is a fixed proportion of Carbon-14 to Carbon-12 in living organisms. Once dead, this proportion falls to about half the former level in approximately 5,700 years (known as 'half life'). By measuring the 14C:12C ratio in organic matter, an approximate date of death may be calculated.

CARBUNCLE *see* ESCARBUNCLE

CARRIAGE OF BUILDING MATERIALS *see* MATERIALS, CARRIAGE OF

CARTS *see* MATERIALS, CARRIAGE OF

CARTULARY An estate register-book containing details of charters, deeds, grants, property and other possessions of an estate. Also one who keeps the register and the place in which it is stored.

CASEMATE (i) A gallery at the foot of a curtain wall to defend against undermining, battering-rams, etc.
(ii) A gun emplacement and/or barrack room located within the ramparts of a post-medieval fortification and protected by a strengthened vault.

CASHEL From the Irish *caiseal*, a strongly fortified dwelling, often constructed within dry-stone ramparts, and dating from the sixth to the twelfth centuries.

CASTELL Welsh for 'castle', though the word may describe a fortified site which is not necessarily medieval.

CASTELLAN The governor or captain of a castle (*see* CONSTABLE *and* HOUSEHOLD).

CASTELLANIES Military estates established by the forced appropriation of property following the Conquest of 1066 as part of William's strategy of ruthless colonisation, the purpose of which was to provide lands for a parvenu Norman aristocracy.

CASTELLATED Descriptive of a building with CRENELLATIONS.

CASTELLOLOGIE An affectedly quaint term for the study of castles.

CASTLE From the Latin *castellum*, meaning 'little fort' or 'refuge', a castle was a fortified feudal residence, a definition that is sufficiently flexible to accommodate both bishops' palaces (*see* ECCLESIASTICAL STRONGHOLDS) and those late medieval residences now described as fortified manor houses (*see* MANOR HOUSE). It is this duality of function – domestic and military – that distinguishes a medieval castle from earlier communal strongholds and later military installations. The military aristocracy lived in castles, which were at once the home and defence of the feudal baronage and the centres of their power. The word 'dungeon' (French *donjon*), used originally to describe such a fortified dwelling, is derived from the Latin *dominium* and expresses lordship. Of course, many castles might more accurately be described as residential fortresses, located, designed and constructed primarily for military purposes, the residential element being an ancillary function. Nevertheless, it should never be forgotten that the majority of castles were more often lived in than fought over (*see* HOUSEHOLD).

The primary military function of a medieval castle was an offensive one, as a base for active operations by which surrounding territory could be controlled. Consequently, it was of considerable value in war and it was the need for impregnability which, above all other requirements, dictated a castle's design and architectural form. A medieval castle was essentially a product and a symbol of the FEUDAL SYSTEM. In a society dominated by the lordship of a military aristocracy a castle was held of the king or of a superior lord in return for loyalty and military service. It is no coincidence that the earliest known castle sites, at Longeais and Doué-la-Fontaine, both date from the second half of the tenth century and are located in northern France where a proto-feudal society was established at that time. The end of feudalism is more difficult to date precisely but by the late sixteenth century military power, which formerly had been delegated to the king's vassals (and to their vassals), had effectively become a monopoly of the sovereign state and the feudal castle replaced by a system of national defences. Sixteenth-century Deal, Walmer, Camber and the other TUDOR COASTAL FORTS were exclusively military installations: they were not castles (*see* DECLINE OF THE CASTLE).

Medieval castles were indeed residences, but magnates who possessed several castles might be in residence only periodically or (in some cases) not at all. Of his many castles Richard, duke of York (1411–60), favoured three: the once-magnificent castle of Fotheringhay in Northamptonshire, with its church, college and library, built on an imposing site above the River Nene; Baynards Castle, a fortified quadrangular 'town house' on the north bank of the Thames (Upper Thames Street); and Ludlow Castle, the ancient stronghold of the Mortimers on the Welsh Marches, which became the chief headquarters of the House of York during the Wars of the Roses. But even when a lord was not in residence, a castle remained a symbol of his power and authority and the instrument of regional domination – administrative, judicial and military. Though the lord's apartments might be vacant, a castle could still accommodate a law court, a prison, an estate office, a barracks and even (in the case of royal castles) a treasury and mint, and for most of the year it would be occupied by a small garrison and administrative staff supervised by a CONSTABLE.

Not all castles were intended to be impregnable in the event of a siege, indeed a castle's offensive capability was as important as its defence, for its principal role was a dynamic one: to command the surrounding territory. Many castles were built as part of a wider defensive system in which they controlled route-ways, bridgeheads, fords and mountain passes, or protected ports and urban centres of trade and commerce (see SITING). Castles varied considerably in size from single towers to vast complexes such as Caerphilly and Kenilworth which covered many acres. Each was essentially an individual structure, located and constructed to meet the strategic offensive and defensive requirements of its owner and the domestic and administrative demands of a household and garrison.

Few castles remain unaltered from when they were first built and none fits neatly into any particular category. For many there is evidence of continuous occupation from the twelfth century; some have been entirely rebuilt and most have been remodelled many times, according to the current military and architectural fashion. Many were severely slighted following civil wars while others have been adapted for domestic purposes.

CASTLE-BOON Obligatory service due to a castle from the owners or tenants of neighbouring properties.

CASTLE-BOTE A levy raised for the repair of a castle.

CASTLE-GARTH A yard or enclosure belonging to a castle.

CASTLE GUARD (i) A military obligation which, in peacetime, was hardly onerous. Important strategic castles may always have been fully garrisoned, but when the kingdom was at peace lesser castles are likely to have been manned only by a watchman and gate-guard, possibly with a local knight acting as constable. In wartime considerable demands were made, particularly of the HOUSEHOLD and those living in the vicinity of a castle.
(ii) A tax originally in commutation of the above military obligation.
(iii) The territory subject to such a tax.

CASTLE-MONGER One who builds or owns a castle.

CASTLERY or CASTELRY The government or jurisdiction of a castle and the territory subject to it.

CASTLES, CATEGORIES OF Many attempts have been made to categorise medieval castles: none has been entirely successful. There were two principal types: (i) the great tower within an enclosure and (ii) an enclosure with gatehouse and flanking towers. To these, historians and archaeologists have added numerous variations. Some categories, such as concentric castles, are reasonably intelligible and certainly concise. But all castles are different. A castle's form is dependent on the topography of its particular site and the site itself may have been selected for a variety of reasons. Castles were essentially functional buildings, but not all castles were built to perform the same function. Furthermore, each castle has evolved (or declined) in response to a variety of circumstances: military, political, domestic and, not least, the financial fortunes of the owner.

The following list of entries includes some that are commonly recognised types of castle (e.g. motte and bailey, pele tower, etc.), while other entries may assist those who wish to categorise castles by reference to particular features (shell-keep, keep-gatehouse, etc):

BAILEY
BRICK BUILDINGS
CONCENTRIC CASTLES
COURTYARD CASTLES (see COURT and COURTYARD)
DOUBLE-COURTYARD CASTLES (see COURT AND COURTYARD)
ECCLESIASTICAL STRONGHOLDS
ENCEINTE
ENCLOSURE CASTLES
FORTIFIED MANOR HOUSES (see MANOR HOUSES)
GATEHOUSES
GREAT TOWER
HALL-KEEP
KEEP

Construction of the motte at Hastings (from the Bayeux Tapestry*).*

CASTLES, CONSTRUCTION OF Many of the earliest castles, those 'perfect instruments of conquest and the rapid occupation of territory' (Brown), were of earthwork and timber and relatively easy to construct by comparison with stone-built fortifications. Once a suitable site was identified, a force of semi-skilled and unskilled labour would construct a MOTTE or RINGWORK and palisade, under the direction of their new Norman lord. The frenetic activity of these building sites is vividly depicted in the BAYEUX TAPESTRY, a scene that was repeated throughout England in the months following the Conquest. Of course, at this time many so-called castles were temporary defensive structures or fortified staging posts, erected while travelling through hostile territory. Nevertheless, according to two reputable chronicles, it took only eight days to construct an earth and timber castle within the existing fortifications at Dover in 1066 and for the raising of a second castle at York in 1069. Whether or not this figure should be taken as literally true, it is clear from the chronicles that such castles could be erected in a relatively short space of time and at minimal expense. Much to the chagrin of the indigenous population, the Conqueror rigorously applied the ancient Anglo-Saxon principle of *burghwork* which ordained that every man could be required to build or repair fortifications: 'Castles he caused to be made, and poor men to be greatly oppressed' (Anglo-Saxon Chronicle). Although it would appear that a reasonably defensible structure could be erected comparatively quickly and cheaply, it is also apparent that the construction of residential accommodation and elaborate timber towers would require more skilled and time-consuming carpentry.

Stone Castles
By contrast, the building of castles in stone was an undertaking of considerable complexity, requiring

detailed planning and more specialised craftsmanship. Inevitably, working in stone was necessarily slower and vastly more expensive, a fact that contributed to a significant decline in castle building in the twelfth century. Indeed, because of the expense of replacing timber fortifications with stone, many earlier earthwork castles became obsolete and were abandoned. The most concentrated period of building in stone occurred in the late twelfth and early thirteenth centuries. A contemporary chronicler described work at the Tower of London in the early years of Henry II's reign (1154–89): 'with so many smiths, carpenters and other workmen, working so vehemently with bustle and noise that a man could hardly hear the one next to him speak'. Fortunately, this was also a time when government was beginning systematically to compile and retain records of its transactions, including those for the building and maintenance of the royal castles (see PIPE ROLLS) which consistently represent the largest items of recorded annual expenditure. Although the castles referred to in the records are almost invariably royal, the information contained therein enables us to establish standards of reference for the construction of seigneurial castles and for the rebuilding in stone of many earlier fortifications.

It is clear from the Pipe Rolls that in the twelfth century the annual cost of building and maintaining royal castles frequently exceeded £1,000 and that on occasions this figure reached £3,000 or even £4,000. In order to appreciate the significance of these figures it is necessary to consider them in context. It has been calculated that annual government revenue during the reign of Henry II (1154–89) averaged £10,000, while the annual income of Roger de Lacy, one of the richest of the king's vassals, has been estimated at £800. Indeed, by 1200 only seven members of the small but immensely powerful ruling class received more than £400 annually. At this time a knight might live comfortably on £15 a year, while his wages on active service were 8d a day in the 1150s, rising to 2s by 1216. The CONSTABLE of a royal castle might receive an annual stipend of £10 to maintain him in his office, while the stipend of a castle chaplain, porter or watchman rarely exceeded 1d per day.

Unlike some early earthwork and timber castles which (it is implied) took little more than eight days to erect, Henry II's castle at Orford took eight years. Orford, on the Suffolk coast, once enjoyed great prosperity as a port and its castle was built on an unfortified site in the years 1165–73. An entry in the Pipe Rolls of 1165–6 refers to the account of the Sheriff of Norfolk and Suffolk 'in the work of

the castle of Orford' and the expenditure of £660 – the largest recorded outlay on a single royal castle since the beginning of Henry's reign. In the following year £323 was spent, and by the autumn of 1167 the building of the keep must have been well advanced for the same roll records payments of £2 for provisioning the castle and 20 marks (see MARK) to a custodian. Work continued over the next six years until 1173 when £58 2s 8d was spent 'in the work of one great ditch round the castle of Orford with palisades and brattices and in the work of a stone bridge in the same castle'.

Unfortunately, at this time the Pipe Rolls provide very few details of construction other than a cursory cash entry: 'In the work of the castle of Orford . . .'. There is no mention of the quarry men and rough masons who worked the stone from the quarries, the freemasons who fashioned it, the woodmen who cut the timber, the carters who transported it, or the carpenters who then worked on it for joists, floors, roofs and hoardings. There are no references to the miners who excavated the ditches and were often required to hack out cellars from solid rock, or to the ironsmiths who (among numerous other tasks) constructed the machinery for portcullises and drawbridges; no mention is made of the humble lime-workers, plumbers and hodmen, the watchmen who guarded the site, or the clerks who checked materials and drew up accounts. Indeed, the occasional reference serves only to add to our curiosity: in 1167–8, for example, we are told that finished timbers were transported from another royal building site at Scarborough, presumably for the joists and flooring of the keep. There is, of course, the evidence of the building itself. When completed, Orford Castle comprised a keep (polygonal, with three projecting square towers and a forebuilding) and a curtain wall with a series of rectangular flanking towers. Today only rough earthworks delineate the former bailey but the splendid (and unusual) keep has survived and this contains dressed Caen stone from Normandy, an indication of the complex organisation required for such a large-scale undertaking. The total cost of building Orford Castle is recorded as £1,413 10s 10d, but it should be borne in mind that, while this figure is a useful indication of costs, it is unlikely to be entirely reliable. Orford provides us with a convenient example of a twelfth-century castle built in its entirety, but the cost of building work elsewhere varied considerably according to the nature of the site and the availability of materials and labour. Furthermore, the more normal practice at this time was to add piecemeal stone buildings and fortifications to an existing site.

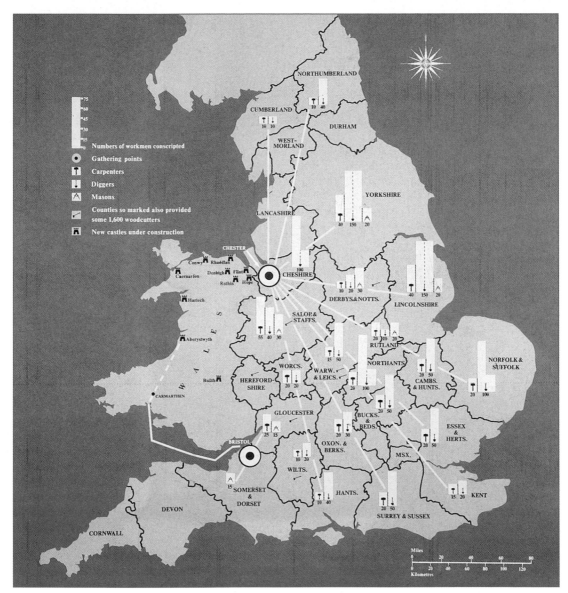

Impressment of workmen for the King's [Edward I] Works in north Wales (1282–3).

The Edwardian Castles of Wales

Work on the greatest of Henry II's castles, at Dover, had cost nearly £7,000 by his death in 1189, and even then it was not complete. But this huge sum pales into insignificance by comparison with that expended by Edward I (1272–1307) on his formidable Welsh castles a century later: a sum exceeding £100,000 in the period 1277–1330, more than 80 per cent of which was committed before 1301 (*see* WALES, CONQUEST OF). The total cost of Harlech Castle is estimated to have been £9,500, while that of Conwy,

for the period 1283–7 when the main work was completed, was £15,000. The town walls, quay and castle at Caernarfon were built for £27,000, though (as at Beaumaris) the castle was never finished. Of the £14,500 expended at Beaumaris between 1295 and 1330, no less than £6,736 was spent in the first six months. In this period carriage of materials alone cost £2,100 as most of the building stone had to be transported from the mainland and a naval force employed 'to keep the sea between Snowdon and Anglesey' (*see* MATERIALS, CARRIAGE OF).

As with Edward's other castles, resources were commandeered from every part of his realm: lead from the Isle of Man, iron and steel from Newcastle-under-Lyme, rope from Lincolnshire and Dorset and timber from Liverpool. At the same time the wages of workmen excavating the moat and erecting a barricade round the site were nearly £1,500, suggesting that their numbers throughout the summer must have averaged some 1,800 men. The quantities of materials used, other than stone, included 2,248 tons of sea-coal for burning lime for mortar, 640 quarters of charcoal, 42 masons' axes, 3,277 boards, eight loads of lead, 160 lb of tin, 314 'bends' of iron and 105,000 assorted nails. In the second year of construction 16,200 freestones were supplied by four contractors and 32,583 tons of stone quarried and transported to the site. At today's prices the unfinished castle at Beaumaris cost in excess of £8 million: and this figure does not include the work at Beaumaris and Caernarfon which continued into the reign of Edward's grandson, Edward III. Only in part may this extraordinary expenditure be accounted for by inflation. Five of the eight castles were integrated with new fortified towns (see TOWN WALLS) and they were all conceived on a scale matched only by Gilbert de Clare's Caerphilly Castle in the southern Marches (1268–71). They also incorporated all the advanced techniques of fortification previously evolved. Described as 'the premium that Edward paid to insure his Welsh conquests against the fire of rebellion', this crippling expenditure effectively postponed Edward's plans for conquering Scotland. The raising of these castles, and the introduction of English settlers into the towns which they protected, was integral to Edward's strategy for the subjugation of the Welsh. Speed was therefore of the essence: Flint Castle was built in eight-and-a-half years (1277–86), Harlech in seven-and-a-half (1283–90), Rhuddlan in four-and-a-half (1277–82) and Conwy in five (1283–7). More to the point, the castles were built simultaneously: Aberystwyth, Builth, Flint and Rhuddlan from 1277, Harlech, Conwy and Caernarfon from 1283. It was a truly formidable undertaking.

For the most part, accurate building accounts have survived for Edward's works, in the Pipe Rolls, in the North Wales Chamberlain's accounts (compiled annually at Caernarfon) and in the detailed rolls of 'particulars' on which the final accounts were based. In addition, many enrolled copies of writs, letters and other documents issued and received by the CHANCERY and EXCHEQUER have also survived. This documentary evidence (although incomplete) graphically illustrates how such a complex operation was carried out. It shows, for example, the personal involvement of the king in the early stages of each project, the seasonal nature of castle-building (work almost ground to a halt from late October to March) and that wages accounted for two-thirds of the total cost. During the building seasons of 1285–7 the three castles of Conwy, Caernarfon and Harlech employed between them an average of 2,500 workers, while at Beaumaris in 1298 there were 3,500 workmen on site. Little wonder that Edward I's architect, Master James of St George, and his clerk of the works, Walter of Winchester, felt obliged to warn the king that: 'In case you should be wondering where so much money could go in a week, we would have you know that we have needed – and shall continue to need – 400 masons, both cutters and layers, together with 2,000 minor workmen, 100 carts, 60 wagons and 60 boats bringing stone and sea-coal, 200 quarrymen, 30 smiths, and carpenters for putting in the joists and floor-boards and other necessary jobs. All this takes no account of the garrison . . . nor of the purchase of materials, of which there will have to be a great quantity.' To mobilise such a force of craftsmen and labourers required considerable administrative organisation. The teams that assembled at Chester were drawn not only from Wales and the Marches but from nearly every English county and even from abroad. It was at this time that impressment for castle-work became a royal prerogative, one that replaced burghwork (see above) with the even older obligation of military service, such service now being demanded by the king of his subjects in the form of labour. From the thirteenth century the Patent Rolls are full of orders for craftsmen and labourers to be enrolled, on pain of imprisonment, for the king's works. Labour was commandeered in the same way as building materials and wagons or boats for their carriage: the king's requirements came before all others. Nevertheless, proper wages were paid and, although we read in the accounts for 1277 of payments to mounted sergeants (each at 7½d per day) for 'guarding the said workmen . . . lest they flee on the way', the only real cause for complaint was a general shortage of skilled labour because 'the king hath taken it all'. Some men worked on piece-work, others were paid by the day and a few, the master craftsmen, earned salaries (see GUILDS). Notable among these were the master masons who, pre-eminent in their craft, were responsible both for designing buildings and for overseeing the construction work, assisted by a clerk of the works (see MASTER MASONS AND ARCHITECTS). Undoubtedly the most influential of the military architects was Master JAMES OF

ST GEORGE, a master mason and 'engineer' (*ingeniator*) brought by the king from Savoy and appointed as 'master of the king's works in Wales'. Of the other masons, the superior class was made up of the *freemasons* who carved the blocks of FREESTONE that were placed in position by the layers, setters and wallers who comprised the second class. The third class of mason, the rough-layers and hardhewers, worked either on site, building rubble walls, or as quarrymen selecting and extracting the stone. The carpenters were expected to undertake every type of woodcraft, from felling timber to carving screens and making tile-pins. There were also the slaters, tilers and thatchers, who were referred to collectively as *helyers*, together with miners, plumbers, glaziers, smiths and painters. Lower in the scale were the plasterers and pargetters, whitewashers and daubers (*see* WATTLE AND DAUB) and, finally, the comparatively unskilled mortarmen, hodmen and barrowmen. When such large numbers of workmen came together the problem of providing accommodation for them must have been considerable and it was often necessary to provide temporary 'lodges' for the respective trades.

Magnate Castles

Of course, in all respects Edward I's 'ring of castles' was exceptional, as were Edward III's improvements at Windsor (1350–77) which cost a prodigious £51,000 – the highest recorded expenditure for any single royal building scheme in the medieval period. Even the greatest of the English magnates could not match the resources available to the crown. Nevertheless, there were far more baronial castles than royal ones (by the end of the thirteenth century there were no fewer than twenty-six masonry castles in the Glamorgan lordship), and several of these were not markedly inferior to their royal counterparts in strength or style. But, unlike Edward's Welsh castles, very few were built from new: most evolved through periods of expansion and refurbishment on existing sites. The builders of Warwick and Kenilworth, Caerphilly and Raglan, Alnwick and Warkworth were all men possessed of considerable resources who relied on a highly competent and organised building industry. Fortunately, although little documentary evidence remains from the earlier centuries, building accounts from the fourteenth and fifteenth centuries have often survived and these show, sometimes in considerable detail, the trials and tribulations experienced by the late medieval builders.

Kirby Muxloe, owned by the prominent Yorkist, William, Lord Hastings (*c.* 1431–83), was a fortified MANOR HOUSE rather than a castle. Typical of its period, it was to have comprised a quadrangular enclosure with four rectangular corner towers and an imposing twin-towered gatehouse at the centre of the north façade, all within a water-filled moat. The building was of brick, and was built on the site of an existing house, part of which was incorporated into the new work. The detailed accounts for the work begin in October 1480 and from them it is possible to trace the scheme's progress. Initially, activity in the winter months was confined to clearing and preparing the site and moat. With the coming of spring, large quantities of stone were transported from neighbouring quarries, timber was cut and prepared, bricks made on site and stacked by the thousand (*see* BRICK BUILDINGS) and increasing numbers of craftsmen and labourers were drafted in. Throughout the summer work proceeded apace, though at the end of May it was considered necessary to engage the services of five men who were paid 1s 8d to watch throughout the night lest the water in the moat should rise and flood the building site. In the autumn preparations were made for the coming of winter. Many of the workmen were paid off and nine cartloads of stubble were brought in from the fields to protect the unfinished tops of walls from frost damage. At the end of the first year total payments of £330 3s are shown in the accounts. The accounts for ensuing years show only minor variations, though as the work neared completion so the number of indoor tasks increased and the contrast between the summer and winter months became less marked. It is clear from the wages columns of the accounts that the workmen (all of whom are named) were largely itinerant and drawn from a wide area, some coming from Wales and many of the specialist bricklayers coming from East Anglia. Most lived on the site where a chaplain was provided for their spiritual welfare. The master bricklayers John Hornne and John Corbell and the master carpenter John Doyle were paid 8d a day, while ordinary craftsmen received 6d and the unskilled labourers 4d. The master mason was John Couper, an experienced architect who regularly visited the site but was not required to be there permanently. The accounts show that in the early summer of 1483 work at Kirby Muxloe suddenly came to a halt. King Edward IV had died in the previous month and Lord Hastings, who had been a loyal supporter of the king and who opposed Richard III's usurpation, was seized and executed. The work was finally put in hand again by Hastings' widow, but it was never completed according to her late husband's original plan. The total recorded cost from the accounts, which were finalised in December 1484, was £1,000 – expended on a building that was never to be enjoyed by the man who commissioned it.

(*See also* FOUNDATIONS; IRONWORK, LOCKS AND NAILS; LEAD; MASTER MASONS AND ARCHITECTS; MATERIALS, CARRIAGE OF; PLUMBING, WATER SUPPLY AND SANITATION; RAM (PILE-DRIVER); SCAFFOLDING AND CRANES; SLATES AND TILES *and* THATCH)

CASTLES, DEVELOPMENT OF Any attempt to set out the development of castles as though it were a systematic evolutionary process is doomed to failure. It is certainly true that development generally occurred in response to changing military, political, domestic and economic circumstances: the introduction of chimney flues, for example, encouraged the provision of apartments and notions of privacy. But circumstances and priorities varied considerably from one area to another, as did the resources available to individual builders. There are elements of evolution evident in most castles, but these should not be overstated.

Earth and Timber Castles

Fortification in Anglo-Saxon England was essentially communal – exemplified by BURHS such as Wareham, Wallingford and Cricklade, the first major settlements to be created since the Roman occupation. These were refuges, surrounded by earth ramparts and ditches, which afforded protection to communities in response to the Danish incursions of the ninth and tenth centuries.

The primary military function of a medieval castle was an offensive one, as a base for active operations by which surrounding territory could be controlled. But as such it was of considerable value in war and it was the need for impregnability which, above all other requirements, dictated a castle's design and architectural form. The castle, and the feudal system of which it was a manifestation (*see* CASTLE), was introduced into England by William I (1066–87) and his Norman and Flemish followers. Soon after the Conquest, castles were erected at key sites (notably at several of the Anglo-Saxon burhs) and by those of Duke William's followers who had been rewarded with land. Undoubtedly the largest concentration (estimated at over 600 castles) was in the marches of Wales, though many of these would have been temporary campaign castles, abandoned once an area had been brought under control (*see* MARCH). For the most part these early fortifications were enclosures (*baileys*) with deeply cut outer ditches and formidable earth ramparts with timber palisades

(*see* BAILEY). These earthwork castles were often dominated by artificial mounds (*mottes*) on which were erected timber stockades and towers (*see* MOTTE). Inevitably, these came to be known as *motte and bailey* castles, though not all early castles had a motte. Many were simply large baileys – ditch, rampart and gate – within which were located all the buildings required by a feudal lord, his household and garrison (*see* RINGWORK). Of course, the common perception of the Norman Conquest is one of numerous motte and bailey castles scattered throughout England and Wales and all conforming to the familiar textbook plan. But what is apparent on the ground is the extraordinary variety of fortifications dating from the immediate post-Conquest period: there were mottes without baileys, baileys without mottes, ramparts surmounted by palisades, ramparts with masonry walls, single ditches or multiple ditches, artificial mounds, cliff-top sites and promontories (*see* SITING).

Masonry Castles

Earthwork castles continued to be built well into the twelfth century, while many earlier ones were reconstructed in stone. The splendid Great Tower at Chepstow Castle is the earliest example in Britain of a HALL-KEEP (1067–75), one that clearly resembles those built in northern France before the Conquest. The best known of these early stone castles is the White Tower (the Tower of London). Intended by William I to be a palace-fortress, it was begun in *c.* 1078 and completed by 1097 when a CURTAIN WALL was constructed around the bailey. Great towers such as these were raised to awe and subdue a conquered people. The walls of the White Tower were 27m (90ft) high and nearly 5m (15ft) thick and were constructed largely of stone transported from Normandy. A number of other castles were strengthened by the rebuilding of bailey walls in stone, though at Richmond Castle the wall and flanking towers of the Great Court or bailey were almost certainly stone structures from the beginning (*c.* 1089).

A prolonged period of internal peace during the reign of Henry I (1100–35) provided an opportunity for the remodelling of many of the earlier castles, particularly those associated with administrative or strategic centres and royal strongholds. Many of the Conqueror's men had gambled and lost all they had won. But others prospered, the de Briouzes and Warennes among them, and it was these men who built the first great stone fortresses such as Bramber, Lewes and Castle Acre. Many twelfth-century magnates constructed magnificent masonry towers or *donjons*, which were entered at first-floor level

Unlike most early castles, Richmond in Yorkshire was probably a masonry stronghold from the beginning. In its original form (1089) there was no keep, the large triangular bailey depending for its defence on a gate-tower, curtain walls on two sides and the cliff edge on the third. The square flanking towers in the vulnerable east curtain are the oldest in any English castle.

and included both military and domestic quarters. William d'Albini's keep at Castle Rising (1138) may have lacked the military sophistication of Henry I's keep at Norwich, but in the provision of private chambers, chapel and garderobes it was its equal (*see* DONJON, GREAT TOWER *and* KEEP). (The separation of a lord from his affinity, which this arrangement implied, was exceptional in the twelfth century.) Not only was a stone keep more easily defended than an earth and timber structure, it was also an unambiguous statement of power and status: both a symbol of subjugation and a bastion of paranoia (*see* NORMANS, THE). Another type of stone keep, the so-called SHELL-KEEP, consisted of a crenellated wall surrounding the summit of a motte, as at Carisbrooke, Cardiff and Brecon Castles, or enclosing the motte itself, as at Carmarthen and Berkeley.

Following the Anarchy of 1135–54 (*see* ANARCHY, THE), Henry II (1154–89) ordered the demolition of many ADULTERINE castles that had been erected during the previous decades, while strengthening his own castles and consolidating his vast empire which stretched from the Tweed to the Pyrenees. It was Henry II who introduced a legal obligation to obtain a *licence to crenellate* before a castle could be built or a residence fortified (*see* CRENELLATIONS). What was clear, even to the mightiest of his subjects, was the prohibitive cost of providing adequate defences against siege warfare. Furthermore, the atmosphere of improved public order that began to permeate Angevin England encouraged not the construction of strongholds but the creation of new TOWNS. For a century or more the building of private castles declined dramatically.

Nevertheless, considerable advances in military architecture are evident in many of the (mostly royal) castles that were built or remodelled in the second half of the twelfth century, mainly because of the experiences of crusaders returning from the Holy Land and Spain. Siege warfare had become more sophisticated (*see* SIEGES) and Norman castles, with their square keeps and low curtain walls, were particularly vulnerable to these techniques. Consequently, curtain walls increased both in height and thickness and projecting TOWERS were added at intervals from which archers and crossbowmen could command the outer face of the wall. The corners of square towers were especially susceptible to undermining and the castle builders responded by

Goodrich Castle, Herefordshire, c. 1425. Built on a rocky outcrop overlooking the River Wye, the massive gatehouse, buttressed drum towers and curtain walls were constructed c. 1300 around an inner courtyard and twelfth-century keep. A series of garderobes project from the wall to the right of the nearest (south-east) tower. The barbican was added in the fourteenth century.

eliminating angles altogether. Circular or semi-circular mural towers became the norm, often with SPUR BUTTRESSES added for increased protection. A number of circular keeps were also built at this time, notable among them the unique great tower of Conisbrough Castle (*c.* 1180) from which projected six tapering buttress-like turrets. Hubert de Burgh, Henry III's chief justiciar, spent prodigiously on the remodelling of Dover Castle following the siege of 1216–17. When completed, Dover was no longer a place of last resort but a formidable 'weapon of aggression' with multiple defences to ensnare the intruder, elaborate sally-ports and a massive residential gatehouse. Thereafter, the message was clear. For those who could afford such expenditure, their castles could indeed be made impregnable.

It was in the late twelfth century that magnates began to withdraw from the communal life of the hall to the relative peace of their privy chambers where much of their business was carried out. The separation of rooms, and their functions within the inner household, was a direct consequence of the expansion of household organisation that is evident in contemporary documents. In the thirteenth century we can observe the growth of a hierarchy of rooms, each located strategically in relation to others, depending on their function, and distinguished by their size, decoration and proximity to the lord's chamber. But it was not until the late thirteenth century that castles began to be designed with suites of rooms integrated according to function, the Edwardian castles in Wales providing some of the best examples (*see* HOUSEHOLD).

By the thirteenth century the concept of the keep as a final refuge had been superseded by that of the ENCLOSURE CASTLE or ENCEINTE, comprising a formidable curtain with mural towers and a self-contained KEEP-GATEHOUSE. Goodrich Castle provides a late but interesting example. Here, in *c.* 1290, a dark and incommodious twelfth-century keep was abandoned for residential purposes and a series of domestic buildings erected against the curtain walls of an almost quadrangular enclosure. These buildings included a gatehouse (with a chapel and chambers above), solar, great hall, kitchen and various service rooms together with a range of lodgings for Aymer de Valence's household knights and officials whose numbers rarely fell below fifty. Goodrich was a compromise: it was both a soldiers' stronghold and an apartment block for which a range of common services was provided. The Norman keep was retained but even today it has the appearance of a military anachronism.

Caerphilly, in East Glamorgan, was undoubtedly the finest castle of the age. Begun in 1268 and covering 30 acres, it had concentric walls with corner towers, seven twin-towered gatehouses and a complex system of water defences, fortified dams and islands called *hornworks* (*see* MOATS AND WATER DEFENCES). At the time of its construction Caerphilly was at the forefront of military technology. For the first time in Britain all the advances in castle design were brought together to create an integrated, interlocking and interlinked defensive system in which every part of the castle assisted in the defence of every other part. And, most surprising of all, it was not a royal but a magnate castle, built by Gilbert de Clare, the 'Red Earl' of Gloucester, who went to the most extraordinary lengths to protect his Glamorgan estates from his recalcitrant Welsh neighbours.

The Edwardian Castles in Wales

Collectively, the castles constructed by Edward I of England (1272–1307) during his subjugation of Gwynedd (1276–96) represent one of the greatest achievements of medieval military architecture (*see* WALES: CONQUEST OF). The disposition and design of each was dictated both by its site – carefully chosen to take advantage of natural features, and its suitability for provisioning by sea – and its function. Conwy (1282) and Caernarfon (1283–92) were citadels, integrated within the defensive walls (*bastides*) of the TOWNS they protected, rectangular and elongated, with adjacent lower and upper wards or courtyards and great flanking towers. At Conwy entry was by means of gate passages protected by BARBICANS at the east and west ends. At Caernarfon the King's Gate (had it been completed) would have contained five gates, six portcullises and numerous murder holes and arrow slits. Harlech Castle (1283) is a combination of keep-gatehouse and concentric castle. It stands on a rocky outcrop 60m (200ft) above the former sea-level and

has a formidable gatehouse, four huge corner towers and walls enclosing a single inner ward. There is also an outer ward protected both by a low curtain wall which encircles the castle and by its precipitous access from the sea. Beaumaris, on Anglesey, is the epitome of CONCENTRIC CASTLES. Begun in 1295 but never completed, it was constructed on a level site that provided none of the advantageous natural features enjoyed by other castles. Because of this, Edward's architect Master James of St George 'perfected the ultimate in symmetrical concentric design'. There is no reliance on a central strongpoint and the castle consists of concentric rings of walls, each higher than that outside it so that both inner and outer wards could be defended simultaneously, and with flanking towers located to eliminate 'blind spots'. There is a wide wet moat with a fortified dock (*see* QUAYS) and two substantial gatehouses to the north and south of the inner ward.

The Fourteenth Century

In the fourteenth century there was a significant divergence between north and south. Raiding and feuding across the Scottish border were endemic (and persisted for three centuries) and were reflected in a proliferation of PELE TOWERS in the northern counties of England; along the south coast, in contrast, the fear of French incursions and possible invasion during the HUNDRED YEARS WAR resulted in the building or strengthening of a number of castles. Notable among these was Bodiam. In 1385 Richard II issued a licence to crenellate to Sir Edward Dalyngrigge, a veteran of the Hundred Years War, which directed him 'to construct and make thereof a castle in defence of the adjacent countryside and for resistance against our enemies'. Those enemies were the French who, in the previous decade, had gained control of the Channel and sacked both Rye (1377) and Winchelsea (1380). Despite its splendid military appearance, Bodiam is typical of several castles of the period that were built or embellished on the proceeds of war (*see* RANSOM). Like the Beauchamp earls' magnificent east façade at Warwick Castle and Edward III's extensive rebuilding of Windsor, Bodiam was a theatrical stage set, an extravagant declaration of accumulated wealth and chivalric superiority. Much of this wasteful exuberance ('dispendiousness') was learned of the French nobility during the Hundred Years War, a 'self-conscious sense of theatre in contemporary chivalry which gave context to the "first great flowering of English domestic architecture"' (Platt, quoting McFarlane). There is also an underlying sense of a social hierarchy (or paranoia?) within the castle itself. The household and garrison were strictly segregated and (significantly, perhaps) the disposition of the lord's quarters ensured that he retained control of the gatehouse. This physical separation of a lord and his personal household from the (potentially disaffected) mercenaries who were hired to protect him is evident in the design of many late medieval castles, even at Thornbury (1511–22) which is generally considered to be the last medieval castle to be built in England (see DECLINE OF THE CASTLE). There is also a clear shift of emphasis in the second half of the fourteenth century with greater concessions made to domestic comfort. Several castles were abandoned as residences while others were extended and refurbished to meet the demand for more commodious accommodation and for the provision of lodgings for ANNUITANTS. New castles (such as Bodiam and Bolton) were often quadrangular, with four ranges of domestic buildings arranged against the surrounding walls and square mural towers which were more conveniently shaped to accommodate domestic apartments (see COURT AND COURTYARD). There was also a revival of the keep, now described as a TOWER-HOUSE to distinguish it from its Norman predecessor. It has been suggested that, unlike the earlier keep which was a refuge against outsiders, the tower-house was intended to defend a lord against his own retainers, many of whom were unreliable mercenaries. Tower-houses are most common in Scotland and the north of England but there are examples elsewhere, such as Wardour Castle in Wiltshire (1393) and Nunney Castle (1373), Somerset.

The effect on military architecture of the introduction of cannon in the fourteenth century has generally been overstated (see FIREARMS AND CANNON). Attempts elsewhere in Europe to adapt fortifications in response to the increasing use of artillery were resisted in England, other than by the insertion of GUN PORTS and the modification of LOOPHOLES. To defend against artillery required a fortification with a squat profile and heavily revetted ramparts and ditches – precisely the type of structure that was unlikely to appeal to the status-seeking English aristocracy.

The Late Medieval Period

The early decades of the fifteenth century witnessed renewed success in the French wars and the return of another generation of war-enriched magnates anxious to advertise their wealth and status through the building and embellishment of castles. However, the emphasis was increasingly on domestic comfort and many of the castles of this period might more accurately be described as fortified mansions. Raglan Castle in south Wales appears to possess all the attributes of a medieval stronghold. But within its crenellated walls and polygonal towers are ranges of private apartments and domestic offices, built in the 1460s to accommodate William Herbert, earl of Pembroke, his family, guests and a substantial retinue. Even so, it is not without significance that the rapacious Herbert retained and strengthened the formidable Great Tower (c. 1435) as a refuge, isolated from the castle by a moat and bascule bridge. Raglan may have been conceived as an aristocratic residence rather than a stronghold, but its defences were sufficient to withstand the bombardment of a Civil War siege.

Some of the finest late medieval BRICK BUILDINGS date from this transitional period,

Raglan Castle in south Wales appears to possess all the attributes of a medieval stronghold. But within its crenellated walls and polygonal towers are ranges of private apartments and domestic offices, built in the 1460s to accommodate William Herbert, earl of Pembroke, his family, guests and a substantial retinue. Even so, it is not without significance that the rapacious Herbert retained and strengthened the formidable Great Tower (c. 1435) as a refuge – isolated from the castle by a moat and bascule bridge.

notably Tattershall Castle (1430–50), Herstmonceux Castle (1440) and Caister Castle (1432–46). At the same time the quadrangular castle was gradually developing into the *courtyard house*: the quadrangular arrangement of domestic buildings remained but with only a token crenellated parapet, gatehouse and moat for protection. It may seem somewhat paradoxical that the castle's decline and a marked proliferation of fortified MANOR HOUSES in the second half of the fifteenth century should coincide with the so-called WARS OF THE ROSES. But these 'wars' were little more than a series of intermittent field campaigns in which castles played only a minor rôle. Unlike the Hundred Years War, the Wars of the Roses were not wars of trenches, protracted sieges and gun batteries. The large windows and thin walls of Tattershall and Herstmonceux are indicative of a society which, despite the poor governance of Henry VI, was relatively prosperous, untroubled by the prospect of war.

Edward IV (1461–83) built his Great Hall at Eltham on the outskirts of London to entertain two thousand guests at a time. By the end of the fifteenth century English kings built palaces not fortresses (*see* ROYAL PALACES). The medieval concept of divine sovereignty was yielding to that of a monarch surrounded by an ever more complex court. Edward was as close to the merchants in the City of London as he was to his feudal magnates and his reign looked forward to the modern world. The medieval castle was a product and a symbol of the feudal system, a system that under the Tudors was as anachronistic as the castle itself (*see* TUDOR COASTAL FORTS). With the suppression of LIVERY AND MAINTENANCE and the abolition of the private army, the English magnate was transformed from war lord to courtier (*see* DECLINE OF THE CASTLE). Nevertheless, many castles continued to be occupied for domestic purposes. At Raglan Castle, from *c.* 1549 to 1589, William Somerset, 3rd earl of Worcester, rebuilt the great hall with a hammerbeam roof and a fine oriel window, and added substantial service and office wings together with a long gallery (a characteristic feature of great Tudor houses) at second-floor level overlooking the Fountain Court. All these major improvements were designed to provide the high standard of accommodation that was expected in the country seat of an Elizabethan nobleman. At Raglan red sandstone was used for this phase of building and this serves to distinguish it from earlier fifteenth-century work for which a pale yellow sandstone was used. Kenilworth Castle was similarly extended and 'improved' by Robert Dudley, earl of Leicester (1533–88), who erected a range of guests' apartments (now known as Leicester's

Building) with further lodgings to the south of the old hall-keep (which he also remodelled), together with a splendid stone and timber-frame stable block, an imposing outer gatehouse and a pleasure garden. Interesting though such later additions may be, there is often something incongruous about them: large, square-headed Elizabethan windows, classical architectural decoration and seventeenth-century parterres do not sit easily in a medieval castle. Similarly, continuous occupation can be a mixed blessing: it is often difficult not to be disappointed when visiting an ancient fortress that has suffered centuries of modernisation and reconstruction and the regular addition of domestic accretions. Somehow, the spell is broken, especially when the interior is noted for its comfort and ostentation – as at Windsor, Bamburgh, Powis, Berkeley and Warwick.

Only in the Civil War of 1642–9 did the castle come into its own again, and then only briefly. Many castles were hastily refortified to accommodate garrisons and consequently the Civil War was remarkable for its many sieges. It is most regrettable that the depredations of artillery, the dismantling of fortifications to prevent their future use (*see* SLIGHTING) and subsequent 'quarrying' for building materials should have resulted in the destruction of so much of our medieval heritage.

CASTLESHIP *or* CASTLEWICKE The privileges or territories of a castle.

CASTLES OF ENCLOSURE *see* ENCLOSURE CASTLES

CASTLES OF LIVERY AND MAINTENANCE *see* LIVERY AND MAINTENANCE, CASTLES OF

CASTLET *or* CASTELLET A small castle.

CASTLE-TOWN A town defended by a castle.

CASTLEWARD (i) The warden of a castle.
(ii) The castle guard (*see* CASTLE GUARD).

CAT *see* SIEGES

CATAPULT A large stone-throwing engine (*see* SIEGES).

CATEGORIES OF CASTLE *see* CASTLES, CATEGORIES OF

CAUSEWAY *or* CAUSEY A raised route-way, often paved, to assist pedestrians, horses and wheeled vehicles when crossing marshy or flooded land.

CAVALIER A raised battery.

CEILINGS *see* MEDIEVAL ARCHITECTURE; PLASTER, WHITEWASH AND PAINT; ROOFS (TIMBER) *and* VAULTING

CELLARER *see* KITCHENS

CEMENT *see* MORTAR AND CEMENT

CENTAINE Militia unit of one hundred men.

CENTRING *see* VAULTING

CERVELLIÈRE *see* HELMETS

CHAIN BOOM *see* BOOM

CHAMBER A relatively private room, used for sleeping and other domestic purposes, in contra-distinction to larger communal rooms such as the HALL.
(*See also* SOLAR)

CHAMBERLAIN An officer of a lord's household, originally responsible for a lord's personal domestic arrangements but ultimately for his financial affairs (*see* HOUSEHOLD).

CHAMFER To cut away the sharp edge (*arris*) of a block of stone or timber beam, usually at 45 degrees to the vertical and horizontal surfaces. A *hollow chamfer* has a concave surface; a *moulded chamfer* is cut in parallel mouldings; and a *stopped chamfer* is one in which the chamfer is carried part-way along the block or beam and is terminated with a carved splay.

CHAMFRON Horse armour, protecting the animal's head (*see* HORSES AND HORSE-HARNESS).

CHAMPION COUNTRYSIDE *see* COUNTRYSIDE

CHANCELLOR An officer of a lord's household responsible for administrative and legal matters such as the drawing-up of charters and the writing of letters (*see* HOUSEHOLD).

CHANCERY Following the Conquest the royal office of Chancellor combined all the duties of the

present-day secretaries of state. The Chancery is the Lord Chancellor's division of the High Court of Justice. It originated in the governmental structure of the early medieval kings and was the department responsible for issuing charters and letters under the great seal, transmitting royal instructions to the sovereign's subjects (*see* HOUSEHOLD). During the reign of Edward I (1272–1307), for example, when the king required letters (in Latin) to be issued by the Chancery under the great seal, he would provide relatively informal instructions (in French) to his chancellor under the privy seal, and these warrants would then be implemented on his behalf. From the reign of Henry II the English Chancery was acknowledged to be the most efficient in the western world. The *Chancery Rolls* record its activities from 1199 to 1937 and in particular royal grants of titles, privileges and land, and details of *Inquisitiones Ad Quod Damnum* – details of commissions convened to investigate such matters as title deeds and the protection of existing rights prior to the granting of fairs and markets. The archives of the Court of Chancery are kept in the Public Record Office (*see* APPENDIX II).
(*See also* STATE RECORDS)

CHANCERY ROLLS *see* CHANCERY

CHANTRY A private mass, celebrated regularly for the repose of the soul of a testator and others nominated by him in his will. The conviction that a regular offering of the eucharist was the most effective means of redemption encouraged medieval man to make financial provision in his will for a chantry or chantries. This was particularly so during the fourteenth and fifteenth centuries when the liturgy of the Catholic Church increasingly emphasised the importance of the mass. Some chantries were endowed during the lifetime of the founder, and the mass-priest would be obliged to celebrate masses for his well-being on earth and his soul after death. Chantries were also endowed by guilds and fraternities for the benefit of their members. They were, in fact, a very cheap form of endowment for even the most humble testator could arrange for one or two masses to be said for his soul. However, it was those with the largest purses (or the heaviest consciences) who were responsible for the erection of the magnificent late medieval CHANTRY COLLEGES and CHANTRY CHAPELS and for the endowment of numerous charitable institutions. Cardinal Beaufort (d. 1447) provided for 3,000 masses to be said at the altar of his magnificent chapel at Winchester while Richard Beauchamp, earl of Warwick, left his heirs with the unwelcome legacy of a trust which, for over forty years, employed the receipts of thirty manors for the benefit of his soul. After his death in 1439 the trust engaged priests to say 5,000 soul-masses and financed the building of the beautiful Beauchamp Chapel at St Mary's church, Warwick, one of the glories of the medieval age. Successive members of the Hungerford family spent vast sums on bequests to the church so that by the end of the fifteenth century they had founded twelve chantries, seven anniversary masses (*obits*), a school and two almshouses. The Hospital of All Saints (now known as Brown's Hospital) at Stamford in Lincolnshire was built by Thomas Brown, a prominent wool-merchant, in the reign of Henry VII to accommodate ten poor men, together with two poor women who were to be 'attentive and useful to the poor men in their necessities'. The residents of the Hospital of All Saints were required to recite three psalms a day for the soul of the home's founder, and it was a condition of admission that a candidate should be not only 'lowly, devout and poor' but also fluent in chanting 'the Lord's Prayer, the Angelic Salutation and the Apostles' Creed'. Men such as Thomas Brown were prepared to make considerable and often posthumous investments to ensure that their souls did not remain too long in the dreadful limbo-land of purgatory, a concept which was popularly established in the twelfth century and which motivated the building of numerous social institutions as well as chantry chapels and other memorials.

CHANTRY CHAPELS By the fifteenth century most large churches, and many smaller ones, had at least one chantry chapel in which a priest was employed to sing masses for the soul of the founder and others nominated by him in his will (*see* CHANTRY). Like other forms of memorial, a chantry chapel does not necessarily mark the place of interment of the person in whose memory it was erected. Rather, it would have been erected at a parish church that was patronised by the deceased's family, often that of a castlery or manor, or sometimes within the castle itself, as at Bolton Castle where a chantry was endowed in 1399 (*see also* CHANTRY COLLEGES). Consequently, the heraldic devices with which a chantry chapel is emblazoned are invariably those of the local magnate or gentry family, the quartered coats of arms providing invaluable information concerning that family's ancestry (*see* MARSHALLING).

Some chantry chapels were large (Henry VII's chapel at Westminster Abbey is the most spectacular example) and often consisted of an aisle or side chapel built on to the main body of the church: the glorious Beauchamp Chapel at the collegiate church of St Mary in Warwick (*c.* 1450), for instance, and Cardinal Morton's chapel (*c.* 1500) in the north aisle of Bere Regis church, Dorset. Other chapels were created by extending an aisle (or aisles) in an eastward direction, parallel to the chancel, or to the north and south to create small transepts. Heraldic embellishment in these larger chapels is often sumptuous and may include badges, cyphers and rebuses (*see* BADGES AND LIVERY, CYPHER *and* REBUSES).

However, the majority of chantry chapels are very much smaller and usually comprise a gilded and painted rectangular PARCLOSE of ornate stone or metal and an intricately vaulted canopy. (The essential difference between a canopied monument and a small chantry chapel is the presence in the latter of an altar at which masses were celebrated.) Such chapels are generally found linking the piers of the chancel arcade or flanking the presbytery and their proximity to the high altar is usually an accurate guide to the status of those they commemorate.

It is significant that the popularity of chantry chapels in the high Middle Ages should coincide with the flowering of the Perpendicular style of architecture for, almost without exception, the decorative detail is exquisite (*see* GOTHIC ARCHITECTURE). At Tewkesbury Abbey in Gloucestershire, for instance, the chapel erected (*c.* 1378) for Edward Despenser (d. 1375) on the south side of the high altar contains the earliest example of fan vaulting in England. From within a lofty canopy on the roof of the chapel the kneeling figure of Edward stares out at the high altar and to where the tabernacle or sacrament house was once suspended. (There is no other known example of an effigial figure in this position.) The chapel is commonly known as the Trinity Chapel because on the east wall of the interior is a remarkable fresco representing the Holy Trinity, with portraits of Edward and his wife (Elizabeth de Burghersh) on either side of the central figures, kneeling behind angels with censers. In the corresponding north bay is a chapel within which stands the tomb of Robert Fitz Hamon, a descendant of William the Conqueror and the abbey's founder, who died in 1107. Fitz Hamon was first buried in the Chapter House of the Benedictine monastery but his body was moved to its present position in 1241 and the chantry erected by Abbot Parker in 1397. The finest of the Tewkesbury chantry chapels is that built by Isabel Despenser in memory of her first husband Richard Beauchamp, earl of Abergavenny and Worcester (d. 1421).

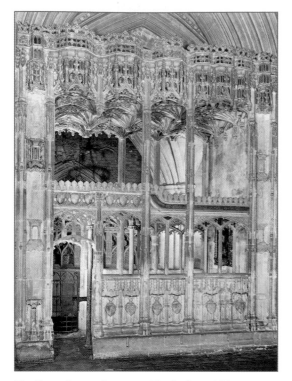

The Beauchamp chantry at Tewkesbury Abbey, Gloucestershire.

Begun in 1422 but not completed until 1438, it has an ornate and spiky canopy and a lovely miniature fan-vault within which is set a carved lady's head – presumably that of Lady Isabella herself. There are traces of original painting in the vault: peacock blue with ribs and pendants in red and gold. There are other notable examples at Newark in Notting-hamshire, Paignton in Devon, Boxgrove Priory in Sussex and Christchurch Priory in Dorset.

With the dissolution of chantries in 1547, many chantry chapels were used for other purposes: the superb Hungerford chantry at Salisbury Cathedral, for example, was converted into an exceptionally ornate mayoral pew.

CHANTRY COLLEGES *and* COLLEGIATE CHURCHES There were two types of college of 'secular priests' in medieval England, the earlier of which was usually created by a religious body and was based on a cathedral model with a chapter of clergy ('secular canons') under a dean or provost. The collegiate chapel in the courtyard of Hastings Castle, endowed by Robert, count of Eu, in *c.* 1070, was of this type. The later, and more numerous, type was known as a *chantry college* because the object

of their foundation was to pray for the souls of the founders and other benefactors (*see* CHANTRY). Their clergy, known as chantry priests, dwelt together in the college precincts presided over by a master, warden or provost, and their constitution ensured a 'perpetual succession' of services. Although many of these colleges were small, some rivalled the cathedrals and monasteries in size and opulence, particularly in the fourteenth and fifteenth centuries when the founding of a chantry college was often the ultimate ambition of the medieval establishment. The very rich, especially those who left no direct heir, might provide for the establishment of a college that was endowed primarily for the celebration of masses in perpetuity for the souls of the founder and his family. Of course, many collegiate churches were also family mausoleums and there can be little doubt that they were intended to be a permanent memorial to a magnate's status and lineage. Thus the late medieval chantry colleges were effectively chantry chapels on a grand scale (*see* CHURCHES). Several, such as St George's Chapel, Windsor, and the (unfinished) collegiate church at Warkworth, were located within the walls of royal or magnate castles, while others, such as Tattershall, Staindrop, Middleham and Fotheringhay, were parish churches which were endowed as chantry colleges by noble patrons whose castles were in close proximity.

Undoubtedly the finest collegiate foundation, and that which inspired many others, is the Chapel of St George at Windsor Castle. The original college was endowed in 1348 by Edward III (1327–77), following the founding of the Order of the Garter in the same year. Henry III's chapel, dedicated to St Edward the Confessor, was repaired and became the collegiate chapel, rededicated to St George and the Blessed Virgin Mary. At the same time the entire lower ward of the castle was converted to house the officials and clergy who were to serve the new college and the Order with which it was to be associated (*see* GARTER, MOST NOBLE ORDER OF THE). St George's Chapel, which now dominates the lower ward of the castle, was begun by Edward IV in 1472 to celebrate his return from exile and was completed by Henry VIII in 1528. It remains the chapel of the Order of the Garter and has been accurately described as one of the greatest achievements of Perpendicular Gothic architecture.

The magnificent collegiate church at Warkworth Castle was erected in the early fifteenth century as a mausoleum for the Percy family. The church, of which only the foundations remain, was never completed but was intended to have a nave and two aisles, transepts, a tower above the crossing and a quire at the east end. The ground slopes upward from west to east so that a pair of crypts could be accommodated beneath the chancel. The larger crypt would have contained the Percy tombs, to which the earl and his family would descend in solemn procession to celebrate the anniversaries of the deaths of their ancestors, while the smaller chamber was probably intended as a vestry. The collegiate church at Warkworth separates the inner and outer wards so that a visitor, having entered through the lofty gatehouse, would see in front of him the south façade and tower of the church and, beyond that, the spectacular mass of the keep. To heighten the dramatic effect, access to the inner ward was through a passageway constructed beneath the east end of the church.

Ralph Neville, earl of Westmorland (1354–1425), was preoccupied with elevating Staindrop church, at the gates of his castle of Raby in County Durham, into a college of priests. His grandfather had endowed three chantries in the church for the repose of his parents and Ralph Neville obtained a licence from the prior of Durham for a further foundation of a warden, twelve clergy, twelve poor gentlemen and six other 'poor persons'. For their support he gave two houses, 12 acres of land and the advowson of the church. Westmorland's splendid alabaster effigy and those of his two wives were placed on a great tomb chest before the altar where 'perpetual masses' were said for their souls.

In 1478 Richard of Gloucester (later Richard III) obtained licences to establish collegiate churches at Barnard Castle and Middleham, only three days after the execution of his brother, the duke of Clarence. The collegiate body at Middleham consisted of a dean, six chaplains, four clerks and six choristers, and (in the words of the king's licence) was charged with the offering of perpetual masses 'for the good estate of Us, and our most dear Consort Elizabeth Queen of England, and of Our . . . brother and Anne his wife, and his heirs, while we shall live, and when we shall depart from this light, for our souls, and for the souls of the most illustrious Prince, Richard, formerly Duke of York, our father, and of our brothers and sisters, and of all the faithful departed . . .'.

Fotheringhay College originated in the chapel of the castle and is described in contemporary documents as 'the Collegiate Church of the Annunciation and St Edward the Confessor within the castle of Fotheringhay'. Towards the end of the fourteenth century Edmund Langley determined to refound the college on a larger scale but his plans were thwarted by his death in 1402. In 1411

Langley's son (also Edward) obtained letters patent for the transfer, and 6 acres of land to the south of the parish church were assigned for the collegiate buildings. However, it was not until 1415 that the parish church and college were formally united and the dean and canons replaced by a master and chantry priests. Edward was killed at Agincourt in the same year and his body buried in the quire of the new collegiate church which was then under construction. The staff of the college consisted of a master, precentor, eleven other chaplains or fellows, eight clerks and thirteen choristers. It was established to pray for the souls of Richard II, Henry IV, Henry V, the founder and other benefactors and their families. A code of statutes was drawn up which consisted of fifty-four sections that had to be recited in the chapter house twice a year. It included legislation regarding the election of fellows, the appointment and payment of officials, the dress to be worn, the administration of corporate lands and property and the preparation of an annual balance sheet. The church building comprised two separate churches: the eastern portion, or quire, was the private collegiate church while the western portion, or nave, was the parish church. The college was transferred into the ownership of the duke of Northumberland following the dissolution of the chantry colleges in 1547. The duke immediately removed the quire roof for the lead and most of the collegiate buildings were demolished, though the nave, aisles and magnificent octagonal tower of the church were retained for parochial use. Intended originally as a family mausoleum, in recent years the church at Fotheringhay has become a shrine to the Yorkist dynasty, though the nearby castle is now little more than a fallen lump of masonry.

CHAPE *see* WEAPONS AND HARNESS

CHAPELS In every castle there would have been at least one chapel, and often two: a private oratory for the lord and his family and a larger garrison chapel in the bailey which often served also as a parish church. Most bailey chapels were originally free-standing timber structures and these were often integrated into domestic buildings when they were extended and rebuilt in stone.

Undoubtedly the most impressive ROMAN-ESQUE chapel is at the Tower of London where the apse of the beautiful Chapel of St John (*c.* 1080) projects from the east wall of the White Tower (there is a similar arrangement at the Conqueror's great palace-keep at Colchester Castle). St John's Chapel, on the second floor of the White Tower, has a nave

The most impressive Romanesque chapel in Britain is at the Tower of London where the apse of the beautiful Chapel of St John (c. 1080) projects from the east wall of the White Tower.

and aisles of four bays and an apse opening by five arches to an ambulatory. The heavy rounded piers carry carved capitals, some of which are engraved with a T-shaped figure (St Anthony's Cross) found only at this early date, and above the arches is a clerestory lighted by a second tier of windows.

At Ludlow Castle the splendid circular nave of the late Norman chapel of St Mary Magdalene remains the most striking feature of the inner ward. Inspired by the church of the Holy Sepulchre in Jerusalem, it is one of only five medieval circular naves to have survived in England. The original apsidal chancel was replaced with a half-timbered structure in the sixteenth century, though this has not survived. At several early castles, such as Dover and Newcastle, the chapel was incorporated within the FOREBUILDING of the Norman keep. Indeed, the forebuilding at Dover Castle contains two chapels, each serving a different storey and each finely embellished with decorative moulding, arcading and well-proportioned round-headed archways.

Most castle chapels are simple, rectangular chambers where a holy water basin (PISCINA) may have survived in the south wall, sometimes within a canopied niche (FENESTELLA) with a shelf (CREDENCE) or recess for a cupboard (AUMBRY). The chapel would have been the most lavishly appointed room in a castle, its stonework richly painted and gilded and its windows filled with STAINED GLASS. Among the chapel furnishings listed after a siege at Caerphilly Castle in 1327 were an altar table with frontal and curtains, nine surplices, chalice and incense, gospel and other service books and four quires of organ music. Today, the presence of a piscina is often the only indication of a former chapel, other than its orientation – it was a liturgical requirement that the altar should be located at the eastern end. At Caerphilly both the

At Ludlow Castle, the splendid circular nave of the late-Norman chapel of St Mary Magdalene remains the most striking feature of the inner ward. Inspired by the Church of the Holy Sepulchre in Jerusalem, it is one of only five medieval circular naves to have survived in England.

piscina and the stone seats (*sedilia*) for the priests who celebrated the mass have survived in the south wall of the chapel. Occasionally there may also be the vestiges of an altar: at Goodrich and Carreg Cennen Castles, for example. The chapel at Carreg Cennen is located in the upper part of a small square tower which projects from the east curtain wall. The vaulted chamber has been identified as a former chapel by the presence of a stone plinth at the east end which is likely to be the remains of an altar. There is a similar arrangement at Kidwelly Castle where the semi-octagonal Chapel Tower projects above a steep river bank on a square base with tall spur buttresses. This fine apsidal chapel, once reached from the (now demolished) great hall and solar, has a double piscina, sedilia, sacristy and, below, a cramped bed-chamber for the priest. At Goodrich Castle the base of the altar and the original piscina may be traced in the recess of the eastern window which was inserted in the fifteenth century. The thirteenth-century chapel is located in the larger, south-western tower of the asymmetrical gatehouse where there is evidence of a later, fifteenth-century,

gallery and the piscinas of two subsidiary altars. GRAFFITI may also provide a clue to a former chapel. At Wardour Castle, for example, two crosses and an INRI symbol (the Latin initials for *Jesus of Nazareth, King of the Jews*) have been carved in the doorway jambs of a chamber which may have been a chapel, together with the names of Roman Catholic recusants and the date 1728. Similar crosses and Christian symbols are sometimes found on or close to buildings associated with the 'old religion'.

In Edward I's Welsh castles the chapel was often located in one of the mural towers. The chapel at Beaumaris Castle, for example, occupies the first floor of the tower on the east side of the inner ward and was intended to have served a range of residential apartments that was never completed. It has an ornately decorated interior, a ribbed stone vault (*see* VAULTING), a ventilator (opened when the smoke of candles and censers became overpowering) and a HAGIOSCOPE or squint cut into the north wall to command a view of the altar. At Conwy Castle the chancel of the tiny chapel royal, located on the first floor of the Chapel Tower, remains the most beautiful feature of the castle despite mutilation and exposure to the weather. The circular chamber formed the 'nave' of the chapel, the chancel being contrived within an apsidal recess contained within the thickness of the eastern wall. The sides of the recess are arcaded in seven bays, the three eastern bays pierced by lancet windows. The delicately carved mouldings and vaulting are of the finest quality and it is likely that the arcades once extended into the chamber to carry a rood beam. At Caernarfon and Harlech Castles the chapel is located in the gatehouse above the gate passage – together with the winding gear for the portcullis! A chapel would be in constant use, both for services and private prayers, which suggests that in these castles the gates were seldom open and then only for the briefest interval. The notion that a besieging force was reluctant to attack a forebuilding or gatehouse for fear of violating a chapel in an upper storey is unfounded. A chapel may have been located above an entrance in anticipation of inviolability, but in practice such considerations rarely deterred a besieging force.

From the early fourteenth century a large domestic chapel was often included in a refurbishment scheme. John de Broughton's chapel at Broughton Castle (a crenellated and moated manor house) was one of the earliest of these (1331). As at Berkeley and Beverston Castles it was but one element in a lavish modernisation of a family's living quarters and was considered necessary despite the close proximity of the parish church. Sir Robert Harcourt's large private chapel at Stanton Harcourt, the Lovell chapel at Minster Lovell and the Hastings chapel at Ashby de la Zouch were all erected within a stone's throw of a parish church. It is clear from these and other examples, such as Bolton and Brougham Castles, that in late medieval England members of the aristocracy 'egregiously privatised religion' (Platt). Anxious to distance themselves from plebeian vulgarity, they built themselves private chapels and oratories in the seclusion of their castles and manor houses. The chapel at Bolton Castle, dedicated to the Virgin Mary, was endowed as a chantry in 1399 – the year in which Richard II was deposed and murdered. It was served by six priests from the abbey of St Agatha at Richmond (now known as Easby Abbey) who were quartered at the castle and required to pray daily for the repose of King Richard's soul (*see* CHANTRY COLLEGES AND COLLEGIATE CHURCHES). Further examples of these exclusive, private chapels are numerous: at Rycote, for instance, where in 1449 Richard Quatremains and his wife founded a chantry chapel in the grounds of their Oxfordshire manor

house; at Sudeley, where Ralph Boteler built himself a private church next to his new castle; and at Cotehele where there are three squints (*see* HAGIOSCOPE), a splendid late medieval oak screen and the earliest clock in England still unaltered and in its original position.

The mid-fourteenth-century chapel at Farleigh Hungerford Castle actually pre-dates the castle which was built in 1370–80. Originally the parish church, it was enclosed within the walls of the castle's outer court in the 1420s when Sir Walter Hungerford commandeered it as a castle chapel and family mausoleum. To compensate the parishioners, Sir Walter built them a new parish church close by. At Raglan Castle the large fifteenth-century chapel was provided with a *closet* or private upper gallery in which Sir William Herbert and his family could participate in services in comfort and raised above the public view. In his will (1469) Sir William gave instructions that window glass should be installed depicting 'the Stories of the passion of Christ and of the nativity and the Saints of mine that be in my Clozett at Ragland'.
(*See also* CHURCHES)

CHARTER A document conferring rights on a body corporate or on an individual. A royal charter was a formal instrument by which a sovereign granted or confirmed lands, liberties, titles or immunities on his subjects in perpetuity. There are two types of *Charter Roll*, the first recording grants and the second confirmations. Both relate to the period 1199–1516 after which charters were succeeded by letters patent (*see* PATENT ROLLS).
(*See also* STATE RECORDS)

CHASE A hunting ground, the administration of which was subject to Common Law rather than Forest Law. The rules that governed a chase were as rigorous in their protection of *vert* and *venison* as were those of a FOREST, but the application of legal sanctions through the chase courts was limited, more serious prosecutions being remitted to the civil courts. The forest courts exercised an independence which could be despotic, for ultimately it was the sovereign or his representative who was both prosecution and judge. The legal status of a chase was not affected by the rank of its owner, even when it was the monarch himself. There were, of course, exceptions to the general rule: chases belonging to the earls of Lancaster were subject to Forest Law, for example. Medieval chases were less numerous than royal forests, twenty-six having been identified. They were defined by topography, taking features such as rivers and rock outcrops as their boundaries.

CHASES *see* DRAWBRIDGE

CHAT CASTEL *see* SIEGES

CHAUSSES *see* ARMOUR

CHEMISE A secondary outer wall surrounding a KEEP with a raised platform that could be reached by means of a POSTERN or DRAWBRIDGE. (*See also* APRON WALL *and* MANTLET WALL)

-CHESTER and -CASTER Borrowed from the Latin *castra*, the Old English word *ceaster* means a city or walled town, originally one which had been a Roman station, e.g. Dorchester. But in many instances the meaning seems to have indicated a prehistoric fort generally: not all *-chester* names in Northumbria can have been Roman stations, for example. It is also found as *Caster-* and *-caster* and corrupted to *-castle* as in Castleford and Horncastle. In other instances former Roman towns were renamed, possibly after the Anglo-Saxon chieftain whose people occupied them: Chichester in Sussex is 'Cissi's ceaster', for example, and Rudchester in Northumberland is 'Rudda's ceaster'. Few Roman names for rural settlements remain, and the use of this element in place-names suggests Anglo-Saxon recognition of a Roman or pre-Roman settlement or fort. Under Norman influence several *-chester* names became *-cester*, as in Gloucester and Cirencester, and even *-(c)eter* as in Wroxeter. *Ceaster* is one of the three classifications of Anglo-Saxon settlement, the others being the BURH and the PORT. (*See also* CAIR-)

CHEVAUCHÉE An armed raid, usually into enemy territory, with the aim of inflicting as much damage as possible on the towns, villages and countryside, rendering them uninhabitable and providing plunder for the victors. They were used most effectively by Edward the Black Prince during his expeditions to France in 1355/6. Many magnificent late fourteenth- and fifteenth-century MONUMENTS, CHANTRY CHAPELS and collegiate churches were financed from the profits of successful *chevauchées* during the HUNDRED YEARS WAR (1338–1453), as were the lavish programmes of domestic and architectural refurbishment evident in numerous castles. (*See also* CHIVALRY *and* RANSOM)

CHEVAUX DE FRISE Wooden stakes or upright stones protecting an outwork or defensive position from a cavalry charge (*see* ARCHERY *and* WARFARE: CONDUCT OF).

CHEVRON One of the most common charges in ARMORY consisting of a broad, inverted V across the centre of the shield (*see* ORDINARY).

CHEVRON MOULDING A zig-zag motif characteristic of late ROMANESQUE ornamentation used especially in the deeply recessed mouldings of arches.

CHIMNEYS AND FIREPLACES In the Middle Ages a fire was the centre of domestic life during a considerable part of the year and was, of course, in constant use in a castle's KITCHENS. Strictly speaking, a chimney (from the Latin *caminus* via Middle English *chimenee*) is a fireplace used both for providing warmth to a room and for cooking. Only in the sixteenth century was the term applied to what is more correctly a *chimney flue* and roof-top *chimney shaft*, capped with a *chimney pot* (*chimney stacks* contain several flues). The structure within which the flue is constructed is the *chimney breast* and the lintel above the fireplace opening is the *chimney bar*. The *chimneypiece* (or *mantelpiece*) is the decorative structure which surrounds the fireplace. This often incorporates a *mantelshelf* or *mantel* which may extend above the fireplace opening to the ceiling as an ornamental framework or *hood*. An *angle-chimney* is a fireplace that is constructed in the corner of a room.

Although the chimney flue was known in the eleventh century, prior to the fourteenth century heating was usually provided in the hall (sometimes described in contemporary documents as the 'fire-house') by an open fire of logs stacked against FIRE-DOGS in a central hearth or against a *reredos*, a wall of earth, stone or brick (often with the additional protection of a FIRE-BACK), the smoke escaping through the windows or by means of an opening or louvre in the roof. In more important buildings (such as Westminster Hall) a louvred lantern structure was often constructed on the roof for this purpose, and this device was later adapted as a means of venting a number of angle-chimneys and flues (as in the late fourteenth-century abbot's kitchen at Glastonbury Abbey in Somerset).

From the thirteenth century fireplaces were sometimes placed against the outside walls of castle chambers though the earliest of these were vented through the walls at a point immediately above the hearth and consequently must have been singularly noisome. By the early fourteenth century stone hoods were provided to direct the smoke into long, vertical flues set within the thickness of the walls, with round or octagonal chimney shafts on gable

Fireplaces in the sixteenth-century buttery range at Raglan Castle, Monmouthshire.

peaks or projecting through the hoardings of castle towers and walkways.

The development of the chimney flue was, perhaps, to have a greater effect on the social history of western Europe than any other factor. It resulted in a previously unknown luxury: privacy. Domestic rooms became smaller and, therefore, greater in number, and allowed for a variety of functions which the old communal hall had not. Excessive draughts were no longer necessary to sustain a large central fire and consequently corridors and stairways were enclosed, external doors provided with porches and windows more extensively glazed. No doubt the health of the occupants improved significantly as a result, as did the efficiency of the kitchens. Even castle guard-rooms were sometimes provided with a simple fireplace. During the fourteenth century fireplaces located on different storeys of new buildings were often connected to common chimney flues set within the walls: one of the most extraordinary sights in any castle is a series of fireplaces suspended at intervals in the walls of a

tower where the floors have disappeared! Fifteenth-century fireplaces had larger hearths and were usually constructed of brick or stone, with wide, four-centre arches (*see* ARCH).

Kitchen fireplaces were often very large indeed: at York Castle in 1364 quantities of plaster and 'walteghell' (wall-tiles) were purchased for the chimney and reredos in the kitchen, as were two great stone mantelpieces into which iron bars had to be inserted because of their size and weight. Indeed, it was common practice for fireplaces to be reinforced with ironwork (*see* IRONWORK, LOCKS AND NAILS). At the Tower in 1335 there is an entry 'for 4 hundredweight of Spanish iron for two pillars and a crossbar made thereof . . . to support the great fireplace in the Queen's chamber, because it broke and stones fell from it while the King's daughters and their nurses were sitting in the room'. At Launceston in 1462 payments were recorded for making 'a great fireplace called mantel and 2 ovens within the said fireplace in the castle kitchen called constabill's kechyn', and stone called 'merestone' was worked for the 'corbelles clavelles dorestones coynestones and vaultyngstones' of the fireplace and oven range. Tiles or bricks were often used for the hearth and, more often, for the backs of fireplaces. At Portchester in 1397 three hundred 'hurthtigel' (hearth tiles) were bought for fireplaces for 3*s*, and a thousand 'white tiles of Flanders' for their reredoses at a cost of 8*s*. Two years later 13*s* 4*d* was paid for '400 large pendantigheles used on the reredosses of fireplaces'. These were almost certainly flanged tiles set upright with their faces outwards. At the palace of Sheen in 1368 a mason repaired two fireplaces in the king's chambers and a plasterer lined four 'pipes' within the walls for the same fireplaces with plaster of Paris. The presence here of four flues suggests that they served two pairs of fireplaces, each back to back, within adjacent rooms. More often there would be a single flue serving 'back to back' fireplaces. As early as 1252 Henry III gave orders for the making of a chimney in his wardrobe at Clipston 'through one mantel and through another mantel in the queen's wardrobe by one and the same flue'.

Accounts for Leeds Castle, dating from 1361, provide details of the building of a complete fireplace:

. . . a linthel containing 9 feet, not worked, for the fireplace; 17 feet of hard stone worked for the flues; 2 baas of hard stone for the same work; 34 feet of hard stone for scheu and lermer, worked for the same; 3 chapitrelles of hard stone worked for the same; 11½ feet of worked hard stone called parpaynassheler; 2 great coygnestons and 6 corbels.

The 'linthel' is the mantelpiece supported on corbels and the two great 'coygnestons' or angle-stones, each standing on a 'baas'. The hood was composed of sections of stone cut with a bevel ('scheu'), projecting mouldings ('larmers') and stones worked on two parallel faces ('parpaynassheler'). The three 'chapitrelles' or capitals were probably brackets to carry lights.

With the rapid development of purely domestic architecture in the final decades of the fifteenth century, chimney shafts, singly or in clusters and usually of stone, were for the first time utilised as decorative features, and by the mid-sixteenth century ornate shafts or stacks had become a characteristic feature of the domestic architecture of the period. These were usually cylindrical or octagonal, constructed of decorative brickwork and terracotta with ornamental crossed beading, zig-zag and honeycomb patterns, scrolls and fluting, and supported on octagonal or square-shaped fluted and moulded bases. There are many examples of sixteenth-century fireplaces inserted into the walls of earlier castles: in Chepstow's lower bailey, for example. Fireplaces were invariably the focal point of any room and many were decorated with heraldry and paintings of allegorical and mythical scenes. At Westminster Henry III ordered a mantel to be painted with 'a figure of Winter, which by its sad countenance and by other miserable contortions of the body may be deservedly likened to Winter itself'. Another, at Clarendon, was painted with the Tree of Jesse and a Wheel of Fortune, while the fireplace in the queen's chamber was to be rebuilt with a marble pier on each side and the mantel carved with the twelve months of the year.

CHIROGRAPH *see* INDENTURE

CHIVALRY Both the code of courage and courtesy which were the ideals of medieval knighthood in western Europe, and the system of knighthood itself. The terms 'chivalry' and 'cavalry' share the same linguistic root, confirming that knighthood was the prerogative of the mounted warrior. His effectiveness in battle (and thereby his reputation) was greatly enhanced by the development of the stirrup and the saddle-bow which provided both manoeuvrability and stability. But the cost of maintaining a horse and equipment was considerable, and membership of such an élite presupposed a man of some position and estate. This exclusive class adopted a code of conduct which aspired to the highest ideals though, as history has shown, few of its members succeeded in attaining them. That none could emulate the perfection of Galahad or Percival did not diminish the code itself which comprised three elements:

1. Belief in the Church and its defence, especially against the heathen, as manifested in the CRUSADES.
2. Courage, and loyalty towards a knight's companions, his feudal lord and sovereign.
3. Respect, pity and generosity in defence of the weak, the poor and women.

To these were added the notion of romantic love which was to inspire much of the literature of chivalry: Roland in France, Arthur in Britain, El Cid in Spain and the Minnesänger in Germany.

The riches and honours which accrued from service in the HUNDRED YEARS WAR (1338–1453) served to promote the notion of an exclusive chivalric brotherhood of knights, exemplified by the institution in 1348 of Edward III's Order of the Garter (*see* GARTER, MOST NOBLE ORDER OF THE). It was this 'self-conscious sense of theatre in contemporary chivalry which gave context to the "first great flowering of English domestic architecture" coincident with the Hundred Years War' (Platt). Edward's new order, although comprising only twenty-six member knights, required a considerable establishment and the king embarked on an extensive rebuilding of the Order's headquarters at Windsor Castle in one of the costliest building campaigns ever undertaken by an English king. In the late 1350s he 'caused many excellent buildings in the castle of Windsor to be thrown down, and others more beautiful and sumptuous to be set up'. But unlike his grandfather, Edward was no builder of fortresses. Windsor, when complete, was more a palace than a castle.

Anxious to emulate their sovereign, magnate society adopted the chivalric ethic with enthusiasm. Thomas Beauchamp, earl of Warwick (1329–69) and Marshal of England (from 1344), participated in nearly every French campaign. He was Edward III's companion at Crécy, was a founding Garter knight and fought at Poitiers where he collected the ransoms of the archbishop of Sens and the bishop of Le Mans. It was ransoms such as these, together with the spoils of war (*see* CHEVAUCHÉE) and the financial benefits of advancement through military service to the crown, that enabled England's aristocracy to express its sense of chivalric

The curtain wall and imposing towers of the north-east façade of Warwick Castle declare the self-esteem of the Beauchamps, their status in aristocratic society and their membership of a chivalric élite.

brotherhood through the erection of heraldry-encrusted MONUMENTS and CHANTRY CHAPELS and through an ostentatious enthusiasm for building and refurbishment. Magnates like Thomas Beauchamp and his immediate successors – Earl Thomas II (1370–1401) and Earl Richard (1403–39) – helped to create the chivalric myth that is reflected in so much building of the period. The curtain wall and imposing towers of the north-east façade of Warwick Castle may be lofty and ornamental but they are of minimal defensive value. Rather, they declare the self-esteem of the Beauchamps, their status in aristocratic society and their membership of a chivalric élite. Magnificent it may be, but Warwick's north-east front is more romantic myth than defensive reality.

(*See also* KNIGHTHOOD AND CHIVALRY, ORIGINS OF *and* TOURNAMENTS)

CHIVALRY, HIGH COURT OF *see* COURT OF CHIVALRY

CHURCHES Castles are often ruinous, churches rarely so. And unlike castles, many parish churches contain MONUMENTS and STAINED GLASS which may be embellished with inscriptions and heraldry that are rich sources of information about the magnate and gentry families who erected them (*see* ARMORY, DONOR AND COMMEMORATIVE WINDOWS *and* HATCHMENTS). Furthermore, the parish church will normally be the oldest building in a village and the obvious starting point for any historical investigation, for it is likely to embody the entire development of a community, often from the Anglo-Saxon period to the present day. Through the architectural development of a parish church the fluctuating fortunes of a community may be assessed. Indeed, we are as much indebted to those parishes whose comparative poverty has ensured the survival of our oldest Saxon and Romanesque buildings as we are to those whose prosperity inspired the endowment of our great medieval churches. Contraction, perhaps in the form of blocked aisles and doorways, is usually indicative of economic decline, whereas expansion, epitomised by ornamentation and the addition of CHANTRY CHAPELS, aisles, transepts and ornate towers, indicates the patronage of a prosperous society.

The scale and complexity of church-building in the century following the Norman Conquest of 1066 was extraordinary. Clearly the Normans considered the simple Anglo-Saxon churches to be inadequate for the needs of a reformed Church and consequently they rebuilt nearly every cathedral and constructed hundreds of new monasteries and thousands of parish churches. Most Norman churches, though built of stone, were fairly modest and they were served by English priests whose education and status were often little better than that of the peasantry. Most were constructed on a simple basilican plan though a small number followed the Rotunda of Constantine's Church of the Holy Sepulchre in Jerusalem, notably those of the Knights Templar and Knights Hospitaller. The Temple Church in London (1185) and the Holy Sepulchre Church at Cambridge (*c.* 1130, restored 1840), for example, are circular with an inner ring of arcaded columns, a central conical roof and a lower roof above the circular, outer aisle. A number of churches were built within castle baileys, at Castlethorpe, Castle Rising and English Bicknor, for example. Many others, including Amberley, Beverston, Kilpeck, Moreton Corbet and St Briavels, were located in the protective shadow of the castle walls (*see also* CHURCH TOWERS).

From the eleventh century onwards many larger churches were constructed or remodelled to a *cruciform* plan with the lower, elongated limb of a *Latin Cross* forming the nave, the upper limb the chancel and the lateral limbs the north and south transepts. During the twelfth and thirteenth centuries many timber roofs were replaced with stone vaults (*see* VAULTING), aisles, transepts and porches were added and nave walls heightened to support aisle roofs and to provide additional windows. Such ubiquitous and innovative activity reflects the prosperity of the period that was coincidental with the first flowering of English GOTHIC ARCHITECTURE. Medieval churches were not only places of worship: they were also community centres where commercial, social and even judicial activities took place. Many were the chapels of trade guilds, fraternities and hospices or the mausolea of the nobility. The great cathedrals exercised considerable regional influence, both ceremonial and commercial. Most were prosperous cult centres, with saints' shrines and reliquaries attracting pilgrims and thereby stimulating local economies. However, it was the corporate ownership of property, and particularly the endowment of land, that ensured the continuing affluence of the cathedrals and monasteries.

The fourteenth and fifteenth centuries witnessed a gradual decline in this support and a corresponding increase in the building or remodelling of parish churches. In part this was attributable to the piety of individual parishioners, anxious by their good deeds to secure eternal rest (*see* CHANTRY). It was also inspired by rivalry, both individual and corporate, as in the wool- and cloth-producing communities of Cullompton and Tiverton in Devon where architectural emulation reached ostentatious proportions, or at Swaffham Prior, Cambridgeshire, where the rival manorial churches of St Mary and Sts Cyriac and Julitta stand within each other's shadow. Inevitably, civic pride reflected that of the individual and *vice versa*: the magnificent churches of East Anglia and the Cotswolds are indicative not only of the prosperity of local industry but also of the pre-eminence of the merchants and manufacturers whose monuments and chantry chapels rivalled those of the nobility. Heraldry in effigies and brasses, and in the fabric of the churches they endowed, advertised the pervasive authority of the medieval magnates, even in death. Some endowed not only churches but also colleges, hospices, almshouses and schools. These are most often found in the vicinity of the parish church and their founders may usually be identified by an heraldic tablet or inscription.

(*See also* CHAPELS *and* CHANTRY COLLEGES AND COLLEGIATE CHURCHES)

CHURCH TOWERS Many communities came to appreciate the defensive advantages of having a tower in their midst, indeed the term *belfry* is of Teutonic origin and means 'a defensive place of shelter'. The name was also given to the movable timber tower used in SIEGES and came to mean a watch-tower, beacon-tower or alarm bell-tower. In the Welsh Marches, where raids and border disputes were a way of life, massive square towers such as those at Bosbury, Clun and Kerry provided refuges for an entire community. The thirteenth-century detached tower at Bosbury is nearly 9m (29ft) square and heavily constructed of red sandstone, while the tower at Clun has a double pyramid timber roof, typical of several medieval churches in the central Marches. Similarly, on the Scottish borders semi-fortified towers such as those at Great Salkeld and Ormside in Cumbria and Bedale (where the grooves made by a portcullis have survived) were clearly intended for defensive purposes.

Round towers are a feature of many East Anglian churches: there are 115 in Norfolk, 40 in Suffolk and 7 in Essex, nearly all located by the coast or a river. Of these, about 20 are of Saxon origin and were probably constructed as refuges from Viking incursions. They may be recognised by the location of a single doorway several metres above ground

In the Welsh Marches, where raids and border disputes were a way of life, massive square towers like that at Clun provided refuges for an entire community.

level, a ladder being required to obtain access. Those that date from the twelfth and succeeding centuries were built as simple belfries in a country where suitable stone for constructing square-cornered towers was scarce. Nevertheless, they would inevitably have been pressed into service as watchtowers and signal stations whenever danger threatened (*see* BEACONS).

There are fifty detached church towers (correctly *detached belfries*) in England of which several are close to the Welsh border and were built for defensive purposes (*see* Bosbury *above*). The immense, fortified thirteenth-century tower of Garway church was once detached but was linked with the main building by means of a low passage-way in the seventeenth century. Unusually (and probably because of the church's TEMPLAR origins) the tower stands at the north-west corner of the present nave and at an angle of 45 degrees to the north wall. A number of detached belfries were sited

so that they could not be used as platforms for siege engines or cannon which would threaten the defences of nearby fortifications, as at Berkeley in Gloucestershire (the tower was rebuilt in 1750). Ironically it was from this tower that parliamentary artillery terminated the three-year siege of Berkeley Castle in 1645. At Richard's Castle in Herefordshire the free-standing bell-tower was (unusually) sited at the east end of the twelfth-century church so that it would not overlook the neighbouring castle.
(*See also* ECCLESIASTICAL STRONGHOLDS)

CINGULUM MILITARE The broad hip-belt of ornamental gold or metalwork from which depended a sword and MISERICORDE. The symbolic sword and belt were strapped to a knight during the dubbing ceremony and remain today, together with his spurs, in the badge of the knights bachelor.
(*See also* ARMOUR *and* HELMETS)

CINQUEFOIL A figure having five radiating stylised 'petals', found both as an architectural motif and an heraldic device (*see* FOILS).

CINQUE PORTS A group of medieval ports in south-east England: originally Dover, Hastings, Hythe, Romney and Sandwich, to which Rye and Winchelsea were later added. The Cinque Ports enjoyed certain trading privileges in return for providing warships in the king's fleet. This arrangement is known to have existed long before they received their first charter from Edward I. Most of the ancient privileges were abolished in the nineteenth century, though the Wardenship of the Cinque Ports remains as a purely honorific office.

CIRCUMVALLATION Entrenchments surrounding a fortification under siege.

CISTERN A reservoir for fresh water, as at Criccieth Castle, where a modern grille at the inner end of the entrance passage covers a cistern fed by a natural spring. This originally had a wooden cover and its somewhat inconvenient location suggests that the spring may have been discovered during the castle's construction. The Cistern tower at nearby Caernarfon Castle contains an open stone-lined rainwater tank above the roof vault from which a stone outlet channel runs through the thickness of the wall, crossing one of the nearby arrow loops, and discharges through a shaft in the adjacent Queen's Gate. In the massive keep of Warkworth Castle water collected in a cistern at the foot of a central LIGHTWELL and could be diverted along a system

of conduits to flush the latrine shafts. At Carreg
Cennen Castle two sunken pits, lined with dressed
stone blocks, were well placed at the rear of the
gatehouse to collect rainwater from adjacent roofs.
(*See also* PLUMBING, WATER SUPPLY AND
SANITATION *and* WELLS)

CITADEL A place of last resort, a self-contained
fortress within the ramparts of a castle or fortified
town. This was often the KEEP, as at Raglan Castle,
where the six-sided Great Tower is located on an
island in the moat, detached from the main body of
the castle and originally approached by means of a
bascule bridge (*see* DRAWBRIDGE). The inner
ward of Conwy Castle, Aberconwy, was separated
from the outer ward by a crossing wall and deep
chasm cut from north to south across the castle rock
and containing a well 27.7m (91ft) deep. Access to
the inner ward (the private apartments of King
Edward and Queen Eleanor) was by means of a
drawbridge across the chasm and through a
projecting gatehouse and gate passage. Clearly the
intention was that the inner ward should be a self-
contained citadel, while the castle was itself a citadel
within the town walls (*see* BASTIDE). At first sight
the wall-walks at Conwy appear to continue
uninterrupted from the outer to the inner ward,
suggesting that the king's apartments were not
entirely self-contained. However, rebates in the
walls of the Stockhouse and Bakehouse towers
indicate that the inner ward could indeed be isolated
at wall-walk level by means of gates.

CIVIC ARMORY *see* ARMORY

CIVIL LIST *see* DEMESNE

CLADDING *see* FACING MATERIALS

CLAYMORE A Scottish two-edged broadsword.
(*See also* WEAPONS AND HARNESS)

CLERESTORY The upper storey of a hall (or large
church) pierced by a gallery of windows to provide
additional light to the space beneath. Because so
many courtyard buildings have been reduced in
height, it is not always possible to identify a former
clerestory. The roof of the Great Hall of Middleham
Castle was removed in the fifteenth century, the side
walls raised, a series of large windows inserted and a
new roof constructed at a higher level. The intention
may have been to create a clerestory, though it is
more likely that a new upper chamber was provided
above the hall.

CLERK OF THE MARKET *see* VERGE

CLERK OF THE WORKS *see* MASONS AND
ARCHITECTS

CLIMATE Rainfall, temperature and air pressure
have been recorded at the Royal Observatory,
Greenwich, since 1840. To chart climatic changes
before that time, climatologists have developed a
variety of techniques including the study of pollen in
peat bogs, growth rings in trees and the distribution
of plants and animals. They have also analysed
personal diaries, military reports, crop records and
letters to crown officials explaining such matters as
the non-payment of taxes because of crop failures.

There has been a series of distinct climatic phases
since the end of the last Ice Age some 10,000 years
ago. A warm epoch following the Ice Age peaked
between 5,000 and 7,000 years ago when sea levels
rose as the ice sheets melted. Average European
temperatures were then 2–3 degrees Centigrade
warmer than they are today. This was followed by a
cold phase during the Iron Age after which a period
of gradual warming continued well into the
medieval period. During the Dark Ages summer
temperatures were about 1 degree warmer than they
are now and in the twelfth century VINEYARDS
flourished 3–5 degrees of latitude further north and
between 100 and 200 m higher above sea-level than
is possible today. A colder phase lasting from *c.*
1210 to *c.* 1320 was accompanied by violent storms
in the North Sea and a reduction in average
temperatures of almost 1.5 degrees. The Thames is
believed to have frozen only once in each century
during the first millennium AD, but from the
beginning of the thirteenth century the pattern
changed. In 1209 the building of the (old) London
Bridge altered the flow of water and encouraged the
formation of ice which was sometimes several feet
thick so that by the winter of 1270 goods which
were normally transported by river had to be hauled
across land. There was a period of warming from
c. 1320 but this was followed by a severe phase
known as the 'Little Ice Age' which lasted from the
end of the fifteenth century until the beginning of
the eighteenth.

CLIPSHAM STONE A honey-coloured stone
quarried in the Clipsham region of the county of
Rutland.

CLOSE HELM A close helm is one which is
designed to protect the whole head and face and with
a movable visor (*see* ARMOUR).

CLOSER Stone cut to complete the bond of a wall at a corner.

CLOSE ROLLS Records of grants from the English crown from 1204–5 to 1903. They contain registered copies of private letters and documents, such as conveyances, writs of summons to parliament and orders to royal officers, directed to particular persons for specific reasons. The first close rolls of 1204–5 dealt with most government business of transitory importance. But as new types of roll developed for recording special documents, the range of business included in the close rolls diminished. Letters close were 'closed' (folded and secured with a seal) unlike letters patent which were 'open' and addressed 'To all and singular . . .' (*see* PATENT ROLLS). Copies of these documents were made on parchment sheets which were stitched together and stored in rolls, one or more for each regnal year. They are housed at the Public Record Office (*see* APPENDIX II).
(*See also* LIBERATE ROLLS *and* STATE RECORDS)

CLOSET (i) A term often applied to a room used as a prison.
(ii) A private gallery in a CHAPEL reserved for the use of a lord and his family.

CLUNCH Chalk for building quarried from the hard, grey-coloured beds of the Lower Chalk, sawn into blocks and dried. Often found used in conjunction with brick dressings or on a footing of SARSEN STONES in buildings dating from the Middle Ages to the nineteenth century.

CLUSTERED DONJON A great tower that is strengthened by a number of projecting towers. In the early fourteenth century Henry Percy rebuilt his twelfth-century shell-keep at Alnwick Castle, enlarging it and adding seven semicircular towers to form a clustered donjon known as the 'Seven Towers of the Percys'.

CNIHTHÁD *see* KNIGHTHOOD AND CHIVALRY, ORIGINS OF

COASTAL DEFENCES *see* CASTLES, DEVELOPMENT OF *and* TUDOR COASTAL FORTS

COAT OF ARMS Correctly, this term should be applied only to the shield of arms, the design of which was often repeated on the SURCOAT or JUPON of the medieval armiger: hence 'coat' of arms (*see* ARMORY).

COAT OF PLATES Protective iron plates riveted inside a fabric or leather coat. In use from the second half of the thirteenth century until it was superseded by the one-piece breast-plate at the end of the fourteenth century.
(*See also* ARMOUR *and* HELMETS)

COB An ancient building material, formed of mud, marl, chalk or gravel with dung and some form of binding material such as hair or chopped straw, used in the construction of domestic and agricultural buildings and walls from the Dark Ages to the present century. Cob walls were built in 'wet' layers of about 60cm (2ft) on a foundation of moorstone or boulders, each layer being allowed to set for at least seven days before the next was applied. Cob was often strengthened by the addition of horsehair or cowhair and the walls limewashed for protection and provided with a water-repellent 'skirt' of tar at the base. A sound roof of THATCH or tile is necessary to prevent a cob wall washing away into the earth whence it came and eaves protrude to ensure that rainwater from the roof is projected away from the surface of the wall and does not accumulate at the base. In the Middle Ages cob was widely used: not only for the 'mud-wall'd tenements' of the poor but also for relatively important buildings such as the fifteenth-century manor house at Trelawse, Cornwall. Many of the ancillary buildings which were erected against the curtain walls of castles would have been of cob construction.

'COCK-UP' *see* ARCHERY

COERL (CHURL) An Old English term for a free peasant, superior in status to a serf who was obliged to do military service. Following the Norman Conquest his status declined to that of VILLEIN.

COFFER DAM A watertight enclosure of piles sunk into the seabed or a riverbed with the water pumped out to facilitate the construction of a building, bridge, etc.

COFFERER *see* HOUSEHOLD

COG A square-rigged sailing ship with a stern rudder.

COIF A close-fitting cap or hood of mail or leather. A *coif-de-mailles* is a Balaclava-type hood of mail.
(*See also* ARMOUR *and* HELMETS)

COINAGE On the eve of the Norman Conquest the English coinage was considered to be one of the strongest in Europe. The pre-Conquest kings had created a sound and stable system of coinage based on a metallic standard: both gold and silver coins were minted but the gold coin was phased out leaving the silver penny.

The silver *penny* was first minted at Canterbury, probably in 760, for King Offa of Mercia who by that time included Kent in his territories. It was then known as the *denier* after the Roman *denarius* and for nearly five hundred years was the only coin struck in England. There were 240 pennies to the Saxon pound weight of silver. In the tenth century a cross was stamped on the reverse so that the coin could be broken accurately into 'broke money', *half-pennies* and quarter-pennies (*farthings*), a practice which continued until 1279. (Hence the use of the word 'broke' in relation to money problems.) From the time of Alfred the Great (871–900) London became the principal mint and his coinage had the London monogram on the reverse. The *mark* and *ora* were not coins but were used as units of accountancy, notably in the DANELAW counties. The mark was a weight of metal initially valued at 128 silver pennies and later revalued. The ora was valued at 16 pennies.

Saxon coinage had such a good reputation that following the Conquest William I (1066–87) ordered his coinage to be issued in the same way and from the same mints, though the number of local mints was reduced. In the early medieval period there was approximately £1 million of currency in circulation. More than 95 per cent of the coinage consisted of silver pennies and the remainder of half-pennies. In 1180 new pennies were minted, known from the reverse design as the *Shortcross* series. In 1247, during the reign of Henry III (1216–72), the number of mints was further reduced to two, at London and Canterbury, both working under the direction of a single official (*moneyer*). In the same year a new type of silver penny was introduced. This was called the *Longcross* and was intended to discourage the illegal practice of cutting pieces from the coinage ('clipping', which was at times a capital offence) by extending the arms of the cross to the edge on the reverse. This type of coin continued to be minted until 1278 when Henry's son Edward I (1272–1307) added silver *groats*, *half-pennies* and *farthings* to the coinage. In 1344 Edward III (1327–77) introduced three gold coins: the *florin*, *half-florin* (or *leopard*) and *quarter-florin* (or *helm*) in addition to the silver coinage. The florin, based on a Florentine gold coin which circulated throughout Europe, was not a success and was withdrawn. (It was reintroduced as a silver coin in 1849 and was translated into the 2-shilling piece and, more recently, the 10p coin.)

Also in 1344 the Royal Mint issued further gold coins: the *noble*, *half-noble* and *quarter-noble*. The noble was a fine coin with a depiction of the king, standing crowned and armed in the midst of a ship, on the obverse and a biblical text inscribed on the edge to discourage clipping. The noble was replaced in 1464 by a gold coin known as the *angel* which had the Archangel Michael depicted on its obverse. The angel was pierced by a hole and was widely used as a 'touch-piece' to induce good health, and there was also a half-angel called an *angelet*. Gold coins called the *ryal* and *half-ryal* were introduced by Edward IV (1461–83) in 1464. Gold coins continued to be minted until the First World War (1914–18) and one of the most splendid of these was the *sovereign* of Henry VII (1485–1509). It weighed 240 grains, was valued at 20*s* and was a large thin coin with a MAJESTY on the obverse and a Tudor Rose and royal arms on the reverse. By the reign of Elizabeth I the sovereign was valued at 30*s*. The Renaissance clearly influenced the design of coins from that time, the portrait of Henry VII on the famous *testoon* coin of 1504 (later called the *shilling*), designed by a German die-sinker called Alexander Bruchsal, being one of the finest royal portraits ever to appear on British coinage.

Mint marks were often depicted on English coins to show where a legend began and to identify where a particular coin was minted. As medieval coins were not dated, the mint mark also had a periodic significance. Other marks may indicate the workshop in which a coin was made or even a particular craftsman.

COKINI Unmounted couriers: unretained messengers working in the English medieval court.

COLDHARBOUR *and* CALDECOTE Originating in the medieval forms of *harbour* and *cote*, meaning places of shelter and refuge, Coldharbour and Caldecote are common place-names, especially in the Midlands of England. Bestowed as an ironical name on a cold and unpleasant place, the term *harbour* (a refuge) may derive from the Old English *here*, meaning an army, and the places where troops were quartered on a HEREPAETH.

COLLAR BEAM A horizontal beam spanning a roof and tying the principal rafters together (*see* ROOFS, TIMBER).

COLLAR PURLIN A horizontal timber running the length of the centre of a roof beneath the COLLAR BEAMS (*see* PURLIN *and* ROOFS, TIMBER).

COLLARS During the fourteenth and fifteenth centuries collars composed of armorial devices were worn as an indication of adherence to a royal house. Some were later adopted by the sovereign as insignia of office, indeed the collar of SS is still worn by certain officers of the crown. This famous collar is of obscure origin. It is composed of, or studded with, *esses* and was probably worn by members of the Lancastrian affinity prior to its adoption as a royal device by Henry IV (1399–1413), sometimes with the swan of De Bohun as a pendant. The Tudors adapted the device, alternating the Lancastrian SS with Beaufort portcullises and with a Tudor Rose or portcullis as a pendant. The corresponding Yorkist collars were composed of alternate suns and roses with a white lion pendant (for Mortimer) and under Richard III a white boar pendant. These collars, and the insignia of the various orders of chivalry, may be found on effigies and monumental brasses throughout Britain.
(*See also* SUMPTUARY LAWS)

COLLEGE OF ARMS, THE The Corporation of the Officers of Arms in Ordinary, comprising the thirteen kings, heralds and pursuivants of arms, exercises authority in England, Wales and Northern Ireland for matters armorial (*see* ARMORY). Royal officers of arms have acted as a corporate body since the early fifteenth century but did not receive a charter until 1483/4. The College was reincorporated in 1555 at Derby House near St Paul's Cathedral, and maintains a magnificent collection of heraldic and genealogical records and documents. It is owned and governed by a Chapter comprising the three *kings of arms*, six *heralds* and four *pursuivants* or junior heralds. The Earl Marshal has jurisdiction over the officers of arms who are members of the Royal Household and receive a (modest) salary from the crown. There is no public access to the records of the College and enquiries should be addressed to the Officer-in-Waiting (*see* APPENDIX II).
(*See also* COURT OF CHIVALRY)

COLLEGIATE CHURCHES see CHANTRY COLLEGES *and* CHURCHES

COLOURS (ARMORIAL) *see* TINCTURES

COMITAL From the medieval Latin, pertaining to a count or earl. The term 'comital class' refers to members of the peerage above the rank of baron.

COMMANDERY A manorial estate and hospice belonging to the military order of the Knights Hospitaller of St John of Jerusalem, usually staffed by a small complement of knights with a chaplain and servants. Such manors enjoyed certain privileges: the parish of the commandery at Dinmore, Herefordshire, is entirely free of tithe, the owners of the estate benefiting from immunities granted to the Hospitallers by Pope Paschal II in 1113. Dinmore is known as an ex-parochial or *peculiar* parish for, although it possesses a parish church (one of only four dedicated to St John of Jerusalem), it forms no part of a diocese, neither do the bishop nor the ecclesiastical authorities have any jurisdiction there; indeed until the mid-nineteenth century the parishioners were exempted from paying local rates. The commandery at Dinmore ranked as third or fourth in importance among the fifty or so similar Hospitaller commanderies established in England and Wales in the twelfth and thirteenth centuries. Each was in the charge of a knight of the Order, the gift of a commandery being the usual reward for outstanding service in the Crusades. In addition to providing income for the Order by the management of the estates, commanderies were regional military training centres and *hospices* or places of rest for those who returned injured or invalided from the Holy Land. They also afforded shelter and refreshment to travellers and sustenance to the sick and needy. Commanderies accumulated extensive tracts of land, acquired both from the Templars following their suppression in 1312 and from the endowments of *corrodians*: those who were not members of the Order but enjoyed residential benefits in return for their generosity. At Dinmore, as at other commanderies, local field-names evoke its past in Friars' Grove, Great St John's Meadow, etc.

The parallel order of the Knights Templar possessed similar establishments called *preceptories*. Following the suppression of the Templars in 1312, these were transferred to the Knights Hospitaller who also adopted the term to describe some of their later commanderies. Typically, the Hospitaller preceptory at Chibburn in Northumberland was built around a central courtyard approached through an arched gateway in a northern two-storey range of domestic buildings, and with a chapel to the south and dwelling house to the west.
(*See also* ST JOHN OF JERUSALEM, ORDER OF *and* TEMPLAR, KNIGHTS)

COMMISSION OF ARRAY *see* MILITIA *and* RECRUITMENT AND ORGANISATION (MILITARY)

COMMOTE *or* **CWMWD** In medieval Wales, an administrative, judicial and fiscal unit comprising a number of townships (*trefi*). A commote was smaller than a CANTREF in which there were one hundred *trefi*.

(*See also* ROYAL PALACES *and* WALES, CONQUEST OF)

COMMUNICATIONS *and* TRANSPORT *see* BEACONS, HEREPAETHS, HORSES AND HORSE-HARNESS, MATERIALS (CARRIAGE OF), MILITARY ROADS, QUAYS *and* ROADS (MEDIEVAL)

COMPOTUS ROLLS Records comprising estate accounts of royal and seigneurial officials. These are housed at the Public Record Office (*see* APPENDIX II). (*See also* STATE RECORDS)

CONCENTRIC CASTLES A concentric castle is one in which there is no reliance on a central strongpoint and the castle consists of an inner courtyard surrounded by concentric rings of walls, each higher than that outside it so that both inner and outer wards can be defended simultaneously. Furthermore, each line of defence was self-contained: a besieging force, having fought its way into the outer ward, would find itself trapped in a narrow KILLING GROUND, vulnerable to archers on the surrounding walls and flanking towers and from where the absence of doorways and window openings prevented escape.

The concept of concentric fortification originated in Crusader castles such as Krak des Chevaliers in the Holy Land. In England there are no truly concentric castles, though the Tower of London is often described as such. However, despite its impressive inner curtain (1238) and parallel outer wall (1275–85), it has a central strongpoint (the White Tower) which true concentric castles do not. Furthermore, if the Tower of London is to be included in this definition, then so should castles with symmetrical plans such as Middleham which, in *c.* 1300, comprised a massive central hall-keep surrounded by a narrow inner ward, a curtain wall with corner towers and a dry moat.

Gilbert de Clare's magnificent Caerphilly Castle, built in 1268–71, is the earliest concentric fortification in Wales. Only the protruding South Tower and (later) kitchen annex disrupt the symmetry of the castle's core; its inner curtain, with twin-towered gatehouses and circular corner towers, is contained within an encircling outer wall (again with a pair of gatehouses), moat and lake (*see* MOATS AND WATER DEFENCES). Four of Edward I's eight Welsh castles are concentric:

Aberystwyth (1277–*c.* 89), Rhuddlan (1277–82), Harlech (1283–9) and Beaumaris (1295–*c.* 1330, but never completed). Of these, Beaumaris is by far the most sophisticated and Harlech the most complete. Of Aberystwyth Castle only fragments remain, but its rhomboid plan is similar to Rhuddlan which was designed and built (in part) by Master JAMES OF ST GEORGE – as were Harlech and Beaumaris. The inner ward of Rhuddlan Castle has twin-towered gatehouses at the east and west corners and circular towers protruding at the north and south corners. The outer curtain surrounds the castle and is strengthened with a series of buttresses and turrets (*see* SALLY-PORT). Beyond the outer curtain on three sides is a dry moat with a stone revetment and, beyond that, an outer wall that was originally surmounted with a timber palisade. While the outer curtain, moat and outer wall are themselves symmetrical on three sides of the castle, they do not follow precisely the rhomboid plan of the inner ward. On the fourth side the outer curtain encloses a large, triangular-shaped area where the land falls away to the River Clwyd on the south-west. Unlike Rhuddlan, the symmetry of Harlech Castle is almost perfect, despite the constraints imposed by building on a massive rock promontory which took two years to level before construction work could begin. The quadrangular inner ward is surrounded by lofty curtain walls that are parallel on the east and west but are splayed on the north and south to accommodate the great twin-towered gatehouse that dominates the centre of the eastern curtain. A lower and less substantial outer curtain wall closely envelops the inner ring of curtain, gatehouse and four corner towers and beyond this, to the south and east (those sides not protected by natural cliffs) a deep dry moat was cut into the rock.

Beaumaris means 'beautiful marsh' and the castle's level, low-lying site overlooking the Menai Strait enabled Master James to construct a perfect concentric castle. Beaumaris, which is considerably larger than Harlech, has four concentric lines of defence: massive curtain walls 10.8m (36ft) high and 4.65m (15½ft) thick surrounding the inner ward; an outer ward which averages 18m (60ft) in width; a lower and less substantial octagonal outer curtain; and a water-filled moat which originally surrounded the castle. The walls of the inner ward have projecting circular corner towers with D-shaped intermediate towers in the east and west walls and twin-towered gatehouses to the north and south. The north gatehouse (the Constable's quarters) is particularly imposing, though it is but a fragment of the building it was intended to be. Had it been

Beaumaris Castle has four concentric lines of defence: massive curtain walls 10.8 m high (36 ft) and 4.65 m thick (15½ ft) surrounding the inner ward; an outer ward which averages 18 m in width (60 ft); a lower and less substantial octagonal outer curtain; and a water-filled moat which originally surrounded the castle.

completed, the height of the two corner turrets would have been twice the height to which they stand today, and the five large windows (a defensive weakness) would have numbered ten. Master James intended that both his gatehouses should be of identical proportions, though why he required two on such a grand scale is unknown: perhaps he was obsessed with architectural symmetry? In the event, the matching south gatehouse was never finished and its GATE PASSAGE is only half the length of that in the north gatehouse, though a BARBICAN was added after 1306 by way of compensation. The outer curtain (completed after 1306) has twelve flanking towers, spaced at regular intervals, and is far more substantial than the outer walls of Harlech or Rhuddlan which merely screened the inner curtain from attack. The outer curtain at Beaumaris was capable of independent defence and was provided with two small gatehouses (the Llanfaes Gate and the Gate Next The Sea), both of which were off-set from the central axis of the castle for defensive purposes (*see* KILLING GROUND). Regrettably, Beaumaris,

the last of Edward's castles, was never completed and today it has a rather squat appearance, accentuated by its concentric plan. It is the inner curtain where this is most noticeable: its flanking towers were intended to be three storeys high with observation turrets and, as we have seen, the scale of both gatehouses was greatly reduced from the original design.

Queenborough Castle in the Isle of Sheppey was the last royal castle to be built in medieval England. Commissioned at considerable expense by Edward III, it was built and furnished as a royal palace but its principal function was to defend the Thames estuary against French incursions and to protect the new town that was founded to support it. Queenborough Castle was uniquely circular in plan with six round towers projecting from an inner *rotunda* and a perfectly concentric outer curtain wall and moat. It was begun in the spring of 1361 and completed in 1377. The accommodation was disposed about the rotunda with the castle well at the very centre of the rigidly geometric plan. At Queenborough the concentric principle was taken to its logical conclusion by locating the entrances to the rotunda and outer ward at opposite points of the compass. Had the outer gate been captured, an intruder would have been obliged to pass through the entire length of the outer ward in full view of crossbowmen on the wall-walks and the many trebuchets and mangonels with which Queenborough is known to have been equipped. In many respects Queenborough anticipated the TUDOR COASTAL FORTS of the sixteenth century, though it was also a residence which they were not. Sadly the castle was demolished in 1650.

CONDUIT A trough or pipe for conveying water (*see* PLUMBING, WATER SUPPLY AND SANITATION).

CONROI A cavalry squadron (*see* HORSES AND HORSE-HARNESS *and* WARFARE, CONDUCT OF).

CONSTABLE (i) The constable (or *castellan*) was a household official responsible for the governance of a castle in the owner's absence. Many castles, especially royal ones, were occupied by a constable and a small caretaker household for long periods, the constable occupying quarters (*maisonette*) which were separate from those of the lord's, often in the keep or in the gatehouse where he could exercise control of the drawbridge and portcullis mechanisms. The constableship of a major fortification such as Dover Castle or Caernarfon was a singularly prestigious office, granted to men of high rank who frequently held it as a sinecure, leaving the day-to-day administration to a deputy or lieutenant.
(ii) The Constable of England (from the mid-twelfth century *Lord High Constable*) was, until the sixteenth century, the seventh of the great offices of state (*see* HOUSEHOLD). Originally, the constable was the quartermaster of the armies and master of the horse, and later (with the EARL MARSHAL) presided over the COURT OF CHIVALRY.
(ii) A manorial officer (*see* LAW AND ORDER *and* MANOR).

CONSTABLEWICK The jurisdiction of a CON-STABLE.

CONSTABULARIA *see* RECRUITMENT AND ORGANISATION (MILITARY)

CONSTRUCTION OF CASTLES *see* CASTLES, CONSTRUCTION OF

CONTRAVALLATION A continuous line of redoubts constructed by besiegers to protect themselves against sorties from the defending garrison.

COPING A protective capping intended to disperse rainwater from the top of a wall.

COPITA Hardened leather protection for a horse's head (*see* HORSES AND HORSE-HARNESS).

COPYHOLD *see* VILLEIN *and* MANOR

CORBEL A projection of stone, wood or brick supporting an arch, beam, parapet or moulding. Corbelling refers to receding courses of stone, brick, etc. supporting a projection such as an oriel window or MACHICOLATION.

CORBEL-TABLE A series of corbels (*see* above) occurring immediately below the roof eaves, both internally and externally. The Normans were especially fond of corbel-tables which were often elaborately carved in the forms of monsters and grotesque figures.

CORNAGE TENANCY *see* RECRUITMENT AND ORGANISATION (MILITARY)

CORNICE A moulded projection surmounting a wall, arch or building.

CORRODIAN A benefactor who is not a member of a religious order but who enjoys residential benefits in return for his or her generosity.

COTSWOLD STONE The band of oolite which runs from the Humber to the Dorset coast is at its widest and reaches its greatest elevation in the Cotswolds, a range of limestone hills largely in Gloucestershire but extending eastwards into Oxfordshire and south-westwards into Wiltshire. Noted for sheep pastures and formerly a centre of the woollen industry, the wide Cotswold landscape is complemented by its buildings as in no other area of Britain. Manor houses, castles, churches, farmsteads and entire villages are constructed of oolitic limestone or 'Cotswold Stone', the colour of which varies from the richest orange-brown in the east to pale creamy greys in the south and west. High quality freestone (*see* ASHLAR) is to be found in deep strata which are accessible only in the steep north-western escarpment. 'Cotswold' is derived from *Cōd's wald* or forest.

COUCHED *see* LANCE *and* WARFARE: CONDUCT OF

COUDES *see* ARMOUR

COULEUVRINE À MAIN *see* FIREARMS AND CANNON

COUNCIL *see* HOUSEHOLD

COUNCIL, ROYAL *see* GOVERNMENT *and* HOUSEHOLD

COUNT Several of the lords who followed Duke William in his conquest of England held substantial territories (*comtés*) in the Low Countries and France and, although granted English lands and titles by the Conqueror, they retained the superior title of *comté*, *county* or count. The English equivalent is EARL, a title which originated in Scandinavia and appeared in England in the early eleventh century as *eorl*, an Old English form of *jarl*. Confusingly, the wife of an earl is a countess.

COUNTER-CASTLE A castle erected by besiegers to protect their operations (*see* SIEGES).

COUNTERPOISE PIT The pit into which the inner end of a movable bridge is lowered in a counterpoise or axle arrangement (*see* DRAWBRIDGE).

COUNTERSCARP The exterior slope of a revetment or ditch.

COUNTERSCARP GALLERY A defensive position on the outer lip of a moat or ditch, usually a passage with loopholes.

COUNTIES Derived from the French *comté*, the county superseded the Anglo-Saxon SHIRE following the Norman Conquest. Many shires conformed with earlier territorial boundaries: in the eighth and ninth centuries the kingdom of Wessex was divided into Berkshire, Dorset, Hampshire, Somerset and Wiltshire, and in the tenth century the kingdom of Mercia was divided into Derbyshire, Gloucestershire, Leicestershire, Northamptonshire, Nottinghamshire, Rutland, Staffordshire, Warwickshire, Worcestershire and parts of Bedfordshire, Buckinghamshire and Oxfordshire. Norfolk and Suffolk were shire divisions of the old East Anglian kingdoms, while the counties of Essex, Kent, Middlesex and Sussex were formed out of Saxon territories. In the north, Yorkshire approximated to the Danish kingdom of York, Cumberland was the land of the Cumbras (from *Cymry* meaning 'the Welsh') and Northumberland was part of the ancient kingdom of Northumbria. The County Palatine of Durham was first granted to Cuthbert in 685 and was held by the bishops of Durham thereafter until 1836 (*see* PALATINATE). Cheshire, which had been a Roman province, also became a county palatine under William I and Lancashire was originally the Honor of Lancaster, the northern part of which extended into Yorkshire. Westmorland was two baronies under the Normans and Rutland was originally a SOKE in Northamptonshire. When the Local Government Act of 1888 created county councils, the Isle of Ely, the Soke of Peterborough, East and West Suffolk, East and West Sussex, the Ridings of Yorkshire and the Isle of Wight all became autonomous administrative divisions while remaining, nominally, part of their original counties. The county of Middlesex disappeared in 1964 when, with parts of Essex, Surrey, Hertfordshire and Kent it was absorbed into Greater London. The Welsh counties were formed after the Act of 'Union' of 1536, Monmouthshire remaining the subject of dispute until its incorporation into the new Welsh county of Gwent in 1974 (*see also* MARCH). Major revisions of administrative boundaries were effected throughout Britain in 1974 as a result of which several new counties were created while others were lost. At the same time the charming but anachronistic vestiges of earlier manorial estates, the isolated 'islands' of one county within another (such as the parish of Holwell in Dorset which was formerly described on maps as 'Somerset Pars'), were absorbed into the new administrative divisions which surrounded them.

COUNT PALATINE *see* PALATINATE

COUNTRYSIDE Lowland England contains two distinctive types of countryside: the *ancient* and the *planned*. Ancient countryside is that which has evolved gradually, whereas planned countryside has the appearance of having been superimposed on the landscape. Medieval writers distinguished between *fielden* and *arden* (field and woodland) and in the sixteenth century the terms *several* and *champion* were coined to describe land held 'in severalty' by a number of small farmers and areas where open fields still predominated. The term *woodland* was also used to describe *several* countryside with its abundance of hedgerow trees.

COUNTY HISTORIES County histories have been compiled for many of the English and Welsh counties, many dating from the nineteenth and early twentieth centuries. These often contain references to castles, crenellated manor houses and other fortifications, and details of architectural features which have not survived or have been badly restored. The county histories are therefore invaluable sources of information, although heraldic references and genealogical charts dating from this period are not always reliable.

COUPLED ROOF *see* ROOFS (TIMBER)

COURSE A single horizontal row of masonry, brick or flint.

COURSED RUBBLE Walling of roughly dressed stone or flints set in courses (*see* COURSE). Uncoursed rubble consists of unhewn stones or flints not laid in regular courses.

COURSIÈRE Timber roofing erected over a WALL-WALK.

COURT *and* COURTYARD A bailey (or ward) is often described as a court or courtyard, although, strictly speaking, a court was an open space, usually paved and entirely surrounded by buildings which many baileys are not (*see* BAILEY). Thus the Upper and Lower wards of Caernarfon Castle and the Inner and Outer wards of Conwy are courtyards, while the Great Court of Richmond and the Outer Court of Farleigh Hungerford are not. The term is most appropriately applied to later castles such as Bodiam and Raglan. Completed in 1388, Bodiam's great hall, kitchens, domestic apartments, chapel, servants' hall

and kitchen, armoury, stables, storerooms and even accommodation for manorial labourers were all contained within its courtyard walls, rather than erected against a curtain wall as in earlier castles (*see* COURTYARD BUILDINGS). At Raglan Castle ranges of apartments were built round the Fountain Court in *c.* 1460–9 and further ranges of domestic and administrative offices round the Pitched Stone Court in *c.* 1549–89. The distinction between a bailey or ward and a court is well illustrated at Old Wardour Castle. Built in 1393 as a fortified TOWER-HOUSE, Wardour has a central hexagonal courtyard, little more than a LIGHTWELL for the rooms looking into it, and is surrounded by a wide, open bailey and curtain wall. There is a similar arrangement at Bolton Castle, though here the courtyard is rectangular and of sufficient size to accommodate tenants and their livestock during Scottish raids. (Lines of raised stones set into the cobbles are believed to be the footings for livestock pens laid down during a Civil War siege.) Although spacious, the courtyard at Bolton is dwarfed by the walls of the surrounding building. Five almost identical doorways lead off into various parts of the castle, each with its own PORTCULLIS and stout wooden door, while the four corner doors are further protected by single MACHICOLATIONS above. At both castles the courtyard is entered through a vaulted GATE PASSAGE, the vault at Wardour being an early example of fan-vaulting. Castles such as these are sometimes referred to as *courtyard castles* or, where there are two conjoined and self-

Apartments and grand staircase built round the Fountain Court at Raglan Castle in c. *1460–9.*

contained enclosures (as at Conwy and Caernarfon), as *double courtyard castles*.
(*See also* QUADRANGULAR CASTLES and SHELL-KEEP)

COURT BARON A manorial court which, unlike the COURT LEET, was a private jurisdiction and effectively the property of the LORD OF THE MANOR. The main functions of the court were to determine ESCHEATS and transfers of land, to enforce manorial custom and to oversee the management of commons and wastes (*see* MANOR). Among several officers appointed by the court was the REEVE who represented the parish and collected manorial dues.

COURT LEET A manorial court of record and public jurisdiction responsible for dealing with minor offences and matters such as the repair and maintenance of highways and ditches and the View of FRANKPLEDGE. It was presided over by the LORD OF THE MANOR or his representative and attendance was obligatory for all males over a certain age (in some areas this was as young as twelve). The court met at least twice a year and appointed officers (*see* MANOR).

COURT OF CHIVALRY In the formative years of ARMORY, namely the end of the twelfth and the beginning of the thirteenth centuries, coats of arms were assumed, probably with the help and advice of the heralds, by the knightly and noble classes. That such a 'system' left much to be desired is evidenced by the establishment of the Court of the Constable and Marshal, sometimes called the Court of Chivalry, in the first half of the fourteenth century. The judges of the court were the Constable and Marshal of England and the court had jurisdiction in causes armorial. Theoretically the Court of the Earl Marshal still exists, though it is rarely called upon to exercise its jurisdiction over matters armorial within England, Wales and Northern Ireland.

COURT ROLL A written record of proceedings in court, usually manorial proceedings such as the administration of wills, grants, the admission and surrender of tenancies and the regulation of common land. Although the court rolls were the property of a LORD OF THE MANOR and were maintained by his steward or agent, they are legally a public record and therefore available for inspection.
(*See also* MANOR)

COURTYARD BUILDINGS It is almost invariably the case that courtyard buildings have been demolished leaving only the remnants of walls or footings to indicate their former extent. This is most unfortunate, for the everyday life of a castle revolved around its servants' hall, the kitchens, buttery, pantry and other domestic offices and, of course, the great hall which, in later castles, was often entered from the courtyard (*see* HALL *and* HOUSEHOLD). At Bodiam, for example, all the courtyard buildings are gone so that the immediate impression, on entering the castle, is one of a very much larger open space than was originally the case. A sense of enclosure is still evident at Middleham Castle, even though the courtyard buildings are in a ruinous condition, while at Conwy the walls of the Great Hall and the King's Hall and Presence Chamber have survived, though the kitchens and stables (opposite the Great Hall) have not. If a visitor can imagine these buildings as they once were, either incorporated within the outer walls (as at Bodiam) or with sloping roofs abutting the curtain, then the confined nature of a courtyard may be appreciated. Even when the courtyard walls were of masonry many of the buildings behind them were of timber, as at Pevensey Castle where, in 1300, the hall and chapel were rebuilt entirely in wood with clay daubing. And even Henry III, that great builder of masonry castles, was not above ordering 'a fair, great, and becoming hall of wood and a kitchen of wood' for his manor at Clipston in 1245. Even so, stables were almost invariably built of stone with slate roofs; horses were extremely valuable and had to be protected from the risk of fire.
(*See also* BAILEY, COURT AND COURTYARD, SHELL-KEEP *and* TIMBER-FRAME BUILDINGS)

COURTYARD CASTLE A castle with a central courtyard surrounded by buildings (*see* COURT AND COURTYARD).

COURTYARD FARMS A traditional quadrangular plan evident in many deserted medieval farmsteads and subsequently adopted in the design of farm complexes through to the nineteenth century. Originally the quadrangle, with its 'blind' outer walls and doorways opening into the courtyard, provided both shelter and a means of defence, particularly in remote areas such as the Welsh Marches. In many instances the farmhouse formed one side of the courtyard which was sheltered on the north by a substantial barn. Stables on the west side faced east into the courtyard so that early morning preparations were illuminated by the rising sun, and timber vehicles in the open-fronted cartsheds to the south were protected from exposure to rain carried

Model of Bodiam Castle, Sussex, as it appeared in the fifteenth century. None of the courtyard buildings has survived so that the immediate impression, on entering the castle, is one of a very much larger open space than was originally the case.

by the prevailing westerly winds. Granaries, reached from the courtyard by exterior flights of stone steps, often formed the second storeys of such buildings. There are also many instances of farmhouses being built away from the courtyard and farm buildings, usually to the south. Such 'detached' dwellings are often of a later date than the original farm complex and may reflect both the increasing prosperity and corresponding social aspirations of a gentleman farmer. Sometimes the original farmhouse was plundered for building materials – thereby removing one side of the quadrangle – or was subsequently adapted for other purposes.

COURTYARD HOUSE *see* CASTLES, DEVELOPMENT OF *and* MANOR HOUSES

COUSINS' WARS *see* WARS OF THE ROSES

COUSTELL *see* WEAPONS AND HARNESS

COUTER Plate armour protection for the elbow. By the end of the fourteenth century the couter had been incorporated into the fully articulated VAMBRACE. (*See also* ARMOUR)

COVE *and* COVING A concave moulding at the junction of a ceiling and a wall.

COVERED WAY In post-medieval fortifications, a continuous passageway on the outer edge of a ditch protected from enemy fire by an earthwork parapet.

CRANEQUIN *see* ARCHERY

CRANES *see* SCAFFOLDING AND CRANES

CREASING A line of projecting stones that trajects rainwater on to a roof below.

CREDENCE *see* CHAPEL *and* PISCINA

CRÉMALLIÈRE In post-medieval fortifications, fieldworks with an indented or saw-tooth pattern to allow greater flanking cover.

CRENEL (*also* CRENELLE) Crenels are narrow gaps between MERLONS in an embattled parapet which were sometimes provided with hinged wooden shutters to afford greater protection for defenders on the wall-walk. At Caernarfon Castle

there is evidence that crenel shutters were held in vertical slots cut into the merlons.
(*See also* BATTLEMENTS *and* EMBRASURE)

CRENELLATIONS Battlemented parapets comprising alternating MERLONS and CRENELS. There is evidence that in the eleventh century the criteria by which a castle was defined included the depth of its ditches and the height of its banks and ramparts together with the design of the walls or stockades which further strengthened them. By the twelfth century the king's officials had evidently settled for the arbitrary criterion of crenellation and thereafter there was a legal obligation to obtain a *licence to crenellate* before a castle could be built or a residence fortified. It would appear that, for the most part, licences were granted to those who applied for them, though Marcher lordships were exempt from this requirement and many ADULTERINE castles were erected without licences. Sometimes a licence was issued as an unsolicited reward for loyal service to the crown but was not acted upon. Licences to crenellate continued to be granted long after there was a need for private fortification, the last ones being granted by Henry VIII.
(*See also* BATTLEMENTS *and* CRENEL)

CRESSET (i) An iron container for a fire beacon mounted on a pole and reached by a ladder (*see* BEACONS).
(ii) The carved holes in *cresset stones* into which cooking fat or grease and floating wicks were placed to provide multiple lamps. Some cresset stones were portable and contained three or four such holes; larger ones were too heavy to move and had perhaps twelve or more cressets.

CREST (i) In the twelfth and thirteenth centuries a simple fan-like projection (the *crista* or cock's comb) was sometimes attached to a HELMET, the sides decorated with armorial devices similar to those on the shield. These early crests were succeeded by *panaches* of feathers which were often arranged in tiers. The ornate tournament crests of the high Middle Ages were moulded in light materials (paste board, cloth or hardened leather over a wooden or wire framework or basketwork) and were fastened to the helm by means of laces or rivets, the unsightly join concealed by a WREATH or coronet, or by the material of the crest itself, the lower edge of which formed a MANTLING, often in the form of a beast's fur or feathers (*see* TOURNAMENT HELM). Crests are depicted on helmets in COATS OF ARMS.
(ii) A ridge-tile (*see* SLATES AND TILES).

CRI DE GUERRE A war-cry, intended to rally troops in the heat of battle.

CROCKET In MEDIEVAL ARCHITECTURE, carved leaf-like decorative features projecting at regular intervals on the sloping sides of gables, pinnacles, etc., and in the capitals of piers.

CROP MARKS William Camden (1551–1623) observed of Richborough, the Fort of the Saxon Shore in Kent: 'Age has erased the very tracks of it. . . . it is at this day a cornfield, wherein, when the corn is grown up, one may observe the draughts of streets crossing one another (for where they have gone, the corn is thinner)'. Such crop marks are produced by variations in the quality of plant growth caused by differences in the soil and subsoil. The presence of buried walls and foundations just beneath the soil's surface will produce weak plants which are vulnerable to dry conditions while deeper pits and silt-filled trenches retain moisture and allow for the

Crest depicting a freeminer of the Forest of Dean in the brass of Robert Greymdour at Newland Church, Gloucestershire.

development of a substantial root structure and more luxuriant growth. From the air such variations of vegetation (usually in a cereal crop) become more evident and may delineate the former walls, buildings and drainage systems of archaeological sites such as castles and abandoned medieval villages. Aerial photography of crop marks is particularly effective when a low sun shines across a field, the different levels of vegetation casting shadows which clearly trace the outlines of the structures beneath.

CROPURE *or* **CRUPPER** Armour for the hindquarters of a horse (*see* HORSES AND HORSE-HARNESS).

CROSSBOW *see* ARCHERY

CROSS DYKES *see* DIKES

CROSSLET *or* **CROSSLIT LOOPHOLE** *and* **CROSSLET WITH FISHTAIL LOOPHOLE** *see* LOOPHOLES

CROSS-WALL An interior dividing wall. These could be external, such as the wall (with ditch, drawbridge and miniature gatehouse) which divides the inner and outer wards of Conwy Castle, or internal, as at Rochester Castle, Kent, where the immense cross-wall within the Norman keep enabled the garrison to take refuge when the keep was undermined in 1215 (*see* KEEP).

CROW *see* SIEGES

CROW STEPS Steps on the coping of a gable.

CROWN POST A vertical post at the centre of a TIE BEAM to support a COLLAR BEAM or COLLAR PURLIN to which it is usually connected by means of diagonal braces (*see* KING POST *and* ROOFS (TIMBER)).

CRUCK A curved and shaped piece of timber extending from ground to roof-ridge to support a roof.

CRUPPER *see* BARDING, CROPURE *and* HORSES AND HORSE-HARNESS

CRUSADES The Wars of the Cross (medieval Latin *cruciata* = cross) waged by feudal Christendom against non-Christians and heretics, notably the Islamic peoples of the Near East, between 1096 and 1271. The Crusades were never envisaged as wars of conversion; rather they were authorised by the Pope for the recovery of Christian lands from the infidel.

Religious fervour pervaded the Crusades: Popes promised redemption for Christians killed in battle while St Bernard of Clairvaux urged criminals to join the Crusades to atone for their sins. But the Crusades were also driven by socio-economic considerations. The increasing inflexibility of the feudal system encouraged young, landless sons of the European nobility to seek their fortunes in war, while the prospect of trade with the East drew many merchants to the Holy Land in the later Crusades. Of equal significance was the emergence of the concept of CHIVALRY among the feudal nobility: by 'taking the cross' even the most humble knight could be admitted to membership of an élite chivalric fraternity. From this arose a spurious romantic interpretation of what was, in practice, one of the most disgraceful blots on the human record. There was nothing remotely noble about these loathsome enterprises which were characterised by pitiless cruelty to all who stood between the crusaders and the recovery of their religious shrines from Islam.

The Crusades began with much optimism and spiritual zeal and occupied the best of western Christendom's military, religious and chivalric leaders for more than two centuries. Yet they achieved virtually nothing, largely because of the lack of organisation arising from jealousies among the leaders, and failure to come to terms with the terrain, the climate and the need for hygiene. The Crusades were essentially about two fundamentalist civilisations, each despising and detesting all values and beliefs that did not coincide with their own.

The *First Crusade* (1096–9) resulted in the capture of Jerusalem, the expulsion of the native population and the founding of a crusader state in the Holy Land. But the fledgling feudal kingdom was never militarily self-sufficient and subsequent Crusades were essentially relief forces sent to assist in its defence. The *Second Crusade* (1147–9) failed to prevent a Muslim resurgence and Jerusalem eventually fell to the sultan Salah ad-Din (Saladin) in 1187. The *Third Crusade* (1189–92) comprised contingents from Germany under Frederick Barbarossa (who died en route); from France under King Philip; and from England and the Angevin lands under King Richard, known as 'Lionheart' (*coeur-de-lion*). The crusaders succeeded in recapturing some lost territory, notably Acre and Jaffa in 1191, but failed to take Jerusalem. Philip and Richard quarrelled and the Crusade collapsed. The *Fourth Crusade* (1202–4) was diverted against the Byzantine Empire and saw the sacking of

Constantinople which fell in 1204. The *Fifth Crusade* (1217–21) was again diverted away from Palestine, this time to Saladin's power base in Egypt. The strategy very nearly succeeded: the sultan offered Jerusalem in return for Damietta which had been captured in 1218. But the crusaders unwisely raised the stakes, the offer was rejected and the Crusade accomplished nothing. The *Sixth Crusade* (1228–9) succeeded in returning Jerusalem to the Christians, though it was lost to the Turks in 1244. The *Seventh Crusade* (1248–54) ended in disaster in Egypt. The *Eighth Crusade* (1270–1) was effectively abandoned when its leader, Louis IX of France, died on his way to the Holy Land and a truce was agreed between Lord Edward of England (later Edward I) and the sultan.

In May 1291 Acre fell and what remained of the Crusader Kingdom ceased to exist. Thereafter Crusades were directed against heretics and schismatics, such as the Albigensians in southern France, who were considered to be as much of a threat to Christendom as the Muslims in the east.
(*See also* ST JOHN OF JERUSALEM, ORDER OF *and* TEMPLAR, KNIGHTS)

CRYPT A vaulted underground chamber, usually constructed beneath the chancel of a church or chapel to accommodate tombs. Not to be confused with an UNDERCROFT, an open (often vaulted) storage chamber beneath the first floor of a domestic building in a castle or monastery.

CUIRASS *or* **CUIRIE** Plate covering for the trunk of the body used throughout Europe from the thirteenth century. By the fifteenth century iron or steel cuirasses were often composed of a number of separate pieces to form a breastplate and backplate, the standard components of a full harness.
(*See also* ARMOUR *and* HELMETS)

CUIR BOUILLI Often (and erroneously) described as 'boiled leather', leather body armour made by soaking in melted wax and hardened and shaped by heating and drying in a mould. Deerskin was considered to be the best leather for this purpose, though in England sheepskin was widely used. Cuir bouilli armour was light yet extremely effective and was in constant use throughout the late medieval period.

CUISSES *or* **CUISHES** Quilted or leather padding for the thigh.
(*See also* ARMOUR *and* HELMETS)

CULVERIN From the French *coulvrine* meaning 'snakelike', the term was originally applied to a

small cannon but was later used to describe a small-bore handgun. Generally the smallest of medieval gunpowder weapons, it was light and portable and was widely used in the fifteenth century, notably by Burgundian troops. The culverin was made of forged iron, affixed to a wooden stock and supported by a rest for firing lead shot.
(*See also* WEAPONS)

CULVERY *see* DOVECOTES

CUPOLA A small circular or polygonal dome crowning a roof or turret.

CURFEW From *couvre-feu*, meaning 'cover the fire', the curfew bell warned townspeople to dowse or cover the fires in their thatched hovels before retiring at the end of each day. Tradition has it that the curfew law, which was devised to minimise the risk of fire, was introduced into England by William the Conqueror who then used it to prevent seditious groups meeting after dark. It is certainly true that in medieval towns the law (and the striking of the bell) was used to restrict nocturnal activity, thereby helping to preserve law and order. At Presteigne in Powys and Midhurst in West Sussex the curfew bell is still rung from the church tower at eight o'clock each night.
(*See also* TOWN WALLS)

CURIA PRIMA *see* MANOR

CURTAIN TOWER *see* TOWERS

CURTAIN (WALL) (i) A general term for the defensive wall surrounding a BAILEY. The term itself dates from the seventeenth century when it was used to describe a wall that fills the space between a pair of towers. Curtain walls had to be of sufficient thickness to withstand the pounding of siege engines (*see* MASONRY *and* SIEGES) and high enough to frustrate attempts at scaling them. Consequently they were often 3m (10ft) thick and up to 12m (40ft) high, with projecting plinths at the base to prevent undermining (*see* BATTER). Stone curtains often replaced earlier timber palisades (*see* BAILEY, MOTTE *and* RINGWORK), the eleventh-century curtains at Richmond Castle (1071–89) and Ludlow Castle (the inner bailey, 1086–95) being exceptional in that they were built in stone from the beginning. Curtain walls are surmounted by wall-walks and BATTLEMENTS and may be pierced by rows of LOOPHOLES: at Caernarfon Castle, for example, shooting galleries within the 4.6m (15ft) thick curtain walls are lined with EMBRASURES.

Windows cut into a curtain wall to provide light to domestic buildings inevitably reduced the defensive capability of a castle, unless it occupied a naturally defended site – as at Warwick and Barnard Castle where the walls are protected on one side by almost vertical cliffs (*see* WINDOWS). 'Blind spots' at the foot of a curtain wall were covered by the provision of MURAL TOWERS (*flanking towers* or *interval towers*) or BASTIONS from which archers and crossbowmen could command the outer face of the wall without revealing themselves. One of the earliest examples is at Chepstow where, in *c.* 1200, William Marshal strengthened his castle with a stone cross wall (the east curtain) flanked by circular towers. Curtain walls were usually filled with rubble, though improved construction techniques and workmanship resulted in thinner walls that were no less defensible. Often there is a second curtain wall, arranged either sequentially or concentrically, beyond the bailey curtain. In CONCENTRIC CASTLES this second or 'outer curtain' was invariably lower than the inner wall so that archers on the parapet of the inner curtain could shoot over it. The wall-walk of a lower, outer wall would also be vulnerable to attack from archers on the inner curtain were it to be occupied by a besieging force. (*See also* TOWN WALLS)
(ii) In post-medieval fortifications, a length of rampart between two bastions.

CURTILAGE, THE *see* KITCHENS

CURVILINEAR STYLE *see* GOTHIC ARCHITECTURE

CUSHION CAPITAL *see* BLOCK CAPITAL

CUSP In architectural decoration, the point at which two curves meet (e.g. in an ogee arch) and the projecting point between small arcs in Gothic tracery (e.g. between the lobes of a trefoil, quatrefoil, etc. (*see* FOILS)).

CUSTOS ROTULORUM *see* LIEUTENANT

CUSTUMAL *see* MANOR

CYCLAS A SURCOAT cut short at the front and long at the back (*see also* JUPON *and* TABARD).

CYLINDRICAL KEEP *see* KEEP

CYPHER A monogram, sometimes ensigned with a coronet to indicate rank, used as a personal or household device. They were particularly popular during the eighteenth and nineteenth centuries when the use of armorial badges was in decline and the new rich of the Industrial Revolution perceived a need for some means of personal identity.
(*See also* GRAFFITI)

DAFYDD'S WAR *see* WALES, CONQUEST OF

DAGGER A short pointed two-edged weapon used for stabbing.
(*See also* WEAPONS AND HARNESS)

DAIS A raised floor to accommodate the principal ('high') table in the great hall.

DAMOISEAU Late thirteenth-century cavalryman, of lower status than a knight.
(*See also* HORSES AND HORSE-HARNESS)

DAMS *see* MOATS AND WATER DEFENCES

DANEGELD A *geld* or land-tax raised in Anglo-Saxon England and paid as tribute to the Danes in order to ward off invasion. Such payments were made throughout the ninth and tenth centuries but, following the catastrophic (though heroic) defeat of the ealdorman Brihtnoth and his local levies at the battle of Maldon (Essex) in 991, the collection and administration of Danegeld was formalised and refined in response to increasing Danish pressure. Immense sums were raised for this purpose during the later years of Aethelred's reign (978–1016) and Cnut (1016–35) levied a similar tax, known as *heregeld*, in order to finance national defence. This was discontinued in 1051 but was revived by William I as a means of raising personal revenues. The term Danegeld persisted in use until its final abolition in 1162.

DANELAW The north-eastern area of Britain occupied by the Danes in the ninth and tenth centuries, comprising the kingdoms of Bernicia, York and East Anglia and the federation of the *Five*

Boroughs of Derby, Lincoln, Nottingham, Leicester and Stamford. It was in the Five Boroughs that the Danes established their administrative and military headquarters. Following the Conquest, the NORMANS attempted to rationalise the often disparate practices of the Danelaw and Saxon administrations. In the Danelaw, divisions had been created out of the former Viking military districts, each with its central borough, wapentake sub-divisions and a Danish lord (*jarl*) responsible directly to the English king. But in the Saxon shires, administrative and judicial practices which originated in the laws of Ine, King of Wessex (688–726) and his successors, were effected through shires and hundreds with an ealdorman and shirereeve representing the king and people.

DAPIFER *see* HOUSEHOLD

DARK AGES, THE A simplistic term denoting the apparent obscurity or barbarity of the period following the withdrawal of Rome from Britain at the beginning of the fifth century to the advent of the MIDDLE AGES. Originally, the term was coined by pre-nineteenth-century historians who tended to disregard everything that was achieved between the fall of the Roman Empire and the Renaissance. It has acquired a more recent significance because of the paucity of contemporary historical information. In the absence of documentary records, archaeological, topographical and other sources (such as place-names) have nevertheless provided us with insights into a period of history in which new elements and new patterns emerged which were to influence the development of medieval and modern Britain. Not least was the introduction of Germanic languages which, with the recedence of the native Celtic tongue, were the ancestral version of modern English. The Emperor Constantine's conversion to Christianity (in AD 312) led to the partial conversion of the Romano-British nobility before Roman rule came to an end in AD 410, and, although Rome had never succeeded in conquering the Irish or the Picts in Scotland, Ireland was converted by Roman missionaries in the fifth century and Irish monks later played a leading rôle in the conversion of the Picts and Anglo-Saxons in Britain. Two major migrations of Germanic-speaking peoples from northern Germany and Scandinavia occurred during this period. The first Anglo-Saxon settlers were mercenaries who overthrew their British masters and founded their own independent states. During the fifth and sixth centuries further settlers arrived and by the end of the seventh century three major

political and military powers had emerged: Northumbria (in north-east England and the south of Scotland), Mercia (in the midlands) and Wessex (in the south and south-west). The annexation of western Britain was a slow process: Cornwall retained its independence until the ninth century and Wales was never subdued.

The second migration, of Vikings from Denmark and Norway, began with sporadic incursions in the late eighth century followed by systematic plundering and colonisation from *c.* 850. The English kingdoms of East Anglia, Northumbria and Mercia were eventually subjugated but during the tenth century the West Saxon kings retaliated and briefly created an English kingdom, theoretically unified but in practice divided into regions approximating to the old kingdoms and ruled by powerful earls. In 1016 this passed to the Danish king Cnut but after 1042 England was again ruled by a West Saxon, Edward the Confessor, until his death in 1065. To the north the kingdoms of the Picts had been replaced in the ninth century by a new kingdom of Scots, and the Vikings in Ireland were finally defeated at the battle of Clontarf in 1014.

It is inevitable that centuries of conquest should acquire the epithet 'barbarous'. The sixth-century British cleric Gildas described the destruction of his country by the German barbarians: 'Swords glinted all around, and the flames crackled. Foundation stones of high walls that had been torn from their lofty base, holy altars, fragments of corpses, covered as it were with a purple crust of congealed blood, looked as though they had been mixed up in some dreadful wine press.' But this is the obverse side of the sun and, obscure though our vision of the Dark Ages may be, that which has been revealed to us is of a brilliant intensity. The ancient kingdom of Northumbria was 'a land of art and culture, a haven of learning and skill' which in the seventh century became the force that first united England into a single realm. Most of this cultural creativity emanated from the Anglo-Saxon church and from the monastic foundations in particular. The monasteries of Northumberland and Kent produced the finest illuminated manuscripts using pigments imported from as far afield as the Himalayas. In churches Anglo-Saxon artists established a unique and highly influential school of sculpture while England's first poets created epic poetry that marked the beginnings of English literature. This was the age of the *Codex Amiatinus*, the world's oldest surviving Latin bible. Weighing 75lb and requiring the skins of 500 calves for its vellum pages, it was (probably) made at the monastery of

Monkwearmouth (Tyne and Wear) as a gift for the Pope in AD 716. This was the age of England's first major historian, the Venerable Bede, who produced his *History of the English Church and People* in AD 731; of the magnificent illuminated *Lindisfarne Gospels* and of the mystical St Cuthbert, whose beautifully carved wooden coffin may still be seen at Durham Cathedral together with an array of superb Anglo-Saxon treasures: the products not of obscurity and barbarity but of a highly sophisticated and cultured people.

'DE' (IN SURNAMES AND TITLES) Individual members of a family were often identified by adding a place-name to a Christian name, prefixed by 'de' (French = 'of'). Simon de Montfort (*c.* 1208–65), for example, was named after his father's estates at Montford l'Amaury, about 30 miles west of Paris. There are many examples of the place-name element being consolidated as a surname: the De Moribrays of the eleventh century became the Mowbrays of the fourteenth, for example. However, the use of this element in titles is fairly modern and, according to Cokayne, 'was presumably adopted to give an air of antiquity to new creations'.
See also FITZ-)

DEBATABLE LANDS, THE A tract of land between the rivers Esk and Sark claimed by both England and Scotland. The term is sometimes applied to other areas of land, ownership of which was disputed. In the absence of any clear authority debatable lands often became the haunt of thieves and vagabonds.
(*See also* MARCH *and* OUTLAWS)

DECLINE OF THE CASTLE It has been argued that the building of Dartmouth Castle between 1481 and 1495 presaged the end of the medieval castle. The first fortification to be built where the Dart estuary narrows, a mile south-east of the town, was commissioned by the mayor and corporation of Dartmouth in 1388 – the earliest known example in England of a castle built by a municipal authority. During the HUNDRED YEARS WAR the piratical 'Sea Dogs' of Dartmouth were causing mayhem in the French channel ports and the castle was built in anticipation of retaliation. The fortification that replaced it a century later may have been modest in scale but it was of considerable military significance. Again, it was the corporation of Dartmouth that built the castle, though maintenance of the garrison was subsidised by the crown. Significantly, it was hardly defended from the

landward side, and was effectively a screen wall facing the estuary. Splayed gun ports in a rock-cut basement were supplemented by further gun emplacements on either side of a central pair of conjoined towers. It is clear that the cannon were intended to sweep the estuary, a revolutionary concept that was to be the rationale for the TUDOR COASTAL FORTS of the mid-sixteenth century. The two floors above the artillery gallery provided basic accommodation for the garrison while an opening at ground-floor level received a chain boom (*see* BOOM) from Kingswear on the opposite bank of the estuary. Dartmouth was far removed from the 'fortified feudal residence' that defines the medieval castle (*see* CASTLE). It was an instrument of national defence and illustrates how military architects responded to the increasing power and range of cannon (*see* FIREARMS AND CANNON).

Although Henry VII (1485–1509) recognised the potential of highly mobile siege artillery and exercised control over the nation's facilities for manufacturing gunpowder, it was not the cannon that brought about the decline of the medieval castle but the abolition of LIVERY AND MAINTENANCE. Livery and maintenance, the practice of maintaining and protecting large numbers of retainers in return for administrative and military services, was common in England in the fourteenth and fifteenth centuries when a magnate's influence was judged by the number of men wearing his uniform (*livery*) and his ability to protect them when necessary in the courts of law. The existence of private armies represented a constant threat to political stability and was one of the chief causes of the WARS OF THE ROSES. By suppressing the practice, Henry VII effectively brought BASTARD FEUDALISM to an end and with it the need for feudal strongholds.

From this follows a second proposition: that it was the Tudors who hastened the demise of the castle by concentrating ownership in their own hands, thereby reducing the ability of over-mighty subjects to challenge royal authority. In 1485 ownership of no fewer than forty English and Welsh castles transferred to Henry VII and during his and subsequent reigns the crown acquired even more. This meant that nearly all the major fortresses were no longer in private hands and could not be used to threaten the peace of the realm. Several of these castles were retained as royal palaces, administrative centres and hunting lodges or for national defence but others were allowed to decay. In 1609 it was found that more than sixty 'of his Majestie's decayed castells' were described as decayed, very ruinous or utterly decayed. This last group included

DECLINE OF THE CASTLE

the great Edwardian castles of Aberystwyth, Beaumaris, Caernarfon, Conwy and Rhuddlan.

The decline of the feudal castle, and the reasons for that decline, is exemplified by one late, stubborn exception. Thornbury is often described as the last private castle in England. Built between 1511 and 1522 it is a testament to the ambition of Edward Stafford, duke of Buckingham (1478–1521), who was executed by Henry VIII on a charge of treason. Buckingham was accused of raising a private army and his castle (which was built without licence) was clearly inspired by nostalgic notions of baronial autonomy. Although (had it been completed) the west façade of the inner curtain would have appeared uncompromisingly defensive, in practice Thornbury was a military conceit concealing a comfortable mansion and with only a token acknowledgement of the increasing power of artillery. Nevertheless, the multiple lodges in its outer courtyards were of sufficient size to accommodate a very large number of retainers – far more than would be needed for purely domestic purposes. After Buckingham's death the castle lay unfinished for almost two centuries, until the Howard family made the inner courtyard habitable.

Whatever the reason for the castle's decline, many fortresses were abandoned and allowed to decay or were quarried for building materials. Others followed the French fashion and were converted into comfortable residences with enlarged WINDOW openings, new and elaborate fireplaces and ranges of domestic buildings extending into pleasure gardens beyond the confines of the bailey. At Raglan and Kenilworth, Warwick and Powis, castles became grand country houses, their towers and machicolated parapets adding a flourish of ancient grandeur to the country seats of Tudor gentlemen (*see* CASTLES, DEVELOPMENT OF). But while curtain walls were sometimes demolished or reduced and drawbridges replaced by more permanent structures of brick and stone, the tradition of the moat and fortified GATEHOUSE lingered on in sixteenth-century England (*see* MANOR HOUSES). Security, of course, remained an important consideration: the gatehouse functioned rather as a wall-mounted burglar alarm does today. It was also necessary to provide a façade with a satisfying architectural climax. But in the sixteenth century there seems also to have been an inherent desire to recollect antiquity, to proclaim architecturally a link with a noble past in an age when 'new men' were everywhere perceived to be usurping the traditional values of the 'old order'. The gatehouse therefore became an architectural symbol of ancestry and status. While the ostentatious

Dating from c. 1520, the great multi-storeyed gatehouse at Layer Marney was built in brick on a scale that was clearly intended to be the showpiece of a great country mansion.

fortified façade (1520) of Compton Castle is thoroughly medieval in character, its function was antiquarian rather than military. The contrast with the great multi-storeyed gatehouse at Layer Marney could not be more pronounced. Also dating from *c.* 1520, it was built in brick on such a scale that it was clearly intended to be the showpiece of a great country mansion. With its eight-storey turrets, multiple tiers of windows, miniature shell-gables and Italianate terracotta ornamentation, Layer Marney belongs not to the Middle Ages but to the dawning northern Renaissance.

Despite the passing of the great medieval castle, England did not entirely abandon its sense of the past. When, in the 1560s, orders were still being given for castles to be repaired 'for the defence of the country' against rumoured rebellion, Tickhill Castle was being preserved for no better reason than its worth as an 'ancient monument'. There was even a brief return to full-blooded castle-building in the early seventeenth century, inspired by new wealth, the inflation of honours under James I and a nostalgic recollection of past glories. Mock-medieval fortresses such as Longford (Wiltshire), Rhiwperra (Glamorgan) and Walworth (County Durham) are from this period. Longford Castle, near Salisbury, was the fantasy creation of Sir Thomas Gorges. Built in 1604 on a triangular plan with three massive corner towers, it conveys an impression of military impregnability that is betrayed by thin walls and large window openings.

But this is not the whole story: north of the Pennines the castle remained an instrument of war well into the seventeenth century (*see* MARCH). Regular incursions along the Scottish border and continued friction between the two countries demanded the constant strengthening and refurbishment of numerous castles, PELE TOWERS and TOWER-HOUSES. The union of the crowns in 1603 did not entirely pacify the region, though by the mid-seventeenth century the Borders had gradually subsided into a more stable and peaceful condition.

DECORATED PERIOD *see* GOTHIC ARCHITECTURE

DEER PARKS Hunting and hawking were the recreations most enjoyed by the medieval nobility. Both involved the conservation of the covert, herbage and game, as the countryside had been so heavily farmed since the eleventh century that little natural habitat remained to satisfy the demands of the hunt. While hawks were flown in wooded or fielden COUNTRYSIDE and falcons worked best in open land, by the eleventh century the hunting of deer and boar needed land to be set aside for it. For the king and members of the aristocracy, the CHASE and the FOREST satisfied this need.

A medieval deer park was a venison farm of some considerable size, enclosed by a substantial earth bank and deer-proof *palisade*: a ring fence of vertical stakes or *pales*. Hunting was an important but ancillary activity, the confines of a park being considered too restricted for good sport. Deer for hunting were therefore maintained within the park and then released into the surrounding countryside for the chase, much to the inconvenience of the local populace. Deer parks undoubtedly existed in late Saxon England but it was the Normans who were the real innovators: by 1086 about forty deer parks had been established and by 1300 this number had increased to 3,200, covering an estimated 2 per cent of the landscape. Most magnate and monastic estates included a deer park and therefore enjoyed a reliable

supply of fresh venison throughout the winter. These parks varied in size but were of at least 30 acres (12 hectares) and normally between 100 and 200 acres (40–80 hectares), though some were very much larger. Deer parks were almost invariably in woodland country, the trees within the park being pollarded to encourage growth above the reach of browsing animals. Emparkment required a (costly) royal licence and this occasionally included a right to construct a *deer leap*, a complex system of banks and ditches which permitted the ingress of wild deer (which were owned by the crown) but prevented their escape. On occasions, a herd was established through a gift of breeding stock from the crown. Inevitably, such high concentrations of captive deer were vulnerable to poaching, though it seems that the king's deer were also lured *into* the parks by means of illegal deer leaps and decoys. The creation and extension of deer parks by the forfeiture of tenanted and common land caused considerable resentment and hardship among the peasantry, further aggravated by the damage caused to crops and livestock by the bloodsports themselves. Parks were sometimes divided into open *launds* (lawns) for grazing and protected areas of young coppice. Before the late eleventh century Britain contained only red and roe deer. The Romans may have attempted to introduce fallow deer to Britain but there is little evidence of their survival and it was the Normans who successfully stocked their parks with fallow deer in the decades following the Conquest. Fallow deer were notoriously difficult to contain and, despite the construction of high stone walls in place of palisades, many escaped from parks to establish wild herds in the open countryside.

By the thirteenth and early fourteenth centuries ownership of a deer park had become a significant status symbol; the acquisition of a royal licence and possession of the resources necessary to maintain a park were considered to be indicative of considerable influence and privilege, as well as wealth. With the decimation of the working population caused by the fourteenth-century plagues (*see* PLAGUE) labour became an expensive commodity and consequently disparking took place on a wide scale during the fifteenth, sixteenth and seventeenth centuries; only the wealthiest of the nobility managed to retain their parks and, in some cases, extended them into land which had been taken out of cultivation following the plagues. Such parks are delineated in the maps of Christopher Saxton (*c.* 1542–1606) and subsequent seventeenth-century cartographers. Some continued as deer parks, others became stud farms or were cultivated. But many were retained to enhance the environment of a great house and it is ironic that out of the misery and squalor of the Black Death was born the great tradition of English landscaped parks.

Clues to the location of former deer parks are legion, both in documentary and cartographical form and in the landscape: in the survival of great perimeter walls or embankments, and in place-names such as Parkend, East Park Farm, North Pale Copse and Park Pale Lodge (all to be found within one square mile of the Dorset countryside) and the even older Dyrham in the county of Avon, *dēor hamm* being an Anglo-Saxon 'deer enclosure'. On Ordnance Survey maps the perimeter embankment of a former deer park may be marked as a '*Park Pale*', though such information should be regarded as a clue requiring further substantiation. Britain's herds of wild deer are now significantly larger than they were during the Middle Ages. No doubt they include many animals of ancient lineage, noble fugitives from England's derelict deer parks.

DEFILADE To design a fortification in order to protect it from enfilading fire (*see* ENFILADE).

DEFILE (i) To march in file.
(ii) A narrow pass or passageway in which troops can march only in file.

DEMESNE Land retained by its owner and not leased out to another. From *dominicus* 'belonging to the lord', a lord's demesne consisted of those manorial lands which were reserved for his personal benefit and on which tenants gave free service or *famuli* were employed. The royal demesne comprised those manors held directly by the sovereign and from which crown revenues were extracted. Similarly, magnates who held several manors would enjoy the revenues of those demesne manors which were not subinfeudated to vassals. Ancient Demesne, defined in Domesday as *terrae regis (Eduardi)*, was land held by the crown during the reigns of Edward the Confessor and William I. Tenure of Ancient Demesne lands was subject to numerous benefits and exemptions and from 1689 the revenues from such land that remained in the direct possession of the crown were surrendered to parliament in return for annual payments of money known as the *Civil List*.
(*See also* MANOR)

DEMI-BASTION A semicircular tower projecting from an outer wall, from which the front of the wall may be defended (*see* TOWERS).

DENDROCHRONOLOGY *see* TREE-RING DATING

DENE In the present context a deeply cut gully, from the Old English *denu* meaning 'valley'. At Barnard Castle a deep dene or gully once protected the castle on the northern side though this was lost as a consequence of massive infilling in the nineteenth century.

DENIZATION The granting of the privileges of naturalisation to an alien, including the right to purchase and devise land (which was forbidden to aliens) but excluding the right to inherit land or to receive grants of land from the crown. Denization records are available for inspection at the Public Record Office (*see* APPENDIX II) and these usually show an immigrant's place of origin.

DENIZEN An inhabitant or occupant of a place. Also a foreigner admitted to residence and to certain rights and privileges.

DESERTED VILLAGES Several deserted villages (or, more correctly, *abandoned settlements*) have been identified in the vicinity of medieval castles. Undoubtedly the most popular reason given for the abandonment of a village, and that which persists most strongly in the received traditions of many communities, is the fourteenth-century pestilence known as the Black Death (*see* PLAGUE). There is no doubting the virulence of this terrifying disease and the debilitating effect it could have on a small, rural community. But documentary and archaeological evidence strongly suggests that very few settlements were abandoned *permanently* and, as in the case of villages decimated by civil war, most were recolonised or replaced by planned villages on adjacent sites. Of course, some villages were lost entirely (such as Tusmore in Oxfordshire which in 1357 was 'void of inhabitance since their death in the pestilence'), but of the two thousand deserted villages that have been recorded, mostly in the Midland counties and eastern parts of England, final abandonment was the result of deteriorating climatic conditions, particularly severe in the fourteenth century, and gradual decline over many decades. Of eighty deserted medieval villages identified in Northamptonshire, for example, only two (Hale and Elkington) are true 'plague villages'.

The real effect of the Black Death, and of subsequent recurrences of the plague which lasted into the seventeenth century, was to accelerate a decline in the rural population which was already evident by the middle of the thirteenth century. It was this decline, and the consequential reduction in the availability of peasant labour, that was to result in the eventual abandonment of many medieval rural settlements. Undeterred by legislation intended to curtail their new-found bargaining power, labourers repeatedly demanded more favourable conditions of service, wages rose substantially and landlords sought means by which they could reduce their labour force and more profitably exploit their lands. Inevitably, in a flourishing wool market they turned to sheep and during the late fifteenth and early sixteenth centuries open fields were enclosed, estates cleared and villagers evicted on an unprecedented scale, creating appalling poverty and almost universal resentment. Hardest hit were the east Midland counties, Norfolk, the Lincolnshire Wolds and the former East and North Ridings of Yorkshire. In the 1480s the priest and antiquarian John Rous noted fifty-eight depopulated villages within 12 miles of his native Warwick.

Amazingly, many medieval village sites have escaped the plough and are still evident in apparently haphazard areas of humps and hollows often covering several acres. Upon closer inspection former streets and back lanes may be identified as hollow ways of varying width, with adjacent house platforms surrounded by low banks and ditches marking the boundaries of closes (the curtilage of a homestead) and tofts (the adjoining paddock). There may be evidence of former ponds or moats, or the artificial mound of a motte and bailey castle (*see* MOTTE) or windmill; and at the village edge the ridge and furrow pattern of ancient open fields is often discernible. Medieval sites in areas of arable cultivation are usually visible only from the air as CROP MARKS. Clues to the identity of a deserted village may be evident in the double-barrelled names of some civil parishes, such as Knayton-with-Brawith in Yorkshire (Brawith is a deserted village); or in an unusual configuration of parish boundaries, particularly those with a 'dumb-bell' shape, indicative perhaps of the annexation of a former parish by its neighbour.

DESTRIER *see* HORSES AND HORSE-HARNESS

DETACHED BELFRY *see* CHURCH TOWERS

DEXTER The left-hand side of a shield of arms *when viewed from the front*. In ARMORY the dexter is considered to be superior to the SINISTER or right-hand side.

DIAPER WORK (i) In medieval architecture, a surface of square and diamond-shaped patterns, usually (but not invariably) worked in brick (*see* BRICK BUILDINGS) or glass (*see* WINDOWS).

(ii) In ARMORY, diaper is a method of decorating plain surfaces by filling them with a pattern, usually in a shade of the background colour. When applied too heavily, diaper may be mistaken for an armorial device.
(iii) The term may also be applied to the artistic embellishment of the interstices in tiles, seals, etc.

DIFFERENCE, MARKS OF *see* CADENCY

DIKES A dike (or *dyke*) is a linear earthwork comprising at least one complementary ditch and bank. Short sections of dike are indicated by the term *Cross Dike* on Ordnance Survey maps, otherwise a local name is usually given. Inevitably, in many areas these earthworks present a confusing lattice-work of varying dates and functions, both on the map and in the field (*see also* CROP MARKS).

The finest post-Roman linear earthwork is Offa's Dyke, constructed during the reign of Offa of Mercia (AD 757–96) to mark the 195km (122 mile) frontier established by his wars with the Welsh. Like many of these later dikes, Offa's was an intermittent earthwork, relying on the terrain to provide a natural boundary for much of its length, with substantial segments of dike filling the 'gaps'. Shorter, but visually more impressive, is the 11km (7 mile) length of Devil's Dyke on Newmarket Heath in Cambridgeshire which is 9m (30ft) high, and the parallel Fleam Dyke, south-east of Cambridge. Although of uncertain date, it seems likely that both dikes were constructed as part of a defensive system designed to prevent Mercian incursions along the Icknield Way which they cross at right angles. The 11km (7 mile) long West Wansdyke (from *Wodnes dic* = 'dike of the god Woden') in Somerset and the 24km (15 mile) long East Wansdyke in Wiltshire are believed to date from the same Dark Age period as the Cambridgeshire dikes and probably served a similar territorial function, the West Dyke being built across the Fosse Way. What all these dikes appear to have in common is a territorial function that is evident even in the apparently agrarian Bronze Age ranch boundaries. In all cases the ditch is on the *outside* of the embankment: that of the Roman Antonine Wall was 12m (40ft) wide and 3.6m (12ft) deep and was clearly intended for defensive purposes. However, as even the Romans discovered, such immense earthworks could not be defended throughout their entire length and they were probably intended as 'passive' or symbolic defences, the ditch being an unambiguous declaration of territorial demarcation: anyone crossing the dike from 'outside' did so knowingly and would be expected to face the consequences of his trespass. Of course, short sections of dike could be defended, especially against cavalry, and they also prevented (or at least deterred) the wholesale rustling of livestock. Dating and function may be difficult to determine, but the immense achievement of the men who built these ancient dikes cannot be denied. They represent an extraordinary degree of organisational skill and corporate energy, and a singular commitment to a fiercely territorial society.

DIMIDIATION *see* MARSHALLING

DINAS Literally 'city' in Welsh but also used to describe a stronghold.

DIPTYCH An altarpiece consisting of a folding pair of pictures or tablets depicting religious themes and sometimes containing genealogical and heraldic information. Many of the finest medieval diptychs originated as portable altars in royal and magnate households.
(*See also* TRIPTYCH)

DISINHERITED, THE (i) Supporters of Simon de Montfort whose estates were forfeited by the crown following the barons' defeat at Evesham in 1265 (*see* BARONS' WARS, THE).
(ii) Those whose estates were forfeited for supporting the English against Robert I of Scotland (1274–1329).

DISTINCTION, MARKS OF In ARMORY, a charge added to a coat of arms to indicate BASTARDY. Contrary to popular belief it is not the *bend sinister* which denotes illegitimacy but the *bordure wavy*, which has been in use since the eighteenth century, and in Scotland the *bordure compony*. The *baton sinister* (erroneously called a 'bar sinister' by fiction writers) has almost invariably been used for this purpose in the English royal family, though there have been notable variations particularly during the Middle Ages when there were few established armorial conventions relating to bastardy. The Beauforts, for example, the illegitimate line of John of Gaunt and Katherine Swinford, following their legitimation in 1397, adopted the royal arms within a border of the Beaufort colours, silver and blue. Care should be exercised regarding the concept of bastardy itself: frequently marks of distinction were intended to indicate that the armiger was not in the legitimate line of succession, not that he was personally illegitimate.

DISTRAINT OF KNIGHTHOOD From the thirteenth century to the seventeenth, payment made by gentry to the crown who qualified for knighthood but did not wish to be knighted.

DIVINE RIGHT OF KINGS Belief that the right to rule emanates from God and that the monarch is answerable to God alone.

DOCKS *see* QUAYS

DOCUMENTARY SOURCES *see* STATE RECORDS

DOG-LEGGED Linear features (e.g. a passage or wall-walk) with right-angled bends.

DOGTOOTH ORNAMENT A form of architectural ornamentation typical of Gothic work of the late twelfth and early thirteenth centuries. It consists of a horizontal band of raised saltires, the four limbs of which are shaped like leaves or pointed teeth.

DOMESDAY BOOK Following the Conquest of England in 1066, Duke William of Normandy was crowned king and most of the lands of the native nobility were granted to his followers. In 1085 'at Gloucester in midwinter . . . the King had thorough and deep discussion with his counsellors about this country, how it was occupied and with what sort of people' and he sent his men 'all over England into every shire . . . to find out . . . what or how much each landholder held . . . in land and livestock, and what it was worth' (Anglo-Saxon Chronicle). Commissioners were instructed to ascertain and record all taxable holdings and anything which added to the annual value of a *manerium* (a manorial estate), a tithing (one-tenth of a HUNDRED) or a township (an administrative division of a parish), including disputed lands. The entire realm, which did not then include Cumberland and Westmorland (present-day Cumbria), was divided into seven circuits and visited county by county, hundred by hundred and township by township. Evidence was taken on oath 'from the Sheriff; from all the barons and their Frenchmen; and from the whole hundred, the priests, the reeves and six villagers from each village'. The *Inquisitio Eliensis* (the Ely volume of returns) also tells us that the Commissioners were required to establish:

The name of the place.
The names of those by whom it was held, before 1066 and since.

The extent of taxable ploughland and the number of ploughs, before and after 1066.
The number of villagers, cottagers, slaves and free men (but not details of their families).
The number of mills and fishponds and the extent of meadow, pasture and woodland (it is unclear whether this was coppiced woodland or open wood pasture).
The extent to which fiscal potential had been reduced or increased since 1066.
The value of holdings enjoyed by each free man.

Details were verified by four Frenchmen and four Englishmen from each hundred, whose names were also recorded, and yet many details were omitted, including several churches. Because the survey was essentially a means by which feudal law and tenure could be maintained, those who were exempt from taxation were generally excluded, in particular lands owned by religious houses. Domesday Book mentions about sixty castles (though, of course, there were considerably more) which were included only because they affected a tax assessment: if houses had been demolished to make way for them, for example. But it was not exclusively a tax assessment: its purpose was that every man 'should know his right and not usurp another's'. A second group of commissioners was charged with the task of checking their predecessors' returns in 'shires they did not know' and 'where they were themselves unknown'. The survey was completed within a year and so pervasive and authoritative was its ambit, establishing every landholder's inescapable liability, that its consequences were likened to those of Domesday itself – the Last Judgement. At Winchester the returns (written in a form of Latin shorthand) were corrected, abridged and catalogued by reference to landowners, before being copied by a scribe into a single volume. The surveys of Essex, Norfolk and Suffolk were also collated and copied, unabridged, into a further volume dated 1086, but those of Durham and Northumberland and of several towns (notably London and Winchester) were not transcribed. Domesday Book – *Liber de Wintonia* – describes, in minute detail, England 'under new management':

LAND OF WALSCIN OF DOUAI
Walscin of Douai holds WINTERBORNE from the King, and Walkhere from him. Alward and Alwin held it before 1066 as two manors. It paid tax for 6 hides. Land for 4 ploughs. In lordship 2 ploughs; 3 slaves. 5 villagers and 3 smallholders with ½ plough. Meadow, 12 acres; woodland, 8 acres; pasture 4 furlongs long and 3 furlongs wide.The value

was £6; now £4. Wimer holds CAUNDLE from William. Alsi held it before 1066. It paid tax for 3 hides. Land for 3 ploughs. In lordship 2 ploughs; 2 slaves. 2 villagers and 2 smallholders with 1 plough. A mill which pays 3*s*; meadow, 10 acres; underwood, 3 acres. The value was and is 40*s*.

The Domesday survey was the product of an experienced and sophisticated administration and was undoubtedly unique in early medieval Europe, both in its scope and in its execution. However, it was the advanced machinery of government inherited from the displaced Anglo-Saxon monarchy which enabled the Normans to complete the survey so quickly and so thoroughly. Inevitably, problems and anomalies exist, especially for the novice who is unaccustomed to interpreting such information and may be unnerved by the complexities of the terminology and format. For example, the listings by landowner often result in references to a single parish being found under a number of owners; and a Domesday reference to a present-day village does not necessarily imply its existence as a *village* in 1086: only the names of manorial estates, tithings and townships were recorded and even these may be concealed in a single entry. The original survey (which has recently been rebound) is at the Public Record Office (*see* APPENDIX II).

DOMESTIC DEPARTMENTS *see* HOUSEHOLD *and* LARDER

DONJON The GREAT TOWER (*magnus turris*) of a castle. *Donjon* is an Old French term derived from the Latin *dominus* meaning 'lord' and it was first used in this context in the fourteenth century, the tower being a powerful symbol of lordship (*see* MOTTE). It is preferred by many historians to 'keep' which does not appear in documents before the sixteenth century (*see* KEEP). 'Donjon' is the archaic form of 'dungeon', a word that has acquired an entirely different meaning: that of an underground cell for prisoners.

A prolonged period of internal peace during the reign of Henry I (1100–35) provided an opportunity for remodelling many of the earlier castles, particularly those associated with administrative or strategic centres and royal strongholds. Many twelfth-century magnates constructed magnificent fortified towers or *donjons*, which included both military and domestic quarters, such as William d'Albini's great HALL-KEEP at Castle Rising (1138) and that of Geoffrey de Clinton at Kenilworth (1180).

There was a revival of the donjon castle in the late fourteenth century, particularly on the Scottish borders (see also PELE TOWERS), and castles such as Nunney in Somerset (1373) and Wardour in Wiltshire (1393) are TOWER-HOUSES, the latter with an enclosed courtyard (see COURT AND COURTYARD) constructed in the French manner for lavish entertainment and domestic comfort but at the same time designed and equipped for defensive purposes.

(See also CLUSTERED DONJON)

DONOR AND COMMEMORATIVE WINDOWS

Many later medieval church windows were *donor windows*, erected both as memorials and to commemorate the generosity of benefactors. For this reason at least half the surviving medieval church glass contains an element of heraldry, usually that of an armigerous family or group of benefactors (see ARMORY). At this time the practice of endowing chantries was particularly popular. These were bequests that enabled priests to pray for the souls of the departed and of relatives, friends and others, including the king and influential lords (see CHANTRY). Shields or other heraldic devices in a chapel window may therefore be those of the people for whom prayers were to be said as well as those of the deceased benefactor. Throughout the medieval and Tudor periods senior churchmen, magnates, guilds and fraternities endowed money for the repair of churches and especially in the fourteenth century groups of citizens would often combine to pay for the refurbishing of their parish church. At Dorchester Abbey in Oxfordshire, for example, the south window of the chancel contains twenty-one heraldic shields to record those who financed the extension of the sanctuary in c. 1340. Perhaps the greatest of all commemorative windows is the magnificent fourteenth-century east window in the choir of Gloucester Cathedral. Constructed between 1347 and 1350 it is 11.6m (38ft) wide and 22m (72ft) high: the size of a tennis court, it is the largest stone traceried window in England. In the lower lights are the shields of the Gloucestershire knights who fought at the battle of Crécy in 1346.

(See also STAINED GLASS)

DOORS

A door was often termed a 'leaf' or in Latin *folium* in contemporary medieval accounts. At Corfe Castle in 1357 we find '2 leaves (*foliis*) for a door at the entry of le Gloriet'. Doors were constructed of timber boards braced vertically within a frame and sometimes with a covering on one or both sides. In 1532 John Ripley supplied a number of doors for the great gallery in Westminster Palace:

Dores of waynscotte lined and doble battened, at 20s.–30s.

Dores of lyke stuffe lined and single battened, at 16s.

Dores of lyke stuffe lined on both sides with draperye pannelle, at 20s.

Pleyne dores of waynescotte with rabettes [rebates] and feelettis, at 6s.8d.

Dores of like stuffe without rabbetius and feelettis, at 6s.

The usual form of bracing was by means of square-sectioned wooden bars known as 'ledges', crossing either at right angles or diagonally on the inside of the door. In the Westminster accounts for 1373 we find '4 pieces of sawn timber called quarteres for legges for the door of the great hall, 8 ft. in length; and a piece of timber for the lynia [the main upright] of the said door, 11 ft. in length, of squared oak 1 ft. in breadth'. This description illustrates the considerable size of many medieval doors. Such a large door or gate was often provided with a smaller *wicket* within or beside it. At the Tower of London in 1278 timber was provided 'for the gate of the tower, with two leaves and a wicket', while at Corfe Castle seven years later the carpenters made wickets for the conduit house and the prison called 'Malemit'. A wicket was commonly found in the outer gate of a GATE PASSAGE where admission to a castle was carefully controlled, the larger gate being opened to admit riders and vehicles. In 1369 two rings, a staple and a hingehook were provided for the wicket of the gate at Hadleigh Castle, while at Clarendon a lock and key were made for the wicket to the great solar in 1316 (*for* latches, keys, etc. *see* IRONWORK, LOCKS AND NAILS). Another small door was the *hatch* or half-door. This appears to have been closely associated with service rooms: in 1352 we find a reference to '4 hinges for the hach of the king's buttery' at Westminster and in 1423 'a Hache for the chamberlain's larder' at Carmarthen. At Dunster Castle one Thomas Pacheboll was engaged for two weeks in 1426, at 18*d* a week and his food, 'making the screen and hatches between the lord's hall and the chapel'. Trapdoors are also referred to in the accounts, for example at Banstead in 1372 where hinges were provided 'for a door called trappedore'. At Westminster in 1352 we find a 'platelok for a folding door' and a sliding door ('rynnyng dore') is mentioned at Windsor Castle in 1311.

In a masonry wall the door-frames were of stone (see ARCH) and in a timber-frame building they

Medieval door at Chepstow Castle, Monmouthshire.

were of wood. The parts of a medieval door-opening are similar to those of a window – sill, jambs and lintel (*see* WINDOWS) – but with certain variations of terminology. At Westminster, for example, jambs were described in 1532 as 'doorsteads' and as 'durnes', as at Launceston in 1461. The carved bosses at the end of a hood-mould, on either side of a door, were known as 'beckets'. In the King's Hall accounts '2 bekettes of the great door' cost 20*d* while '2 beketts of smaller size' cost 12*d* in 1417.

The porch, which was a natural accessory to the doorway of an important building, served as a shelter from inclement weather and provided a dignified entrance. In 1244 Henry III commissioned the building of a great porch at Westminster Hall 'so that the king may dismount from his palfrey in it at a handsome façade'.
(*See also* SHUTTERS)

DORMER A projecting upright window in a sloping roof, having also its own independent roof.

DORSE The reverse side of a document (*see* ENDORSEMENT).

DOUBLE-COURTYARD CASTLES *see* COURT AND COURTYARD

DOUBLE CRUCIFORM LOOPHOLE *see* LOOPHOLES

DOVECOTE or PIGEON-HOUSE There is evidence that the Romans obtained fresh protein from birds which nested in tower-like dovecotes similar to those introduced into England from Normandy in the eleventh century. They were commonly found in the precincts of castles: at Denbigh, for example, where a pigeon-house was located in the middle of the bailey and at Bodiam where there was a dovecote in a mural tower, adjacent to the KITCHEN. Medieval dovecotes are usually square or rectangular free-standing buildings of stone or brick or, from the thirteenth century, cylindrical with a conical roof and 'lantern' through which the pigeons (domesticated rock-doves with an instinct for nesting on cliff faces) could come and go as they pleased. The cylindrical shape accommodated a ladder (or pair of ladders) which revolved on central pivots to provide access to the rows of nesting holes that lined the walls. This mechanism, or *potence* (from Old English *potent* meaning 'crutch'), was often so well-balanced that it could be turned at the touch of a finger and enabled the culverer to remove the *squabs* (young birds not fully fledged) with a minimum of fuss. The general impression inside a dovecote was of a circular brick wall with alternate bricks removed from floor to roof level. In fact, each hole was larger than two bricks and was several feet deep to provide ample space for roosting and nesting accommodation for the succession of two-egg clutches produced through most of the year. Many cotes contained more than a thousand nesting holes, and with two pigeons and two young to each there could be up to four thousand birds feeding freely on the tenants' crops! This no doubt accounts for the fact that dovecotes in the medieval period were restricted to DEMESNE and monastic lands where they represented a significant element in the domestic economy by providing fresh meat and eggs during the winter and a constant supply of droppings (*guano*) which was used as fertiliser.
(*See also* FISH PONDS *and* WARRENS)

DOWER *and* DOWAGER Originally a dower was a gift (*dowry*) from a husband to his bride on the morning of their marriage, but from the twelfth century the term came to mean a portion of an estate (generally one-third) claimed by a widow in her lifetime or until she remarried. Similarly a residence assigned from an estate to a widow for life is a *dower house*. A *dowager* is a woman with property and/or a title derived from her late husband.

DRAINS *see* PLUMBING, WATER SUPPLY AND SANITATION

DRAW-BAR A stout timber bar securing a gate or pair of gates on the inside, which had to be drawn back into the porter's lodge or guardroom at the side of the GATE PASSAGE before the gates could be opened.
(*See also* JAMB)

DRAWBRIDGE A drawbridge is a timber platform that can function either as a bridge when lowered or as a barrier when raised. It is more complicated, both in its construction and its operation, than the simple 'sliding bridge' which could be hauled in when necessary. At Conwy, for example, several of the drum towers in the town walls contained plank bridges that could be removed whenever a section of the wall-walk appeared to be under threat (*see* TOWN WALLS *and* WALL-WALK).

Medieval castles were almost invariably protected by a water-filled moat or dry ditch that was partially spanned by a drawbridge or a series of drawbridges. Clearly, a drawbridge would not be of sufficient length to span the full width of a moat and its outer edge would be supported by a permanent structure projecting from the bank. Some of the larger castles included BARBICANS, causeways and other outworks (*hornworks*), and these were often defended with extraordinary ingenuity. The approach to the inner ward at Carreg Cennen Castle was dictated by the construction of an elaborate barbican consisting of a long, sloping ramp along the north side of the castle ditch. The first section of the barbican was set at right angles to the main axis so that an attacker approaching it from the outer gate would be forced to turn on to the ramp in full view of archers in the north-east tower. The next section of the ramp, over 30m (100ft) in length, was heavily defended by two pivoting drawbridges, the lower bridge protected by a small gate-tower and the upper by the formidable Middle Gate Tower where the ramp turned again at right angles and crossed a third drawbridge before entering the gate passage of the castle's principal gatehouse. Bodiam, one of the last castles to be built in medieval England (1388), is now approached from the north by means of a wooden bridge that crosses the wide moat via an artificial octagonal island or 'platform'. Originally, a wooden causeway linked this island with a drawbridge on the west bank so that an enemy would

have been exposed on its right flank to archers on the castle's battlements. Turning through 90 degrees, a second drawbridge provided access from the island to a two-storey, crenellated barbican and a third bridge that linked the barbican with the castle's gatehouse.

Inside a castle deep *bridge pits* were often inserted in the FOREBUILDINGS of keeps and at vulnerable gateways in a castle's defences. At Conwy, for example, the outer (public) ward of the castle was separated from the king's quarters in the inner ward by a strong lateral wall. The Middle Gate, which gave access from the outer ward to the inner court through the dividing wall, was protected by a small projecting gatehouse and a drawbridge which spanned a pit hollowed out of a natural cleft in the rock.

Various mechanisms were used to raise bridges. The least sophisticated, the *lifting bridge*, comprised a barrel capstan or pair of capstans located in a room above a GATE PASSAGE, the chains or ropes passing through slits in the outer wall to where they were attached to the bridge below. Such a drawbridge pivoted on its inner end and could be raised slowly to an almost vertical position, thereby providing additional protection to the portal. At Caerphilly Castle pairs of elongated sockets carved in the walls of the main outer gatehouse once supported a series of drawbridges that linked both the eastern approach to the castle (through a barbican) and access to the north dam from the first floor. The windlass mechanism used for raising a lifting bridge was similar to that for a PORTCULLIS and was usually located in the same chamber of the gatehouse or barbican.

Another type of drawbridge, dating from the thirteenth century, was the *turning bridge* which pivoted on an axle (*trunnion*) located slightly closer to the front of the bridge than the back. When a pin was removed, the counterpoised rear section revolved rapidly into a deep pit (*counterpoise pit*) within the floor of the gate passage while the lighter front end swung upwards to form a barrier across the gateway. The movement, which was finely balanced, was controlled from a PORTER'S LODGE adjacent to the gate passage. In the Middle Tower at the Tower of London a turning bridge is pivoted off-centre with a counterweight at one end. In the wall of the pit there are three curving slots or *chases* in which the counterweights run. Once released, the bridge would swing up rapidly revealing the pit beneath. In most castles a modern bridge provides access across the ditch and counterpoise pit, though an operational turning bridge may be seen at Castell Coch (1875).

A variation of the turning bridge, the *pivot bridge*, had pits on both sides of the wall on which the

When raised, the beams of a bascule bridge would be drawn upward through 90 degrees into vertical grooves in the face of the tower and the deck of the bridge seated in a rectangular housing containing the gate arch, thereby ensuring that it was flush with the wall. At Raglan Castle, Monmouthshire, there were two such drawbridges side by side: the larger one for horses and vehicles and the smaller (raised by a single beam) for daily domestic use.

bridge pivoted at its centre point. Unlike the turning bridge, the pivot bridge was raised and lowered by means of a windlass located in a chamber above the entrance. Thus, each bridge would present three obstacles to an assailant: first, the outer pit had to be crossed, then the bridge in its vertical position, and finally a second pit. Furthermore, this arrangement of pits frustrated any attempt to set fire to the barrier formed by the raised timber bridge. The series of bridges in the barbican at Carreg Cennen Castle were of this type (see above), presenting a total of nine obstacles to the enemy before the main gatehouse was reached.

The Great Tower of Raglan Castle, a massive fifteenth-century detached hexagonal KEEP, known from the colour of its ashlar as the Yellow Tower of Gwent, was originally entered by means of a pair of bascule bridges spanning a wet moat. The *bascule bridge* worked on the counterpoise principle. It was raised by two horizontal beams (*rainures*) that pivoted within the building. Counterweights were attached at the inner end of the beams and the deck of the bridge was suspended by chains at the other. So precisely was the mechanism balanced that only a finger's pressure was required to operate it. When raised, the beams would be drawn upwards through 90 degrees into vertical grooves in the face of the tower and the deck of the bridge seated in a rectangular housing containing the gate arch, thereby ensuring that it was flush with the wall. At Raglan there were two such drawbridges side by side, the larger one for ceremonial occasions and the smaller (raised by a single beam) for daily domestic use. This twin bascule arrangement is unique in British castles and it seems likely that Sir William ap Thomas (d. 1445) based his lofty free-standing keep on Breton models, several of which have bascule bridges. Many drawbridges were replaced by permanent structures from the late fifteenth century and the bascule bridges at Raglan were no exception. In *c.* 1460 Thomas's son, Sir William Herbert, had them dismantled and erected two stone bridges, one above the other, which allowed direct access from both floors of the castle's new solar block to a three-storey forebuilding abutting the keep. Only the foundations of the forebuilding remain but the new doorways which were created within it have survived, their apparently illogical location serving only to confuse the observer. A stylised bascule bridge was a favourite heraldic device of the Herbert family and may be seen carved in the fabric of the castle's state apartments (*see* ARMORY).
(*See also* IRONWORK, LOCKS AND NAILS)

DRESSED STONE Worked and smoothly finished stone used in architectural features such as doorways and window openings.

DRESSING Dressed stone around openings and along edges.

DRIP COURSE A projecting course to catch and throw off rainwater.

DRIPSTONE also DRIP-MOULDING, HOOD-MOULD and LABEL A projecting moulding above an arch, doorway or window to throw off rain. The dripstone corbels (*label-stops*) of exterior windows are often carved as human heads and may assist in dating that part of the building.

DRUM A common term used to describe a cylindrical artefact or architectural feature e.g. a receptacle for liquids or a DRUM TOWER.

DRUM TOWER Characteristic of the thirteenth century, mural towers that are either circular or D-shaped with the flat side facing inwards (*see* TOWERS). Several of the twenty-one bastions in Conwy's town wall are D-shaped and are open on the inward-facing side. The towers could act as 'circuit-breakers' between one section of wall-walk and the next, the temporary plank bridges which spanned the open interior of each tower being removed whenever a section of wall appeared to be under threat.

DRYSTONE A method of building without mortar.

DUBBING *see* KNIGHTHOOD AND CHIVALRY, ORIGINS OF

DUELLING From the archaic Latin *duellum* meaning 'war', single one-to-one combat was a generally accepted legal means of settling disputes throughout medieval Europe. Culturally the nobility claimed the right to defend their honour by means of a duel. A knight could throw down his gage (a personal item such as a glove or hat) as a token of defiance and demand combat with an accuser. The challenge was accepted when the gage was picked up. The medieval and Tudor tournament joust was effectively a duel but without the judicial element (*see* TOURNAMENTS).

DUKE The senior rank of the British peerage. Derived from the Latin *dux* meaning 'leader', the rank was introduced into England in 1337 although the style had been known before that date, William the Conqueror being referred to as *Ducis Normannorum et Regis Anglorum*, for example. The first English non-royal dukedom was granted to Henry, earl of Lancaster, Derby, Lincoln and Leicester, in 1351, while in Scotland David, the eldest son of Robert III, became duke of Rothesay in 1398. The wife of a duke is a *duchess*.

DUNGEON *see* DONJON *and* PRISONS

DURHAM, PRINCE BISHOPS OF *see* PALATINATE

DYKES *see* DIKES

EALDORMAN Prior to the Conquest, a high-ranking royal official responsible for civil matters at shire courts and the king's chief representative in a county. After the Conquest the duties and responsibilities of the ealdorman were transferred to the office of SHERIFF.

EARL The third rank in the British peerage (corresponding with the Latin *comes* and the French *comte*). The title 'earl', which is quite different from the Saxon *ealdorman*, came originally from Scandinavia and appeared in England in the early eleventh century as an English form of *jarl*. It is thus the oldest title and rank of the English nobility and was the senior until 1337 when the Black Prince was made a duke. The earliest known charter creating an hereditary earl is that by which King Stephen bestowed the earldom of Essex on Geoffrey de Mandeville in *c.* 1140. The wife of an earl is a countess (*see* COUNT).

EARL MARSHAL Now known as the Earl Marshal and Hereditary Marshal of England, one of the great Officers of State responsible for the organisation of state ceremonies (though not 'royal' occasions such as weddings) and hereditary judge in the COURT OF CHIVALRY, being ultimately responsible for all matters relating to HERALDRY, precedence, honour, etc.

Before 1386 the office was known simply as Marshal and was held by a member of the household whose responsibilities included supervision of the royal stables (*see* MARSHALSEA). In 1385 the office, which by that time had acquired considerably greater significance, was granted to Thomas Mowbray, earl of Nottingham, who a year later was given the title Earl Marshal.

In the Middle Ages the Marshal was, with the Lord High Constable (*see* CONSTABLE), the first in military rank beneath the sovereign, and it was he who was responsible for marshalling the various contingents in battle, assisted by attendant heralds whose business it was to be conversant with the devices borne on the FLAGS and uniforms of an assembled host. The Marshal was also responsible for the organisation of state ceremonies and, with the Constable, presided over the Court of Chivalry.

EARLY ENGLISH *see* MEDIEVAL ARCHITECTURE

EAVES Underpart of a sloping roof overhanging a wall.

ECCLESIASTICAL STRONGHOLDS In the twelfth century a number of parish churches were located within castle baileys, such as English Bicknor and Castle Rising, while others were drawn to the protection of a castle or manor house, or were themselves the rationale for its location, as at Beverston, Kilpeck, St Briavels and Moreton Corbet. Religious houses relied heavily for protection on their status and on the principle by which 'The precincts of monks' houses and granges . . . like cemeteries and churches are all by apostolic authority to be free and undisturbed by any invasion, terror or violence.' But principle was a poor defence against the unprincipled, and in 1235 the Cistercian house of Holmcultram, near the Scottish border, was permitted to arm its servants and later to erect a small castle to protect its grange at Raby, County Durham. Most monastic sites were enclosed within a hedge or low wall and ditch, and had a gatehouse at which visitors could be interrogated by a gate-keeper or porter (*portarius*) before entering or leaving the precinct. At the Cistercian abbey of Cleeve in Somerset, the gatehouse wall is inscribed with the words: 'Stay open gate and close to no honest person.' But in the more volatile regions of the Borders, gatehouses were heavily fortified (as at Alnwick) and many outlying monastic estates were provided with PELE TOWERS (Nunnikirk, West Ritton and Greenleighton in Northumberland) and even castles (Carrycoats, Filton and Rytton) for their defence. The monastery of Tynemouth was the largest to be located within the walls of a castle. In 1296 the monks obtained a licence to enclose and crenellate their precinct which occupied a naturally defended promontory, washed on three sides by the ocean. With a garrison to maintain they were brought to the brink of bankruptcy many times, though (with a keep-gatehouse added in the 1390s) the castle was considered to be one of the strongest in the north. Monastic sites at Hulne and Lanercost were also heavily defended, as was the priory of Ewenny in the southern March of Wales, a dependency of the Benedictine abbey of Gloucester. The nave of the priory church remains in parochial use, while its great defensive walls, with gates and towers, have also survived.

Bishop's Palaces

Bishops and mitred abbots were, of course, senior members of the medieval aristocracy with their own retinues, and many episcopal castles, such as Llandaff and Llawhaden in Wales, are indistinguishable from those of secular lords. Roger de Caen, bishop of Salisbury (c. 1065/70–1139), was Henry I's chancellor and the greatest prelate of his day. He accumulated a huge personal fortune and built prodigiously, rebuilding his cathedral at Old Sarum (Salisbury), founding Kidwelly Castle in Wales, rebuilding Sarum and Malmesbury Castles in England and creating a fortified palace at Sherborne that was later the model for the 'sumptuous palaces' of Henry of Blois, bishop of Winchester (c. 1100–71). Sherborne Castle stood in a large deer park on the banks of the River Yeo. Typical of several Norman palace-fortresses, it consisted of a residential quadrangle surrounded by a defensive outer bailey. The inner quadrangle comprised a square keep with four ranges of buildings around a small courtyard. The outer bailey was protected by a deep ditch and curtain wall with square flanking towers and a long, narrow barbican crossing the ditch. In King John's reign a tower on the north side of the curtain was enlarged to form a new gatehouse. (An earthwork to the west of the castle was probably a Civil War siege platform.) Another major project was Roger's castle at Devizes, described by Henry of Huntingdon as 'the most splendid in Europe' and which included a church for the garrison. Despite his calling, Bishop Roger built castles more readily than churches.

A century later Robert Burnell, bishop of Bath and Wells from 1275 to 1292, was denied the archbishopric of Canterbury by his fathering of numerous illegitimate offspring and the acerbic comment that his proclivity attracted. Nevertheless, he was an extraordinarily wealthy man: he controlled eighty-two manors, either in his own right or through his episcopal see, and he built a splendid residence for himself at Acton Burnell in Shropshire, in addition to his bishop's palace at Wells. Acton Burnell, with its corner towers and crenellated walls, has the appearance of a castle, but it is unlikely that defence was ever a serious consideration, despite its proximity to the Welsh border. It was essentially a defensible MANOR HOUSE, a residence built for comfort and as an ostentatious manifestation of the bishop's status and influence. In addition to his own lavish quarters, provision was made for a constable and other senior officials with smaller attic rooms for clerks and secretaries.

Gaol delivery records clearly illustrate a significant increase in criminal activity during the first decades of the fourteenth century. One cause was undoubtedly a devastating rise in the price of wheat and the Great Famine of 1315–17. But, although destitution and violence were clearly linked, it was certain members of the gentry (and even the parish clergy) who were chiefly responsible for organised crime, in some cases aided and abetted by patrons and maintainers among the aristocracy. It was these well-born bandits who recruited OUTLAWS and vagabonds to their service and accelerated the breakdown of law and order that was already evident in the late thirteenth century. Furthermore, from 1294 pardons had been granted for service in the royal armies, emptying the king's gaols with violent and predictable effect. Discontent was further inflamed by a widespread failure of manorial discipline, exacerbated by the unrealised aspirations of the peasantry and the determination of manorial lords to frustrate them. And it was the Church and its senior prelates who were most often accused of avarice and sharp practice.

It was against this background of lawlessness that many abbots and bishops were obliged to defend their precincts and palaces. Henry Gower, bishop of St Davids (1328–47), fortified his country residence at Lamphey and extensively refurbished his palace next to the cathedral. Even so, there is no evidence in the palace gatehouse of a portcullis, suggesting that defence was not a major consideration. Bishop Henry's ambitious programme of works included a double set of spacious apartments on two sides of a courtyard. The eastern range appears to have been planned as private accommodation while the south wing comprised an even grander suite of apartments focused on a great hall (see HALL and HOUSE-HOLD). This double arrangement is evident at several other episcopal palaces such as Lincoln, Wells and Wolvesey. Whereas the one range would have been occupied by the bishops as their lodgings, the other would have been used to accommodate and entertain distinguished guests. The great hall may also have been used for judicial and administrative purposes: the bishop of St Davids was a Marcher Lord (see MARCH) whose tenants were obliged to appear in the episcopal courts.

Disputes between ecclesiastical corporations and their burgesses were commonplace. In 1326–7 the townspeople of two of the richest monastic boroughs, St Albans and Bury St Edmunds, had risen violently against their lords, besieging and plundering both abbeys. Consequently, monastic communities became ever more reliant on their precinct walls and GATEHOUSES. At St Albans Abbot Thomas de la Mare rebuilt the huge fortress-like gatehouse in the mid-fourteenth century, while the (second) gatehouse at Bury St Edmunds at first appears to possess few military pretensions but was provided with a portcullis and arrow loops concealed by the statuary on the outer façade. A monastic precinct would have been impossibly large to defend, and these buildings should, perhaps, be considered as a type of keep-gatehouse, normally serving as a court house and exchequer but capable of independent defence in an emergency. In 1340, for 'the security and quiet of the canons and ministers resident there', Bishop Ralph of Bath and Wells (1329–63) secured a royal licence 'to build a wall round the precinct of the houses of him and the canons and to crenellate and make towers in such a wall'. The walls, moat, drawbridge and gatehouse that guard the Bishop's Palace at Wells comprise one of the most formidable episcopal defensive systems ever built.

Lordship and Patronage

The abbots and priors of many religious houses grasped the opportunity both to enhance their status through architectural display and to dominate and overawe those over whom they exercised lordship. The massive Great Gate at St Augustine's, Canterbury, rebuilt by Abbot Thomas Fyndon between 1300 and 1309, is a wonderful confection of turrets and crenellations. Only eight years after its completion six hundred men of the nearby manor of Minster

having gathered to themselves a still greater number of malefactors, approaching the manors of the abbot at Minster and Salmstone in hostile fashion with bows, arrows, swords and sticks, several times besieged them and made sundry attacks thereon, and placed fire,

which they had brought with them, against the doors to burn down those manors.

Throughout the thirteenth century Battle Abbey had acquired numerous holdings of lesser landowners and had tightened its grip on the activities of its increasingly resentful burgesses. The abbey's huge, crenellated and turreted gatehouse, erected in 1338 ostensibly as a defence against French pirates, was in fact an unequivocal statement of lordship that dominated the town's market place and overawed its populace. Arrays of heraldic ornament on the façades of many contemporary monastic gatehouses were clearly intended to invoke the protection of the great and good. At Butley Priory no fewer than five tiers of shields above the entrance include the arms of the Holy Roman Emperor, the French and English kings and many of the most illustrious baronial families of East Anglia, all implying royal and noble patronage. Of course, this was not always the case. Worksop Priory's fourteenth-century gatehouse, although imposing, was essentially domestic in character, while the gatehouse at Tor Abbey on the south Devon coast is unambiguously defensive, intended to protect its community against piratical incursions.

By the end of the fourteenth century every major monastery was furnished with a precinct wall and gatehouse. But decades of pestilence (see PLAGUE) and the PEASANTS' REVOLT of 1381 fermented discontent that proved to be even more violent than that which had preceded it. The criminal elements in the post-plague years were not the poor and desperate but people of substance: the yeomen, craftsmen and manorial officials who had led the Great Revolt and were markedly more dangerous than any previous rebel leadership. Immediately after the rebellion the abbot of Thornton obtained a licence to crenellate 'the new house over and about the gate' of his abbey. Although Thornton's 'new house' was primarily residential it bristled with loopholes at several levels, each served by a purpose-built gallery. The portcullis was so large that the mechanism had to be located on the second floor while the precinct was enclosed within a substantial wall and, in front of the gate, a moat. However, what makes Thornton unique among monastic sites is a long BARBICAN that was added in 1389. Built entirely in brick, it comprises parallel walls, each pierced by thirteen arrow-slit embrasures and terminating in a round turret.

As at Battle and Tor Abbeys and at Michelham Priory, proximity to the coast was undoubtedly a factor. Like his neighbour Abbot Hamo of Battle, Prior Leem of Michelham was a commissioner for

coastal defence and was able to combine this responsibility with the need to secure his priory against civil unrest, for he was also a receiver of rents for the singularly unpopular John of Gaunt. Other late medieval defended monastic sites include Brecon, Hulne, Lanercost, Lindisfarne, Tavistock and Ulverscroft.
(*See also* CHURCH TOWERS)

ECHAUGETTE In post-medieval fortifications, a sentry box projecting from the angle of a bastion.

ÉCHIELLE *see* HORSES AND HORSE-HARNESS *and* WARFARE: CONDUCT OF

EDWARDIAN CASTLES *see* CASTLES, CONSTRUCTION OF *and* WALES, CONQUEST OF

EDWARDIAN CONQUEST OF WALES *see* WALES, CONQUEST OF

EDWARDIAN GATEHOUSE *see* GATEHOUSE and KEEP-GATEHOUSE

EFFIGIES *see* MONUMENTS

ELEANOR CROSSES Wayside memorial crosses constructed to mark the progress of the body of Queen Eleanor of Castile, first wife of Edward I, who died at Harby in Nottinghamshire on 29 November 1290 and was buried at Westminster Abbey (though her bowels were first removed and interred at Lincoln Cathedral). From 1292 to 1294, in accordance with her will, a series of elaborate crosses was erected by the king's masons at her coffin's resting places along the route to Westminster, the best known being Charing Cross in London. Only three crosses survive of the original twelve: at Geddington and Hardingstone in Northamptonshire and at Waltham Cross in Hertfordshire.

EMBLAZON To depict coats of arms, badges, etc., in colour. Not to be confused with BLAZON, which is to describe a coat of arms using the language of ARMORY.

EMBRASURE (i) The recess within a wall behind an arrow loop or window. The stone walls of major castles were of considerable thickness with intra-mural passageways (*galleries*) providing access to a series of embrasures, the outer walls of which were pierced with splayed LOOPHOLES for archers and crossbowmen. The finest examples are in the south curtain wall at Caernarfon Castle in North Wales (1283–92).

A loophole must be of sufficient height to allow for a variety of trajectories and of sufficient width to allow an arrow or bolt to be released without impediment. Furthermore, it must provide a wide field of vision while keeping the loop as narrow as possible in order to protect the defender. All four objectives were achieved by the use of embrasures: the larger an embrasure, the easier it was for a defending crossbowman to release his bolts close to the loophole, thereby avoiding the possibility of a deflection on the embrasure walls.

A longbow should be approximately the height of the archer and half of this height will be above eye-level when taking aim. Traversing with a longbow is difficult because it requires a whole body movement. The crossbow may be traversed more easily, but the weight of the bow is difficult to support unaided for any length of time and it is more easily used in a kneeling position. Therefore a high embrasure is required for a standing longbowman, while a crossbowman requires a low embrasure, preferably with support for his weapon at waist height.
(For window embrasures *see* WINDOWS)
(ii) In post-medieval fortifications, an opening in a parapet or wall through which a gun may be fired.
(*See also* BATTLEMENTS, CRENEL *and* LOOP-HOLE)

ENARMES Straps for the forearm and hand on the inside of a shield. Enarmes are evident in the eleventh-century Bayeux Tapestry and were the usual method of carrying heater- or flat-iron-shaped shields and circular targets throughout the medieval period (*see* GUIGE *and* SHIELDS).

ENCAUSTIC TILES Decorated floor tiles dating from the thirteenth to the sixteenth centuries may occasionally have survived in castles, usually in former private chambers which have been protected from the elements.

During the thirteenth century several methods were developed for the decoration of plain clay tiles. The pattern could be engraved in outline on the surface of the tile or the design could be carved in relief or counter-relief on a wood-block which was then pressed into the tile. In both instances the tile was then glazed and fired to produce a patterned tile of one colour. A third method was to fill the matrix of a stamped tile with white pipeclay before it was glazed and fired. This produced the familiar brown and yellow encaustic tile. (Occasionally the design was reversed with a dark pattern set into a light coloured tile.) Early encaustic tiles are usually 12½–15cm (5–6in) square and as much as 2½cm (1in) thick with a 2mm inlay.

By the mid-fourteenth century a flourishing English tile manufacturing industry had been established in the Chilterns with its centre at Penn in Buckinghamshire. 'Penn' tiles were smaller, only 11½cm (4⅓in) square and 2cm (¾in) thick. It seems likely that by this time the various stages of manufacture were combined in a single process, the stamp being dipped into the white slip clay before it was pushed into the malleable tile so that the slip remained in the impression when the stamp was removed. This would explain why the slip is very thin and some edges of the inlay may be smudged or missing. The inlay was usually flush with the surface of the tile but a later development in technique resulted in the pattern being slightly concave.

Many designs were used in encaustic relief and counter-relief tiles including Christian symbols, rebuses and armorial devices associated with royal or dynastic establishments (*see* ARMORY). Armorial tiles are a considerable aid to research but not all lions, eagles and fleurs-de-lis are of heraldic significance. Confusingly, it is not unusual to find

that an armorial design has been carved correctly on the wood-block but the resultant impression is back to front.

(*See also* SLATES AND TILES)

ENCEINTE *and* ENCEINTE CASTLES The enceinte – 'the body of the place' – is the main defensive enclosure of a fortification. The term 'castles of enceinte' is sometimes applied to fortresses which had no keep and depended for their strength on the integrity of their walls and mural towers. These towers were interconnected not from the wall-walk of the curtain wall but by means of intra-mural passageways, while ground-floor entrances were provided only where absolutely necessary. In this way each tower could be shut off from the next and each could be defended independently should the wall be breached and the castle penetrated. Framlingham Castle is one of the best examples of this type of castle. Erected by Roger Bigod in 1189 on an earlier motte, the lofty stone curtain wall and thirteen square mural towers

The enceinte is the main defensive enclosure of a fortification. The term 'castles of enceinte' is sometimes applied to fortresses which had no keep and depended for their strength on the integrity of their walls and mural towers. Framlingham Castle, Suffolk, is one of the best examples of this type of castle. Erected by Roger Bigod in 1189, the lofty stone curtain wall and thirteen square mural towers surround a courtyard in which a great hall, chapel, stables, accommodation and storehouses were erected against the inside of the wall.

surround a courtyard in which a great hall, chapel, stables, accommodation and store-houses were erected against the inside of the wall. The square towers were the castle's weakness: had Bigod planned his defences a decade later he would almost certainly have built rounded flanking towers which were better able to resist attack. Two of the thirteen towers are open-backed and were originally crossed by wooden bridges which could have been removed were an enemy to occupy an adjacent section of wall. The brick chimneys which surmount several of the towers are ornamental Tudor additions.

Several castles acquired outer wards which were effectively enceintes: at White Castle, Monmouthshire, for example, an outer BAILEY was added in 1256 to (what was then) the rear of the castle. This comprised a dry ditch and stone curtain wall with a formidable outer gatehouse and four projecting mural towers: a defended enclosure where armies in the field could camp without fear of a surprise attack – like that which had routed Henry III's army as it camped outside the walls of nearby Grosmont Castle in 1233.
(*See also* LIVERY AND MAINTENANCE, CASTLES OF)

ENCLOSURE CASTLES *or* CASTLES OF ENCLOSURE A generic term descriptive of a castle which depended for its defence on encircling curtain walls and mural towers in contradistinction to those, mostly early, castles which relied on the strength of their keeps for security (*see* CASTLES, DEVELOPMENT OF and GREAT TOWER).
(*See also* BAILEY, CONCENTRIC CASTLES, CURTAIN WALLS, ENCEINTE CASTLES, LIVERY AND MAINTENANCE, CASTLES OF)

ENDORSEMENT Something written on the back (*dorse*) of a document, usually an archival reference or related notes.

ENFILADE Flanking fire which sweeps the length of a fortification (*see* DEFILADE).

ENGAGED Descriptive of piers which are attached to, or partly sunk into, a wall (*see* PIER).

ENGINE TOWER Indicative that defensive engines (espringals, great crossbows, etc.) were mounted on the platform of this tower, or that it contained a mechanism of some sort, e.g. for raising a portcullis or drawbridge. The North Tower at Criccieth Castle was also known as the Engine Tower because, from the late thirteenth century, it appears to have had a stone-throwing trebuchet or a catapult (*espringal*) mounted on its roof (*see* SIEGES).

ENGLISH ROMANESQUE *see* ROMANESQUE

ENGLISHRY That area of south-west Wales which, in the Middle Ages, was subject to the authority of the Marcher lords (*see* MARCH).

South-west Wales comprises two distinct landscapes. That to the south of Fishguard, known as the Englishry, is a landscape shaped by post-Conquest settlement (notably farmers from the English West Country), a land of castles, nucleated villages, broad fields and church towers. To the north, the landscape of the *Welshry* is very different: small, irregular fields, scattered settlements and squat churches hidden in the folds of the hills. The castles of the Englishry date from the early 1090s when they were established to hold down the southern MARCH and to secure the sea-ways to Ireland and the west. The Englishry was effectively a Norman colony governed from a string of castles along the southern coast, each with a 10- to 20-mile radius of influence and located on sea inlets and navigable rivers so that they were easily provisioned and relieving forces could be brought in whenever danger threatened.

Dating from the reign of Henry I (1100–35), the law of Englishry distinguished between English and Normans and, in the Marches of Wales, between Anglo-Normans and Welsh. This was necessary in order that payment of a *murder fine* might be avoided. The fine, which was introduced by William I to prevent the killing of Norman settlers, was paid by the hundred in which the murder took place unless the murderer could be presented within five days. Originally the king received 40 marks and the victim's family 16. Henry I amended the law so that a hundred would be excused payment of the fine if it could be proved that the victim was English!

ENGROSS (i) To copy a document in a formal hand or in distinct characters.
(ii) To write out a document in legal form for signature.
(iii) To name in a legal list or document.

ENGROSSMENT The combining of two or more holdings.

EN SOLEIL In ARMORY, a device surrounded by the rays of the sun (*see* BADGES).

Escarbuncle or carbuncle.

ENTAIL To bequeath an estate inalienably to a specified succession of beneficiaries. Although the making of conditional family settlements of freehold property (*entails*) was common practice in the Middle Ages, it was not until 1285 that legislation was enacted which provided a legal basis for such transactions (Statute of Westminster II). Writs, known as *Formedon in Descender*, were made available to enable a donor to recover his lands where the conditions were not kept, though in practice this often led to fictitious legal actions so that the property could be sold.

ENTOURAGE Those in attendance on a lord.

ENTRENCHED CAMP A protected area in which troops muster.

ENTRESOL A low storey linking two main storeys of a building.

EORL An Anglo-Saxon magnate, often also an EALDORMAN.

EQUILATERAL ARCH *see* ARCH

ERMINE One of two principal furs used in ARMORY consisting of black ermine tails (drawn in a variety of stylised forms) on a white field (*see* TINCTURES *and* VAIR).
(*See also* SUMPTUARY LAWS)

ESCALADE The climbing of ramparts by means of scaling ladders.

ESCARBUNCLE *or* **CARBUNCLE** A decorative and heraldic motif in the form of ornamental spokes, normally eight in number, radiating from a central boss. It is likely that this was originally the boss of a shield.

ESCARP In post-medieval fortifications, the outer slope or revetment of a rampart.

ESCHAUGETTE A turret projecting from the top of a wall or tower.

ESCHEAT The reversion of a FIEF to the lord following the death of a tenant without heirs (*see* INQUISITIONES POST MORTEM).

ESCUTCHEON (i) In ARMORY, a shield.
(ii) Any shield-shaped decorative motif.
(iii) A small metal plate pierced by a key-hole.

ESCUTCHEON OF PRETENCE *see* MARSHALLING

ESPALIER *see* ARMOUR

ESPIONAGE *see* INTELLIGENCE AND ESPIONAGE

ESPLANADE The open space between the buildings of a town and its CITADEL.

ESPRINGAL *or* **SPRINGALD** *see* SIEGES

ESQUIRE *or* **SQUIRE** In the Middle Ages, an attendant (*escutifer* = shield-bearer) to a knight. An esquire's feudal service required him to maintain his master's shield and armour, though his responsibilities and duties were considerably wider than this and were, in part, intended to train him in the martial and courtly arts and chivalric code. Many esquires were themselves of noble birth and in practice pages tended to perform the more menial duties (*see* PAGE). By 1400 sons of peers and the eldest sons of knights were deemed to be esquires and in the sixteenth century the title was applied to officers of the crown. It was thereby considered superior to that of GENTLEMAN, though only by association with a royal office which provided added distinction. The rural '*Squire*' is generally a LORD OF THE MANOR or major landowner, and the term is entirely colloquial.
(*See also* KNIGHTHOOD AND CHIVALRY (ORIGINS OF), MILITARY TRAINING, NOBILITY AND GENTRY *and* YEOMAN)

ESTATE (i) Landed property. A medieval estate comprised DEMESNE lands together with wide areas of general jurisdiction: an assemblage of customary manorial rights and revenues rather than a physical unit. During the fourteenth century demesne farming was replaced by an economy based on the payment of rents in lieu of free service.
(ii) A person's liabilities and assets, especially at death.
(iii) The three *Estates of the Realm*: the Lords Spiritual, the Lords Temporal and the Commons (though *see also* FEUDAL SYSTEM).

EXCHEQUER The Norman kings created two departments to deal with financial matters: the TREASURY and the Exchequer, which was itself divided into the lower Exchequer and upper Exchequer. The lower Exchequer was responsible for receiving moneys and was connected to the Treasury; the upper Exchequer was a court of law which dealt exclusively with fiscal matters until it was merged with the High Court of Justice in 1880. The sheriffs were required to attend the twice-yearly meetings of the upper Exchequer at Easter and Michaelmas in order to pay the income (*farms*) due from their shires. The office of Chancellor of the Exchequer was created in the reign of Henry III (1216–72) and was originally that of assistant to the treasurer of the Exchequer. By the end of the thirteenth century the PRIVY SEAL was used to transmit orders from the sovereign to the Exchequer. The term Exchequer now denotes the account at the Bank of England into which public revenues are paid. The word is believed to derive via Old French from the Latin *scaccarium* = 'chess board', a reference to the practice of keeping accounts on a chequered table-cloth, the ranks and files of which served in the manner of an abacus. Many of the numerous Exchequer records (*see* PIPE ROLLS), which are maintained in the Public Record Office, have been published, notably by the Stationery Office and the Pipe Roll Society (*see* APPENDIX II). (*For* the Wardrobe *see* HOUSEHOLD)

EXTENT *see* MANOR

EXTRAORDINARY RETAINER A retainer who was not a member of a household or an official who received a knight's fees or an annuity from a lord.

EYRE, IN From the Latin *itinere* meaning 'on a journey', eyres were judicial circuits undertaken by the king's justices who sat (somewhat infrequently) at sessions of county courts in order to hear crown pleas and to standardise the administration of justice which, in the Middle Ages, tended to be localised. They were also responsible for auditing royal revenues and inspecting county administration. The system of justices in eyre was introduced in 1166 but was effectively abandoned in 1294 when general eyres were replaced by judicial commissions.

FACING MATERIALS Facing is a finish applied to the surface of a building. When a building is described as *cased* the facing is of high-quality material, usually finer than that of which the building is constructed. *Rendering* is a covering of plaster mixed with mortar (and sometimes animal hair to facilitate bonding) and is usually applied in two coats. White Castle in Monmouthshire was known as Llantilio Castle in the thirteenth century but acquired its new name as a consequence of the white 'daub' rendering which is still visible on small sections of the exterior walls. Similarly the walls and towers of Conwy Castle were limewashed when building was completed in 1287. The gleaming whiteness of the immense building must have made it a striking landmark – and, for the Welsh, a singularly intimidating one. *Limewash* is quicklime (unslaked lime) which boils with intense heat when water is added. For centuries limewash was made by packing coarse waste fat in a tub of quicklime and adding water, the effect of which was to heat and distribute the fat. When used as an external wall-covering, the fat content of limewash did not dissolve in the wet, thereby making the coating waterproof. Traces of the whitening may still be seen at Conwy, notably on the southern towers and on the north-west curtain wall. Gravel, shingle or similar material may be cast on render before it hardens. This is known as *rough-cast* and is intended both as decoration and to provide protection. *Pebbledash* is similar but requires an additional layer of rendering in order that the pebbles or flints may be affixed to it before it dries. *Cladding* is a thin covering of stone, tiles or slate applied to the exterior of the building.

FAIRS Medieval fairs were generally annual occasions and of greater significance to a local populace than MARKETS. They usually took place (or commenced) on the *feriae*, the feast or holy days of the local church to whose patronal saint the fair was often dedicated. On such days men were freed from labour ('holy day' became 'holiday') to engage in both the business and the sociability of the fair. Most fairs originated in the thirteenth and fourteenth centuries in the new TOWNS and seigneurial boroughs and were concerned not only with trade and commerce but with entertainment and the propagation of news and ideas. Many fairs grew to national, even international importance, lasting for several days and sometimes weeks and, because they were held regularly at a fixed time and fixed place, many became centres of banking and commerce and contributed to the intellectual and cultural development of medieval Europe. The exclusive right to hold a fair was established through a royal or magnate charter which specified the day or days on which it was to be held. Enterprising manorial lords or burgesses who obtained charters profited from the revenues which could be raised through farming out stalls or 'pitches' to lessees. Often, booths, utensils, etc., were provided and these were stored in a 'Fair House' or market hall when not required. Fairs inevitably attracted merchants who were able to offer exotic and high-quality goods not normally available at markets and for this reason many continued to be held until the distribution of merchandise was transformed by the advent of the railway age and an efficient postal service in the nineteenth century. Several fairs outgrew their market squares and were removed to a more suitable site on the periphery of the town, sometimes within the ramparts of an ancient earthwork such as that on the summit of Woodbury Hill near Bere Regis in Dorset which was in constant use as a fair ground from the early Middle Ages to the 1950s. But the anticipated profits which encouraged many medieval magnates to apply for charters did not always materialise: establishing a fair was a speculative business and while many fairs flourished or specialised others became moribund.

FALCHION From the Latin *falx* meaning 'sickle', a curved dagger or short sword with a blade wider towards the point. They were favoured by medieval archers.
(*See also* WEAPONS AND HARNESS)

FALCON A small cannon of 60cm (2½in) bore, capable of firing a 700g (1½lb) ball (*see* FIREARMS AND CANNON).

FALCON AND FETTERLOCK *see* BADGES AND LIVERY

FALDSTOOL An occasional stool with folding legs. The term is also used (erroneously) to describe a litany desk or PRIE-DIEU.
(*See also* BACKSTOOL)

FAMILIA *see* HOUSEHOLD

FAMILIA REGIS The military household of the Angevin kings which provided a large and effective fighting force and included a unit of professional archers or crossbowmen. Other household troops garrisoned important royal castles. The *Familia Regis* was more than a standing army: it provided a source of skilled and loyal men from whom the king could select sheriffs, constables, governors and other key officials (*see* HOUSEHOLD).

FAMULI Paid estate workers as opposed to manorial tenants whose labours formed part of their service.

FAN VAULT *see* GOTHIC ARCHITECTURE *and* VAULTING

FARM The annual payment due for an estate.

FARTHING *see* COINAGE

FAULD Dating from the early fifteenth century, a hooped plate skirt attached to the lower edge of the CUIRASS in a full set of plate armour.
(*See also* ARMOUR *and* HELMETS)

FAUSSART *see* WEAPONS AND HARNESS

FAUSSE-BRAYE (i) A line of defences on the floor of a ditch at the base of a wall.
(ii) In post-medieval fortifications, an outer rampart lower than the principal rampart.

FEALTY An oath of allegiance made by a VASSAL in recognition of obligation and fidelity to a feudal lord. In medieval England feudal tenants were required to take such oaths when doing LIEGE HOMAGE.

FEET OF FINES Records containing judgments regarding the ownership of land and property, usually as a consequence of actions brought by the parties to establish a title in the absence of documentary evidence. The judgment or fine (Latin *finis* = 'end') effectively terminated any dispute and registered ownership. It was written three times on the same parchment sheet: two sections going to the disputants and the third being lodged with the Court of Common Pleas. The records are housed in the Public Record Office where indexed calendars for 1509–1798 may be consulted (*see* APPENDIX II). (*See also* STATE RECORDS)

FELONY A generic term formerly applied to a class of crimes which were regarded by the law as being of greater severity than those described as *misdemeanours*. The class (which included murder, wounding, rape, arson and robbery) comprised those offences for which the penalties formerly included forfeiture of land and goods. Forfeiture was abolished in 1870 but in English law procedural differences were maintained until the distinction between felonies and misdemeanours was abandoned in 1967.

FENESTELLA *see* CHAPEL *and* PISCINA

FENESTRAL A small WINDOW or window-frame. Also a frame containing a glass substitute such as oiled linen (*see* GLASS).

FENESTRATION The disposition of WINDOWS in a building.

FERRAMENTA Metal ornaments and furniture, e.g. of a door.

FERRULE A metal ring or cap affixed to the foot of a pole to provide additional strength and protection.

FETTERLOCK A manacle (*see* BADGES AND LIVERY).

FEUDAL AIDS Medieval lords enjoyed an entitlement (set out in *Magna Carta*) to financial aid which could be exacted from their free tenants for ransoming the lord's person, for knighting his eldest son and for the marriage of his eldest daughter. Such were the abuses of the system that in 1275 minimum ages were specified: fifteen for the eldest son and seven for the eldest daughter! Kings often exercised this right (which was not abolished until 1660) and in addition they might obtain aid for other purposes, usually when a state of necessity existed and funds were required 'for the common good'. Initially, such taxation, known as '*gracious aids*', was authorised on an individual basis and limited to 20*s* for a KNIGHT'S FEE or 20*s* for rented land with an annual value of £20. But during the thirteenth century a formula evolved which enabled the crown

to raise taxes (or enact other legislation) by means of the concept of *plena potestas* ('full power') derived from Roman law. This was based on the need to obtain a full measure of consent for taxes which were to be paid by all subjects, irrespective of tenurial status. From 1268 representatives – knights, burgesses and citizens – were summoned to (some) parliaments on the basis of *plena potestas* and had to bring with them letters of authority giving them 'full power' to act on behalf of the communities they represented. Records are maintained at the Public Record Office and six volumes entitled *Feudal Aids*, containing details of assessments and inquisitions during the period 1284 to 1431, were published between 1899 and 1921.

FEUDAL INCIDENTS Occasional aspects of feudalism that were of financial benefit to a lord, e.g. wardship.

FEUDAL SYSTEM A medieval European political-economic system based on the relationship of VASSAL and superior, the former holding land of the latter on condition of homage and military service or labour. Medieval society was divided into three estates: the clergy, the nobility and the (predominantly agricultural) workers. Each estate was dependent on the others: theoretically the Church, under the Pope, was charged by God to attend to mankind's spiritual needs, while the nobility received their lands from the king on condition that they fulfilled certain obligations to those above and below them. When a noble received land (a FIEF) he became the vassal of the lord who bestowed it and owed him military service and attendance. In return the lord offered his vassals justice and protection, and he received their sons into his own household where he educated them and prepared them for knighthood. Large fiefs were usually subdivided and the clergy often administered Church lands held in fief from nobles. The VILLEINS or serfs rendered service by working the land of the noble or Church or by pursuing a craft for the benefit of the manor in return for security, justice and protection. Villeins were given a share in the common lands and pasture, sufficient for their own needs.

A feudal system was already established in Anglo-Saxon England before the Conquest of 1066. Norman 'feudalism' may have meant different emphases in the conditions of upper-class land-holding, but the principle that lords were obligated to the king and responsible for the rights and obligations of their subordinates was unchanged. Many aspects of feudalism were superseded by BASTARD FEUDALISM, though English law continued to recognise feudal tenures until their abolition in 1660. (*See also* CASTLE)

FEUDAL TENURE Tenure of land in return for military service. Almost inevitably such service was eventually commuted to money payments.

FIEF An estate held in return for homage and service.

FIELDEN COUNTRYSIDE *see* COUNTRYSIDE

FIGHTING CASTLE Timber structures on the prow and stern of larger ships where marines were concentrated for action (hence *fo'c'sle* = 'forecastle').

FIGHTING GALLERY An intra-mural passage or wall-walk with EMBRASURES, LOOPHOLES and GUN PORTS, usually accessed by means of newel stairs (*see* STAIRS) and often with evidence of HOARDINGS which may once have been affixed to the parapets (*see* WALL-WALK). The triple fighting galleries in the south curtain of Caernarfon Castle are among the most formidable medieval defences in Britain. Within the 4.6m (15ft) thick wall, continuous galleries with deep embrasures and loopholes extend the full length of the curtain at first- and second-floor levels, circling the outer sides of the mural towers. At parapet level the wall-walk is not continuous (unlike other Edwardian castles) but is punctuated by the towers so that attackers who gained one section of wall-walk would have been isolated and vulnerable until they could batter down the door of an adjacent tower.

FIGHTING TOP Strong timber 'crow's nest' high on a warship's masts.

FILLET (i) A narrow band between mouldings or running down a shaft.
(ii) A narrow head-band.

FINE or OBLATE ROLLS Records concerned with fines imposed by the crown on subjects who received particular advantages such as a CHARTER or the holding of the wardship of an heiress (*see* HEIR). The rolls also record the appointment of royal officials. They are held at the Public Record Office (*see* APPENDIX II) and some have been published or calendared.
(*See also* STATE RECORDS)

FINIAL A carved ornament on top of a pinnacle, gable or spire, for example a sphere (*ball finial*) or a foliated fleur-de-lis.

FIREARMS AND CANNON
The following terms are most commonly used when describing firearms and cannon of the medieval period (* *see also* individual entries).

BOMBARD*	short-barrelled cannon
COULEUVRINE À MAIN	hand-held gun
CULVERIN*	long-barrelled cannon or handgun
FALCON*	medium-sized late medieval gun
HANDGONNE	English term for hand-held gun
RIBAUDEQUIN	a cart carrying RIBAUDS
RIBAUDS*	lightweight multi-barrelled cannon
SERPENTINE	fifteenth-century cannon
TAMPION	wooden disc separating powder from shot
THUNDER-BOX	separate breech-chamber
TOUCHE	heated metal rod used to fire cannon
TOUCHE-HOLE	aperture to which touche is applied
TRUNNION	studs on either side of barrel enabling it to be elevated or lowered

Gunpowder is an explosive mixture of potassium nitrate, charcoal and sulphur. 'Villainous salt petre' is generally believed to have been introduced into English warfare in the first half of the fourteenth century by Edward III against the Scots but may have been used even earlier at the siege of Stirling in 1297 by Edward I. Cannon first appeared in England in the early fourteenth century, though these early weapons (known as *pots de fer*) were singularly unstable. The first cannon were quite small, firing a stone, bolt or garrot; they had a limited range and were considerably less accurate than the siege weapons of the period such as the *mangonel* from which the word 'gun' is probably derived. One suspects that their effect was more psychological than physical: the thunderous roar of primitive cannon must have been a terrifying experience for those under siege, as were the terrible crushing wounds they could inflict. Guns of various kinds were more widely used from the first quarter of the fourteenth century, the *bombard*, a short-barrelled, large-calibre weapon, being commonly used throughout Europe. While bombards were only occasionally used by the English at SIEGES for both attack and defence (the English are known to have used bombards at the battle of Crécy in 1346), the French may have used some form of cannon during a raid on Southampton in 1338. This may have been a *falcon*, a medium-size cannon which was more easily transported than the heavier bombard. Larger forms of the bombard ('great guns') were transported by carts from which they had to be removed before firing. By 1386 the port of Southampton was defended by sixty large-bore cannon, the largest of these having a calibre of more than 50cm (20in). The *culverin* or 'snake' was a small, long-barrelled gun used in open battle or (later) as a handgun. The first true 'field artillery' piece was the *ribaudequin*, a cart on which several small-bore, long-barrelled guns (*ribauds*) were mounted. Cannon with separate breech-chambers (*thunder-boxes*) were first used in the late fourteenth century. Several of these could be placed in the

breech one after the other to provide a brief burst of rapid fire. In the late fifteenth century the development of guns and cannon was rapid. The 'great iron murderer Muckle Meg' (now at Edinburgh Castle) dates from 1450, though she blew up in 1680 and was later restored. Such cannon were undoubtedly effective but were notoriously slow and difficult to move and were rarely available when and where they were needed.

Cannon were relatively cheap, particularly after metalworkers had mastered the craft of smelting and casting large quantities of metal. Most fourteenth-century guns were made of brass or latten and the cannon-makers not only supplied the barrels, shot, tampions, carriages and powder but also established themselves as highly paid gunners. The earliest guns were either bedded in the ground at a pre-determined angle or mounted on boards. *Trunnions*, studs on either side of the barrel that enabled it to be elevated or lowered on a frame, were not introduced until the fifteenth century. An iron ramrod (*drivell*) was used to load the gun, while circular wooden *tampions* separated the shot from the powder. The gun was fired

Bombard at Bodiam Castle.

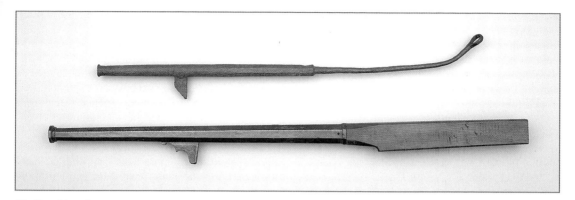

Medieval handguns.

by placing a metal *touche* (pre-heated in a brazier) against the *touche-hole* (hence the later expression 'touch-paper'). The science of artillery developed in the fifteenth century when iron cannon balls were first used and longer barrels were introduced. In order that the barrels of these guns should not burst, the ballistic force of the powder used was deliberately low. Even so, early cannon were probably as dangerous to their users as they were to the enemy.

The earliest hand-held guns (*couleuvrines à main*) were first used in fourteenth-century France and were later known in England as *handgonnes*. Rare before *c.* 1360, they were effectively miniature cannon attached to the ends of long poles and held beneath the arm or against the shoulder. Firearms were often operated by men working in pairs, one supporting the gun and the other firing it. Some early handguns also had a hook beneath the barrel to counter the shock of recoil when the gun was supported on a wall. By the end of the fourteenth century handguns were cheaper to manufacture than the highly sophisticated and expensive crossbows of the period (*see* ARCHERY). Longer barrels increased muzzle velocity, the long supporting pole being replaced by a shorter stock that facilitated more accurate aiming.

The only effect that firearms had on castle design in the fourteenth and fifteenth centuries was the introduction of GUN PORTS, suggesting that they were used more often in defence than attack. Typically, the Byward Tower at the Tower of London was adapted in the late fifteenth century to accommodate cannon mounted in embrasures within the thickness of the outer walls, each embrasure marked externally by a small gun port. It has recently been discovered that the late thirteenth-century portcullis in the Byward Tower was also modified in the sixteenth century to provide a solid

barricade for hand-gunners and a secure gun port for larger cannon (*see* PORTCULLIS). With the exception of a small number of well-documented occasions, cannon played very little part in medieval siege warfare in England and were not a determining factor in the decline of the medieval castle. The lofty towers and elaborate embattled parapets of many late medieval castles such as Warwick and Warkworth were aristocratic conceits, intended to convey an image of magnate superiority. They were the very antithesis of the broad, squat ramparts, revetments and bastions required to withstand an artillery bombardment (*see* TUDOR COASTAL FORTS). Only by the mid-sixteenth century had guns become generally effective and extensively employed, and nearly all the damage inflicted on medieval castles by cannon occurred during the English Civil War in the seventeenth century. Even so, medieval defences that had been designed to withstand the pummelling of siege engines were very often found to be equally effective against artillery. Firing a cannon at close range did not invariably bring the walls tumbling down. Corfe Castle, for example, withstood nine pieces of heavy artillery during a three-month siege in 1643.
(*See also* GREEK FIRE *and* INCENDIARY DEVICES)

FIRE-BACKS The gradual introduction of the enclosed chimney flue and fireplace from the late thirteenth century resulted in a number of innovations including the cast-iron fire-back which both protected the stone wall at the back of the hearth and reflected heat into the room. It was also found that because the metal absorbed and conserved heat (effectively an early storage radiator) the up-draught in the chimney flue could be

maintained, thereby improving the efficiency of the grate. Many fire-backs incorporated traditional designs such as religious symbols, floral motifs and scroll-work; others bear the royal arms, though these are not always contemporary and usually have no particular significance. Other fire-backs were made for specific fireplaces and included armorial devices appropriate to the family who commissioned them. Care should be exercised, however, for it should not be assumed that a fire-back has remained in its original location and the heraldry may not relate to the house in which it is found. There are also many modern (usually inferior) imitations.
(*See also* CHIMNEYS AND FIREPLACES)

FIRE-DOGS A fire-dog or *andiron* is a metal stand (usually one of a pair) used for supporting logs in a fireplace. This ancient method was intended to raise the burning logs above the hearth-bed so that an up-draught of air was maintained. From the late thirteenth century, when enclosed chimney flues and fireplaces began to replace the central open hearths of earlier communal halls, shallow fire-baskets were sometimes slung between the andirons. With the importation of coal in the seventeenth century these baskets were adapted to accommodate the new fuel but fire-dogs continued in use and were later incorporated into the design of free-standing grates (*see* CHIMNEYS AND FIREPLACES). Because wood burns at a lower temperature than coal, many pre-seventeenth-century fire-dogs were embellished with intricate silver or brass finials. In many vernacular buildings fire-dogs were used for wood-burning until the late nineteenth century.

FIREPLACES *see* CHIMNEYS AND FIREPLACES

FIRST POINTED PERIOD *see* GOTHIC ARCHITECTURE

FISH PONDS The medieval method of preserving meat in brine was so unreliable (and the results so unpalatable) that many castles and manors and most religious houses possessed their own sources of fresh protein, notably DOVECOTES, WARRENS and fish ponds. Of these the fish pond was of singular importance for it provided a reliable source of food on the numerous 'fish days' that were observed throughout the year and on which no 'flesh' (i.e. red meat) could be eaten. Today most medieval fish ponds are dry, their leats silted and their sluices long abandoned. Typically, they are rectangular and flat-bottomed with retaining embankments raised 1m (3ft 3in) above ground level and with two or three

adjacent *stew ponds* where young fish were raised. The main pond sometimes contained an artificial island for wildfowl. Another type of pond, similar to those created for fish farming and angling today, was the *scoop pond*, which was formed by digging out or damming a small coomb just below the spring line on a scarp face. Carp were the most popular fish, though pike, perch, bream, roach, tench, trout and elvers were also farmed, although pike were kept in separate ponds to prevent them from eating each other. The earthworks of decayed fish ponds are most often found in the vicinity of domestic buildings where they could more easily be observed and protected. They were also incorporated in the water defences of some medieval castles and moated homesteads (*see* MOATS).

FISHTAIL LOOPHOLE *see* LOOPHOLES

'FITZ-' Surname element meaning 'son of', often applied in the Middle Ages to illegitimate children. (*See also* 'DE' IN SURNAMES AND TITLES)

FIVE BOROUGHS *see* DANELAW *and* TOWNS

FLAGS From the inception of ARMORY in the twelfth century until forbidden by the army regulations of 1747, personal flags (*banners* and *pennons*), on which were displayed the same devices as those in the shield of arms, accompanied armigerous commanders in battle. By the fifteenth century mustering and rallying functions were performed by *livery flags*: the *standard* and *guidon* (*see* BATTLEFIELDS).

Personal Flags
The *pennon* was a medium-size personal flag, about 1m (3ft 3in) in length, swallow-tailed or triangular and emblazoned with the arms of an armiger below the rank of BANNERET. Unanticipated promotion in the field of battle to the rank of banneret could be signified by the removal of the pennon's tails to form a small banner (*banneret*). Both Sir John Chandos (1367) and Sir Thomas Trivet (1380) were promoted in this way.

A square or oblong *banner* was the principal personal flag of the nobility down to the knights banneret. It was (and is) indicative of the physical presence of an armiger and consequently to raise one's banner in the field of battle was an unequivocal indication of commitment to a particular cause. Unlike the livery flags (*see below*) only one banner or pennon was carried into battle and this accompanied the owner wherever he went.

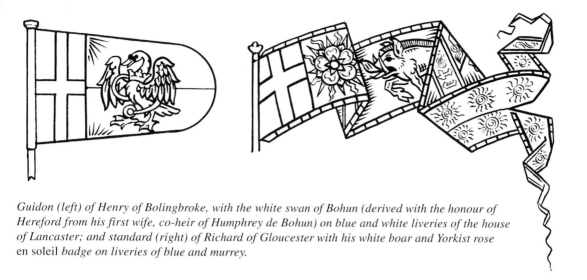

Guidon (left) of Henry of Bolingbroke, with the white swan of Bohun (derived with the honour of Hereford from his first wife, co-heir of Humphrey de Bohun) on blue and white liveries of the house of Lancaster; and standard (right) of Richard of Gloucester with his white boar and Yorkist rose en soleil *badge on liveries of blue and murrey.*

In the Middle Ages the banner was also known as the *lieutenant* and was the responsibility of an officer of that name. Banners of member knights are hung above their stalls in the chapels of the orders of chivalry, at St George's Chapel, Windsor (the Most Noble Order of the Garter) and Henry VII's Chapel at Westminster Abbey (the Most Honourable Order of the Bath), for example.

Livery Flags

The *standard* bore, on a background of the livery colours, the various badges familiar to a commander's retinues, together with a motto and the national device: in England the red cross of St George. Standards were used for mustering purposes in the battlefield and at tournaments. The medieval English standard was usually 2.4m (8ft) long and about 0.6m (2ft) wide, though in the sixteenth century the Tudor heralds determined that flags of specific lengths should be prescribed to different ranks of the nobility. Also known as the *ancient*, the standard's maintenance was the responsibility of an officer of that name. The *guidon* was a small version of the standard, carried before a contingent of retained men and essential as a rallying point in the heat of battle. It too was composed of the livery colours and bore one (or sometimes two) badges but no motto.
(*See also* BADGES AND LIVERY *and* GONFANON)

FLAIL *see* IRONWORK, LOCKS AND NAILS

FLAMBOYANT The final phase of French Gothic architecture in which window tracery is composed of wavy undulating lines. It is found in English buildings of the Perpendicular period where the resulting motif resembles interwoven curves ('flames').
(*See also* GOTHIC ARCHITECTURE)

FLANCHARD Side protection for a horse. From the fourteenth century pairs of flanchards were standard elements in a full set of plate armour for horses (*see* HORSES AND HORSE-HARNESS).

FLANK (i) The left or right side of a body of troops.
(ii) The principal defensive element of a post-medieval bastion fortification: the side of a construction (e.g. a bastion) between the face and the curtain.
(iii) To be posted to, or to move along the flank or side of.

FLANKER A gun emplacement commanding a CURTAIN WALL or RAMPART from the flank of a BASTION.

FLANKING TOWER *see* TOWERS

FLASHING *see* STAINED GLASS

FLAUNDERSTILE The medieval word for a brick (*see* BRICK BUILDINGS).

FLÈCHE (*also* SPIRELET) (i) A slender wooden spire at the centre of a roof.
(ii) In post-medieval fortifications, a small arrow-shaped outwork at the foot of a GLACIS.

FLETCH The feathered flight of an arrow or crossbow bolt (*see* ARCHERY *and* BOWYER). Fletches were made by *fletchers*.

FLETCHER *see* FLETCH

FLEUR-DE-LIS (*also* FLEUR-DE-LYS) *see* ROYAL ARMS, THE

FLIGHT *see* ARCHERY

FLINT A variety of quartz consisting of irregular nodules of nearly pure silica, dark grey or black in colour, and occurring in association with chalk which provides it with its white coating. Despite its apparent ordinariness, this extremely hard and fissile mineral was of singular importance in the development of civilisation: it provided Neolithic man with implements and, when struck, it would produce fire. The Anglo-Saxons knew it as *firestone*.

Because of its strength and durability flint is frequently found as a building material in chalk districts of south and east England and has continued in use for this purpose from the Iron Age to the present day. The Romans used it, in conjunction with brick and mortar, in the construction of the walls of Silchester (near Reading, Berkshire) and the forts of the Saxon Shore. Before the fourteenth century whole flints were embedded in the mortar of walls which were further strengthened with stone and flint rubble and lacing courses of stone or brick. But from the late thirteenth century split and shaped (*knapped*) flints, with their dark facets outwards, were often used in conjunction with brick or stone to form chequer-work and other geometrically patterned surfaces. A special decorative technique called *flushwork* also developed at this time. Knapped flint set in mortar within the matrices of intricately carved freestone facings was a feature of many East Anglian buildings and continued, there and elsewhere, into the sixteenth century, by which time a high standard of craftsmanship had evolved.

FLORIN *see* COINAGE

FLUSHWORK Knapped flint set in mortar within the matrices of carved freestone facings to form a decorative pattern.

FLUTING *see* PIER

FLYING BUTTRESS *see* BUTTRESS *and* GOTHIC ARCHITECTURE

FOILS (i) Decorative figures in Gothic tracery consisting of a number of leaf-shaped curves (*lobes*) formed by small arcs separated by CUSPS. Most commonly used are the *trefoil* (three lobes), *quatrefoil* (four) and *cinquefoil* (five).
(ii) Similar figures in ARMORY which include also the *sexfoil* (six) and the *octofoil* (eight). These may be plain or *slipped* (having a stem).

Trefoil (top), quatrefoil (left) and cinquefoil (right).

FOLLIES *see* ARTIFICIAL RUINS

FOREBUILDING Early tower keeps were usually entered at first-floor level by means of an external flight of steps. In many cases the entrance was defended by a stone forebuilding which encased (or partially encased) the stair and entrance vestibule (*see* KEEP). The best surviving examples are at Dover Castle (1180–90), Newcastle (1168–78), both of which rise (unusually) to entrances on the second floor, and Castle Rising (*c.* 1139).

The Dover forebuilding is a complex L-shaped structure with three projecting turrets, one of which contains a small Romanesque chapel. At Newcastle the forebuilding has survived in its entirety, the broad stair rising (past a modern entrance at first-floor level) to an elaborate Norman portal on the second floor. A chapel was incorporated within the space beneath the grand stair. The Great Tower of Castle Rising is more accurately a HALL-KEEP than a tower. Its forebuilding, perhaps the finest surviving in England, comprises a square entrance tower rising the full height of the keep, with a first-floor vestibule and a narrower annexe enclosing a great flight of stairs. The entrance vestibule was originally an open arcaded loggia and still contains a splendid Romanesque portal, now blocked by a Tudor fireplace and nineteenth-century glazed tiles. The open arcading of the vestibule is now a series of glazed windows, all but one of which have fifteenth- or sixteenth-century mullions and transoms. The vaulted ceiling was inserted in the early fourteenth century when a storey and (somewhat incongruous) pitched roof were added to the forebuilding.

There are also instances of forebuildings serving other types of keep. At Orford in Suffolk (1165–73), for example, an open stair leads to a vestibule in one of three square towers attached to a circular (polygonal) keep, and at Berkeley Castle in Gloucestershire (c. 1155) the forebuilding enclosing a narrow stair was added as an afterthought to the shell-keep. In Wales several of the early thirteenth-century castles of the princes of Gwynedd were tower keeps with the principal chambers entered at first-floor level. At Dolwyddelan Castle, Aberconwy, the apartment was reached by means of an external flight of steps with a drawbridge (which closed against the door) and a modest forebuilding protecting the doorway and drawbridge pit. At nearby Dolbadarn a cylindrical keep, similar to those of southern Marcher lords, had a small, square forebuilding enclosing the entrance that was defended by a portcullis. Several forebuildings were modified by the addition of a chamber or CHAPEL as an upper storey: at Rochester Castle (1127–36), for example, an unusually tall forebuilding contains a vaulted prison beneath the entrance vestibule and an austere chapel above. However, the romantic notion that an attacking force was often reluctant to attack a forebuilding for fear of violating a chapel is unfounded.

A forebuilding which was erected for defensive purposes, often with the roof-space open so that assailants could be exposed to attack from the wall-walk of the keep and from the surrounding parapet, is normally termed a BARBICAN.

FOREST MARBLE A limestone ideally suited to the manufacture of stone roofing slates. The name is derived from the Forest of Wychwood in Oxfordshire.

FORESTS The popular perception of a forest is of 'a large tract covered with trees and undergrowth' (*Oxford Dictionary*). This is far removed from the medieval definition which was strictly a legal one, concerned with the protection of VERT AND VENISON and the administration of Forest Law. Hunting forests encompassed a wide variety of countryside: woodland, moor and heath, wastes and even cultivated land. One of the most satisfactory definitions of a forest is that of the eighteenth-century writer James Lee, quoted in Thomas Hearne's *Curious Discourses on English Antiquities*:

> The word *forest* . . . doth signify . . . all things that are abroad, and neither domestical nor demean [demesne]: wherefore *foresta* in old time did extend into woods, wastes and waters, and did contain not only *vert* and venison, but also minerals and maritimal revenues. But when *forests* were first used in England I find no certain time of the beginning thereof; and, although that ever since the Conquest it hath been lawful for the

The keep and forebuilding at Scarborough Castle, c. 1175.

King to make any man's land (whom it pleased him) to be *forest*, yet there are certain rules and circumstances appointed for the doing thereof. For, first, there must issue out of Chancery a writ of *perambulation*, directed unto certain discreet men, commanding them to call before them XXiiij Knights and principal freeholders, and to cause them, in the presence of the officers of the forests, to walk or perambulate so much ground as they shall think to be fit or convenient for the breeding, feeding and succouring of the King's deer, and to put the same in writing, and to certify the same under the seals of the same Commissioners and Jurors unto the Chancery.

It is clear that forest territory was originally that vast 'no man's land' which extended beyond those areas which had been cleared, enclosed, cultivated or grazed. These wildernesses were possessed by (or of) the crown and several were used by the late Saxon kings for hunting (notably the New Forest). But it was the Normans who recognised the advantages of combining sport with exploitation and it was they who created the bureaucratic framework within which the forests were defined, extended and protected by law. Where definition of a forest was considered necessary a formal procedure of perambulation and registration was used and, where possible, it was delineated by topography, taking features such as rivers and rock outcrops as its boundaries.

There can be little doubt that an inherent love of the chase stimulated the creation of vast hunting forests under the Norman kings. But this should not conceal the fact that a regular and substantial supply of fresh protein was also an essential requirement of a numerous and often itinerant court and, because hunting was enjoyed by a privileged few, membership of that élite could be manipulated as a form of patronage at minimal cost to the crown. The distribution of forests corresponded closely with that of royal manors so that the king could progress from one estate to another, assured of a constant supply of meat for his legion companions and retainers as well as a day's sport (bucks were hunted in summer and autumn and does from early September to the beginning of February, after the breeding season). The forests also provided *largesse* in the form of gifts of beasts for the stocking of DEER PARKS and income could be derived from the imposition of fines, from the granting of assarts (licences to clear woodland) and from the sale of privileges and exemptions from the Forest Law. In 1204, for example, the people of Devon paid 5,000 marks so that the Forest Law (which at that time applied to the entire county) should be limited to the forests of Exmoor and Dartmoor. Woodland within the forests was managed commercially and special enterprises were sometimes permitted, such as cattle farms (*vaccaries*), mining and quarrying – always providing that such activities were not detrimental to the vert and venison. 'The breeding, feeding and succouring of the King's deer' had precedence over every other consideration and from this principle developed a system of regulation known as Forest Law, applicable to the royal forests and those chases held by the earls of Lancaster (*see* CHASE). Not only were the beasts (known generically as *venison*) protected but so was their habitat and any form of vegetation which could be serviceable to the deer (the *vert*). Nevertheless, there existed certain rights which could be acquired and which could be exercised without detriment to the deer. Each 'right' was defined with great precision, often as a consequence of protracted negotiation, and could be suspended under certain specific circumstances: in a hard winter, for example, when a period of *heyning* would be declared during which the grazing of domestic animals would be curtailed to the benefit of the deer.

Forest Law was undoubtedly effective in the context from which it evolved, but inevitably it became oppressive and ultimately the cause of almost universal resentment. In particular, the special authority of the courts which administered the Forest Law outside the Common Law, the arbitrary (and often unlawful) extension of forest limits and the frustration caused by constant disputes and bureaucratic procrastination over individual rights, led to organised resistance and ultimately contributed to *Magna Carta* in 1215 and the Charter of the Forest two years later. This effectively brought to an end the institution of new forests which had grown in number from about twenty-five at the time of Domesday Book in 1086 to almost one hundred and fifty in 1217.

At the heart of each forest was a refuge in which the deer (fallow, red and roe) lived and bred. This was surrounded by an area of marginal land, often cultivated or grazed and containing farmsteads and settlements (Colchester was within the bounds of Essex Forest), in which the deer were protected and over which hunting might take place. Although technically within the forest 'bounds' (and therefore subject to Forest Law), marginal land was not necessarily in the ownership of the crown. But the game within the forest was, and land-holders were powerless to control the depredations of browsing deer or the ravages of the huntsmen and their followers. Contrary to popular belief, *poaching* or the unlawful removal of timber was punishable by fine (or imprisonment for habitual offenders) and not by mutilation. Dogs could be 'lawed' (mutilated) to prevent their use for hunting, or 'humbled' (their claws were clipped) so that they should not harm the deer, but even this could be avoided by payment of a fine. Deer were permitted free access to land and enclosure fences had to be low enough to allow for this or provided with 'leap-gates'. Only foresters had the authority to drive deer from land, even when herds were discovered grazing in growing crops. The forests were administered by two justices, responsible for the forests to the north or to the south of the River Trent, and each forest had its VERDERERS and warden who controlled a large contingent of foresters (*free-foresters*), the more senior of whom were often from well-to-do local families, and woodmen (*woodwards*). Several hereditary offices were established: in 1148 the earl of Oxford was the Hereditary Steward of the Royal Forests in Essex and in *c.* 1270 the earl of Norfolk and Suffolk, as well as being Hereditary Marshal of England, Hereditary Steward of the Household and Hereditary Bearer of the Banner of St Edmund, was also Hereditary Warden of Romford Forest and Hereditary Forester of Farnedale.

FORT Any building or position designed primarily for defensive purposes. The term is generally applied to post-medieval fortifications which (unlike castles) were not designed primarily as residences.

FORTALICE A small fort or defended site.

FORTIFIED MANOR HOUSES *see* MANOR HOUSE

FORTRESS Any fortified place capable of accommodating a large force.

FOSS *or* FOSSE From the Latin *fossa* meaning 'long ditch' or 'trench', especially one associated with a fortification (*see* MOTTE).

FOSSATORES The excavators of moats, ditches, etc. There is documentary evidence that no fewer than 1,800 of these early 'navvies' excavated the moat at Flint Castle during the month of August 1277. The records show that they came not only from Wales but from Lancashire, Leicestershire, Lincolnshire, Warwickshire and Yorkshire, and that

at least one gang comprised pressed men doing forced labour.

FOUGASSE A small mine comprising explosive and rocks.

FOUNDATIONS Once the master mason had staked out the lines of a wall or building his next task was to oversee the construction of the foundations (*see* MASTER MASONS AND ARCHITECTS). At Woodstock in 1256 six workmen were paid 'for searching for and making the foundation'. It would appear, therefore, that it was normal practice for bore-holes to be dug in order to locate a solid stratum on which to build and this would dictate the depth of the foundations. Unless the castle was to be built on rock, trenches would be excavated and filled to a variable depth with rough stone and other material to form a footing that would be of somewhat greater width than the wall to be raised on it. At Nottingham twenty-four loads of 'fyllingstones' were supplied for this purpose in 1367, while at Shene in 1369 Robyn of Greenwich was paid 18*s* for two freightages of his ship: 36 tons of 'stones called Shalke [a form of chalk] for the foundations of the walls'.

Where there was neither rock nor reasonably firm ground to build on, piles were often used. At York in 1327 trunks of alder were bought 'to make piles for the foundations of the cellar underneath the Queen's private chamber and of the cellar below the new chapel and also for the foundation of the latrine'. In 1348 nine elms were purchased 'for piles for the foundation of the postern [gate]' at the Tower of London, and in 1363 twenty elms 'for piles whereof to make the foundation of the King's chamber' at Hadleigh Castle. There is a reference in the Calais accounts for 1468 to an engine or 'gynne called Ram, used for fixing piles' while 'a machine called a Fallyng Ram' is found in 1473 at Shene. The *ram*, or pile-driver, consisted of a hoisting apparatus of two or more poles which carried a pulley by means of which a heavy block of wood or iron (the 'ram') could be raised and let fall on the head of the pile. Rams were most often used in connection with bridge works: over ten thousand timber piles were driven into the riverbed in order to provide foundations for the piers of Rochester bridge in 1383. At the Tower in 1324 men were 'driving piles in the foundation with a great engine called "ram"' and there can be little doubt that they were used at castles such as Caerphilly and Kenilworth where dams, weirs and artificial lakes formed part of the formidable defences. At a number of castles (notably Rhuddlan), watercourses were diverted and major engineering works undertaken to allow for the provisioning of the castle by ship. When a contract was made in 1432 for the construction of a wharf at Norwich the mason was instructed to 'take the ground pile it and plank it with englyssh oke . . . of reasonable thickness . . . and thereupon begynne the seyd kaye [quay] of freston', the void behind the stone facing to be filled and rammed with marl and gravel.

FOUR-CENTRE ARCH *see* ARCH *and* GOTHIC ARCHITECTURE

FRAISES Stakes embedded horizontally in the outer slopes of a rampart.

FRANCE ANCIENT *and* **FRANCE MODERN** *see* ROYAL ARMS, THE

FRANCHISE A liberty, privilege or exemption by grant or prescription.

FRANKLIN A free tenant or farmer, usually enjoying reasonable prosperity and often a manorial steward or bailiff.
(*See also* MANOR *and* YEOMAN)

FRANKPLEDGE In many areas of Anglo-Saxon and early medieval England each *vill* or *township* was subdivided into *tithings* of ten households. Each tithing was charged with a corporate responsibility for the conduct of its members and for ensuring that anyone accused of an offence was available to answer the charge at the COURT LEET. The system was known as frankpledge and was administered in each tithing by a *tithingman*. Some classes of society (e.g. knights and clerks) were exempt.

FREESTONE Easily sawn stone, usually oolitic limestone or particular types of sandstone. Freestone has a fine grain, does not possess strongly marked laminations and may be 'freely worked' with a saw and chisel.
(*See also* MASONRY *and* RAG *and* RAGSTONE)

FRET (i) A decorative motif, sometimes described as a *key* or *lattice* motif, consisting of continuous combinations of straight lines joined at right angles.
(ii) In ARMORY, a device consisting of a voided diamond interlaced by two diagonal lines.

Fret.

FROSTERLEY MARBLE *see* MARBLE *and* MASONRY

FULLER *see* WEAPONS AND HARNESS

FUNERARY HERALDRY Funerals of the late medieval and Tudor nobility were often magnificent spectacles, not least the processions which preceded the committal in which the deceased's 'achievements' were paraded. These included his spurs, gauntlets, crested helm, shield, sword, tabard and banner which was retained for display in the church, the best known example being those of Edward, the Black Prince (d. 1376), at Canterbury Cathedral. Several less grandiose examples of funeral achievements have survived in parish churches, mostly from the sixteenth century, and from these may be traced the gradual evolution of funeral heraldry from the practical equipment of medieval warfare and tournament through the stylised artificial helms, crests and tabards of the Tudor period to the heraldic substitute, the funeral HATCHMENT of the seventeenth, eighteenth and nineteenth centuries. Banners of members of the various orders of chivalry will also be found in many British churches. These are invariably 1.5m (5ft) square, embroidered with the knight's arms and fringed in two or more colours. The banner of a deceased knight is the perquisite of the king of arms of the order to which he belonged but, in practice, it is normally conveyed to the family and displayed in their parish church.

FYRD *and* **FYRD-BOTE** *see* MILITIA *and* TRINODA NECESSITAS

1. Fotheringhay, Northamptonshire, was a collegiate foundation. Its patron, Edward duke of York, died at Agincourt in 1415 before his college was completed and the choir and collegiate buildings were demolished following the dissolution of the chantries in 1547. Richard of Gloucester (later Richard III) was born in the nearby castle (now only an earthwork) in 1452 and in recent years the church has become a shrine to the Yorkist dynasty.

2. Several ringworks have erroneously been described as shell-keeps. Restormel Castle (Cornwall), for example, comprises a perfectly circular bailey with internal buildings arranged concentrically against a crenellated curtain wall. From the outside, the stone curtain appears to crown a motte and for this reason it is often described as a shell-keep. But the inner bank of the ringwork was removed when the curtain was built in c. 1200 and the living quarters added in c. 1280.

3. Archbishop Corbeil's keep at Rochester Castle, Kent. With a height of 35 m (115 ft) it is the tallest keep in Britain. Five storeys high, including a 'double' storey containing the hall and solar, a well shaft rises the full height of the keep so that water could be drawn at each level. The round corner tower replaced an earlier angle tower that was brought down by King John's sappers in the siege of 1216.

4. Extensive remodelling of Dover Castle following a siege of 1216–17 included the construction of a huge gatehouse which thrusts forward across the dry moat from the outer curtain. Known as the Constable's Gate, it comprises a cluster of rounded towers of different sizes, the whole curving backwards and dominating all angles of approach. The Constable's Gate has been accurately described as the most elaborate gateway to any British castle.

5. *Goodrich Castle, Herefordshire, stands on the summit of a hill above the River Wye in a naturally defendable position further protected by a deep rock-cut moat on two sides. The original earthwork castle, erected shortly after the Conquest, was rebuilt in stone in the twelfth century. In the late thirteenth century the castle was almost entirely rebuilt by the earls of Pembroke who retained the keep within a new rectangular inner ward with drum towers at each of the angles. In the fourteenth century an outer curtain and elaborate barbican were added to the already formidable defences.*

6. *The hall at Winchester Castle is, after Westminster, the finest surviving medieval hall in England. Reconstructed by Henry III in 1222–36, it measures 35.5 m in length (110 ft) and is exactly half as wide as it is high.*

7. At Kenilworth, Warwickshire, the first Norman earth and timber fortress was rebuilt in stone in the twelfth century to provide a formidable keep (centre) and curtain wall. King John enlarged the castle at the beginning of the thirteenth century and constructed a fortified dam (centre right) to form a vast shallow lake (the Great Mere) upstream from the castle island. John of Gaunt (1340–99) further improved the castle, creating a magnificent palace overlooking the lake. In the Tudor period, yet more buildings were added by Robert Dudley, earl of Leicester (1533–88), together with a pleasure garden (centre left). The castle was slighted and the Great Mere drained in 1649.

8. *A painting by the late Dan Escott of the principal knights and nobles who fought at the battle of Crécy in 1346. This was the first major English victory of the Hundred Years War. An invading English army under Edward III was attacked in a strong defensive position near the village of Crécy in Ponthieu by a French force of considerable size. English longbowmen wrought havoc in the ranks of the mounted French knights, whose reckless and undisciplined charges made little impact on the English lines. After repeated assaults, lasting well into the night, the French retreated in confusion leaving thousands of their dead on the field, to be identified and recorded next morning by the English heralds. The valley below the ridge is still called* La Vallée aux Clercs. *The chronicler Froissart tells us that King Edward established his command post in a windmill from where he watched his sixteen-year-old son, Edward Plantagenet, later called the Black Prince, win his spurs. Incredibly, the English are said to have lost fewer than fifty men.*

9. A triangular castle with an enclosed timber bridge linking the barbican and drawbridge. From the magnificent Très Riches Heures du Duc de Berry, *painted by the Limbourg brothers in the early fifteenth century.*

10. At Flint, in north-east Wales, town and castle were combined in a single defensive unit, with the castle located on a low promontory on the shores of the River Dee. This was the first of Edward I's great Welsh fortifications, begun in 1277 (when nearly three thousand men were employed to excavate the ditches round the castle and the new town) and completed in 1286.

11. Originally, the gleaming whiteness of the lime-washed castle of Conwy must have been a startling sight against the dark cloud-capped mountains of Snowdonia. Inevitably, the native Welsh loathed the massive structure – an instrument of subjugation and a symbol of English strength, dominion and permanence.

GABIONS Cylindrical wicker baskets packed with earth or sand to absorb cannon shot. Used to protect emplacements and as temporary parapets.

GABLE The triangular upper part of a wall supporting the end of a ridged roof.

GAD *see* IRONWORK, LOCKS AND NAILS

GAFELUC *see* WEAPONS AND HARNESS

GALLERY (i) Strictly speaking, a gallery is a colonnaded walkway – enclosed except for an open arcade along one side. However, in the present context the term is often applied to a narrow passageway or chamber. Galleries were provided in castles for a variety of purposes. For example, an arcaded gallery between the Great Tower and the river cliff at Chepstow Castle served to divide the castle into a number of self-contained units, each of which could be defended independently. At Raglan Castle a fifteenth-century gallery above the gate passage is believed to have housed a library and was lit by a range of windows overlooking an inner court. In 1549, at the same castle, William Somerset, 3rd earl of Worcester (d. 1584), incorporated an elegant first-floor long gallery, typical of Elizabethan 'great houses', comprising a long, narrow apartment for 'promenading' and taking exercise during inclement weather.
(ii) A FIGHTING GALLERY may be an intra-mural passage with loopholes and embrasures or an open crenellated wall-walk, possibly with an overhanging timber HOARDING.
(iii) A *minstrels' gallery* or platform was often provided above the SCREENS PASSAGE in late medieval halls (*see* MINSTRELS).

GALLETING *see* SLATES

GALLOGLASS AXE *see* WEAPONS AND HARNESS

GAMBESON A quilted coat, larger than the AKETON and with longer sleeves, worn beneath chain or plate armour in order to reduce chafing and the effect of blows to the body. In use from the twelfth century, some gambesons were made of very fine materials and were worn over armour for sartorial effect. By the thirteenth century the padding of the gambeson had become so effective that it replaced the old mail HAUBERGEON worn by infantry.
(*See also* ARMOUR *and* HELMETS)

GAOLS *see* PRISONS

GARDE DE LA MERE Fourteenth-century coastal MILITIA.
(*See also* RECRUITMENT AND ORGANISATION, MILITARY)

GARDENS Horticultural practice declined following the withdrawal of Rome in the late fourth century AD, though it is known that leeks, cabbages and dried peas and beans formed some sort of subsistence diet during the so-called Dark Ages that followed. In the sixth century St Benedict decreed that all Benedictine monasteries should become self-sufficient. The domestic buildings of monasteries were laid out on the Roman court and cloister plan and within the cloister garth the monks cultivated medicinal plants, herbs and vegetables, sometimes in a series of raised, rectangular beds. Plans exist from the early twelfth century of the monastery gardens at Canterbury which included a *herbarium* (herb garden), orchards and vineyards, all watered by an elaborate irrigation system. It is generally assumed that British medieval gardens remained essentially utilitarian until the early sixteenth century. This was certainly true of the average villager whose natural preoccupation with the production of food was to be subject to the vestigial obligations of the Norman feudal system for several centuries. But from the second half of the fourteenth century, as the residences of the nobility became less defensive, so areas of cultivation began to extend outwards to provide orchards and vegetable gardens and the delightful 'pleasure grounds' (*pleasaunces*) illustrated in contemporary HERBALS and books of poetry such as the *Romance of the Rose*. Typically, these show a series of walled and trellised gardens connected by arched openings, with close-clipped hedges, turf seats, mulberry bushes and water-fountains. From these evolved the *knot garden* of flower beds and gravel pathways. Beds were small, usually raised and laid out in intricate geometric patterns with dwarf shrubs such as box or thrift or herbs like rosemary forming low, neatly clipped edges. Spaces were filled with washed or coloured gravel or earth, and beds planted with flowers such as lilies, lavender, marigolds, roses, primroses and gillyflowers.

Probably the earliest garden in any English castle was that which was created for Henry II at Arundel in 1176–89 but very few details have survived. The east barbican of Conwy Castle is described as a 'herbarium' in an account of 1316. Overlooked only by the state apartments and shielded to the east by a low curtain wall, it would have provided privacy for King Edward and his queen whenever they were in residence. It is known that when the castle was under construction a new chamber was built for Queen Eleanor with a private stair leading to the garden where a lawn was laid, with turf shipped up the river at a cost of 16s. The lawn was fenced with the staves of an empty wine tun and was watered for the first time on a July evening in 1283 by one of the queen's esquires who received 3d for his trouble. A remarkable pleasaunce was created by Henry V in 1414 to the west of Kenilworth Castle. Known as 'the Pleasaunce in the Marsh' it comprised a timber-frame pavilion or banqueting house within a walled courtyard with corner towers. The courtyard was surrounded by concentric water-filled moats and was approached from Kenilworth's Great Mere by a wide harbour channel up which the royal barge could be rowed, almost to the pavilion door. The buildings were removed by Henry VIII and only the earthworks and moats remain.

During the sixteenth century English gardens followed those of Renaissance Italy and France, with stone staircases, terraces and elaborate water features, fountains and cascades. But the English horticultural Renaissance was less rigorously formal: the climate was more conducive to mixed planting and the style more whimsical than grand. The garden at Hampton Court Palace was to provide a model for the gardens of the Tudor nobility. Mazes, labyrinths, pavilions, arbours, sundials and elegant topiary characterised the gardens of the period which remained formal and geometric in character with separate (usually walled) areas designated for growing fruit and vegetables, including many introduced by adventurers returning from the New World (notably the potato and maize).

(See also DEER PARK)

GARDEROBE A garderobe was a latrine or privy, usually a single cell at the end of a short, crooked passage within the thickness of a wall, from which a shaft vented to a cesspool beneath. These would require periodic cleansing, though in a few fortunate cases the foot of the wall would be washed by a river (a water-filled moat must have been particularly noisome when stagnant!). Most castles were liberally supplied with latrines: any intra-mural passage that comes to a dead end is likely to have been one, though many latrine shafts have been plugged and the seats (sieges) lost long ago. Being located in the outer walls, latrine chutes were considered to be a vulnerable area of a castle's defences and were often designed so that they could not be used to gain access during a siege. Other types of latrine consisted of benches in stone cubicles (gonges) supported on corbels that projected from a wall or simple timber cabins built out over a moat. The largest of the three town gates at Conwy was fitted out as an office for Edward I's private secretariat who benefited from the last word in thirteenth-century staff lavatories: twelve separate cubicles projecting from the town walls and discharging into the stream below. At Brecon Castle an entire tower served as a latrine block.

Private chambers almost invariably had a garderobe and these were sometimes located next to a chimney flue for warmth and were reached by means of a doorway in the side of a window embrasure. These 'privy' latrines were marginally more sophisticated (though just as draughty) as those used by the household and garrison, with provision for braziers to heat water for washing and a degree of privacy. It was believed that fumes from a privy assisted in the preservation of fabrics and clothing was often stored in the immediate vicinity of a latrine. Indeed, in the Middle Ages the term 'garderobe' more accurately described a dressing room or ante-chamber, literally a 'cloak-room' where clothes were kept. Nevertheless, expert advice at the time recommended that 'a wyse builder will set a sege house [latrine] out of the wey from syght and smellynge'. It has been suggested (by R. Allen Brown) that the arrangement of garderobes in the twelfth-century keep of Castle Rising represents 'the earliest distinction between Ladies and Gents'.

Unique in their complexity were the curtain wall latrines provided for the garrison at Beaumaris Castle (begun in 1295): sixteen in all, each pair located at intervals on the wall-walk with a further sixteen accessible from the intra-mural passages beneath. Eight large rectangular pits, extending from below ground level to the wall-walk, were constructed within the 4.65m (15½ft) thickness of the curtain walls. Above these, at each level, back-to-back latrines were separated by a rectangular ventilation shaft rising from the centre of the pit. It is likely that the pits were scoured by water directed from the moat along channels beneath the outer ward, a system that depended for its effectiveness on the castle's location at sea level. On the wall-walk each cubicle was approached down a flight of six or more

The last word in thirteenth-century staff lavatories: twelve separate cubicles project from the town walls at Conwy and once discharged into the stream below.

steps at the bottom of which a door was rebated against the wall. Beyond the door was the latrine, the grooves for its wooden seat set in the walls of the recess and the ventilation shaft separating it from its neighbour. A survey of 1306 reported that 'the little houses' required roofs (confirming that originally they were open to the sky as they are today), that their drains were in need of repair and that 'the said houses should be cleansed of refuse, the ducts of the latrines being full of water and filth'.
(*See also* PLUMBING, WATER SUPPLY AND SANITATION)

GARGOYLE From the Old French *gargouille* meaning 'throat', a gargoyle is a projecting gutterstone, sometimes (though not necessarily) incorporating a lead water-spout and often carved to depict a grotesque visage, beast or figure. Its function was to traject rainwater away from the walls and footings of a building. This was particularly important when, in the fourteenth

century, ornamental traceried parapets were developed as a means of finishing off a wall. With no eaves to carry rainwater away from the building, it was necessary to provide lead bow-gutters behind the parapets and gargoyles to discharge the rainwater at regular intervals.

GARRISON Under the Norman kings, service as a member of a castle garrison was a feudal obligation (*see* CASTLE GUARD). A magnate owed a specified number of men for duty in the royal castles and could claim similar services from his own vassals. But in practice the system was singularly inflexible, feudal levies being free to return to their homes once a tour of duty was completed. Consequently the feudal levies were supplemented by mercenaries and by the fifteenth century most members of the comital class were capable of raising substantial retinues through the practice of LIVERY AND MAINTENANCE – a system which came to be known as 'Bastard Feudalism'.

Many castles are so large and their defences so complex that it is easy to imagine that they were once permanently garrisoned with large numbers of armed retainers. But in peacetime a large garrison would have been an expensive and unnecessary affectation, especially for those of the comital class who possessed more than one castle and whose households were peripatetic. Indeed, even in wartime too large a garrison could have been a liability, consuming valuable resources and provisions which might be required to resist a lengthy siege (*see* SIEGES). It follows, therefore, that there must have been an optimum number of men required to maintain an effective defence, depending on the size and complexity of a particular castle. Following Edward I's conquest of Wales in 1284, Caernarfon Castle was garrisoned by forty men and Conwy and Harlech by thirty. Indeed, thirty men succeeded in withstanding sieges at Caernarfon in 1403 and 1404. In peacetime garrisons were sufficient to attend to a castle's security: to mount a watch and to control access. Lesser castles are likely to have been manned by no more than a pair of watchmen and two gate-guards working in shifts, while Caernarfon, the capital of Edward I's new principality, had a peacetime garrison of between twenty and thirty-seven men in addition to the constable and his administrative and domestic staff (*see* HOUSEHOLD). Even during Glyn Dŵr's rising of 1400–13 the garrisons of the Welsh castles rarely exceeded in size those of the Edwardian period. Caernarfon, for example, withstood a prolonged period of isolation when it was often under siege. In 1403, at the height of the blockade, a garrison of thirty-seven archers succeeded in repulsing two fierce attacks by Glyn Dŵr's French allies.

GARTER, THE MOST NOBLE ORDER OF THE Edward III (1327–77) and his court rejoiced in the chivalric ethos of the Arthurian legends (*see* CHIVALRY). Pageants (called 'Round Tables') included TOURNAMENTS at which two teams, each of twelve knights, fought under the leadership of the king and his eldest son, and these were followed by feasting at a circular table. It is likely that from these festivities evolved the notion of a brotherhood of young men, a fellowship in which all were equal, 'to represent how they ought to be united in all Chances and various turns of Fortune, co-partners in both Peace and War, assistant to one another in all serious and dangerous Exploits and through the whole Course of their Lives to show Fidelity and Friendliness towards one another'. The informal creation of the Round Table after the great tournament at Windsor in 1344 was translated, probably on St George's Day 1348, into the Order of the Garter: twenty-four young men together with the king and his eldest son, Edward Plantagenet, the Black Prince. These were the founder knights 'foreshadowing a distinguished line of noble successors throughout the history of English chivalry'. The symbol of the blue garter is traditionally said to have been suggested by an incident at a ball at Calais in the autumn of 1347 when the young countess of Salisbury, Joan of Kent (later to be princess of Wales), dropped her garter which the king retrieved and tied below his knee with the now famous words *Honi soit qui mal y pense* – 'Shame on him who thinks evil of it' – and a promise that the garter would become highly honoured. There may be an element of truth in this, but the garter was not an exclusively female accoutrement (there are numerous contemporary illustrations of its use by men) and it seems likely that it was adopted because of its suitability both as a device (in stylised form) and for its prominence when worn below the knee of a mounted knight. The chapel of the Order, where the knights' banners and crests are displayed above their stalls, and where former knights are commemorated in heraldic stall-plates, is St George's Chapel at Windsor Castle. By the time the chapel was completed by Henry VIII in 1528 the 'flower of English chivalry' had already been decimated on the battlefields of the WARS OF THE ROSES and by the executioner's axe. The idea of a brotherhood of knights enshrined in the Order of the Garter was no longer the reality it had once been. Although modelled on principles of chivalric egalitarianism and humility, it had become a tool to be used for international diplomacy and political alliance. (*See also* KNIGHTHOOD, ORDERS OF)

GARTH Derived from the Middle English *garth* meaning 'enclosed ground used as a yard, paddock, etc.', as in courtyard.

GASCONY *see* AQUITAINE

GATE HALL An atrium within or at the end of a gate passage (*see* GATEHOUSES). Sometimes used as a synonym for GATE PASSAGE.

GATEHOUSES The Romans recognised that the entrance to a fortification was its weakest point. They erected timber towers over the gateways in their rampart forts (there is a convincing replica at Chesterholm) and substantial stone gatehouses at permanent military centres such as Cardiff where the twin-towered North Gate of the castle is, again, an impressive replica. A gatehouse was far more than a simple entrance gate in a castle wall. It was a substantial building intended to make the entrance as impregnable as possible while providing a means of controlling access to the castle. It was therefore the gateway to an earthwork castle or town rampart that was usually the first element of the defences to be rebuilt in stone. Norman curtain walls were usually pierced by arched openings, closed with pairs of stout timber gates and sometimes overlooked by an adjacent tower, a characteristic of several early castles in south Wales including Hay, Ogmore and Newcastle (Glamorgan). (The gateway at Newcastle has been described as the finest example of Romanesque architecture in any Welsh castle.) The Romans had understood that an entrance could be strengthened by lengthening it into a passage with a gate at each end. Several early medieval castles, such as Ludlow, Richmond and Exeter, were provided with square *gate-towers* with a passage leading through the ground floor to the inner ward. In Wales, Carew and Llansteffan Castles have the

earliest examples, the latter (the inner gatehouse) being particularly well preserved. Although stone gate-towers such as these were markedly stronger than a simple gate in a curtain wall, they were still vulnerable to attack because the outer gateway was not visible from the battlements above. The development of the mural tower solved this problem. By positioning flanking towers at either side of the entrance the 'blind spot' at the gate could be observed without the defender revealing himself (*see* TOWERS). The King's Gate and Palace Gate in the inner curtain at Dover Castle are the earliest examples of this type in England, the simple gateways flanked by shallow, square towers.

From this principle there developed the thirteenth-century B-plan or twin-towered gatehouse. This consisted of a pair of round-fronted towers linked above a long stone-vaulted GATE PASSAGE by a chamber in which were the mechanisms for portcullises (*see* PORTCULLIS). Medieval castles, and gate passages in particular, were designed on the principle of retreating defence. As an attacking force succeeded in overcoming each obstacle (barbican,

Cutaway reconstruction of the gate passage at Harlech Castle (c. 1283) showing the complex arrangement of double doors with drawbeams, portcullises and murder holes.

drawbridge, doors, portcullises, etc.) so they would be drawn into successive KILLING GROUNDS and attacked through loopholes in the side walls of the passage and MURDER HOLES in the floor of the chamber above. (At Caernarfon Castle the passage in the King's Gate contained five pairs of doors, six portcullises and numerous murder holes.) However, the principal function of a murder hole (or *meurtrière*) was for the rapid discharge of water to extinguish fires set by assailants at the foot of a wooden gate or portcullis or in a drawbridge pit (*see* DRAWBRIDGE). (It was also to protect against fire that gate passages were almost invariably vaulted with stone.) On either side of the gate passage were GUARDROOMS and a PORTER'S LODGE, often accessible only from within the gatehouse, with fireplaces and GARDEROBES and containing the DRAW-BARS which secured a series of stout double doors. The twin-towered gatehouse of Montgomery Castle was probably the earliest example of its type in Britain (*c.* 1223), though in this case the bases of the flanking towers were constructed of solid masonry. There were similar early thirteenth-century gatehouses at Pembroke (effectively an early KEEP-GATEHOUSE) and at Chepstow (replacing an even

earlier single tower), while the twin-towered gatehouse at the native Welsh castle of Criccieth is now believed to be a later Edwardian addition (*see* WALES: NATIVE CASTLES).

One of the earliest residential gatehouses, and one that undoubtedly influenced later designs, was Hubert de Burgh's massive edifice at Henry III's castle at Dover. De Burgh, the king's chief justiciar, extensively remodelled the castle following the siege of 1216–17 during which King John's gatehouse had been undermined, causing one of its flanking towers to collapse. The remodelling included the closing of this vulnerable northern gate with a group of three substantial towers (the Norfolk Towers) and the creation of a new opening on the steep western slope with a huge gatehouse which thrusts forward across the dry moat from the outer curtain. Known as the Constable's Gate, it comprises a cluster of rounded towers of different sizes, the whole curving backwards and dominating all angles of approach. The spurred base of each of the front-facing half-round towers descends deep into the moat while the entrance to the gate passage was protected by projecting flanking towers. The towers at the rear of the gatehouse incorporated a suite of residential

The massive gatehouse, known as the Constable's Gate, at Dover Castle, Kent (c. 1216).

The Eastern Inner Gatehouse at Caerphilly dominates the castle and was clearly conceived both as a heavily fortified entrance and a self-contained residence for the constable, capable of independent defence should insurrection or mutiny threaten.

chambers for the constable and his household. The Constable's Gate could only be approached along the crest of the rampart beyond the moat and was further protected by an elongated BARBICAN. It has been accurately described as the most elaborate gateway to any British castle.

The twin-towered gatehouse reached its apogee in the late thirteenth century when its various elements (towers, passage and upper chambers) were brought together in a unified whole. There can be little doubt that when he was charged with designing Edward I's castles in north Wales (*see* WALES, CONQUEST OF) Master JAMES OF ST GEORGE was influenced by Gilbert de Clare's revolutionary concentric castle at Caerphilly (begun in *c.* 1268) and by his massive gatehouse at Tonbridge which was visited by Edward shortly after its completion in 1275. Tonbridge is a perfect example of a *keep-gatehouse* that could be isolated from the rest of the castle and defended independently if necessary. Its two half-cylindrical towers were built on square plinths and flank a long gate passage that was protected by two portcullises, three rows of murder holes and two pairs of gates. Inner gates prevented access from the bailey and doors to the wall-walks were protected by portcullises. Caerphilly Castle was provided with concentric rings of water defences, curtain walls,

mural towers, barbicans and no fewer than seven twin-towered gatehouses (*see* CONCENTRIC CASTLES *and* MOATS AND WATER DEFENCES). The larger of two great gatehouses in the inner curtain (the Eastern Inner Gatehouse) is almost identical to that at Tonbridge. It dominates the castle and was clearly conceived both as a heavily fortified entrance and a self-contained residence for the CONSTABLE, capable of independent defence should insurrection or mutiny threaten. At the inner end of the passage a pair of stout timber doors closed against the courtyard while at the outer end another pair of doors closed against the raised drawbridge. The only doorways led into guardrooms on either side of the passage while stairs to the upper floors were enclosed within turrets. Again, the doorways leading to the curtain wall-walks were provided with portcullises. First-floor windows were uniformly small, the only large windows (two) being in the hall which was located on the upper floor so that the drawbridge and portcullis mechanisms did not intrude. Undoubtedly this major residential keep-gatehouse was the model for the Edwardian masterpieces at Harlech (1283–9) and Beaumaris (1295–6), though both were compromised defensively by the insertion of large first-floor windows in the Constable's Hall (*see* KEEP-

GATEHOUSE). Had they been completed, the twin gatehouses at Beaumaris would have been the largest keep-gatehouses of all. Each would have contained a gate passage, porter's lodge and guardrooms on the ground floor while on the first and second floors there would have been residential suites each comprising a hall, offices and chambers. But why was it considered necessary to provide two halls and two lavishly appointed suites of rooms in each of the gatehouses? Assuming that the constable of Beaumaris would have occupied one of the four gatehouse suites, who would have occupied the other three? At Caernarfon there is evidence that various of the king's officials were provided with accommodation in the vicinity of the castle. Perhaps the sheriff of Anglesey and the king's chamberlain were to have enjoyed similar privileges at Beaumaris? Or perhaps the architect, James of St George, anticipated the castle being used by the king and his considerable entourage more frequently than it was. Had it been completed, the castle would have housed five self-contained suites and nineteen other rooms, each with a fireplace and private latrine. In the event Edward's rapidly diminishing resources were increasingly directed towards Scotland and the great gatehouses of Beaumaris were never completed.

The gatehouse at the Marcher stronghold of Denbigh is an extraordinary triangular complex of three formidable hexagonal towers, each measuring more than 12.2m (40ft) in diameter, similar to that which was intended for the King's Gate at Caernarfon. The upper floors of the gatehouse incorporated a hall and chambers for the constable while the gate passage gave access to a large hexagonal atrium or *gate hall* from which a further passage led past the third of the towers to the courtyard beyond. Originally, there were no other doors leading off the central atrium which would have been a death-trap for any attacker who succeeded in penetrating that far. At Dunstanburgh Castle in Northumberland the presence of the drawbridge and portcullis mechanisms rendered the first-floor chambers of the gatehouse so incommodious that in the 1380s John of Gaunt blocked the gate passage and created a new entrance, defended by a barbican, in an adjacent curtain wall. Dunstanburgh's keep-gatehouse effectively became a *donjon*, used both as a residence and as a final refuge.

This type of twin-towered gatehouse was also constructed, on a smaller scale, in the walls of several towns, notably at Caernarfon and at Conwy where the upper chambers of the Mill Gate were occupied by the Controller of the Wardrobe, the royal secretariat (*see* TOWN WALLS). (It is interesting to note that, because of the limitations of its site, the castle at Conwy was entered not by a major gatehouse but by a heavily protected barbican.)

In many respects an *outer gatehouse* performed precisely the same function as a gatehouse in a town wall. As the term suggests, it was a secondary gatehouse, intended as a preliminary line of defence and as a means of checking the credentials of those who wished to enter the outer BAILEY but not the *inner sanctum* of the castle itself. At White Castle, for example, a simple twin-towered gatehouse guarded the entrance to the inner ward, while the large outer ward was entered through a gatehouse with square flanking towers, a gate passage and a chamber above for the portcullis and drawbridge mechanisms. Outer gatehouses are sometimes described erroneously as barbicans but they are invariably located at too great a remove from a principal gatehouse for this term to apply (*see* BARBICAN).

Simple gate-towers (*see above*) continued in use throughout the medieval period, often as secondary gates, while the fourteenth century saw a return to the rectilinear gatehouse in which the flanking towers were retained but only as subsidiary elements in the overall design. In gates such as Bootham Bar and Micklegate Bar in York's city walls the twin towers were reduced to ineffectual buttresses and turrets.

Nevertheless, gatehouses had their part to play in the ostentatious embellishment of several late fourteenth-century castles, refurbished from the proceeds of the French wars (*see* HUNDRED YEARS WAR). The gatehouse of Warwick Castle, for example, is the quintessence of the twin-towered design, the centre-piece of the Beauchamp earls' remodelling of the castle's glorious west front in which the emphasis is on height and dramatic effect. The towers on either side of the gateway are bound together into a solid building that rises for three storeys above the entrance passage with tall, embattled turrets at each corner and a heavily crenellated parapet. In front of the entrance is a massive projecting barbican with parallel embattled walls, each terminating in a polygonal turret. The long, narrow gate passage was defended by its gates, portcullises, murder holes and two drawbridges, while the approach was further protected by strategically disposed triple battlements on the barbican, the gatehouse and the gatehouse turrets which are linked by arched embattled bridges. The whole façade is a majestic piece of chivalric theatricality, the splendid Caesar's Tower financed by ransoms collected by the earl of Warwick after the English victory at Poitiers in 1356.

Whatever the reason for the castle's decline, many fortresses were abandoned and allowed to decay or were quarried for building materials (*see* DECLINE OF THE CASTLE). Others followed the French fashion and were converted into comfortable residences, the lofty towers and machicolated parapets of Raglan and Kenilworth, Warwick and Powis adding a flourish of ancient grandeur to the country seats of Tudor gentlemen. But while curtain walls were sometimes demolished or reduced and drawbridges replaced by more permanent structures of brick and stone, the tradition of the fortified gatehouse lingered on in sixteenth-century England (*see* MANOR HOUSES). Security, of course, remained an important consideration. It was also necessary to provide a façade with a satisfying architectural climax. But in the sixteenth century there seems also to have been an inherent desire to recollect antiquity, to proclaim architecturally a link with a noble past in an age when 'new men' were everywhere perceived to be usurping the traditional values of the 'old order'. The great multi-storeyed gatehouse at Layer Marney (*c.* 1520) was built in brick on such a scale that it was clearly intended to be the showpiece of a great country mansion. With its eight-storey turrets, multiple tiers of windows, miniature shell-gables and Italianate terracotta ornamentation, Layer Marney belongs not to the Middle Ages but to the dawning northern Renaissance.

(*See also* ECCLESIASTICAL STRONGHOLDS, POSTERN, QUAYS (*for* water gates) *and* SALLY-PORT)

GATEHOUSE-TOWER *see* KEEP-GATEHOUSE

GATEKEEPER'S LODGE *see* PORTER'S LODGE

GATE PASSAGE In the gatehouse or barbican of a castle or fortified town, the principal entrance passage through which entry and egress were controlled (*see* BARBICAN, GATEHOUSES, GUARDROOM, MURDER HOLES, PORTCULLIS *and* PORTER'S LODGE).

GATE-TOWER A tower containing a GATE PASSAGE (*see* GATEHOUSES).

GAUNTLET Protective covering for the hand, wrist and lower forearm, usually of plate (*see* ARMOUR).

GENTLEMAN In the Middle Ages the word *gentil* meant 'noble' and no social distinction existed between the English nobility and gentry prior to the emergence of a parliamentary peerage (*see* NOBILITY AND GENTRY). It was in the early fifteenth century that persons of some social standing began describing themselves as 'gentlemen' and it is likely that this was associated with ARMIGEROUS status. A statute of Henry V (1413–22) required that in certain legal documents the 'estate, degree or mystery' of a defendant must be stated, and the style 'gentleman' came into use to signify a condition between ESQUIRE and YEOMAN. The term *les gentiles* was used in an act of parliament of 1429 to describe men holding freehold property of 40*s* a year or more. From the sixteenth century the term seems to have been applied to all those who were not required to labour and therefore employed servants.

GENTRY *see* GENTLEMAN *and* NOBILITY AND GENTRY

GEOMETRIC STYLE *see* GOTHIC ARCHITECTURE

GIPON *see* JUPON

GISARME *see* WEAPONS AND HARNESS

GLACIS *or* TALUS (i) The outward slope of a wall. (ii) In post-medieval fortifications, the outward-sloping parapet of a covered way.

GLACIS RAMPART A rampart constructed of stone, earth or spoil.

GLASS *see* GLAZING, STAINED GLASS *and* WINDOWS

GLAZING Glass for WINDOWS was manufactured throughout the Roman Empire and many Romano-British houses had glazed windows. But after the withdrawal of Rome in AD 410 the craft of glass-making was all but lost and domestic window glass became a rare and costly luxury enjoyed only by those who could afford to import glass from continental Europe. By the mid-twelfth century the majority of church windows were glazed (often with pictorial glass), but the window openings of domestic chambers were often filled with ingenious substitutes such as thin sheets of alabaster or horn, oiled linen, paper or parchment treated with gum arabic and pieces of mica (*see also* SHUTTERS). An unusually elaborate example occurs in the Windsor Castle accounts for 1426–7: 'To John Horstede, joiner, of Windsor for making a fenestral of wood for a window in the chapel called Gaille on the south, 4d.

For linen cloth bought of Isabel Northfolke for the said fenestral, 8½d. Paid to Thomas Fletcher for the waxing of the said fenestral, 14d. Paid to Thomas Stanynour of Windsor for painting the fenestral like a glass window, 4d.' However, at this late date and in such an important building, it is likely that this was a temporary measure, intended to fill a space while a glass window was being repaired. In the chapels, halls and private apartments of royal and magnate castles white or pictorial glass was used from at least the second quarter of the twelfth century (*see* STAINED GLASS). Indeed, glazing was not confined to large windows: in 1238 Henry III ordered that a garderobe window at Westminster should be glazed 'So that the chamber may not be so draughty as it has been.' By the sixteenth century window glass was more widely used but was still an expensive commodity which had to be protected by wooden lattices and sometimes even removed when the occupants were away from home.

Techniques
The small quantities of glass made in medieval Britain were generally of inferior quality to that which could be obtained from Europe, especially from northern France (*Normandy Glass*), north-west Germany (*Rhenish Glass*) and Flanders where quantities of pure white sand were readily available. Contemporary English glass was usually manufactured locally using immediately available materials and producing glass of a grey or green-brown colour, mostly for bottles and inferior glazing.

The ingredients required for glass-making were soda ash, pure silica sand and lime. The presence of a minute quantity of an impurity would affect the transparency, consistency and colour of the glass. Producing and sustaining the extremely high temperatures required for the successful fusion of the ingredients must have been a formidable problem and melting was generally carried out in two or more stages in stone or brick furnaces.

Prior to the eighteenth century *cylinder glass* (also known as *broad glass, green glass* and *muff glass*) was hand-blown by the cylinder method. The molten glass (*metal*) was gathered on to the blowpipe and blown into a sphere. Then, by swinging and twisting it in the air, the craftsman would blow the sphere into a hollow cylindrical 'sack' which was then cut open (with the 'ends' removed) and flattened and cooled into a rectangular panel. Cooling took place in an *annealing oven* which permitted the glass to cool gradually, thereby avoiding unnecessary stresses that would make the finished glass brittle.

Medieval panels of cylinder glass were small, generally 63 by 38cm (25 by 15in).

An account of 1287 for the Tower of London provides an indication of the cost of glazing: 'For 2 new glass windows in the great hall, made in colours, being of 66 ft., at 10d. the foot, 55s.; also for 160 ft. of glass for 10 windows in the said hall and in the small hall and the king's chamber, at 4d. the foot, 53s. 4d.; also for 4 windows of coloured glass, containing 40 ft., at 6d. a foot, 20s.' The glass quoted at 4*d* was white (clear) glass, that at 10*d* elaborate picture work, and that at 6*d* may have been GRISAILLE, glass to which a delicate silver-grey coating of paint was applied, often with lightly painted leaf and stem patterns on a background of cross-hatching and interlaced strapwork. There are many references in contemporary accounts to so-called stained-glass windows: the thirteenth-century Guildford windows, referred to above, were to be 'closed with white glass . . . and in one half of the glass window a king sitting on a throne and in the other half a queen, also sitting on a throne'. Typical of the fifteenth century is an account of 1402 for the royal palace of Eltham: 'For 91 square feet of new glass, diapered and worked with broom flowers, eagles and scrolls inscribed *Soueraigne*, bought of William Burgh, glasier, for 3 bay windows and side lights, each of 2 lights, at 3s. 4d. a foot. And for 54 square feet of new glass worked with figures and canopies, the field made in the likeness of cloth of gold, bought from the same William for 3 windows, each of 2 lights, in the new oratory, at 3s. 4d. the foot.' Sometimes windows were bought 'ready made'. At the palace of Westminster in 1322 John de Walworth supplied windows of white glass at 4*d* the foot and payments were made 'for land and water carriage of the said windows and glass from Kandelwekstrete [now Cannon Street] to Westminster'. In 1351–2 a team of glaziers from a Westminster workshop was engaged to glaze a series of windows in the chapel at Windsor Castle. When these were completed, boards and nails were purchased 'to make cases for carrying [by water] the glass panels from Westminster to Wyndesore', and 14*d* paid 'for hay and straw to put in the said cases for safe keeping of the glass panels'.

GLAZING BARS *see* WINDOWS

GLORIETTE A local name given to a range of residential buildings set round an open courtyard in the inner bailey of Corfe Castle, Dorset. These royal apartments (1200–5) included the kitchens, the Queen's Chamber and Parlour to the north and west, the Long Chamber to the south and the Great Hall or King's Chamber to the east. In the corner between the Long Chamber and the Great Hall was the King's Chapel. The Gloriette Tower in the south-east corner of the inner ward was also named 'Plenty'. Corfe was one of King John's favourite residences and the few surviving window mouldings suggest that his Gloriette was an embryo courtyard house of considerable sophistication and elegance (*see also* HOUSEHOLD).

Another Gloriette is to be found at Leeds Castle in Kent. The castle was rebuilt by Edward I (after 1278) on two islands, the smaller one (the *parva mota*) consisting of a plinth on which stands an unusual D-shaped open tower known as the Gloriette. Edward may have built this tower as an 'inner sanctum' of private apartments, linked with the main island by a timber causeway and drawbridge (long since replaced with stone). The tower is similar in structure to a miniature SHELL-KEEP enclosing a tiny courtyard and was much extended and improved first by Edward III and later by Henry VIII.

GNOMON *see* SUNDIALS

GOAT'S-FOOT LEVER *see* ARCHERY

GONFANON *or* **GONFALON** A flag supported by means of a horizontal pole suspended by cords from the top of a staff. Probably (in shape) a descendant of the Roman *vexillum*, in Britain the gonfanon has generally been associated with the church and with guilds and fraternities and was widely used for processional purposes.
(*See also* FLAGS)

GONGES *see* GARDEROBE *and* PLUMBING, WATER SUPPLY AND SANITATION

GONGFERMOR One who was responsible for scouring and cleansing cess-pits (*see* PLUMBING, WATER SUPPLY AND SANITATION).

GOOD LORDSHIP The obligation of a lord to support the 'just cause' of a feudal inferior, often a member of his AFFINITY.

GORGE The rear of a fortification, e.g. the neck of a BASTION.

GORGET A collar of plate armour designed to protect the neck, shoulders and chest. In use from the fifteenth century, the gorget was usually made in two pieces and was either hinged or pivoted on a rivet and secured by means of a stud and keyhole. (*See also* ARMOUR *and* HELMETS)

GOTHIC ARCHITECTURE The architectural style current in medieval Europe from the late twelfth century to the mid-sixteenth. Although the term is widely used in the context of church architecture, it is equally applicable to those parts of a castle which were used primarily for domestic and religious purposes (*see* CHAPEL, GREAT CHAMBER *and* HALL), though the ornate window tracery and VAULTING by which Gothic architecture is now defined have rarely survived because of the depredations of warfare, weather and dereliction. Complete examples of vaulting, for example, are most often found in UNDERCROFTS and cellars which, because of their location, have survived the ravages of time. Inevitably, the best preserved examples of Gothic architecture are to be found in ecclesiastical buildings rather than castles, and it is to these that the reader is referred.

The term 'Gothic' was first used by the sixteenth-century painter, architect and historian Giorgio Vasari (1511–74) to imply disapprobation of all things medieval. To the post-Renaissance mind, Gothic architecture symbolised barbarism, while classicism represented the intellect: the verticality of faith versus the horizontality of enlightenment.

There were four phases of the Gothic style, each dependent on that which preceded it and fashioning that which followed. Each phase grew further away from the solidity which characterised ROMAN-ESQUE architecture and closer to the 'seemingly ethereal fragility' (Yarwood) of the late fifteenth century. Above all, the medieval architect was attempting to achieve an appearance of lightness and elegance in direct contrast to the heavy sturdiness of the Romanesque, and unlike Classical and Renaissance buildings the great medieval monastic and collegiate churches were therefore conceived from the inside outwards. It was this relentless quest for unattainable perfection (equated in the medieval mind with the greater glorification of God) that inspired architecture of the most extraordinary ingenuity and audacity and in particular the development of the stone vault and abutment. The 'heavenward thrust' of glass and stone created that feeling of ascension which is the essence of Gothic architecture. And yet these great medieval buildings are essentially functional: every piece of stone is critical to the equilibrium of the building and (as at Richard Rogers' twentieth-century Lloyd's building in London) no part of the structure is deliberately

GOTHIC ARCHITECTURE

concealed. Like a house of cards, weight is distributed and structural stability maintained by translating the outward thrust of an ARCH into the downward thrust of a corresponding pier or BUTTRESS. Nothing is superfluous: even a pinnacle is part of the structural equation, adding its weight to a buttress or corner tower. As the Middle Ages progressed so too did man's understanding of structure and his ability to apply new engineering techniques. Buildings became larger, higher, lighter and the geometry ever more complex.

The familiar Gothic classification of *Norman*, *Early English*, *Decorated* and *Perpendicular* was devised by Thomas Rickman (1776–1841) and first published in his book *An Attempt to Discriminate the Styles of English Architecture from the Conquest to the Reformation*. Other forms of classification have been advocated but those which attempt to apply specific dates to what was essentially an evolutionary process ignore both transitional elements, which are present in the gradual movement of one architectural phase to the next, and significant regional variations. Furthermore, architectural features were often added to those of an earlier period: at Gloucester Cathedral, for example, a fourteenth-century remodelling of the eleventh-century choir resulted in the construction of a spectacular perpendicular stone-ribbed 'cage' which masked the original Romanesque arcade and was extended upwards into a magnificent new clerestory and vault.

Rickman's *Norman* period is that which is now described as English ROMANESQUE and is easily recognised through the builders' preoccupation with solidity, exemplified by massively thick walling, small window openings and arcades of immense pillars supporting 'rounded' (semicircular) arches (though experimentation with the pointed arch and ribbed vault began in *c.* 1130).

The *Early English* period (also *First Pointed* or *Lancet*, from the characteristic narrow, pointed *lancet window*) is endowed with a certain austerity of form and a beauty of proportion best seen (in its most developed form) at Salisbury Cathedral in Wiltshire, built between 1200 and 1275. Typically, the vaulting has plain quadripartite ribbing; tiers of lancet WINDOWS pierce the walls of the aisles, clerestory and transepts in pairs and threes; and the tall piers of the nave have clustered shafts (of black Purbeck marble) and simple moulded capitals in a characteristic inverted bell form. The Early English period established the form of Gothic architecture. Later periods expanded on it, in particular through the development of complex vaulting and buttressing which enabled larger areas of wall space to be devoted to glass.

The need for *window tracery* (ornamental stone mouldings within a window) arose from the Early English practice of grouping two or more lancet windows beneath a single arch head (*hood-mould* or *dripstone*) which was intended to direct rainwater away from the openings. This created an awkward space (*spandrel*) between the window openings and the arch head, which at first was carved and pierced to provide the earliest form of tracery (*plate tracery*). From this simple device developed a variety of forms by which the Gothic phases are most readily identified. From the mid-thirteenth century single windows were divided by slender stone 'bars' (*bar tracery*) to provide larger areas of glass, one of the earliest forms being *Y-tracery* in which a Y-shaped mullion divided the window into two narrow vertical lights and a smaller top light. This later developed into *intersecting tracery* in which two or more mullions intersect each other in curves at the head of the arch.

The *Decorated* period (also *Curvilinear*, *Flamboyant* or *Geometric*) refers to the *Middle Pointed* style of window tracery which lasted from *c.* 1275 to *c.* 1375. The increased width of buildings, achieved through advances in vaulting, had created a need for greater internal illumination: windows became larger and wider and clerestories higher. This in turn increased the height of the building and resulted in the development of the *arch buttress* (or *flying buttress*) which conveys the thrust of the vault and main roof over and beyond the outer walls (*see* BUTTRESS). The increase in window size was accommodated by an equilateral arch and several mullions giving three, five, seven and even nine lights and ever more complex tracery. At first this was essentially geometrical with circles, quatrefoils and trefoils, but in the fourteenth century *flowing* or *curvilinear tracery* evolved, based on the OGEE form of double-curving lines producing flowing flame-like shapes. *Reticulated tracery* was a development of this, circles forming a lattice of ogee shapes. Decoration also became more elaborate in the form of stone carving, coloured window glass and painted and gilded stonework. The nave of Exeter Cathedral in Devon (1275–1369) is a superb example of this period.

The final, and by far the longest, of Rickman's periods was the *Perpendicular*, which lasted from the late fourteenth century to the end of the fifteenth (when it became *Tudor Gothic*). Characteristic of the period is the delicate vertical tracery of windows and stone panelling (from which the term 'perpendicular' is derived) with regular horizontal divisions and slender fluted pillars leading upwards into an

Gothic Window Tracery
1 Y-tracery (13th century)
2 Intersecting tracery (13th century)
3 Geometrical tracery (early 14th century)

4 Reticulated tracery (14th century)
5 Panel tracery (late 14th century)
6 Panel tracery (late 15th and early 16th centuries)

exuberance of intricate fan-shaped vaulting (known as *fan vaulting*), as exemplified in the magnificent Chapel of King's College, Cambridge (1446–1515), and Henry VI's Chapel in Westminster Abbey (1503–19). Windows of the period are significantly wider and the arches flatter, those of the late Perpendicular and Tudor Gothic periods being of the *four-centre* type (*see* ARCH). *Reticulated* or *panel tracery* features both in windows and in wall panels and is characteristic of British architecture of the period. This form of tracery incorporates both mullions and transoms thereby creating rows of small glass 'panels', with more complex tracery confined to the upper tiers within the arch.

Many earlier buildings were remodelled at this time (*see* Gloucester *above*) including both Winchester and Canterbury Cathedrals where the naves were rebuilt. These late Gothic builders very nearly achieved the perfection sought by their thirteenth-century predecessors. Their buildings are lofty, spacious and brilliant with a minimum of masonry supporting a maximum of glass. But in the over-elaboration of detail they fall short of that ideal.
(*See also* BALL-FLOWER ORNAMENTATION *and* TUDOR ARCHITECTURE)

GOTHICK (NEO-GOTHICK) A derogatory term used to describe the excesses of romantic medievalism in late eighteenth- and nineteenth-century literature, architecture, etc.

GOTHIC REVIVAL Despite a preoccupation with 'authenticity', Gothic Revival (post-1840) restorations of castles do not possess the vitality of their prototypes and are immediately recognisable. Gothic architecture took over four hundred years to evolve: the setting in place of every stone was innovative and dependent on the cumulative experience of generations of skilled craftsmen. The Gothic Revival was based on inflexible precepts: rigid guidelines for Gothic design which were set out in *The Ecclesiologist*, the journal of the ecclesiological movement which promoted the 'Middle Pointed' period of the late thirteenth and early fourteenth centuries as the only pure architectural style (*see* GOTHIC ARCHITECTURE).

GOTHIC TRACERY *see* GOTHIC ARCHITECTURE

GOVERNMENT In medieval England the government of the country was carried out by the king's Council which sat almost continuously and was composed of lords temporal and spiritual as well as able men of lesser rank. Although all the business of the Council was carried out in the king's name, his presence was not necessary for it to function. Its chief duties were to assist the king in the formulation of policy and to conduct the day-to-day business of government. Parliament had a subsidiary function, although its powers increased throughout the fifteenth century. It comprised the *three estates of the realm*: the lords spiritual, the lords temporal and the commons who were represented by the *knights of the shires* and burgesses from the boroughs. Elections were frequently manipulated by the magnates who attempted to pack parliament with members of their affinities. Parliament's chief functions were the granting of taxation and the consideration of petitions. It was also the supreme court of justice. The king could summon and dismiss parliament at will and it could be called upon to meet anywhere in the kingdom. New laws could not be enacted without the consent of parliament, neither could the king go to war. 'The king declares his intentions and asks for aid from his subjects; he cannot raise any tax in England except for an expedition to France or Scotland or some other comparable cause. They will grant them very willingly, especially for going to France!' (Philippe Commines).

GRAFFITI Graffiti – writing or drawings scratched on walls and glass – come in a variety of shapes and sizes and from all periods. Graffiti are a useful, though as yet incoherent, source of historical evidence which includes glaziers' marks, masons' marks, merchants' marks and carpenters' and plumbers' marks. The value of MASONS' MARKS is in the contribution they can make to detailed studies of individual buildings, and the various phases of construction. Carpenters' marks, both signatures and assembly marks, are invaluable when considering the construction of a timber roof or floor, while plumbers' and glaziers' marks serve to identify individual craftsmen and workshops and to date their work. Such marks are commonly found in churches, where the fabric is generally better preserved, but less often in castles.

Perhaps the most common graffiti found in castles are the initials, dates and (often enigmatic) patterns engraved on the walls of chambers and in the stonework of window openings by generations of visitors – demonstrating that vandalism is not a recent phenomenon. Some graffiti are of genuine artistic merit (*see* CHAPELS) while most are simply vernacular and a few are deliberately vulgar and offensive. Undoubtedly the most interesting are graffiti carved in the walls of former prisons. The best known examples (and the best preserved) are in the Beauchamp Tower at the Tower of London, used almost exclusively to lodge prisoners of rank during the fifteenth and sixteenth centuries (*see* PRISONS). The Beauchamp Tower consists of three storeys and dates from the reign of Edward I (1272–1307). It is entered at the south-east corner and a circular stair ascends to the middle chamber where are found most of the graffiti, some of which have been brought from other chambers. There are others in the entrance passage and on the stairs. All are numbered and catalogued, and most are of sufficiently high quality to be described as *mural inscriptions* rather than graffiti. They include, to the right of the fireplace, an

Elaborate plaque and mural inscription in the Beauchamp Tower at the Tower of London.

elaborate piece of sculpture which is effectively a memorial to the five brothers Dudley: Ambrose (created earl of Warwick in 1561), Guildford (beheaded in 1554), Robert (created earl of Leicester in 1564), and Henry (killed at the siege of St Quentin in 1557), carved by the eldest, John (called earl of Warwick), who died in 1554. Beneath a bear and lion supporting a ragged staff is the name 'JOHN DVDLE' and surrounding them is a wreath of roses (for Ambrose), oak leaves (for Robert, *robur* = 'oak'), gillyflowers (for Guildford) and honeysuckle (for Henry). Below are four lines of text (one incomplete) in which the meaning of the various devices is explained. There are many other heraldic shields, cyphers and rebuses in the Beauchamp Tower, including the letter A surmounting a bell for Dr Thomas Abell, chaplain and faithful servant of Queen Catherine of Aragon, first wife of Henry VIII, who championed her cause with such determined advocacy that he offended the king, was condemned for denying the royal supremacy and was executed in 1540.
(*See also* CYPHER *and* REBUS)

GRAND SALLE The 'great hall' of a castle, used for ceremonial purposes (*see* HALL).

GRANGE An outlying farm usually, though not invariably, monastic.

GREAT CHAMBER *see* SOLAR

GREAT CROSSBOW *see* ARCHERY

GREAT GATEHOUSE-TOWER *see* KEEP-GATEHOUSE

GREAT HALL *see* HALL

GREAT HELM *or* **HEAUME** Also referred to as a *barrel helm*, a large cylindrical helmet of plate metal riveted together with a flat or rounded top, eye slits (*sights*) and ventilation holes (*breathes*). The great helm first appeared in Europe in the early thirteenth century, when it was worn over an arming cap and mail COIF, and was superseded by the visored BASCINET in the early fifteenth century. The early, flat-topped style of great helm is sometimes referred to as a *pot-helm*.
(*See also* ARMOUR *and* HELMETS)

GREAT REVOLT *see* PEASANTS' REVOLT

GREAT ROLLS OF THE EXCHEQUER *see* PIPE ROLLS

GREAT SEAL The first 'great' seal of England was probably that of Edward the Confessor (1003–66) but it is more practicable to trace the development of the Great Seal from the reign of William I (1066–87) who used a seal with the *majesty* copied from that of Henri II of France (a depiction of the king seated in state) and on the obverse an equestrian figure, also of the king. Subsequently, the faces were reversed, the majesty becoming the obverse and the equestrian the reverse. The Great Seal is used to authenticate important documents issued in the name of the sovereign and the matrix is held by the Lord Chancellor who was sometimes also referred to as the Lord Keeper (of the Seal).
(*See also* CHANCERY, PRIVY SEAL *and* SEALS)

GREAT TOWER A medieval tower was effectively a horizontal residence built vertically for reasons of security. From the sixteenth century the term KEEP was used to describe the great tower (*magnus turris*) or DONJON of a castle. The great tower was a fortified residence, up to six storeys in height, with thick walls, battlemented parapets and a well-protected entrance (*see* FOREBUILDING), all surrounded by a walled enclosure (*see* BAILEY). A great tower could be square, rectangular, triangular, cylindrical, polygonal or D-shaped in plan and built of timber (*see* MOTTE), stone or brick (*see* BRICK

BUILDINGS). It was a final refuge into which a garrison could retreat should the outer defences of the castle be captured and occupied by an enemy. Another type of castle, the ENCLOSURE CASTLE, depended for its defence on encircling curtain walls, mural towers and a formidable GATEHOUSE rather than a single great tower.
(*See also* HALL-KEEP)

GREAVES Plate armour protecting the lower leg. In use from the second half of the thirteenth century, *demi-greaves* were single 'shin pads' which protected only the front and sides of the leg, while the later *grèves closes* comprised a pair of hinged plates which completely enclosed the lower leg.
(*See also* ARMOUR)

GREEK FIRE A combustible material used in medieval warfare, especially against timber ships and fortifications. Possibly first used by the Greeks when besieged in Constantinople (673–8), it was widely used by the Byzantine Empire. Almost certainly the main ingredient was naphtha (crude oil) though the recipe was a closely guarded secret. Greek fire could be projected through a tube (like a modern flame-thrower) and would explode on impact.

GREENSAND A Cretaceous sandstone carrying the green iron-bearing mineral glaucomite.

GRISAILLE Thirteenth- and fourteenth-century window glass to which a delicate silver-grey coating of paint was applied often with lightly painted leaf and stem patterns on a background of cross-hatching and interlaced strapwork. Such glass remains translucent and enhances the coolness and tranquillity of an interior. In the fourteenth century colourful painted and STAINED GLASS motifs, including human figures and armorial devices, were often inserted in the grisaille.

GROAT *see* COINAGE

GROIN The junction of two curved surfaces in a vault.

GROIN VAULT *see* GROIN *and* VAULTING

GUARDROOM The quarters of a castle guard. A garrison would comprise a number of units, one of which would always be on guard duty. In many castles the guardroom was adjacent to the gate passage in a gatehouse so that access and egress could be controlled.
(*See also* PORTER'S LODGE)

GUETTE A watch-tower.

GUIDON *see* FLAGS

GUIENNE *or* **GUYENNE** *see* AQUITAINE

GUIGE A strap fitted to the inside of a shield so that it could be carried over the shoulder.
(*See also* ARMOUR, ENARMES *and* SHIELDS)

GUILDS (*also* GILDS) Guilds derive their twelfth-century origins from the religious fraternities that evolved round a church, monastery or hospice to which they attached themselves and whose saint they adopted as their patron. Members of those fraternities who lived together often worked together in a common trade or craft, and they developed into mutual protection societies making provision for the poor, sick and needy in their communities and promoting the interests of their crafts including apprenticeship and the power of search which gave each company the right to inspect all goods handled by its members. This gave craft guilds an effective weapon against competition from strangers to their city and a constructive measure to keep their own members in line and maintain high standards of work and so make the guild stronger. The medieval guilds were concerned with the welfare of their members' families in this world and the next and many enjoyed the patronage of influential magnates who supported financially the provision of guild chantries, hospices and alms-houses (*see* CHANTRY). Craft guilds were strictly local: the fact that a man was a member of a guild in his own town gave him no right to exercise his craft elsewhere. This was an inconvenient form of organisation for many craftsmen (notably the masons) who were constantly moving from one site to another. Consequently we find that the local, permanent guild was often replaced by temporary associations of craftsmen centred on a 'lodge' or workshop where they were employed.

GULES The heraldic term for red (*see* TINCTURES).

GUN EMBRASURE An opening in a wall, splayed on the inside, to accommodate a gun (*see* EMBRASURE, FIREARMS AND CANNON *and* GUN PORTS).

GUN PORTS, GUN-LOOPS *and* SHOT-HOLES Early gun ports for hand-guns are simple circular openings (*loops*) in curtain walls, towers and gatehouses. They first appeared in southern England

Gunports at Raglan Castle, Monmouthshire.

An arrow loop in the north-east tower of Carreg Cennen Castle was blocked and converted to a gunport in the fifteenth century.

in the fourteenth century, probably in response to French raids, and resemble in shape an inverted keyhole: a circular opening with a vertical sighting slit above. There are many examples including those at Bodiam Castle, Canterbury, Southampton and the Byward Tower at the Tower of London. Cruciform LOOPHOLES were sometimes modified for this purpose by the addition of a circular opening at the foot of the lower limb, or by the enlargement of an existing opening in an OILLET. Fifteenth-century Raglan Castle in Monmouthshire has a series of small, circular gun ports beneath the ground-floor windows and at basement level in the gatehouse range. These could not have been particularly effective and were probably intended as a deterrent. Floor-level gun ports in the Kitchen Tower pierce the back wall of the kitchen fireplace! The brick-built Great Tower at Caister Castle, Norfolk, has circular gun ports at several levels and these were employed on at least two occasions, one of them in 1458 against French incursions. Portcullises were sometimes modified to incorporate a gun port or a barricade for hand-gunners, as at the Byward Tower at the Tower of London (*see* PORTCULLIS). *Gun embrasures* for larger cannon were incorporated into Dartmouth Castle, Devon, in the 1480s and were

widely used in Henry VIII's coastal forts (*see* TUDOR COASTAL FORTS). Medieval gun ports should not be confused with later musket loops such as those in a parapet of the lower bailey at Chepstow Castle which date from the seventeenth century. Some historians differentiate between the openings for early hand-guns (*shot-holes*) and larger embrasured openings (*gun ports*).
(*See also* EMBRASURE, FIREARMS AND CANNON *and* GUNPOWDER)

GUNPOWDER *see* FIREARMS AND CANNON

GUNS *see* FIREARMS AND CANNON

GUYENNE *or* **GUIENNE** *see* AQUITAINE

H

HABERGEON *see* HAUBERK

HAGGADAY *see* IRONWORK, LOCKS AND NAILS

HAGIOSCOPE *or* **SQUINT** Squint is a term coined by Victorian ecclesiologists to describe a rectangular opening cut obliquely through masonry to afford a limited view of the high altar in a church or CHAPEL from a subsidiary altar. This enabled a chantry priest to synchronise his celebration of the mass with that at the high altar, especially at the Elevation of the Host. Others, such as that at Beaumaris Castle, also allowed the Sanctus bell to be rung at precisely the right moment.

HAKETON A padded garment intended to protect the body from the chafing of the heavy HAUBERK. (*See also* ARMOUR *and* HELMETS)

HALBERD A 'three-in-one' infantry weapon in common use from the fourteenth century. The halberd consisted of a wooden shaft with a thrusting spike and a double-sided blade, one side an axe and the other a pick. The shaft was usually 1.8m (6ft) in length though halberds used for ceremonial purposes were often longer (*see* WEAPONS AND HARNESS).

HALBERDIER An infantryman armed with a HALBERD.

HALF SHAFT *also* **ENGAGED SHAFT** A PIER partially attached to, or let into, a wall.

HALL The humble 'hall' or entrance lobby of a modern house is all that remains of what was once the most important room in a dwelling. In the Middle Ages the hall was the focus of family life, a central hearth providing warmth and a sense of shared experience. In a medieval castle or manor house the hall was both a refectory and the court and nucleus of an estate (*see* MANOR). Mealtimes were particularly important for it was on these occasions that a lord shared a common meal with the members of his household, thereby confirming publicly their mutual commitment and enhancing his reputation as 'a good lord' (*see* HOUSEHOLD *and* WORSHIP). Indeed, in the 1240s Bishop Grosseteste advised the countess of Lincoln not to allow the members of her household to eat anywhere but in the hall for to do so would be wasteful of food and their absence would bring 'no honour to lord or lady'. At these times the lord, his family and personal guests occupied a platform or *dais* at one end of the hall while at the other a wooden screen reduced the draughts from the SCREENS PASSAGE, from which doors led to the *service rooms*: the BUTTERY, PANTRY and KITCHEN. This triple-door arrangement became the norm, even when (as was often the case) the kitchen was located at some distance from the hall, as in the Great Hall of Goodrich Castle. The screen itself was sometimes

movable and a number of these have survived, that at Rufford Hall being 'carved with uninhibited exuberance' (Platt). Quite often the chamber above the service rooms was assigned to a member of the household, such as the butler or domestic steward (the *chamberlain*). A lord's retainers, and those of his guests, sat 'below the salt' at long trestle tables in the body of the hall.[*] The serving of food on great occasions was the most complicated of the activities carried out in the hall. For the high table food would be brought on dishes. Elaborately decorated and presented, it would be carved at the table before the lord and his guests. Those sitting at tables in the body of the hall ate from dishes shared with two or three others. The dishes were called *messes* and those who shared a dish were therefore *mess-mates*. There being no forks (until the seventeenth century), meat on the messes was already carved into small digestible portions and would be eaten with the fingers, a trencher of stale bread serving as a plate. Grain and other foods would be pounded into a soft mash that could be sipped from a spoon. Similarly, those sitting at the high table drank from individual cups while others shared a communal jug. The serving, replenishing and clearing away of dishes and jugs required service rooms separate from the kitchens. Indeed, it is evident from the location of many kitchens that it was considered undesirable for them to be adjacent to the hall, presumably because of the risk of fire (*for* details of meals *see* KITCHENS).

Throughout the Middle Ages halls retained their public as well as their domestic functions and were used for periodic festivities and ceremonial as well as being the administrative and business centre of a manor and, often, its courtroom. The development of the chimney flue in the late thirteenth century (*see* CHIMNEYS AND FIREPLACES) encouraged notions of privacy and the creation of small, private chambers as bedrooms and parlours, and these, together with specialised rooms for food preparation and storage (and, in larger households, accommodation for servants who had previously occupied the hall) were obtained by constructing cross-wings at right angles to the original hall. In castles, where defensive considerations prevailed, it was not always possible to follow this plan, though the general principle of locating service quarters and kitchens at one end of the hall and the solar and private apartments at the other was adhered to wherever

[*] This was not a medieval expression: the earliest reference to sitting 'above the salt', which implied a place of distinction above the *saler* or saltcellar, occurred in 1597.

possible. In castle and manor house alike the ratio of public space (the hall) to private space (chambers) steadily decreased, reflecting a desire for greater personal comfort and convenience and an increased appreciation of the concept of private family life.

Many castles had two halls. As we have seen, the larger or *great hall* was used as a refectory by the household and for festive and ceremonial purposes. It has been suggested that a smaller or *lesser hall* was sometimes provided so that a visiting nobleman might house and feed his retinue independently. However, the proximity of so many lesser halls to a constable's quarters suggests that they were reserved for the use of a constable and his reduced household when a lord was away. At Harlech Castle, for example, the constable's lodgings in the gatehouse included a hall that was clearly intended for his use (*see below*), while the 1373 accounts for Caerphilly Castle refer to a 'constable's hall' on the second floor of the inner east gatehouse. At Bodiam Castle (1385) there was both a Great Hall and a 'servants' hall', each with its own kitchen and service rooms. It has been suggested that the servants' hall was provided for the benefit of estate workers rather than the household who would have eaten in the Great Hall. However, it is more likely that it was the castle garrison who ate in the lesser hall, a strict segregation of household and garrison being evident in the disposition of other buildings within the castle. Sometimes a lesser hall was provided for the private use of a lord and his immediate household. When a new keep was built at Warkworth in the 1380s the design included a lesser hall for the earl's personal use, while the great hall in the outer bailey was retained and refurbished for communal purposes. Even where two halls were provided, there is little doubt that the lord would take some of his meals in the great hall, especially on feast days and holidays, so that his household would be 'graced by his presence' and the social contract renewed.

As the focal point of a castle community the hall invariably received particular attention and was often refurbished or even rebuilt several times. The walls of a hall would have been plastered and whitened and were often lavishly decorated with wall paintings and heraldry, while WINDOWS might be glazed with coloured glass (*see* GLAZING). If the wall of a hall served also as a defensive curtain then any windows on that side would have been small and inserted at a level where they would hardly affect a castle's defensive capability.

The Buildings

Early motte and bailey castles (*see* MOTTE) soon proved inadequate for domestic purposes and

timber-frame halls were often erected in a BAILEY to accommodate a Norman lord and his household. For the most part these were simple, rectangular *aisled halls* with a pitched roof of thatch or shingles. Window openings were 'glazed' with thin sheets of horn or oiled linen, while smoke from a central hearth drifted upwards to a hole or *louvre* in the roof. Archaeological evidence now suggests that internal divisions in domestic ranges, which were commonplace by the thirteenth century, were in fact present in some twelfth-century timber-frame halls. These might consist of a kitchen at one end of the hall and the lord's private apartments at the other (*see* SOLAR). There were also double-aisled halls in which arcades of posts or piers and horizontal beams (*wall-plates*) carried the roof trusses over flanking aisles in the manner of a church, thereby creating greater internal space (*see* TIMBER-FRAME BUILDINGS). Timber-frame walls were often replaced with stone and later incorporated into ranges of domestic buildings, though the use of timber-framing persisted throughout the medieval period. Inevitably no timber-frame courtyard buildings have survived, though the stone-built twelfth-century halls at Oakham and Winchester Castles serve to illustrate how splendid these double-aisle halls could be. Of Oakham Castle very little remains except for the wonderful Romanesque hall,

Plan and cutaway drawing of the thirteenth-century hall at Ludgershall Castle, Wiltshire.

divided by a four-bay arcade into a 'nave' and side aisles, the capitals and corbels positively bristling with sculptural decoration. The hall at Winchester Castle is, after Westminster, the finest surviving medieval hall in England. Reconstructed by Henry III in 1222–36, it measures 35.5m (110ft) in length and is exactly half as wide as it is high. The hall is Early English (*see* GOTHIC ARCHITECTURE) with five-bay arcades and Purbeck marble piers dividing the main body of the hall from its aisles. (For the Round Table in the hall of Winchester Castle *see* ARTHURIAN BRITAIN.) Westminster Hall was, of course, one of the largest enclosed spaces in medieval Europe. Its floor covers an area the size of six tennis courts and measures 73m (240ft) by 27.4m (90ft). With the Jewel Tower, it is all that remains of the original Palace of Westminster which was destroyed by fire in 1834. The side walls are of Norman origin but the hall was remodelled in 1394–9. The timbers of the great double hammer-beam roof were prefabricated at Farnham in Surrey and transported by barge down the Thames to Westminster. For six centuries it was the hub of the kingdom, not only as a venue for royal ceremonial and state trials but also for the king's courts once they had ceased to be peripatetic.

A further type of hall, built at first-floor level over a stone-walled UNDERCROFT and reached by an exterior flight of steps, may have originated in the claustral buildings of monasteries. These first-floor halls were comparatively exclusive, the best surviving example, from *c*. 1190–1200, being at Boothby Pagnell. Originally surrounded by a moat, the hall comprised a first-floor chamber, lit by two double-light Norman windows, above an undercroft for storage on the ground floor. The essential difference between these first-floor halls and the more conventional timber-frame hall was size. At the manor house at Alsted in Surrey, for example, accommodation within the twelfth-century first-floor hall was considered to be so restrictive that it was replaced before 1250 by a more commodious aisled hall, timber-built on stone foundations and with a detached stone-built solar and kitchen that were later incorporated into the hall itself.

It has been suggested that this type of first-floor hall, with the hall built above an undercroft, was effectively a modest form of HALL-KEEP in which the hall and private chambers occupied the upper storey (or storeys) and which relied for its defence on the height and thickness of its walls and, in some cases, a FOREBUILDING. By *c*. 1000 these formidable hall-keeps were being constructed in many parts of western Europe, both as symbols of

magnate prestige and independence and as a defence against internecine aggression following the disintegration of the Carolingian Empire. In Britain the earliest example is William fitz Osbern's Great Tower at Chepstow (1067–75) which comprised an immense rectangular two-storeyed hall-keep, entered at first-floor level from an external (timber?) stair and located within a stone-walled bailey. By 1270 the facilities of Chepstow's Great Tower were considered to be inadequate and a new hall was built at first-floor level against the north wall of the Lower Bailey. This had a screens passage at one end beyond which were doors to a pantry and buttery, together with stairs and a service passage from the kitchens on the ground floor. Nevertheless, the Great Hall continued in use throughout the medieval period, indeed it was heightened by the addition of a further storey in 1290.

Unlike Chepstow's hall-keep, which was designed for both defensive and domestic purposes, the function of the tower-keep was purely defensive and its chambers were almost invariably cramped and

Interior of William fitz Osbern's Great Tower at Chepstow (1067–75).

poorly lit (see KEEP). Consequently, as fortifications became more sophisticated so halls were constructed within the protecting walls of an inner ward or courtyard, the tower-keep being reserved as a final refuge for use only *in extremis*. These courtyard halls were usually placed against a curtain and, where the site allowed, window openings could be provided without affecting security: at Pembroke, Barnard Castle and Chepstow, for example, where the hall windows overlook steep cliffs (see WINDOWS).

The eleventh-century Scolland's Hall at Richmond Castle is the earliest of these courtyard halls, though in this case the hall was built before the keep. Named after a steward to the first earl, the hall is a two-storey building located in the south-east corner of Richmond's Great Court, some 90m (300ft) from the keep. The ground floor provided storage space and once served as an entrance lobby to the east gate, while the hall itself, on the first floor, was approached by external stairs leading to a fine doorway and was lit by ten two-light windows. The buildings to the west of the hall date from the twelfth century when openings were made in the west wall to provide for the usual arrangement of triple entrances to the buttery, pantry and kitchen passage. The hall was originally partitioned at the east end to provide a solar.

More typically, at Goodrich Castle a twelfth-century keep survives in close proximity to an early thirteenth-century great hall, built at ground level against the north-west curtain of the courtyard, and measuring 19.8 by 8.4m (65 by 27½ft). At Pembroke Castle William Marshal's lofty but incommodious keep (c. 1200) was complemented by a great hall (the Norman Hall) which may even pre-date the keep. This hall was later converted to a solar and an impressive new hall (the Northern Hall) built next to it (1280–90), together with a second hall that was used as a chancery and courthouse. Uniquely, steps descend from the Northern Hall directly to a subterranean cavern by which access could be gained to the sea.

The massive keep-gatehouses of Edwardian castles such as Harlech and Beaumaris incorporated suites of rooms for the constables and other senior royal officials (see KEEP-GATEHOUSE). Each gatehouse had its own spacious lesser hall, that in the north gatehouse of Beaumaris being 21m (70ft) long and 7.5m (25ft) wide, though it may have been divided into two smaller chambers (as at Harlech). These were supplemented by great halls and chambers set against the curtain walls of the courtyards: at Harlech the end (north) wall of the hall still stands, ROOF-CREASING and a series of

BEAM-HOLES and corbels marking the position of its inner and outer roofs.

One of the most evocative medieval halls is the Great Hall at Stokesay Castle which has retained its magnificent timber roof and central open hearth. Built in c. 1285 to replace an earlier wooden hall, the Great Hall is 15.8m (52ft) long, 9.5m (31ft) wide and 10.4m (34ft) high and comprises four bays with separate gables above each window and the doorway. The builder, Lawrence of Ludlow, could afford glass in the upper lights of his windows, but the lower lights were shuttered. The roof was originally supported by three pairs of CRUCKS, each pair braced by two collar beams (see ROOFS (TIMBER)). Each cruck was 10.3m (34ft) long and rested on a stone corbel 2.4m (8ft) above the hall floor. In time the lower sections of the crucks became damp and had to be replaced by stone pilasters. In the late thirteenth century the hall was provided with a solar at its southern end and private chambers above an earlier tower (c. 1240) to the north. It was essentially the hall of a prosperous wool-merchant who, in 1291, obtained from Edward I a licence to fortify and crenellate his home, adding a substantial keep-like tower (c. 1291–1305), linked to the solar by a fortified passage-way.

The Great Hall of Stokesay Castle, Shropshire, one of the most evocative of medieval halls.

HALL-KEEP Many historians dislike the term 'keep', preferring to describe the principal tower or *donjon* of a castle as the GREAT TOWER. Others argue that a minority of keeps cannot accurately be described as towers for they are somewhat longer than they are high. Consequently, these formidable buildings are often described as *hall-keeps*, a not entirely satisfactory definition for (other than their proportions) they have much in common with other large residential keeps, such as those at Dover, Colchester and Norwich Castles and the Tower of London (the White Tower), which were of sufficient size to provide a considerable degree of comfort and convenience and which also contained halls (*see* KEEP). Significantly, keeps of this magnitude were seldom attempted again.

Unlike the vertically arranged chambers in a TOWER-KEEP, which were often cramped and poorly lit, the hall, solar and private apartments of a hall-keep were located side-by-side on an upper storey and, because of their height above ground level, could be generously lit. This type of fortified residence originated in northern France in the tenth century, following the disintegration of the Carolingian Empire. In Britain the earliest example is William fitz Osbern's Great Tower at Chepstow Castle (1067–75), an immense rectangular two-storeyed hall-keep entered at first-floor level from an external stair. It has recently been suggested that the Great Tower was built by William I as an audience chamber in which to meet with his Marcher lords.

The White Tower at the Tower of London was begun in 1078 and took twenty years to build. It was by far the tallest building in London and its psychological effect on the populace must have been profound, indeed 'the Tower' is still used today to describe the entire castle. Its walls were 27m (90ft) high and 4.6m (15ft) thick, erected by William I 'against the fickleness of the huge and fierce population'. Initially the upper storey was left empty so that, while the stone exterior of the building looked intimidating, it was in fact only three-quarters filled. The White Tower was the prototype in England for other great hall-keeps and contains one of the most perfect examples of ROMANESQUE architecture in Britain, the beautiful Chapel of St John (*c.* 1080) which projects from the east wall (*see* CHAPELS).

The twelfth-century hall-keep of Middleham Castle (1170) dominates the inner courtyard just as it must have dominated the surrounding countryside before the encircling curtain wall was built in *c.* 1300 and courtyard buildings added in the fifteenth century. Measuring 32m (105ft) by 24m

The hall-keep at Castle Rising (1138–40) has survived almost in its entirety, except for its roof and floors, and is the finest example of its type in Britain.

(78ft), and with walls 3 to 3.7m (10 to 12ft) thick, it is one of the largest keeps in England. Divided longitudinally into two by a central wall, it was a self-contained fortified residence with stone-vaulted kitchen and cellars on the ground floor and a hall, chapel, great chamber, inner chamber and latrines on the first. The doorway, at first-floor level, was approached by a well-defended stair, enclosed within an open-roofed forebuilding. Two gates, one at the foot and one half-way up the stair, would have been controlled by a gatekeeper whose guardroom was built into the side of the keep. A third gate gave access to an ante-room at the head of the stairs where those seeking an audience would assemble outside the doorway to the hall. Originally the only access to the ground-floor kitchen and cellars was by means of a spiral stair from the floor above, though a more convenient opening was later formed at ground level. This same stair ascended from the hall to the battlements and corner turrets on the roof.

The hall-keep at Castle Rising (1138–40) has survived almost in its entirety, except for its roof and floors, and is the finest example of its type in Britain. It is considerably longer than it is high, measuring 24m (78ft) in length, 21m (68ft) wide and 15.2m (50ft) high, and the disposition of its rooms is more sophisticated than at Middleham. The undercroft was used only for storage while the first floor, which rises through two storeys, contains all the principal public and private chambers, divided (as at Middleham) by a longitudinal cross-wall which separates the hall, kitchen and pantry from the solar or Great Chamber and chapel. There is the usual first-floor entrance reached by an elaborate forebuilding (for details *see* FOREBUILDING).

HAMMER BEAM *see* ROOFS (TIMBER)

HAMMER POST *see* ROOFS (TIMBER)

HAND-AND-A-HALF SWORD A sword that could be used with one or two hands.
(*See also* WEAPONS AND HARNESS)

HANDGONNE *see* FIREARMS AND CANNON

HARBOURS *see* QUAYS

HARNESS A complete suit of plate armour (*see* ARMOUR).

HARRYING OF THE NORTH (1069) From Old English, the verb *harry* means 'to ravage and despoil' and this is precisely what William I visited on the north of England in 1069. In August of that year a fleet of 240 vessels, carrying perhaps ten thousand Danes, Frisians and Saxons, landed in the Humber estuary where they were joined by local chieftains and 'an immense multitude of common men riding and marching gladly'. Clearly, the people of Lincoln and Northumbria, mindful of their Danish ancestry, received the nephew of Cnut the Great (d. 1035) with far greater enthusiasm than that which they had afforded Harold or the Atheling. By the end of September the Danes and English poured into the city of York without encountering any resistance; the castles were abandoned by the Normans and 'for the last time on English soil the English axe and foot-soldier made good their ancient reputations'. According to tradition, the Norman fugitives who brought the disastrous news to William were rewarded by the severing of their noses and right hands. English success in the north inspired rebellion elsewhere: the men of Devon and Cornwall marched on Exeter to expel the Norman garrison while the castle at Shrewsbury was threatened by Eadric the Wild and his Welshmen. William's response was swift and severe. Leaving the minor rising to be quelled by his lieutenants, he led a mounted force to the Humber where the Danes had beached their ships and established their winter quarters. At news of the king's approach they fled. William wheeled his forces and at Stafford crushed a Mercian insurrection which threatened his communications and, after a long blockade, recaptured York from the Danes and English. It only remained to make an example of the province that had harboured his enemies and for two months William was engaged in harrying the cultivated lands between the rivers Ouse and Tyne. In the upland dales and river valleys there were numerous villages and wealthy churches, while on the coast ports such as Whitby could boast a measure of prosperity. These William determined to destroy with method and deliberation, sparing neither land nor men. In Yorkshire every settlement through which he passed became a scene of massacre. A few miserable refugees fled to the hills where they supported themselves on the flesh of horses, dogs and cats. Others sold themselves into slavery and 'bowed their heads for meat in evil days'. The devastation was complete: from York to Durham not a single inhabited village remained. Two decades later *Domesday Book* recorded the extent and lasting nature of the desolation.

HATCH *see* DOORS

HATCHING To represent colours in ARMORY using a system of lines and dots (*see* TINCTURES).

HATCHMENTS A hatchment is a diamond-shaped heraldic panel, of wood or of canvas within a wooden frame, usually found in a church where it may be affixed to a wall or removed to a ringing chamber, vestry or some other equally inaccessible quarter. Although post-dating the medieval period, hatchments are often useful indicators of a family's lineage (*see* CHURCHES). The word itself is a corruption of 'achievement' and suggests that hatchments originated in the FUNERARY HERALDRY of the medieval nobility and were therefore erected in churches following interment.
(*See also* ARMORY)

HAUBERGEON A lighter form of the HAUBERK worn by poorer troops in the twelfth and thirteenth centuries (*see* ARMOUR).

HAUBERK *or* **BYRNIE** A sleeved shirt of mail. In early medieval Europe long-sleeved hauberks were rare, though not unknown. However, there is evidence that two hauberks, one with long sleeves and the other with short, could be worn at the same time. The hauberk usually weighed slightly more than 10kg and, contrary to popular belief, was reasonably comfortable when worn with a padded garment beneath, even in hot weather. Hauberks came in a variety of forms including the *jazerenc* of Middle Eastern origin which incorporated a quilted lining and fabric cover. From the fourteenth century the term *habergeon* was used in inventories, possibly to describe a short hauberk.
(*See also* ARMOUR *and* HELMETS)

HAWGABLE *see* BURGAGE

HAWKING *see* DEER PARK *and* MEWS

HEADER The narrow face of a brick. A *bull header* is made especially for circular work and has one end wider than the other.
(*See also* BRICK BUILDINGS)

HEARSE *also* **HERSE** A barrel-shaped metal cage erected above an effigy and intended to support candles and a pall which was removed only on special occasions (*see* MONUMENTS). One of the most magnificent examples is that above the gilded bronze effigy of Richard Beauchamp, 5th earl of Warwick (d. 1439), at St Mary's, Warwick.

HEART BURIAL The medieval practice of interring a man's heart, the seat of love and piety, in a place other than that in which his body was buried was particularly common during the thirteenth and fourteenth centuries. In many localities tradition links these miniature effigies with the heart burial of a local crusading knight: a not unreasonable assumption when the difficulties of transporting a rapidly deteriorating corpse from the Holy Land are considered. There are good examples at Mappowder in Dorset, at Horsted Keynes in Sussex (probably the work of the same artist), at Bottesford in Leicestershire and Halesowen Abbey in Worcestershire. At Tenbury, in the same county, a half-size effigy is depicted clasping a heart in his hands.

HEATER SHIELD A shield shaped like the base of a flat-iron, with a straight or slightly curved top and two curved sides meeting at a point, covering the body from shoulder to mid-thigh. This type of shield was usually held by means of ENARMES and secured by a GUIGE over the shoulder (*see* SHIELDS).

HEAUME *see* GREAT HELM

HEIR One who has inherited, and enjoys possession of, a title, property or arms. The term is often mistakenly used to mean an *heir apparent* who is one whose right of succession is inalienable. An *heir presumptive* is one whose right of succession is dependent on the absence of an heir apparent.

HEIRESS (HERALDIC) An heraldic heiress is a daughter who has inherited arms from her deceased father, there being no brothers or surviving issue of brothers. The arms of an heraldic heiress are shown on an *escutcheon of pretence*, a small shield at the centre of her husband's shield. Both her arms and those of her husband are transmitted to their children as QUARTERINGS, her husband's arms being in the first quarter. When there is more than one daughter, all are co-heiresses and all transmit their father's arms on equal terms. An *heiress in her issue* is one through whose issue arms descend when all male lines of her father have failed. In this way it is possible for descendants of the daughter of an armiger to inherit his arms several generations after her death.
(*See also* MARSHALLING)

HELM (COIN) *see* COINAGE

HELMETS
The following terms are most commonly used when describing helmets of the medieval period (* *see also* individual entries). For body armour *see* ARMOUR.

ARMET*	helmet with cheek pieces and visor
ARMING CAP	padding worn beneath helmet
AVENTAIL	a mail fringe attached to edge of helmet
BARBOTE	alternative name for BEVOR
BARBUTE*	helmet with T-shaped opening at front
BARREL HELM	see GREAT HELM
BASCINET*	pointed steel helmet
BEVOR*	plate armour to protect lower front of face
BURGANET	light helmet with cheek-pieces (sixteenth century)
CAMAIL*	mail protection for neck and shoulders
CERVELLIÈRE	close-fitting round helmet
CHAIN MAIL	a pleonasm for MAIL
CHAPEL DE FER	see KETTLE HAT
CHAPLET	an iron skull-cap
CLOSE HELM*	enclosed helmet with a movable visor
COIF*	mail hood
CUIR BOUILLI*	hardened leather
GORGET*	plate armour form of CAMAIL
GREAT HELM*	cylindrical helm with eye slit
HEAUME	see GREAT HELM
HOUNSKULL	a snout-like visor on a BASCINET
KETTLE HAT*	plate helmet with a broad brim
LAMBREQUIN	see MANTLING
MAIL*	armour formed of circular links
NASAL	protective nose-piece
PANACHE	crest of feathers
PIG-FACE VISOR	see HOUNSKULL
POT HELM	early form of GREAT HELM
SALLET*	domed helmet with neck extension
TILTING HELM	see TOURNAMENT HELM
TORSE	see WREATH
TOURNAMENT HELM*	a 'close' helmet for jousting
VENTAIL	a mail flap to protect the lower face
VISOR	hinged frontpiece of helmet
WAR HAT	see KETTLE HAT

By the eleventh century one-piece iron helmets with face-protecting *nasals* (nose-pieces) were in common use throughout Europe. Nasals could be remarkably broad: according to tradition, the helmet worn by Duke William at the battle of Hastings (1066) had such a large nasal that it obscured his features, causing panic in the ranks when it was rumoured that he was dead. In the twelfth century the increasing threat of the crossbow (*see* ARCHERY) resulted in significant improvements in helmet design. Nasals became even larger while the sides and lower part of the face were protected by a mail *coif*.

The *great helm* first appeared in France in the mid-twelfth century. This was usually a flat-topped helmet with a face-mask which, at that time, took a variety of forms. The true *heaume* or *great helm*, which completely enclosed the head, was in evidence by 1220, while documentary references to visored helms (*heaume à vissere*) first occur in the late thirteenth century. The earliest thirteenth-century great helm is sometimes described as a *pot helm* because of its flat top and cylindrical shape, later great helms having a domed top and more rounded profile. The infantryman's *chapel de fer* or brimmed *kettle hat* with a slightly bulbous bowl was increasingly popular from the end of the twelfth century. At the same time the simple, round helmet of earlier centuries evolved into the *cervellière*, a close-fitting iron cap which was worn by all classes of soldier over or beneath a mail *coif*. It could also provide additional protection beneath a great helm (the combination being described in some sources as a 'doubled helmet') and eventually evolved into the *bascinet* (*see below*). Little wonder that a knight was required to trim his hair before putting on his helm!

Although the great helm continued to be worn into the fourteenth century, its use was confined almost exclusively to the TOURNAMENT where it was eventually replaced by the *tilting helm* or *tournament helm* which was permanently 'closed', forward vision being by means of an eye-slit which was only effective when leaning forward in the tilting position. The early fourteenth century was a time of considerable experimentation which produced the *bascinet*, a relatively lightweight, close-fitting metal helmet which afforded protection to the neck and the sides of the head. The bascinet, which first appeared in mid-thirteenth-century Italy, had a mail *aventail* and in later versions a *visor*. This was often of the *hounskull* or *pig-face* type, a singularly distinctive projecting 'snout' with an eye-slit (*sight*) and ventilation holes (*breathes*), which was hinged at the sides of the helmet.

The broad-brimmed *chapel de fer* continued in use by infantry, many examples no doubt handed down from father to son over several centuries. Increasingly, however, these were replaced by the *sallet*, the most popular of fifteenth-century helmets, similar in shape to a 'sou'wester' with a pronounced neck extension and domed crown. Most examples have an eye-slit and were worn in conjunction with a *bevor* to protect the lower front of the face. There were several types of sallet, some of which had movable visors and articulated neck guards. Dating from the fifteenth century, the *armet* was a *close helm* (intended to protect the whole head and face and with a movable visor) with a bevor formed of two cheek-pieces fastened together at the chin.
(*See also* ARMOUR, ARCHERY, SHIELDS *and* WEAPONS AND HARNESS)

HELMETS (HERALDIC) In late medieval ARMORY, a TOURNAMENT HELM was depicted in a COAT OF ARMS in order that a CREST could be displayed. The crest was attached to the helmet, together with a MANTLING, by means of rivets or laces, the unsightly join being concealed by a WREATH. Since the early seventeenth century various stylised helmets have been indicative of rank when depicted in coats of arms.

HELYERS *see* CASTLES, CONSTRUCTION OF

HENRICIAN Fortresses dating from the reign of Henry VIII (1509–47), principally a series of artillery forts along the south coast of England. By definition, these should no longer be accounted castles for they are not fortified residences in the medieval sense.
(*See also* TUDOR COASTAL FORTS)

HEPTARCHY A misleading term often applied to the seven kingdoms of Anglo-Saxon England: Wessex, Sussex, Kent, Essex, East Anglia, Mercia and Northumbria. Its use in this context erroneously implies the existence of a unified system of government.

HERALDIC BEASTS *see* BEASTS (HERALDIC)

HERALDIC COLOURS *see* TINCTURES

HERALDIC HEIRESS *see* HEIRESS (HERALDIC) *and* MARSHALLING

HERALD OF ARMS An officer of arms of the middle rank between kings of arms and pursuivants of arms. 'Herald' is generally used as a generic term for all officers of arms (*see* ARMORY *and* COLLEGE OF ARMS).

HERALDRY All matters relating to the duties and responsibilities of the kings, heralds and pursuivants of arms. The term is frequently and erroneously used as a synonym for ARMORY, that aspect of a herald's work which is concerned with the marshalling and regulation of coats of arms and other devices and insignia.

HERALDRY OF THE DECADENCE *see* ARMORY

HERALDS *see* ARMORY *and* COLLEGE OF ARMS

HERALDS' VISITATIONS By the fifteenth century the use and abuse of coats of arms were becoming widespread. At that time the English kings of arms were required to survey and record the devices and pedigrees of those using arms and to correct any irregularities. Occasional tours of inquiry were held but it was not until the sixteenth century that heralds' visitations were undertaken in a regular and systematic way. In England major visitations took place throughout the country in 1580, 1620 and 1666, minor visitations being conducted at other times. The original heralds' notebooks were used as a basis for manuscript copies, most of which have been published. These are a very useful source of early pedigrees, though it should be borne in mind that they may occasionally contain unauthorised additions or alterations which may not be immediately apparent. Many of these volumes have been published by the Harleian Society (*see* APPENDIX II) and others by county record societies. Many of the manuscripts on which the printed versions are based are held in the British Library in London. There are also good collections of printed visitation records at the Guildhall Library in London, the Society of Genealogists and the Institute of Heraldic and Genealogical Studies (*see* APPENDIX II).
(*See also* ROLLS OF ARMS)

HERBALS 'There is no herbe or weede but God hath gyven vertue them to helpe man.' In the Middle Ages the culinary uses of herbs were so taken for granted that they were hardly ever mentioned in *herbals*, treatises which were almost entirely devoted to the medicinal properties of herbs and spices. Many of the herbs we know today were introduced into England by the Romans and particular areas of the country gradually established reputations for growing specific herbs: mint at Mitcham, Surrey, saffron at Saffron Walden, Essex, and lavender at Market Deeping in Lincolnshire, for example. Many of London's streets still bear the names of their medieval and Tudor herb markets: Camomile Street, for example, was once a market for the surplus produce of the great houses in the St Paul's area. In the last decades of the fourteenth century Richard II established a fashion in the experimental use of herbs for culinary purposes. He employed innovative cooks and encouraged them to catalogue successful dishes in 'herballs'. The herbs used at that time were stronger in flavour than those used today as they had to temper the pungent taste of salted meats and game. One consequence of the Dissolution of the Monasteries (1536–9) was to transfer many monastic gardens into the hands of private owners. The monasteries had previously been the chief source of horticultural innovation but from that time the initiative was taken up by the nobility and gentry. (*See also* GARDENS)

HERCE Fourteenth-century 'harrow' formation in which archers fought with dismounted men-at-arms within a thicket of sharpened stakes (*see* WARFARE: CONDUCT OF).

HEREDITARY OFFICES A characteristic of feudalism was the creation of numerous hereditary (or heritable) offices by which service to the nobility or to the crown was rewarded. Such offices were by no means sinecures, however, and were concerned with the administration of those aspects of society which appertained directly to the crown or to the running of magnate estates. The earliest recorded offices date from the eleventh and twelfth centuries: in 1119, for example, Robert, earl of Gloucester, was Hereditary Governor of Caen and Hereditary Banner-bearer of Bayeux Cathedral and in the 1190s the earl of Arundel was Hereditary Chief Butler of England and Hereditary Patron of Wymundham Abbey. Several hereditary offices were often the prerogative of one man: in 1270, for example, the earl of Norfolk and Suffolk was Hereditary Marshal of England, Hereditary Steward of the Household, Hereditary Bearer of the Banner of St Edmund, Hereditary Forester of Farnedale and Hereditary Warden of Romford Forest. Such offices are legion and were by no means confined to the upper echelons of society. Numerous hereditary foresters, falconers and farriers; stewards, sewers and sheriffs; constables and chamberlains; warders and keepers of castles, almoners and patrons of religious houses embellish the pedigrees of prince and yeoman alike.

Many hereditary offices have been extinguished and others are now held for purely ceremonial purposes.

HEREPAETHS *or* HEREPATHS Several Saxon land charters refer to *wegs* or trackways along territorial boundaries of which the most common road name is *herepaeth*, probably meaning a trackway used for military and administrative purposes: for border patrols, for government officials and their armed escorts and for the rapid movement of troops (Old English *here* meaning 'army'). No doubt they were also used by the populace for journeys beyond their immediate locality. Perhaps the best known *herepaeth*, on the Marlborough Downs, runs for 7 miles between Avebury and Marlborough on the line of a prehistoric trackway and is still known as 'Herepath' or 'Green Street'. A similar *herepaeth* in the Vale of Pewsey, also in Wiltshire, is commemorated in Harepath Farm near Bishops Cannings. The city of Hereford was a place on a *herepaeth* where armies were quartered before fording the River Wye and proceeding into Wales.

HERRINGBONE A characteristic of Norman work, herringbone masonry is a decorative zig-zag pattern in a wall or floor, similar in appearance to the bones of a herring, formed by alternate rows of diagonally laid stones, bricks or tiles. This type of brick bonding was commonly used in the backs of fireplaces.

HERRISON A wooden palisade, presumably named after the medieval term for a hedgehog with which it shares certain physical characteristics.

HILT *see* WEAPONS AND HARNESS

HIP The external angle formed by the junction of two sloping surfaces. A *hipped roof* has sloping ends instead of gables (*see* GABLE).

HISTORIATED INITIAL In documents, an initial capital letter within which is an illustration, usually associated with the text.

HOARDING *or* HOURD *also* BRATTICE, BRETACHE, BRETESCHE *or* BRETÈCHE Overhanging timber galleries (*war-heads*) which projected from the parapet of a curtain wall, gatehouse or tower. Hoardings enabled the 'blind' areas at the base of a wall to be observed and defended by means of openings or trapdoors in the floor of the projecting gallery. It was otherwise

A timber fighting-platform viewed from the inside of the north curtain wall at Caerphilly Castle.

impossible for archers to shoot vertically from a parapet, or to drop missiles on attackers at the base of the wall, without exposing themselves to danger. Hoardings were supported on joists (*putlogs*), had sloping roofs and were similar in function to the very much more sophisticated (and permanent) stone-built MACHICOLATIONS of later castles, though unlike machicolations temporary hoardings could be dismantled when not required (*see* PUTLOG HOLES). More substantial hoardings, such as the conical structures which surmounted towers, are generally termed PENTISES.

Although the term *brattice* is now generally applied to a hoarding, it has been used for a variety of other purposes: to describe the wooden tower of a motte and bailey castle, for example, or a temporary timber fortification at the end of a bridge or an open-floored latrine within a machicolation. When a breach was made in a castle wall, a brattice or timber breastwork could be erected as a temporary defence. Similarly, the term *bretache* (and its variants) has been used specifically to describe a defensive wooden or stone structure protruding from a window part-way up a wall.

HOBELAR Effectively 'mounted infantry' – lightly armed medieval troops who travelled on horseback but fought on foot. From the early fourteenth century Irish hobelars became an increasingly important and highly regarded form of light cavalry, based on the Celtic traditions of warfare.
(*See also* HORSES AND HORSE-HARNESS)

HOLY WATER SPRINKLER *see* MACE *and* WEAPONS AND HARNESS

HOMAGE The ceremonial acceptance of inferiority to a lord as a condition of feudal tenancy.

HONOR A collection of estates, often distributed over a large area, occupied by a TENANT-IN-CHIEF of the crown.

HONOUR A group of KNIGHT'S FEES or manors administered by a superior and an honorial court comprising honorial barons as principal under-tenants. Such groupings were often (though by no means invariably) regional and based on a particular magnate castle.

HOOD-MOULD see DRIPSTONE and GOTHIC ARCHITECTURE

HORNWORK In post-medieval fortifications, a detached outwork beyond the main ditch with the front elevation forming two demi-bastions on either side of a curtain. The term is sometimes used erroneously to describe a medieval outwork, often crescent-shaped (hence the name) and surrounded by a lake or water-filled moat and detached from the principal defences of a castle except for a bridge. An earthwork at White Castle is so described though it was effectively a detached bailey, separated from the original motte by an encircling moat and defended by a timber palisade and towers.

HORSES AND HORSE-HARNESS The following terms are most commonly used when describing horses and horse-harness of the medieval period (* see also individual entries).

BARD or BARDING*	horse-armour (generic)
BATAILE	cavalry division
CAPARISON*	heraldic horse-covering
CHAMFRON	protection for a horse's head
CONROIS	cavalry squadron
COPITA	protection for a horse's head
CRUPPER or CROPURE	protection for the hindquarters
DAMOISEAU	cavalryman
DESTRIER	heavy 'war horse'
ÉCHIELLE	cavalry squadron
FLANCHARDS	armour protecting flanks
HOBELAR*	mounted infantryman
JENNET	small Spanish horse
MAN-AT-ARMS*	fully armoured cavalryman
PALFREY	ordinary 'riding horse'
PEYTRAL	armour for the front of the horse
POITRAL	breast strap attached to saddle
POMMEL	upward projecting front of a saddle-bow
SERGEANT À CHEVAL	non-noble cavalryman
STIRRUP*	support for rider's foot
TRAPPER	abbreviated caparison

Armoured cavalry dominated warfare throughout the medieval period, though in the twelfth and thirteenth centuries infantry began to play an increasingly important rôle (see WARFARE: CONDUCT OF).

The terms 'cavalry' and 'chivalry' share the same linguistic root, confirming that knighthood was the prerogative of the mounted warrior (see CHIVALRY). His effectiveness in battle (and thereby his reputation) was greatly enhanced by the development of the stirrup and the saddle-bow which provided both manoeuvrability and stability when wielding a weapon in the saddle.

In Anglo-Norman warfare cavalry advanced in close order with infantry archers and crossbowmen positioned on the flanks to bring down as many enemy horses as possible. In defensive positions against a cavalry attack, the infantry were supported by dismounted but fully armoured knights who might advance against the enemy on foot. Traditionally the cavalry were deployed in large divisions or battalions (batailes) and these, in turn, were divided into operational units or squadrons (échielles or conrois). Each conrois comprised about twenty knights riding in close formation in two or three ranks. The function of these densely packed cavalry units was to act as 'shock cavalry', the 'shock' being a relatively slow charge aimed at breaking an enemy's formation followed by a close-combat mêlée, a re-grouping and, if practicable, a further charge at the enemy's rear.

The muscular destrier or 'war-horse' was used only in battle, the élite cavalry of knights and their mounted esquires and sergeants (sergeant à cheval or damoiseau) riding lighter palfreys at other times. By the late thirteenth century the arms, armour and (above all) the horses required of a knight were extremely expensive. A knight was generally expected to have five horses, though not all of these would be destriers, while a sergeant à cheval would have three: a destrier for battle, a palfrey for ordinary riding and a pack-horse to carry his equipment. In the fourteenth century there were several categories of cavalry: increasingly heavily armoured mounted men-at-arms, less well-equipped but more mobile light-cavalrymen and mounted infantry (hobelars), and archers who travelled on horseback but fought on foot. Indeed, it has been suggested that in the fourteenth- and fifteenth-century chevauchées of the Hundred Years War the hobelars were tactically more effective than the famous English longbowmen. A war-horse needed strength, not size, to carry a fully armoured cavalryman: horse mail and plate armour could weigh over 32kg (70lb) and that of a knight 27kg (60lb). It is fallacious, therefore, to assume that destriers were large, heavy animals: they were bred for strength and stamina. Until the late Middle Ages English horses were relatively heavy-boned, slow and unresponsive, and the finest destriers were often Spanish and Andalusian breeds with Arabian blood (a really fine destrier could be worth more than seven ordinary horses). Pack-horses and draft-horses were just as important to a medieval army and were used in large numbers. In twelfth-century France the king's élite troops had one wagon for every forty or fifty infantry sergeants, the knights and other cavalry having pack-horses to carry their equipment.

Bard or *Barding* is a generic term to describe both the armour and the trappings of a horse. Early barding consisted of a heavy covering of mail with four 'skirts' to protect the animal's legs. Later horse armour consisted of a series of plates protecting the head and neck (the plate *chamfron* or leather *copita*) to which, at a later date, were added the *peytral* (covering the front of the horse), *flanchards* (protecting the sides) and the *crupper* or *cropure* (covering the hindquarters) made of leather, wood or plate. A *poitral* or breast-strap was attached to the saddle to prevent it from sliding backwards. The *caparison*, a richly embroidered or painted cloth covering the body of the horse, was a favourite means of heraldic display in the medieval and Tudor periods, particularly at TOURNAMENTS and for ceremonial processions. In battle the abbreviated (and more practical) *trapper* was sometimes used for the same purpose.

HOSPITALLER, KNIGHTS *see* ST JOHN OF JERUSALEM, ORDER OF *and* COMMANDERY

HOSTAGE A person seized or held by an enemy as security, his release being contingent on the fulfilment of predetermined conditions.
(*See also* RANSOM)

HOUNSKULL *see* BASCINET *and* HELMETS

HOURD *see* HOARDING

HOURS (BUILDERS') *see* ORGANISATION (BUILDING)

HOUSECARL A professional soldier in the retinue of an eleventh-century Anglo-Saxon king.

HOUSEHOLD A castle was not merely a stronghold: it was the home of a lord and his family. But it was the lord, not his family, who provided the rationale for a castle's existence. In the arrangement of its accommodation, his castle reflected both his status in medieval society and his requirements as head of a substantial household and estate. In order to conduct his business and to maintain control of

his estates a lord needed a body of officials to carry out or enforce his decisions and a secretariat to support them. Corporately, the lord, his family and his officials comprised the inner household. Beyond them was the outer household, the multitude of minor officials and servants who attended to his personal and domestic needs and those of his family and guests. Throughout the medieval period the nature and structure of the magnate household (the *familia*) became increasingly complex, as did the disposition of the buildings in which its various departments were accommodated.

Not only were members of the household corporately and individually responsible for the personal needs of the noble and his numerous relations and guests, they were also charged with the administration of his estates or, in the case of the sovereign, with that of his realm. In return for his patronage, they were expected to take up arms on their lord's behalf, both in times of war and in defence of his territories and rights (*see* LIVERY AND MAINTENANCE). The sons of noble and knightly families were expected to serve in the households of superiors where they received academic as well as military and courtly training. Even the younger brothers of kings were not exempt: in 1461, for example, the young Richard, duke of Gloucester (the future Richard III), joined the household of Richard Neville, earl of Warwick, at Middleham Castle in Yorkshire.

The household of a magnate who held several estates, or who spent much of his time overseas, was often peripatetic and in the lord's absence each of his castles would be governed by a *Constable* or *Castellan* (*see* CONSTABLE), a small residential staff and garrison. At the royal castle of Harlech in 1284 the establishment comprised a constable 'together with 30 fencible men of whom 10 shall be crossbowmen', one chaplain, an artiller, a smith, a carpenter and a mason, 'and from the others shall be made janitors, watchmen, and other necessary officers'.

Little remains in British castles of the COURTYARD BUILDINGS that accommodated the various divisions of a household, though evidence of rooms in towers and gatehouses has often survived. In general terms the more opulent the accommodation and the finer the architectural detail, the higher up the social scale were its occupants. A chamber with good windows, a fireplace and access to a garderobe was invariably that of a lord, his family or one of his senior officials. Despite the increasing efficiency of household administration, the arrangement of rooms within a castle may appear haphazard, its effectiveness constrained by the physical limitations of a site and by military considerations. It was not until the late thirteenth century that castles began to be designed with suites of rooms integrated according to function, the Edwardian castles in Wales providing some of the best examples (*see below*). In all castles the HALL was pivotal, both physically and socially, to the kitchens and service rooms and to the domestic quarters. It is usually the largest and grandest structure in the castle and was splendidly furnished with tall windows, a dais and fireplace(s) and with access to a sufficiency of garderobes. Even with the development of private apartments, the lord would continue to take some of his meals with his household in the hall, thereby confirming publicly their mutual commitment one to the other and enhancing his reputation as 'a good lord' (*see* WORSHIP). Suites of private (*privy*) chambers were generally located to take advantage of natural light (*see* SOLAR) and ease of access to public rooms. Those in close proximity to the lord's chamber were clearly of greater importance than those that were at some remove from it, while chambers located in a gatehouse were likely to be those of the constable (*see below*).

The Twelfth Century

As will be seen, terminology changed with function but in the twelfth century the provision of food and drink was the responsibility of the *seneschal* (also called the *steward* or *dapifer*) and the *butler*, under whose authority were the controllers of the *larder* (responsible for provisions, including meat), the *pantry* (bread) and the *buttery* (wines and ale), together with the staff in the kitchens and hall (*see* KITCHENS). The lord slept in a chamber where he kept his most valuable possessions in chests beneath his bed. The official responsible for the chamber, and for the security of its contents, was the *chamberlain* with a staff of door-keepers and valets to attend to the personal needs of the lord, including his wardrobe. (Also in the twelfth century a *chancellor* was appointed to the royal household with responsibility for the chapel and the crown's written records – and hence, the law. This was the first 'department' to leave the peripatetic court and to be given a permanent office at Westminster.) These men formed the 'inner core' of the twelfth-century household. Next came the CONSTABLE and MARSHAL who were responsible for the castle's security, for supervising and training the lord's military retinues, for deploying the garrison, and for overseeing the stables and MEWS. A lord's wife and children, together with their own servants, might form an additional 'department' if they accompanied him.

Major household officials were generally only slightly below their lord in status: it was their duty and privilege to attend him and to offer their advice when requested, either individually or as members of his council (*see below*). Royal officials were drawn from the upper echelons of the baronage, supplemented by men of lesser rank whose experience and intellect marked them out. The barons consulted their senior tenants just as a king consulted the barons as his tenants-in-chief. The system was not in any sense democratic; nevertheless, medieval lordship could rarely operate effectively without, at least, the tacit approval of those on whose feudal obligations a lord depended.

Domestic accommodation in eleventh- and early twelfth-century castles such as William fitz Osbern's Great Tower at Chepstow (1067–75) was starkly simple, comprising a hall that filled two-thirds of the interior space of the tower and two rooms, one above the other, in the remaining third. Here the household lived in the hall while their lord and his family occupied a chamber next to it. In the following century the inner household continued to be accommodated within a HALL-KEEP, as at Rochester, Winchester, Orford and Dover Castles, or in buildings erected in the inner BAILEY, the magnate family occupying the keep or great tower. Almost invariably a lord eventually built more comfortable quarters for his household in the bailey, while retaining the keep as a final refuge, and the garrison was removed to a second or outer bailey, also known as a *base court*. The majority of castles therefore have two baileys: a strongly fortified inner bailey containing the lord's chambers, great hall, chapel, lodgings and domestic offices, and an outer bailey in which the ancillary buildings were located and in which the day-to-day activities of a garrison took place.

The Thirteenth Century

As the life of the English aristocracy became more complex, so too did the bureaucratic and financial machinery of the magnate household. By the mid-thirteenth century the single office of steward had been divided into two, reflecting the development of estate management and the need for financial control and detailed record-keeping. Land management and the relationships between a lord and his tenants were now the responsibility of the *steward*, while the *treasurer* was responsible for his lord's financial affairs. In the thirteenth-century household there would also be a second or domestic steward who would oversee the acquisition and distribution of provisions. The cook, butler and *pantler* were responsible to the domestic steward, while a further official (sometimes described as a *marshal*) organised the serving staff in the hall. In major households the *marshal* was a senior household official responsible for a lord's horses, soldiers, weaponry and general military organisation.

From *c.* 1200, the lord began to distance himself from his larger household. In 1200–5 King John spent over £1,400 improving his castle at Corfe where he built a suite of rooms (known as the *Gloriette*) in the inner courtyard. These comprised a great chamber leading to a smaller PRESENCE CHAMBER, a chapel, kitchens and suites of rooms for John and his queen. Corfe is significant in that it provides an early example of the physical separation of a lord (in this case the king) from the great hall and the more public areas of the castle. It also illustrates the designation of discrete suites of rooms for both private and administrative purposes. The separation of rooms and their functions within the inner household was a direct consequence of the expansion of household organisation that is evident in contemporary documents. In the thirteenth century we can observe the growth of a hierarchy of rooms, each located strategically in relation to others, depending on their function, and distinguished by their size, decoration and proximity to the lord's chamber.

Nevertheless, even in newly built castles where the opportunity existed to accommodate the needs of a household within a coherent plan, it is clear that military considerations were invariably given priority over domestic ones. At Caerphilly Castle, a masterpiece of military architecture built by the earl of Gloucester after 1270, the hall abuts one side of the inner curtain while lodgings are distributed among the towers without any apparent planning. Similarly, at Denbigh Castle, begun in 1282 by Henry de Lacy, the kitchen, hall and lord's chamber are accommodated within mural towers or sited in a range of buildings against the curtain wall with no attempt at integrating them according to function. Of course, there are exceptions: Conwy Castle (1283–7), for example, is one of the most elaborate of all the Edwardian castles in Wales and, although built on a difficult narrow site, its architect (Master JAMES OF ST GEORGE) succeeded in planning accommodation that satisfied all the requirements of a royal household, administrative centre and garrison. The castle was divided into two wards or courtyards by a strong lateral wall. The main gate, which incorporated the constable's lodgings, led into an outer (public) ward in which were the great hall, kitchens and service rooms. The Middle Gate, which gave access to the inner (private) court through the dividing wall, was protected by a drawbridge and a small, projecting gatehouse. Within the inner ward the rooms for the king's principal officials were on the ground floor with the royal apartments above. There were two entrances to the king's suite from the courtyard below, both leading to outer chambers. One of these was the Presence Chamber where the King's Council met and where he received important visitors. A passage from the Presence Chamber led to the king's private chapel in the adjacent Chapel Tower. The other, smaller, chamber was probably used for more private business for it was provided with an outer lobby or 'waiting room'. Doors from both the outer chambers gave access to the inner or King's Chamber from which stairs led to bed chambers on two levels in the adjacent King's Tower. A further stair from the King's Chamber descended to the east barbican which was used as a private garden (*see* GARDENS). Two important design principles are evident at Conwy: the division of public and private spaces (the outer and inner wards) and the careful integration of chambers according to function.

The so-called KEEP-GATEHOUSE evolved as a consequence of the declining effectiveness of the KEEP in the thirteenth century and the development of the ENCLOSURE CASTLE in which the gate was the weakest point. The keep-gatehouse developed in response to that weakness, a manifestation of the principle, established at Dover Castle after 1216, whereby the most vulnerable element of a castle's defences should also be its most strongly fortified nucleus (*see above*). These great GATEHOUSES contained suites of rooms that were ideally suited to the residential and administrative needs of the CONSTABLE and it is not surprising therefore that it was the constable who almost invariably occupied a gatehouse. Not only could he maintain control of the drawbridge and portcullis mechanisms, but his suite of rooms often included a lesser hall which, in the lord's absence, would be used for judicial and other purposes.

The Fourteenth Century

By the beginning of the fourteenth century the office of domestic or household steward, now generally referred to as the *chamberlain*, was of increasing importance and may reasonably be considered to be one of the inner circle that included also the steward and treasurer. This was a consequence of the tendency, noted in the previous century, for lords to withdraw from the communal life of the hall to the relative peace of their privy chambers where much of their business was carried out. The purchase of provisions was now the responsibility of a specialist clerk with the butler overseeing the preparation and serving of food.

Thus, by the fourteenth century the magnate household comprised three distinct elements: the inner circle of household officials and their staffs; a wide network of supporting staff who managed a lord's estates; and the retainers upon whom he could call for military or political support (also described as his 'riding household') and who were required to attend their lord for ceremonial and other purposes (see CASTLE GUARD and LIVERY AND MAINTENANCE).

At the same time the magnate *council* became more formalised in its composition. It too consisted of three components: the senior household officials; professional lawyers who were paid members of the council; and the heads of senior tenant families who were usually of only slightly inferior status to the lord himself. It was the council's responsibility to advise the lord on the administration of his estates and to consider the implications of proposed actions, particularly those that might affect his relationships with his tenants and his standing in society. The council was not part of the household and was convened only when needed. It was by no means democratic: advice was given and the lord then either acted on that advice or disregarded it.

At Barnard Castle in the 1320s John de Baliol built a new hall with service rooms and kitchen at one end and a great chamber and round tower at the other for his own accommodation. This particular arrangement of rooms is common to many castles and fortified MANOR HOUSES and in many cases formed the nucleus of later additions. Quite often the physical constraints of a site meant that accom-modation could only be added or improved by sacrificing efficiency, though medieval architects were capable of finding ingenious solutions: at Chepstow Castle, for example, in the late thirteenth century Roger Bigod extended the domestic accommodation. By exploiting the slope on which the new range was to be built, Bigod's master mason was able to add two halls, a great hall and a lesser hall at a lower level, and to combine the service rooms and kitchens of the two halls with a common service passage.

The Fifteenth Century
By the fifteenth century the structure of a medieval magnate's *familia* or household was usually modelled on that of the sovereign (see below), the principal officials being:

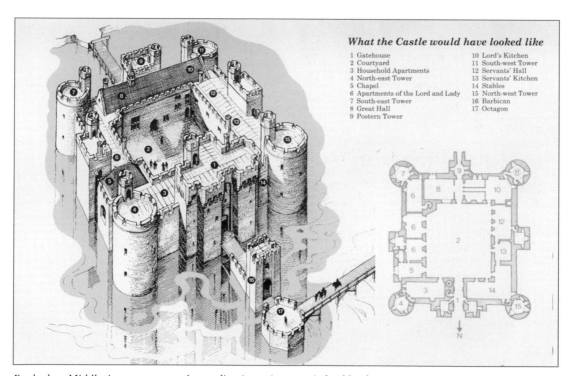

What the Castle would have looked like

1 Gatehouse
2 Courtyard
3 Household Apartments
4 North-east Tower
5 Chapel
6 Apartments of the Lord and Lady
7 South-east Tower
8 Great Hall
9 Postern Tower
10 Lord's Kitchen
11 South-west Tower
12 Servants' Hall
13 Servants' Kitchen
14 Stables
15 North-west Tower
16 Barbican
17 Octagon

By the late Middle Ages, a magnate's standing in society was judged by the size and efficiency of his household. Completed in 1388, Bodiam Castle's great hall, domestic apartments, kitchens, offices, chapel, servants' hall and kitchen, armoury, stables, storerooms and suites of rooms for guests and numerous household officials were all contained within its courtyard walls, rather than erected against a bailey wall as in earlier castles.

Seneschal A lord's senior officer and deputy, responsible for the administration of justice in a lord's absence.

Chamberlain Originally responsible for a lord's personal domestic arrangements but ultimately for his financial affairs.

Chancellor Responsible for administrative and legal matters such as the drawing-up of charters and the writing of letters.

Marshal Responsible for a lord's horses, soldiers and weaponry.

Steward Responsible for the administration of a lord's estates.

In a lord's absence, responsibility for his castle remained with the constable but its administration was delegated to a *receiver* who attended to financial matters including maintaining the profitability of an estate and the collection of taxes, rents and dues.

Each of these officials was responsible for a household department often comprising large numbers of junior officers with specific areas of responsibility such as the larder, the audit, the almonry, etc. (*see* ALMONER *and* AUDITOR). Of course, not all households demanded such a large staff: that of a knight, for example, may have comprised a steward, a receiver and a few retainers and domestic servants. On the other hand, Richard Beauchamp, earl of Warwick, the greatest and wealthiest of all medieval nobles, had two almost entirely separate entourages, one for his domestic affairs and one for his activities in the French wars. His receiver-general managed the income of his estates while a second official, a *cofferer*, looked after his diplomatic and war incomes together with those from the sales of timber and mining rights. Surviving household accounts record payments to messengers travelling between the earl in France, his council in London and his wife Elisabeth, who was supervising his affairs at Berkeley Castle. The accounts give details of the ordering of the Berkeley household for each day. First is a list of guests and the number of meals served in the hall. This is followed by records of purchases and provisions taken from the stores listed under Pantry (bread), Buttery (wine and ale), Kitchen (meat and fish), Wardrobe (wax for candles, spices, etc.) and Marshalsea (provisions for horses, transport, etc.). Elisabeth's daily charitable donations are also recorded as 'oblations'. Each time a new barrel of wine or herring was opened it was recorded by a small drawing in the margin of the account. Even at a time when Warwick and his entourage were away from home, a total of ninety-four guests and members of the household were provided with meals on the

fourth Sunday in Lent, 1421. The accounts record that on that day 196 fish and 300 oysters were eaten (no meat, for it was Lent) together with 146 large loaves and an average of one bottle of wine and six pints of ale for each person present (*see* KITCHENS).

The need to accommodate a rapidly expanding secretariat is evident in work that was carried out at Middleham Castle by Ralph Neville, the 1st earl of Westmorland, from *c.* 1405 to *c.* 1410. It was Neville's intention that his castle should be both his principal residence and the administrative centre of his vast estates. The new buildings provided offices and lodgings for his substantial retinue in two ranges abutting the south and west curtain walls (*c.* 1300) and these were linked by timber bridges, spanning the courtyard at first-floor level, to the twelfth-century keep which contained the great hall and principal residential chambers (*see* CLERESTORY). Richard Neville, Ralph's eldest son by Joan Beaufort, inherited Middleham in 1440 and it was during his ownership that the scheme was completed by the addition of a further range of offices against the north curtain that included an auditor's chamber and kitchen (though these facilities may have been added after the castle ceased to be a major residence and was used primarily as an estate office).

It may seem remarkable that so many early medieval great towers were retained for residential use at a time when the keep had become an incommodious military anachronism. Indeed, several new towers were constructed in the late fourteenth and fifteenth centuries, several of them in brick (*see* BRICK BUILDINGS). But there can be little doubt that the great tower remained an enduring symbol of lordship, a declaration of feudal permanence and prestige. Indeed, the French *donjon*, which is often used in English as a synonym for 'great tower', is derived from the Latin *dominium* and expresses 'absolute ownership' or lordship. At Warkworth Castle, for example, a magnificent new tower-house was built in the late fourteenth century by Henry Percy, 1st earl of Northumberland, to provide a self-contained suite of apartments, hall and domestic offices for the earl and his family. Not only was this accommodation extraordinarily well designed, but the tower was clearly intended to amaze all who saw it, not least the earl's illustrious guests. Even at Raglan Castle, with its sophisticated late fifteenth- and sixteenth-century ranges of domestic and administrative offices, its suites of guests' apartments, its long gallery, library and Fountain Court, the lord chose to live in the Great Tower of Gwent, a splendid hexagonal keep, detached from the main body of the castle by a water-filled moat.

Was it paranoia, as some have suggested? Or was it simply a spectacular gesture?

The Royal Household

In government, the administration was essentially that created by the Norman kings. The office of the EXCHEQUER oversaw the finances of the realm following long-established bureaucratic procedures, and the CHANCERY issued charters and letters under the GREAT SEAL, thereby transmitting instructions to the king's subjects. But at the heart of the governmental system was the household: a flexible, personal instrument consisting at one level of the sovereign's domestic entourage or *domus* (with departments such as the kitchen, the saucery, the pantry and the scullery) and at another the *Wardrobe*. This was a central department which, from the mid-thirteenth century, effectively annexed the responsibilities formerly associated with another department, the Chamber. During the reign of Edward I (1272–1307) the Wardrobe enjoyed increasing financial autonomy and, unlike the Exchequer, was capable of expanding to meet changing national demands, such as war. It became the chief spending department of central government, indeed the PRIVY SEAL was retained by the Controller of the Wardrobe so that letters of instruction, authenticated by this seal (*warrants*), could be sent to the Exchequer and the Chancery and to royal officials throughout the realm. The officials of the household, and especially those of the Wardrobe, were essential to the effective government of the country in both peace and war. It also provided the core of the royal army (the corps of royal household knights and esquires) which could be expanded rapidly in time of war and was retained through the Wardrobe. In the mid-1280s lists of those receiving the royal livery include some 570 names, ranging from high-ranking officials to scullery boys.

Many of the great English offices of state originated in the households of the dukes of Normandy well before the Conquest and there is little doubt that the ducal establishment itself was modelled on that of the kings of France. The *Constitutio Domus Regis*, compiled for King Stephen in *c.* 1136, indicates that at that time there were four principal ranks of officer in the royal household:

First: Chancellor, Steward, Master Butler, Master Chamberlain and Constable.
Second: Master Dispenser of the Bread, Master Dispenser of the Larder, Master Dispenser of the Buttery, Master of the Writing Desk, Clerk of the Spence of the Bread and Wine and Duty Chamberlain (deputy to the Master Chamberlain).
Third: Deputy Constables, Master Marshal and Chamberlain of the Privy Purse.
Fourth: Dispenser of the Pannetry, Dispenser of the Larder, Keeper of the Butts, Chamberlain of the Candle and four Marshals of the Household.

The stewards were responsible for the hall and those departments connected with food over which the butler had no jurisdiction (*see* LARDER *and* STEWARD). In England the butler was responsible for the buttery, wine selection, the dispensers, etc. (in France the office was of far greater importance, controlling the royal vineyards, collecting taxes from certain abbeys and sitting as a judge in the king's court). The chamberlain was in charge of the royal bed chamber and, immediately after the Conquest, was also the royal treasurer. Towards the end of the Norman period a separate office of treasurer was created and by 1135 this was considered to be as important as that of chancellor and other offices of the first rank. The constables (*comes stabuli*) initially controlled the stables from which their title derives, the kennels, the MEWS and anything relating to the king's sporting activities. They were also quartermasters, responsible for the payment of the king's soldiers, and each royal castle was governed by a constable in the king's absence. Initially the marshal's duties included supervision of the royal stables, though by 1385 the office had attained considerable military and judicial importance comparable with that of the constable (*see* MARSHALSEA).

From these household offices evolved the eight great officers of medieval government, each responsible for his own department: Lord High Steward, Lord High Chancellor, Lord High Treasurer, Lord President of the Council, Lord Keeper of the Great Seal, Lord Great Chamberlain, Lord High Constable and Earl Marshal. (As the influence of the Wardrobe grew during the thirteenth century so too did that of its controller so that a further office, the Lord Privy Seal, was eventually established.) In time many of the lesser household offices became sinecures, granted as royal patronage and perceived by recipients as a means of advancement. As the functions of monarchy and government diverged, so many of the major offices became offices of state while others remained as offices of the royal household. Most still exist, though in much modified and often ceremonial form. (*See also* FAMILIA REGIS *and* VERGE)

HOUSEHOLD BADGES *see* BADGES AND LIVERY

HUE AND CRY The pursuit of a felon was the responsibility of the parish in which he was discovered or to which he was known to have fled. Parishioners were obliged to 'raise the hue and cry' by shouting and the blowing of horns.
(*See also* LAW AND ORDER)

HUNDRED A tenth-century administrative division of a SHIRE, administered by a reeve, who served writs on behalf of the sheriff of the shire, and later by a constable, who was responsible for the apprehension of criminals. These administrative divisions may have originated as units of a hundred taxable hides, each *hide* being the amount of land required to maintain an extended free family, or else as units of ten *tithings*. In Kent hundreds were known as *lathes* (the subdivisions of which were hundreds), in Surrey *rapes*, in East Anglia *lets*, in the Isle of Wight *liberties* and in Cumberland, Durham, Northumberland and Westmorland *wards*. In the Danelaw counties (principally Derbyshire, Leicestershire, Lincolnshire, Nottinghamshire and parts of Yorkshire) they were known as *wapentakes* (Old Norse for 'weapon-taking'), each subdivision being a hundred.
(*See also* LAW AND ORDER)

HUNDRED ROLLS Corruption in local administration, particularly the usurpation of liberties, was endemic in the second half of the thirteenth century. The Hundred Rolls record the findings of an investigation into local government conducted in 1274/5 on the direct instruction of Edward I. In 1278 the Statutes of Gloucester required all holders of franchises to prove their titles through *quo warranto* proceedings. Both sets of records are maintained by the Public Record Office and contain invaluable details of thirteenth-century local administration. Two volumes of *Rotuli Hundredorum* were published in 1812 and 1818, together with an *Index*. *Placita de Quo Warranto* was also published in 1818 and this contains transcripts of many of the proceedings which followed the survey of the hundreds.

HUNDRED YEARS WAR, THE The period of Anglo-French hostilities which opened with the confiscation of Gascony by Philip VI in 1337 and ended with the expulsion of the English from France (with the exception of the Calais pale) in 1453. The war had several causes, concerned (as previous Anglo-French conflicts had been) with the demarcation of English territorial possessions in France and the extent of English sovereignty in those possessions. But the principal cause was the English king's claim to the French throne. In 1340 Edward III (1327–77) assumed the title *Rex Angliae et Franciae* at a ceremony in Ghent and emphasised his claim by quartering the French royal arms with his own (*see* ROYAL ARMS). His claim was well-founded. In 1328 Charles IV had died without issue, his nearest heir being his sister Isabella, widow of Edward II of England. However, the French council determined that the crown should pass to Charles's cousin Philip of Valois, who became Philip VI of France.

The Hundred Years War consisted of five phases. The first, from 1337 to 1340, was a period of lengthy diplomacy, over-ambitious alliances, broken treaties and a refusal of the French to face the English in battle. It was brought to a close in 1340 by the truce of Esplechin and the return to England of Edward and his army with only the naval victory off Sluys (1340) to show for their efforts.

The second phase, to 1360, was a period of outstanding success. Edward abandoned his previous strategy of attacking from the north-east (where several of his intended allies had proved singularly unreliable) and decided instead to launch a series of assaults from bases in Gascony, Brittany and Normandy, exploiting the resentment of the local nobility against the centralising policies of the Capetian and Valois monarchs. There followed two decades of military success with crushing English victories at Crécy (1346) and at Poitiers (1356) where the French king was taken captive. In 1359 Edward embarked on an expedition which he hoped would culminate in his coronation at Rheims, but the city resisted his assault and at Brétigny he was obliged to come to terms with the French. By this treaty he was granted full sovereignty over an enlarged Aquitaine in return for surrendering his claim to the French throne. For most of this period the initiative lay with the English and the war was fought almost exclusively on French soil. Consequently, it was the French who suffered the devastation of war and the English who, for the most part, benefited from the spoils. In particular, the ransoming of aristocratic prisoners (*see* RANSOM) and the financial benefits of advancement through military service to the crown enabled England's comital class to express its sense of chivalric brotherhood through an ostentatious enthusiasm for building and refurbishing castles (*see* CHIVALRY *and* GARTER, THE MOST NOBLE ORDER OF THE).

When hostilities resumed in 1369 Edward's powers were already in decline and the advantages of strong leadership passed to the French. Gradually the English gains of the previous decades were lost until only the coastal strip of Gascony remained. Protracted negotiations, begun in the 1370s, resulted in a draft treaty by which the English surrendered their claim to hold Gascony in full sovereignty. But the treaty was rejected by parliament and in 1396 a 28-year truce was agreed instead. This was confirmed by a marriage alliance between Richard II (1377–99) and Isabella, the six-year-old daughter of Charles VI of France.

The fourth phase, from 1396 to 1420, was a time of cumulative French disaster. The madness of Charles VI, combined with civil war in France and the rise of Burgundian power, provided the opportunity for Henry V (1413–22) to revive his claim to the French throne. When, as he had anticipated, his excessive demands were rejected by both the Armagnacs and the Burgundians, he landed at the mouth of the Seine, captured Harfleur and embarked on a devastating CHEVAUCHÉE to Calais. Although heavily outnumbered, in 1415 Henry won a famous victory near Agincourt in the Pas de Calais (*see* ARCHERY). In 1417 he began the systematic conquest and settlement of Normandy which, by 1419, had fallen into English hands. As a consequence of the murder of the duke of Burgundy in 1419 and the capitulation of the Burgundian party, Henry was able to conclude the Treaty of Troy in 1420 by which the dauphin was disinherited and Henry was recognised as heir to the French crown.

Only two years later Henry V died, followed in the same year by Charles VI of France. The heir to this dual monarchy was Henry's nine-month-old son Henry VI (1422–61), during whose thirteen-year minority John, duke of Bedford (1389–1435), acted as Regent of France. Bedford was well aware that continued political stability depended on the Anglo-Burgundian alliance and maintenance of the bitter dispute between the dauphin (now Charles VII) and Duke Philip of Burgundy. But with the revival of Charles's fortunes (inspired by Joan of Arc), Philip's influence in French affairs waned and at the Congress of Arras (1435) he abandoned his English allies and joined his kinsman. The collapse of the Burgundian alliance, the death of Bedford and the incompetence of Henry VI sealed England's fate in France. Even so, it took a further sixteen years for

the French to regain Normandy (in 1450) and to take Gascony (1451). The war veteran John Talbot, earl of Shrewsbury (*c.* 1387–1453) led an army into Gascony in 1452 but was defeated and killed at Castillon in 1453. Talbot's memory lived on: his name was anathema to the French who chided their errant children with a dreadful warning – 'the Talbot cometh!'. But of England's possessions in France, only Calais remained.

HUNTING *see* CHASE, DEER PARK, FOREST *and* HUNTING LODGE

HUNTING LODGE Medieval forests were vast and long distances were covered by a hunting party and its attendant officials and servants in the course of a day. Hunting lodges, strategically distributed throughout a FOREST or CHASE, were necessary both as places of refuge during and after a long day's sport and as centres of operation for the various foresters and woodmen who were responsible for the maintenance of the vert and venison. Lodges and keepers' dwellings were also provided in many of the larger DEER PARKS and often occupied vantage points on high ground from which spectators might observe a ceremonial hunt. Regrettably, hardly any ancient hunting lodges remain, though the decaying earthworks of their former moats and fishponds may still be discernible. These suggest that a typical medieval lodge was a castle in miniature: a square, central tower containing a hall and kitchens (and sometimes a chapel) set within a rectangular moated enclosure entered by means of a bridge and gatehouse. Perhaps the best example is the Barden Tower, one of six lodges constructed in the Clifford hunting grounds in Wharfedale, Yorkshire. The original tower was enlarged in 1485 and remodelled in 1658. In Wales a late medieval hunting lodge at Hen Gwrt near Abergavenny is traditionally associated with Dafydd Gam, a kinsman of the Herberts of Raglan, who was killed at Agincourt in 1415. But there is no evidence for this tradition and it was almost certainly the Herberts themselves who established a park for red and fallow deer at Hen Gwrt when they came into possession of the manor of the bishops of Llandaff in the late fifteenth century. The hunting lodge, which comprised an almost square stone building within a walled enclosure, was built on the site of the bishop's timber-frame manor house. Within the two-storey building there was a hall with a fireplace, an adjoining chamber and several latrines. Today only the water-filled moat and rectangular grassy island have survived.

I

ILLEGITIMACY *see* BASTARDY

IMBREX *see* SLATES AND TILES

IMPALEMENT *see* MARSHALLING

IMPOST A wall bracket on which rests the end of an ARCH.

IMPRESSA *see* BADGES

INCENDIARY DEVICES References to oil-based incendiary devices are found in sixth-century manuscripts. These included fire-pots, which were thrown by hand (*see* PETARD) or shot from *ballistae* (*see* GREEK FIRE *and* SIEGES).

INDENTURE A formal inventory or agreement. The term derives from the practice of repeating the text of an agreement on a single sheet of vellum and separating the two identical texts by cutting in an irregular manner so that the indentations of each party's document complemented those of the other, thereby making it impossible to substitute a forged agreement or to alter the original. Medieval indentures were often prepared for a number of parties to an agreement and sometimes the word *chirograph* was written across the indented line to show that there were several copies of the same text. An *indenture of retainer* bound a retainer to service (not necessarily military service) for life in peace and war, while an *indenture of war* bound a retainer to military service on a particular campaign.

INDICTMENT The formal accusation of a crime made by a jury.

INDULGENCE The remission of punishment for sin following absolution and penance, usually in return for payment or service (e.g. taking part in a Crusade).

INESCUTCHEON In ARMORY, a small shield placed at the centre of a larger one.

INFANGENTHEOF The right of a manorial lord to try and punish a thief arrested in his manor.
(*See also* OUTFANGETHEOF)

INFEUDATION The granting of land to a VASSAL.

INN The private town house of a noble or bishop, for use when attending the court or parliament. The term was also applied to retainers' lodging houses, usually located in towns associated with castles.

By the late fourteenth century many of the senior aristocracy owned or leased a London residence and these were often provided with modest defences, perhaps a gatehouse (similar to that of an Oxbridge college) and exterior walls in which windows were inserted only on the upper floors. In the late 1470s the duke of Gloucester's town house, Crosby Place in Bishopsgate, was leased from the widow of its builder, Sir John Crosby, a prosperous grocer. The Elizabethan antiquarian John Stow described Crosby Place as a 'great house of stone and timber, very large and beautiful, and the highest at that time in London'. It was built round a courtyard and had a solar, chapel, great chamber, garden and a wonderful great hall with an oriel window, marble floor and a painted and gilded arched roof.

INQUISITIONES AD QUOD DAMNUM *see* CHANCERY

INQUISITIONES POST MORTEM An inquest held on the death of one of the crown's tenants-in-chief to determine the date of death and the lands held at that time, and to confirm the identity and age of the heir. The process was conducted by the official *escheator* who was responsible for deciding how much tax (known as *relief*) should be paid by the heir on entering his estate. If the heir was a minor, the estate reverted to the crown until he came of age. Records began in the reign of Henry III (1216–72) and many are indexed at the Public Record Office (*see* APPENDIX II).
(*See also* STATE RECORDS)

INTELLIGENCE AND ESPIONAGE By the late thirteenth century the development of professional bureaucracies enabled governments to maintain intelligence-gathering networks. One of the most effective was that which operated on both sides of the English Channel during the HUNDRED YEARS WAR (1337–1453). Advance warning of French raids was essential and it was the government's task to gather and coordinate intelligence from abroad through its network of spies and informers and through counter-espionage measures in the English ports and those under English control in France. In fact, the crown's French possessions were a major source of military intelligence, as were the diplomatic officials who shuttled between the English, French and Burgundian courts. The majority of English spies were Frenchmen and other foreigners, though English merchants were also engaged to gather information while abroad on business. Other agents worked as *provocateurs*, spreading disinformation and rumour to confuse the enemy. By the end of the fourteenth century a particularly effective spy network was operating out of CALAIS. The French, too, had their spies, as did the Scots, and both countries engaged in economic sabotage, flooding England with inferior bullion coinage. Fear of agents and saboteurs resulted in a close watch being kept on foreigners, particularly clergy and mendicant friars. Edward III required that inn-keepers should search all foreign guests and report their activities to the authorities. Captured spies were interrogated and imprisoned but, surprisingly, they were only rarely subjected to harsh punishment. Presumably there was tacit agreement on all sides that allowed for leniency. At a more local level magnates looked to their networks of retainers and to members of their wider affinities to report on any matter that might affect their security (*see* LIVERY AND MAINTENANCE).

INTERCLOSE *see* SCREENS

INTERREGNUM A period during which normal government is suspended, especially between successive reigns.

INTERSECTING TRACERY *see* GOTHIC ARCHITECTURE

INTERVAL TOWER One of a number of towers set along the length of a CURTAIN WALL (*see* TOWERS).

INTRA-MURAL Within the body of a wall, for example a stair, gallery or passageway.

INTRA-MURAL CELL A small room within the thickness of a wall.

INVENTORY A list of possessions, goods and chattels, often with a valuation.

INVEST In the present context, to lay siege to a castle or fortified town.

IRONSTONE Limestone or sandstone which has been coloured brown or green by the presence of iron oxide.

IRONWORK, LOCKS AND NAILS Considerable quantities of ironwork were used in the construction and maintenance of medieval castles, not only for accessories such as the stanchions and glazing bars of windows and door furniture but also for constructional purposes. Various types of rods, clamps and anchors and prodigious quantities and types of nails were required and the smith was, therefore, an important member of the building establishment, one whose responsibilities included making and repairing workmen's tools. Contemporary accounts show numerous purchases of iron, much of it imported from Spain. At Leeds Castle in 1370 home-produced iron (presumably from the Weald) cost between 5s 6d and 7s while Spanish iron cost from 9s 3d to 10s, suggesting that the imported product was considered to be of such superior quality that the additional expenditure could be justified. The accounts include numerous references to a variety of measures: in the 1323 catalogue of stores for the castles of north Wales, for example, we find 11,729 'pieces of iron' which included '24 seams of iron, each seam containing 72 pieces' and also '10 byndynges of iron, each byndyng containing 25 pieces'. The *gad* of iron was a common measure, equivalent to approximately three-quarters of a hundredweight (38kg). The Wealden (*Waldis*) iron-fields are mentioned in 1278 when Master Henry of Lewes, the chief smith at the Tower of London, bought '75 rods in Waldis' for 65s 7½d and paid £4 3s 4d 'to a smith in Waldis for 100 iron rods'. Steel, which was required for the edges of workmen's tools, was too costly a material to be wasted. Consequently, pieces of steel were welded on to the edge of iron tools: at Portchester Castle in 1397 42kg (94lb) of Spanish steel were used 'for the hardening of the axes and other tools of the masons'.

Medieval references to constructional ironwork are generally unhelpful, consisting of lists of the manufacture or purchase of bars, clamps, crampons and other devices without any indication of their intended use. The Westminster accounts for 1532 mention 66 'crampettes of iron made for the cramping and joining of harde stone togethers', presumably for use in a spire or gable where stones projected at an angle at which they were likely to slip. Iron pins were used for fastening the 'king's beasts' on the roofs and gables of Hampton Court and for the stone *types* or domical caps at the gable ends of the tennis court, two special tools ('ston persers') being provided 'for the masons to make holys to yowte in the sayd pynnys'. Similarly, in 1282 the smith at Caernarfon Castle made 'three crampons to hold a stone eagle upon the great tower'. At Leeds Castle in 1370 there is an entry of two irons and four crampons for reinforcing the stone brackets of the machicolations, while at York Castle 'four stays of iron to support the hoarding called le bretesse within the tower' are mentioned in 1362. Iron was frequently used in the construction of CHIMNEYS AND FIREPLACES: an entry for Westminster of 1259 records payments 'to smiths employed on making the ironwork which supports the shaft from the fireplace of the king's chamber against the force of the winds'. At the Tower in 1335 there is an entry 'for 4 hundredweight of Spanish iron for two pillars and a crossbar made thereof . . . to support the great fireplace in the Queen's chamber, because it broke and stones fell from it while the King's daughters and their nurses were sitting in the room'.

The term *dog* is frequently used for a band of iron used for strengthening woodwork, as at Gloucester Castle in 1442 where 'two iron dogges [were] used on the repair of the drawbridge'. Large quantities of iron were required for the construction of DRAWBRIDGES, as is evident from details of the ironwork made for a bridge at the Tower in 1324:

> To Walter de Bury, smith, 2 iron bolsters to carry the bridge, – 2s. To the same for 2 iron goiouns to lie on the said bolsters, – 2s. For 2 iron hoops for binding the axle-tree at either end, – 2s. For 6 iron bands to bind the weights called ballokis, – 6s. For 3 great iron pins to fasten the bridge to the axle, – 18d. For 2 rings with staples, 1 pin, 1 hinge for raising the bridge, 2 haspes with 4 staples, – 21d.

Huge quantities of charcoal were required to power the forges from which were produced nails and ironmongery. During the construction of Harlech Castle, during an eight-month period, 419 tons of charcoal were consumed, equivalent to 1,200 tons of sawn wood.

Windows

Iron was used in WINDOWS for strengthening the construction, for supporting glazing and for frustrating intruders. The ironwork of a window consists of upright and transverse bars, with small iron wedges (*keys*) driven in where the uprights pass through the crossbars. Where a window was of one or more lights it was usual to have a horizontal 'stay-bar' running through the mullions and a number of smaller bars parallel to it. The small bars to which the glazing was wired or soldered were

called *soudlets*. When glazed windows were intended to be opened it was necessary to set the glazing in an iron frame (*casement* or *case*). In 1365 no fewer than 160 'iron cases with their hinges for glazing the windows of the castle' were purchased at 5s each at Sheppey. In accounts, the word 'double' probably implies that the glazed frame was hinged into an outer metal frame, as at Westminster in 1532 where reference is made to 'a doble case sette in a windowe within a jakis in the Ladye Wilshire's lodgeing'. Window frames were often blackened or varnished to arrest the rusting process. At Windsor, for example, in 1352 we find 'a barrel of pitch for blackening various ironwork'. But more often ironwork was whitened by dipping it in tin. At Queensborough in 1375 there is an entry of 'half a pound of fresh fat, with which to grease nails, bolts and other ironwork to keep them from rust until they are tinned'.

Fastenings and Locks

Iron was also required for hanging doors, shutters and windows. The earliest method of hanging a door was by means of a *pin-hinge*, the back beam (*hartree*) of the door having at its end an iron spindle which turned in a socket (*har*) in the threshold. From the late thirteenth century the majority of doors were hung by two or more *hook hinges*, still commonly found in the doors of medieval churches. A hook hinge comprises an iron 'wedge' inserted in the door-frame, from the broader end of which a round iron pin rises vertically to carry an eyed plate attached to the door. Another type of hinge was the *garnet*, a T-shaped hinge, the short cross-bar of which was attached to the door-frame. There is mention in 1348 of a 'pair of gernettes for a trappedore of a prison' at the Tower. The simplest way of closing a door or window is by means of a latch and catch operated by a 'snatch' (or 'sneck') and references to these are numerous in contemporary documents. The circular handle by which a latch was raised was known as a *haggaday*. 'Rings with plates, tinned, called hagodayes, for doors' occurs in the 1383 accounts for Windsor, while '79 bolts, 38 wrestlacchis [latches lifted by turning the ring] and 12 hauegodaies of iron' were supplied to Sheppey Castle in 1365.

For fastening doors, bolts and various types of lock were used. The 1348 accounts for Nottingham Castle include the entry: 'For making a prison under the high tower to keep the Scots safely, namely for double doors with bands and hasps, locks and iron shuttles, with wooden bars.' The 'shuttles' were bolts which were inserted into 'shutting plates' or 'staples' when a door was secured. Bolts are also referred to as *slots*: at Westminster in 1353, for example, we have '12 staples and 2 slottes for dores', while at Clare in 1347 we read of 'a sleet with 3 stapelles of iron with fittings for a new door by the Lady's chamber' and 'for 6 small sletes of iron with fittings for windows'. 'Running' or sliding bars were often used to secure the inside of a door or pair of doors. These went right across the back of the door(s) and could be withdrawn into deep sockets on either side of the passage when not in use. (These sockets have often survived in gate passages and several still contain at least part of the draw-bar *see* GATEHOUSES.) Entrance gates could also be fastened by a *flail* or *sweep*, an iron bar that pivoted in the centre and was turned into the horizontal position when the gates were closed, each end fitting into an iron plate with a hasp that could be secured by a padlock. An exceptionally large flail was provided for the Watergate at the Tower in 1324. John de Thorney was paid 42*s* for 'a thousandweight of iron for a great bar of iron by way of a fleyl for closing and fastening the great gates of the Watergate'. A team of smiths worked for seven weeks to complete the task, though the iron must have been of poor quality for we are told that 'two thirds of the same iron was wasted in the fire and the working'.

Various types of lock were used in the medieval period, the simplest being the *clicket lock*. In 1425 'a klyketlok for the door of a latrine' is mentioned at Eltham. When the action was spring-assisted, the lock was known as a *spring lock*, a device that was known to the Romans and was probably used in early medieval Britain. In 1532 the door between the king's bedroom and dining room at Westminster was provided with a 'sprynge locke with a staple and flappe', the 'flap' being a hinged plate (*scutcheon plate*) to protect the keyhole. Locks of this type, where the outer plate was visible, were known as *plate-locks*, while those that were concealed beneath a block of wood fastened to the door were called *stock-locks*. At Corfe Castle 'four stoklokkes with keys for setting on doors' were purchased in 1357, while at Havering 'six locks called stoklokkis and two clyketlokkes' are recorded in the accounts for 1374 and 'locks called platelok and stoclock' in 1376. Considerable use was made of padlocks, though they were rarely described as such, the earliest reference being at Windsor in 1438 when 'two padlockes' cost 16*d*. One variety of the padlock was the *terret* or *turret*, which was similar in appearance to the *fetterlock* or manacle, and was used principally for restraining birds of prey.

Nails

Huge quantities of nails were used in medieval building and at first sight it would appear from the accounts that these were carefully graded by size and function. However, medieval business was characterised by a contradiction between apparent exactitude and haphazard casualness. The nomenclature of nails depended on the purpose for which they were to be used, their shape or their price. But examination of the accounts frequently reveals that two dozen different terms may have been applied to an identical article while quantities were often measured by weight or (in the fifteenth century) by their cost per hundred. Thus, the stores at Calais in 1390 included '494,900 nails of various kinds' which (as nails were often counted by the 'long hundred' of six score) may actually have been 593,880. So numerous (and so inconsistent) were the terms used that an inventory of nails purchased at York Castle in 1327 will have to suffice as an example of the names attributed to different types of nail at that time:

220 braggenayl	at 15*d* the hundred, 'by the great hundred'		
100 knopnayl	" 6*d*	"	"
3,260 doublenail	" 4*d*	"	"
1,200 greater spyking	" 4*d*	"	"
5,200 spyking	" 3*d*	"	"
3,250 thaknail	" 3*d*	"	"
1,800 lednail	" 2*d*	"	"
300 grapnayl	" 2*d*	"	"
7,760 stotnayl	" 2*d*	"	"
1,100 smaller stotnayl	" 1½*d*	"	"
300 tyngilnayl	" 1*d*	"	"
18,600 brodd	" 1*d*	"	"

The largest types of nail were *bragges*, *gaddes* and *spikes*, diminishing through various grades of *spikings*, *spikenails*, etc., but even these terms implied no standardisation and were, in practice, generic. Ordinary nails are often termed *board nails* or *plank nails*, the fixing of boards or planks being the most common purposes for which nails were used. *Door nails* were secured by a process of clinching or riveting: at the Tower in 1323 'Richard Spark, clincher, working on the gates at clinching and riveting great nails' was paid 4½*d* a day. Of the various nails used for roofing, *lath nails* were the most common: as early as 1208 we read of 21,000 'nails for laths' bought for repairs at Farnham Castle. *Clout nails* were used for securing patches of iron and are particularly associated with the repair of carts, ploughs and other machinery, as well as use for building purposes. At Rockingham Castle in 1375 '14,700 clouthnayl' were purchased 'for fastening laths and lead' at 2s 6d per thousand. Of the smaller nails in common use, *prigs* and *sprigs* were almost certainly identical. The Westminster accounts for 1532 refer to 'one bagge of sprigge' costing 9d while later entries show 'sprigges' purchased at 7s 6d 'the bagge' of 20,000. The heads of nails used on doors (*head nails*) and for similar purposes were often shaped and faceted: a payment is recorded at the Tower in 1278 for '280 large nails with square heads for the gate of the turret'; while, again at the Tower, fifty large *dicehead* nails were ordered 'for the bars of the lion house' in 1350. At the royal palace of Sheen in 1447 '300 tinned nails called dicehedenayles, used for naylyng the rayle newly made for the aras [wall-hanging]' were supplied for Queen Margaret's manor of Pleasance near Greenwich.

ISSUE ROLLS A series of rolls dating from 1240 to the end of the seventeenth century (but with omissions from 1480 to 1567) recording payments made from crown revenues. These are maintained at the Public Record Office (*see* APPENDIX II) and a number have been published.
(*See also* STATE RECORDS)

J

JACK (i) A small flag flown at the bow of a ship.
(ii) A colloquial term for a medieval retainer.
(iii) An infantryman's garment of rough canvas strengthened with plates of metal or horn (*see* ARMOUR).

JAMB The side of a doorway, window, archway or fireplace. Pairs of vertical jambs projecting from the side walls of a GATE PASSAGE mark the position of former doors. The reinforced double doors closed on to the stone jambs, protecting the vulnerable hinges and rendering it almost impossible to force them open from the outside. The doors were secured on the inside by massive draw-bars, the ends of which rested in deep recesses in the passage wall. These were drawn back through holes in the opposite wall, into the adjacent guardroom or porter's lodge, when the gates were open.
(*See also* WINDOWS)

JAMES OF ST GEORGE (c. 1235–1308) Possibly the most famous of all castle builders and principally responsible for the design and construction of the great Edwardian castles of North Wales (*see* MASTER MASONS AND ARCHITECTS).

In the 1260s Master James had learned the arts of castle-building and the techniques of the military engineer (*ingeniator*) working with his father for the counts of Savoy, a region partly in south-east France, partly in western Switzerland and partly across the Alps in northern Italy. Count Peter and Count Philip of Savoy were Edward I's kinsmen and by a feudal technicality several castles and towns on the routes to the Alpine passes were held by them as Edward's vassals. Furthermore, Count Amadeus V, who succeeded Count Philip in 1285, was in King Edward's service in Wales in the war of 1277 and in 1282 led an expedition from Chester to relieve the siege of Rhuddlan Castle. James acquired the surname 'St George' from the castle of St George-d'Espéranche, near Lyon, which he had built for Count Philip and at which King Edward had briefly stayed on his return from the Holy Land in 1273. Thus, Master James of Savoy came to the attention of King Edward of England and entered his service as *ingeniator regis*.

Having worked on the castles at Builth and Aberystwyth, Master James completed Rhuddlan Castle in 1282 (it was begun, in 1277, by another notable *ingeniator* the Gascon Master Bertram). He then went on to complete the construction of Flint Castle before embarking, after 1283, on the castles of Conwy, Caernarfon, Harlech and Beaumaris. Contemporary records show that Master James was paid 2s a day, as much as an average craftsman could earn in a week, and that his services were rewarded with a pension and a grant for life of the manor of Mostyn near Holywell. He died in 1308 and is generally acknowledged to have been the greatest architect in the history of English castles.

JAVELIN *see* WEAPONS AND HARNESS

JAZERENC *see* HAUBERK

JEDDART AXE *see* WEAPONS AND HARNESS

JETTY Projecting floor joists in a timber-frame building, usually supporting an overhang.

JEWS Large numbers of Jews came to England in the decades following the Norman Conquest but they were not permitted to trade or to practise agriculture and were acceptable only as money-lenders at a time when usury was forbidden to Christians by Canon Law (though it was undoubtedly practised privately). Although of use to the crown and nobility, the Jews were singularly unpopular and many were massacred in 1189–90. In the following century their usefulness declined and they were finally expelled in 1290. In part, medieval anti-Semitism was the result of religious prejudice and resentment against the Jewish community, which tended to maintain a separate and distinctive identity. But more particularly it reflected an almost universal suspicion and jealousy of Jewish commercial success which came to be associated in the common mind with sharp practice; thus the persecution of Jews was the inevitable reaction to every economic or social crisis.

JOUSTING *see* TOURNAMENTS

JOUSTING CHEQUES *see* TOURNAMENTS

JUPON *or* **GIPON** The successor to the SURCOAT: a short, sleeveless coat worn over ARMOUR and often emblazoned with a coat of arms. Popular from the mid-fourteenth to the mid-fifteenth century, at which time plate armour became so highly embellished and valuable that it was fashionable for it to be worn without covering (*see* ALWITE). The later TABARD was worn for purely heraldic purposes.
(*See also* CYCLAS)

JUSTICES OF THE PEACE *see* LAW AND ORDER *and* QUARTER SESSIONS

JUSTICIAR From the eleventh to the thirteenth century, the viceroy of the Norman and Angevin kings who governed as the monarch's deputy while he was overseas. The office lapsed in 1234, was revived in 1258 in the Provisions of Oxford and was abolished after the justiciar Hugh le Despenser sided with Simon de Montfort at the battle of Evesham in 1265 (*see* BARONS' WARS, THE). In the localities justiciars were appointed by the king to hear cases referred to them by him. They were men of standing in the community whose loyalty to the crown was beyond question.

KEEP A sixteenth-century term for what is referred to in medieval documents as the 'great tower' (*magnus turris*), the most important tower in a castle and usually its strongest point. The fourteenth-century term DONJON is also used synonymously for great tower. The keep was effectively a castle within a castle: a horizontal residence built vertically for reasons of security. It contained the principal domestic chambers, at least during the Norman period, and was a final refuge in the event of a siege – barracks, workshops, stables and other garrison buildings being located in a BAILEY.

Many historians dislike the term 'keep' and it is used here reluctantly for the simple reason that it cannot be ignored. Its use in reference books and guidebooks is ubiquitous. Furthermore, a number of other terms are derived from it and these require further explanation (*see* HALL-KEEP, KEEP-GATEHOUSE, SHELL-KEEP *and* TOWER-KEEP). The truth is that each keep, great tower or donjon is different and an understanding of how their function and design evolved in response to changing military and domestic circumstances is of greater importance than any attempt at a rigid classification.

In the decades following the Conquest, the earth and timber motte and bailey castle (*see* MOTTE) remained the most common form of fortification. Several timber towers were rebuilt in stone but mottes were often found to be unstable and were abandoned in favour of more suitable natural sites (*see also* SHELL-KEEP). Nevertheless, the strength of early earth and timber fortifications was demonstrated in 1075 when the formidable motte of Norwich Castle held out against a three-month siege.

During the eleventh and twelfth centuries a number of large stone keeps were constructed, usually within an existing fortified enclosure. The earliest of these was the magnificent HALL-KEEP of Chepstow Castle in Gwent. Built by William fitz Osbern, palatine earl of Hereford, shortly before his death in 1071, it was modelled on similar eleventh-century hall-keeps in the Loire Valley and in Normandy and is the earliest datable secular stone building in Britain. Other major eleventh- and twelfth-century keeps include the White Tower at the Tower of London (1077–80), Colchester (the largest keep in England, *c.* 1085), Norwich (1125–35 and restored in the nineteenth century), Rochester (1127), Castle Rising (1138), Duffield (*c.* 1165), Bamburgh (*c.* 1165), Middleham (1170), Bowes (1171–8), and Dover (1180). Unlike the vertically arranged chambers in a TOWER-KEEP, which were often cramped and poorly lit, the hall, solar and private apartments of these large keeps were located side-by-side on an upper storey and, because of their height above ground level, could be generously lit. At Hedingham Castle (*c.* 1130–40), for example, the upper level of the two-storey hall is surrounded by an open mural gallery, similar to the triforium of an abbey church. These large keeps were usually divided internally down the middle, or slightly off-centre, by a *cross-wall* which often ran the full height of the building. Depending on the function of a particular storey, this might be a solid wall, an arcade or an immense flying arch. Not only did a cross-wall strengthen the structure of the building, it also meant that floors could be spanned more easily, without the need for exceptionally long timbers. Again at Hedingham, the massive walls of the undercroft support internal arches, that in the hall measuring nearly 9m (30ft) in width, the widest Norman arch in England. Significantly, keeps of this magnitude were seldom attempted again – until the

late fourteenth century when great towers such as Warkworth were erected to proclaim the status and wealth of the late medieval aristocracy (*see p. 167*).

The square tower-keeps at castles such as Goodrich (*c.* 1160), Richmond (*c.* 1170), Peveril (1174) and (the native Welsh) Dolwyddelan (*c.* 1200), are more typical of the period than the large keeps referred to above and must have been dark and incommodious places in which to live. Indeed, Peveril's keep (which cost £184 to build) may have been used only intermittently for domestic purposes, while at Dolwyddelan a second, rectangular, tower was later added to accommodate a first-floor hall (*see* HALL). Nevertheless, at the time they were considered to be virtually impregnable and so fulfilled their primary function. Typically, a stone vaulted UNDERCROFT or cellar was used for storage and above this the ground floor would house the garrison with the hall taking up the entire first floor. On the second floor were the principal private chambers which often included a CHAPEL, and above was a battlemented open platform. Fireplaces were sometimes set into the thickness of the outer walls, with tapering flues rising diagonally to vent at the outer face (*see* CHIMNEYS AND FIRE-PLACES). Access to the keep would normally be at

The square tower-keeps at castles such as Goodrich, Herefordshire, (c. 1160), must have been dark and incommodious places in which to live.

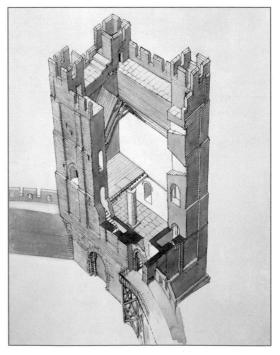

The keep of Richmond Castle (c. 1170) is 30.6 m (100 ft) high with an entrance chamber on the first floor and a hall on the second.

first-floor level by means of a flight of steps enclosed, in most cases, within a FOREBUILDING. In some castles a pit at the top of the forebuilding was spanned by a wooden floor that could be withdrawn or destroyed if required. At ground level the walls of a keep could be 3 to 3.5m (10 to 12ft) thick, and in some cases, such as Dover, up to 6m (20ft) thick. They were built of cut stone blocks or rubble and mortar faced with dressed stone, and rose to 25m (80ft) or more, often with splayed buttresses at the corners and at the centre of each face. The floors were connected by STAIRS, either flights of mural stairs or newel stairs contained within a corner turret. Sometimes the stair entrances were located at opposite corners of a chamber so that, were one level to be captured, an attacking force would be obliged to fight its way across the chamber before attempting to climb to the next floor. Window openings were generally confined to secure upper storeys and were small on the outside but splayed on the inside to admit more light and to improve ventilation from open hearths. Within the thickness of the walls were passages, chambers and GARDEROBES (latrines) that vented to a cesspool or pit below or on to the outside of the walls.

The keep of Richmond Castle is 30.6m (100ft) high with an entrance chamber on the first floor and a hall on the second, opening to the roof. Typically, the roof is pitched beneath parapet level and set within a crenellated WALL-WALK with two-storey turrets at each corner. At Ludlow Castle the keep doubled as a gatehouse, one of the earliest examples of a KEEP-GATEHOUSE in England (c. 1175), with a separate hall and unique circular chapel located within a stone-curtained bailey with flanking towers (see TOWERS). Because of the enormous weight of masonry tower-keeps had to be constructed on solid ground, usually on a natural eminence, either within an earlier bailey or RINGWORK or on an entirely new site. The need for a solid foundation often conflicted with the other essential requirement: a reliable water supply within the walls of the castle. It was often necessary to excavate deep well-shafts in order to reach water, though such measures helped to prevent pollution during periods of siege (see WELLS).

So successful were these formidable great towers that the civil war known as the ANARCHY (during the reign of Stephen (1135–54)) was essentially a succession of sieges, resolved as often by starvation or treachery as by the use of projectile machines such as the *mangonel* and *trebuchet* (see SIEGES). These strongholds had been designed primarily for defensive purposes, but military architects, no doubt influenced by experiences in the CRUSADES,

perceived a need to provide a besieged garrison with a means of retaliation. Rows of PUTLOG HOLES, still visible just below the CRENELS (openings) of battlements, once supported timber *hourds* (projecting galleries – see HOARDING) and larger PENTISES or 'penthouses' (projecting wooden turrets) that were built over battlements both for added protection and so that projectiles could be dropped into the vulnerable area at the foot of a wall. These timber structures were later superseded by MACHICOLATIONS – permanent projecting stone parapets carried forward on corbels between which the offensive material could be thrown.

The first cylindrical keep, at New Buckenham, was built in the 1140s for William d'Albini who was also responsible for the magnificent hall-keep at Castle Rising (1138–40). From this and other examples, it is evident that there was no sudden preference for cylindrical rather than rectilinear towers, and that both continued to be built, together with the occasional polygonal tower, throughout the medieval period. One of the earliest cylindrical keeps, and undoubtedly the finest, is at Conisbrough Castle (c. 1180). Built of ashlar masonry, it rose to nearly 30m (100ft) in height from a tall plinth (to frustrate undermining) with six tapering buttress-like turrets projecting from the outer face. These projections, which enabled defenders on the wall-head to observe 'dead ground' at the foot of the wall, are unique in England. Defensively, a cylindrical tower was ideal: it had no corners that could more easily be battered by siege engines or undermined by sappers. Nevertheless, rectangular rooms were very much more convenient for domestic purposes and military considerations often took second place when decisions had to be made. Indeed, the round tower at New Buckenham may have been no more than a pragmatic solution in the absence of good quality stone which was necessary for strengthening corners. It was built entirely of flint and, somewhat incongruously, was constructed with a cross-wall that divided the interior into two semicircular chambers. There were also regional trends: in the Marches of Wales twelfth- and thirteenth-century towers tended to be cylindrical (at Bronllys, Longtown, Tretower and Skenfrith, for example), while on the Scottish borders rectilinear towers (such as Belsay, Chipchase and Prudhoe) continued to be built in the sixteenth century and beyond (see PELE TOWERS). One of the finest cylindrical keeps, at Pembroke Castle (c. 1200), rises through four levels to a height of 24m (80ft) with walls 5.8m (19ft) thick at the base which is battered (splayed) to provide greater stability and to frustrate undermining. A row of putlog holes just below the

One of the earliest cylindrical keeps is at Conisbrough Castle (c. 1180). Built of ashlar masonry it rose to nearly 30 m (100 ft) from a tall plinth (to frustrate undermining) with six tapering buttress-like turrets projecting from the outer face. These projections, which enabled defenders on the wall-head to observe 'dead ground' at the foot of the wall, are unique in England.

parapet once secured a timber hoarding. As is generally the case, the openings in the walls increase in size towards the top of the tower: at the lower levels they are mere LOOPHOLES while larger windows illuminate the secure top floor with its magnificent stone dome. As with most other Welsh keeps, Pembroke's great tower was intended for occupation only during emergencies (it had no built-in latrines!), the residential and domestic buildings in the east corner of the inner ward being contemporaneous.

The cost of building these great towers was often prodigious. A simple tower, such as that at Bridgnorth Castle, cost less than £400 while more complex structures, such as Newcastle and Scarborough, cost between £500 and £1,000 in the period 1167–77. At the other end of the scale, Henry II's magnificent keep at Dover Castle was built at a cost of some £4,000 – just part of the estimated £7,000 that was spent on improving the castle's defences

between 1181 and 1191 (*see* CASTLES, CONSTRUCTION OF.)

With the exception of the hall-keep at Bowes Castle (1171–8), all eleventh- and twelfth-century keeps were constructed within a surrounding rampart or rudimentary curtain wall that contained other buildings. (There were exceptions: the twelfth-century stone curtain walls and flanking towers of Ludlow Castle were by no means rudimentary.) But while the keep remained the final refuge, its strength had become its weakness. It was the immediate target for the concentrated efforts of an attacking force and, with the increasing effectiveness of siege weapons and new mining techniques, it became necessary to keep attackers as far away from it as possible. Consequently, further lines of defence were added and existing ones improved. Substantial crenellated CURTAIN WALLS with mural towers and fortified gatehouses replaced earlier earthen ramparts and rudimentary enclosure walls, compelling a besieging force to capture each obstacle before progressing to the next. In time, these outer defences proved so effective that the keep became obsolete; indeed, the notion of the great tower being the 'final refuge' was superseded by the need for a garrison to emerge from its defences at a time of its choosing – what today might be described as 'proactive defence'. When, in 1180, Henry II built his massive keep at Dover Castle it was 'like a conventional battleship in the atomic age . . . obsolete almost as soon as it was built' (*The King's Works*). In the siege of 1216–17 the French had succeeded in bringing down one of Dover's gate-towers and thereafter considerable royal expenditure was devoted to making the castle truly impregnable. Of greatest significance, and the key to Henry III's reorganised defences, was the formidable gatehouse which was built on a new site and incorporated the constable's lodgings. The Constable's Tower at Dover is an early example of the KEEP-GATEHOUSE principle whereby the most vulnerable element of a castle's defences should also be its most strongly fortified nucleus (*see also* ENCLOSURE CASTLES).

There were, of course, later great towers and these are frequently (and erroneously) described as 'keeps'. It has been argued that they provided a secure and self-contained refuge for a lord and his family at a time when many castles were garrisoned by mercenaries whose loyalty could not be guaranteed. There may be an element of truth in this, but they possessed few of the defensive characteristics of early keeps and were essentially grandiose residential tower-houses, intended to provide privacy away from the day-to-day activities of the bailey and the great hall (*see* TOWER-HOUSE). One of the finest

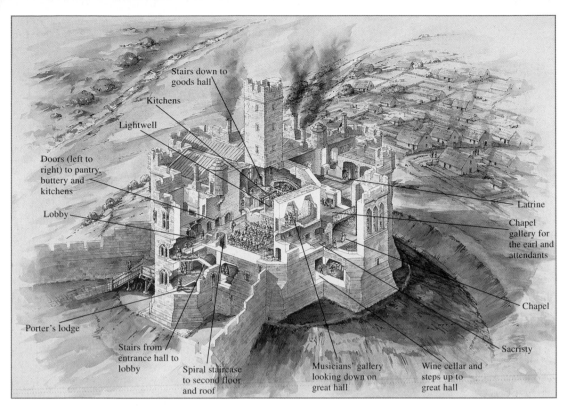

The Great Keep at Warkworth Castle, c. 1500.

examples is the 'Keep' at Warkworth Castle which was commissioned by Henry Percy, earl of Northumberland, and constructed in 1380–90. Built on a truncated twelfth-century motte, Warkworth's tower was clearly intended to celebrate the status and wealth of its builder, a spectacular declaration of self-confidence and the permanence of the Percy dynasty. Like other large tower-houses of the period, Warkworth was a self-contained residence enjoying lavish standards of comfort and convenience and with minimal defensive capabilities. Its plan is unique: square, with semi-octagonal towers projecting from the centre of each of its four sides in a cruciform arrangement that dictated the disposition of its chambers and services (*see* LIGHTWELL). The ground floor comprised a number of vaulted cellars and storage chambers, a guardroom and a splendid entrance hall and stair. On the first floor were the great chamber, chapel, buttery and pantry, together with the hall, kitchens and the sanctuary of the chapel, all of which rose into the second storey where there was a solar and a suite of private apartments.

A notable late medieval anomaly, and one that may reasonably be described as a *magnus turris*, is the Great Tower of Raglan Castle (*c*. 1435–45), a massive hexagonal keep known from the colour of its ashlar as the Yellow Tower of Gwent. The tower, which was originally entered by means of a pair of bascule bridges spanning a wet moat, was once five storeys high and crowned with machicolated battlements. In the seventeenth century it was observed that: 'At some distance on the left side [of the main castle] stood the Tower of Gwent, which for height, strength, and neatness surpassed most, if not every other tower of England or Wales.' This is no exaggeration and its function is clear: while it was ostensibly intended to provide a refuge, a place of safety with its own kitchen and water supply, its true purpose was ostentatious display. Unlike contemporary tower-houses such as Tattershall (1430–50) and Caister (1432–46), which were essentially brick-built conceits with few concessions to defence (*see* BRICK BUILDINGS), Raglan's Great Tower was a military anachronism that very soon revealed its domestic limitations. With the building of a gatehouse and new domestic offices and residential apartments in the 1460s, it became a magnificent folly, a structure with no apparent

rationale other than the aggrandisement of its builder. Nevertheless, it continued in residential use until the seventeenth century when the upper chambers were considered by the marquis of Worcester to be the 'most esteemed of all in the castle'.
(*See also* CLUSTERED DONJON)

KEEP-GATEHOUSE, GATEHOUSE-TOWER or GREAT GATEHOUSE-TOWER As the term suggests, a keep-gatehouse combined the defensive and residential characteristics of a KEEP with those of a GATEHOUSE. Many historians dislike the term 'keep' (which was unknown before the sixteenth century), preferring instead the medieval 'great tower' (*magnus turris*) or DONJON. Consequently, the term 'keep-gatehouse' is also controversial, and 'gatehouse-tower' or 'great gatehouse-tower' are sometimes preferred.

There are also problems of definition. The term 'keep-gatehouse' suggests that it was a building that could be isolated from the rest of the castle and defended independently against an enemy, should they capture the inner ward, or against a garrison of rebellious mercenaries. The magnificent gatehouses at Harlech and Beaumaris Castles, for example, are often described as keep-gatehouses. But in both cases rows of large windows overlook the inner ward and were clearly vulnerable to attack from within the castle (*see* WINDOWS). Some historians have proposed a more precise definition of a keep-gatehouse. This requires that the inner pair of gates should be barred from within the GATE PASSAGE, not the courtyard, and that they should be protected on the courtyard side by a PORTCULLIS. In such cases, it is argued, the intention is clear: the gatehouse was a final refuge, secure from attack from within the castle as well as from outside. This may be true in a small number of cases, such as Tonbridge Castle (*see below*), but these features are also to be found in a number of major gatehouses where the security of the building is otherwise compromised. Furthermore, it was not uncommon

The massive keep-gatehouse, curtain walls and corner towers of Harlech Castle (1283–9) dominate the skyline above Tremadog Bay.

for a portcullis to be positioned at the inner end of a gate passage in order to trap an enemy in the intervening space (*see* KILLING GROUND).

The term 'keep-gatehouse' is a difficult one to sustain. 'Gatehouse-tower' is preferable, but even so it implies a single tower whereas one of the characteristics of this type of gatehouse is that there are at least two (the gatehouse at Denbigh Castle has three polygonal towers). It has been argued, convincingly, that the term 'gatehouse' is sufficient, for it implies both a strengthening of the entrance and the provision of residential accommodation. It also allows for a variety of forms and may be qualified: the term *Edwardian gatehouse*, for example, implies a twin-towered gatehouse with a central gate passage and residential accommodation above. Nevertheless, the term 'keep-gatehouse' is commonly found in reference books and guidebooks where it is generally used to denote a large, heavily fortified residential building protecting an entrance. Whatever the definition, the term cannot be ignored.

It is generally acknowledged that the keep-gatehouse evolved as a consequence of the declining effectiveness of the keep in the thirteenth century (*see* KEEP) and the development of the ENCLOSURE CASTLE in which the gate was the weakest point. The keep-gatehouse developed in response to that weakness, a manifestation of the principle, established at Dover Castle after 1216, whereby the most vulnerable element of a castle's defences should also be its most strongly fortified nucleus. However, several early keeps served also as gatehouses: the Norman keep at Ludlow Castle (*c.* 1175), for example, the doorway of which was blocked in the fourteenth century, and the magnificent twelfth-century keep at Richmond Castle which was erected over an eleventh-century gatehouse.

Examples of keep-gatehouses in England are rare. That at Tonbridge Castle (*c.* 1275) was built by Gilbert de Clare who, at Caerphilly, also erected one of the most remarkable defensive complexes in Britain (*see below*). The Tonbridge gatehouse has a pair of massive half-cylindrical towers on square plinths flanking a long gate passage which was protected by two portcullises, three rows of MURDER HOLES and two pairs of gates. Accordingly, it is a true keep-gatehouse that could be isolated from the rest of the castle, the inner gates preventing access from the bailey and the doors to the wall-walks being protected by portcullises. The keep-gatehouse at Dunstanburgh Castle is one of the largest: two storeys high, its twin five-storeyed D-shaped towers flank a gate passage above which a great hall occupies the second floor. When the castle

passed to John of Gaunt in 1322, the entrance was closed with a stone wall and FOREBUILDING and a new entrance made in the curtain (protected by a BARBICAN) so that the gatehouse could be turned into a residential great tower.

In Wales keep-gatehouses are more numerous. Pembroke's splendid cluster of interconnected barbican and gatehouse towers was the first (*c.* 1237) while Caerphilly Castle (*c.* 1268–71) provided the prototype. Caerphilly was constructed with concentric rings of water defences, curtain walls and mural towers (*see* CONCENTRIC CASTLES *and* MOATS AND WATER DEFENCES), and two great gatehouses in the inner curtain, the larger of which (the Eastern Inner Gatehouse) is almost identical to that at the other de Clare castle at Tonbridge (*see above*). It dominates the castle and was clearly conceived both as a heavily fortified entrance and as a self-contained residence for the constable, capable of independent defence from within (the front façade was rebuilt in the 1930s but the rest of the gatehouse is original except for the crenellations). Gates at both ends of the gate passage prevented access from the courtyard and from outside, and the only doorways led into guardrooms on either side of the passage. Stairs to the upper floors were enclosed within turrets while doorways leading to the curtain wall-walks were provided with portcullises. First-floor windows were uniformly small, the only large windows (two) being in the hall which was located on the upper floor so that the drawbridge and portcullis mechanisms did not intrude. It is likely that this major residential keep-gatehouse was the model, several decades later, for the Edwardian masterpieces at Harlech (1283–9) and Beaumaris (1295–6), though (as has already been noted) both were compromised by the insertion of large first-floor windows in the Constable's Hall.

In all keep-gatehouses living accommodation must have been seriously inconvenienced by the raising and lowering of the portcullises and (in some instances) the drawbridge. Even though only one or two pairs of gates would normally be used to control access and egress to the castle, the presence of the portcullis mechanism and murder holes in the chambers above the gate passage must have been a constant source of annoyance to the constable and his family.

KENTISH RAG A grey-green sandy limestone quarried in Kent and used extensively for architectural dressings and as facing stone because of its hard, impervious characteristics.
(*See also* MASONRY)

KETTLE HAT, CHAPEL DE FER *or* WAR HAT
An iron helmet with a spherical crown and broad
brim. Kettle hats first appeared in the late twelfth
century and continued in use throughout the medieval
period, principally (in England) by men-at-arms.
(*See also* ARMOUR *and* HELMETS)

KETTON STONE A cream-coloured limestone
quarried in Rutland.

KEY ESCUTCHEON The pierced metal plate
affixed to a door to protect the keyhole.

KEYSTONE *see* ARCH *and* BOSSES

KILLING GROUND The late Iron Age people of
Maiden Castle, Dorset, understood that the gateway
that pierced the triple ramparts of their massive
hillfort was the most vulnerable point in its
defences. They therefore protected the entrance with
a series of interlocking defiles that had to be
negotiated by anyone approaching the gates. These
deep alleys, commanded on all sides by almost
vertical earthen ramparts, were an early form of
killing ground: in order to attack the gate, a
besieging force would be drawn into a disorientating
series of constricted enclosures while the defenders
attacked them from above.

Thirteen centuries later the same principles
applied. The vulnerable entrances to medieval
castles were strengthened with BARBICANS and
GATEHOUSES and killing grounds provided to
ensnare and hold the intruder. Most castles were
designed on the principle of retreating defence: as an
attacking force succeeded in overcoming each
obstacle (drawbridge, doors, portcullises, etc.) so
they would be drawn into successive killing grounds.
Beaumaris, perhaps the finest CONCENTRIC
CASTLE in Britain, provides an example. First, the
outer gatehouse ('the Gate next the Sea') could only
be approached by a drawbridge across the moat, the
entrance guarded by MACHICOLATIONS. Then,
within the outer gatehouse, two wide MURDER
HOLES or slots protected the gate passage and its
heavy, two-leaved door and massive draw-bar (*see*
JAMB). The next obstacle, a barbican, is set at right
angles and out of alignment with the outer gatehouse
so that attackers were forced to turn into an open
killing ground, overlooked on all sides by the curtain
wall of the outer ward and the towers of the
formidable south gatehouse. The roofless interior of
the barbican was itself a killing ground with a
shooting platform running round three sides of the
wall-head; should the barbican be taken, a further

right-angled turn was required in order to attack the
south gatehouse passage. This, again, provided a
series of killing grounds with no fewer than seven
parallel murder holes (again, the wide 'slot' variety)
through which the gate passage could be defended
from above should attackers succeed in advancing
through three sets of heavy two-leaved doors with
double draw-bars and three portcullises. It has been
suggested (not convincingly) that portcullises were
sometimes partially raised in order to entice
intruders into the killing ground where they would
be imprisoned when the portcullis was dropped
behind them. At Beaumaris, should the attackers
have turned away from the barbican and into the
outer ward they would have been trapped in a long,
narrow killing ground between the outer curtain and
the walls and mural towers of the inner ward where
the absence of doorways and window openings
prevented escape. And even if the inner ward was
reached, the surrounding walls and towers could be
isolated and secured by the defenders.

The term 'killing ground' is also applied to the
open ground surrounding a castle – that which was
within the range of a defending archer. The entire
area would be covered by tiers of LOOPHOLES in
curtain walls and towers, the sight-lines from each
loophole and crenellation forming overlapping arcs
so that there were no 'blind spots' in which an
attacker could seek refuge. It follows, therefore, that
a hill-top location was not necessarily the best site
from which to defend a castle. In many instances a
site was selected precisely because it lay at the
centre of a natural 'bowl', the sides of which formed
a sloping killing ground within bowshot of the walls
and afforded no protection to a besieging force (*see*
SITES).

KING OF ARMS An officer of arms senior to the
heralds and pursuivants (*see* ARMORY *and*
COLLEGE OF ARMS).

KING POST A central vertical post rising from a
tie beam to the ridge piece of a timber roof (*see*
ROOFS (TIMBER)). The term *queen post* is used
where there are two vertical posts instead of one.

KINGS AND QUEENS *see* RULERS OF
MEDIEVAL AND TUDOR ENGLAND

KING'S BENCH The royal court of common law at
Westminster which was concerned with both
criminal and civil cases.

KING'S PEACE, THE *see* LAW AND ORDER

KITCHENER *see* KITCHENS

KITCHENS

> His bread, his ale were finest of the fine
> And no one had a better stock of wine.
> His house was never short of bake-meat pies,
> Of fish and flesh, and these in such supplies
> It positively snowed with meat and drink
> And all the dainties that a man could think.
>
> Chaucer, *Canterbury Tales* (N. Coghill)

The kitchen was a vital feature of a medieval castle. An overflowing table in the great hall, with a surplus to distribute to the poor at the castle gate, was an essential symbol of a lord's prestige (*see* WORSHIP). 'Conspicuous consumption was expected of them and conspicuous consumption is what they got' (Saul). Meals were also important ceremonial occasions, designed to emphasise a lord's pre-eminence and to reinforce the bond between him and his HOUSEHOLD. In late medieval households the kitchen was the core of a complex of departments that included the *pantry* (bread), the *buttery* (wines and ales), the *napery* (table linen), the *poultry* (poultry and game), the *saucery* (spices and dressings), the *scullery* (utensils and equipment) and the *curtilage* (fruit and vegetables). In the domestic hierarchy the *cellarer* was responsible to the STEWARD for all these departments, together with the produce of the dairy, bakehouse and brewhouse, while the *larderer* administered the acquisition and storage of provisions in the *larder* and the *kitcheners* managed the serving of meals. During meals the serving and replenishing of dishes and jugs required a room separate from the kitchens and this is sometimes referred to as a *servery*. Two further departments frequently referred to in household accounts were the *wardrobe* (wax for candles, spices, etc.) and the *marshalsea* (provisions for horses, transport, etc.).

In some of the larger royal and magnate castles there were often two kitchens, one serving the great hall and the other the lesser hall in the lord's quarters, as in the great towers of Raglan and Warkworth Castles (*see* HALL). There are also instances of kitchens being provided for senior members of a household such as the steward and constable, though some of these may be later additions. In the accounts for Launceston in 1462 we read of payments for making 'a great fireplace and two ovens within the said fireplace in the . . . constabill's kechyn'. However, the 'auditor's kitchen' in the north range of Middleham Castle may have been added in the sixteenth century when the

castle had ceased to function as a principal residence and had become an administrative centre and estate office. At Westminster in the late fifteenth century there was an additional or *privy kitchen*, described in contemporary documents as 'the place where the chief cooks prepared delicious and elaborate dishes'.

In early castles the kitchen was usually detached from other buildings because of the risk of fire. Later, when service rooms were integrated within the domestic buildings, the kitchens were often provided with a stone vault and isolated from the hall by a substantial wall and a corridor entered from the SCREENS PASSAGE. Even so, in some cases the risk of fire must have been considerable, especially where the kitchen was located in a keep: at Raglan, for example, the basement kitchen in the Great Tower had a timber ceiling, poor ventilation and only one means of escape. Although the majority of kitchens were reasonably accessible to the hall and service rooms, there is no consistent pattern. At Weobley Castle the kitchen was in an undercroft beneath the hall, while at Caerphilly, Denbigh and Raby Castles the kitchens were located in mural towers. The hall kitchen in the fifteenth-century north tower at Raglan had a larder beneath and in the sixteenth century was linked with a pantry, buttery and other service rooms by means of a long passageway that terminated in a servery at the west end of the Great Hall. At Beaumaris Castle, which is often cited as being the most advanced example of military architecture in Britain, domestic arrangements were obliged to take second place and the kitchens were located on the west side of the wide inner ward while the hall was some distance away on the opposite east side. In some cases a single kitchen served two halls: at Chepstow Castle, for example, in the late thirteenth century Roger Bigod extended the domestic accommodation by exploiting the slope on which the new hall range was to be built. Bigod's master mason was able to construct two halls, a great hall and a lesser hall at a lower level, and to combine the kitchen, buttery and pantry of the two halls with a common service passage and stairs. A further stair leads down to a large vaulted cellar with an opening in the end wall overlooking the River Wye. From a natural cleft at the foot of the cliff supplies could be hauled up by a light crane, and in the nineteenth century the wooden door and iron bracket for the pulley mechanism were still in place. Halfway down the stairs a landing led to a platform that projected over the cliff face and this may also have been used to haul up provisions. At the head of the stairs a double cupboard of dressed stone once contained the knives and other implements used by waiters in the halls, and next to it was a two-seater garderobe that discharged into the river below.

Castle kitchens were often impressive chambers, with lofty ceilings and massive fireplaces and ovens, the remains of which may still be seen embedded in a curtain wall where otherwise only the foundations of the kitchen remain (*see* IRONWORK, LOCKS AND NAILS *and* REREDOS). At Lincoln Castle the kitchen was a four-sided building with a great hearth in each of the corners, facilitating the construction of the canopies and flues (*see* CHIMNEYS AND FIREPLACES). As at Launceston (*see above*) it was usual to build one or more circular domed ovens into the side walls of the hearth for the baking of bread and pies. Together the hearth and ovens formed a *range*, a term that remains in use today to describe an oven with hotplates for cooking. Separate *brewhouses* and *bakehouses* were sometimes provided, as at Middleham where ovens were built into a cross-wall in the west range of buildings in the late fifteenth or early sixteenth century. (There are further ovens in the south range together with the remains of a sixteenth-century horse-mill.) Kitchens were usually ventilated by means of chimney flues and sometimes by a central shaft with a louvred opening above the roof. At Eltham in 1369 a weather cock, costing 3*s* 4*d*, was affixed above the kitchen 'to know how the wind lies' so that the louvres could be adjusted to take advantage of the prevailing wind. Even so, some kitchens must have been singularly unpleasant places in which to work: the only natural light admitted to the basement kitchen of the Great Tower at Raglan Castle came from narrow gun ports and cross-slits.

The scale, both of the operation and of the facilities required to prepare meals for a lord's family, his household and guests, is evident in an instruction issued by King John for the construction of new kitchens at Ludgershall and Marlborough Castles: 'in each kitchen shall be made a hearth for the cooking of two or three oxen'. The castle kitchens at the late-medieval castle of Bodiam again illustrate the lavish scale of castle catering. Two huge fireplaces in the kitchen adjoining the Great Hall, and two more in the servants' kitchen, provided roasted or boiled food for an establishment that often exceeded one hundred at a single meal. A constant supply of water was, of course, essential and at Bodiam the well in the adjoining tower is fed by a spring (*see* WELLS). Elsewhere, water might be conducted to the kitchens from fresh-water cisterns by means of stone or lead pipes and conduits, waste products being removed by drains directly into a moat or cess-pit. Such drains were sometimes referred to as *swallows* and most of the numerous legends concerning underground tunnels in castles are due to the existence of such arrangements (*see* PLUMBING, WATER SUPPLY AND SANITATION). The Westminster accounts for 1260 include a payment for 'making a conduit through which the refuse of the King's kitchens at Westminster flows into the Thames, which conduit the King ordered to be made on account of the stink of the dirty water which was carried through his halls, which was wont to affect the health of people frequenting the same halls', while at the Tower of London in 1386 a payment was made for 'making a pit with stone walls by way of a swallow beside the Lieutenant's kitchen for the receiving of all water falling there'. Water was not drunk in its raw state but was first boiled and made into ale – even children drank diluted or *small ale*. At Bodiam a DOVECOTE at the top of the (south-west) well tower provided meat for the table and feathers for cushions and mattresses, while the lodgings below the dovecote were occupied by the Clerk to the Kitchen who supervised a large staff of cooks, brewers, bakers, gardeners and kitchen boys (*scullions*). Between the kitchen and the Great Hall were the usual buttery and pantry, and beneath the buttery was the wine cellar.

The household accounts for Richard Beauchamp, earl of Warwick, provide a fascinating insight into the daily life of Rouen Castle during 1431. The document was written in Latin on 410 sheets of watermarked paper by Nicholas Roudy, Warwick's steward in France. The six headings for each day's provisions are always the same: pantry, buttery, kitchen, poultry, wardrobe and marshalsea. At the end of each month an account was made of the provisions used and of money spent, in this case noted in both English and French currency. Each day there is a list of those dining, always beginning with the name of the head of the household (frequently Lady Talbot, Warwick's daughter) and then the names of diners in the order in which they entered the hall. For this reason nobles (and even the king) are often listed below a visiting merchant or nun.

In affluent medieval households there were two principal meals during the day: dinner, which was taken mid-morning, and supper, which was taken at about 4.00 in the afternoon. In most households an early breakfast seems to have been taken only by a small number of children. At Rouen catering must have been a constant headache, for the number of those attending at dinner varied between 60 and 210, while between 60 and 70 regularly took supper. From the accounts, and the descriptions of tradesmen who are listed as dining in the hall, it is possible to follow the rhythm of the seasons. In September and October grape-pickers are listed (we would now describe them as 'wine merchants'). In November there are furriers to prepare skins for winter clothing. Minstrels arrive in June and falconers in February. On 19 November a marriage was recorded between two members of the household, James Dryland and Alice Lyghtwood, and ninety guests were entertained in the hall following the ceremony.

KITE-SHAPED SHIELD Dating from the eleventh and twelfth centuries, an elongated and slightly convex shield with a rounded or flat top, handgrip and neck-strap so that it could be slung across the back. Designed to protect both infantry and mounted knights, it was used at the battle of Senlac in 1066 and is illustrated in the Bayeux Tapestry (*see* SHIELDS).

KNAPPING *see* FLINT

KNIGHT *see* KNIGHTHOOD AND CHIVALRY, ORIGINS OF

KNIGHT BACHELOR The lowest degree of knighthood but perhaps the most ancient. Knights were originally required to perform military service in exchange for the lands granted to them (*see* KNIGHT'S FEE) but this duty was gradually commuted to a money payment (*scutage* = 'shield money'). Knights bachelor were often bound by indenture of retainer and resided in a lord's household. In the medieval army the knight bachelor would command the smallest unit – perhaps consisting of a few personal retainers – and would display his arms on a pennon (*see* FLAGS). There was not an order of knights bachelor, though many of their number belonged to military and fraternal orders (*see* KNIGHTHOOD AND CHIVALRY, ORDERS OF).
(*See also* KNIGHTHOOD AND CHIVALRY, ORIGINS OF)

KNIGHT BANNERET *see* BANNERET *and* KNIGHTHOOD AND CHIVALRY, ORIGINS OF

KNIGHTHOOD AND CHIVALRY, ORDERS OF The medieval chivalric orders were fraternities of like-minded men of the appropriate social class, bound together in common purpose. That of the Knights Hospitaller, for example, was to succour pilgrims in the Holy Land, the Trinitarians ransomed Christian captives, and the knights of the Most Noble Order of the Garter pledged themselves to 'a Society, Fellowship, College of Knights' of equal status 'Co-partners in Peace and War, assistant to one another in all serious and dangerous Exploits and thro' the whole Course of their Lives to shew Fidelity and Friendliness towards one another' (*see* GARTER, THE MOST NOBLE ORDER OF THE).

Many members of the early crusading orders were simply adventurers, often the impecunious younger sons of the aristocracy, no doubt motivated as much by the security of fellowship and the concept of exclusive pre-eminence as by religious or chivalric idealism (*see* ST JOHN OF JERUSALEM (ORDER OF) – also known as the Knights Hospitaller – *and* TEMPLAR, KNIGHTS (THE POOR KNIGHTS OF CHRIST AND OF THE TEMPLE OF SOLOMON), known as the Knights Templar).

Several chivalric orders lay claim to very early dates of foundation: the Order of Constantine St George of Naples, for example, claims a fourth-century foundation and reconstitution in 1190. However, the majority of the early orders can justifiably claim to have been founded during the period of the First Crusade (1196–9), though papal recognition may have been considerably later: the Knights Hospitaller, for instance, received recognition of Pope Pascal II in 1113, though their foundation undoubtedly pre-dates it by some thirty years.

Many of the later medieval orders of chivalry, such as the Garter and the Burgundian Order of the Golden Fleece (founded in 1429/30), were exclusive foundations, membership being strictly limited and usually in the gift of a sovereign. Although modelled on the concept of chivalric egalitarianism and humility, these orders were essentially élitist, membership being the ultimate reward for service to the sovereign, or were utilised for the purposes of international diplomacy.
(*See also* BATH, THE MOST HONOURABLE ORDER OF THE)

KNIGHTHOOD AND CHIVALRY, ORIGINS OF The word 'knighthood' is the modern form of the Old English *cnihthád*, the period between youth and maturity, while the word 'chivalry' derives from the Old French *chevalerie* meaning 'gallant horsemen equipped for battle' (*see* CHIVALRY). By the mid-twelfth century the two words were virtually synonymous, describing both the personal attributes of a mounted warrior and the code which governed his conduct.

In England *cnihtháds* were originally the retainers of Anglo-Saxon magnates, young land-holders who in the time of Edward the Confessor had pledged themselves to the service of some 'lord' (ealdorman, bishop or greater thegn). By the mid-eleventh century there seems to have evolved some form of initiation ceremony by which a young man of noble birth would gain admission to the warrior class. This almost certainly involved being presented with a sword or a lance and shield. After the Conquest the term *cnihthád* seems to have been applied to military tenants who, as vassals of earls, major barons and bishops, held their estates in return for forty days' military service (*see* KNIGHT'S FEE). But by the time of the Fourth Crusade (1202–4) this form of service was already being replaced by the paid man-at-arms and the emergence of a seasoned international warrior class able and willing to fight in any cause.

It was perhaps only to be expected that in this climate of holy war, augmented by a release from feudalism, a concept of knighthood with codes of honour should gain ground and find expression in both military and religious orders of chivalry. The first group, under the command of a king or royal nominee, often richly endowed, evolved into late medieval orders such as the Garter, the Golden Fleece and the Annunziatta of Savoy. The second fraternal group comprised orders under grand masters, of which the Teutonic Order, the Knights Templar and the Knights Hospitaller were the pre-eminent examples (*see* TEMPLAR, KNIGHTS (THE POOR KNIGHTS OF CHRIST AND OF THE TEMPLE OF SOLOMON) *and* ST JOHN OF JERUSALEM, ORDER OF).

It is apparent that there were four stages through which an aspiring knight could pass: those of page, squire, knight bachelor and, for some men, knight banneret, the latter being of considerable distinction (*see* BANNERET, ESQUIRE *and* KNIGHT BACHELOR). From their very earliest years boys of the appropriate social class were schooled, through military exercises, in the arts of war. Every feudal court and castle was effectively a school of chivalry and the knight-to-be progressed from toy weapons made of wood to more demanding tilting exercises as he moved from the first stage to the second. The conditions of page and squire were normally passed through during boyhood and early teens, and the stage of knighthood was reached at the very threshold of maturity. Pages were never combatant but squires were, and some men (by reason of poverty) stayed as squires all their lives, voluntarily serving knights – looking after their horses and armour, following them into battle and aiding them in tournaments. More generally, however, knighthood was attained after a suitable period as a squire.

The earliest records suggest that there were two methods by which knighthood could be conferred on an aspirant. The first was extremely simple and was used mainly in time of conflict: the candidate knelt before a senior knight or field commander who struck him three times with the flat of a sword. The

second procedure was much more elaborate. Writing in 1614 the historian Seldom stated that: 'the ceremonies and circumstances at the giving of this dignity in the elder time were of two kinds especially, which we may call courtly and sacred. The courtly were the feats held at the creation, giving of robes, arms, spurs and the like. The second were the holy devotions and what else was used in the church at or before the receiving of the dignity.' These elaborate solemnities seem to have been superseded at an early stage by the practice of *dubbing* alone, so much so that Garter Segar in the reign of Elizabeth I wrote: 'He that is to be made a knight is stricken by the prince with a sword drawn upon his back or shoulder, the prince saying Soys Chevalier.' Significantly, Segar does not mention a holy vigil, the presentation of golden spurs or any form of complex ceremonial event such as that which (apparently) accompanied admission to the Knighthood of the Bath (*see* BATH, THE MOST HONOURABLE ORDER OF THE).

(*See also* GARTER, THE MOST NOBLE ORDER OF THE *and* KNIGHTHOOD AND CHIVALRY, ORDERS OF)

KNIGHT SERVICE *see* KNIGHT'S FEE *and* MILITIA

KNIGHT'S FEE Also known as *Knight Service*, a feudal obligation to provide military service to the crown in the form of a fully armed and equipped knight, together with his retainers, for forty days each year. The system of knight service was introduced by Henry II in 1181 and was intended to provide the king with a readily available military reserve, raised by his tenants-in-chief as part of their feudal obligation. In practice, knight service was often commuted to the payment of a fine (*scutage*) and was abolished in 1660.

(*See also* FEUDAL AIDS, MILITIA *and* TRINODA NECESSITAS)

KNIGHTS HOSPITALLER *see* ST JOHN OF JERUSALEM, ORDER OF

KNIGHTS TEMPLAR *see* TEMPLAR, KNIGHTS (THE POOR KNIGHTS OF CHRIST AND OF THE TEMPLE OF SOLOMON)

KNOTS Various knots are known in ARMORY, most of which originated as badges worn by retainers, the best known being the Stafford knot badge of the dukes of Buckingham (*see* BADGES AND LIVERIES).

L

LABEL (i) A small, stylised 'scroll' inscribed with a religious aphorism or prayer and located, for example, near the head of a figure in a monumental brass.
(ii) *For* architectural label *see* DRIPSTONE.
(iii) *For* heraldic label *see* CADENCY.

LABEL STOP Carved architectural decoration at the termination of a label (*see* DRIPSTONE).

LADDERS *see* SCALING LADDERS

LADY CHAMBER *see* PRIVY CHAMBER

LADY DAY *see* MICHAELMAS

LAMBREQUIN *see* MANTLING

LAMES (LAMELLA) Thin metal plates, laced together and used in ARMOUR for articulation.

LANCE A long wooden spear, used by cavalry and by mounted knights in the tilt (*see* TOURNAMENTS). Eleventh-century lances were about 1.8m (6ft) long and, in a cavalry charge, were carried in the horizontal *couched* position: held tightly beneath the horseman's upper right arm. By the end of the thirteenth century they had increased in length to 2.4m (8ft) and by the mid-fourteenth century to 3m (10ft). The lance of an armiger would often have carried a triangular pennon or small banner emblazoned with his coat of arms (*see* FLAGS). The 3.6m (12ft) long tilting lance was carried in the couched position and across the neck of the horse. In the later medieval period it could be supported by a *lance rest* affixed to the breastplate or a notch in an *à bouche* shield. The hand and forearm were protected by a raised conical guard, designed to deflect an opponent's lance. When tilting, the point was usually blunted with a *coronel*, a crown-shaped termination to prevent the piercing of armour.

LANCET *see* ARCH, GOTHIC ARCHITECTURE *and* WINDOWS

LANDGABLE *see* BURGAGE

LANGUAGE 'English' was originally the dialect of the Angles but the term has subsequently been extended to include all the dialects of the vernacular, whether Anglian or Saxon. Old English (or Anglo-Saxon) is the language which developed from the composite dialects of Germanic-speaking tribes of Angles, Saxons and Jutes who settled in Britain from the mid-fifth century. It was an inflected language, though these endings gradually decayed until most of them had been lost by the fifteenth century. It was also essentially a spoken language, although by the time of Alfred the Great (849–99) a standard literary version was emerging. In addition to native Celtic elements and words surviving from the Roman occupation, vocabulary expanded through the spread of Christian culture and the influence of Scandinavian invaders in the ninth and tenth centuries. By the late tenth century the Wessex dialect had become dominant.

Following the Norman Conquest of 1066 Anglo-Norman was quickly established as the language of the aristocracy and Latin as that of the administration. It has been estimated that some 33,000 Old French words were absorbed into the English language in the centuries following the Conquest, but from the fourteenth century English was again the standard and, despite the influence of French, the Germanic nature of the language has been maintained, even though the original native English element is probably now a minor one. By the sixteenth century most vowels were pronounced as they are today. The traditional historical phases of linguistic development are *Old English* (up to *c.* 1150), *Middle English* (*c.* 1150–*c.* 1500) and *Modern English* (from *c.* 1500) which derives from the east Midland dialect and that of London. But in practice the language evolved gradually and with considerable regional variations.

LAPS AND ROLLS The usual method for constructing a lead roof is for lengths of LEAD to be laid vertically with their edges overlapping. The 'laps' (overlapping edges) are then 'rolled' to make them waterproof.

LARDER A storeroom for meat and provisions. In medieval households the *larderer* was responsible for the acquisition and storage of provisions including meat which was, of course, cooked in the KITCHENS. Bread was the province of the *pantry* and there were other departments responsible for the preparation of poultry and game (the *poultry*) and spices and dressings (the *saucery*). Utensils and equipment were maintained by the *scullery* and table linen by the *napery*. Wine and ale were the concern of the *buttery* and vegetables were provided by the *curtilage*. In the domestic hierarchy the *cellarer* was

responsible to the STEWARD for all these departments, together with the produce of the dairy, bakehouse and brewhouse, while the *kitcheners* managed the serving of meals.
(*See also* HOUSEHOLD)

LARDERER *see* KITCHENS *and* LARDER

LARGESS (*also* LARGESSE) The liberal bestowal of gifts (from the Latin *larga* meaning 'abundant' and 'bountiful'). Liberality, and in particular the regular distribution of gifts to the poor, was considered to be both chivalrous (*see* CHIVALRY) and one of the qualities by which contemporary society assessed a magnate's esteem (his 'worship'). Of course, largess was not confined to the poor: regular gifts of rare and valuable items (such as illuminated books) to patrons and dependents were a prerequisite of anticipated preferment – both on earth and in the afterlife.

LATH AND PLASTER Material used for ceilings and the internal walls of timber-frame buildings, consisting of a framework of interlaced or parallel laths (usually split hazel or willow) covered with layers of plaster which often contained a bonding agent such as horsehair.

LATRINES *see* GARDEROBES

LAVATORIUM (LAVER) A washing-place.

LAW AND ORDER Within the numerous communities of the Anglo-Saxon and Danelaw kingdoms, a variety of judicial systems evolved, based on custom and administered through people's courts whose elected officials were responsible for the day-to-day regulation of a community's affairs and for the enforcement of its court's rulings. By the mid-tenth century the kingdom of Edgar the Peaceful was divided into *shires*, each with its SHERIFF (shire-reeve) who was responsible through the shire courts for 'keeping the peace' and, in an emergency, could call out the *posse comitatus*: all the available men in the shire. The shires were themselves divided into HUNDREDS, each with its own court and consisting of a number of *tithings* of ten households which stood security for one another and were led by a tithingman in a system known as FRANKPLEDGE. Crime was committed not against an individual but against a community: it was a crime against the peace, eventually defined as the *King's Peace*, and it was therefore the responsibility of all male members of the community between the ages of twelve and sixty to bring the offender to justice. If they failed to do so, the tithing could be punished.

Minor offences were brought before the local *moot court*. More serious cases were taken to the hundred court, where they were heard by a REEVE, or to the shire court to be determined by the sheriff.

Few changes were effected by the Norman administration following the Conquest of 1066. Shires became COUNTIES with Norman sheriffs and officials and the duties of tithingmen were defined in law and made obligatory, but for the most part the system of tithings, hundreds and shires was considered to be effective and was adapted rather than replaced.

In 1133 Henry II introduced full-time judges and annual judicial circuits from which evolved the English system of Common Law. Keepers (or Conservators) of the Peace were appointed to each county in 1277 and 1287 and these became *Justices of the Peace* in 1361: 'one Lord and with him three or four of the most worthy in the County with some learned in law'. The Statute of Winchester of 1285 reaffirmed the obligation of a locality to attend to its own law and order with a High Constable in each hundred and under him petty constables in each tithing. In towns a system of *Watch and Ward* was introduced which required up to sixteen watchmen to guard a town's walls and gates during the hours of darkness (the *watch*) and to convey all strangers and wrong-doers to the wardens at sunrise on the following day (the *ward*). The statute also revised the Anglo-Saxon system of HUE AND CRY, whereby anyone attempting to make an arrest could summon others of the parish to join him in pursuit. It also established the *Assize of Arms* which required all men between the ages of fifteen and sixty to maintain weapons with which to keep the peace. The system of parochial or borough self-regulation continued, with some modification, through the Tudor period. The vestry of a parish appointed one or more *constables* who were to assist the justices in maintaining the King's Peace as well as carrying out numerous other duties. Constables were ordinary citizens who rarely wanted the job – which was unpaid and unpopular – and the more prosperous citizens often paid deputies to do the work for them. In 1663 the City of London began to pay night-watchmen to guard the streets at night. These 'Charlies', as they came to be called, carried a bell, a lantern and a rattle and were armed with a staff but were badly paid and were often too decrepit to be effective. It was not until the eighteenth century that other towns promoted their own acts of parliament, enabling them to levy rates for lighting and watching streets, and for many centuries the justices of the peace, the constables and the watchmen carried the responsibility for maintaining law and order.

(*See also* COURT BARON, COURT LEET, OYER AND TERMINER, QUARTER SESSIONS, STAR CHAMBER *and* TRAILBASTON)

LAZAR HOUSE A hospital for lepers. The term is derived from St Lazarus, the patron saint of lepers, and from the nursing order of that name.

LEAD A heavy, soft, grey-coloured metallic element widely used in glazing, as a roof covering or sealant, as piping and as linings in cisterns (*see* CISTERN). In Britain lead was first used by the Romans for water pipes because of its durability and resistance to corrosion. In the medieval period it was used in the complex plumbing systems of castles and religious houses (the Franciscans were acknow-ledged to be expert in the use of lead piping) and to replace the vast timber roofs of abbey churches and castle halls which were especially vulnerable to destruction by fire (*see* ROOFS (TIMBER)). When laid correctly, a complete lead roof formed an impervious sheet and it could therefore be used on a low-pitch or flat roof (*see* LAPS AND ROLLS). Unlike tiles, a lead roof did not require constant repairs and, unlike thatch, it was not inflammable – though many fires were caused by the carelessness of plumbers. The chief deterrent was cost: in 1300 the *char*, *fother* or cartload – sufficient to cover about 160 sq ft – cost as much as £3 and this rose to £7 following the Black Death. Some 12½ tons of lead were required in roofing the great tower at Flint Castle and a ton of cordwood was needed to smelt each ton of ore. Of course, the cost fluctuated according to locality. Thus, in the Winchester Castle accounts for 1222 we read of '20 chars of lead brought by Elyas Westman at Boston Fair, £27 6*d*. For carriage of the same by sea to Southampton, 32*s*'. For Corfe Castle in 1367 four 'foudres' of lead were bought in London for £30, a further 4*s* was paid for their carriage from Cannon Street to the Thames, and 13*s* 4*d* for their carriage thence to the castle. In 1363 lead was carried from Yorkshire to London for repairs at Windsor Castle: 'For hire of two wagons, each with ten oxen, carrying 24 fothers of lead from Caldstanes to Nidderdale by high and rocky mountains and by miry ways to Boroughbridge, more or less 20 leagues, namely for 24 days, each wagon with the men for it taking three shillings a day – £7 4*s*. Carriage from Boroughbridge to York by land and water at 2*s* 4*d* the fother. Carriage by water from York to London, of forty fothers, £26 13*s* 8*d*.'

Although the initial expense of supplying and fitting a lead roof was considerable, it could easily be stripped and recast when necessary. There is evidence that lead was just as susceptible to theft in the medieval period as it is today. One of the ordinances of the London plumbers, drawn up in 1365, required that: 'None shall buy stripped lead from the assistants of tillers, bricklayers, masons or women, who cannot find warranty for it.' Sometimes lead was bought in sheets (*webs*) which were, of course, more expensive than the raw materials. At York Castle in 1365, 'half a fother and forty stone of wrought lead, at 10*d* the stone, was bought for re-roofing the turret beside the chapel and for making the gutters for the kitchen'. When lead is laid directly on unseasoned timber it may be affected by the vegetable acids contained in the wood, while the timber is also affected by changes of temperature in the lead. Layers of earth and sand were therefore inserted between the wood and the lead, as at Dover in 1227 where 4*d* was paid 'for 100 horseloads of earth called arzille [clay] bought from the land of a poor old woman to put on the towers between the planks and the sand which lies under the lead to prevent the material rotting'. At Rhuddlan Castle in 1302 payments were made for 'removing the earth placed between the joists and the lead of the upper storey of the tower, making new joists, putting them in place, and placing earth afresh between them and the lead'.

(*For* the use of lead for gutters, spouts, pipes, etc. *see* PLUMBING, WATER SUPPLY AND SANITATION)

LEADED LIGHTS *see* WINDOWS

LEADS The flat areas of a castle roof.

LEGISLATION *see* BARONS' WARS (*for* the Dictum of Kenilworth, 1266), CALAIS (*for* the Act of Retainer, 1466), CRENELLATIONS (*for* licence to crenellate), ENGLISHRY (*for* Murder Fine), HUNDRED ROLLS (*for* Statutes of Gloucester, 1278), LAW AND ORDER, LIVERY AND MAINTENANCE, LORD OF THE MANOR (*for* Quia Emptores), MAGNA CARTA, MAGNUM CONCILIUM, MILITIA (*for* Assize of Arms and Militia acts), PARLIAMENTARY ACTS, PEASANTS' REVOLT (*for* Ordinance of Labourers), RECRUITMENT AND ORGAN-ISATION (MILITARY) (*for* Assize of Arms, 1181), SCOTLAND: ENGLISH WARS IN (*for* the Treaty of Northampton, 1328), STATE RECORDS, SUMPTUARY LAWS, TRAILBASTON, WALES (*for* the Treaty of Montgomery, 1267, the Statute of Rhuddlan, 1284 *and* the Act 'of Union', 1536) *and* WALES, CONQUEST OF (*for* the Treaty of Woodstock, 1247, the Treaty of Montgomery, 1267 *and* the Treaty of Aberconwy, 1277).

LEOPARD (COIN) *see* COINAGE

LESENE A shallow pier, with neither capital nor base, attached to a wall. Also known as *pilaster strips*, they are a characteristic feature of Anglo-Saxon architecture.

LESSER HALL *see* HALL

LETTERS CLOSE *and* **LETTERS PATENT** *see* CLOSE ROLLS *and* PATENT ROLLS

LIBERATE ROLLS Writs under the authority of which royal officers made certain payments on behalf of the crown. They originated in the CLOSE ROLLS but after 1226 constituted a distinct type of document which remained in use until 1426. They are of particular interest in that many of the earlier documents itemise purchases made in specific localities. Liberate rolls are maintained at the Public Record Office and a *Calendar of Liberate Rolls* in six volumes, covering the period 1226 to 1272, was published by HMSO from 1917 to 1964. *For* addresses *see* APPENDIX II.
(*See also* STATE RECORDS)

LIBERTY (i) A group of manors, to the lord of which were granted certain privileges of the crown and from which the sheriff's authority was excluded.
(ii) An area located outside a borough in which freemen exercised certain rights, e.g. of pasture.

LICENCE TO CRENELLATE *see* CRENELLATIONS

LIEGE HOMAGE The duty of a tenant (VASSAL) to his principal (*liege*) lord who was usually the landlord of the vassal's largest estate or that which had been held for the longest time (*see* FEUDAL SYSTEM). The liege lord had a prior claim on his vassal's loyalty and feudal obligations in any dispute with another landlord. By the thirteenth century the notion of military service which liege homage implied was of little significance and its main purpose was to identify which of several landlords had a prior claim to the pecuniary profits due from a particular tenant.

LIERNE *and* **LIERNE VAULT** *see* VAULTING

LIEUTENANT (i) In the Middle Ages, a military officer responsible for the maintenance of the banner (*see* FLAGS). The banner was a personal flag on which was emblazoned the coat of arms of a military commander. Consequently its use was restricted to those of noble or knightly rank (*see also* BANNERET). A mounted lieutenant would accompany his lord in battle and carry his banner before him. To raise one's banner in the field of battle was an unequivocal indication of commitment to a particular cause; and, because the banner represented the person of the commander, the lieutenant was expected to defend it to the death. Banner-bearers to the most eminent commanders may themselves have been knights: Henry V's lieutenant was Sir John Codrington, for example. By the fifteenth century mustering and rallying functions were performed by *livery flags* (the *standard* and *guidon*) which were the responsibility of an officer known as the ANCIENT (*see* BADGES AND LIVERY *and* BATTLEFIELDS).
(ii) Since the sixteenth century, a *Lord Lieutenant* has been appointed as the crown's representative in each county of the United Kingdom. Before the Tudor period the office was that of the sovereign's 'lieutenant' who was usually a nobleman and in time came to be known as 'Lord Lieutenant'. A Lord Lieutenant was custodian of the county records (*Custos Rotulorum*) and was charged with the sheriff's former responsibilities for the county MILITIA and defence (e.g. signal beacons).
(*See also* SHERIFF)

LIGHT A section of a glazed window or an opening for light.

LIGHTWELL A central shaft in, for example, a KEEP, open to the sky and pierced by windows which admit air and a little daylight to parts of the building which would otherwise be dark. Water was collected in a CISTERN at the foot of the lightwell in the massive keep of Warkworth Castle and could be diverted along a system of conduits to flush the latrine shafts.
(*See also* COURT AND COURTYARD)

LIMEWASH *see* FACING MATERIALS

LINEAR EARTHWORKS *see* DIKES

LINENFOLD *see* PANELLING

LINTEL A horizontal stone or wooden beam spanning an opening and supporting the wall above.
(*See also* ARCH *and* WINDOW)

LIST The interval between two lines of concentric walls.

LISTS The scene of a contest (*see* TOURNA-MENTS) and the palisades surrounding a TILTYARD.

LIVERIES *see* BADGES AND LIVERIES

LIVERY Distinctive clothing and/or badge that identified membership of a particular retinue or affinity.

LIVERY AND MAINTENANCE Livery and maintenance, the practice of maintaining and protecting large numbers of retainers in return for administrative and military services, was common in England in the fourteenth and fifteenth centuries when a magnate's influence was judged by the number of men wearing his uniform (*livery*) and his ability to protect them when necessary in the courts of law.

Livery, in the form of distinctive clothing or badges, was distributed at Christmas and Midsummer, its purpose being to impose a group identity on the members of an AFFINITY and to focus their loyalties on the lord by whom they were retained. 'For the upwardly mobile there can be little doubt that [livery] was a status symbol which legitimized aspirations of respectability. Acceptance of livery placed donor and recipient under obligation to each other. The latter was expected to serve his lord faithfully in peace and war, while the former was expected to stand by his man and to support him in all causes and disputes' (Nigel Saul). The wearing of livery defined status and was a visible expression of the bond that was created between lord and man. It enabled the retainers of one affinity to be distinguished from those of another. It located the wearer both politically and in terms of social standing.

BASTARD FEUDALISM was a characteristic of the period 1115–1650 and (contrary to the popular view) was generally a source of stability rather than abuse. Nevertheless, the practice of livery and maintenance (though not of retaining) was the subject of numerous complaints to parliament during the late thirteenth and early fourteenth centuries. When describing the statute of 1399, Adam of Usk reported that 'it was ordained that the lords of the kingdom should not give their livery or suit of cloth, or badges, or more especially of hoods, to anyone, except their familiars dwelling constantly with them, on account of several seditions in the kingdom caused by this'. In 1377 the Commons complained that men of lesser estate were giving liveries to men from whom they then demanded money in return for a promise to maintain any 'reasonable or unreasonable quarrel'.

By far the most contentious form was *livery of badges*, also described as 'liveries of company' or 'marks of fellowship' (*see* BADGES AND LIVERIES). In the parliament of 1384 the Commons protested that these were being distributed by lords in their localities in order to 'establish petty tyrannies over their neighbours'. Typically, the retainers of John of Gaunt, duke of Lancaster, believed that their badges 'would give them the earth and sky' and there arose numerous complaints concerning the perversion of justice when the magnates influenced and corrupted in their favour the whole working of the legal system.

An ordinance of 1390 restricted the right to grant 'liveries of company' to dukes, earls, barons and bannerets, while only knights and esquires, retained for life by indenture, and domestic servants in residence were permitted to receive them. But it is evident that the legislation was not entirely effective. Petitions of 1393 and 1397 complained that yeomen and others below the estate of esquire were wearing 'livery of signs'. Indeed, the practice of maintenance was spreading down the social scale and so too was livery – to those who were not concerned with permanent obligations and gave livery with only criminal intent.

It is also clear that from 1397 the king himself was abusing his authority by developing large retinues of liveried lesser servants, notably the Cheshire *vigilia*, in contravention of the ordinance of 1390. Consequently, in 1399, at the first parliament of the new reign, an amending statute was enacted which prohibited lords of any degree from giving badges. Only the king was excepted: he was permitted to give his badge to any lord, or to any knight or esquire who was a member of his household or one of his life retainers, but the knights and esquires were only to wear them in the king's presence, and in particular they were not to wear them in their own localities. A further exception permitted the constable and marshal to distribute livery badges to knights and esquires serving with them on the borders in times of war. In the parliament of 1401 the Commons once again demanded that all livery badges should be prohibited, excepting those of the king (described as the 'Coler'), which was to be subject to the same rules as in 1399. In fact, this was something of a victory for the king, for he gained two concessions when compared with the 1399 statute. Firstly, he insisted that his knights and esquires should be permitted to wear his livery badge not only in his presence but also when they were travelling to and from his household; and secondly, he insisted that Prince Henry should be permitted to use his livery of the swan as a pendant to the Lancastrian collar of esses (*see* COLLARS).

A Statute of Livery of 1429 marked a significant shift in policy. Lords, knights and esquires were permitted to give livery 'in times of war'. This was later confirmed in 1461 when the new Yorkist regime reinforced the prohibition on the giving of liveries for other purposes: 'The king . . . charges and commands that no lord, spiritual or temporal, shall from henceforth give any livery or cognizance, mark or token of company, except at such times as he has a special command from the king to raise people for the king's aid, to resist his enemies and to repress riots within his land.'

The Statute of Livery of 1468 explicitly outlawed retaining for life, including indentured retaining by the peerage. It would appear that the act was necessary because of the misuse of legal retainers for violent feuding and private war in the north Midlands in 1468. It was aimed at the peerage and was immediately used to prosecute the dukes of Norfolk and Suffolk and their private armies for offences committed in East Anglia. Indeed, throughout the second half of the fifteenth century problems arose because of the difficulty of distinguishing between legal and illegal retaining. Maintenance and private war could result from livery that was entirely legal: very large retinues could be mustered by legal means, and the legitimate categories of household officials and councillors could accommodate large numbers of men. Nevertheless, indentured retainers had all but disappeared by 1470, and ultimately it was the Tudors who were successful in suppressing livery and maintenance, though by that time the practice encompassed several distinct offences and it is unlikely that any one act actually solved all the problems.

LIVERY AND MAINTENANCE, CASTLES OF

A somewhat spurious term descriptive of late medieval magnate castles with enceintes capable of accommodating large numbers of retainers. Dunstanburgh Castle, Northumberland, was built in 1313–16 by Thomas, earl of Lancaster (*c.* 1278–1322), as 'the remote refuge of a defiant magnate' (Pettifer). Its broad, open enceinte was clearly intended as a barracks for Lancaster's vast retinue and is a striking contrast to the compact quadrangular courtyards of the period. Similarly, Thornbury Castle in Gloucestershire, one of the last castles to be built in England, includes accommodation for a substantial number of armed retainers. The ambitious Edward Stafford, duke of Buckingham (1478–1521), began building in 1511, without licence and at a time when the practice of

maintaining private armies was vigorously suppressed by the Tudor administration (*see* LIVERY AND MAINTENANCE). The castle consists of a comfortable residence behind a defensive façade and is provided with an outer courtyard in which two long ranges of retainers' lodgings abut the outer curtain. Buckingham died before his castle could be completed: executed for treason in 1521, he was charged with raising a private army in the Welsh Marches. Even in its unfinished and truncated state, much of Thornbury appears uncompromisingly defensive. But closer inspection will reveal both its defensive limitations and a Tudor inclination towards luxurious living. (*See also* ENCEINTE and ENCEINTE CASTLES)

LIVERY BADGES *see* BADGES AND LIVERY

LIVERY FLAGS *see* BADGES AND LIVERY *and* FLAGS

LLYS The residence and court of a Welsh prince or lord (*see* ROYAL PALACES).

LOCKS *see* IRONWORK, LOCKS AND NAILS

LOGGIA A gallery, one side of which comprises an arcade of open arches to catch the sun.

LONG AND SHORT WORK Typical of Anglo-Saxon structures, alternate long vertical and short horizontal stones set in the termination of a wall to provide additional strength, to the corners of a square tower or a doorway jamb, for example. (*See also* QUOIN)

LONGBOW *see* ARCHERY

'LONG HUNDRED' One hundred and twenty. A method of calculation based on units of six scores ($6 \times 20 = 120$).

LOOPHOLE, ARCHÈRE, ARROW LOOP *or* **ARROW SLIT** A narrow vertical opening in a defensive wall through which an arrow or bolt was shot. Loopholes are found throughout a castle's defences: in the MERLONS of parapets, in the EMBRASURES of intra-mural galleries and towers, and in the inner walls of GATE PASSAGES and BARBICANS where they were sometimes provided with rebated wooden shutters (as in the east gatehouse of Rhuddlan Castle). Beside the loopholes in the towers at Corfe Castle there is evidence of lockers in which spare arrows and bolts were kept.

Dunstanburgh Castle, Northumberland, was built in 1313–16 by Thomas, earl of Lancaster (c. 1278–1322), as 'the remote refuge of a defiant magnate' (Pettifer). Its broad, open enceinte was clearly intended as a barracks for Lancaster's vast retinue.

These were on the right side of the archer to ensure a rapid rate of reloading.

Although a vertical slit is a common feature of loopholes, the characteristics of the different types of bow (*see* ARCHERY) require different styles and size of loophole. A loophole must be of sufficient height to allow for a variety of trajectories and of sufficient width to allow an arrow or bolt to be released without impediment. Furthermore, it must provide a wide field of vision while keeping the loop as narrow as possible in order to protect the defender. (It has been demonstrated that a skilled archer can shoot one arrow in three through a 5cm (2in) wide arrow slit from a range of 25m (82ft)). All four objectives were achieved by the use of EMBRASURES: the larger the embrasure, the easier it was for a defending crossbowman to release his bolts close to the loophole, thereby avoiding the possibility of a deflection on the embrasure walls. A

longbow, on the other hand, should be approximately the height of the archer and half of this height will be above eye-level when taking aim. Traversing with a longbow is difficult because it requires a whole body movement. The crossbow may be traversed more easily, but the weight of the bow is difficult to support unaided for any length of time and it is more easily used in a kneeling position. Therefore a high embrasure is required for a standing longbowman, while a crossbowman requires a low embrasure, preferably with support for his weapon at waist height. A loophole can measure from 0.9 to 2.7m (1 to 3yd) in height and 3.7 to 10.1cm (1.5 to 4in) in width. A common form of arrow loop is the *fishtail* which has a triangular splay at the foot, intended to increase the field of vision at the base of a wall.

Cruciform or *crosslet loopholes* came into use in the thirteenth century, almost certainly to accom-

Unusual loophole, known as displaced traverse slots, at White Castle, Monmouthshire.

modate crossbows. The addition of a horizontal sighting slit made it possible for an archer to line up his target before it entered the target area (*killing ground*) defined by the vertical arrow slit. Crosslet loopholes may be found in a variety of styles including the *crosslet with fishtail*, similar to the fishtail (*see above*) but with a cross-loop; the *top crosslet with fishtail*, a loop with a broad horizontal cross-loop near the top of the vertical opening and a fishtail at the foot; and the *double cruciform* which has two horizontal cross-loops. The *oillet* loophole (literally, an 'eyelet') has circular sight-holes at the ends of the cruciform loop to improve a defender's line of sight. In some cases the oillet at the foot of a vertical loop may have been enlarged to accommodate firearms (*see* GUN PORTS). There are also examples of rectangular oillets, as at Pembroke Castle. One of the most unusual forms of cruciform loop is to be found at White Castle where the arms of the cross-loops are offset, one higher than the other – known as *displaced traverse slots*. It has been suggested that this arrangement was intended to compensate for the steep slopes outside the moat – so that an attacker could be kept in the

sighting slits for as long as possible. If so, the system failed to find favour elsewhere. Vertical loops were sometimes inserted in the angle formed at the conjunction of adjacent walls or (as at Conisbrough, South Yorkshire) where a wedge-shaped buttress meets the cylindrical wall of a tower.

The location of loopholes was determined by two principles: first, that the target areas of individual loopholes should overlap in order to avoid 'blind spots', especially at the foot of a wall; and secondly that a wall was most effectively protected by a flanking counter-attack from projecting towers (*mural towers*) (*see* TOWERS). In the Avranches tower at Dover Castle (*c.* 1190) the loopholes are so arranged that two or three crossbowmen could shoot through a single loophole simultaneously: these are often described as *multiple arrow slits*, though in practice they are single loops with triple, converging embrasures. A similar arrangement is found in the King's Gate and north curtain wall of the upper ward at Caernarfon Castle (1290), where the crossbowmen were required to shoot down slits only 5–10cm (2–4in) wide and at least 3m (10ft) long! Also at ground level in the north curtain wall is a second range of experimental arrow slits, this time comprising triple loopholes emanating from a single embrasure, clearly intended to increase an archer's field of vision.
(*See also* BATTLEMENTS *and* GUN PORTS).

LORD In the Middle Ages the term, which was synonymous with 'sire', was applied to a feudal superior and to anyone of noble rank, including royal dukes and male members of the sovereign's family. Since then the term has acquired a more specific application:
(i) The abbreviated style of a peer below the rank of duke.
(ii) An honorary prefix used by the younger sons of dukes and marquesses.
(*See also* NOBILITY AND GENTRY)

LORD HIGH CONSTABLE *see* CONSTABLE *and* EARL MARSHAL

LORD LIEUTENANT *see* LIEUTENANT

LORD OF THE MANOR Following the Conquest of 1066, England was divided among the followers of William I who remained, in theory, the owner of the kingdom. The smallest holding within these granted estates has subsequently become known as the MANOR. The highest level of tenancy, held of the king, was the tenancy-in-chief (*lordship in fee*).

Multiple loopholes in the north curtain wall of the upper ward at Caernarfon Castle (1290).

Magnates in this category sometimes let to lesser lords (*mesne tenants*) who, on occasion, let to *their* followers who thereby became *tenants-in-demesne*. The 'lord of the manor' could belong to any of these categories but was always the tenant on whom the actual feudal obligation rested. Thereafter, overlordships of manors tended to become forgotten and after 1290, when the statute of *Quia Emptores* forbade further subinfeudation, qualifying clauses were inserted in conveyances to prevent future claims of overlordship. The term itself means 'landlord' and a lord of the manor was not necessarily titled or even armigerous.

The identities of manorial lordships and the services (*fees*) by which the manors were held may be obtained from the *Book of Fees* (see FEUDAL AIDS) and INQUISITIONS POST MORTEM. Since 1926 all matters relating to the ownership of manors and the location of manorial records have to be reported to the Master of the Rolls and this information may be obtained from the National Register of Archives (see APPENDIX II). (*See also* FEUDAL SYSTEM *and* VILLEIN)

LORD PARAMOUNT In England, the sovereign (*see* VASSAL).

LORDSHIPS IN FEE *see* LORD OF THE MANOR

LORDS SPIRITUAL AND TEMPORAL In the Middle Ages the Lords Spiritual comprised the archbishops, bishops and certain senior abbots while the Lords Temporal comprised the members of the PEERAGE. Although this distinction was made, the Lords Spiritual were just as likely to take up arms and to fortify their residences as were the Lords Temporal. It has been suggested that war-like bishops, in order to avoid spilling blood in battle, preferred the blunted mace and battle-hammer to the sword and battle-axe.

LOUVRE *or* LOUVER A ventilator in the roof of a hall or kitchen through which smoke escapes.

L-PLAN A particular form of TOWER-HOUSE in which a wing has been added at right angles to the main tower for additional protection from covering fire.

LUNETTE (i) In post-medieval fortifications, a substantial advanced work comprising two faces, two flanks and an open rear (*see* TUDOR COASTAL FORTS).
(ii) *See* CAPITAL

M

MACE A heavy club, usually having a metal head comprising four or six protruding flanges or a spherical head with spikes, the latter sardonically named 'Morning Star'. A particular type of flanged mace, known as the 'Holy Water Sprinkler', was similar in appearance to the asperges used by a priest for sprinkling consecrated water over the altar during the mass. Metal strips below the head protected the shaft of a mace from a lopping blow while guards were often fitted to protect the hand from blades sliding down the shaft. Intended for crushing rather than piercing, it has been suggested (not convincingly) that the mace was the weapon favoured by warrior churchmen for 'it draweth not blood'.
(*See also* WAR HAMMER *and* WEAPONS AND HARNESS)

Ornate machicolations at Raglan Castle, Monmouthshire.

MACHICOLATIONS Most often found on the gateways and towers of late medieval castles and town walls, machicolations are crenellated parapets which project on corbels from the head of a wall, the gap between each corbel allowing defenders to observe and defend the vulnerable base of a wall. It was otherwise impossible for archers to shoot vertically from a parapet, or to drop missiles on attackers at the base of the wall, without exposing themselves to danger. Machicolations are effectively a reworking in stone of wooden HOARDINGS, though usually without a roof: the covered fighting gallery at Tattershall Castle (1434–46), being an exception in England. Occasionally the entire parapet of a gateway, keep or flanking tower was machicolated, as at Lancaster and Warwick Castles and Raglan, though expense dictated that most curtain walls were not. Some of the best examples are found in Wales, the earliest being in the gateway from the west barbican to the inner ward of Conwy Castle (1283). Those in the gatehouses of Beaumaris and Carmarthen and Kidwelly are better preserved. A rare example of a fortified town bridge, the thirteenth-century Monnow Gate at Monmouth, is also provided with machicolations, while in the same county, at Caldicot Castle, the corbels which carry the machicolations are ornately sculpted. In the inner ward of Rhuddlan Castle, *box-machicolations* once projected from the centre of each of the four curtain walls, at the vulnerable area midway between the towers. These were effectively rectangular turrets, large corbelled MERLONS with EMBRASURES and machicolation holes. None of the box-machicolations have survived, but the position of those on the south-west and south-east walls can be clearly seen. As with crenellations, machicolations may be found in several late medieval houses where their function is purely decorative. The term is sometimes strictly applied to the openings themselves, to a single wide machicolation slot within the outer archway of a gatehouse (*see also* SLUICE), or to MURDER HOLES in the vault of a GATE PASSAGE.
(*See also* BATTLEMENTS)

MADOG, THE WAR OF *see* WALES, CONQUEST OF

MAGNA CARTA The Great Charter sealed by King John following his meeting with the barons at Runnymede on 15 June 1215. Violent baronial opposition to John's arbitrary rule and his disastrous foreign policy was channelled by Archbishop Langton into a demand for constitutional restraints of royal power. Subsequently regarded as a milestone in British constitutional history, though in practice not a particularly radical document, the resulting charter ('great' because of its unusual length) redefined many feudal practices and laid down what the barons considered to be the recognised and fundamental principles for the governance of the realm, and bound both the king and the barons to maintain them. Magna Carta comprises a preamble and sixty-three clauses, the most famous of these guaranteeing every free man security from illegal interference in his person or property (39) and justice to everyone (40). No man was to be punished without trial before his peers and ancient liberties were to be preserved. No demands, other than those recognised, should be made of a vassal by his lord without the sanction of the MAGNUM CONCILIUM. Furthermore, the king was not to levy scutage or aids without reference to the 'common council' of the realm (12), the Church was to be 'free', the authority of sheriffs restricted and the liberties of boroughs confirmed. The Charter was to be enforced by a council of twenty-five barons which, should the king renege on his oath, was empowered to declare war on him. Although the Charter failed to prevent the first BARONS' WAR of 1215–17, it was later amended and reissued in 1216, 1217 and 1225. The four extant copies of Magna Carta are held at the British Library (2) and Lincoln and Salisbury Cathedrals.

MAGNATE The term was first used in the fifteenth century to describe eminent persons of wealth and influence. Most pre-nineteenth-century documents refer to the Latin plural *magnates*.

MAGNUM CONCILIUM The 'great council' of post-Conquest England that replaced the Anglo-Saxon *witan* and was the forerunner of the modern parliament. It comprised the king's great vassals who, with the king, exercised legislative functions and initiated taxation. The terms of reference and composition of the Magnum Concilium were prescribed in MAGNA CARTA in 1215.

MAGNUS TURRIS *see* TOWERS

MAIL Armour formed of circular metal links (usually iron) arranged so that each link passes through two similar links in the row above and two in the row below. The most common type of link comprised a length of wire with its flattened ends overlapping and riveted. Rows of riveted links were often alternated with rows of welded links, the ends of which were forge-welded together. A quilted or padded jacket would always have been worn beneath a mail HAUBERK, otherwise a blow from a weapon would have driven the mail links into the flesh. Tests have shown that mail can absorb arrows shot from

some distance, though it could not prevent minor wounds. The term 'mail' should be applied to all forms of mail armour, 'chain mail' being a pleonasm. (*See also* ARMOUR)

MAINTENANCE Unlawful support of another person in a law suit by word or deed. The practice of protecting and defending retained men in the courts in return for service was a characteristic of the fourteenth and fifteenth centuries (*see* LIVERY AND MAINTENANCE).

MAISONETTE A suite of rooms within a castle, such as those allocated to the constable and chaplain at Carew Castle, Pembrokeshire.

MAISON FORTE *see* MANOR HOUSES

MAJESTY A depiction of the king seated in state (*see* COINAGE, GREAT SEAL *and* SEALS).

MAN-AT-ARMS Any fighting man when equipped with a full harness – a knight, a banneret, an esquire, a member of the lesser gentry or a sergeant (*see* WEAPONS AND HARNESS). In fourteenth-century England the term was applied specifically to a fully armoured cavalryman.
(*See also* HORSES AND HORSE-HARNESS)

MANGONEL *see* SIEGES

MANOR A feudal estate (from the Latin *mansus*) and for five hundred years after the Conquest the essential unit of local government, though it is likely that several important elements of the 'manorial system' had been established long before 1066. A fundamental of the *land law*, introduced, applied and expanded by successive Norman kings, was 'no land without a lord and no lord without land'. A manor was held of the king by a LORD OF THE MANOR (literally 'landlord') either directly or through one or more *mesne lords* (*see* SUBINFEUDATION). Many held several, often widely dispersed, manors, the day-to-day management of each being entrusted to an elected officer known as the REEVE and the administration of a manorial court (or group of courts) to a STEWARD.

In practice, the term *manorial system* is fallacious, for there was no such thing as a 'typical' manor. Generalisations are inevitably misleading, and historians prefer to study individual manors, recognising that each was possessed of characteristics and customs which rarely conformed to a 'system' and were often unique. A manor itself might encompass a number of townships or *vills* (administrative divisions) and farmsteads; it may have been reorganised around a new and more substantial village; or it may have retained the boundaries of an earlier Saxon (or even Roman) estate. A manor could be part of a parish (the smallest unit of ecclesiastical administration), contiguous with its boundaries or spread over a number of parishes. It would usually comprise the lord's DEMESNE lands and the common ploughland, meadowland and waste (peripheral land on which tenants exercised their rights of commonage). Over much of England the arable land of a manor consisted of three or more large open fields in which the inhabitants held scattered strips according to their relative *tenements*. The lord's demesne land might similarly be distributed within the open fields or contained in a consolidated block of the most fertile strips. From the produce of these demesne lands was derived the wealth of the manor, together with a variety of feudal dues, rents and fines exacted by the manorial court. The earliest manors were worked by VILLEINS who laboured on the demesne lands in return for their tenements (known as *villein tenure*, together with one or more FRANKLINS who were free tenants. As the feudal system decayed, villein tenure increasingly became commuted to money payments, a form of tenure known as *copyhold*.

The manor was governed by a manor court, a periodic meeting of tenants convened and presided over by the lord of the manor or his steward, who was usually a man of some substance and often trained in law. Manorial custom determined both the frequency and conduct of these meetings which were usually held at intervals of between six weeks and six months. Though the procedure was judicial, the manorial courts considered both judicial and administrative matters, such as the transfer of property (*alienations*), sitting either as COURTS BARON or COURTS LEET (*see also* LAW AND ORDER). The overriding principle was that of custom by which the rights and responsibilities both of the lord and of the tenantry were determined: 'Justice shall be done by the lord's court, not by the lord.' Many customs were already of 'ancient foundation' at the time of the Conquest and were to form the basis of Common Law. The manor court was not entirely autonomous, however, for it was subject to the authority of the royal courts in certain areas such as the rights of free tenants. All tenants were obliged to attend manorial courts and were eligible for election as jurors. Defaulters who failed to attend or refused to serve as jurors were fined unless they were able to demonstrate 'good cause' to the satisfaction of the court. Manorial

officers (other than the *bailiff* who was appointed by the steward as his manager) were elected at an annual meeting of the court. These included the REEVE, BEADLE, CONSTABLE, hayward (responsible for ensuring that cattle did not stray from the common), ale-taster (responsible for testing the quality and measurement of ale) and two affeerors (responsible for administering fines). When the lordship of a manor changed hands a special Court of Recognition (*Curia Prima*) was held, at which the new lord was formally 'seized' of his tenants' service and received their renewed oaths of fealty. A Court of Survey was also convened, at which were recorded all the manorial lands and the customary dues by which they were held.

The records of manorial courts are an invaluable source of information for historians. Of these, the most significant are the *Court Rolls* which were compiled by the steward's clerk as minutes of proceedings, including disputes and changes in the occupancy of holdings. The customary rights and responsibilities of a lord and his tenants were set out in the *Custumal* and details of the location and size of the various holdings were recorded in the *Terrier*. Jury verdicts were retained in a separate record and details of rents due and paid were kept in the *Rental*. In the *Valor* were recorded the financial value of holdings and the *Extent* was a document in which were summarised the customs, valuations and tenancies of a manor at a given time. Since 1926 all manorial records and changes of ownership of lordships of manors have to be reported to the Master of the Rolls. The Royal Commission on Historical Manuscripts (*see* APPENDIX II) maintains a *Manorial Documents Register* from which may be ascertained the names of the manor or manors in each parish and the last-known location of manorial records. In many cases these are held by the solicitors of families holding lordships of manors but many have been deposited at county record offices. There are also notable collections of manorial records at the Public Record Office, the British Library and Birmingham Reference Library (*see* APPENDIX II).

MANOR HOUSES A manor house was the administrative centre of a manorial estate (*see* MANOR) and the dwelling of a feudal lord or (more often) his steward. Many so-called 'manor houses' are not what they seem, having acquired the name to accommodate the social aspirations of a previous owner, together with the acquisition of a manorial lordship which may, even today, be bought and sold at auction (*see* LORD OF THE MANOR). The definition of a castle as a fortified feudal residence (*see* CASTLE) encompasses those manor houses that were crenellated and protected by a gatehouse and moat: commonly described as *fortified manor houses*. The French term *maison forte* is also used.

Fortified homesteads are described in the DOMESDAY BOOK as *domus defensabiles* and there can be little doubt that, even before the Conquest, the manorial *caput* was, of necessity, both a residence and a stronghold. At Goltho in Lincolnshire the earliest of a series of fortified manor houses has been dated to the mid-ninth century, its encircling rampart and deep outer ditch confirming that the Anglo-Saxons were familiar with the defensive RINGWORK. In the 1080s Goltho's fortifications were substantially remodelled, the ramparts raised, the moat re-cut and a new castle mound constructed across one corner where its timber tower could command the gate (*see* MOTTE).

Anxious that the crown should exercise control over the building of non-royal castles, twelfth-century government officials evidently settled for the arbitrary criterion of CRENELLATION and thereafter there was a legal obligation to obtain a *licence to crenellate* before a residence could be fortified.

Manor houses, with varying degrees of defensibility, co-existed with castles from before the Conquest to the end of the sixteenth century (*see* HALL *and* TIMBER-FRAME BUILDINGS). Moats did not necessarily enclose high-status buildings: from the late thirteenth century many modest farms and homesteads were encircled by a moat, reflecting an almost obsessive concern for domestic security at a time of increasing public disorder (*see* MOATS AND WATER DEFENCES). At this time many monastic and episcopal communities were obliged to attend to their defences (*see* ECCLESIASTICAL STRONG-

HOLDS), as were the gentry and wealthy merchants such as John de Vaux, a man of considerable substance but of the 'second rank', who built Little Wenham in Suffolk, and Lawrence of Ludlow, a wool-merchant and financier, who in the 1290s rebuilt his home at Stokesay in Shropshire. Aware of his vulnerability to the violence of the MARCH, Lawrence obtained a licence to build a tower next to his hall and private chambers in 1291. His Great Tower was in all respects a personal stronghold, a massive masonry polygon, sophi-sticated in plan, strongly crenellated and with a drawbridge that separated it from a walled and moated enclosure. Stokesay was, for its day, a very modern building, combining domestic comfort with defences that were more than adequate to deter an intruder. This combination of residence and stronghold is evident in numerous manor houses dating from the thirteenth and fourteenth centuries, and it is apparent that there was often a conflict between a desire for domestic convenience and privacy and the need to defend against widespread lawlessness.

Gaol delivery records clearly illustrate a significant increase in criminal activity during the early decades of the fourteenth century. One cause was undoubtedly a devastating rise in the price of wheat and the Great Famine of 1315–17. But although destitution and violence were clearly linked, it was certain of the gentry (and even the parish clergy) who were chiefly responsible for organised crime, in some cases aided and abetted by patrons and maintainers among the aristocracy. It was these well-born bandits who recruited OUTLAWS and vagabonds to their service and accelerated the breakdown of law and order that was already evident in the late thirteenth century. Furthermore, from 1294 pardons had been granted for

Stokesay Castle (1290s) was, for its day, a very modern building, combining domestic comfort with defences that were more than adequate to deter an intruder.

service in the royal armies, emptying the king's gaols with violent and predictable effect. Discontent was further inflamed by a widespread failure of manorial discipline, exacerbated by the unrealised aspirations of the peasantry and the determination of manorial lords to frustrate them. This general disorder explains the fortification of many manor houses, such as Boarstall in Buckinghamshire in 1312, the digging of a moat at Broughton in Oxfordshire, and the provision of strong residential towers at, for example, Longthorpe, Northamptonshire and Halloughton, Nottinghamshire.

The decades that preceded the Black Death (*see* PLAGUE) witnessed a flowering of extravagant building unparalleled at any other time in the medieval period (*see* CASTLES, DEVELOPMENT OF). But by the end of the fourteenth century decades of pestilence frustrated the further enrichment of church and manor house while the PEASANTS' REVOLT of 1381 fermented discontent that proved to be even more violent than that which had preceded it. The criminal elements in the post-plague years were not the poor and desperate but people of substance: the yeomen, craftsmen and manorial officials who had led the Great Revolt and were markedly more dangerous than any previous rebel leadership. In such a climate, security could not be left to chance.

The traditional perception of the fifteenth century as a time of political instability and internecine warfare (*see* WARS OF THE ROSES) is in sharp contrast to the self-assurance and optimism evident in the architectural activity of the period. Numerous castles and fortified houses were remodelled and new houses built to provide greatly improved standards of domestic comfort and convenience as well as providing opportunities for lavish architectural detail and flamboyant displays of heraldry. The QUADRANGULAR CASTLE gradually developed into the *courtyard house*, the quadrangular arrangement of domestic buildings remaining but with only a token crenellated parapet and gatehouse for protection. Buildings were often raised from one to three storeys and provided with tall chimney stacks and gables. New ranges of buildings containing private apartments and improved domestic arrangements were erected against the curtain walls of courtyards. Outer defensive walls were pierced with windows and doorways in the contemporary Gothic style and new fireplaces and flues set within the walls. Many private CHAPELS date from this period, as at Cotehele in Cornwall, Bramall in Cheshire and Compton in Devon. Features such as gatehouses and moats were not always abandoned, however, for by their 'antiquity' they declared both the owner's prosperity and his lineage (*see also* PROSPECT TOWER). Nevertheless, drawbridges were often replaced by permanent bridges of brick or stone and portcullises removed (though the portcullis grooves in the walls of gate passages often remain). The great hall was also retained as the administrative and social centre of the manor and the venue for the manor court. Good examples of late medieval manor houses are Lytes Carey, Somerset (1450), Mannington, Norfolk (1460), Great Chalfield, Wiltshire (*c.* 1480), Cotehele, Cornwall (1485), and Athelhampton, Dorset (1485).

The Great Hall at Athelhampton, Dorset, was built in 1485 – the year in which the Wars of the Roses reached their denouement at Bosworth Field. Intended as a comfortable residence, the crenellated parapets served a decorative rather than a military purpose. The gatehouse (left) was demolished in 1862.

Comfortable fifteenth-century manor houses such as Lower Brockhampton, the home of a Herefordshire farming family, were ubiquitous. The gatehouse, half-timbered and with a jettied upper chamber, provided a formal entrance to a moated enclosure but was hardly capable of serious defence.

Sir Edmund Bedingfeld obtained a licence to crenellate Oxburgh Hall, Norfolk, in 1482, though it is likely that construction had already begun for the licence pardons him for work already undertaken. As one might expect at this late date, Oxburgh was essentially a residence, with four domestic ranges of buildings round a courtyard and a lofty brick gatehouse that dominates the north front. Oxburgh's wide moat and gatehouse are pretentious rather than defensive, their function to define private space. Nevertheless, in some cases, such as Baconsthorpe Castle in Norfolk, moats, gatehouses and towers were still built of necessity. Baconsthorpe was the work of John Haydon (d. 1480) who rose to prominence during the Wars of the Roses when he demonstrated an aptitude for backing the winning side, frequently changing his allegiance and making many enemies in the process. He was an aggressive, self-seeking lawyer with a distinctly unsavoury reputation and it is not surprising that his house was heavily defended by a deep moat and quadrangular curtained courtyard with flanking towers and a substantial three-storey gatehouse in the south wall.

Ralph, Lord Cromwell's great house at Tattershall was built on the fortune he acquired as Treasurer of England from 1439 to 1450. Although described as a castle, Tattershall was a spectacular country house, not a fortress. It had two quadrangles, each with its own gatehouse, a great hall, a large audience chamber and a magnificent High Tower that served as Cromwell's private residence. Of particular significance were the numerous lodgings that filled the ranges of buildings on every side of the two courtyards. Cromwell had been a trusted royal councillor for most of Henry VI's reign, but he had made many enemies. And yet, unlike John Haydon, Cromwell realised that his best security lay not in his walls but in the vigilance of his large household. Tattershall was built on too grand a scale to be described as a manor house, but neither was it a castle. Already, in 1448, the boundaries of definition were becoming blurred (*see* BRICK BUILDINGS).

Very much lower down the social scale, comfortable fifteenth-century manor houses such as Lower Brockhampton, the home of a Herefordshire farming family, were ubiquitous. The gatehouse of Lower Brockhampton, half-timbered and with a jettied upper chamber, provided a formal entrance to a moated enclosure but was hardly capable of serious defence. But such modest defence was not necessarily a reflection of lower status. Ockwells, Berkshire, was the purpose-built home of Sir John

Norreys (d. 1466), Master of the Wardrobe to Henry VI and a successful household official whose motto was 'Feythfully Serve'. His new house was close to Windsor and was clearly intended as a base for his political ambitions and for entertaining friends from court. Ockwell's prodigious display of expensive timber-framing, heraldic glass and brickwork declare the rank and affluence of its owner. But it was virtually undefended.

Many medieval and Tudor manor houses were refortified and strengthened in the Civil War, often with earth ramparts constructed behind the medieval curtain walls to absorb the impact of bombardment. (*See also* PELE TOWERS)

MANOR HOUSES, FORTIFIED *see* MANOR HOUSES

MANTLET *or* MANTELET In siege warfare, a covering of toughened hide or wood used as a mobile shelter beneath which defensive walls could be approached in comparative safety. Mantlets were sufficiently light to be carried overhead by a troop of men and could be erected, like a protective skirt, round a siege engine (*see* SIEGES).

MANTLET WALL (i) A wall protecting or covering an entrance-way or courtyard.
(ii) A secondary defensive wall surrounding a tower, known also as a CHEMISE. The mantlet or *apron wall* which surrounds the early fifteenth-century Great Tower at Raglan Castle was added in *c.* 1465 and includes six turrets, one of which contains a latrine and another a postern gate to the moat. When completed the mantlet wall obscured the gun ports in the walls of the tower, rendering them useless.
(iii) An outer defensive wall (without towers) beyond a curtain wall: at Denbigh Castle, for example, a mantlet was added to the earlier defences after the castle had been captured by the Welsh in 1294. This is joined to an elaborate sloping barbican which protects a postern gate. At Denbigh the space between the mantlet and the town walls is known as the 'lists', which suggests that it may once have been used as a tilt-yard.

MANTLING (*also* LAMBREQUIN) A protective cloth affixed to a helmet by means of a WREATH. In a coat of arms the mantling is depicted as flowing from beneath the CREST, sometimes terminating in tassels and scalloped or 'slashed' in a stylised form. Almost certainly the mantling originated in the Holy Land where it was worn by crusading knights to deflect the sun's heat.

MANUMISSION *see* VILLEIN

MAPS (MEDIEVAL) The term 'map' is derived from the Latin *mappa* meaning 'napkin'. Fascinating though Hereford Cathedral's *Mappa Mundi* (Richard of Haldingham, *c.* 1290) may be, such early maps are of little direct relevance to the local historian other than to facilitate one's understanding of the medieval mind. At that time there were three entirely dissimilar images of the world, each with its own origin and serving different sections of medieval society. The first, the humanist *Ptolemaic* maps of the twelfth century, exemplified the world view of ancient Greece based on geographical data gathered by the second-century astronomer and geographer Ptolemy of Alexandria. These maps were drawn according to Ptolemy's perception of a world 'held together by an astronomically determined mathematical grid' that was to become the standard reference of the Renaissance. (Unfortunately, Ptolemy's calculations were so inaccurate that Columbus mistook eastern America for Japan!) The second, the *mappae mundi*, were fantastic compendia of God's creation, sanctioned by the Church and constructed round the symbolic core of a T (life) within an O (eternity), the latter representing the hemisphere and the T the Mediterranean with the rivers Dom and Nile forming the cross-piece. In such maps Paradise is depicted at the top and Jerusalem at the centre with Asia filling the upper (eastern) half and Africa and Europe the lower quarters. The third category consisted of the mariners' or *portolan* charts which were devised from first-hand experience to aid navigation in the Mediterranean and Black Sea in the thirteenth century and gradually expanded so that by the sixteenth century all the coastlines of the known world were delineated. It is interesting to note that a belief in a 'flat earth' is evident in none of these early maps, not even in the *mappae mundi*. In 1569 Garardus Mercator devised a projection that both presented a curved surface in two dimensions and endeavoured to satisfy the requirement of navigators for a chart on which a compass course could be laid down as a straight line. The earliest maps of Britain are also of little value to the local historian: the Matthew Paris map of 1250, for example, is intrinsically interesting but contains little accurate information.

MAPS (MODERN) *see* ORDNANCE SURVEY

MARBLE A granular crystalline limestone, though the term is loosely applied to any stone of a similar appearance which takes a high polish. A rich and

costly material, marble was frequently used for embellishing major medieval churches, notably in altars, colonettes, flooring and screens. While little evidence of its use has survived in castles it must be assumed that marble was similarly employed in the architecture of chapels, halls and high-status chambers. Both imported and local English marbles were used, the best known being *Touch*, a black marble quarried near Tournai in Belgium (hence *Tournai Marble*) which, from the twelfth century, was imported into Britain, usually as finished tomb slabs and decorative mouldings. Tournai marble is similar in appearance, though by no means identical, to Purbeck marble and other cheaper 'marbles' by which it was replaced. *Purbeck marble* is not a true marble but an almost black, fossiliferous limestone which occurs in two narrow strata in quarries on the Isle of Purbeck, Dorset. Its northern equivalent is *Frosterley marble*, a black or dark grey limestone extracted from quarries in County Durham.
(*See also* MASONRY)

MARCH From the Old English *mearc* meaning 'boundary', from which are derived place-name elements such as Marcle (Herefordshire) meaning 'boundary wood', a march is a tract of land on the borders of two territories, such as the medieval Calais March (or *Pale*) and the Marches of Wales and Scotland.

Following the Conquest most of Duke William's followers received dispersed estates, thereby avoiding a potentially dangerous concentration of magnate power, but on the remote borders of Wales and Scotland he created counties palatine whose overlords were charged with the defence of the realm. In the north a Prince Bishop ruled over the vast territories of his PALATINATE of Durham while in the Marches of Wales the king created the palatine earldoms of Hereford (William Fitz Osbern), Shrewsbury (Roger de Montgomery) and Chester (Hugh d'Avranches). William also selected the most rapacious and unruly of his followers, who might otherwise have threatened his authority, and gave them licence to annex any lands they could wrest from the Welsh. In time these Norman 'adventurers' (*see* ADVENAE), men of 'extreme arrogance and presumption', were to overrun nearly half of Wales, taking advantage of the disunity of the Welsh princes and minimal interference from their sovereign (*see* WALES *and* WALES, CONQUEST OF). They mounted expeditions to seize the territories of any native ruler too weak to resist them and what they gained 'by the power of their swords and of fortune' they passed on to their descendants as Marcher

lordships, private kingdoms in all but name that were to last until the Act of 'Union' in 1536.

William II (*r.* 1087–1100) also encouraged the Marcher lords (the *domini marchearum*) and their subtenants to conquer what they could, and in the Welsh borderlands they planned their strategy with care. Inevitably, there was a proliferation of castles, each serving to protect its neighbour, and the whole system forming a network that guarded every important river crossing and gap in the hills. By the mid-twelfth century this fiercely independent warrior aristocracy occupied much of eastern Wales together with the south coast from Chepstow to St David's and had established a triple line of defences along the border. It has been calculated that there were at least six hundred earthwork and timber castles in Wales and the Marches at this time, some of which would have been temporary structures, occupied for the duration of a campaign and then abandoned. In the Marcher zone, some 50 to 80km (30 to 50 miles) deep, the Normans introduced their own laws and culture (though in some areas Welsh communities which had submitted to Norman overlordship were allowed to live by their ancient laws and customs) and exercised judicial authority over the population for whom access to the crown courts was effectively denied (*see* ENGLISHRY).

By the fifteenth century two distinct forms of government were to be found to the west of the English shires: in the counties of the Principality and in Flint and the Welsh Marches or Marcher lordships. The principality shires, organised in two groups centred on Carmarthen and Caernarfon, and with Flint attached to Chester, were governed directly by the king (independently of the English shires) through his appointees, and each was administered by a justiciar and chamberlain. The Marcher lordships, on the other hand, although ultimately held of the crown (into whose hands they occasionally fell by escheat, forfeiture or wardship) were independent franchises. Every function of government in each lordship was the sole responsibility of its Marcher lord: his courts had power of life and death over his tenants, he could impose his own taxes and royal officials from neighbouring Welsh or English shires had no authority there. No real attempt was made to restrict the power of the Marcher lords, whose lands had become a refuge for fugitives and dissidents, until in 1471 Edward IV instituted the Council of the Marches of Wales which was maintained as an administrative authority until its abolition in 1689. The Marcher lordships themselves were finally abolished in 1536 when the five new counties of

Denbigh, Montgomery, Radnor, Brecon and Monmouth were created. The political pattern of the Welsh Marches was constantly changing throughout the Middle Ages as families failed in the male line, heiresses married into other families (sometimes forming alliances with the Welsh nobility) or lands were confiscated by the English kings. Of the 136 Marcher lordships mentioned in the Act of 'Union' in 1536, 41 had reverted to the crown either through forfeiture, conquest or marriage.

The Scottish *Borders*, although not named as such until the thirteenth century, were from the earliest times the disputed territory of contending races or nations (*see* SCOTLAND: ENGLISH WARS IN). Indeed, the Anglo-Scottish frontier was the major factor determining the political and social character of the north, not simply because of the feuding and raiding over the border that were a constant threat to life and property, but because the English crown entrusted responsibility for guarding the frontier to those whom parliament in 1388 described as 'les seignurs marchers del north'. The exigencies occasioned by the constantly recurring Border wars and incursions of the thirteenth to the sixteenth centuries resulted in the building of numerous castles and PELE TOWERS, each strategically placed to control routeways and river crossings and almost invariably in sight of one another to facilitate the rapid communication of signals of invasion or alarm. In 1460 Northumberland alone possessed thirty-seven castles and seventy-eight towers and the Scottish side was equally well defended. By the fifteenth century the Borders had effectively become ungovernable (*see* REAVERS) and the two kingdoms agreed that an element of control should be exercised through the creation, on both sides of the border, of divisions known as the East, West and Middle Marches. Salaried officials (*Wardens*) were appointed by their respective sovereigns to each division and endowed with considerable administrative and judicial authority. The wardens represented their sovereign in their respective divisions and the office was at one time hereditary, being the prerogative of a few of the senior magnates who held estates on the Borders and who recognised the potential for aggrandisement. At certain times a day of truce was held when the English and Scottish wardens met, examined each other's credentials, and attempted to settle any matters that might be in dispute among their followers. As may be imagined, not all such meetings ended amicably! One district which was the cause of considerable trouble to the wardens of the West March was that known as the *Debatable*

Land which lay partly in England and partly in Scotland. First mentioned in 1449 as 'the lands called Batable or Threep lands', its chief families were the Grahams and the Armstrongs, clans of 'desperate thieves and freebooters', whose constant antagonism was finally concluded in the seventeenth century when the Grahams were transported to Ireland and forbidden to return on pain of death. Other districts of the Borders periodically required the armed intervention of the Scottish commissioners and as late as 1606 the earl of Dunbar seized and hanged 140 brigands. The character and way of life of Borderers were similar on both the Scottish and the English sides. The magnates lived in large, heavily fortified castles while the lesser nobles and gentry occupied pele towers and fortified farmsteads. The feudal bond between chiefs and the principal men of their clans was that implied in the term 'kindly tenant': a tenant being of the chieftain's family or having held his lands in succession for several generations. This tie was not dependent on the payment of rent, either in money or in kind, but on kinship, and bound the leading members of the clan to corporate self-interest and self-defence. The union of the crowns in 1603 removed some obvious grounds of contention between the border clans and from the middle of the seventeenth century the Borders gradually subsided into a more stable and peaceful condition.

MARCHER LORD *see* MARCH

MARCHIONESS *see* MARQUESS

MARCLE *see* MARCH

MARK In early medieval England, an economic unit used originally in the DANELAW when it represented 128 silver pennies or 10*s* 8*d*. It was later adopted for use throughout the country and its value rose to 13*s* 4*d*.
(*See also* COINAGE)

MARKETS In the centuries that followed the withdrawal of Rome, Saxon chieftains built their strongholds and the monks their abbeys and such places inevitably attracted a scattered but increasingly gregarious populace, anxious to join with others in the celebration of saints days and holy days or to witness the administration of justice and the settlement of disputes in the lord's courts. For itinerant merchants travel was both slow and dangerous, so that these large gatherings of people, enjoying the security of monastic or magnate patronage, provided ideal opportunities for trade. Edward the Elder (900–25) decreed that all buying and selling should take place openly in a market place and within the jurisdiction of a town-reeve. As permanent communities developed round many abbeys and castles so markets and fairs flourished and by the late tenth century tolls were being exacted, both by the Saxon kings and by the nobles and clerics who organised and controlled the movement of goods between their estates.

In the early Middle Ages 'markets' and 'fairs' were similar occasions and quite distinct from the religious feast days and holy days which had their own traditions and ceremonies. Gradually FAIRS emerged as more seasonal gatherings, often on the periphery of TOWNS or at prominent sites in the surrounding countryside, whereas markets were held weekly and always in towns or villages. Royal mints were also established at various centres to provide an authoritative and standardised coinage for a rapidly expanding commerce.

After the Conquest many of these customary markets and fairs were recorded in the DOMESDAY Book and eventually regularised under the Norman kings by the granting of charters which permitted the receipt of revenues. The acquisition of a market charter was obviously of great financial advantage, to both a manorial lord (who would receive the tolls and taxes levied on his markets and fairs and the fines exacted for breaches of trading regulations) and the crown (from whom the privilege was almost invariably purchased). Many charters were granted by sovereigns to their own estates in anticipation of future prosperity and others were granted as gifts in recognition of service to the crown.

As commercial expertise increased so foreign merchants were attracted to the larger English markets, bringing with them oriental spices, wines from Bordeaux and pottery, silks and glass from the Mediterranean. Restrictions aimed at alleviating the problems of inequitable competition included the staggering of market days throughout a week in a particular area; the prosecution of *forestallers* (or *regrators*), merchants who traded before reaching a market and sold on at a profit; and the imposition of limits on the proximity of markets. (A reasonable day's journey for an unmounted man was considered to be 32km (20 miles) which, when allowing time to walk to market, time to do business and time to walk home again, was divided by three to give 11km (6⅔ miles): the statutory distance between markets in the fourteenth century. 'And all these things it will be necessary to do by day and not by night on account of the snares and attacks of robbers.')

While many markets have been held on the same weekday for 500 or 600 years, the aspirations of numerous medieval entrepreneurs exceeded the commercial potential of their markets, which eventually foundered, usually because they were geographically unsustainable or as a result of intense competition or the ravages of plague. Consequently, there are numerous tiny boroughs whose medieval charters have guaranteed continuing political and legal privileges not enjoyed by larger and more prosperous communities. Bishops Castle in Shropshire, for example, was the smallest borough in England until 1967 when it lost that distinction but none of its quaintness. Many market charters were granted by the Norman kings, but the greatest proliferation took place during the thirteenth century when some 3,300 markets were authorised, with a further 1,560 grants in the fourteenth century before the advent of economic decline. A fair or market usually fell within the jurisdiction of a lord of the manor whose steward presided over the Court of Pie Powder (a corruption of *pieds poudreux*, meaning 'dusty footed' travellers). This court met in a building called a *tollbooth* or *tolsey* and was responsible for both the general administration of the market and the maintenance of law and order for the duration of the market. Local traders often traded first, outsiders (known variously as *stallingers*, *censers* or *chensers*) either waiting their turn or paying a supplementary fee in order to jump the queue.

At first, parish churches were often used as repositories for documents and valuables, and trading took place in the porch and precincts. In 1285, however, a statute was passed forbidding the holding of fairs in churchyards and by 1448 the clergy was so incensed by 'the abominable injuries and offenses done to Almighty God because of fairs and markets upon their high and principal feasts', that trading was finally removed into the space beyond the churchyard wall and fairs were prohibited on Good Friday, Ascension Day, Corpus Christi, the Assumption of the Virgin Mary, All Saints and on any Sunday except the four at harvest time.

As England prospered, rows of semi-permanent stalls were erected in the larger markets and may be evident in street names today: the *shambles*, for example, being the area of a market where fish and flesh were sold. Names such as Cheap Street and Sheep Street are also indicative of early markets. So too is Chipping in place-names, derived from the Old English *cēping* or *ciēping* meaning 'market' or 'market town', as in Chipping Norton in Oxfordshire. Any dwelling beside a market square could buy a licence to serve ale on market day.

Official market halls were erected as administrative offices in which goods were weighed by the *Ponderator* and scrutinised and stored by the Overseers of the Market and other officials. From 1640 the senior official was the Clerk of the Market, appointed by the lord of the manor or the town mayor. On market days the Clerk announced the commencement of trading at ten and its cessation at sunset. (The Clerk of the Market was originally a crown official, responsible within the VERGE for supplying market goods to the royal household and for the examination of weights and measures.)

A market's success depended on its accessibility: roads to and from markets had to be maintained and in several instances special roads or *portways* were built. Portway is a term derived from the Latin *porta*, the port or gate of a market town at which borough officials scrutinised traders' credentials and collected tolls and rents (*see* PORT). In some cases the word *port* became synonymous with 'market', as at Langport, Somerset.

MARKS, MASONS' *see* MASONS' MARKS

MARKS OF DIFFERENCE *see* CADENCY

MARKS OF DISTINCTION *see* DISTINCTION, MARKS OF

MARQUESS (*or* MARQUIS) The second rank of the British peerage, introduced (from Europe) in 1385, though from an early date the term was sometimes applied to lords of the Welsh and Scottish Marches (*see* MARCH). The wife of a marquess is a marchioness.

MARSHAL A senior household official responsible for a lord's horses, soldiers, weaponry and general military organisation (*see* MARSHALSEA).
(*See also* EARL MARSHAL, HOUSEHOLD *and* MEWS)

MARSHALLING The practice of arranging armorial devices on a shield to signify marriage, inheritance or the holding of an office (*see* ARMORY).

Early forms of marshalling are evident in a number of twelfth-century seals where a figure is depicted between shields bearing arms of alliance or where a geometrical arrangement of related shields surrounds that of a principal house. Another early method was to combine charges from several different shields to form an entirely new one: John de Dreux, duke of Brittany and earl of Richmond, whose mother was a

daughter of Henry III, bore a shield charged with the gold and blue chequers of de Dreux within a red border charged with the gold lions of England and *over all a Canton Ermine* for Brittany.

From *c.* 1300 different coats were marshalled in the same shield, at first by means of *dimidiation*, the dexter half of a husband's arms (those to the left when viewed from the front) being joined to the sinister half of his wife's. But this practice often resulted in alarming visual ambiguities and it was abandoned in favour of *impalement* by which two complete coats were placed side by side in the same shield (again, with those of the husband to the dexter).

Impalement generally signifies a temporary or non-hereditary combination of arms such as those of a husband and a wife who is not an heraldic heiress but whose father is armigerous. But a woman who has no brothers living and no nephews or nieces from deceased brothers becomes her father's *heraldic heiress* upon his death. While he lives her arms are impaled with her husband's, but when her father dies they are displayed on an *escutcheon of pretence*, a small shield placed over the centre of her husband's shield. If she has sisters, each is a co-heiress, and each transmits her father's arms on equal terms.

After a woman's death her husband ceases to bear his wife's escutcheon of pretence and her children quarter their arms by dividing the shield into four and placing the paternal arms in the first and fourth quarters and the maternal arms in the second and third (*see also* CADENCY). Thereafter, further inherited arms may be added as *quarterings*, usually in order of acquisition though not invariably so.

Arms of John de Dreux

1. Dimidiation, 2. Impalement, 3. Inescutcheon of Pretence, 4. Quartering.

Many armigers accumulated large numbers of coats, sometimes adding ones which were already present in their arms through earlier marriages with heiresses of the same family. It is not necessary to retain all the coats (*quarterings*) that have been acquired in this way, indeed it is often impracticable to display more than four. Nevertheless, proof of *seize quartiers* (i.e. that all sixteen of an armiger's great-great-grandparents were entitled to bear arms in their own right) was sometimes proposed as a means of defining true ancestry, 'true blood' and, therefore, undisputed gentility. In Britain the proposal has always been regarded with considerable scepticism and has nothing to do with marshalling.

MARSHALSEA In the thirteenth century the marshalsea was the department responsible for the royal horses: not only those actually with the household, but also the numerous studs and farms where they were bred and kept. The senior officer of the marshalsea was the *Marshal*. In 1385 the office, which by that time had assumed considerably greater significance, was granted to Thomas Mowbray, earl of Nottingham, who a year later was given the title EARL MARSHAL. In the late Middle Ages the Marshal was, with the Lord High Constable, the first in military rank beneath the sovereign, and it was his responsibility to marshal the various contingents of troops and retainers in battle, to organise state ceremonies and to judge matters armorial brought before the COURT OF CHIVALRY. In the performance of his various duties he would undoubtedly have depended on the advice of the heralds and today the Earl Marshal continues to exercise jurisdiction over the officers of arms as hereditary judge in the High Court of Chivalry. (*See also* HOUSEHOLD)

MASONING *see* PLASTER, WHITEWASH AND PAINT

MASONRY The following terms are most commonly found in contemporary documents where there are references to medieval masonry (* *see also* individual entries). All are subject to the vagaries of spelling and several are still in use today, though not always with precisely the same meaning.

ANGELL	angular opening in a window
ASHLAR*	worked stone
BATEMENT	vertical light in the head of a window
BECKET	carved boss at end of DRIPSTONE
BOS	a vessel for carrying mortar
BOWTEL	convex moulding
CASEMENT	concave moulding
CATER	a quatrefoil (*see* FOILS)
CHAUMERE	window jamb
CLIBANUS	a lime kiln or hearth
CORBEL*	a stone bracket
CRESTE	moulding on (e.g.) a parapet
FEATHERS	pairs of metal plates to split rock
FENESTRAL	stones composing a traceried window
FILLET*	flat narrow strip
FORME	complete set of window tracery
FORME-PIECE	a section of window tracery
FREE-MORTAR	covering for an exposed wall
GARGOYLE*	carved stone water spout
KATUR	a quatrefoil (*see* FOILS)
KEY	a boss (*see* VAULTING)
LEDGEMENT	horizontal course of stone slabs
LINTEL*	top member of window frame
LORIMER	undercut with rounded upper face
MOLDS	stones composing moulded window frame
MULLION*	vertical division of window frame
NOWEL	central pillar (*see* NEWEL)

OGIVES	ribs in VAULTING
OYLEMENT	small opening in window tracery
PACE	a stone step
PARPAYN	stone dressed on parallel faces
PENDANTS	stone infill in VAULTING
QUARREL	opening in tracery for a quarry
QUARRY	single piece of window glass
RESPOND	semi-pillar attached to a wall or PIER
RESSAUNT	inflected moulding
RETOURNE	angle of DRIPSTONE
SCONCHON	splayed stone
SEVEREY	a single bay in a vault
SKEWES	stones cut at an angle
SPELUNCA	the tower of a lime kiln
TABLE	horizontal course of stone slabs
TRANSOM*	horizontal division of window frame
TRANSOUM	as above
TYLEPOUDRE	crushed tiles
VICE*	a spiral stair
VOUSSOIR	wedge-shaped stone forming an ARCH
WATER TABLE	stone gutter

In Britain most of the stone structures that have survived from before the sixteenth century are of rubble construction. *Rubble* is not a derogatory term but describes stones of different sizes, laid in a variety of ways and bound with lime mortar. *Squared coursed rubble*, for example, is walling of roughly square stone laid in horizontal courses (also described as *regular coursed rubble*), while *square-necked rubble* is walling in which small stone blocks (*snecks*) are inserted to prevent a wall being weakened by long, vertical joints. The term *random rubble*, on the other hand, describes stones of different shapes and sizes laid without any discernible pattern, while *coursed random rubble* consists of similar unshaped stones laid in horizontal courses. Cut and squared (*dressed*) stone was exceedingly expensive and was generally used only for facings and dressings such as mouldings, quoins, sills, merlons, window tracery, lintels and arches (*see* ARCH). *Ashlar* is masonry made from smooth, finely cut blocks of stone that are tooled on one external face. Rare in most early castles, ashlar was used for several later keeps and gatehouses: the magnificent late medieval castle of Raglan, Monmouthshire, is built throughout of ashlar. Thin walls, such as those of parapets or screens, might be constructed of ashlar blocks dressed on both faces which were known as *through stones* or, more commonly, as *parpains*. While the walls of many castles were often faced with dressed stone, in practice it was the thickness of the random rubble and the quality of the mortar which provided strength and stability. Walls were constructed with a soft core of rubble and quicklime between outer skins of masonry, the lime remaining flexible and enabling the wall to absorb the shock of bombardment.

It has been estimated that in the Middle Ages the cost of transporting stone for a distance of 19km (12 miles) was equal to the cost of the stone itself, though clearly this depended on the terrain and on whether movement by water was an option. For repairs to Tutbury Castle in 1314 the cost of hewing nearly six thousand freestones in the quarry at Winshill was £11 7s 8d while the cost of transporting them to the castle, some 8km (5 miles) away, was £15 19s 2d. Wherever possible local stone was used and many castles were built from quarries opened in the vicinity of the site. Where stone was not immediately available, or there were insufficient quantities, the builder was obliged to buy or hire a quarry for his operations or to buy his stone from privately owned commercial quarries. When the quarry was in the neighbourhood of the site, the same men would be employed first as quarrymen and then as masons. But if the stone had to be brought to the site from a distance, it was usually bought ready cut. Most stone was supplied in blocks, rough-hewn (*scappled*) to convenient sizes. Normally stones were sold by the hundred though sometimes sizes were specified, as at Harlech Castle in 1286 where two quarrymen were paid £25 10s for 'quarrying and cutting 2,040 stones, each containing 2 feet [60cm] in length, 1½ feet [46cm] in breadth and 1 foot [30cm] in thickness, at 25s. the hundred'. Another measure was the *ton* or *tonne-tite* which was based on the weight of a tun of wine (90kg or 2,000lb).

Stones in standard shapes and sizes and dressed stone for ornamental work were usually supplied from quarries ready worked and cut to measure according to a master mason's specifications. Indeed, it is likely that from early in the fifteenth century mouldings were increasingly purchased 'off the shelf', even for the finest applications. Consequently, much late medieval moulding of the Perpendicular period is of uniform craftsmanship and lacks individuality (*see* GOTHIC ARCHITECTURE).

When a quarry was opened the soil strata would be removed together with the top layer of inferior stone (*rag*) which might be used for filling walls. Beneath this was the *freestone*, usually oolitic limestone or particular types of sandstone. Freestone has a fine grain and does not possess strongly marked laminations and may therefore be 'freely worked' with a saw and chisel. (Medieval builders were expected to lay stone in a wall in the same position as it lay in the quarry, though there is ample evidence that they did not always bed their stone correctly.) Heavy steel-tipped iron wedges and *malls* were used to extract blocks of stone and these were then reduced by further splitting (*plugging and feathering*) and sawing to the required dimensions. The final tooling was performed either at the quarry or on site in the masons' lodge. Considerable effort was expended on ensuring that stone was of the right quality: an entry in the 1442 accounts for Gloucester Castle records 'Wages of John Hobbys, mason, riding to the quarry of Upton and the quarry of Freme to pick out and prove good stones from bad stones called cropston, and marking and scappling and proving the stones so picked out, so that the King should not be deceived therein, at 6d.' Hobbys was assisted in this task by his servant, William, who received 4*d* a day.

As one would expect, certain sources of stone were more highly prized than others. London drew largely on quarries in Kent and Surrey, the Maidstone district in particular supplying large quantities of hard *Kentish rag* which had been used by the Romans for the walls of Londinium. For finer work freestone was extracted from quarries in the neighbourhood of Reigate and Mersham in Surrey, while Windsor Castle also used stone from Totternhoe in Bedfordshire. In 1477 '9,755 feet of Teynton [Oxfordshire] stone, measured by Henry Jenyns, chief mason' were bought at 2*s* a foot for St George's Chapel at Windsor, while in 1360 over 1,000ft of 'crestes' and 'tables' were brought down by water from quarries near Stamford to Surfleet and Lynn and shipped from there to Windsor. Barnack stone was considered to be the best in East Anglia, while stone from Yorkshire quarries was widely used from at least the middle of the fourteenth century. In 1395 the walls of Westminster Hall were heightened with stone from the Yorkshire quarry of Marr, while stone from Huddleston was recorded in the accounts for 1442. This was no doubt transported to London by barge, as was Devonshire stone from quarries in the Beer district. In 1347 William Hamele of Weymouth supplied sixty-eight 'great stones of Bere' for the king's chapel at Westminster for £11, while two years later the Tower accounts show a payment of £4 6*s* 8*d* for '100 great stones of Bere, whereof fifty were worked as voussoirs for the heads of doors and windows . . . and 50 were in the rough'. Stone from Portland in Dorset was also widely used: at Westminster in 1347 and at the Tower in 1349, for example. But of far greater significance in the medieval period was Purbeck marble (*see*

MARBLE). This is not a true marble but an almost black fossiliferous limestone that occurs in two narrow strata in quarries on the Isle of Purbeck, Dorset. Purbeck marble, which came into fashion at the end of the twelfth century, is capable of receiving a very high polish and was used for high-status decorative work, notably in monumental effigies and the shafts of clustered piers (*see* MONUMENTS *and* PIER). Two marble stones, 'one subtly worked with columns for the slab of the lavatory', are mentioned in the Westminster accounts for 1288. The northern equivalent of Purbeck marble is *Frosterley marble*, a black or dark grey limestone extracted from quarries in County Durham. Undoubtedly the finest building stone in Europe was the pure white stone from the quarries at Caen in Normandy which was in constant demand throughout the medieval period, especially from the mid-thirteenth century. No less than seventy-five shiploads of Caen stone, comprising 89,200 'parpayns' or stones dressed on two parallel faces, were delivered to the Tower of London in 1278 at a cost of £332 2*s*. The quality of Caen stone made it particularly suitable for mouldings and it was used, for example, on Edward I's ELEANOR CROSSES, both for the statues of the queen and for other decorative features.

Mortar and Cement

Mortar, composed of lime and sand, was used to bind together the stones or bricks of a wall. The usual proportions were one part lime to three parts sand. Lime, which is produced by burning limestone or chalk, was either obtained from kilns constructed near the building site or purchased ready-burned. For major building works, kilns could be of considerable size: a kiln built at York in 1400 required 3,300 bricks and 33 loads of clay for its construction. Huge amounts of timber were needed to feed the kilns: at Windsor in 1275 the Hundred Rolls complain that five hundred oaks in the forest of Wellington had been used to fire the king's two lime kilns, while in 1229 the abbot of Abingdon permitted the king to clear the timber from 26 acres of woodland for three kilns producing lime for work on Oxford Castle and the town walls. Coal was also used where it was available, either from pits or from the sea. In 1278 huge amounts of 'sea-coal' were used to make lime for work on the Tower of London, leading to complaints from the citizenry, while in 1291 coal from Newcastle upon Tyne was used to fire the kilns at Corfe Castle in Dorset. Old mortar was often reused, either by reburning or by pounding it with new. At Pevensey Castle in 1288 we find men 'digging stones and old mortar where the wall had been thrown down' while others carried material from the keep to the gate for 'making old mortar and new'.

Whereas the preparation of lime was a comparatively skilled task, sand could be dug, sieved and carried by unskilled labourers. It is self-evident that even larger quantities of sand were required than of lime: the Dover accounts for 1226 record payments of over £20 for 11,160 seams of sand and 11,000 'loads'. The mixing of mortar by 'mortermen' was also unskilled work that was sometimes carried out by women. There is a reference in the Westminster accounts for 1399 to 'a sieve in which to sift burnt lime for the making of free mortar', which was probably a type of mortar that was used for plastering the exposed surfaces of walls. But where a wall was particularly exposed to the elements, a cement composed of wax and pitch or resin was applied in a molten condition. The medieval mortermen were not averse to experimenting with a variety of supplements – including, at Silverston in 1279, sulphur and 'a pennyworth of eggs'. In 1349 at the Tower of London the foundations of 'the turret beside the Thames opposite the King's Exchange' was in urgent need of repair. The accounts for the works include references to 'an iron pan in which to heat cement', 'a caldron bound with iron in which to make cement', and 'an iron ladel and an iron slice, with a tripod, to serve the masons for making cement'. There is also a reference to 'tylpuodre for making cement fore the foundations of the turret' which confirms that the Roman practice of pounding crushed tiles in with the mortar continued into the medieval period. When used on the outer face of a wall, this type of mortar was believed to be less pervious to rain.

(*See also* BRICK BUILDINGS; CASTLES, CONSTRUCTION OF *and* PLASTER, WHITEWASH AND PAINT)

MASONS' MARKS Devices used by stone masons to mark their work. Each mason had his distinctive mark which was often passed from father to son. They were usually hastily and shallowly incised and measure about 5cm (2 in) in height. The marks were numerous and varied and included simple ciphers. Registers of marks were maintained by the medieval masons' guilds both to avoid duplication and to ensure that bad workmanship could be traced. Most medieval masons were peripatetic craftsmen who often worked in teams. It is therefore possible to trace the movements of a particular mason or group of masons from one commission to the next through the identification of their marks. Masons' marks may also assist in the dating of buildings and in studying the various phases of construction – though because they are so easily eroded and effaced, few marks have survived in the fabric of castles which are generally more exposed to the elements than churches or domestic buildings.

Warkworth Castle has an unusually rich collection of masons' marks. Some common marks appear on nearly all parts of the castle without respect to date, while others, such as the pentagrams on the keep, the upper-case E on the foundations east of the gatehouse and the distinctive zig-zag device on the collegiate church, are peculiar to different parts of the building.

MASTER MASONS AND ARCHITECTS Castles were constructed by teams of master craftsmen, skilled workmen and general labourers. But who designed a castle and who was responsible for ensuring that the builders translated vision into actuality? Documentary sources for the medieval period are comparatively scarce and most of the available records are for royal castles (*see* PIPE ROLLS). It is often stated that a particular king or magnate 'built a castle' and it is self-evident that they would be closely involved in identifying the site and drawing up a specification. Henry III provided elaborate directions for the decoration of his palaces but was content to leave everything else (except, occasionally, the overall dimensions, the number of windows and the position of fireplaces) to those in charge of the operations. Typically, Henry VI drew up minutely detailed instructions for his colleges at Eton and Cambridge (King's College) – and then demolished the Eton chapel after seven years of construction in order to build it on a larger scale.

For the building or refurbishment of royal and baronial castles a *Clerk of the Works* was usually appointed to oversee operations, an office that was often identical with (though sometimes additional to) that of Supervisor or Surveyor of the Works. As his title suggests, the Clerk of the Works was head of the clerical staff, responsible for the payment of wages and the provision of materials and workmen. But he was not the architect. Medieval building accounts almost invariably show that the work was supervised by a chief, or master, mason, though the actual mason in charge may have changed during the course of the work. Many of these chief masons (often described as '*masters of the compass*') can be traced to a succession of building projects, military, ecclesiastical and domestic, in different parts of the country, and some obtained official positions. In 1157, for example, we find that one Ailnoth 'the engineer' was Surveyor of the King's Buildings at

Westminster and the Tower, receiving a substantial salary of £10 12s 11d. From 1167 to 1173 he supervised the purchase of stone and lead for work at Windsor Castle and after the rebellion of 1174 was in charge of the dismantling of Walton and Framlingham Castles. Richard the engineer was involved in the building of Bowes Castle in 1170 while also employed by Bishop Pudsey at Norham Castle, being described as 'vir artificiosus . . . et prudens architectus'. Wulfric and Ives, both described as engineers, supervised work at Carlisle and Berkhamstead respectively in 1172–3, and Maurice the engineer was engaged at Newcastle in 1174 and at Dover in 1181–2. The use of the word 'engineer' (ingeniator) in this context is significant, for all these men were primarily concerned with military engines such as mangonels and trebuchets (see SIEGES) and with designing defences which could both accommodate their own artillery and resist that of a besieging force. Indeed, when the west wall of the lower bailey at Windsor Castle was built in 1228, a 'master trebucheter' was one of two men appointed to supervise the work.

In 1245 Henry de Reins, 'master of the King's masons', and Martin Simon, a master carpenter, were sent to inspect the site of a new royal castle at York and to determine how it should be built. There they were met by the sheriff of York, accompanied by other master craftsmen, and they debated, in the great tradition of 'site meetings', how best to implement the king's instructions (one can almost see the hard hats and clipboards!). Henry was succeeded as king's mason by Master John of Gloucester (1254–61) and Master Robert of Beverley (1262–80). It was at this time that Master JAMES OF ST GEORGE was appointed as 'Master of the King's Works in Wales' (ingeniator regis). Master James, pre-eminent among military architects, was responsible for designing one of the finest groups of medieval fortifications in Europe, notably the castles at Conwy, Caernarfon, Harlech and Beaumaris (see CASTLES, CONSTRUCTION OF and WALES, CONQUEST OF). But like other medieval architects, he did not work alone. In Wales Master James was assisted by Stephen the Painter from Savoy, Master Bertram the military engineer from Gascony, Master Manasser, who was responsible for the diggers at Caernarfon, and Master Walter of Hereford – each an expert in his craft and collectively a 'management team' of advisers.

In the second half of the fourteenth century the office of royal mason was filled for more than thirty

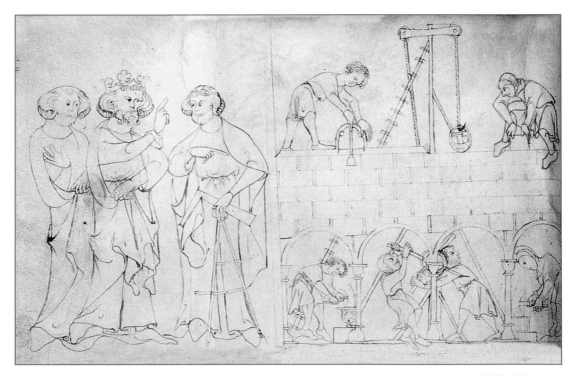

A king and his master mason discuss work in progress. From a drawing by Matthew Paris (c. 1200–59).

years by Henry Yevele, who in 1356 was already sufficiently respected in his craft to be involved in drawing up the regulations for the Masons' Guild of the City of London. In 1365 he was 'master of the masons, controlling their work' at Westminster. In the following year he supervised repairs at Baynard's Castle while arranging also for the supply of stone, plaster and tiles – apparently combining the rôles of master mason and contractor. In 1385 Hugh Kynton is described as master of the masons at Portchester Castle, 'arranging the work of the masons there under the instructions of Master Henry Yeveley', while in the same year his appointment as 'deviser of masonry works at Westminster and the Tower' was confirmed at a salary of 12d a day. In 1386 Yevele was joined by John de Cobham at York where they supervised the construction of the city walls, and in 1393 he advised on repairs to the eleventh-century keep ('Dongeon') of Canterbury Castle. In 1395 he supplied the 'forme et modle' for the raising of the walls of Westminster Hall and in 1399 he advised on the erection of a vault above the entrance. Henry Yevele died in 1396 and was succeeded in the office of king's mason by his erstwhile business partner Stephen Lote who had been warden of the masons at St Paul's in 1382. Yevele's career shows that a highly skilled and experienced master mason could reasonably anticipate royal or baronial patronage and employment as a consultant on a variety of projects. But to what extent should he, and other master masons, deserve the title of architect?

Very few architectural drawings have survived from the medieval period. They were, by their nature and use, fragile documents and it is hardly surprising that most were disposed of (or, if drawn on vellum, erased and reused) once a building was finished. Nevertheless, there is abundant evidence that the master masons of the period did indeed make such drawings. In 1380, for example, William de Wyntringham of Southwark undertook to build a chapel and other buildings at Hertford Castle 'as set out in a design made in duplicate', though it is far from clear whether this 'design' included a ground plan. Indeed, a ground plan was the least important element of the architectural drawings, for the marking out of the walls on the ground was the first stage of building, whether a plan existed or not. (It is for this reason that in medieval illustrations architects are often shown holding a large pair of dividers suitable for this work.) In 1519, when Horman published his *Vulgaria*, a Latin–English phrase book, he included a section of technical terms and phrases such as 'He drewe out a platte [working

drawing] of the house with a penne' and 'He is not worthy to be called maister of the crafte, that is not cunnyng in drawynge and purturynge.'

The rules of the Strassburg masons are likely to be an accurate indication of practice throughout Europe at the end of the fifteenth century: 'If anyone contracts for a work and gives a plan for it . . . the work shall not be cut short of anything in the design, but he shall execute it according to the plan which he has shown to the lords . . . so that nothing be altered in the building.' Furthermore, 'No one who has not served his time as a craftsman or been employed in a lodge, and does not know how to execute carved or designed stonework from the ground plan shall undertake such work' and 'No craftsman . . . shall teach anyone that is not of our craft to make extracts from the ground plan, or other usages of masonry.' From this, it is evident that a qualified mason was expected to be able to draw and interpret a plan and to carve mouldings from a sectional drawing (*see* MOULDING). The work of making these drawings was carried out in the *trasour* or 'tracyng house' – the drawing office of the master mason. These were then converted by carpenters into wooden templates for use by the masons working on the carved mouldings of a building. In 1350 John Leycestre, chief mason at the Tower, was making moulds for the postern and sixteen masons were 'shaping and working stones according to moulds given to them by John Leycester'. An entry in the accounts for Corfe Castle in 1376 records the delivery of '4 planks called waynescotes for moulds for the mason' while at Langley in 1372 '2 sawn ryngoldbord' were bought to make moulds.

There can be little doubt that a medieval master mason performed a dual rôle. In consultation with his patron he was responsible for the overall design of a building and thereafter for preparing working drawings (*plattes*) that could be interpreted by those working under him. In the majority of cases he superintended the execution of his own designs, but if his employer was the crown or a major magnate then he could usually rely on a Surveyor and Clerk of the Works to attend to day-to-day supervision. As a senior freemason, he was also responsible for much of the detail, supervising the preparation of the sectional drawings (*moulds*) for architectural features such as the mouldings of arches and window tracery. Despite their professional status, master masons were not always entirely dependable. In 1316 Masters William de Hoo, John de Hardingham and John de St Omer were sued for breach of contract to build a wall round the royal manor of Eltham. The jury found that the wall and buttresses were deficient in thickness and, whereas they ought to have been made of stone and good 'cement', they had been constructed of chalk, soft stone and 'false cement'. The cost of replacing this wall was estimated at £305 15s 7d – a substantial sum. The masons were committed to prison but released after undertaking to carry out the work properly.

MASTER OF THE COMPASS *see* MASTER MASONS AND ARCHITECTS

MATERIALS, CARRIAGE OF The cost of transporting materials to a building site was always a significant item in the accounts (*see* CASTLES, CONSTRUCTION OF). Clearly, this figure would vary considerably depending on the availability or otherwise of materials locally, the distance they had to be carried and the means and availability of transport. Unfortunately, contemporary accounts usually record only the number of cartloads and the rate paid per cart; they rarely refer to the sources of materials or to the distance they were carried. Only when the accountant felt the need to explain an apparent discrepancy is any detail given. The 1363 accounts for Windsor, for example, include an explanation of excessive expenditure: 'For hire of two wagons, each of 10 oxen, carrying the said 24 fothers [tons] of lead from Caldstanes in Nitherdale by high and stony hills and miry ways to Burghbrigge, about 20 leagues, namely, for 24 days, each wagon with the men for it taking 3s. a day – £7 4s.' Whenever possible, stone and heavy timber were carried by water. The type of cargo boat most frequently referred to in the late medieval accounts was the *farecost* which was designed specifically to carry heavy loads of stone and timber. In 1350 John Lorkyn was paid 'for a ship called farcost bringing timber from the wynwarf to the Tower [of London], for making the lion house', and in the same account there is mention of Purbeck stone being conveyed from Westminster to the Tower in a 'dong boat', a type of barge commonly employed on the Thames at that time for the removal of waste materials. Timber for the splendid roof of Westminster Hall (1395) was prefabricated near Farnham and sent by land to the Thames and thence to Westminster, the accounts recording payments of £19 1s 4d for the carriage of 26 half-beams and 26 'pendant posts' to Hamme on the river. Also recorded are the carriage of 26 corbels and 263 cartloads of timber at 4s per load, 76 at 3s 4d and 69 at 3s, the variation in price probably reflecting the number of horses required. For shorter distances stone and other heavy materials would be transported on sleds pulled by oxen or horses. Pack-horses with panniers were occasionally used to carry rubble and smaller items, but most materials were conveyed by carts that varied considerably both in capacity and construction. A cartload of timber, for example, was reckoned to be 18m (60ft) in London in 1425 and 12m (40ft) at Cambridge in 1532. The *biga* was a 'shortcart', a two-wheeled cart drawn by one or two horses, while a four-wheeled cart was usually referred to as a *wagon* or *wain*. The records show that 28s 8d was expended at Gloucester Castle in 1406 for 'bread, ale and cheese given various men coming from the park and doing 88 cartings of timber from the park to the castle, with their own horses and with a brakke, or cart, of the king's, appointed for the carriage of the said great timber. . . . And for the brakke, or cart, bound with iron in the fashion of a wain [wagon], bought for the carriage of great timber, 33s. 6d. And for grease for the easier running of the said cart, 6d.' Another type of wagon for carrying timber was the *tug*, a simple four-wheeled frame similar to that recorded in the accounts for Leeds Castle in 1370: '2 pairs of wheels for a tugge whereon to carry timber'. Handcarts were used for lighter work and these are often referred to as (for example) 'croudewayns', 'handwayns' or 'thrustewayns'. Barrows of various kinds were in constant use in and around a building site: Edward I is even known to have wheeled a barrow on the fortifications of Berwick but this was undoubtedly a symbolic gesture. In the stores at York in 1399 there were '10 beringberwes and 2 whelebarwes'. The former (also described as a 'handebarwe') comprised a flat base, often strengthened with bars or rods, with projecting handles carried by two men. A larger version, the 'bayard', was used by 'bayarders' to carry heavy loads of mortar or particularly large stones to the workshops for carving. The bayarders must have been chosen for their strength, for additional support was provided by straps from the handles attached to a yoke worn across the shoulders. At Harlech in 1286 we find 'girths bought for the bayarders' and at Caernarfon in 1320 'three pairs of collars for the bayarders'. Wheelbarrows were similar in appearance to those used today and were usually made of ash or oak boards and willow, the wheel being lubricated regularly with grease. In the Windsor accounts for 1532 is an entry for the purchase of two hundreds of 'sesoned elmyn borde' to make 'hoddis, bossis and whele barowes'. 'Bossis' were receptacles for mortar, while 'hoddis' (hods) were wicker panniers carried on the back. 'Hodmen carrying sand for the making of mortar' are referred to in the Dover accounts for 1295, while the modern type of hod, carried on the end of a long staff and used for carrying bricks, may be inferred from an entry in the Westminster accounts for 1532.

MATRIX A cavity within which a thing is embedded, e.g. the recess in a slab to receive a monumental brass (*see* MONUMENTS).

MAUSOLEUM (i) A large and magnificent dynastic tomb or monument. The term is derived from the marble tomb of Mausolus, a fourth-century king of Caria in Asia Minor, which was accounted one of the Seven Wonders of the World.
(ii) A chapel containing a collection of family tombs.

MEALS *see* HOUSEHOLD *and* KITCHEN

MEDIEVAL ARCHITECTURE *see* GOTHIC ARCHITECTURE *and* ROMANESQUE

MEMORANDA ROLLS These rolls were kept by the King's Remembrancer and the Lord Treasurer's Remembrancer and are concerned with EXCHEQUER business, particularly moneys owing to the crown. They supplement the PIPE ROLLS and contain many items of local interest. Memoranda Rolls are maintained at the Public Record Office and several have been published (*see* APPENDIX II).

MERLON (*also*** COP)** Merlons are the solid upright sections of a crenellated parapet (*see* BATTLEMENTS). They alternate with CRENELS, may incorporate a shallow EMBRASURE and may be pierced by a LOOPHOLE. The merlons of the late thirteenth-century Marten's Tower at Chepstow Castle are topped with carved human figures, described (in the guidebook) as 'a garrison in stone', though their function is unclear. There are similar figures on the merlons of Edward I's Eagle Tower at Caernarfon Castle at York and several Northumbrian castles. From the fifteenth century crenellations are found as decorative features on the walls of domestic buildings and churches. But these are very different from the defensive crenellated parapets of castles, the merlons of which were of sufficient height to protect a man's head and considerably wider than the adjacent crenels.

MESNALTY An estate held directly of the crown by a mesne lord.

MESNE TENANT *see* LORD OF THE MANOR

MESNIE A military retinue.

MESS-MATES *see* HALL

MESSUAGE A dwelling house with an attached court or yard.

METALS In ARMORY, the TINCTURES *Or* (gold) and *Argent* (silver), often represented by yellow and white.

MEURTRIÈRE *see* MURDER HOLE

MEWS A *mew* was a cage where hawks were kept while moulting. From this, the word came to be used for a building or yard where hawks were kept in cages (*mews*).

MEZZANINE In a building, an additional storey between two others, usually entered from a half-landing.

MICHAELMAS (i) A quarter day: the Feast of St Michael and All Angels on 29 September. The other *quarter days*, which are often referred to in medieval documents, were Lady Day (25 March), Christmas (25 December) and Midsummer (6 July). Until 1752 Lady Day (the Annunciation of the Blessed Virgin) was also New Year's Day.
(ii) The academic and law term beginning near Michaelmas.

MIDDEN A rubbish tip.

MIDDLE AGES, THE For the purposes of this book, the medieval period is taken to be the five centuries from Duke William's victory at Senlac Hill in 1066 to the dissolution of the greater monasteries in 1539.

Traditionally, the Norman Conquest of 1066 is taken to be the 'beginning' of the Middle Ages in England and the accession of the Tudor dynasty in 1485 to be the 'end'. But, 'unlike dates, historical periods are not facts. They are retrospective conceptions that we form about past events, useful to focus discussion, but very often leading historical thought astray' (G.M. Trevelyan). It is undoubtedly true that medieval society (or that of any historical 'period') may only be studied fruitfully if it is considered, not as a static order, but as a complexity of continuous and evolving processes and relationships without any definable beginning or end. Nevertheless, our common perception of medievalism would lead many to agree with Robert Fossier (*The Cambridge Illustrated History of the Middle Ages*, 1986) when he suggests that: 'We should tread carefully; Henry V was medieval, Henry VIII was not: these are our limits.'

Today, definitions are as diverse as they are numerous. Archaeologists now use the term 'medieval' to describe the period, of about 1,000 years, from the end of the Roman occupation to the time of the Tudors, with the Norman Conquest separating the 'early medieval' period from the 'high medieval'. Fossier considers medievalism in a European context beginning in 1250 and lasting until 1520. H.R. Loyn's *The Middle Ages: A Concise Encyclopaedia* (1989) encompasses the eleven centuries from *c.* 400 to *c.* 1500, while the *Oxford Reference Dictionary* (1986) defines the Middle Ages as being 'the period in Europe after the Dark Ages (*c.* 1000–1400) or in a wider sense *c.* 600–1500'. Some historians have argued that the introduction of printing in 1476 marked the end of the medieval period in England, or that it ended with the final battle of the Wars of the Roses at Stoke Field in 1487 and the suppression of LIVERY AND MAINTENANCE. Others point to the diversion of resources from defence to domesticity, 'from castles to palaces', which was apparent during the reign of Edward IV (1461–83).

An essential characteristic of the Middle Ages was feudalism, which in the late medieval period evolved into 'Bastard Feudalism' (*see* FEUDAL SYSTEM *and* BASTARD FEUDALISM). The earliest castles of Dové-laontaine and Langeais in northern France date from the second half of the tenth century which is where one would place the first establishment of a feudal society and therefore the beginning of the Middle Ages in Europe.

As to its close, Henry VII (1485–1509) is often credited with transforming England into a 'new monarchy' and thereby guiding the kingdom into a new age. But he did little more than revitalise government machinery which had changed little in its essentials since Edward I (1272–1307). Indeed, it was Edward IV (1461–83) who was chiefly responsible for rendering that machinery effectual and there is very little political or constitutional significance attached to the date 1485. The Dissolution of the Monasteries (1536 and 1539), the Dissolution of the Chantries (1545–7) and the introduction, through the *Book of Common Prayer*, of a revised liturgy had a profound effect on the people and institutions of England. It was Thomas Cromwell and Archbishop Cranmer, not Henry Tudor, who brought the Middle Ages to a close.

MIDDLE POINTED STYLE *see* GOTHIC ARCHITECTURE

MILES *and* MILITES Professional soldiers in early medieval western Europe: usually cavalry and therefore the forerunner of the KNIGHT.

MILITARY ORDERS *see* COMMANDERY; ST JOHN OF JERUSALEM (ORDER OF) also known as the Knights Hospitaller; PRECEPTORY *and* TEMPLAR, KNIGHTS (THE POOR KNIGHTS OF CHRIST AND OF THE TEMPLE OF SOLOMON)

MILITARY RECRUITMENT AND ORGANISATION *see* RECRUITMENT AND ORGANISATION (MILITARY)

MILITARY ROADS The Roman roads were, of course, constructed principally to facilitate the rapid and efficient deployment of large numbers of men and equipment throughout the province as well as to encourage commerce and trade. Similarly, the Anglo-Saxon HEREPAETHS were trackways used for military and administrative purposes as well as by ordinary travellers. These old roads continued to be used for military purposes in the Saxon and medieval periods and often influenced the site of a battle. In 1066 Harold moved south towards Hastings by the Roman road from London to Rochester and Maidstone, while roads from Castleford and York, which intersected at Tadcaster, brought together the Yorkist and Lancastrian armies at Towton in 1461. In 1485 the decisive battle of Bosworth was fought close to a Roman road out of Leicester where it crossed the angle of the Fosse Way and Watling Street.

MILITARY TRAINING Documentary evidence deals principally with cavalry training rather than infantry, the cavalry forming the dominant military élite of the medieval period. In the early Middle Ages it was said that if a boy had not learned to ride a horse before he reached puberty then he would be suited only for the church. Training was intended to improve individual skills, both as a horseman and in the use of weapons, and to teach individuals to work with others as a military unit. These basic drills were modified to accommodate the adoption of the *couched lance* technique by cavalry (*see* LANCE) and the crossbow by infantry (*see* ARCHERY). From the eleventh century those who were destined by rank to join the military élite began their training at the age of twelve. They were trained in age peer-groups, learning to use a variety of weapons (*see* QUINTAIN), to ride and to care for their horses, and increasing their strength and stamina through weight-lifting, wrestling and other sports. They also learned the skills of scouting, stalking and moving in hostile territory by hunting wild animals and taking part in youthful 'war games'. Learning horsemanship within a closely packed group of riders (*conrois*) developed a team spirit and loyalty to one's companions. The initial training was usually completed by the early twenties when groups of aspirants were dubbed knights, often in anticipation of joining a military campaign.

By the thirteenth century a boy was expected to begin his training at the age of five, serving his elders, helping to care for their horses and receiving religious instruction. At seven he was removed from the company of women and became a PAGE whose education included training in the arts of war, through hunting and the use of small weapons, and CHIVALRY. When he reached the age of twelve he would normally be sent away from home to join a magnate household where, if his service was satisfactory, he might be given additional responsibilities and eventually become an ESQUIRE. In theory an esquire's feudal service required him to maintain his master's shield and armour but in practice his responsibilities and duties were considerably wider than this and were, in part, intended to train him in the martial and courtly arts and the chivalric code. Not all esquires became knights: much depended on an individual's circumstances, his family's status and wealth and his ability to promote himself (*see* KNIGHTHOOD AND CHIVALRY, ORIGINS OF).

For a fully fledged knight, the TOURNAMENT combined entertainment and self-aggrandisement with military training. And, for senior commanders (those who could read) there was a growing number of practical and theoretical treatises on the arts of war and associated subjects such as armory and courtly behaviour: *L'Arbre de Batailes*, 'The Tree of Battles', for example, a French treatise on the conventions of war written in *c.* 1382–7 by Honoré Bonet; *De Officio Militari et Insigniis Armorum*, a Latin treatise on the laws and practice of war compiled by Nicholas Upton in *c.* 1446; and *Blasons des Batailes*, a late fifteenth-century French manuscript comprising notes on the conduct of war, heralds' duties and so on.

MILITIA A military force, usually raised from the civil population to supplement regular troops in an emergency.

The *Fyrd* of the Anglo-Saxon period was a force comprising thegns who owed *fyrd-bote* or military service as one of their obligations under the TRINODA NECESSITAS. King Alfred divided the Fyrd so that one half was resting while the other was on duty. From 1070 a system (now known as *Knight Service*) was introduced whereby the king's tenants-in-chief agreed to provide a number of knights

equipped and available for service for a specified period. In peacetime this was usually an annual commitment of forty days. By 1100 tenants were able to commute their military service by payment of 'shield-money' (*scutage*) which was fixed at 20s per knight's fee and was recouped by the tenant-in-chief from his tenants. (Scutage was last levied in 1327.) In 1181 Henry II issued an *Assize of Arms* which determined the weapons and equipment required of each knight, freeman and burgess. Juries from each town or hundred were charged with assessing the degree of military obligation. Each possessor of a knight's fee and each free layman owning effects or receiving rents valued in excess of 16 marks was required to provide a coat of mail, a helmet, shield and lance. Likewise, a free layman whose property did not exceed 10 marks was obliged to provide a mail jacket (*haubergeon*), an iron skull-cap (*chapelet*) and a lance. Justices were sent out to enforce the assize and sheriffs were responsible for raising the levy. By the thirteenth century unfree peasants were also liable for military service, an obligation which was confirmed in 1285 and not repealed until 1558. *Commissions of Array* were appointed by the crown to compile *Muster Rolls* which listed, by counties, all those who were available for military service.

In the Tudor period a LORD LIEUTENANT was nominally responsible for the *posse comitatus*, or county militia, though in practice it was usually the Deputy Lieutenant who ensured that parish constables raised the required levies. All able-bodied men between sixteen and sixty were liable for service and formal inspections (*general musters*) were held in each shire at least once every three years. The Tudor militia was divided into ten classes, the equipment for each being prescribed by law: some were required to keep only a longbow, helmet and JACK while, at the other extreme, others had to provide sixteen horses, eighty suits of light armour, thirty longbows and forty pikes. It was at this time that TRAIN BANDS were established, forces who were liable for specialist military training and acquired a justifiable reputation for public indiscipline and lawlessness. Before 1660 there was no standing army and the county militias represented the principal means of defending the kingdom. But the system was essentially feudal, both in the way in which troops were levied and in the way the militias were financed. Its deficiencies became even more apparent during the Civil War of the 1640s when many militia troops refused to serve beyond their county borders. Volunteer companies (the first of which was formed in 1537 as the Guild of

St George) were far more flexible and were, by definition, disciplined mercenaries. Following the Restoration, the Militia Act of 1672 established a system of military service based not on a feudal obligation but on a statutory one.
(*See also* RECRUITMENT AND ORGANISATION, MILITARY)
For the Military History Society *and* the Society for Army Historical Research *see* APPENDIX II.

MILLS Many castles had their own corn mill: the early sixteenth-century horse-powered mill in the south range of service buildings at Middleham Castle, for example, provided sufficient corn for the daily needs of the castle's establishment. In the Middle Ages every manor, or group of manors, had its own mill which was either water-powered or wind-powered, depending on the topography of the area.

Watermills
It is likely that watermills were introduced into Britain by the Romans. They were numerous in the Saxon period and some six thousand mills were recorded at the time of the DOMESDAY survey, though there were undoubtedly many more. *Milling soke* was a feudal monopoly exercised by most (though not all) lords of the manor. In practice many mills were leased to tenant millers and manorial custom required that the peasants should have their corn ground in the lord's mill on payment of a toll (*multure*), usually one-sixteenth of the grist ground. (From the thirteenth century the toll was usually commuted to a money payment.) The lord, who was responsible for major repairs, had first claim on his mill for grinding corn from the DEMESNE lands while the peasants could be fined for grinding their corn at home or for patronising a rival mill. The right of a miller to receive a constant and unimpeded supply of water remains today.

Watermills were of four types, all of which harnessed the power of falling or running water to turn the grind-stones between which the grain was milled. In the *horizontal mill* (or *click mill*), which was of Saxon origin, the wheel was positioned horizontally across a stream from which water was directed to the paddles by means of a chute. There was no gearing and the grinding stone, which was on the floor above, was driven directly by the shaft of the wheel. The *undershot mill* was a Roman innovation and was reintroduced into Britain towards the end of the Saxon period. It consisted of a vertical wheel with flat blades at its circumference, the lower section of which came into contact with the water. The flow of water to the blades could be regulated by

means of a weir and sluice gate set within a leat. The *overshot mill*, introduced in the Middle Ages, was more efficient and was particularly well-suited to hill country. Again, water was directed and controlled by means of a leat but was supplied, at the top of the wheel's circumference, to a series of containers which caused the wheel to revolve by the downward motion and weight of the water. A rare example has survived (in ruinous form) in the south dam platform at Caerphilly Castle. This overshot mill, which was in continuous use from the thirteenth century to the seventeenth, was powered by a constant head of water from the castle's south lake. Such a flow would have made the castle mill particularly efficient when compared with mills which depended on the unpredictable flow of ordinary streams and rivers. So valuable was this resource that it was afforded protection by a tower in the massively buttressed south dam. The *breastshot mill* was similar, but the water was directed into the containers at a point level, causing it to turn in an anti-clockwise direction. *Tidemills*, dating from the late fourteenth century, were a type of undershot mill driven by the flow of water from a large but shallow mill-pond constructed on the landward side of the mill. Water was impounded at high tide by means of sluice gates and released when the tide had dropped sufficiently to provide an adequate fall of water. The *mill race* is the often turbulent stretch of water immediately downstream from a mill. In all but the horizontal mill, the millstones were driven (at approximately 150 revolutions per minute) by a series of wooden cogwheel gears.

From the thirteenth century water power was also used to drive *fulling mills* in which hammers, fitted to a moving beam, removed the grease and grime from woven cloth by pummelling the fabric under water. In the same century water-powered *forge hammers* were also introduced in the Weald of Kent and other iron-producing areas and in the fifteenth century water wheels were used to drive the bellows of the first blast-furnaces. Water-powered paper mills are known to have operated on the River Lea near Hertford in the late fifteenth century and there were gunpowder mills in south-east England from the seventeenth century.

Windmills
The earliest authentic record of a windmill is that of an 'adulterine' mill (one which operated unlawfully in direct competition to manorial mills) at Bury St Edmunds in 1191. It is likely that windmills were numerous by the end of the twelfth century and had been introduced from mainland Europe by crusaders

returning from the Holy Land. There are many references to thirteenth-century mills in contemporary documents and several illustrations in manuscripts such as the *Windmill Psalter* of *c*. 1270. The earliest windmills were primitive fixed structures which could only be operated when the wind was blowing from a particular quarter. These were followed by *post mills* in which a weather-boarded body, on which the sails were carried, revolved on a strong central post so that it could be orientated to catch the wind. This was effected by means of a long tail pole and wheel which projected from the rear of the mill and was pushed into position by hand. This tail pole also increased the structure's equilibrium and sometimes carried a flight of steps by which the mill was entered. The central post was secured at the base by cross trees which were embedded within the raised mill-mound. Such mounds may be mistaken for tumuli both in their configuration and their location which was usually on an exposed or hill-top site. The machinery for driving the grinding stones was contained within the body of the mill and the trestles on which this was supported were later protected by the provision of a *roundhouse* which also provided storage space. Towards the end of the medieval period the roundhouse was sometimes extended upwards to form a rigid structure on top of which a conical cap and sails revolved on a circular track. These *smock mills* were constructed of wood and were usually octagonal in plan, had battered (sloping) sides and were sometimes provided with a brick base, as at Cranbrook in Kent.

There were two types of sail (*sweep*) in medieval Britain: *common sails*, the earliest type, consisted of sail-cloth stretched over a wooden framework, while *spring sails* were series of movable shutters, pivoted at right angles to the length of the sweep and connected by a rod to a spring which was adjusted by the miller so that the shutters opened automatically when the strength of the wind reached a predetermined level. Regrettably, no medieval mills have survived though there are many examples of later types which may be seen both as ruins and as restorations.

MILL TOWER A tower in which a small corn mill was located. This may have been hand-driven or powered by a horse or donkey, either walking in continuous circles round the grinding stones (as at Middleham Castle) or within a geared, oak-framed wheel similar to that at Carisbrooke Castle which is still used for raising water from the castle well (*see* WELLS).

MINERALS AND MINING Tin, lead and coal were the principal commodities mined in late medieval England and investment in mining supplemented the incomes of men of all classes. In the Middle Ages the miner enjoyed rights and privileges derived from ancient usage and he was, therefore, a free man – unlike the feudal peasant. Wage-labour was common and most miners were probably poor; but, except in some of the crown mines, where a system of impressment was used, miners generally enjoyed free-tenure of their small mining properties and in some areas (such as the south-west) were exempt from tallages, tolls and subsidies.

In the tin-mining districts of Cornwall and Devon (*see* STANNARIES) there were more than a thousand men who were entitled to the rank of tinner in the fourteenth century: free-men with extensive rights of prospecting, with their own courts and in most civil matters answerable only to the warden. When control of the Stannaries was vested in the Duchy of Cornwall in 1338, the annual output of tin had reached 700 tons and crown revenues exceeded £2,000. Despite the debilitating effects of the Black Death, one Abraham the Tinner was said to have employed three hundred miners in 1357.

Lead was mined chiefly for its silver, principally in the neighbourhood of Bere Alston in Devon and in the Mendip Hills of Somerset where the mines were leased to the bishop of Bath and Wells. By 1340 the Devonshire lead mines were in decline and by the end of the century it was the mines of Derbyshire, Nottinghamshire and Yorkshire that were contracted to provide lead for the repair of the Great Hall at Westminster. In the Middle Ages the Forest of Dean was the most important iron-producing area, though London was again turning to the Weald of Kent for its supplies. Most of the English coalfields were already being worked to some extent, though open-cast extraction continued until the mid-fourteenth century when the first vertical shafts were sunk. Coal (*secole* because it was usually transported by sea) was used mainly for smelting and working metals, but with the increase in chimney flues towards the end of the fourteenth century it began to be used for domestic purposes also. The free-miners of the Forest of Dean in Gloucestershire continue to enjoy certain rights of ancient usage to this day.

The late Tudor period was a time of expansion in lead, copper and tin mining. The Mendips continued to yield large quantities of lead for export through the nearby port of Bristol, innumerable small tin mines flourished in Cornwall and Devon and untapped supplies of copper in the remoter parts of the north-west attracted miners from Germany. In particular, English iron was acknowledged to be of the finest quality. In 1543 an iron cannon was cast at Buxted in Surrey. This was the first casting in Britain and was effectively the first tentative step towards the Industrial Revolution. It was significant because it represented an entirely new way of making iron. Instead of the ancient, low-temperature method of producing blooms which had to be worked into wrought iron, the high temperatures of the new 'blast'-furnace actually melted the iron, thereby enabling it to be cast as finished objects. The development of the blast-furnace meant that considerable quantities of iron could be produced as a continuous process: iron ore and charcoal were added at the top and the molten iron tapped from the bottom. The need for a constant supply of timber for charcoal and the availability of fast-flowing water to provide motive power inevitably determined the location of iron-works. There were, of course, substantial supplies of coal available, but at this time coal produced iron that was 'red-short' and brittle and of little use to a rapidly expanding market for iron goods.

(*See also* MASONRY *for* stone quarries)

MINING (MILITARY) *see* SIEGES

MINSTRELS A *minstrels' gallery* or platform was often constructed above the SCREENS PASSAGE in the great halls of late medieval castles. The minstrels of medieval and Tudor society provided a service equal in importance to that which is available through television today: music, drama and entertainment; the dissemination of news and information; political comment; and popular songs and ballads – the 'soap operas' of medieval England. These lengthy tales of familiar personalities (such as the ubiquitous Robin Hood) had fresh sub-plots and characters grafted on to them as they passed from one generation to the next.

The minstrels made up a diverse profession. Many were permanent members of royal or magnate households, established men of substance with rich patrons and the status of esquire, while others were independent, itinerant professionals or casual entertainers who counted minstrelsy as an occasional service among many. Wardrobe accounts, many dating from the thirteenth and fourteenth centuries, contain contracts of employment together with details of the allowances, duties and status afforded to minstrels. Some were accomplished musicians, singers and players of the harp, vielle or psaltery; others were acrobats, jugglers or magicians; actors, story-tellers (*fabulators*) and declaimers of

momentous events and stirring deeds: 'Sitteth alle stille ant herketh to me . . .'.

In an ordnance of 1315 it was maintained that 'indolent persons, pretending minstrelsy', were seeking payment and hospitality, and rules were set out for the proper conduct of the profession. Nevertheless, in 1469 Edward IV incorporated the royal minstrels as a guild, declaring that 'no minstrel of our kingdom . . . shall in any way exercise this art or occupation within our kingdom henceforth unless he be a member of the guild' for 'rough peasants and craftsmen of various mysteries . . . have pretended to be our own minstrels . . . and although they are not intelligent or expert in that art or occupation, and are occupied in various activities on week-days . . . on feast-days they travel from place to place, and take all the profits on which our aforesaid minstrels . . . ought to live' (A. Myers, *English Historical Documents*, 1969). But the legislation proved ineffectual and many a 'rough peasant' who had built up a repertoire and could attract an audience continued to supplement his meagre income by entertaining the local populace on feast-days. Many minstrels belonged to companies who toured the great magnate and monastic households. The bursar's account for Fountains Abbey, Yorkshire, in the 1450s records payments to (among others) the minstrels of Beverley (16*d*), the players of the Earl of Westmorland (2*d*) and the minstrels of Lord Arundel (16*d*) as well as a story-teller 'whose name was unknown' (6*d*), the Boy Bishop of Ripon (3*s*) and a fool called Solomon ('who came again') (4*d*). During the reign of Elizabeth I (1558–1603) the already stringent laws against vagabonds were extended to include itinerant musicians who, unless vouched for by noblemen by whom they were regularly employed, were ostracised by the musical establishment and could be severely punished.

The earliest bodies of musicians not directly subsidised by royal or magnate patronage were the town or city *waits*, a word of Nordic derivation meaning 'watcher' or 'guard'. These were members of the watch and ward (*see* LAW AND ORDER) who formed themselves into bands of instrumentalists both to entertain the local populace and to perform at civic functions. Proud of their municipal or guild livery, these groups claimed a musical monopoly in their neighbourhood and jealously urged the authorities to outlaw wandering buskers and entertainers. In sixteenth-century York, for example, a strict apprenticeship was required under the jurisdiction of the fellowship of musicians and a 'searcher of the waits' appointed to enforce their monopoly. In time, the terms 'minstrel' and 'musician' were used to

differentiate between vagabond entertainers and those entitled to perform music exclusively with a royal, magnate or civic warrant.
(*See also* MUSICAL INSTRUMENTS)

MINT-MARKS *see* COINAGE

MISDEMEANOUR *see* FELONY

MISERICORDE Longer than an ANELACE, the misericorde was a thrusting dagger, carried on the right hip and used especially for the *coup de grace* through a visor – hence the ironic *misericordia* or 'Mercy!'. A straight dagger without a guard, the blade had a triangular section and only one cutting edge. Often found depicted in brasses and effigial figures dating from the late fourteenth and fifteenth centuries, misericordes were sometimes engraved with grisly scenes such as the 'Dance of Death'.
(*See also* WEAPONS AND HARNESS)

MITRE ARCH *see* ARCH

MITRED ABBOT Mitred abbots and bishops were ecclesiastical magnates who exercised considerable political (and sometimes military) influence. It is hardly surprising, therefore, to find that many of their palaces were protected by walls and gatehouses, some of which (the moated Bishop's Palace at Wells in Somerset, for example) have defensive devices comparable with those of contemporary castles. They also provided an ostentatious manifestation of an abbot's status and influence.
(*See also* ECCLESIASTICAL STRONGHOLDS)

MOATED HOUSES *see* ECCLESIASTICAL STRONGHOLDS, MANOR HOUSES *and* MOATS AND WATER DEFENCES

MOATS AND WATER DEFENCES A moat is a steep-sided defensive ditch, either dry or water-filled. Its purpose was to frustrate a direct attack and prevent undermining of the castle walls. Many moats have been cut into natural rock or have their sides revetted in stone. *Segmented moats* are those in which one section of a ditch was water-filled and the other was dry. Castles were invariably enclosed within a moat on those sides where they were not protected by natural cliffs, and many had sequential baileys that were separated by internal cross-ditches (*see* BAILEY). Without the outer protection of a moat, a wall on level ground would have been vulnerable to close-quarter attack from siege towers, battering and undermining (*see* SIEGES). Almost invariably moats were traversed by means of DRAWBRIDGES, though many of these were later replaced by permanent stone structures. It should be borne in mind when visiting castles that many water-filled moats have subsequently been drained.

Although at some Norman castles natural water features were adapted for defensive purposes, the majority of early fortifications were either located on elevated ground or on mottes that were constructed from the spoil of a surrounding ditch (*see* MOTTE). In some instances these ditches were water-filled, as at Pleshey, a mighty motte and bailey castle raised during the ANARCHY, and Berkhamsted Castle, a motte and bailey fortification dating from the eleventh century, where the inner ditch was water-filled until the 1950s. Castles such as Goodrich, Harlech and Carreg Cennen were deliberately built on solid rock (to provide a firm foundation and to frustrate undermining) and excavating their moats must have been an exhausting task for the *FOSSATORES* who would have been recruited in large numbers. There is documentary evidence that no fewer than 1,800 of these early 'navvies' excavated the moat at Flint Castle during the month of August 1277. Flint was, of course, one element in Edward I's strategy for the invasion of Gwynedd and the records show that he recruited workmen not only from Wales but from Lancashire, Leicestershire, Lincolnshire, Warwickshire and Yorkshire and that at least one gang comprised pressed men doing forced labour (*see* CASTLES, CONSTRUCTION OF). In Wales, Beaumaris and White Castle have retained their water-filled moats, as have the keeps at Raglan and Cardiff and the site of a stone-built, late medieval hunting lodge at Hen Gwrt near Abergavenny (*see* HUNTING LODGE). Some moats contain raised platforms or 'islands' that are sometimes described (erroneously) as *hornworks*. There is a good example at White Castle where a crescent-shaped detached bailey was separated from the original motte by an encircling water-filled moat and was defended by a timber palisade and towers.

Most medieval manor houses and numerous homesteads were moated; indeed, lowland England is scattered throughout with moated sites mostly dating from the decades before and after 1300, a time of widespread disorder and social change (*see* MANOR HOUSES). The lawlessness and rapacity of those times are reflected in the ubiquitous activity of those who possessed property that was worthy of protection. Licences to crenellate multiplied significantly while new moats were excavated or existing ones reinforced and curtain walls and gatehouses were erected or strengthened. In 1270, for

The moat at Beaumaris Castle, North Wales, formed the outer ring of the castle's concentric defences. The distinctive horizontal line of masonry in the wall of the tower marks a pause in the construction of the outer curtain from 1295 to some time between 1306 and 1330.

example, Weoley Castle was a lightly defended manor house protected only by a ditch, bank and palisade. And yet by 1320 it had acquired a moat and timber drawbridge, a substantial stone curtain wall with interval towers and several other buildings located within the new compass of the walls. And it was against this background that many abbots and bishops were obliged to defend their precincts and palaces (*see* ECCLESIASTICAL STRONG-HOLDS). At Wells, for example, Bishop Ralph of Bath and Wells secured a royal licence to fortify his palace with walls, a gatehouse and a moat 'for the security and quiet of the canons and ministers resident there'.

Leeds Castle was built on two islands in a broad artificial lake and was the favourite residence of at least three kings: Edward I, Edward II and Henry VIII, all of whom spent considerable sums on extending and refurbishing the accommodation. The extensive water defences narrow to form a moat between the gatehouse and an unusual triple-gated BARBICAN. The smaller island to the rear was connected to the larger island by means of a timber causeway and drawbridge (long since replaced with stone) and

contained a D-shaped open tower of royal apartments enclosing a tiny courtyard (*see* GLORIETTE). Several of the low-lying quadrangular castles of the late medieval period had water-filled moats: Bodiam Castle (1385), for example, is surrounded by a broad lake that was intended to keep siege engines at a distance and (more importantly, one suspects) to emphasise the grandeur of the castle (reflected romantically on the water's surface) and the status and good taste of its owner. Even the approach to the castle was 'a carefully contrived conceit to match the formality of the . . . architecture' (McNeill). Of Kirby Muxloe, 'one of the saddest sites in England', little has survived. The castle was begun in 1480 by William, Lord Hastings but, following his arbitrary execution in 1483, it was never completed. Today, its principal feature is a broad, rectangular water-filled moat, typical of several fortified manor houses of the late medieval period such as Mannington Hall (1460) and Oxburgh Hall (1482).

Undoubtedly the most impressive medieval water defences were those at Kenilworth Castle in England and Caerphilly in Wales. The first Norman castle at

Kenilworth was surrounded by a dry moat but at the beginning of the thirteenth century King John radically extended the castle, building an outer perimeter wall beyond the ditch. A fortified dam was constructed to create an enormous shallow lake, later known as the Great Mere, which effectively surrounded the castle on its 'island'. This dam served as a causeway to the castle and as a means of controlling the water level in the lake – and, incidentally, as a TILTYARD. Kenilworth's strength, and its formidable reputation for withstanding sieges, derived from these water defences which, again, were intended to prevent undermining of the walls and to keep siege engines as far away from the castle as possible. The lake washed its south and west curtain walls, where mural towers were (apparently) considered unnecessary, while the more vulnerable north side was protected by a double moat. But Kenilworth was not just a military stronghold. In 1414 a remarkable garden was created by Henry V to the west of the castle. Known as the 'Pleasaunce in the Marsh', it comprised a timber-framed pavilion or banqueting house within a walled

courtyard with corner towers. The courtyard was surrounded by concentric water-filled moats and was approached from Kenilworth's Great Mere by a wide harbour channel up which the royal barge could be rowed, almost to the pavilion door. Most regrettably, the castle was slighted and the Great Mere drained in 1649.

Gilbert de Clare's Caerphilly in the southern Marches (1268–90) has some of the most extensive water defences of any castle in western Europe, and indeed it can justly claim to be the finest medieval stronghold in Britain. The fact that Caerphilly was not a royal but a baronial castle is indicative of the power and wealth of the thirteenth-century aristocracy. Gilbert de Clare (1243–95), earl of Gloucester, known as 'the Red Earl' because of his colouring, expended vast sums of money in order to defend and extend his Glamorgan estates against the native Welsh led by Llywelyn ap Gruffudd of Gwynedd (d. 1282) (*see* WALES, CONQUEST OF). Caerphilly was the first major CONCENTRIC CASTLE in Britain and, when complete, the whole site extended to more than 30 acres. The castle is

Gilbert de Clare's Caerphilly in the southern Marches of Wales (1268–90) has some of the most extensive water defences of any castle in western Europe, indeed it can justly claim to be the finest medieval stronghold in Britain.

Reconstruction of Caerphilly Castle showing the water defences and, in particular, the massive barrage or dam (left). As an example of military architecture its scale is extraordinary, as were the wealth and ambition that created it.

situated on a narrow spit of land between the marshy valleys of the Nant y Aber and Nant y Gledyr. Ditches were excavated across the gravel spit in order to create a central island on which the body of the castle was to be built. The spoil from the ditches was then used to create curved counter-scarp banks to the north and south of the platform that were intended to retain a water-filled moat. But having created this central island it was then decided not merely to channel water into the surrounding moat but to flood the entire valley on the southern side of the castle. (De Clare had been present at the siege of Kenilworth Castle in 1266 and was undoubtedly influenced by Kenilworth's Great Mere.) The raised gravel areas to the east and west of the central island were now ditched and revetted in stone, in order to provide solid foundations for bridgeheads to the castle, and their corners formed into semicircular salients. To the west, an irregular-shaped island platform (sometimes described as a *hornwork*) was linked by drawbridges to the castle island and to the shore. Known in Welsh as *Y Weringaer* or *Caer y Werin*, 'the people's fort', it may have been intended as a refuge for Caerphilly's townspeople though there is no evidence that the surrounding revetment was ever raised to form a wall. On the eastern side, where the land fell away, a heavily buttressed barrage was constructed, 152m (167yd) in length, to form a wide platform that incorporated a water-mill (*see* MILLS) and a gatehouse at the southern end. This twin-towered gatehouse provided access to the

town and protected the main sluice-gates which operated like the lock-gates of a canal. The northern lake dates from after 1276 when the barrage was extended northwards for over 130m (142yd) and a twin-towered gatehouse built at the northern end. This was linked by a massive wall, with three projecting interval towers, to another twin-towered gatehouse located on the central platform where the north and south dams met. This became the principal entrance to the castle (the Main Gatehouse) and could only be approached across two drawbridges, supported on an intermediate pier, that spanned a wide moat on the outside of the dam. Water levels in the inner and outer moats were maintained by means of a spillway (with a portcullis and watergate) beneath the stair wing (the Wassail Tower) of the Main Gatehouse. (It would appear that this portcullis was *raised* to block the passage – *see* PORTCULLISES.) The north dam platform was considerably narrower than the earlier, southern, platform and was provided with pairs of loopholes and deep traps behind each of the three interval towers. These were traversed by wooden planks that would have been removed by defenders as they retreated along the wall-walk when under attack.

The barrage at Caerphilly is a remarkable structure and is quite unique. As an example of military architecture its scale is extraordinary, as were the wealth and ambition that created it. The combined length of the south, central and north platforms exceeds 300m (328yd). It served four purposes: to hold back, control and protect the waters of the lakes; to shield the eastern side of the castle from direct assault; to control access to the castle through the dam platform which was, effectively, a BARBICAN; and to make a dramatic architectural statement of feudal superiority and invulnerability. The south dam platform may also have been used as a tiltyard. Because Caerphilly depended heavily on its water defences, it was imperative that the lakes should not be drained during an assault. It is for this reason that the north and south dams were provided with such massive and sophisticated defences. Each segment of the castle – barrage, central core and western hornwork – was separated by a moat and connected by drawbridge to the next, the north bank of the original moat providing a link between the hornwork and the barrage that by-passed the central island. As at Kenilworth, the shallow lakes were intended to keep an enemy's siege engines at a distance and to frustrate undermining. Even so, siege engines would have been brought within range of the main body of the castle had a besieging force succeeded in occupying the western hornwork or the barrage platform.

Caerphilly owes much to the 4th marquess of Bute (1881–1947) who undertook extensive restoration work from 1928 to 1939. By then the castle had suffered badly from slighting after the Civil War and from centuries of dereliction during which the sluice-gates and island revetments had been neglected and the lakes drained. When John Leland visited Caerphilly in 1539 he described the castle as a ruin surrounded by a marsh, a clear reference to the fact that by that date the lakes had been drained. It was only in the 1950s that they were reflooded. (*See also* QUAYS)

MONARCHY Literally, 'rule of one'. Hereditary kingship or queenship. A king was deemed to rule 'by the grace of God', whose lawful representative he was on earth. The ceremony of crowning, established in the reign of Edgar in the tenth century, conferred sanctity and a form of priesthood upon a king. Once crowned and anointed he was invested with divine authority to rule.

MONASTIC GATEHOUSES *see* ECCLESIASTICAL STRONGHOLDS

MONEY *see* COINAGE

MONEYER *see* COINAGE

MONOGRAM Two or more letters interwoven to form a symbol.

MONUMENTS A particular manifestation of the wealth created by the HUNDRED YEARS WAR was a proliferation of magnificent church monuments erected to celebrate the achievements of a deceased magnate and to commemorate his status and lineage. These monuments were sometimes contained within ornate chantry chapels where masses would be said for the soul of the deceased and others named in his will (*see* CHANTRY *and* CHAPELS). Such monuments do not necessarily mark the place of interment but were erected in the parish churches of a magnate's estates or in the great monastic and collegiate churches that he and his family had endowed.

Medieval effigial monuments and brasses developed from the practice of carving designs on stone coffin lids and on slabs which were exposed in a church floor. The earliest surviving lids are from the eleventh century and are carved in shallow relief with simple decorative designs, usually foliage or Christian symbols. It is likely that depiction of the human form was reserved, in the twelfth century, for eminent ecclesiastics, the earliest known example in England being that of Abbot Gilbert Crispin (d. 1117) at Westminster Abbey. In these early monuments the image was recessed into the slab, but from the beginning of the thirteenth century it gradually assumed a more three-dimensional effigial form and was usually gilded and painted. One of the earliest knightly effigies is that of William Longespée, earl of Salisbury (d. 1226), in Salisbury Cathedral. This effigy provides evidence of the early systematic use of hereditary armorial devices (*see* ARMORY). During the Middle Ages the three-dimensional effigy was widely used by the nobility and by eminent knights and clerics and was normally placed on a tomb chest. Through the thirteenth to the fifteenth century most effigial monuments were carved in stone, often Caen stone or ALABASTER, but there were some notable exceptions including the late twelfth-century oak effigy of Robert, duke of Normandy (d. 1134), at Gloucester Cathedral. The effigy of Henry III (d. 1272) at Westminster Abbey was the first of a series of gilt bronze effigies created for members of the English royal family, a fashion later emulated by the nobility, including Richard Beauchamp, earl of Warwick (d. 1439) in his effigy at the collegiate church of St Mary's, Warwick. This magnificent tomb still retains its gilded *hearse* or barrel-shaped metal cage, originally intended to support a pall cover which was removed only on special occasions.

Two-dimensional figures were engraved on incised slabs and *monumental brasses*, flat metal plates made of an alloy of copper (75–80 per cent)

Effigy of William Longespee, earl of Salisbury (d. 1226) at Salisbury Cathedral.

with 15–20 per cent zinc and small amounts of lead and tin. In the Middle Ages this material was known as *latten* and later *cuivre blanc* (white copper). English brasses comprised a number of separate pieces cut from a single sheet of metal, each of which was engraved and set within an indentation (matrix) carved out of the stone slab so that the brass was flush with the surface. Each section was secured within its matrix in a bed of black pitch which also protected the metal from corrosion, though later brasses were often fixed by means of brass rivets driven into lead plugs which were compressed within holes in the slab. In many instances coloured enamels were let into the concave surfaces of the brass to provide heraldic decoration and this practice continued well into the sixteenth century. Slabs were generally of local stone or Purbeck marble. By far the most interesting category is the 'military brass', so called because figures are depicted in armour. Invariably, these brasses contain heraldic devices which facilitate dating and identification and often provide genealogical and personal information not included in an inscription. Indeed, it was for this reason that armory was considered to be such a necessary component in memorials. Tomb chests, with effigies (and, occasionally, brasses), could be

free-standing or placed against a wall and were sometimes surmounted by a canopy.

The development of ARMOUR and costume may be traced through such figures, though it should be remembered that memorials are not necessarily contemporary with the death of those they commemorate, for many were prepared years (or even decades) beforehand while others were commissioned retrospectively and may be in a later style (*for* dating *see* SHIELDS). The figures in effigies and brasses are stylised: it was the accompanying heraldry which announced the identity, lineage and status of the deceased. It became the practice to place man and wife (or wives) side by side but children were not usually represented, except as weepers (small figures) around the base of the tomb or by shields, illustrative of marital alliances. Many effigies and brasses also include the insignia of chivalric orders, of which the most common is the Order of the Garter. During the first half of the fifteenth century the SS collar of the House of Lancaster appears on many figures, and again during the early Tudor period, often with a pendant of the Portcullis badge or Tudor Rose. The collar of suns and roses of the House of York is found on effigies dating from the latter half of the fifteenth century, though many were defaced after Tudor's victory at Bosworth in 1485 (*see* COLLARS).

(*See also* DONOR AND COMMEMORATIVE WINDOWS, HATCHMENTS, HEART BURIAL *and* PETRA SANCTA)

For the Church Monuments Society, the Royal Commission for Historic Monuments and the Monumental Brass Society *see* APPENDIX II.

MOOT COURT *see* LAW AND ORDER

MORNING STAR *see* MACE *and* WEAPONS AND HARNESS

MORTAR AND CEMENT *see* MASONRY

MORTISE (*also* MORTICE) A cavity in a wooden member cut with precision to receive the projection (*tenon*) of another member, thereby forming a *mortise and tenon* joint.

MOS MAJORUM The code of conduct of the late medieval nobility.

MOS MILITUM The code of conduct of the late medieval knightly class.

MOTTE A flat-topped conical mound with a fortified superstructure. In the *motte and bailey castle* the larger area of the BAILEY was enclosed within a ditch and palisaded rampart while the *motte* rose above it and was connected to it by a timber bridge. The *motte* fortification depicted in the BAYEUX TAPESTRY (*c.* 1080) originated in the Rhineland and France some two decades before the Conquest. It consisted of a flat-topped, conical mound of earth and rubble, excavated from a surrounding ditch, on top of which was erected a wooden tower (*donjon*) or a timber stockade enclosing a HALL. The word 'motte' is derived from the Old French for 'mound' and shares the same etymology as 'moat' (which could be a dry ditch) confirming that the one was dependent on the other for its construction. The motte was built up layer upon layer using compacted material excavated from a surrounding ditch and was often surrounded at its base by a further palisaded bank. The sides of the earthwork may have been coated with a slippery layer of clay and the base revetted with timber or (later) with stone. There is evidence to suggest that palisades were sometimes painted white or grey in imitation of masonry. Occasionally a stream or lake was diverted to fill the ditch (*fosse*) with water as at

New Buckenham Castle (1146) and Pleshey, a mighty motte and bailey castle raised during the ANARCHY (1135–54) (*see* MOATS AND WATER DEFENCES). Sometimes a naturally defensible site was selected, as at Beaudesert Castle near Henley-in-Arden, where an elongated hill-top was 'sculpted' to form a ditch and bank and the summit levelled to accommodate a timber hall (*see* RINGWORK). Quite often, earlier defensive sites were adopted: at Montacute in Somerset, for example, Robert of Mortain (*c.* 1031–90) excavated the earthworks of his bailey within the ramparts of an Iron Age hillfort. In some instances the tower was built first and the motte added afterwards, as at Geoffrey de Mandeville's castle at South Mimms which was constructed at ground level and a substantial motte thrown up around it (*see* BERGFRIED). Similarly, the motte of Farnham Castle encased a 11.3m (37ft) square substructure that extended downwards through the mound to ground level and supported a square stone tower on a 15.5m (51ft) plinth. There are similar stone cores within the mottes at Aldingbourne, Lincoln, Saffron Walden and Totnes Castles. At Abinger, a timber tower rose from four stout posts embedded in the motte, presumably so that defenders could move freely beneath it within the narrow confines of the stockade.

There can be little doubt that the motte with its towering DONJON was far more than a stronghold: it was a statement of a lord's authority, its legitimacy and permanence. For the indigenous population it was a symbol of ruthless colonisation and subjugation. But, of course, size is relative. That which was considered overpowering in the eleventh century may now seem modest in scale, especially when compared with the great castles and cathedrals of later centuries. However, it should be remembered that many mottes would have been temporary structures, occupied for the duration of a campaign and then abandoned, while other rapidly erected 'proto-castles' were often replaced by more permanent strongholds once Norman authority had been established. A number of motte and bailey castles, such as Berkhamsted and Helmsley, had double banks and ditches and it has been suggested (by R. Allen Brown and others) that this feature may have been a royal prerogative.

There are numerous motte and bailey sites throughout England and Wales. Large numbers of strongholds were needed quickly to render Norman colonisation permanent and the motte and bailey castle was ideally suited to this need. Others date from the Anarchy (1135–54) when the building of adulterine castles was rife. Wessex was clearly a

The motte and bailey, Rayleigh Mount, Essex, c. 1172.

problem area for the Conqueror: no fewer than thirty-seven motte and bailey castles have been identified in Somerset alone. In the Welsh Marches (*see* MARCH) mottes are known as *tumps* and in Wales as *tomen*, which can also mean 'heap' or 'dunghill'. It has been calculated that by the end of the eleventh century there were at least six hundred earthwork and timber castles in Wales and the Marches of which some two hundred have survived in recognisable form, notably Castell Nanhyfer, Trecastle and Twmbarlwm. Abergwyngregin, Castell Aberlleiniog and Tomen-y-Mur remain as relics of Hugh d'Avranches's brief occupation of Gwynedd, while Brecon, Builth Caerleon and Cardiff were centres of new Norman lordships in the south (*see* WALES, CONQUEST OF). Of native Welsh motte and bailey castles, Mathrafal, Tomen-y-Rhodwydd and Tomen-y-Faerdre are the best preserved (*see* WALES: NATIVE CASTLES).

Most castles were located for strategic reasons, as the caputs of military estates (*castellanies*) and to control routeways and river crossings. Some were deliberately erected on sites that were known to be of symbolic significance to the native population: at Montacute the local Saxons believed that a piece of the 'true cross' was buried in the hill on which Mortain erected his stronghold. Such fortifications could be constructed relatively quickly: one was built immediately the invasion army disembarked at Hastings in 1066 and mottes at Warwick, Nottingham, York, Lincoln, Huntingdon and Cambridge were constructed during a single campaign (*see* CASTLES, CONSTRUCTION OF). Mottes varied considerably in size and not all were circular in plan. The largest known motte, at Thetford in Norfolk, had a height of 24m (80ft) and a base diameter of 110m (360ft). Other large mottes include those at Arundel, Cardiff, Warwick and Windsor. Most were considerably smaller and often comprised a low mound with a broad, flat summit and were undoubtedly the fortified 'homesteads' of minor knights who had staked their claim to a piece of land. In some cases the palisade surrounding the summit would be rebuilt in stone to create a SHELL-KEEP, which, because of its shape, spread the downward thrust of the masonry evenly around the summit of the motte. Conversely, stone towers were only rarely erected on mottes, the concentration of weight often causing subsidence and eventual collapse. Some mottes, such as those at Warkworth Castle in England and Bronllys, Caldicot and Hawarden Castles in Wales, were truncated and strengthened in order to accommodate later stone keeps, that at Warkworth being a massive, late fourteenth-century tower-house. However, it should not be imagined that earth and timber fortifications were invariably replaced with stone. As late as 1301 Edward I, that great builder of masonry castles, wrote to his architect concerning 'gates and towers of stone' which he had ordered at Linlithgo Castle, saying 'The King . . . has changed his mind and intends that instead of these works, good gates and towers shall be made entirely of timber. . . . And the King also wills that the said Peel [tower] be made well and strongly of whole trunks or of great trunks hewn without much reducing them.' Brinklow, Haughley, Pleshey and Thetford Castles survive as good examples of mottes that were not disturbed by masonry, while timber palisades and buildings have been reconstructed at Mountfichet Castle in Essex. Of all the castles in England, only Lewes and Lincoln Castles have two mottes each. At Lincoln they stand in close proximity, the larger being crowned with a twelfth-century shell-keep. At Lewes they are located at either end of an oval bailey, the larger motte having a circular shell-keep while there is also evidence of early masonry on the smaller Brack's Mount. It has been suggested (by R. Allen Brown) that twin donjons, of which there are examples in France, represent dual lordships, the donjon being a powerful symbol of feudal authority. In 1146 King Stephen granted the castle and city of Lincoln to Ranulf, earl of Chester, until he should recover for him his Norman lands and castles. When this had been accomplished, the castle was to be restored to the crown except that the earl might 'fortify one of his towers of the castle of Lincoln' and have the lordship of it. The shell-keep on the larger motte is almost certainly that tower.

Not all early castles had a motte. Many were simply baileys – ditch, rampart and gate – within which were located all the buildings required by a feudal lord and his household (see RINGWORK and TIMBER-FRAME BUILDINGS). There is no motte at Dover Castle, or at Pevensey, Ludlow, Old Sarum, Richmond or Rochester or, indeed, at the Tower of London.

MOTTE AND BAILEY CASTLE *see* BAILEY; CASTLES, CONSTRUCTION OF; CASTLES, DEVELOPMENT OF; *and* MOTTE

MOTTO An aphorism, the interpretation of which is often obscure but may allude to a charge in a coat of arms or to some event in a family's history: 'TOUCH NOT THE CAT BOT A GLOVE' (referring to the cat crest of Mackintosh) and 'I SAVED THE KING' (Turnbull), for example. Mottoes accompanying signatures will be found in medieval documents and first appear in ARMORY in the fourteenth century.

MOULDING A modelled surface of a building. Many mouldings are decorative while others project from vertical surfaces to protect them from rain and snow. The form and ornamentation of mouldings are characteristic of certain periods of building and often facilitate the identification of architectural styles (*see* GOTHIC ARCHITECTURE *and* MASONS AND ARCHITECTS).

MOUNTING BLOCKS *and* **MOUNTING STONES** *see* UPPING STOCKS

MUFFLERS Integral mail mittens which were added to the HAUBERK in the twelfth century (*see* ARMOUR).

MULLION A vertical bar dividing the lights of a window.
(*See also* TRANSOM *and* WINDOWS)

MULTIVALLATE An earthwork having more than two encircling ramparts. Those which had two are *bivallate*, and one *univallate*.

MUNIMENT A title deed. Documentary evidence of a right or privilege.

MUNITION Military weapons, ammunition and equipment.

MUNTIN A vertical framing piece between door panels, openings (*lights*) in screens, etc. Not to be confused with a window MULLION.

MURAGE A tax levied by boroughs to pay for the building and maintenance of their TOWN WALLS.

MURAL INSCRIPTIONS *see* GRAFFITI

MURAL STAIRS A (usually straight) flight of stone stairs contained within a wall (*see* STAIRS).

12. Edward I's choice of Caernarfon as the capital of his new principality was almost certainly motivated by a belief, still current at the time, that the nearby Roman fortress of Segontium was once the seat of the emperor Magnus Maximus who had dreamed of coming from Rome to a far-away land of high mountains and to an estuary facing an island where there was a fortified city, 'the fairest man ever saw', surrounded by towers of many colours, each tower bearing upon it eagles of gold. When Edward came to build Caernarfon as his own fortress palace, he appears to have deliberately appropriated the legend in order to add legitimacy to his occupation, making it both a fulfilment of the past and a statement of future policy.

13. Beaumaris Castle was begun (but never completed) in 1294 both as a dramatic reassertion of English authority and to complete the chain of castles that extended along the north Wales coast from Flint to Aberystwyth. The castle and English borough were constructed on the site of Llanfaes, at that time the principal port on the island of Anglesey and the most flourishing urban centre in north Wales. Edward I evicted the entire native population and moved them to a new town (Newborough) 12 miles away.

14. In the early fourteenth century Henry Percy rebuilt his twelfth-century shell-keep at Alnwick Castle, Northumberland, enlarging it and adding seven semi-circular towers to form a clustered donjon known as the 'Seven Towers of the Percys'.

15. In 1385, Richard II issued a licence to crenellate to Sir Edward Dalyngrigge, a veteran of the Hundred Years War, directing him 'to construct and make thereof a castle . . . for resistance against our enemies'. But, despite its splendid military appearance, Bodiam Castle was in reality a theatrical stage set, an extravagant declaration of accumulated wealth and chivalric superiority.

16. In the late fourteenth century, Henry Percy, 1st earl of Northumberland, built a magnificent new tower-house at Warkworth Castle to provide a self-contained suite of apartments, hall and domestic offices for himself and his family. The tower was clearly intended to amaze all who saw it, not least the earl's illustrious guests who would enter the inner bailey through a passage beneath the collegiate church. Of this structure only the entrance passage has survived (lower centre right).

17. The Garter Ceremony at Windsor Castle, Berkshire. The informal creation of a 'Round Table' after a great tournament at Windsor in 1344 was translated, probably on St George's Day 1348, into the Order of the Garter: Edward III and his eldest son, Edward Plantagenet, the Black Prince, together with twenty-four young men – the founder knights 'foreshadowing a distinguished line of noble successors throughout the history of English chivalry'.

18. Stall plates of former Garter knights at St George's Chapel, Windsor Castle (left to right): Sir John Grey of Ruthin (d. 1439), Walter, Lord Hungerford (d. 1449) and Henry Bourchier, earl of Essex (d. 1483).

19. Banners, helms and crests of the senior Knights Grand Cross of the Most Honourable Order of the Bath above their stalls in Henry VII's chapel, Westminster Abbey.

20. Bamburgh Castle occupies a lofty basalt crag that rises 45.7 m (150 ft) above the wind-swept Northumbrian coast. Its site could not be more dramatic and yet, of the castle itself, little that is original or authentic remains. The rectangular tower-keep is twelfth century but is severely altered, while Lord Armstrong's 'restoration' of 1894–1905 is said to have 'combined the acme of expenditure with the nadir of intelligent achievement.'

21. The earliest castle at Arundel in Sussex was a substantial motte (c. 1088) with an elevated bailey on each side – similar in plan to that at Windsor. A masonry shell enclosure was added in the late twelfth century. Palatial residential buildings, mostly dating from the 1890s, surround the inner bailey on three sides. Since the sixteenth century Arundel has enjoyed continuous occupation by the Howard dukes of Norfolk, the indirect descendants of William d'Abini (d. 1176) who built the shell keep.

22. Deal, in Kent, was the largest of the sixteenth-century coastal forts built by Henry VIII. It consists of a central circular 'keep', from which radiate six semi-circular bastions (lunettes), within a 'curtain wall', also with six lunettes, and a broad dry moat and outer wall. The heaviest artillery was mounted in three tiers on the reinforced roofs and was intended for long-range use against ships.

23. In 1340, for 'the security and quiet of the canons and ministers resident there', Bishop Ralph of Bath and Wells (1329–63) secured a royal licence 'to build a wall round the precincts of the houses of him and the canons and to crenellate and make towers in such a wall'. At this time many religious houses were accused of avarice and sharp practice and this friction often turned to violence. The walls, moat and gatehouse that guard the Bishop's Palace at Wells comprise one of the most formidable episcopal defensive systems ever built.

MURAL TOWERS 'Blind spots' at the foot of a CURTAIN WALL were covered by the provision of mural towers (*flanking towers* or *interval towers*) from which archers and crossbowmen could command the outer face of the wall without revealing themselves (*see* TOWERS).
(*See also* BASTION)

MURDER FINE *see* ENGLISHRY

MURDER HOLE *or* **MEURTRIÈRE** Meurtrières are openings in the vault of a gateway or GATE PASSAGE. They are popularly believed to have been used for dropping missiles on besiegers, but the principal function of a meurtrière was for the rapid discharge of water to extinguish fires set by assailants at the foot of a wooden gate or portcullis. Of course, murder holes would undoubtedly have been used for offensive purposes but the notion that boiling oil was poured on to the heads of besiegers is fallacious: oil was far too valuable a commodity! Murder holes could be any shape and size: many comprise a narrow slot that extends across the full width of a passage while others are simply small apertures in the vault (*see* SLUICE). The gate passage in the south gatehouse of Beaumaris Castle is divided into a series of KILLING GROUNDS by seven parallel murder holes (of the 'slot' variety) through which the passage could be defended from above should attackers succeed in advancing through three portcullises and three sets of heavy two-leaved doors with double draw-bars. Even more impressive is the gate passage within the King's Gate at Caernarfon Castle which contained five great timber double-doors and six portcullises, all defended by arrow loops and spy-holes at various levels, and no fewer than nine meurtrières. Murder holes could be inconvenient for those using the rooms above the passage: at Kidwelly Castle, for example, a murder hole runs across the floor of the constable's hall.
(*See also* GATEHOUSES)

MUSICAL INSTRUMENTS Musical instruments (notably trumpets) are known to have been used by the Carolingians in order to maintain morale in battle and to help troops reassemble after a defeat. The Normans used trumpets to control the movement of troops on the battlefield in the eleventh and early twelfth centuries, as did early crusader armies who also introduced drums to assist foot-soldiers when marching and to intimidate an enemy. The musical traditions of the Turks and Muslim Arabs had a profound effect on European music generally, especially that of the magnate élite.

Several musical instruments were introduced from the Middle East, notably the Arab *ūd*, which evolved into the European lute, mandolin and guitar.
(*See also* MINSTRELS)

MUSTER An assembly of armed forces for inspection or payment, details of those present being recorded in muster rolls.

MUSTER ROLLS *see* BADGES AND LIVERY, MILITIA *and* RECRUITMENT AND ORGANISATION (MILITARY)

NAILS *see* IRONWORK, LOCKS AND NAILS

NAME AND ARMS CLAUSE A clause in a will requiring a beneficiary to assume the name and coat of arms of the testator as a condition of inheritance.

NAPERY *see* KITCHENS

NASAL The protective nose-piece of a HELMET.

NATIONAL MONUMENTS RECORD (NMR) Previously a section within the Royal Commission on the Historical Monuments of England, the National Monuments Record is now run by English Heritage. It is England's national archive of heritage information and contains over twelve million items covering architecture, archaeology, aerial photographs and maritime sites in England. The NMR collections include three million photographs of buildings; almost total coverage of the country in aerial photographs; data on most known archaeological sites; textual records for buildings including the Listed Buildings Information Service; fifty thousand measured drawings; and an extensive reference library. The NMR offers a wide range of services which are freely accessible to the public. There are research rooms and other facilities at Swindon in Wiltshire and London.
For address *see* APPENDIX II

NECKING *see* CAPITAL

NEWEL The central support for a spiral stair (*see* NEWEL STAIR).

NEWEL POST *see* STAIRS

NEWEL STAIR, TURNPIKE STAIR *or* **VICE** A spiral stair, the steps of which radiate from a central pillar (*newel*) (*see* STAIRS).

NOBILITY AND GENTRY, THE In late medieval England there was a deep-rooted belief that society was ordered by God for the good of humanity. This was reflected in a hierarchy in which anointed kings were closest to God and beneath them, in descending order, were the nobility and the princes of the Church, knights, gentry, the professional classes, merchants and yeomen and, at the bottom, the multitude of peasants. Before the emergence of a parliamentary PEERAGE the social distinction between the nobility and the gentry hardly existed. In the early fourteenth century aristocratic society consisted of some three thousand landowners whose estates were worth at least £20 a year. Among these noblemen the earls were pre-eminent by reason of their rank; the rest were 'lords', specifically barons, bannerets, knights and esquires, all of whom were recognised by their ARMIGEROUS status. It was not until the early fifteenth century that persons of some social standing began to describe themselves as 'gentlemen'. At first this implied nobility but as usage spread so the meaning of the term changed (*see* GENTLEMAN). With the establishment of a House of Lords (an assembly of lords summoned by the king to discuss judicial, financial and other important matters), only peerage families could describe themselves as 'noble'. With acceptance, in the thirteenth century, of the principle that taxation required consent, knights and burgesses who represented their shires and boroughs were occasionally summoned to parliament and the practice developed of a 'Commons' assembly meeting separately, though it did not have its own meeting chamber until the sixteenth century. Recognition that the peerage had come to constitute a separate estate of the realm led many historians to regard all landowners below the rank of baron and above that of yeoman as belonging to the gentry class. The term 'peerage' now includes the degrees of DUKE, MARQUESS, EARL, VISCOUNT and BARON, all of which are hereditary.
(*See also* BANNERET, COMITAL, COUNT, ESQUIRE, KNIGHTHOOD AND CHIVALRY (ORIGINS OF), LORD, MAGNATE *and* YEOMAN)

NOBLE (COIN) *see* COINAGE

NOGGING *see* BRICK NOGGING *and* TIMBER-FRAME BUILDINGS

NORMAN ARCH *see* ARCH

NORMAN ARCHITECTURE *see* ROMANESQUE

'NORMAN' SHIELD *see* KITE-SHAPED SHIELD *and* SHIELDS

NORMANS IN SCOTLAND *see* SCOTLAND, NORMANS IN

NORMANS IN WALES *see* MARCH, NORMANS *and* WALES

NORMANS, THE The great conquering people from Normandy in northern France, who from 1050–1100 subjugated England, southern Italy and Sicily. The duchy of Normandy evolved from territory around Rouen granted to the Viking chieftain Rollo in 911 which, despite its origins and continuing Scandinavian immigration during the first half of the tenth century, developed in the eleventh century as a characteristic French territorial principality. Norman warriors seem to have been present wherever warfare was taking place but there does not appear to have been a coherent policy of conquest: England, for example, was the victim of the political opportunism of a reigning duke.
From *c.* 1025 Normandy had been convulsed by internecine warfare and Duke William's eventual pacification of the duchy after 1050 appears to have been achieved principally through a strategy of diverting aggression against neighbouring states. The childless King Edward ('the Confessor') of England (*r.* 1042–66) nominated Duke William as his successor and in 1064 Earl Harold, who had effectively dominated Edward's court during the last years of his reign, reluctantly swore homage to William and promised to support his claim to the English throne. But on Edward's death in January 1066, Harold was elected king – thereby precipitating two invasions within months of his accession. He defeated his half-brother Tostig and the Norse king Harald Hardrada at Stamford Bridge but was himself slain by the Conqueror's army at Senlac ('the lake of blood') in Sussex.
William retired to nearby Hastings, to the motte and bailey castle he had already constructed there, and waited for the English capitulation (*see* MOTTE). But, 'when he saw that no one would come, he went up with all the army . . . and ravaged all the parts he went over' (Anglo-Saxon Chronicle).

Hundreds of villages appear to have been ransacked as William rapidly established control over southern England while in London 'fortifications were erected against the fickleness of the huge and fierce population for he perceived that to crush the Londoners under heel was his first objective'. William was crowned at Westminster on Christmas Day 1066. Northern England proved more recalcitrant and Norman rule only became effective there following the ruthless suppression of a major rebellion in 1069 (see HARRYING OF THE NORTH). The invasion had been carried out with the Pope's blessing, and many of the native English believed that the 'lake of blood' at Senlac was evidence of God's displeasure. The great men of the realm 'from necessity submitted when the greatest harm had been done; and it was very imprudent that it had not been done earlier, as God would not better it for our sins' (Anglo-Saxon Chronicle). No doubt Harold's duplicity incurred William's indignation, but the duke must also have recognised that invasion, and the prospect of territorial conquest, would serve to concentrate the energies of his rancorous aristocracy. In the event, 1066 was an opportunity which was ably taken.

The conquest of England offered unlimited scope for the personal aggrandisement of ambitious warriors through service to the Norman kings and magnates and through the acquisition of new lands from bases securely under Norman control or through marriage to Anglo-Saxon heiresses. The Norman system of lordship provided cohesion to these often disparate groups of warriors who were not exclusively Norman but included large numbers of Flemings, Bretons, Poitevins and other Frankish mercenaries. The acquisition of land by a lord was invariably followed by the granting of constituent estates to vassals: thus men from Montgomery in Normandy are named in DOMESDAY as holding land in Shropshire of their lord, Roger de Montgomery, for example. During the decade of Norman settlement following the Conquest, the native English aristocracy was almost entirely replaced in positions of secular and ecclesiastical authority by a new ruling class that established and maintained control through the sword, the stirrup and the keep. All land belonged to the Conqueror whose followers held their estates by his pleasure and in return for specified services. Estates were confiscated and redistributed to the Norman lords and their dependents, many of whom already held lands in Normandy, so that by 1080 only 8 per cent of estates held directly of the king remained in native hands.

Over a thousand castles were built in the century following the Norman Conquest: 'Castles he [Duke William] caused to be made, and poor men to be greatly oppressed' (Anglo-Saxon Chronicle). Most were constructed in the wake of the Conquest itself by the Norman lords and their allies as they took possession of their lands. These conquerors in a hostile land numbered only a few thousand and their castles became both symbols of subjugation and bastions of paranoia. Before the Conquest hillforts, Roman *castelli* and Anglo-Saxon BURHS were constructed for communal defence but, with the exception of a very small number of castles built by Anglo-Norman favourites of Edward the Confessor (such as Richard FitzCrob's stronghold at Richard's Castle, erected in 1032), the concept of the private fortified residence was new in England. Unlike the Saxon English, the Welsh never entirely succumbed to the Norman invader, though it was the inability of the Welsh principalities to unite against the common enemy that frustrated any aspirations of independence (see WALES). The extraordinary number of Norman strongholds, both large and small, permanent and temporary, that are scattered throughout the Marches is testimony to the toughness and resilience of the Welsh (see MARCH). Indeed, over the next two centuries a number of major Norman castles, including Cardiff and Laugharne, were successfully invested by the Welsh, though native resistance was never entirely successful for neither the Normans nor their Anglo-Norman successors were ever driven out.

Latin replaced English as the language of administration and French became the language of the aristocracy. An archaic English Church was also reformed and by the time of William's death in 1087 only one English bishop, Oswald of Worcester, remained, the rest having been replaced by foreigners. In the parishes English priests continued to preach in the vernacular in churches built by native craftsmen, but the larger churches, abbeys and cathedrals, built in stone and in the alien ROMANESQUE style, were almost exclusively staffed by foreign clergy. The highly developed and distinctive Wessex and DANELAW systems of administration and justice were rationalised, exploited and centralised by the new management.

Norman England was essentially a colonial society, with the immense new cathedrals and castles symbolising the invaders' power and the *Domesday Book* Duke William's ruthless efficiency (see DOMESDAY BOOK). But *Domesday* also reveals that the Norman Conquest had little real effect on the peasantry, indeed some actually enjoyed greater

freedom, for slavery, a common phenomenon in Anglo-Saxon society, was abolished under Norman rule. While most peasants continued to cultivate their holdings and to provide service on their lord's demesne, the new aristocracy consolidated their estates and constructed their castles. Some endowed monasteries which at first tended to be English dependencies of Norman foundations but in the twelfth century were more often new Cistercian houses. At this time there was a significant increase in population and commercial and economic expansion which led both to the development of new towns as regional centres of administrative, political and mercantile activity and to the colonisation of many of the more remote regions by individuals and communities. But perhaps the most significant change was a cultural one: England now looked towards France and no longer to Scandinavia. Amalgamation of the two territories was never on the political agenda, however: under the Normans England had its own institutions and government as did Normandy. Henry II (1133–89) ruled from the Scottish border to the Pyrenees but the Angevin 'Empire' remained essentially a confederation in which England and Normandy were linked more closely to each other than they were to Anjou, Maine, Touraine, Aquitaine, Poitou or Auvergne. The independent existence of the duchy of Normandy ended in 1204 when it was conquered by the Capetian kings of France, though successive English dynasties continued to press claims to the ducal territories and exercised limited military and political authority in the duchy, notably during the so-called HUNDRED YEARS WAR of the late Middle Ages (1340s–1450s).
(*See also* BAYEUX TAPESTRY)

O

OBLATE ROLLS *see* FINE

OBTUSE ARCH *see* ARCH

OEILLET *see* OILLET

OFFA'S DYKE *see* DYKES *and* WALES

OFF-SET A horizontal or sloping break in the face of a wall, often delineated by a ledge, caused when the upper part of the wall is reduced in thickness. A *buttress off-set* (or *set-off*) is sloped.

OGEE A double continuous curve (like an S). An *ogee arch* has two ogee curves meeting at the apex. (*See also* ARCH *and* GOTHIC ARCHITECTURE)

OGIVE (i) A diagonal ogee-shaped rib in a vault (*see* VAULTING).
(ii) An OGEE arch above a door or window opening.
(iii) An ogival compartment is a space delineated by a border consisting of two ogees.

OILLET, OILET *or* **OEILLET** Literally, an 'eyelet', a type of arrow loop with circular sight-holes at the ends of the loop to improve the defender's field of vision and to increase the amount of natural light entering a chamber (*see* LOOPHOLE).

ONAGER *see* SIEGES

OPE An opening.

ORATORY A chapel licensed for private use.

ORDER The sequence of recession in a doorway or window.

ORDERS OF KNIGHTHOOD *see* KNIGHTHOOD AND CHIVALRY, ORDERS OF

ORDINARY (i) In ARMORY an ordinary is one of a number of bold rectilinear charges also known as the Honourable Ordinaries.
(ii) An ordinary of arms is a reference book which lists the heraldic descriptions (*blazons*) of shields of arms alphabetically by the charges they contain. Proficiency in the use of blazon is essential if an ordinary is to be used to identify arms. The best known ordinary is J.W. Papworth's *Ordinary of British Armorials*, first published in 1874 and reprinted in 1977 (published by Five Barrows).

ORDNANCE SURVEY Ordnance Survey maps are essential tools of the historian and always a joy to possess. In particular, they assist in understanding the location of a castle and its strategic significance, relating it to topographical features and to other castles in a locality. Today, all information is stored in digital form on computer and may be used to draw out any part of a map required by a customer. Large-scale mapping is available at over forty Ordnance Survey agents throughout the United Kingdom in both digital form (*Superplan Data*) and paper (*Superplan Plots*).

The following map series and services are of particular interest to the historian:

Urban areas are surveyed at 1:1250 scale (50 in to 1 mile) while rural areas are surveyed at 1:2500 scale (25 in to 1 mile). Mountain and moorland areas are shown in maps at the scale 1:10000 (6 in to 1 mile), as are several towns and cities.

The *Landranger* series covers the whole country in 204 maps at a scale of 1:50000 (2cm to 1km or 1¼in to 1 mile) and is the most appropriate scale for studying networks of castles and how these relate to topographical features such as river crossings and routeways.

The excellent *Explorer* series at 1:25000 (4cm to 1km or 2½in to 1 mile) gives more detailed information such as field boundaries, medieval park-pales (*see* DEER PARKS) and the earthworks of castle sites and abandoned settlements.

Superplan is the Ordnance Survey's 'tailor-made' large-scale, site-centred mapping system. Each *Superplan* plot is individually produced to order which means that plots can be up to A0 size or even larger, and at any scale from 1:200 to 1:10000. Every plot includes all the latest available information together with ground areas and parcel numbers. *Superplan Data* provides similar information in a form that is intended for computer-aided design (CAD) in DXF format on a standard floppy disk, CD-ROM or via e-mail. A *Siteplan* pack provides six copies of a project site and may be precisely centred on any property address in the country.

Landplan is the first graphic product to be digitally derived from a variety of thematic and topographical databases. It is a 'plot on demand' service on paper or film at 1:5000 or 1:10000 scales.

The *Historical Data* service is available in a range of formats. Map data is scanned from the Ordnance Survey's historical archive of County Series and superseded National Grid mapping back to the mid-nineteenth century.

ORGANISATION (BUILDING) *see* CASTLES, CONSTRUCTION OF and MATERIALS, CARRIAGE OF

ORGANISATION (MILITARY) *see* RECRUITMENT AND ORGANISATION (MILITARY)

ORIEL A projecting window on an upper floor (*see* WINDOWS). The term *oriel* is also found in medieval documents where it is used to describe a porch, gallery or ante-room, again on an upper floor.

ORILLONS The twin spurs of an ARROWHEAD BASTION, protecting the flankers.

OUBLIETTE (i) From the French 'oublier' meaning 'to forget', an underground prison cell entered by means of a hatch in the ceiling. Also known as a *bottle dungeon* because of its shape and narrow entrance, prisoners were 'consigned to oblivion' (*see* PRISONS).
(ii) A pit beneath the wall of a tower, once covered by a pivoted trapdoor which was operated by a garrison in retreat.

OUTER GATEHOUSE *see* BARBICAN *and* GATEHOUSE

OUTFANGETHEOF The right of a manorial lord to apprehend a thief beyond the boundaries of his estate and to return him for trial in his own court. (*See also* INFANGETHEOF)

OUTLAWS Those who were literally 'outside the law' were usually men or women who had either absconded or escaped from custody before being brought to court in order to answer criminal charges. If thereafter they failed to appear before a court, having been summoned to do so on four occasions, they were declared outlaws and their goods forfeited; denied the protection of the realm, they could be killed on sight. With nothing to lose, most fugitives joined with others to form outlaw bands living by petty crime in remote areas where they were effectively beyond the law. Of course the archetypal outlaw was Robin Hood, but in answer to the question 'Who was he?' the answer must be 'There were more than one'. This still allows for an original, but his identity is lost in the 'obscurity created by his own fame. Real people move in the shadows, their crimes revealed before the courts, but by borrowing [Robin Hood's] reputation they dissolved his identity' (Holt). From 1547 many vagrants turned to outlawry as an alternative to branding and servitude. Outlawry was abolished as recently as 1879.
(*See also* LAW AND ORDER *and* TRAILBASTON)

OVENS see CHIMNEYS AND FIREPLACES and KITCHENS

OYER AND TERMINER Commissions of Oyer and Terminer were royal commissions of *ad hoc* appointees charged with authority to 'hear and determine' specific cases of treason, insurrection, murder, coining and other serious crimes within a particular county. The records were kept by Clerks of the Peace.
(*See also* LAW AND ORDER)

P

PAGE A non-combatant liveried attendant of a knight. Service included training in the arts of war and chivalry and was the first stage of training for knighthood, followed by that of a squire (*see* ESQUIRE *and* KNIGHTHOOD AND CHIVALRY, ORIGINS OF).

PAINT see PLASTER, WHITEWASH AND PAINT

PALACES see BISHOPS' PALACES and ROYAL PALACES

PALATINATE The word *palatine* means 'pertaining to a palace' and the Palatine Counties were those over which Norman magnates and their successors exercised royal jurisdiction. The original Palatine Counties were those of the Welsh MARCH (ruled by the earls of Chester, Shrewsbury and Hereford) and the Scottish Borders (ruled by the Prince Bishop of Durham). The palatinates were necessary for the defence of the Conqueror's new realm but elsewhere holdings were dispersed to prevent the concentration of magnate power.

The *prince bishops* of Durham are unique in the history of England. They were appointed by the king as *counts palatine*, head of Church and state in a vast territory which included all the lands between the Rivers Tyne and Tees, land around Crayke and Northallerton in Yorkshire and an area along the River Tweed in Northumberland known as 'North Durham': Norhamshire, Islandshire, including Holy Island, and Bedlingtonshire. This was St Cuthbert's

diocese: the seventh-century bishopric of Lindisfarne which from 995 was administered from Durham, the customary dues of its vast estates recorded in 1183 in what is now called the *Boldon Book*. The palatinate was effectively a kingdom within a kingdom, and as defenders of the realm in the north the prince bishops were charged with the defence of the Scottish border. By the fourteenth century the palatinate was at the height of its military power, its warrior-bishops uniquely commemorated in the ducally crowned mitre and sword in the coats of arms of all subsequent bishops of Durham. They had their own chancellors, exchequer and mint; they administered the civil and criminal law; they granted charters for markets and fairs and they exercised rights of forfeiture. Inevitably the bishops' authority was reduced under the Tudor kings, but even so in 1585 the bishop of Durham was the largest land-holder in the country with eighty manors worth £2,500 annually. The failure of the Northern Rising in 1569 succeeded in suppressing local opposition to the bishops' traditional domination of local affairs and single-faction politics continued in County Durham until the mid-nineteenth century. The bishops' powers were finally vested in the crown in 1836 and the palatinate courts abolished by the Courts Act of 1971.

PALE (i) A stake used in a fence (*see* PALISADE).
(ii) A boundary.
(iii) A district or territory subject to a particular jurisdiction or confined within agreed boundaries (*see* MARCH). The *English Pale* was the hinterland of CALAIS, the only part of France to remain in English possession at the end of the HUNDRED YEARS WAR in 1453. In Ireland the *Pale* was that area which was settled by the English during the 1170s. By the fourteenth century the area subject to English law and royal government consisted of Meath, Trim, Louth, Dublin, Kildare, Kilkenny, Waterford, Wexford and Tipperary. However, this area was subject to gradual Irish encroachment and was only re-established by Henry VIII's reconquest in the sixteenth century.
(iv) In ARMORY, an ORDINARY consisting of a broad vertical stripe.

PALFREY see HORSES AND HORSE-HARNESS

PALIMPSEST A manuscript on which the original writing has been effaced to make room for new material. Also a monumental brass which has been re-engraved on the reverse.

PALISADE (*also* PEEL) A stockade or protective fence of pointed stakes (*pales*); also (as a verb) to enclose within a palisade. The timber palisades of early castles were often painted white in imitation of stone (*see* MOTTE).

PANACHE A crest of feathers worn on a helmet.

PAND A vaulted passage.

PANELLING From the thirteenth century the interior walls of larger chambers were often lined with wooden boards (*wainscoting*) which were placed vertically and overlapping one another as in a clinker-built ship. (Wainscot was usually oak imported from the Baltic coast and used also for wagons or 'wains'.) During the fifteenth century panel and frame construction (*joined* woodwork) was introduced from Flanders. The panels, thin sheets of wood, were tapered on all four sides and fitted into grooves within a framework of thicker wood. The horizontal and vertical strips of the frame (*rails* and *stiles*) were united by mortise and tenon joints and fastened by square oak pegs inserted into round holes. This type of panelling was used for centuries on walls and ceilings and in doors and furniture. Early panelling was rarely carved but was sometimes painted in coloured designs. From the late fifteenth century until about 1550 *lignum undulatum* ('wavy woodwork') decoration was popular, each panel being carved with a representation of a piece of material folded vertically. (From the nineteenth century this style of decoration has been described as *linenfold*). Later examples may have a decorative 'punched' border to represent embroidery and a further variation of the design, known as *parchemin*, resembles a curled piece of parchment. Early sixteenth-century panels were often decorated with a central roundel, incorporating heraldic and other devices, and from about 1550 a profusion of English Renaissance motifs appeared.
(*See also* WALL HANGINGS)

PANEL TRACERY *see* GOTHIC ARCHITECTURE

PANTLER *see* HOUSEHOLD

PANTRY Strictly, the domestic department of a HOUSEHOLD responsible for the making of bread (*see* LARDER), though the term is also used to describe a service room, generally adjacent to a hall, where food was prepared.

PAPAL BULL *see* SEALS

PARADE Ground on which musters and exercises are held.

PARALLEL A wide trench dug parallel to the walls of a besieged fortification to provide protection for the attackers.

PARAPET (i) A low wall erected at the edge of a structure for reasons of safety or to conceal guttering, etc. A *crenellated parapet* is an embattled wall affording protection for defenders on the outer edge of a castle wall-walk (*see* BATTLEMENTS).
(ii) In post-medieval fortifications, a wall or earthen embankment for the protection of troops on the forward edge of a rampart.

PARCLOSE *see* SCREENS

PARISH CHURCHES *see* CHURCHES *and* CHURCH TOWERS

PARK-PALE *see* DEER PARKS

PARKS *see* DEER PARKS

PARLIAMENT *see* GOVERNMENT

PARLIAMENTARY ACTS The records of Public and Private Acts since 1500 are housed in the House of Lords Library (*see* APPENDIX II). Many have been published as *Statutes of the Realm* or *Statutes at Large*.
(*See also* STATE RECORDS)

PARLOUR From the Old French *parleur* meaning 'to talk', a room set aside for private conversation. Parlours are found in some late medieval castles (at Nunney, for example) and are generally small chambers located in the vicinity of the hall. Later parlours were very much larger and served many of the functions of the hall.

PARPAIN *see* MASONRY

PATENT ROLLS In 1516 letters patent replaced CHARTERS as the form in which royal grants are made. They are 'open' documents intended for public consumption (Latin *patere* = to open), often addressed 'To All and Singular to whom these Presents shall Come'. Armorial bearings, for example, are granted by means of signed letters patent to which the seals of the granting kings of arms are appended. Patent rolls, which contain copies of letters patent, were begun in 1201 and are still

maintained today. Private documents may be described as letters *close* and, unlike letters patent, may only be opened by the breaking of a seal. Copies of these documents were made on parchment sheets which were stitched together and stored in rolls, one or more for each regnal year. They are housed at the Public Record Office (*see* APPENDIX II).
(*See also* CLOSE ROLLS *and* STATE RECORDS)

PATINA An encrusted or glossy surface acquired by an object as a result of age or chemical changes following burial.

PAULDRON Plate shoulder ARMOUR with extensions to protect the upper chest and back. First used at the end of the fourteenth century, pauldrons were thereafter incorporated into complete suits of plate armour.

PAVILION A circular tent supported on a central pole, the canvas or material of the outer skin often decorated with the colours and armorial devices of the occupant. During the medieval and Tudor periods pavilions were much in evidence at TOURNAMENTS, pageants, the scenes of diplomatic negotiations and military camps.

PAVING The use of tiles for paving the interior of buildings was well established by the thirteenth century. In 1250 Henry III ordered that his chamber at Clarendon was to be 'paved with plain tiles', while in 1256 'a pavement of tiles' was laid on the dais in his hall at Winchester. 'Plain tiles' could be glazed in a variety of colours and were sometimes painted after firing: in 1308 Hugh le Peyntour and Peter le Pavier were employed for a month 'making and painting the pavement'. Tiles, both patterned and plain, were purchased in large numbers. At Shene, for example, in 1385, 15*s* were paid to Katherine Lyghtfote for two thousand painted tiles 'for the room set apart for the King's bath'. In high-status chambers ENCAUSTIC TILES were the most common form of paving. Flemish tiles were particularly fine: in 1368 Henry Yevele supplied a thousand tiles for the pavement of the wardrobe at Eltham and three years later '8,000 tiles of Flanders for the paving of floors and other work' at Westminster Palace. Kitchens, service rooms and lobbies were usually paved with stone 'flags' and occasionally floors were plastered: the floor of the queen's chamber at Winchester in 1268, for example. But for the most part they were covered with compacted earth: the 1453 accounts for New College, Oxford, give details of the boarding and levelling of a chamber floor with 'a cartload of red earth for earthing the flore'.

PAVISE A large, rectangular shield used by medieval infantry. Dating from the fourteenth and fifteenth centuries, it was sometimes fitted with a prop so that it could stand by itself, thereby affording protection to archers and crossbowmen. (*See also* MANTEL *and* SHIELDS)

PEASANTS' REVOLT The 'Great Revolt' of English artisans and peasants, notably from the counties of Kent and Essex, caused by poor economic conditions, unpopular taxation and repressive legislation. In 1381 the rebels marched on London, killing several unpopular ministers and occupying the city. They even succeeded in entering the Tower of London where they rampaged through the royal apartments (at that time the Yeomen Warders of the Tower paid 'base men from the streets' to undertake their duties so that infiltration would have been easy). After the death of their leader Wat Tyler, the young Richard II acceded to a number of the rebels' demands and they were persuaded to disperse. However, the government immediately revoked the concessions and re-established its authority. The principal cause of peasant unrest, which was to re-emerge throughout the following century, was the *Ordnance of Labourers*, a series of reactionary labour laws which sought to reverse the improved conditions enjoyed by labourers as a consequence of depopulation following the Black Death (*see* PLAGUE). Although the Peasants' Revolt failed to attain its immediate objectives it stimulated an almost universal resistance to serfdom which ultimately rendered it uneconomic.

PEBBLEDASH *see* FACING MATERIALS

PEDIGREE A genealogical table illustrating descent through the male line. The term is said to have originated in the practice of writing the names of forebears in groups of circles which, when joined by curved lines, resemble the imprint of a crane's foot, a *pied de gru* in French. A chart which records all direct-line ancestors, both male and female, is termed a Birth Brief, Blood Descent or Total Descent.

PEEL *see* PALISADE

PEERAGE, THE Derived from the medieval Latin *paragium*, peerage simply means 'a company of equals' and was applied to those of similar rank within the nobility. From 1321 the term was used to describe those senior barons of England who were accustomed to receive a writ of summons to parliament, and later also referred to the lords

spiritual. In order of precedence the peerage now comprises the ranks of DUKE, MARQUESS, EARL, VISCOUNT *and* BARON.
(*See also* NOBILITY AND GENTRY, THE)

PELE TOWERS Derived from the Latin *palus* meaning 'stake', the term *pele* originated in the palisaded enclosure (hence 'beyond the pale') and was probably introduced in the present context by nineteenth-century antiquarians. Although 'pele' implies enclosure, it is used to describe a type of small fortified tower-house dating from the mid-fourteenth century to the seventeenth. Whereas in England and Wales the need for fortification began to diminish in the fourteenth century (*see* CASTLES, DEVELOPMENT OF), in the Scottish MARCH numerous pele towers continued to be built by the gentry and lesser nobility as protection against armed incursions across the border in the centuries before the Act of Union in 1707. A typical stronghold, such as the Vicar's Pele at Corbridge in Northumberland (*c.* 1300), consisted of a rectangular tower with immensely thick stone walls pierced by small window-openings and entered at first-floor level by means of a stone flight of steps or (in early examples) by a ladder that would be hauled inside whenever danger threatened. The ground floor usually contained store-rooms, and in most towers these

Pele tower at Corbridge, Northumberland.

would originally have been stone-vaulted and accessible only from the floor above, thereby reducing the risk of attack by fire or explosion from beneath. On the first floor was the SOLAR and above that a further floor of bed chambers and an upper platform with a parapet and sometimes a corner observation turret which may also contain the chimney flues. Several pele towers had an attached hall, and sometimes a second tower at the service end of the hall. In most examples a walled courtyard (*barmkin*) protected livestock from marauders. Other pele towers were more sophisticated: the imposing fourteenth-century Chipchase and Belsay towers in Northumberland, for example, had crenellated and machicolated parapets and projecting wings containing the stair, entrance and small chambers. Chipchase Tower has four storeys, with a turret rising at each corner and a projecting wing with an entrance at first-floor level defended by a portcullis. The top storey contained the great chamber and kitchen and there was a chapel within the wall of the third floor. There are ninety pele towers in Cumbria alone, of which Sizergh Castle is perhaps the best example. Dating from *c.* 1340, the tower (with an attached hall) dominates the castle which was largely rebuilt in the second half of the sixteenth century. At that time two large projecting wings were added together with a lofty turret (the Deincourt Tower) in which a suite of latrines once served the three upper floors. One of these wings (the Barracks Wing) is reputed to have accommodated a garrison of armed retainers – indicative, perhaps, of the turbulent nature of the Borders at that time. Several other pele towers were extended and remodelled to provide substantial dwellings: Nappa Hall in Wensleydale, for example, has an additional west tower linked to the original pele tower by a mid-fifteenth-century hall. The larger pele towers, such as Belsay and Dacre, are better regarded as self-contained tower-houses (*see* TOWER-HOUSE).
(*See also* BARMKIN *and* BASTLE)

PENDANT Dependent or suspended from. For example, an armorial device suspended from a collar (*see* COLLARS).

PENNON *see* FLAGS

PENNY *see* COINAGE

PENTHOUSE *see* PENTISE *and* SIEGES

PENTISE *also* **PENTICE** *and* **PENTHOUSE** The term has acquired a number of definitions, the common element being the presence of a sloping roof. In this context, a penthouse is literally 'a sloping house':

(i) A subsidiary structure (e.g. a covered way or gallery) with a sloping roof attached to the wall of a main building. The courtyard at Goodrich Castle was surrounded on three sides by a pentise which must have been similar in appearance to a monastic cloister. Similarly, a pentise along one side of the inner ward of Harlech Castle provided shelter from the elements for people walking from the chapel to the great hall and its kitchen and service rooms.

(ii) A projecting wooden turret on a curtain wall (*see* HOARDING).

(iii) A large, conical hoarding on a tower.

(iv) When used in a siege, a penthouse was a large movable wooden 'shed' (known colloquially as a *cat* because of its stealthy approach to the foot of a wall), the reinforced roof of which provided protection from arrows and bolts and from missiles dropped from above (*see* SIEGES).

PERPENDICULAR PERIOD *see* GOTHIC ARCHITECTURE

PERRIER A siege machine designed to be used by unskilled soldiers and comprising a throwing arm with a net at one end into which the missile was placed. Three or more men would pull the arm back with ropes before releasing the missile. The machine had an effective range of up to 230m (250yd). (*See also* SIEGES)

PETARDIER *or* **PETARD** From the French *péter* meaning 'to break wind', a petardier was a medieval grenade comprising an earthenware casing filled with 'Greek Fire', inflammable materials and explosives (sulphur and saltpetre), and with a cotton thread fuse, which was thrown in the face of the enemy, to breach a gate or to clear a trench. It is known that petardiers were used by Edward I at the siege of Brechin in 1303. This was probably the first time that gunpowder had been used in a siege in Britain, though as yet its potential for mining was unrealised. The substance was singularly unstable and no doubt many an Edwardian soldier was 'hoisted with his own petard'.

PETRARIA *see* SIEGES

PETRA SANCTA, SYLVESTER (SYSTEM) *see* TINCTURES

PEWTER From the Old French *peutre*, a grey alloy: usually twenty parts of tin to three of lead and one of brass. It was widely used during the medieval period for drinking vessels, plates, etc. In 1348 a number of reputable pewter-makers, anxious to maintain the standards of their craft, formed themselves into a GUILD which for one and a half centuries regulated the lead content in pewter. Later legislation required that each pewterer should have his own mark which was to be recorded on a *touch-plate* at the Pewterers' Hall.

PEYTRAL Armour for the front of a horse (*see* BARDING *and* HORSES AND HORSE-HARNESS).

PIEDS POUDREUX *see* MARKETS

PIER A solid support of brick or masonry carrying a LINTEL or the downward thrust of an ARCH. A pier is composed of four parts: the ABACUS (from which the arch springs), the CAPITAL (immediately below the abacus), the shaft (which may be oval, rectangular or multiform) and the base. An arch which springs from a pier is called a *pier arch* while a *half pier*, which is set within a wall and carries one end of an arch, is known as a *respond*. *Fluting* is vertical channelling in a shaft and a pier which is surrounded by clusters of attached or detached shafts is a *compound* or *clustered pier*. An *engaged pier* (also *applied* or *attached*) is one where part of its surface is in contact with a wall. A slender pier dividing a wide doorway is a *trumeau*. In ROMANESQUE and GOTHIC ARCHITECTURE the term is synonymous with *pillar*. (*See also* HALF SHAFT)

PIG-FACED BASCINET *see* BASCINET

PIKE *see* WEAPONS AND HARNESS

PILASTER *see* LESENE

PILASTER BUTTRESS A shallow vertical BUTTRESS often used with other similar buttresses for ornamental purposes.

PILLAR *see* PIER

PILLOW MOUNDS *see* WARRENS

PIPE ROLLS The earliest and most important royal records, the *Great Rolls of the Exchequer* (known as the Pipe Rolls) were introduced in 1120 and survive in an almost unbroken sequence from the second year of Henry II (1155–6) to their abolition in 1832. The rolls, made up annually (at Michaelmas) in duplicate by the EXCHEQUER, contain the annual accounts rendered by the sheriff of each county and certain other royal officials, and thus contain (at least from the twelfth to the early fourteenth century) records of most of the king's receipts and payments – including those for the building and maintenance of royal castles. The Pipe Rolls are so called because they were rolled around a rod or pipe. *For* the Pipe Roll Society *see* APPENDIX II. (*See also* STATE RECORDS)

PIRATAE Marines: sailors trained to fight at sea.

PISCINA A stone basin in which a priest rinsed the chalice and paten after Mass. The presence of a piscina in the south wall of a chamber is almost certainly indicative of a former CHAPEL. A piscina may be set within a *fenestella* (a canopied niche) together with a *credence* (shelf) and an AUMBRY (cupboard).

PIT PRISON An underground cell which was entered by means of a hatch in the ceiling. Also known as a 'bottle dungeon' because of its shape, and an 'oubliette' because those who were imprisoned therein were invariably forgotten (French 'oublier' = 'to forget'). (*See also* PRISONS)

PIVOT BRIDGE *see* DRAWBRIDGE

PLACKART *or* PLACKET The lower half of a fifteenth-century two-part breastplate in a full suit of ARMOUR.

PLAGUE During the first decades of the fourteenth century climatic changes resulted in a series of poor harvests causing starvation and malnutrition which, by the 1330s, had debilitated the peasant population of Europe. Recent evidence has shown that by 1341, eight years before the arrival of the *Black Death* in England, many villages were already depopulated and their lands left uncultivated. It is now clear, therefore, that climatic change, famine and depopulation preceded the plague and, by reducing immunity to disease, contributed to its virulence.

The Black Death of 1349/50 first arrived in Britain through ports in the West Country (traditionally Melcombe Regis in Dorset) and is generally believed to have been a form of bubonic plague, though some scholars have suggested that it was anthrax. The initial symptoms, a blackish often gangrenous pustule at the point of a flea bite, was followed by an enlargement of the lymph nodes in the armpits, groin or neck. Haemorrhaging occurred beneath the skin causing the purplish blotches called *buboes* from which the bubonic plague is named. Cells died in the nervous system, which may explain the *danse macabre* ritual which often accompanied the Black Death, and between 50 and 60 per cent of victims died. The disease was carried by fleas living in the fur of black rats (*Rattus rattus*) and would have passed to humans only when so many rats had died that the fleas were forced to adopt unfamiliar human hosts. (Female black rats were capable of producing two hundred offspring a year. In Britain the species is believed to have become extinct in the wild in 1988.) The fourteenth-century pandemic probably originated in Mongolia in the 1320s and reached Europe by *c.* 1347. Amazingly, there was no attempt to prevent its spreading across the English Channel or even to discourage contact with the stricken continent. Indeed, two weeks before the plague's arrival the archbishop of York was warning of its inevitability, and of 'the sins of men, whose prosperity has made them complacent and who have forgotten the generosity of God'. Presumably he was not referring to the emaciated peasantry. When the disease finally struck, the only provision made by the establishment was the excavation of mass grave-pits. At Clerkenwell, outside the walls of London, fifty thousand corpses were buried in a 13-acre cemetery established by Walter de Manny, who later founded a Carthusian monastery on the site as a memorial to the dead. This later became the Charterhouse, the cloister, chapel and gatehouse of which have survived, as have the foundations of the original cemetery chapel in which penitential services were held during the Black Death. At Clerkenwell a small lead cross was placed on the chest of each victim before burial. Estimates of the numbers who died during the Black Death vary enormously but at least 20 per cent of the population must have perished in this way and some historians have proposed figures of 40 or even 50 per cent. 'To our great grief the plague carried off so vast a multitude of people that it was not possible to find anybody to carry the corpses to the cemetery,' wrote a fourteenth-century monk of Rochester in Kent, '. . . mothers and fathers carried their own children on their shoulders to the church and dropped them in the common pit . . . such a terrible stench came from these pits that hardly anyone dared to walk near the cemeteries.' The nobility and gentry, with a more reliable diet and a marginally greater perception of hygiene, fared somewhat better, though neither rank nor privilege brought immunity: at Crich in Derbyshire a local knight, William de Wakebridge, erected a tiny chantry chapel to the memory of his wife, father, two sisters and three brothers, all of whom had been cut down by the plague in the summer of 1349. At Gloucester the terrified inhabitants barred the city gates to refugees fleeing from plague-stricken Bristol, while at Winchester the populace was urged to parade barefoot round the market place and to recite the seven penitential psalms three times a week – but to no avail, for well over half the population perished. In the late fifteenth century the population of England was scarcely larger than it had been in the twelfth. The effects of depopulation are evident in the commercial and agricultural decline of many communities and in a deterioration in craftsmanship. At Ledbury church in Herefordshire, for example, the mid-fifteenth-century decorative capitals of the north arcade are of significantly inferior workmanship to those of the south arcade which were carved in c. 1340. Many settlements became moribund, although (contrary to popular belief) only a small number of villages were abandoned as a direct result of the plague (see DESERTED VILLAGES). The severity of England's post-plague decline has been questioned by some authorities and it is certainly true that there is an opulence in much of the domestic architecture of the time which is difficult to reconcile with economic collapse. The name Black Death dates from 1833 and is a translation from the German.

PLAISTOW (*also* PLASTOW *and* PLASTER) Derived from the Old English *pleg-stow* meaning 'a place for sport', plaistows were medieval playing fields where a community enjoyed its recreation. Some plaistow sites may also have been the meeting places of manorial and hundred courts.

PLANTAGENET Geoffrey, count of Anjou (1113–51), was nicknamed 'the Fair' because of his handsome appearance, and Plantagenet because of the sprig of broom flower (*planta genista*) which he is said to have worn in his hat. Although, following Shakespeare, the dynasty founded by Geoffrey's son, Henry II of England (r. 1154–89), came to be known as the Plantagenets, the name was not used again by his descendants until Richard, duke of York, adopted it in c. 1460 in order to emphasise his claim to the throne. (*See also* ANJOU *and* AQUITAINE)

PLANTATION TOWNS By the Statute of Wales (1284) the principality of Gwynedd was brought under English rule and divided into three counties: Caernarfon, Merioneth and Anglesey. Castles and fortified boroughs were constructed and populated with English merchants, to the exclusion of the native Welsh (*see* TOWNS, TOWN WALLS *and* WALES, CONQUEST OF). These colonial settlements are sometimes referred to as 'plantation towns'. Increasing prosperity under English rule could not conceal widespread Welsh resentment of the commercial privileges enjoyed by the burgesses of the English plantation towns such as Conwy and Caernarfon, and it was this continuing resentment that fanned the flames of insurrection, notably the Glyn Dŵr rebellion of 1400–9.

PLAS Welsh for 'hall', 'mansion' or 'palace'.

PLASTER, WHITEWASH AND PAINT Medieval plaster, for both interior and outdoor use, was made from lime, sand and water together with various other materials which were added to prevent cracking and to encourage binding. These included straw and hay, animal hair, feathers, dung and blood. *Plaster of Paris* was introduced into England in c. 1255. This was made by burning calcium sulphate (*gypsum*, obtained from the Montmartre area of Paris) which was mixed with water to produce a hard, high-quality plaster. Initially, Plaster of Paris was expensive and was used only in important buildings, but when gypsum deposits were discovered in England (notably in the Isle of Purbeck in Dorset and in the Trent and Nidd valleys) its application became more widespread. The best material was used for sculpting monumental effigies (*see* ALABASTER) but the inferior deposits were burned to form plaster. 'Plastre de Nower' (from the gypsum deposits at Nore Down in Purbeck) was used at Clarendon in 1288, while 'Plaster of Corfe' (also in Purbeck) occurs in the Windsor accounts for 1362. In 1303, at Knaresborough in Yorkshire, we read of payments made for 'hewing 53 cartloads of plaster in the quarry' and it was probably local gypsum that was used in 1284 at Scarborough when Richard le Plasterer of York and his colleagues made the partition walls in the queen's chamber of 'plastre de Parys'. Plaster of Paris was not only used for making and finishing walls, it was also used for CHIMNEYS AND FIREPLACES where it could withstand heat more readily than mortar plaster.

In the medieval period the whitening of interior walls with a wash of whiting and size was commonplace: at Westminster in 1351, for example, John Cripelegate supplied 'a bushel of chalk dust and 4 gallons of size for whitening the walls of the chamber'. *Albacio* or whitewash (a solution of lime) was used lavishly both for decorating internal walls and for external finishes. The White Tower at the Tower of London was so called because of its resplendent coating of whitewash and it was provided with gutters and downpipes to protect its whiteness from rainwater. Corfe Castle's lofty keep was whitewashed in 1243, as were the hall, chapels and other buildings at Guildford Castle in 1255. Llantilio Castle in the southern March of Wales was first referred to as White Castle in the thirteenth century. The white rendering to which the name refers is still visible on parts of the external walls. Similarly, it is known that the walls and towers of mighty Conwy were limewashed when the castle was completed in 1287. The gleaming whiteness of the castle must have been a startling sight against the dark cloud-capped mountains of Snowdonia. Traces of the limewash can still be seen, especially in the southern towers and on the curtain wall near the modern entrance.

Paint was a very much more expensive material, though more permanent. At Melbourne Castle the accounts for 1314 record 34s 9d paid for 'the wages of a painter whitening the lord's chamber below the lantern, with white lead, varnish, oil and other things purchased' and at Windsor in 1356 'for 66 pounds of white lead for painting the vaulting of the Treasurer's house – 22s. And for 12 gallons of oil for the same – 24s. And for 4 earthen pots and 2 bottles for putting the oil in to carry it from London to Windsor – 15d.' A common form of decoration was *masoning*, the marking of a whitewashed wall with red liner to resemble the joints in masonry. In the late thirteenth-century Great Hall of Chepstow Castle, for example, traces of cream plaster are picked out with red lines to imitate blocks of expensive squared freestone. Quite often the 'blocks' were decorated with heraldic and other devices. In 1238 Henry III ordered that the walls of the queen's chamber in the Tower should be 'whitewashed and pointed, and within those pointings to be painted with flowers'. Timbers were sometimes decorated: at the Tower in 1337 Simon Rabos was paid 'for the pargetting and whitening of the whole of the great hall, together with the ochreing of the posts and beams, using his own supplies of chalk, size and ochre'. In 1245 Henry III ordered that the posts in his chamber should be painted to imitate marble and ten years later that the arches and pillars of the hall at Guildford Castle should be 'marbled'. For some obscure reason Henry seemed to be obsessed with gold stars scattered on green paintwork. In 1233 his chapel at Kennington was to be painted with 'histories' – 'so that the field shall be of a green colour spangled with gold stars'. In 1252 two chapels and the king's chamber at Geddington were to be similarly decorated, as were the royal chambers at

Windsor a decade later and the ceiling at the great chamber at Guildford in 1255. In 1236 Odo the Goldsmith was ordered to remove paintings of lions, birds and beasts from panels in the king's great chamber at Westminster and to paint them green 'in the fashion of a curtain', while in the following year the panelling of the chamber at Winchester was to be painted green with gold stars. What may appear to be an obsession may in fact be an accurate reflection of practice at the time. It is almost certain that the gold star is a reference to the 'star and crescent' badge borne by King John and Henry III and that the colour scheme was heraldic. Painted and gilded heraldry was a ubiquitous feature of medieval castles and it is little wonder that particular colours and devices prevailed in the halls, chambers and chapels of particular families (*see* ARMORY). Unfortunately, so little decorative paintwork has survived that we are unable to appreciate the extent of this practice. Above the doorway to the Great Hall at Chepstow Castle two painted shields have survived, suspended by painted ribbons from painted nails – a common medieval motif. At nearby Raglan a series of finely carved panels above the windows of the state apartments (*c.* 1469) provides evidence of the prominence given to heraldic display at that time. Although they are no longer painted, the late fifteenth-century shields once bore the arms of Sir William Herbert who was created earl of Pembroke in 1468 as a reward for capturing Harlech Castle – the last Lancastrian stronghold of the Wars of the Roses. Alternate panels contain the Herbert badge of a bascule drawbridge (*see* DRAWBRIDGES). In North-umberland a carved heraldic façade above the entrance to the Great Hall of Warkworth Castle declares the power and magnificence of the Percy dynasty, but regrettably it is no longer painted and gilded. It was not only the walls that were painted: in 1240 Henry III ordered his great chamber in the Tower 'to be entirely whitewashed and newly painted, and all the windows [shutters] of the same to be made anew . . . and to be painted with our arms' (*see* SHUTTERS).

Of course, not all decorative paintwork was heraldic. At Clarendon in 1245 one chamber was to be painted green with a border depicting the heads of kings and queens, and in another the walls were to be painted with the figures of the four Evangelists and the story of St Margaret. Again at Clarendon, this time in 1248, Henry III gave orders for a new hood to be made for the fireplace in his chamber on which were to be painted the Wheel of Fortune and the Tree of Jesse. Two years later he ordered a painting of 'the story of Antioch and the battle of King Richard', while in 1251 'the history of Alexander' was painted on the walls of the queen's chamber at Nottingham Castle. In 1265 'the twelve months of the year' (another favourite medieval subject) were painted round a fireplace at Kennington.

Decoration of this standard was expensive, as illustrated by a payment made during Richard II's reign: 'To Thomas Prynce for the painting of five chambers assigned to the King and 2 small chapels, as well as a great chapel 70 feet in length, painted with stags with golden antlers [Richard's badge], by contract, including finding colours and gold – £299 16s. 6d.' The high cost of painting was generally due more to the cost of materials than to the ability or reputation of the artist. The use of fine-quality gold leaf was particularly expensive and was therefore indicative of superior status and wealth. When ten painters were engaged at Westminster in 1252, under the direction of Master Peter of Spain, to 'paint behind the table in the great hall', 24s 11d was paid 'for 51 dozen [leaves] of gold for the painting'. (See also WALL HANGINGS)

PLATE TRACERY see GOTHIC ARCHITECTURE

PLATFORM A hard level surface on which guns or siege engines may be placed.

PLEASAUNCE or PLEASANCE A pleasant and agreeable place, often a small garden (see GARDENS).

PLENA POTESTAS see FEUDAL AIDS

PLINTH A sloping projection at the base of a wall providing increased stability against undermining. As a further means of defence, objects dropped on to a plinth from the walls would ricochet on to besieging troops. Also an artificial platform on which walls were built to counteract direct attack at the foot of wall.

PLUMBING, WATER SUPPLY AND SANITATION In contemporary documents the medieval plumber is sometimes referred to as a *ledder* for he was responsible for making and installing lead roofs as well as gutters, spouts and pipes (*for* lead roofing *see* LEAD). Sometimes gutters were made of wood and lined with lead, as at Pevensey in 1300 when gutters from the hall and the castle wall were cut out of timber and plumbers employed to cast the lead covering. In other instances they were made entirely of metal, soldered with tin or pewter and supported by iron brackets. In the 1390 accounts for Guildford Castle there is mention of '2 gutters of lead,

containing in length 72 feet [22 metres] and in breadth two feet [0.6 metre], and a gutter for the end of the same chamber, 34 feet in length [10 metres] and two feet in breadth'. While most gutters discharged their contents by means of spouts, stack pipes were also used: as at the Tower of London in 1248 where Henry III ordered 'all the leaden gutters of the Keep, through which rainwater should fall from the top of the same tower, to be carried down to the ground; so that the wall of the said tower, which has been newly whitewashed, may be in no wise injured by the dropping of rainwater'. In 1444 at Pevensey Castle a plumber was employed for the 'melting and casting of new lead and of old torn and holey lead sheets taken by him from roofs . . . for making a leaden pipe reaching from the top of the tower called the Dungeon down to the ground on the west side of the same tower to carry off the water from its wall'.

Castles were rarely built without a reliable and secure water supply (*see* WELLS). Nevertheless workmen had to dig 'in a place in a field called Chereshethe' in search of freshwater springs during the construction of Queenborough Castle in 1375. This would have required a conduit 'from the said place to the castle' which would have been extremely vulnerable should the castle have been invested. Consequently, one Robert Man was also employed 'mending and binding the water casks [cisterns] appointed to receive the rain water coming down through leaden pipes within the castle enclosure' (*see* CISTERN). At Wardour Castle a secure well in the courtyard was supplemented by a freshwater supply carried into the castle by lead piping from a source 3.2km (2 miles) away. (The piping was cut into short lengths and sold by parliamentary soldiers following the Civil War siege in 1643.) Settling tanks or *spurgels* are sometimes referred to in contemporary documents. It would appear that these were intended to clear incoming water and to reduce pressure in the pipes. Reduction of pressure might also be effected by means of a *suspirail* or 'wind-vent', an upright pipe soldered into the water main and with a stopcock that also functioned as a standpipe for drawing off water. Stopcocks and taps were known as *keys* and were often decorative. At Dover in 1227 two 'bronze heads' were purchased for the cisterns 'without which the cisterns could not well be made safe'. At Westminster in 1288 Master Robert the Goldsmith was paid 40s for 'the working of five heads of copper, gilded, for the laver [wash-place] of the small hall' and for 'the images of the said laver, and for whitening the laver and gilding the hoops'. (Here, 'whitening' probably means lining with tin.)

In 1348, again at Westminster, 2s was paid for 'a quilet [small pipe] of latten set in the mouth of a leopard made of stone, on the wall beneath the hall . . . pouring water into the cistern'.

Systems for the supply of water and the removal of waste were usually more complex in medieval monasteries than they were in castles which were, of course, more compact in plan. A number of towns benefited from royal and episcopal benevolence. In 1451 Thomas Beckington, bishop of Bath and Wells, entered into an agreement with the burgesses of the city of Wells for water to be piped from within the palace precincts to a conduit house from where it would be distributed to various parts of the palace and to reservoirs in the city (see ECCLESIASTICAL STRONGHOLDS). The first conduit, for the bishop's water, comprised a stone reservoir 3m (10ft) in diameter and contained a circular lead cistern. Pipes from the head of this cistern, measuring 30cm (12in) in circumference, fed water to the bishop's palace and to the high cross in the city market and elsewhere. The conduit had a door with two keys: one for the bishop and the other for the burgesses. The reservoir was to be cleaned twice a year and when the palace moat was scoured all the water was to be turned into the reservoir until it was refilled. In return, the master and burgesses were to make an annual pilgrimage to the bishop's tomb in the cathedral and pray for his soul.

In 1447 the citizens of Westminster were given the overflow from the king's conduit in the palace with permission to convey it to their own conduit. This seems to have been a consequence of a major reconstruction of the palace water system when an elaborate vaulted conduit house was built 'towards the great door of the hall' in 1443–4. It is apparent that the palace of Westminster had long enjoyed its own water system. In 1260 there is a reference to repairs to 'the conduit of water which is carried underground to the King's lavatory and to other places there', while in 1233 one Master William the conduit-maker was sent 'to bring water to our court of Westminster in accordance with what we have told him'. In 1341 there is mention in the accounts of the purchase of 'five fathoms' of wire for cleansing the conduit pipe in the king's mews, and in 1373 five workmen were engaged to examine the pipes 'because the water was lacking in the hall and the kitchens and did not come through'.

Water was sometimes piped to *baths*: in the Westminster accounts for 1275 we read of payments made to Robert the Goldsmith for keys (taps) to the laver in the bathroom, some of which had heads fashioned in the shape of leopards. Most unusually,

Edward III appears to have enjoyed hot and cold water on tap: in 1351 (again, at Westminster) one Robert Foundour was paid 56s 8d 'for two large bronze keys for the king's bath-tub for conducting hot and cold water into the baths'. The English term for a bath-house was *stew*: at Langley in 1368 'a square lead for heating water for the stews' is mentioned. This may imply that hot water was conducted to the bath by a lead pipe, though the more usual method was to carry it to the tubs in large earthenware jugs. The Westminster account for 1325 provides a vivid description of a high-status medieval bathroom:

> William de Wynchelse for 3 boards . . . for crests and filetts of the bathing tub. For 3 oak boards . . . for making the covering of the said tub, 6 ft. long [1.8 metres] and 2½ feet broad [0.76 metres]. For 100 fagetts for heating and drying the stuwes. For a small barrell, 2 bokettes and a bowl for carrying water to the stuwes . . . carpenters working on the covering of the bathing tub and the screen in front of the said tub . . . for 6 pieces of stone for making a slabbing in front of the screen of the said tub in the King's ground-floor chamber . . . for 24 mattis, at 2d. each, to put on the flore and pavement of the King's chamber on account of the cold.

Drains were often referred to as *swallows* and most of the numerous legends concerning the presence of underground tunnels in castles are due to the existence of such arrangements (see TUNNELS AND SECRET PASSAGES). Most 'tunnels' were drainage systems by which effluent was removed from the precincts of a castle. (However, it is undoubtedly true that many sieges were concluded when attackers succeeded in gaining access to the drains.) KITCHENS were almost invariably provided with drains. Reference is made at Leeds Castle in 1369 to 'an iron grate fixed in the pavement to receive water', while at the Tower of London in 1386 26s 8d was paid 'for making a pit with stone walls by way of a swallow beside the Lieutenant's kitchen for the receiving of all water falling there'. In 1260 payment was made for 'making a conduit through which the refuse of the King's kitchens at Westminster flows into the Thames, which conduit the King ordered to be made on account of the stink of the dirty water which was carried through his halls, which was wont to affect the health of people frequenting the same halls'.

Drainage channels were often made of stone and set within the thickness of walls: at Wardour Castle, for example, a number of stone-lined drains from the various latrine chutes all converged into a main drain sloping down towards the lake. (It was in this drain, where it passed directly beneath the south wall, that a mine was fired during the siege of 1643.) The original meaning of the word *garderobe* was 'cloak-room' or 'wardrobe' – a chamber in which clothes were kept. However, it was frequently used in the medieval period to describe a latrine. These were often located in close proximity to a wardrobe: the 1365 accounts for Hadleigh Castle record a payment of *2d* 'for mending a latrine within the King's wardrobe'. (It has been suggested, not convincingly, that fumes from a privy assisted in the preservation of fabrics in the adjacent wardrobe.) The term 'privy chamber' may also imply a small chamber containing a latrine, though it is more commonly used to describe the private apartment of a lord in contradistinction to the great or public chamber (*see* PRIVY CHAMBER). In 1248 Henry III instructed the sheriff of Wiltshire to 'cause the fireplace of our wardrobe at Clarendon to be pulled down and a new one built, and renovate and enlarge the privy chamber of the same and make a wardrobe thirty feet in length [nine metres] in front of the said privy chamber'. The terms *withdraught* and *draught* were commonly used to describe latrines, as was *gong* or *gonge*, a *gongfermor* being a man whose job it was to scour and cleanse (*fey*) cess-pits. Castles were usually liberally provided with garderobes, the majority of which comprised a single cell at the end of a short, crooked passage within the thickness of a wall from which a shaft vented to a cesspool beneath. These would required periodic cleansing, though in a few fortunate cases the foot of the wall would be washed by a river (a water-filled moat must have been particularly noisome when stagnant!). Other types of latrine consisted of benches in stone cubicles supported on corbels that projected from a curtain wall or simple timber cabins built out over a moat (*see* GARDEROBE).

POINTED ARCH *see* ARCH

POITRAL *see* HORSES AND HORSE-HARNESS

POLE ARM Any hand-held weapon incorporating a variety of axe blades, hammer heads, beaks and spikes. The term *pole* refers to the 'poll' or head of the weapon, not to the shaft (*see* WEAPONS AND HARNESS).

POLE AXE The weapon of the foot-soldier: a combined cutting blade, hammer and thrusting spike,

set on a wooden shaft between 1.2m and 1.8m (4ft and 6ft) in length, which was capable of shattering plate armour. Metal strips below the head protected the shaft from a lopping blow while guards were often fitted to protect the hand from blades sliding down the shaft (*see* WEAPONS AND HARNESS).

POLEYNS Plate armour to protect the knee. Poleyns were first used in the mid-twelfth century when they were attached to quilted thigh protectors (*cuisses*). By the mid-fourteenth century they had acquired small projecting wings, and from 1370 they were joined by articulated lames to plate cuisses. (*See also* ARMOUR *and* HELMETS)

POLISSOIR Stones or masonry in which grooves have been made by the sharpening of tools, weapons and arrow-heads. They are usually found as a series of straight, parallel grooves and have the appearance of being highly polished, quite unlike the smoothest natural rock surface. (*see also* ARCHERY)

POMMEL (i) The round end of a sword hilt, often decorated with an heraldic device.
(ii) The upward-projecting front of a saddle bow.

PONS *see* ARMOUR

PORT From the Latin *porta* meaning 'gate' and *portus* meaning 'harbour' or 'port of entry', a place-name element which in Old English could mean 'harbour', 'town' or 'gate'. Portchester in Hampshire was 'the Roman fort by the harbour', while Langport in Somerset means 'long market-place'. The term *port* suggests that some form of control was exercised over those who wished to enter a harbour or market for commercial purposes (*see* MARKETS *and* TOWNS). When applied to castles, the term clearly implies a gateway or entrance passage through which movement was strictly controlled (*see* SALLY-PORT).

PORTCULLIS A grille that could be lowered to block an entrance passage. Portcullises were usually made of wood reinforced with iron and had iron spikes that dropped into an earthen surface below. A portcullis was intended to form a barrier within the GATE PASSAGE, against which a ram would have little effect, and to protect a pair of gates that could not be forced open when the portcullis was lowered. Keep-gatehouses that were designed to be defended independently would have portcullises and doors at both ends of the passage and these would be closed against an attack from outside the castle and from within the bailey (*see* GATEHOUSE). Most gate passages contained at least two sets of gates and portcullises, with so-called MURDER HOLES in the stone vault through which water could be poured to extinguish fires set at the foot of the timber gates. In many castles there were more than two portcullises: at Caernarfon, for example, the passage in the King's Gate contained five pairs of doors, six portcullises and numerous murder holes. SALLY-PORTS and the entrances to towers were often protected by portcullises or hinged iron grilles (*see* YETT). Marten's Tower at Chepstow Castle was built by Roger Bigod in 1285–93. Internally it comprised a suite of self-contained apartments on three floors above an unlit basement, a refuge for Bigod and his family that could be isolated by means of portcullises at the doorway from the bailey and the two entrances from the wall-walks on either side of the tower. (Marten's Tower was later used as a PRISON.) At St Briavel's Castle in the Forest of Dean the doorways to the PORTER'S LODGES on either side of the gate passage were provided with small portcullises which isolated the lodges from the passage.

Portcullises were raised and lowered by means of a windlass located in a chamber above the gate passage, the movement assisted by counterweights. This arrangement could be singularly inconvenient when the chamber was used for residential and domestic purposes. At Harlech Castle, for example, the mechanism was located in the gatehouse chapel, while at Kidwelly the raised inner portcullis occupied one end of the constable's hall and the winding gear for the outer portcullis and drawbridge were located in a small chamber between the flanking towers. The capstan and lifting gear were constructed of timber, the joints and moving parts strengthened with iron. The complex defensive arrangements at Caerphilly Castle include an unusual portcullis that was *raised* to block the entrance passage to the Watergate. When 'opened', it would be lowered into the channel of the spillway.

Only a small number of original portcullises remain *in situ* (at Warwick and Windsor Castles, for example) though the grooves into which they slotted have survived in the gate passages of most castles. A late thirteenth-century portcullis, installed by Edward I in the Byward Tower at the Tower of London, was recently lowered for the first time for several centuries. It was found to be 3.5m (11ft 6in) high and to have been modified, possibly in the early sixteenth century, to accommodate firearms. The lower section had been boarded to form a barricade to protect hand-gunners and a round cannon port inserted which could be closed with a horizontal

Portcullis mechanism in the Byward Tower at the Tower of London.

cross-bar and vertical iron bolt. Although portcullises are mentioned in contemporary accounts, details are rarely given. One exception is in the 1374 accounts for Leeds Castle where '8 portecolys, to which belong 20 pukes with 20 plates of iron, 14 long iron plates, and transverse iron plates, and 188 nails for re-ironing the same portecolys' were listed in the castle's stores.

PORTER'S LODGE *or* GATEKEEPER'S LODGE

A chamber adjacent to the GATE PASSAGE in a GATEHOUSE or BARBICAN from which access to and egress from a castle were controlled by a gatekeeper or porter. A porter's lodge was usually (though not invariably) positioned at the outer end of the gate passage so that the porter could inspect the credentials of anyone wishing to gain access before admitting them beyond the first (outer) gate. A loophole in the outer wall enabled the porter to observe anyone approaching the castle and a second loophole in the wall of the gate passage allowed for closer inspection. These loopholes were often provided with external wooden shutters that could be secured from within: rebates for the shutters in the walls of the east gatehouse at Rhuddlan Castle are particularly well preserved. In many cases a small fireplace and GARDEROBE were provided so that the porter was not obliged to leave his post. The draw-bars of the outer gates often intruded into the chamber through holes in the walls and sometimes the mechanism of a turning bridge was controlled from within the lodge (see DRAWBRIDGE). One of the best surviving examples of a porter's lodge is at Wardour Castle (1393). On either side of the entrance passage are vaulted rooms below the hall, one of these being the porter's lodge, a self-contained chamber with a garderobe and loophole. Significantly it is the only room that could be entered directly from the gate passage.

In larger castles the outer gate passage is often controlled by a *guardroom*. At Warkworth Castle there are two, one on either side of the passage, each with three cruciform loopholes in the outer walls that enabled the guard to survey the approaches to the castle and the south curtain walls on either side of the projecting gatehouse. There are three further loopholes in the walls of the passage itself but no doorways: the guardrooms could only be entered from the courtyard. Access to the keep at Warkworth was also controlled by a porter's lodge. In an emergency the keep could be isolated from the rest of the castle by withdrawing a bolt that would release a hinged wooden walkway to reveal a pit beneath. At St Briavel's Castle the doorways to the porter's lodges on either side of the gate passage were provided with small PORTCULLISES which isolated the lodges from the passage. Beneath one of these lodges is a 'bottleneck prison' or OUBLIETTE.

PORTLAND STONE Hard oolitic limestone from the Isle of Portland, Dorset.

PORTMANMOOT A meeting of the burgesses (the *portmen*) appointed to administer the affairs of a borough.

PORTS *see* QUAYS

PORTWAY *see* MARKETS

POSSE COMITATUS *see* LAW AND ORDER, MILITIA *and* RECRUITMENT AND ORGANISATION (MILITARY)

POSTERN A pedestrian gateway in the curtain wall of a castle, fortified town or monastic close. The term SALLY-PORT is often used synonymously, though this had a specific military purpose.
(*See also* QUAYS *for* water gates)

POT HELM *see* GREAT HELM

POULTRY, THE *see* KITCHENS

POURPOINT *see* ARMOUR

PRECEPTORY *see* COMMANDERY

PRESENCE CHAMBER The reception room in which a lord conducted the formal business of his office. In a royal castle the presence chamber was a state apartment where councils were held and in which the king would receive distinguished guests, ambassadors, emissaries and delegations. At Conwy Castle the king's pentagonal presence chamber (distinguished by fine window tracery) was approached through a series of three rooms, the first of which was a small ante-chamber or 'waiting room'.

PRICK SPURS *see* WEAPONS AND HARNESS

PRIE-DIEU From the French 'pray God', a small prayer-desk for private devotions.

PRIMOGENITURE The state or fact of being first-born; the custom of right of succession and inheritance by a first-born child. *Male primogeniture* further restricted inheritance to a first-born son. *Ultimogeniture* was inheritance by the youngest son.

PRINCE BISHOP *see* PALATINATE

'PRINCE OF WALES'S FEATHERS' The so-called 'Prince of Wales's Feathers' device, which comprises three white ostrich feathers enfiling a gold coronet, is the badge of the heir apparent to the *English* throne, not all of whom have been invested as princes of Wales. It is likely that the ostrich feather badge was first used by Edward, the Black Prince, who inherited it through his mother, Philippa of Hainault.

PRINTING Although printing was known in China it probably developed independently in western Europe and emerged late in the medieval period, stimulated by an increased demand for books and a corresponding increase in manuscript production. The mechanical problems of producing 'artificial' script were resolved by the Mainz-born goldsmith Johann Gutenberg (*c.* 1400–68) whose method of printing was to remain the standard for three-and-a-half centuries. In 1455 he completed the first printed book, the *Gutenberg Bible*, in an edition of two hundred copies printed with hand-cut lead type-fonts on paper and vellum in the German Gothic script of contemporary manuscripts. By 1500 some sixty printing centres had developed in Germany while in England the first press was established in the precincts of Westminster Abbey in 1476 by William Caxton (*c.* 1422–91) who had learned his trade at Bruges. The first dated printed English book, *The Dictes or Sayengis of the Philosophres*, was produced in the following year. Caxton went on to produce more than eighty texts including the works of Malory, Gower and Chaucer as well as translations of Virgil's *Aeneid* and the French romances.

PRISONS For some reason the word 'dungeon' seems always to have been associated with a dark, dank, subterranean prison. In fact, the term is derived from the Latin *dominus* meaning 'lord' from which evolved the Old French *donjon* or 'lord's tower' (*see* DONJON). The term implies feudal authority of which the great tower or keep was a powerful and enduring symbol. It was in the donjon that a Norman lord dispensed justice and in many cases it was in the donjon that malefactors were imprisoned 'at the lord's pleasure'. But in practice, most dimly lit undercrofts were storerooms, secured against theft and stone-vaulted to prevent the spread of fire.

Surprisingly few castles in England had purpose-built prisons, high-ranking prisoners enjoying comparative comfort in secure apartments or even suites of rooms that had usually been built for purely residential purposes. Undoubtedly the most important royal prison was at the Tower of London where the Beauchamp Tower was used almost exclusively to lodge prisoners of rank during the fifteenth and sixteenth centuries (*see* GRAFFITI). At the Tower and elsewhere, prisoners were often detained for long periods. Llywelyn ap Gruffudd imprisoned his elder brother Owain for twenty-two years (from 1255) in the tower of Dolbadarn Castle in north Wales, while the regicide Henry Marten was confined for over twenty years in the south-east tower (Marten's Tower) at Chepstow Castle, ending his days there in 1680. Although not intended as a prison, Marten's Tower was ideally suited for the purpose. Built by Roger Bigod III from 1287 to 1293, internally it provided a suite of accommodation arranged on three storeys above an unlit basement. The ground floor was lit by three arrow loops and would have served as a guardroom while the upper floors were well lit and provided with fireplaces, latrines and a private chapel. Ironically, the PORTCULLISES that were originally intended to secure the tower as a refuge for Bigod and his family may later have been used to frustrate escape.

The traditional perception of a dungeon is reinforced by the grim basement chamber at Warwick Castle (Caesar's Tower), the rock-hewn *pit prison* at Newark and the sinister *oubliette* in the Dungeon Tower of Pembroke Castle. From the French '*oublier*' meaning 'to forget', the oubliette was an underground prison cell entered by means of a hatch in the floor above. It was also known as a *bottle dungeon* because of its shape and single narrow entrance. Anyone lowered into the oubliette knew that he was being 'consigned to oblivion'. All the Edwardian castles in north Wales were provided with prisons – presumably on the assumption that all Welshmen were recalcitrant and would remain so. At Harlech both the north-east Prison Tower and the south-east Mortimer Tower had deep circular oubliettes, each with only a narrow slit for light and air, sloping upward steeply through the thickness of the wall. The Prison Tower at Conwy Castle (1283) is differently arranged from the other towers in the outer ward. Here there are four floors, while the others have only three, and it is almost as if the existence of the prison was deliberately concealed. The entrance to the basement of the tower was by a narrow doorway inconspicuously located in the side of one of the window embrasures in the adjoining Great Hall. From here an intra-mural passage behind the hall fireplace leads to the foot of the tower staircase and from here five steps lead down through two doors and a right-angled turn to an opening in the wall. This opening was about 1.2m (4ft) above the floor which was almost certainly of stone flags, supported on ten massive close-set timbers. This floor conveyed the illusion that this was the bottom of the tower. But below the level of the beams was a circular pit with smooth walls and a narrow ventilation shaft barely 46cm (18in) square inserted just below the ceiling in a wall 3.7m (12ft) thick. Again, this was an oubliette, entered by means of a trapdoor in the floor above.

At Corfe Castle the entire west bailey appears to have been used for custodial purposes. This may have been the prison referred to as 'Malemit' in the royal accounts for 1285. Triangular in shape, it is divided into two courts: the Inner Gaol Court (where executions took place – the remains of a 'hanging stone' or gallows have been identified on the inner face of the curtain wall) and the Outer Gaol Court which was separated from the rest of the castle by a curtain wall. There is a tower at each corner of the triangular bailey: that to the north is believed to have contained a prison chapel, the south tower is still known as the Gaoler's Tower, and in the western corner the octagonal Butavant or Dungeon Tower once contained an oubliette. It was at Corfe, in 1211, that King John incarcerated Maude de Braose and her son, committing them to a long and painful death by starvation. Near the outer gatehouse, and at the opposite end of the castle, there is also the Correction Cell Tower. There is no evidence here of an oubliette and it is likely that the tower contained a cell in which members of the garrison were held on charges of indiscipline and for minor misdemeanours.

Many medieval castles were used as prisons and courtrooms long after they were abandoned as fortresses or residences. The gatehouse of St Briavel's Castle in the Forest of Dean served as a prison for those who failed to observe the harsh FOREST laws, while the main gatehouse of Caerphilly Castle has survived remarkably intact because of its long use as a BRIDEWELL. Guildford Castle was used as the county gaol for nearly four centuries (c. 1200–1600) and in 1381 was a clearing house for prisoners taken during the PEASANTS' REVOLT. At Lincoln the castle bailey is still disfigured by assize and prison buildings (the County Gaol closed in 1878) while the shell-keep encloses the graves of hanged prisoners. The keeps of Carmarthen and Haverfordwest also housed county gaols, while Lancaster Castle remains in use as a courthouse and prison, the oldest working penal institution in Europe.

PRIVATUM SIGILLUM *see* PRIVY SEAL *and* SEALS

PRIVY A latrine (*see* GARDEROBE).

PRIVY CHAMBER First referred to in c. 1400, the private chamber of a lord or constable, in contradistinction to the Great Chamber which was reserved for the public everyday life of a lord (*see* SOLAR). More private than the HALL, but not used for sleeping, the privy chamber could be occupied without interruption or disturbance. Confusingly, the term is sometimes found in contemporary documents as a synonym for 'latrine' or GARDEROBE. As the name suggests, the *Lady Chamber* was a privy chamber designated for use by the ladies of the lord's family.

PRIVY KITCHEN *see* KITCHENS

PRIVY SEAL The *privatum sigillum* was, in England, a twelfth-century innovation and was held by the clerks of the king's chamber. It was attached to documents that were afterwards to pass the GREAT SEAL, particularly instructions to the

Exchequer or CHANCERY. It was also appended to lesser documents which nevertheless required royal approval. By the fourteenth century the authority of the privy seal rivalled that of the Great Seal and in the reign of Edward II (1307–27) a *secretum* was introduced for the sovereign's personal use (*see* SEALS).

PROOFING Testing a piece of plate armour by shooting at it (*see* ARMOUR).

PROPRIETARY CHAPEL *see* CHAPELS

PROSPECT TOWER *or* **VIEWPOINT TOWER** A late medieval tower erected to 'command the prospect' or distant view of a lord's DEER PARK and estates. These towers were usually attached to MANOR HOUSES and provided both additional accommodation and a reminder of a family's chivalric past. Lord Lovell's fifteenth-century prospect tower at Minster Lovell and the tower at Stanton Harcourt, built by Sir Robert Harcourt in the 1460s, are good examples. Typically, Harcourt's tower had a fine chamber on the top storey, beneath a crenellated parapet, with a private chapel on the ground floor. The term was later used to describe towers that were built for similar purposes in the eighteenth and nineteenth centuries.

PROVISIONS OF OXFORD (1258) *see* BARONS' WAR, THE

PURBECK MARBLE *see* MARBLE

PURLIEU (i) Disafforested land on the periphery of a forest.
(ii) Land added to an ancient forest without authority.

PURLIN A horizontal beam running parallel to the ridge of a roof and carrying the common rafters.

PURSUIVANT A junior officer of arms beneath the rank of herald (*see* ARMORY *and* COLLEGE OF ARMS).

PUTLOG HOLES A *putlog* was a beam inserted into a hole in the masonry of a wall to support a HOARDING or scaffolding for building or repairs. Putlog holes are often visible in a castle's masonry, either in horizontal lines immediately below a parapet (where they supported a hoarding) or ascending diagonally across a wall (where they supported scaffolding). It has been suggested that

Putlog holes in the keep of Ludlow Castle, Shropshire. The larger, square holes in the foreground are beam-holes which supported the cross members of a floor.

building materials were hauled up inclined planes of planks that were affixed to a wall by means of putlogs. Putlog holes should not be confused with drainage holes or with BEAM-HOLES which are of similar appearance but larger and perform an entirely different function.
(*See also* BATTLEMENTS *and* SCAFFOLDING AND CRANES)

Q

QUADRANGULAR CASTLES A term applied by some historians to castles, mostly dating from the thirteenth and fourteenth centuries, of rectilinear plan: usually delineated by a masonry curtain wall, corner towers and a gatehouse located at the mid-

point of one side. The quadrangular plan was particularly suited to level ground where MOATS AND WATER DEFENCES compensated for an absence of natural protection. A fine thirteenth-century example is Barnwell Castle, built (without licence) by Berengar le Moine in *c.* 1264. It has an unusually thick curtain wall surrounding a rhomboidal courtyard, with four round corner towers, two of which have smaller round towers (containing latrines) projecting from them. The gatehouse, in this case adjacent to a corner tower, anticipates later Edwardian GATEHOUSES with its long, vaulted gate passage flanked by a pair of strong U-shaped towers. There is rarely a KEEP in this type of castle, residential and domestic buildings being ranged around the courtyard and supported by the curtain wall. At Barnwell and many other thirteenth-century quadrangular castles these buildings were almost certainly of timber construction, though the towers were also used for residential purposes (*see* TIMBER-FRAME BUILDINGS). In Wales Kidwelly was originally built as a quadrangular castle (1274), comprising a square courtyard with curtain walls and uniform, cylindrical corner towers and containing a stone-built range of hall and solar. Within a few years a semicircular outer bailey was constructed on three sides of the original castle, with a magnificent gatehouse and a replacement hall. Courtyard buildings were rarely integrated into the curtain walls that supported them, not even at Maxstoke Castle which was built as late as *c.* 1346. However, by the end of the fourteenth century there was a marked degree of integration between domestic buildings and defences. Quadrangular castles were by then effectively four ranges of buildings surrounding a courtyard, as at Bodiam and Bolton Castles which are sometimes described as courtyard castles (*see* COURT AND COURTYARD).

QUARREL *see* ARCHERY *and* MASONRY

QUARRIES *see* MASONRY *and* SLATES AND TILES

QUARTER DAYS *see* MICHAELMAS

QUARTERING *see* MARSHALLING

QUARTER SESSIONS The quarterly meetings of the justices of a county, riding or county town which originated in 1361 when Keepers of the Peace became Justices of the Peace with authority to determine cases (*see* LAW AND ORDER). From

1363 they began to meet four times a year, at Easter, Midsummer, Michaelmas and Epiphany. In 1461 indictments that had previously been heard by the Sheriff's Tourn were transferred to quarter sessions. These were criminal cases concerning offences such as riot, murder, assault and poaching, and the quarter sessions were not concerned with civil matters or with cases of treason or forgery. The Tudors gave the justices wide-ranging new powers and responsibilities, and in carrying out these duties they gradually replaced the sheriffs in the administration of local affairs.

QUATREFOIL A figure having four radiating stylised 'petals', found both as an architectural motif and as an heraldic device (*see* FOILS).

QUAYS A *water gate* is a fortified gate leading from the interior of a castle or walled town directly to a river or the sea. In some cases boats could be unloaded inside a water gate passage: at Newport Castle, for example, a remarkable fourteenth-century water gate has survived within a square tower with flanking turrets and an outer archway that opens on to the River Usk. Vessels could enter at high tide and unload their cargoes which were stored in cellars beneath the castle courtyard. The best known (and most infamous) water gate is the so-called Traitors' Gate at the Tower of London which was accessed directly from the Thames. St Thomas's Gate, as it was originally known, would have been in constant use as an entrance to the Tower throughout the medieval period. It assumed its sinister appellation in the sixteenth century when various traitors (beginning with the duke of Buckingham in 1521) were conveyed by water from trial at Westminster to the Tower for imprisonment or execution. A second 'privy' water gate was built in *c.* 1350 for Edward III beneath his chambers to the east of the Wakefield Tower.

Many castles were provisioned by river craft and sea-going vessels, water-borne transport being the most efficient means of carrying bulky goods. Indeed, Edward I's strategy for the conquest and colonisation of Gwynedd depended on the creation of a ring of coastal castles all of which could be supplied by ship (*see* WALES, CONQUEST OF). Rhuddlan Castle (1277–82) was built on the site of an earlier Norman fortification, but in order to make it accessible to supplies and relief by sea Edward ordered the construction of a new deep-water canal, 'a great dyke leading from the sea to the castle', some 3km (2 miles) long, together with a fortified quay designed to take a 40-ton vessel. The diversion of the River Clwyd was an extraordinary under-

taking for the time, and one that would have required an average of seventy-five FOSSATORES working continuously for six days a week throughout the first three years of the castle's construction. A POSTERN (now called the River Gate) and landing stage provided access to the outer ward from rowing boats, while another larger gate (the Dock Gate) was constructed next to the quay where it was protected by a self-contained, four-storey tower (Gillot's Tower) that projected from the south-west corner of the outer ward.

Harlech (1283–9), where the sea once lapped at the foot of the great rock on which the castle stands, was serviced by a narrow flight of steps known as the 'Way from the Sea'. This ascended the rock face from a dock with a water gate, drawbridge and glacis and was protected by a parapet wall. From the water gate 118 shallow steps climb to an intermediate turret with a drawbridge, skilfully sited within an awkward re-entrant of the rock and protected from above by the south-west tower of the castle. From this Upper Gate, a further flight of 19 steps leads to a gate at the foot of the north-west tower. Siege engines, located on platforms carved into the cliff-top in the outer ward, protected the water gate and sea-approaches below.

The Castle Dock at Beaumaris (1295–*c.* 1330, but never completed) is the most perfect of all British medieval quays. Beaumaris means 'beautiful marsh' and the castle's level, low-lying site overlooking the Menai Strait enabled Master JAMES OF ST GEORGE to construct a dock that allowed fully laden sea-going vessels to approach the castle at high tide. The quay was located immediately to the side of the castle's main entrance gate (the 'Gate Next the Sea') while a second gate, in the outer curtain, enabled smaller ships to be unloaded directly into the outer ward. A 3.6m (12ft) wide spur wall (known since the nineteenth century as Gunners' Walk) enclosed the eastern side of the dock. Within this wall a passage led to a water mill in a projecting turret and sluice gates that controlled the flow of tidal water into the castle moat. It also provided a shooting platform overlooking the dock, with crenellations and arrow loops on either side, while a raised machicolated deck at one end may have housed a siege engine. On the western side the town wall terminated at the end of the quay which was protected at its northern end by a tower attached to the outer gatehouse. (The town wall was not built until the beginning of the fifteenth century though it was evidently envisaged in the original plan.) What is most striking about the Castle Dock at Beaumaris is its size: to modern eyes it appears almost to have been constructed in miniature.

In order to make Rhuddlan Castle (1277–82) accessible to supply and relief by sea, Edward I ordered the construction of a new deep-water canal, 'a great dyke leading from the sea to the castle', some 3 km (2 miles) long, together with a fortified quay (entered to the right of the square tower) designed to take a 40-ton vessel.

This, in turn, illustrates just how small a medieval 40-ton vessel could be!

Conwy and Caernarfon Castles (both begun in 1283) were served by harbours, though both also had water gates. The Caernarfon water gate, located at the foot of the Eagle Tower, led via a passage with portcullis and strongly barred double doors to a basement ante-chamber through which anyone travelling by water would enter the castle. However, there is clear evidence that a far more ambitious entrance was planned. The intention of the thirteenth-century builders was to erect a wide arched gateway against the side of the Eagle Tower through which water-borne supplies could have been carried into the castle ditch at high tide to a quay at the foot of the Well Tower, and thence via a doorway in the tower to the storerooms and kitchens beyond. To the left side of the Eagle Tower may be seen the slot that was intended for a portcullis, the springers

and jambs for the great archway and two doorways in the face of the tower, one above the other, which would have provided access to the chambers above the gate. The water gate at Conwy Castle was a very much more modest affair. Although little has survived the building of Telford's suspension bridge (1826), it is clear from early illustrations that a stepped ramp once curved down and round the wall of the East Barbican to the rocks below where (presumably) there would once have been a timber landing-stage for use at high tide. Unlike Caernarfon, the Conwy water gate would have been used only as a private entrance to the suite of state rooms at the east end of the castle.

At both towns supplies for the castles and merchandise for the English boroughs (*see* PLANTATION TOWNS) would have been landed at quays located between the TOWN WALL and the foreshore. At Conwy this section of town wall

The castle dock and 'Gate Next the Sea' at Beaumaris Castle, Anglesey.

incorporated four open-backed mural towers (all now converted to dwellings) and a crenellated wall-walk. A POSTERN enabled travellers from the river ferry to gain access to the town, while a twin-towered gatehouse (the Lower Gate), with its portcullis and great double doors, served for many centuries as the principal entrance to Conwy for water-borne goods and travellers. The harbour was enclosed to the north within a substantial spur wall that projected into the river and acted both as a defence and a breakwater. The 1286 building account indicates that this wall terminated in a round tower at the seaward end. The effects of erosion on these walls must have been considerable for within twenty years of their construction the 'poor burgesses of Conwy' were petitioning the king for an annual grant of £20 'to save the wall and towers of the town which are in great peril from the tides of the river'.

The quay at Caernarfon was originally a timber structure but was rebuilt in stone in the early fourteenth century following the rising of 1294–5. It occupies the space between the town wall and the Menai foreshore and is protected by two open-backed mural bastions and a substantial twin-towered gatehouse (the Porth-yr-Aur or Golden Gate) and small projecting BARBICAN. In the gatehouse the portcullis grooves have survived, as has a fragment of a projecting latrine at wall-walk level, but the windows and battlements date from the nineteenth century and the building now houses the Royal Welsh Yacht Club. When viewed across the Seiont estuary from the west, the quay, with its unbroken stretch of town walls, splendidly retains its medieval atmosphere.

(*See also* FOUNDATIONS *and* TOWN WALLS)

QUEEN POST *see* KING POST

QUIA EMPTORES *see* LORD OF THE MANOR

QUILLIONS The arms of the cross-guard of a sword handle.
(*See also* WEAPONS AND HARNESS)

QUINTAIN, QUINTIN *or* **QUINTAL** An upright pole with pivoted cross-beam, at one end of which was affixed a shield and on the other a log of wood or sand-filled sack suspended from a chain. It was used for tilting practice – the target being the shield and the punishment for tardiness being a firm clout on the back of the head from the log or sack! A more basic form, the *quintin*, comprised a tall board fixed in the earth, and used as a target for tilting practice.
(*See also* MILITARY TRAINING)

QUIVER A case for holding arrows or crossbow bolts. Crossbow quivers were usually made of wood covered with rawhide, with an opening (and sometimes a lid) made of hardened leather and a back reinforced with an iron plate.
(*See also* ARCHERY)

QUOIN From the French *coin* meaning 'corner' or 'angle', a quoin is the external angle of a building and *quoins* or *quoin stones* are the dressed stones forming the angle.

R

RAFTER Any of the sloping beams within the framework of a roof. *Principal rafters* are those which carry the PURLINS.

RAG *and* **RAGSTONE** A hard, coarse stone which is not FREESTONE (*see* MASONRY).

RAGGLE The remains of a roof line preserved in the stonework of an adjacent building.

RAGMAN A parchment document with seals appended.

RAGWORK Rubble walling composed of polygonal stones (*see* RUBBLE *and* MASONRY).

RAINURES Beams for raising a DRAWBRIDGE.

RAINWATER HEAD A box-shaped metal structure (usually of lead or cast iron) in which water from a gutter is collected and discharged into a down-pipe.

RAM (BATTERING) A battering ram for use against a gate or at the base of a wall, often contained within a timber shed, from the ridge beam of which it was suspended, or protected by a layer of earth (*see* SIEGES).

RAM (PILE-DRIVER) *see* FOUNDATIONS

RAMP In post-medieval fortifications, an inclined track on the rear slope of a rampart to facilitate the movement of troops and guns on to the level surface of the TERRE-PLEIN.

RAMPANT Of an heraldic beast when standing on one hind leg and with the other legs waving fiercely in the air (*see* BEASTS, HERALDIC).

RAMPANT ARCH *see* ARCH

RAMPART A broad-topped defensive wall of masonry or excavated earth surrounding a settlement, castle or other fortified site.
(*See also* BATTLEMENTS)

RANSOM There were three ways of gaining financially from war. The least lucrative was pay: a retainer of whatever rank would receive a daily wage, together with the expenses of maintaining his retinue, and those magnates who held military or administrative offices would be rewarded accordingly. Secondly, there were the 'spoils of war': a conquering army considered itself free to take anything of value from the enemy – armour, weapons, clothing, stores and, especially prized, jewels, plate and even furniture and livestock. In the eleventh and twelfth centuries booty was a vital source of income, helping a knight to maintain his increasingly expensive horses, weapons and armour. However, the most important source of income was a ransom. The capture of important prisoners could result in massive rewards: Thomas Beauchamp, earl of Warwick (1329–69), demanded an £8,000 ransom for the archbishop of Sens, captured during the HUNDRED YEARS WAR. This was the largest ransom paid in the fourteenth century and is the equivalent of millions of pounds today. There was a constant stream of noble and knightly prisoners to English castles during the French wars and most of these were exchanged for ransoms, though negotiations could be protracted. The most illustrious prisoner of the period, the duke of Orléans, captured at Agincourt in 1415, was lodged in considerable comfort in the Tower of London for more than twenty years while his huge ransom was being raised and paid off. During the Hundred Years War the English troops' lust for booty was such that special regulations had to be introduced to stop men brawling over their 'perquisites'. The king retained the most important castles, land and prisoners while the contracts and sub-contracts of the indenture system were applied to the rest (*see* RECRUIT-MENT AND ORGANISATION). Usually the senior party took one-third, an ordinary soldier paying a third of his plunder to his officer, and so on up the chain of command.

This accumulated wealth, a direct consequence of the wars in France, is evident in the remodelling of many castles and in the magnificent church MONUMENTS, CHANTRY CHAPELS and collegiate churches which were financed from ransoms and the profits of successful *chevauchées*. Sir Hugh Calveley (d. 1393), for example, a freebooting captain of the Hundred Years War, used the profits of his notorious raiding parties to re-found his parish church at Bunbury, Cheshire, as a college in 1386. It was no coincidence that the 'first great flowering of English domestic architecture' (McFarlane) coincided with the Hundred Years War, or that the chivalric notion of a brotherhood of knights should have found expression in the founding of the Order of the Garter in 1348 (*see* CHIVALRY *and* GARTER, THE MOST NOBLE ORDER OF THE). The English nobility, anxious to proclaim its wealth, influence and self-esteem, indulged in an orgy of building. Thomas Beauchamp was at Crécy and Poitiers. From 1344 he was Marshal of England and participated in nearly every French campaign. There is no surviving record of his total profits but from Poitiers alone he collected the ransoms of two wealthy priests, the bishop of Le Mans and the archbishop of Sens (*see above*). It was these ransoms that financed the rebuilding of the gatehouse and east façade of Warwick Castle, not to improve the castle's defences but as a public declaration of his wealth and status – 'less a barrier than a stage set' (Platt).

RATH From the Gaelic *ràth*, meaning 'circular fort', a defended Irish farmstead usually contained within a circular rampart and ditch. Examples date from the Bronze Age to the early medieval period, though many are recognisable only from the air or from the common *rath* place-name element.

RAVELIN In post-medieval fortifications, a triangular detached work in the ditch between two bastions.

RAVENS It is probable that there have always been ravens at the Tower of London: they were once common in London's streets and were protected for the service they rendered as scavengers. There is a legend that the Tower will fall should the ravens leave and six of their number are therefore carefully guarded by the Yeoman Quartermaster. Each bird receives a weekly allowance of horseflesh and they have their own quarters in a cage by the Lanthorn Tower. Ravens can live to a good age: one, James Crow, resided in the Tower for forty-four years. Until their wings were clipped they would wander from the Tower's precincts; one in particular used to fly off to perch in St Paul's Cathedral and in 1890 took up residence in Kensington Gardens!

READEPTION, THE Henry VI's brief restoration to the English throne, usually given as October 1470 to March 1471. Edward IV's return from exile and his victory at the battle of Tewkesbury in May 1471 led to the final overthrow of his Neville and Lancastrian enemies, the deposition of Henry VI and his recovery of the throne (*see* WARS OF THE ROSES).

REANS *or* REINS Boundary land.

REAVERS Infamous gangs of Scottish marauders whose frequent incursions brought terror to the northern borders of England (*see* MARCH).

REBUS A rebus is a pictorial pun on a name (*non verbis sed rebus*). Many early SEALS include simple rebuses and the concept therefore pre-dates ARMORY. Rebuses were especially popular in medieval circles and were widely used as personal devices and to decorate the fabric of buildings and tombs. At Milton Abbey, Dorset, for example, a stone corbel is carved and painted in the form of a windmill on top of a wine barrel (*tun*), the rebus of Abbot William of Milton. Rebuses should not be confused with armorial badges which served a different purpose (*see* BADGES AND LIVERY), though many badges are effectively rebuses: the Talbot (hound) of the Talbots, for example, and the *hirondelle* (swallow) of the Arundels.
(*See also* GRAFFITI)

RECEIVER A castle administrator in charge of financial affairs, who was responsible for ensuring that taxes, rents and dues were collected and for making the estates profitable (*see* HOUSEHOLD).

RECORDS *see* STATE RECORDS

RECOVERY ROLLS Records relating to property conveyances since the fifteenth century. They are housed at the Public Record Office (*see* APPENDIX II). (*See also* STATE RECORDS)

RECRUITMENT AND ORGANISATION (MILITARY) The Norman element of the army that invaded Anglo-Saxon England in 1066 comprised both the *mediae nobilitatis*, vassals of Duke William and his principal followers, and the *stipendiarii*, cavalrymen who served for wages and whose obligations were defined by less formal oaths of allegiance (*see* FEUDAL SYSTEM). In addition, there were significant numbers of infantry archers and spearmen. Together with the allied forces of Flanders and Brittany, the invading army was one of the most efficient and cohesive military units to have been mustered in the eleventh century. The colonising forces included Normans, French, Flemings, Bretons, assimilated Anglo-Saxons and Welshmen, disinherited noblemen and adventurers, and assorted mercenaries. This apparently disparate group was held together by the force of Duke William's authority and the success of the centralised military and governmental system that he had imposed on his duchy. The military aristocracy had strongly supported his policy of conquest, attracted by the prospect of exercising authority in England on the duke's behalf. By the late 1070s a remarkable degree of stability had been achieved and this led to the gradual demilitarisation of the new Anglo-Norman aristocracy so that only the royal household (the *Familia Regis*) remained as an efficient military structure. This group provided guards and escorts and, when required, would form the nucleus of a larger army. The king's CONSTABLE was responsible for discipline and for the administration of the royal guard and the stables. The baronage also had their military *familia* of household knights under the command of a MARSHAL or constable. On the remote borders of Wales and Scotland William created counties palatine whose overlords were charged with the defence of the realm. In the north a Prince Bishop ruled over the vast territories of his PALATINATE of Durham while in the Marches of Wales the king created the palatine earldoms of Hereford, Shrewsbury and Chester (*see* MARCH). Even though the Anglo-Saxon military élite had been decimated in the aftermath of the Conquest, in some areas the old local military levy (the *fyrd*) survived (*see* MILITIA).

In the twelfth and thirteenth centuries the knights of the royal HOUSEHOLD consisted, for the most part, of young men (*bacheliers*) who held no land of their own and were in receipt of pay, and so were not considered to be members of the feudal aristocracy (*see* KNIGHT BACHELOR). Neither were those, of more lowly origins, who formed an élite corps of mercenaries within the *Familia Regis*, men drawn from throughout the Angevin Empire and beyond who provided an essential professional element in the king's army. Units of the *Familia Regis* served at court (*see* VERGE) and garrisoned the royal castles (*see* CASTLE GUARD) while senior members were often appointed as sheriffs, governors and constables of castles and to other key offices. As the threat of invasion diminished, so feudal military obligations declined and were commuted to money payments (*scutage* = 'shield money'). This enabled the king to hire well-trained and disciplined mercenaries who could serve for longer periods than knights whose obligation to serve with the feudal host was limited to a specific number of weeks. Even so, a theoretical military obligation remained enshrined in law and the Anglo-Norman feudal aristocracy continued to provide military leadership. Again, exceptions were to be found in the Marches of northern England where defence appears to have remained the responsibility of local Anglo-Saxon thanes – indicative, perhaps, of a successful system that required little or no modification. There also existed an ancient form of non-knightly military service that obliged those holding land under *cornage tenancy* to accompany the king whenever he chose to enter Scottish territory. Because of their local knowledge, these men led the vanguard when advancing into Scotland and the rearguard when returning across the border. In the Welsh March non-knightly mounted infantry, known as *'riding men'*, served under the palatine lords.

Toward the end of his reign Henry II (1154–89) carried out a comprehensive review of military obligations in England and in his possessions in France. The *Assize of Arms* of 1181 attempted to impose a degree of uniformity on the obligations of feudal service and in particular to define the equipment that each group was expected to provide. This in turn was assessed according to an individual's wealth rather than his social or military status (*see* ARMOUR (BODY) *and* WEAPONS AND HARNESS).

The system of feudal military obligations continued, in a somewhat *ad hoc* form, into the late thirteenth century. Only on the Scottish border did it remain relatively intact. But it was an entirely inadequate method of raising élite cavalry forces and it was gradually replaced by a system of contract and indenture that developed into BASTARD FEUDAL-ISM. Nevertheless, the old statutory obligation to serve in a local levy remained, every man being assigned a particular task according to his wealth and where he lived: infantry spearman, axe-man, archer and so on. By the mid-thirteenth century the men of Sussex and Kent were considered to be the best archers and many were recruited into the military households of the nobility. The fourteenth century was, of course, the age of the longbow when archers were considered to belong to a professional élite (see ARCHERY). But there was also a corresponding decline in the quality and numbers of those who were recruited to the infantry, even for Edward I's Scottish campaigns. As a result men of highly dubious reputations were recruited: criminals or suspected criminals, vagrants and outlaws – 'the sweepings of the country's stews and gaols'.

By the fourteenth century English military forces were clearly divided into the king's army, based on the royal household, and a very much larger defensive force in the localities. During the fourteenth century the *fyrd* levies were replaced with royal *Commissions of Array*, though the obligations continued to be based on wealth and status. Commissioners now toured the country to select specified numbers of suitable men from each shire or hundred to serve in the local levies. During the HUNDRED YEARS WAR, when the south and south-eastern coasts were especially vulnerable to raids by French privateers, all men aged between sixteen and sixty who lived or held land in the coastal strip (the *terre maritime*) could be summoned to array. They were not normally expected to serve outside their localities and their numbers could be supplemented by men from neighbouring inland shires (see also BEACONS). This coastal militia (the *garde de la mer*) consisted of units (*posse comitatus*) of local men-at-arms, light cavalry and infantry, led by constables under the overall command of the royal commissioners. The cavalry was grouped into units called *constabularies* and the infantry into *millenaries* (1,000 men), *centaines* (100) and *vintaines* (20).

At the beginning of the fourteenth century the knights of the royal household formed a small but effective standing army of élite experienced soldiers, selected to provide both military leadership and managerial acumen. Each knight was usually served by four men-at-arms who operated in units

(*constabularies*) of about twenty men (see MAN-AT-ARMS). For international duties, the boroughs were obliged to provide the king with the numbers of troops specified in their charters and these were supplemented by voluntary groups and specialists such as the Irish *hobelars*, miners from the Forest of Dean and expert longbowmen from the southern counties of England. Military commanders were able to negotiate with the government the number and type of troops the king required and to engage them by means of *indentures of war* which specified the conditions and length of service (see INDENTURE). These troops generally consisted of heavily armoured cavalry, light cavalry, archers and infantry, and recruitment was usually sub-contracted to junior commanders, the lesser nobility and local gentry. Attendance was checked by means of *muster rolls* on which were listed the names of those who had undertaken to provide troops, including the retinues of the nobility and gentry whose heraldic badges (by which their contingents were identified) appeared in the margin of the roll (see BADGES AND LIVERY). Magnate retinues were enlisted through the practice of LIVERY AND MAINTENANCE while foreign mercenaries were often engaged in specialist rôles and as senior commanders in royal and magnate retinues.

RECTANGULAR KEEPS *see* KEEPS

REDAN In post-medieval fortifications, an outwork with two faces forming a projecting angle.

REDOUBT In post-medieval fortifications, a small enclosed defensive position without bastions.

REDUIT A small self-contained defensive position intended to protect a town independent of its CITADEL.

RE-ENTRANT An inward-facing angle, the opposite of SALIENT.

REEVE A man of villein status elected or nominated by his fellow tenants to arrange the day-to-day business of a MANOR and to undertake other duties which varied according to the customs of a particular manor or area. Because of his position the reeve usually represented the tenants in negotiations with the lord of the manor or his steward and, in the absence of specially appointed officers, he was also responsible for the general agricultural policy of the manor and for its livestock.
(*See also* COURT BARON *and* LAW AND ORDER)

REGNAL YEARS In the Middle Ages it was the custom for documents to be dated by reference to the year of a monarch's reign: for example, 3 Henry III would indicate a date of 1218/19, the king's third regnal year beginning on 28 October 1218 and ending on the following 27 October.

REGULATIONS (BUILDING) *see* ORGANISATION (BUILDING)

REIVERS *see* REAVERS

RELIEVING ARCH An arch constructed within a wall in order to relieve the thrust on an adjacent opening (*see* ARCH).

RENDERING *see* FACING MATERIALS

RENTAL *see* MANOR

RERE-ARCH An internal arch to a Gothic window supporting the inner part of a wall's thickness, characteristic of thirteenth-century lancet windows.

REREBRACE *see* ARMOUR *and* VAMBRACE

REREDOS (i) A decorative stone or timber screen, usually supported on a shelf (*predella*), behind and above an altar.
(ii) A wall of earth, stone or brick at the back of a fireplace, sometimes with the additional protection of a fire-back (*see* BRICK BUILDINGS *and* CHIMNEYS).

RESPOND *see* PIER *and* MASONRY

RETAINING To secure the services of a person (*retainer*) by means of a contractual payment (*see* AFFINITY, BASTARD FEUDALISM *and* LIVERY AND MAINTENANCE).

RETARDATAIRE A piece of work executed in the style of an earlier period.

RETICULATED TRACERY *see* GOTHIC ARCHITECTURE

RETINUE A medieval lord surrounded himself with a liveried retinue for political, social, administrative and military purposes and in order to increase his prestige in society and to strengthen his relationship with the local gentry (*see* AFFINITY, BASTARD FEUDALISM *and* LIVERY AND MAINTENANCE). The most important retainers throughout the medieval period were members of a lord's household and the tenants of his estates. Indentured retainers were the exception, and had all but disappeared by 1470. Some late medieval retinues were of considerable size: John of Gaunt, for example, had nearly 100 knights and 200 esquires in his pay, together with significant numbers of other indentured retainers.

RETRENCHMENT Defensive works designed to protect the rear of a fortification, to provide defence in depth and to make good any breach.

RETURN The point at which a length of wall or moulding changes direction, e.g. in the DRIPSTONE of a doorway or window opening.

REVEAL The side surface of a recess, or of an opening of a doorway or window, between the frame and the outer surface of a wall.

REVET To face with masonry.

REVETMENT The retaining wall of a rampart or ditch.

RHAGLAW *and* **RHINGYLL** In medieval Wales, the equivalent of the English steward and bailiff.

RHINGYLL *see* RHAGLAW

RIB *and* **RIBBED VAULT** *see* VAULTING

RIBAUDEQUIN *see* RIBAUDS

RIBAUDS A common fourteenth-century term used to describe guns in general and, more specifically, a lightweight multi-barrelled cannon carried on a cart (*ribaudequin*). It is known that Edward III had several guns clamped together so that they could be fired simultaneously. Undoubtedly the most remarkable example was recorded in 1387, at Verona in Italy, where 144 guns were placed together in three tiers and four sections, each of twelve tubes. Four horses pulled the 6m (20ft) high ribaudequin in which they were placed, with a gunner responsible for each tier. (*See* FIREARMS AND CANNON)

RIDGE PIECE The principal timber running along the apex of a roof (*see* ROOFS, TIMBER).

'RIDING HOUSEHOLD' *see* HOUSEHOLD

'RIDING MEN' *see* RECRUITMENT AND ORGANISATION (MILITARY)

At Restormel Castle the stone curtain appears to crown a motte and for this reason it is often described as a shell- keep. But the inner bank of the ringwork was removed when the curtain was built in c. 1200 and the living quarters added in c. 1280.

RINGWORK A comparatively recent term describing an ancient form of fortification, a ringwork comprised a defensive bank and ditch, generally circular or oval in shape, surrounding a hall. At Goltho in Lincolnshire the earliest of a series of fortified MANOR HOUSES has been dated to the mid-ninth century, its encircling rampart and deep outer ditch confirming that the Anglo-Saxons were fully acquainted with the ringwork. Not all Norman castles had a MOTTE, the inner BAILEY being the last line of defence: effectively a bailey within a bailey. These defences are also described by some archaeologists as ringworks. There are several notable ringworks in Wales: at Aberrheidol, for example, where the ramparts were originally lined with timber and later cased in stone; at Dinas Powys, located on a commanding summit which it shares with a sixth-century hillfort; and at Walwyn's Castle, where a large outer bailey incorporates the ramparts of an Iron Age fort. Some ringwork fortifications were later provided with stone curtains, as at Coity,

Cilgerran and Kidwelly, while Loughor's ringwork was later built up into an oval-shaped motte on which stood a SHELL-KEEP. Several ringworks have erroneously been described as shell-keeps. Restormel Castle, for example, comprises a perfectly circular bailey with internal buildings – hall, solar, guests' quarters and kitchen (all now ruined) – arranged concentrically against a crenellated curtain wall. From the outside the stone curtain appears to crown a motte and for this reason it is often described as a shell-keep. But the inner bank of the ringwork was removed when the curtain was built in *c.* 1200 and the living quarters added in *c.* 1280. Several ringworks were constructed at naturally defended sites, such as Beaudesert Castle near Henley-in-Arden, where an elongated hill-top was 'sculpted' to form a ditch and bank. By 1141 a keep had been constructed within the ringwork and the timber palisade replaced by a stone curtain.

RIVER GATE *see* QUAYS

ROADS, MEDIEVAL Most Roman roads were strategically planned and brilliantly engineered and, following the Norman Conquest of 1066, they formed the foundation of a communications network that again radiated from an administrative base at London. The Roman Fosse Way, Watling Street and Ermine Street, together with the earlier Icknield Way, were given royal protection, and in the mid-fourteenth century some 40 per cent of routes were of Roman origin. In contrast, most medieval roads 'made and maintained themselves' (C.T. Flower) and were essentially ancient trackways which developed in response to changing circumstances while others regressed. So-called drove-roads and pack-horse roads were used by a variety of travellers and acquired their designations only because they functioned primarily (though by no means exclusively) as routes for the movement of livestock or pack-horse trains. At this time most bulky goods were transported by means of a comparatively efficient water-borne trading system, the hinterland of each coastal or river port being serviced by roads, the standard and reliability of which improved as they converged on their destination. Similarly FAIRS and MARKETS depended for their commercial success on the safe arrival of customers from surrounding settlements and on the ability of merchants and traders to travel conveniently from one engagement to the next. Pilgrims and magnate retinues also travelled by road, both on foot and on horseback, and many wayside inns were established at this time to accommodate them, particularly along the more popular pilgrimage routes. But travel could be dangerous: in 1285 a statute of Edward I required that where a road passed through woodland an area extending to 18m (60ft) on either side of the highway should be cleared of vegetation in order that robbers and outlaws should not find concealment there. Few medieval roads were actually created, other than Fenland causeways around Ely and a number of Edwardian military roads in North Wales. The repair and maintenance of roads, bridges and causeways was largely in the hands of monastic houses and borough authorities, anxious to attract commercial investment and trade. Medieval legislation was principally concerned not with the fabric of a road or track but with its legal status as the King's Highway, a right of way, established by custom, over which the traveller was at liberty to 'pass and repass'. As is the case today, this right of way was variable: obstructions could be circumnavigated by entering on to neighbouring land. Manorial courts were obliged to attend to matters which might impede or cause annoyance to

'the passers-by in the King's Way' but it was not until 1555 that parishes were obliged to appoint an unpaid officer, the *Surveyor of the Highways*, who was required to inspect roads and bridges in the parish three times a year and to organise the statute labour to repair them.

ROCHET Long-armed naval axe used to cut enemy rigging.

ROLLS OF ARMS A roll of arms is any collection of ARMORY, whether painted, tricked (drawn in outline with colours indicated by abbreviations) or listed in written form using BLAZON, the language of armory. The term is most often applied to strips of vellum or parchment, sewn together and rolled up or bound into books, on which rows of shields or armorial figures have been painted or tricked and identified. Most of these manuscripts are of medieval origin, though there are many later copies and compilations and they illustrate both the development of armory, its terminology and conventions, and the mobility of the knightly classes throughout medieval Europe. The study of rolls of arms dates from the thirteenth century when heralds exchanged information concerning armorial devices and compiled their own armorials – manuscripts or books concerned with armory. In their simplest form, rolls of arms are little more than hastily illustrated lists which were compiled on the spot, at a tournament for example. Others, such as the Rous Roll (compiled 1477–85), are pictorial records of historical characters and events. There are some 350 surviving European medieval rolls of arms, of which 130 are English. (*See also* HERALDS' VISITATIONS)

ROMANESQUE A style of art and architecture prevalent in Europe from about 1050 to 1200, which reached its fullest development in central and northern France. In England architecture of the period is often referred to as *Norman*. Although the term is widely used in the context of church architecture, it is equally applicable to those parts of an eleventh-century masonry castle which were used primarily for domestic and religious purposes.

As the name suggests, Romanesque architecture was inspired by the classical buildings of ancient Rome and the basilican plan with its nave, aisles and apsidal termination which was adopted in Romanesque churches. In central Europe Romanesque masôns developed variations of classical themes, using the semicircular arch, arcading and tunnel vaults, and their buildings were vigorously decorated with foliated and other motifs. In northern and western Europe a more austere Romanesque style reflected Carolingian influences rather than those of classical Rome, and from this a distinctive Norman style developed in the tenth century.

Following the Norman conquest of England in 1066 there was a significant cultural decline from the achievements of the Anglo-Saxon period: with the notable exception of architecture. The chapel of St John (c. 1080) in the White Tower of the Tower of London, for example, is undoubtedly the most perfect and best preserved example of Romanesque architecture in any British castle (see CHAPEL). Eleventh-century Romanesque masonry was massive with walls up to 7.3m (24ft) wide at the base for safety and to compensate for poor-quality mortar and wide jointing. Window openings were small, so that the walls should not be weakened, and decoration minimal.

The twelfth century was a period of intense building activity and experimentation: walls became less substantial, the masonry was more finely jointed and there was an increasing use of carved ornament. Early mouldings had been cut very sparingly with shallow hollows, fillets and chamfers but later Romanesque work was often profusely carved, mostly in geometrical forms the most common of which were the familiar zig-zag (chevron) decoration used in the deep mouldings of round arches and cylinder-shaped stones (billets) which alternated with spaces in hollow moulding. Sculptural decoration in doorway arches, capitals and tympana included floreated and animal forms, human figures, biblical scenes and monsters. Typically English is beak-head ornament in which the heads of birds and beasts were carved in hollow mouldings so that the beaks or tongues overlapped into adjacent round mouldings. Anglo-Norman sculpture was an extraordinary pot-pourri of influences, from Scandinavian to Levantine and from French to Byzantine. Many of the sinuous and diabolical creatures depicted in Romanesque carvings are of Celtic origin, while others were introduced through bestiaries (see BESTIARY) and the importation of highly decorated eastern silks. This merging of Christian and pagan mythology, which was to continue well beyond the Romanesque period, is best observed in the ornamental carving of smaller Romanesque churches such as Kilpeck in Herefordshire (c. 1140) where a local school of sculpture produced carvings of extraordinary vigour and imagination. Romanesque design continued in England until the advent of the Gothic style in the last decades of the twelfth century (see GOTHIC ARCHITECTURE).

ROOF BOSSES see BOSSES

ROOF-CREASING A line cut into the fabric of a wall where a roof was once attached. Most commonly found where the lean-to roofs of buildings once abutted a curtain wall (see BEAM-HOLES).

ROOFING TILES see SLATES AND TILES

ROOFS (TIMBER) While stone vaulting is commonly found in medieval churches, in castles its use was generally restricted to chapels, gate passages, mural chambers and areas where there was a risk of fire, such as kitchens, undercrofts and cellars. These were usually simple barrel, groined or quadripartite vaults, the more ornate late medieval styles being confined to the chapels and state chambers of royal and high-status castles (see VAULTING). The roofs of large castle buildings, such as the HALL, were almost invariably of timber construction, though stone was sometimes used to strengthen a roof, as in the Great Hall of Conwy Castle where eight immense stone arches were inserted in 1346–7. The smaller circular, rectilinear or polygonal roofs of towers would also be of timber construction and, like the roofs of larger buildings, these would usually be covered with lead, shingles, tiles or slates (see below).

In its simplest form the medieval trussed roof consisted of a long beam (ridge-piece) which extended horizontally along the length of the apex of the roof and was supported at each end by the gables of the building. From either side of the ridge-piece, parallel timbers (principal rafters and less substantial common rafters) were carried downward to timbers (wall plates) laid along the tops of the side walls of the building and secured by means of stone CORBELS set into the walls. Further horizontal beams (purlins) were incorporated at intervals between the ridge-piece and the wall plate and, to counteract the outward thrust of the roof on the wall, massive beams (tie beams) spanned the interior space at wall-plate level. These were pinned or tenoned to the wall plates and often curve upwards at the centre where a vertical post (king post) or pairs of posts (queen posts) secured the structure to the ridge-piece. Further tie beams (collar beams) were sometimes incorporated above the wall-plate level and curved arch braces or straight struts added for reinforcement. Coupled roofs have neither tie beams nor collar beams, and braced collar roofs were constructed with collar beams and arch braces but no tie beams.

Horizontal rows of wooden battens were affixed to the outside surfaces of the rafters from which overlapping or interlocking tiles, slates or

SHINGLES were hung, to provide a weather-proof outer surface (*see* SLATES AND TILES). These materials were not always effective, however, and were often replaced by LEAD. At Conwy Castle, for example, it was reported in 1321 that 'in the Hall . . . several of the roof trusses have failed, and in other buildings and towers many of the trusses and much of the rest of the timber have perished for want of a covering of lead'. (This was only thirty-four years after the castle's completion.) In 1322 a further report stated that 'the king understands they [his Welsh castles] are ruinous and not fit for him to dwell in if he should go there'. Nothing was done until a detailed survey carried out in 1343 concluded that, at Conwy, the roofs in six out of the eight towers, as well as in many of the courtyard buildings, were unsafe because of the rotting timber. Three years later major reconstruction took place and lead roofs were substituted throughout the castle. In order to bear the increased weight (and that of the clay membrane that was customarily inserted between the lead and the wood), fifteen great stone arches replaced the original timber trusses in the Great Hall and royal apartments.

In the last decades of the fourteenth century the *hammer-beam* roof evolved. Hammer beams are abbreviated tie beams which project at wall-plate level and are supported from corbels by arch-braced *wall posts*. Vertical *hammer posts* rise from the inner ends of the hammer beams and are secured to collar beams and purlins (*collar purlins*). This structure enables the weight of a roof to be carried across a much wider span than would otherwise be possible. At Westminster Hall, for example, an immense hammer-beam roof, constructed in 1399 of Sussex oak, spans a floor space measuring 88m by 21m (290ft by 68ft) on walls 28m (92ft) high. Hammer-beam roofs and double hammer-beam roofs (those with two tiers of projecting beams) reached decorative perfection in the fifteenth century, particularly in East Anglian churches. The projections often terminate in carved angels, sometimes exceeding one hundred in a single roof, and these may bear emblazoned shields or other armorial devices. The wall plate or cornice may also be richly carved with painted and gilded figures. In some medieval halls and churches the wooden equivalent of the stone vault may also be found: the *wagon roof*, a continuous timber roof of half-cylindrical section.
(*See also* TIMBER-FRAME BUILDINGS)

ROSES, WARS OF THE *see* WARS OF THE ROSES

ROSE WINDOW A circular window with a complex traceried design, usually located in the gable wall of a large building such as a hall (*see* WINDOWS) or the transept of a major church. As early as 1243 we read of Henry III ordering a round window, 9m (30ft) in diameter, to be inserted in the gable end of his new hall at Dublin Castle, similar to the 'one great and handsome window' that replaced four windows in the east gable of his hall at Woodstock. One of the first references to a 'rose window' is found at Westminster Abbey in 1451 when there was a payment to one 'Northinstone for le rose' in the south transept, a project that took ten years to complete. This type of window is often confused with a *wheel window* which is also circular but contains a design of 'spokes' radiating from a central hub.

ROTUNDA A circular room or building, often with a domed roof.

ROUGH-CAST *see* FACING MATERIALS

ROUNDEL (i) A circular moulding usually containing a decorative motif.
(ii) In ARMORY, a flat coloured disc of a specified colour.
(iii) Circular metal plates, usually strapped to the shoulder gussets to protect the armpit (*see* ARMOUR (BODY)).

ROUND TOWERS *see* TOWERS

ROUTIERS Ruthless mercenaries whose lives were dedicated to fighting and plunder.

ROWEL A star-shaped piece of metal which revolves at the end of a spur where it is applied to a horse's flank.

ROYAL ARMS, THE It was the thirteenth-century heralds who assigned retrospectively the gold 'leopards of England' on a red shield to the Norman kings. But it is likely that Henry I (1100–35) was the first English king actually to adopt the lion as a personal device and it was during his reign that the first lion was seen in England – at the royal menagerie at Woodstock. Henry was known as the 'Lion of Justice' and his descendants through his illegitimate children bore one or more lions in a variety of attitudes, and sometimes accompanied by other devices. Where the second lion of England originated remains a mystery, though it has been suggested (not convincingly) that it was acquired through Henry's marriage with Adeliza, the daughter of Godfrey of Louvaine who is also believed to have used a lion device on his seal. The seal of Eleanor of Aquitaine, wife of the first Angevin king, Henry II (1154–89), bears three lions, while a shield of *three lions passant guardant* later appears on the second great seal of Richard I (1198) and was used thereafter by successive English sovereigns (*see* SEALS).

Llywelyn ap Gruffydd (d. 1282) and successive native princes of Wales bore a shield of gold and red quarters, each quarter charged with a *lion passant guardant counterchanged*. These arms were first borne by Gruffydd ap Llywelyn (d. 1244) whose mother Joan was the illegitimate daughter of King John of England. It may be, therefore, that the adoption by the Welsh princes of *lions passant* in red and gold was intended to emphasise their familial relationship with the Plantagenets.

When Edward III of England laid claim to the French throne, in 1337, declaring himself *Rex Angliae et Franciae*, he quartered the royal arms of France (*Azure semy-de-lis Argent*) with those of England. The silver *fleurs de lis*, scattered on a blue field, were first borne by Louis VII (1137–80) and became the emblem of French sovereignty – 'the flower of Louis'. The heraldic fleur-de-lis is a stylised lily, probably the Madonna Lily (*Lilium candidum*), a symbol of purity generally associated with the Blessed Virgin Mary. In 1376 Charles V of France reduced the number of *fleurs-de-lis* in his arms to three, and when a new great seal was struck for Henry IV of England in 1405 it too bore the new French arms in the first and fourth quarters – arms which became known as 'France Modern' to distinguish them from the earlier (and more attractive) 'France Ancient'. These arms continued in use until 1603 when James VI of Scotland succeeded Elizabeth I as James I of England, the fleurs-de-lis of France remaining in the royal arms of British sovereigns until 1801. By the Treaty of Amiens (1802) George III finally surrendered his title to the crown of France.

ROYAL BADGES *see* BADGES AND LIVERIES, 'PRINCE OF WALES'S FEATHERS' *and* WARS OF THE ROSES

ROYAL COMMISSION ON THE HISTORICAL MONUMENTS OF ENGLAND (RCHME) *see* NATIONAL MONUMENTS RECORD (NMR)

ROYAL HOUSEHOLD *see* HOUSEHOLD

Royal arms: 1. The Norman kings (attributed); 2. 1195–1337; 3. 1337–1405; 4. 1405–1603

ROYAL PALACES Numerous palaces were built or acquired by monarchs and bishops during the medieval period and many of these were fortified (*see* ECCLESIASTICAL STRONGHOLDS). In the early thirteenth century King John accumulated the largest collection of palatial residences of any medieval English king: twenty-nine in all. Later in the thirteenth century Henry III and Edward I were conspicuous builders, though many of their sites are more precisely regarded as castles and the number of royal residences was reduced to twenty. By 1485 most royal palaces were concentrated around London and the Thames valley: Baynard's Castle, Eltham, Greenwich, Sheen and Westminster in the south-east with King's Langley, Woodstock and Clarendon (the most popular of all royal medieval palaces) in Hertfordshire, Oxfordshire and Wiltshire respectively. Locations were chosen for a variety of reasons: as the administrative centres of estates, as convenient stopping places on regularly taken journeys or as hunting lodges, for example (*see* CHASE *and* FOREST). Although used primarily for private residential purposes, royal palaces often provided the settings for public judicial and ceremonial occasions – for receiving foreign heads of state, distinguished guests and ambassadors, and for celebratory banquets, festivals and TOURNAMENTS. And, of the utmost importance, by their magnificence they declared the authority and pre-eminence of the English king. In such politically uncertain times it was imperative that the king and his queen should be seen by their subjects and the palaces provided accommodation during their travels. As residences, they were visited periodically by the court which might stay for several nights or for longer periods (*see* VERGE).

Residence implies a greater degree of privacy, comfort and convenience than was generally found in a royal castle. Although lavish suites of rooms were built and furnished for residential and state purposes at fortresses such as Conwy and Caernarfon, the dark confines of the Edwardian conquest castles must have been dispiriting and oppressive at times and they were rarely visited by the English kings. Windsor Castle, on the other hand, was clearly intended as much for palatial accommodation as it was for defence. It was much favoured by Henry III who stayed there regularly from 1224, while Edward III spent over £51,000 on refurbishing the castle in 1350–77, the most expensive secular building project of the entire medieval period in England.

Henry III's expenditure on buildings was prodigious, especially during the decades of his personal rule between 1234 and 1258. Each of his buildings was more 'seemly' and 'sumptuous' than that which had preceded it, but Clarendon, near Salisbury, was the finest of them all. It had expensive tile-mosaic floors (among the first in medieval England) and its chambers were painted with frescos of the king's favourite romances, saints and moralities (*see* PLASTER, WHITEWASH AND PAINT). Its state chambers had glazed windows, wainscoted walls, chimney-pieces embellished with statuary and rich blue ceilings that sparkled with golden stars. Henry risked everything for building. His extravagance brought him permanent debt and the distrust of his barons.

To a large degree, court and government moved with the king and accommodation was provided for the HOUSEHOLD and for royal departments such as the Exchequer and the Wardrobe, before they ceased to be peripatetic at the end of the medieval period. The notion of palaces as pleasure-grounds was firmly established by the early fifteenth century. Freedom and relaxation, albeit transitory, could be found in the GARDENS, DEER PARKS and sumptuous interiors of the royal palaces by those who wished to escape from the responsibilities of government and the rigours of public office.

The Palace of Westminster was the chief royal residence and the administrative centre of government. Within the palace were to be found the Exchequer, the Court of King's Bench and the Court of Common Pleas. But it was also a luxurious home, noted for its beautiful chapel of St Stephen, Henry III's Painted Chamber and the Star Chamber, built by Edward III who decorated its dark blue ceiling with gilt stars. The private chambers had beds hung with cloth of gold and satin, and made up with deep feather mattresses and coverlets furred with ermine. The palace of Westminster was, in fact, three palaces: the Great Palace, the official seat of government; the Privy Palace, which housed the royal apartments; and the Prince's Palace, where the royal family was usually accommodated. There were two halls: the White Hall, which housed the Court of Chancery, and the magnificent Westminster Hall, which, together with the fourteenth-century Jewel Tower, is all that survived the fire of 1834 (*see* HALL).

In medieval Wales the princes of Gwynedd established a system of land tenure based on a number of townships (*trefi*) that together formed administrative districts (*commotes* or *cwmwd*) or larger *cantrefi*. Two townships in each commote were held directly by the prince: the *maerdref* and the *fridd*. The hub of the maerdref was the *llys*, a complex of royal buildings which the prince and his

Edward IV's Great Hall at Eltham Palace (1480).

household would visit periodically in order to dispense justice, collect taxes and attend to the administrative business of the commote (*see* WALES: NATIVE CASTLES). Within the *llys* the native rulers lived in large timber-frame halls (*neuadd*) with thatched roofs and (in some cases) adjoining stone chambers, protected by lightly defended enclosures. According to the twelfth-century chronicler Gerallt Gymro (Gerald of Wales), the three principal Welsh royal courts were located at Rhosyr on the island of Môn (Anglesey), Dinefwr in Carmarthenshire and Penwern in Shropshire. There were, of course, other courts and commotal residences, many of which occupied strategically important sites, and a number of these were later rebuilt as castles. By 1283 the system had effectively collapsed for the Welsh royal estates had passed to the English crown and the *maerdrefi* had ceased to function (*see* WALES, CONQUEST OF).

RR Abbreviation for *regni Regis*, meaning 'in the —th year of King —'.

RUBBLE The term does not necessarily imply inferior construction. Walls built of roughly cut stones of different shapes and sizes, bound with lime mortar and sometimes laid in courses, are singularly durable. (*See also* MASONRY)

RULERS OF MEDIEVAL AND TUDOR ENGLAND

Saxon

Edward the Confessor	1042–66
Harold II (Godwinson)	1066

Normandy

William I	1066–87
William II	1087–1100
Henry I	1100–35
Stephen	1135–54

Plantagenet

Henry II	1154–89
Richard I	1189–99
John	1199–1216
Henry III	1216–72
Edward I	1272–1307
Edward II	1307–27
Edward III	1327–77
Richard II	1377–99

Lancaster

Henry IV	1399–1413
Henry V	1413–22
Henry VI	1422–61
Readeption	October 1470 – March 71

York

Edward IV	1461–83
Edward V	1483
Richard III	1483–85

Tudor

Henry VII	1485–1509
Henry VIII	1509–47
Edward VI	1547–53
Mary I	1553–58
Elizabeth I	1558–1603

RYAL *see* COINAGE

S

SABATON *see* ARMOUR (BODY)

SABLE The heraldic term for black (*see* TINCTURES).

SADDLE BARS *see* WINDOWS

ST JOHN OF JERUSALEM, ORDER OF Among the many new religious orders which came into being in the eleventh and twelfth centuries were the military-religious orders of the Knights Templar and Knights Hospitaller. Both originated in the decades following the capture of the Holy City by the crusaders in 1099 and the establishing of a Christian Kingdom of Jerusalem which stretched from northern Syria to the Sinai desert (*see* CRUSADES). The Knights of the Hospital of St John of Jerusalem provided shelter and care for the sick, poor and weary pilgrims who visited the holy places, while the Templars guarded the holy places of Jerusalem, protected travellers and lived according to the rule of Bernard of Clairvaux. Both orders were endowed with substantial revenues, property and lands in the new kingdom and throughout Catholic Europe. Within a few years of their foundation most of their brethren, while living under vows of religion, were conventual knights (their priests were known as *chaplains*) and the two orders played an increasingly significant rôle in the defence of the Christian settlements in Palestine and Syria and in the administration of the Kingdom of Jerusalem. They constructed and garrisoned castles and fought alongside crusading forces in the perennial wars against the Egyptians and Turks. The convent of each order was situated in the Holy Land, with dependent priories and estates throughout Europe. Each order had about fifty PRECEPTORIES or COMMANDERIES in the British Isles, many commemorated by place-names such as St John's Jerusalem in Kent, St John's Wood in London, Templecombe in Somerset, Temple Guiting in the Gloucestershire Cotswolds and Fryerning in Essex, 'the place of the brothers'. Driven from Palestine with the rest of the Catholics in 1291, the Hospitallers took over the island of Rhodes, off the coast of Asia Minor, which became their base for naval operations against Muslim shipping. The island was ruled as a semi-independent state until 1522 when it was seized by the Ottoman Turks and the knights removed to the island of Malta which they held as a sovereign power from 1530 until 1798. Following the persecution and papal suppression of the Templars in 1312 (*see* TEMPLAR, KNIGHTS), most of their properties were transferred to the Hospitallers. From 1312 to their dissolution by Henry VIII in 1540, the English Knights Hospitaller comprised a minor, though well-endowed, branch of an international order, drawn (as required by its statutes) from the armigerous families of the noblesse. Discipline was firm and a knight's vow of obedience to the rule was strictly observed. Chastity and poverty were also required, though in practice a successful knight could enjoy his possessions until they were claimed by the order at his death. The Hospitallers' headquarters were at St John's Priory, Clerkenwell, in London and it was there that an aspiring knight would undertake his novitiate before travelling to Rhodes where several years of military service against the Mohammedans would normally lead to promotion to the rank of commander. As a senior member of the order he would be responsible for the administration of its estates and finances, serve as a diplomat or be seconded into royal or magnate service. The arms of the order were a plain white cross on a red background and its habit was black with the badge of a white 'Maltese' cross on the shoulder.
(*For* the Order of St John Library and Museum *see* APPENDIX II)

SALIC LAW The law of the Salic Franks which barred dynastic succession through a female line. In the fourteenth century, Edward III's claim to the French throne, based on descent from his mother, a

Capetian princess, was denied by the French who cited the Salic Law as authority. The resulting military and political conflict has since been described as the HUNDRED YEARS WAR. In medieval England there was no statutory impediment to prevent a woman succeeding to the throne or transmitting a claim to her descendants. In practice the issue was never put to the test because, until the fifteenth century, the house of Plantagenet had produced a sufficiency of male heirs.

SALIENT (i) An outward-projecting angle (*see* RE-ENTRANT).
(ii) In ARMORY, descriptive of a beast when springing or leaping.

SALLET The most popular of fifteenth-century helmets, the sallet was similar in shape to a 'sou'wester' with a pronounced neck extension and domed crown. Most examples have an eye-slit and were worn in conjunction with a BEVOR. The term includes similarly shaped helmets with movable visors and articulated neck guards.
(*See also* ARMOUR *and* HELMETS)

SALLY-PORT A type of POSTERN, usually a passageway or narrow gateway in a castle's outer wall, by which troops undertook a 'sally' or sortie against a besieging force. Surprise and speed of retreat were of the essence and an attack would often take place under cover of darkness. In the event of the flat space (*berm*) between the foot of a curtain and the edge of a moat or ditch being occupied during a siege, defenders could counter-attack by emerging from a sally-port. Most sally-ports were protected by a small but sturdy portcullis which remained closed at all other times. Some were contained within a turret: at Rhuddlan Castle, for example, where each of a series of turrets in the outer wall once contained a stair and sally-port leading to the dry moat, though three of these were afterwards blocked and the stairs filled in. At Denbigh Castle a substantial sally-port was added (next to the Postern Tower) in 1295. This comprised an upper gate in the curtain wall with a drawbridge and portcullis and a staircase that descended through three right-angled turns to a complex BARBICAN with a drawbridge and portcullis.
(*See also* QUAYS *for* water gates)

SALTIRE A broad, diagonal cross, familiar as the cross on which St Andrew, the patron saint of Scotland, is said to have been crucified, though its use in early Celtic art clearly pre-dates Christianity.

SANCTUARY (i) From the Latin *sanctus* meaning 'inviolable' is derived the Right of Sanctuary which in medieval England was of two kinds, ecclesiastical and secular. Ecclesiastical sanctuary developed through usage from the Saxon period and originally applied only to that area in the immediate vicinity of a bishop's throne (*cathedra*), though this was later extended to the curtilage of a church, from which a criminal could not be removed. Within forty days he was permitted to take an oath before a coroner by which he confessed his crime, swore to *abjure the realm* and submitted to banishment. Some churches possessed sanctuary knockers (*hagodays*), large brass escutcheons adorned with the head of some monstrous beast. By grasping the ring of the hagoday, a fugitive could claim sanctuary from his pursuers. Contravention of the laws of sanctuary was a serious crime, punishable by excommunication. Secular sanctuary relied upon a royal grant and in theory might be applied to any franchise where a lord exercised *jura regalia*. For this reason secular sanctuary is often confused with ecclesiastical sanctuary, for fugitives frequently sought refuge in a church in franchise, especially in ecclesiastical liberties such as Durham. The privileges of sanctuary were restricted to seven cities in 1540. Sanctuary for crime was abolished in 1623 and for civil purposes in 1773.
(ii) That part of a church containing the ALTAR or, if there are several altars, the high altar.

SANITATION *see* PLUMBING, WATER SUPPLY AND SANITATION

SAP The undermining of a wall, above or below ground, and the construction of covered trenches to conceal an assailant's approach to a besieged fortification – hence 'sapper' and 'to sap (weaken) one's strength'.
(*See also* SIEGES)

SAPPER One who digs saps (*see* SAP).

SARSEN STONES Immense sandstone boulders of the Eocene period that occur in southern England and are a particular feature of the Marlborough Downs in Wiltshire. The term is probably derived from 'Saracen', a convenient aphorism that was often applied prior to the seventeenth century to objects of incongruous appearance for which there was no rational explanation. Many thousands of sarsens were removed for building materials, notably in the Middle Ages when large blocks of undressed sarsen were used as foundations for church towers, castle walls and buttresses. Sarsen was rarely used for domestic buildings, however, for the exceptionally hard silica surface of split stones caused condensation.

SAUCERY, THE *see* KITCHENS

SAXON BURHS *see* BURHS

SCABBARD *see* WEAPONS AND HARNESS

SCAFFOLDING AND CRANES Scaffolding used in the construction of castles usually consisted of a platform supported on trestles for low-level work and more elaborate structures, not dissimilar to those used today, for working above head-height. The uprights (*spars*) were most often of alder, though other types of timber were used. These and the horizontal ledgers (sometimes described as *putlogs*) were lashed together with ropes of bast (or some other fibrous material) or withies, and the lashings tightened by driving in wedges (*see* PUTLOG HOLES). In 1368 185,000 'twists' of withies were obtained for the scaffolding at Windsor Castle. Hurdles formed both the platform 'for the masons to stand upon' and 'the way onto the scaffold'. Employers often undertook to provide the necessary scaffolding and the temporary timber or wicker structures (*centering*) required to keep an arch or vault in place during construction (*see* VAULTING). To avoid the expense of erecting a scaffold when undertaking repairs, a platform was often bracketed out from a wall or a cradle lowered from above. At Hadleigh Castle in 1365 a 'cradel' was hired 'for taking down the scaffolding round two towers and blocking up the holes' – presumably the putlog holes in which the ledgers of the scaffolding had rested.

A variety of baskets, barrels and other receptacles for carrying materials are to be found in medieval illustrations, while large blocks of stone were lifted separately using rope 'slings' or pincer-like iron 'grips' which were attached to lifting ropes. While the hodmen were capable of carrying small quantities of material on to the scaffolding, it was necessary to have some sort of machine for hoisting heavier loads. In 1222 we find tallow bought 'for greasing the machines for lifting timber and water', while at Westminster in 1333 tallow was used 'for greasing the pulleys and beams for lifting up great blocks of marble'. This type of mechanism, known as a 'gin' or *verne*, consisted of a rope running over a wheel fixed above the position to which the stone was to be delivered, one end of the rope ending in a hook and the other passing round an axle rotated by

a wheel. At Corfe Castle in 1292 a log of alder was supplied 'for the machine which is called verne', while the accounts for 1329 give details of the making of a 'verne or machine built for lifting or winding up timber' at the Tower. Among the stores at Westminster in 1399 were 'a machine called wynde, a machine called brokke, and 4 vernes'. The 'brokke' or *brake* was a type of capstan, while 'wynde' probably refers to a *windas* or windlass mechanism, both of which were turned by hand. Other lifting machines were powered by treadmills: in 1488 the sum of 6s 8d was paid at Clarendon 'to four workmen running in the great wheel for 4 days'. This type of wheel features in several medieval illustrations of cranes.
(*See also* CASTLES (CONSTRUCTION OF), MASTER MASONS AND ARCHITECTS, MATERIALS (CARRIAGE OF), IRONWORK, LOCKS AND NAILS *and* RAM (PILE-DRIVER)

SCALING LADDERS The walls of many late medieval castles were so high that any attempt to attack them by means of ladders would have been impractical. Nevertheless, there is documentary evidence to suggest that scaling ladders continued in use throughout the medieval period and that these would have been affixed to a wall by means of pegs and secured at the foot by iron spikes to prevent them from slipping. Both attackers and defenders would use forked poles either to raise the ladders or to push them away, though the notion that large quantities of extremely expensive oil were boiled and poured down on the besiegers is fallacious. However, boiling water and heated sand were used for this purpose, the latter apparently penetrating the slightest gap in armour.
(*See also* SIEGES)

SCAPPLED *see* MASONRY

SCARCEMENT A ledge formed by the setting back of or cutting into a wall, possibly to support a floor.

SCARP The outer slope of a RAMPART (*see* REVETMENT) or the inner face of a ditch or moat.

SCHILTRON A medieval Scottish term for a body of spearmen in close formation, making a circular, outward-facing 'hedgehog' of their weapons as a defence against English knights. Although efficient at repelling cavalry, the formation lacked mobility and was vulnerable to archery. At Falkirk (1298) the English archers decimated schiltrons pinned down by the threat of a cavalry charge. Even so, Robert Bruce (king of Scotland 1306–29) succeeded in defeating the English at Bannockburn (1314) using precisely the same tactic.

SCONCE A wall-bracket holding a candle-stick.

SCOOP POND *see* FISH PONDS

SCOTLAND, ENGLISH WARS IN A series of conflicts between England and Scotland precipitated in 1293 when John Balliol, king of Scots (1292–6), renounced his allegiance to Edward I of England. Balliol (*c.* 1250–1315) had been selected by Edward (as his feudal overlord) from among a number of competing claimants to the Scottish throne, even though he had little previous contact with Scotland. Ominously, Edward had demanded not only the homage of all claimants during this process but also custody of all the major Scottish castles. Balliol swore fealty to Edward before and after his investiture at Scone in 1292 but he found himself caught between the excessive demands of the English king as his feudal superior and the determination of his advisers to defy English demands. By 1295 a council of twelve magnates had effectively taken control of the Scottish government and concluded a treaty with France, then at war with England, undertaking to attack England should Edward ever venture abroad. In March 1296 armies were mustering on both sides of the border. The Scots attacked Wark Castle and besieged Carlisle. Edward responded by sacking Berwick-upon-Tweed, then Scotland's largest and most prosperous town, which he later converted into a fortified borough. On 27 April 1296 he defeated the Scots at Dunbar before moving on to Edinburgh Castle, which fell to Edward's siege engines in three days, and to Stirling where the garrison capitulated. After just three weeks Edward controlled Scotland: Balliol was stripped of his crown, the highly symbolic Scottish coronation stone was removed from Scone to Westminster and every important castle was occupied – 'stuffyt all with Inglis men'.

In 1297 William Wallace (*c.* 1274–1305), the second son of a Scottish knight, emerged as leader of the opposition to English rule. After defeating the English at Stirling Bridge in 1297, Wallace recaptured Berwick-upon-Tweed and invaded northern England, his unruly followers committing atrocities wherever they went. As a consequence of his exploits, and despite his comparatively modest ancestry, he was knighted and appointed as guardian of Scotland. Wallace succeeded in recovering a number of castles, but crucially the strategically pivotal fortresses of Edinburgh, Stirling, Roxburgh and Berwick remained in English hands. At Falkirk on 22 July 1298 Wallace unwisely decided to face the English in open battle but his spearmen were no match for the longbow and his cavalry fled in disarray (*see* SCHILTRON). He continued briefly to wage a guerrilla war before escaping to France in 1299. In the same year the English garrison at Stirling Castle was starved into submission while, in July 1300, Edward invested the castle of Caerlaverock, a siege that was famously described by a chronicler as though it were a chivalric spectacle. He tells how the attackers, having failed to storm the castle, bombarded its walls with three great siege engines. And how, when the garrison of sixty men surrendered, the king pardoned them and gave them new clothes. (In reality they were all hanged!) Wallace returned to Scotland in 1303. Arrested near Glasgow in 1305, he was taken to London to face a traitor's death. He was hanged, drawn and quartered and his body parts sent to Berwick, Newcastle, Perth and Stirling Castles where they were displayed as a grisly warning to others.

In May 1303 Edward launched a further full-scale invasion. He planned to march up the east coast of Scotland, relieving or recovering the fortresses on his way. In order to cross the Forth he had to secure Stirling Castle, 'the key of Scotland', which guarded the only bridge. Rather than commit himself to a prolonged siege, he commissioned the building of three prefabricated bridges, complete with drawbridges at each end and *espringals* (large crossbows) mounted on towers. These were brought by sea from Norfolk and were so successful that by the time Edward set up his winter quarters at Dunfermline most of his objectives had been achieved. The exception was Stirling, which remained in Scottish hands. So important was this castle that Edward gathered together the most formidable collection of siege engines ever seen in Britain. Woods were felled to provide timber for their construction, church roofs were stripped of their lead for counterweights and hundreds of stones, weighing up to 140kg (300lb), were brought in from the surrounding countryside for the *trebuchets* and *mangonels* (*see* SIEGES). After twelve weeks the garrison surrendered but Edward insisted that it remain in the castle so that he could test his latest siege engine, nicknamed 'War Wolf', which succeeded in demolishing an entire wall with a single missile. With the surrender of Stirling, Scottish resistance effectively came to an end. Although Edward allowed the Scottish nobility a rôle in government, an English lieutenant was appointed and all the major castles were occupied by English garrisons. Some were repaired but Scotland was not to be subjugated as Wales had been by the building of magnificent new castles and fortified boroughs (*see* WALES, CONQUEST OF). The still incomplete Welsh castles had almost bankrupted the Exchequer and a scheme of new Scottish castles, considerably greater in extent and number than those which encircled Gwynedd, was not a practicable proposition.

The struggle for Scottish independence was revived by Robert the Bruce (1274–1329), King Robert I of Scots (1306–29). The son of Robert Bruce, earl of Carrick, and grandson of one of the competitors for the Scottish throne, he fought for the English against John Balliol but joined the Wallace uprising in 1297, having previously renewed his oath of fealty to Edward I in the same year. In 1298 he was appointed one of the four guardians of the Scottish realm but submitted to the English in 1302–5. In 1306, having killed John Comyn (a nephew of Balliol and a rival to the throne), Bruce asserted his own rights and, following a carefully planned *coup d'état*, was crowned king of Scotland at Scone. Following two defeats in June and July 1306, one by the English at Perth and the other by the lord of Argyll (a kinsman of the Comyns), Bruce fled the country, leaving many of his supporters to face execution and his female relations exile in English nunneries or imprisonment in iron cages in English castles. By February 1307 Bruce had returned to Galloway. Acknowledging his enemy's superiority in castles, cavalry and siegecraft, he decided to fight a guerrilla war. An English force was defeated at Loudoun in May 1307 and in July of the same year the 68-year-old Edward I, 'the Hammer of the Scots', died of dysentery and exhaustion while leading a new invasion force through Cumbria. He was succeeded by his feckless son Edward II (1307–27), whose campaigning in Scotland resulted in a series of disasters. By 1309 Bruce was able to convene his first parliament, though this was attended only by his own supporters. He won control of the north of Scotland with a series of military victories between 1310 and 1314 and, in so doing, established his credentials once and for all as a national leader. A series of castles was captured, leaving only Lothian outside his control, and in early 1314 Edinburgh and Roxburgh Castles fell, leaving Stirling as the only English fortress north of the Forth. The Scots' famous victory at Bannockburn on 24 June 1314 (near Stirling, where the English were attempting to relieve the castle) did not end the Anglo-Scottish war but it did settle the Scottish civil war, leaving Robert I unchallenged. For ten years the north of England was subjected to constant raiding. On the very night of Edward III's coronation (1328) a Scottish force crossed the border and laid siege to Norham Castle. When news reached the English court of a plan to launch a combined Scottish, Irish and Welsh invasion, preparations for a campaign were immediately put in hand. But when the two armies eventually met at Stanhope Park near Durham, the Scots launched a surprise night attack and then withdrew before battle could be joined. The campaign proved an expensive fiasco (the English government had to pawn the crown jewels to pay for it) and Edward was left with no choice but to sue for peace. By the treaty of Northampton (1328) Edward III (1327–77) renounced all claims to feudal suzerainty and to lands in Scotland. For the young king the terms of the treaty were an unmitigated disaster and, although he resumed hostilities in the 1340s, his increasing preoccupation with the French wars (*see* HUNDRED YEARS WAR) diverted his resources away from Scotland and he ceased to prosecute the war with any real commitment. Conflict on the Borders remained endemic, however (*see* MARCH *and* PELE TOWERS).

SCOTTISH BORDERS *see* MARCH

SCREENS Wooden screens and *spurs* were often placed near doors to reduce draughts. The terms were used synonymously, though strictly speaking a *spur* was a (hinged?) screen that projected from a wall and did not reach across the full width of a chamber. An account for 1333 at Nottingham Castle mentions the provision of 'three great spurs, one opposite the door of the King's wardrobe, another at the door of the chamber, and the third at the King's head', and also 'boards for a screen hanging over the fireplace between the hearth and the King's bed'. At Cambridge Castle in 1295 there is an entry for 'ten deal boards for making a spere in front of the seat of the latrine of the wardrobe of the hall. . . . Also for hooks and hinges for the door of the said speer.' In this instance, it is clear that the spur was, indeed, a complete partition that required a door. This type of screen is often referred to as an *interclose* or *parclose*. All screens were ideally suited to painted and gilded decoration, particularly allegorical, chivalric and biblical motifs and heraldry. In 1260 Henry III required Richard Freemantle 'to make an interclose of board on each side of the high altar in the King's chapel at Windsor, with proper doors, and to paint the interclose and doors as the King had instructed him'. The SCREENS PASSAGE was a characteristic feature of high-status medieval halls (*see* HALL).

SCREENS PASSAGE A passageway separated from a medieval HALL by a decorative timber or stone screen (*see* SCREENS). The courtyard door usually opened into one end of the screens passage with doors to the domestic chambers at the other. On one side of the passage three doorways led to the PANTRY, the BUTTERY and (in the centre, via a corridor) the KITCHENS. On the other side, and running across the width of the hall, was a screen, pierced by a single doorway or pair of doorways and often with a gallery above as at Berkeley Castle and Haddon Hall (*see* MINSTRELS). This was the standard arrangement, though in castles it would often be modified in order to accommodate the confines of the site. The screen was intended to reduce draughts from these doorways and enabled the domestic staff to carry out their duties unobserved by guests in the hall. Although essentially a medieval feature, screens passages were provided in several great houses of the Elizabethan and Jacobean periods. The late sixteenth-century screens passage at Montacute House in Somerset, for example, served as an ante-chamber to the great hall which by that time was both a communal living room and a reception area.

SCULLERY *see* KITCHENS

SCULLION *see* KITCHENS

SCUTAGE *see* KNIGHT BACHELOR, KNIGHT'S FEE *and* MILITIA

SEALS A seal (*sigil*) is a piece of wax, lead or paper attached to a document as a guarantee of authenticity or affixed to an envelope or receptacle to ensure that the contents may not be tampered with other than by breaking the seal. The piece of stone or metal upon which the design is engraved, and from which the impression is taken, is called the *matrix*. The Keeper of the Seal was a royal official who was responsible for the security of the matrix. Even before the development of ARMORY, seals bore distinctive devices which often alluded to the names of their owners: thus a man called Raven might use a raven on his seal. From the twelfth century sigillary devices first appear on shields, the various shapes of which provide clues for the dating of seals. The first occurrence of a shield of arms in the seal of an English monarch is to be found in the second seal of Richard I (*c.* 1191) which shows on the reverse an equestrian figure bearing a pointed shield charged with three lions. From this time also magnates and knights began using equestrian figures of themselves

in armour, with their arms depicted on the shield and horse-cloths (*caparison*). These official seals were large, and sovereigns and magnates generally used a PRIVY SEAL (*privatum sigillum*) to authenticate warrants to their clerks who would then issue documents on their master's behalf under a GREAT SEAL. A personal seal (*secretum*) was used for private matters. The continued use of the same seal by succeeding generations of a family contributed to the development of the hereditary nature of armory. Whereas a simple shield was ideally suited to a circular seal, the elongated fourteenth-century coat of arms, with its helm and CREST, created awkward spaces between the motif and the surrounding legend. These were filled with decorative patterns (*diaper*) and the figures of beasts or chimerical creatures, many of which were armorial badges which, from the fifteenth century, were often adopted as SUPPORTERS. In England the Great Seal of the realm has always been two-sided, like the coinage, with a different device on each side. Typically, the principal side (*obverse*) depicted the enthroned sovereign (the *majesty*) and the reverse his equestrian figure. The Great Seal of Edward IV (1461–83) shows the quartered arms of France and England with fleurs-de-lis and the Yorkist badges of roses and suns interspersed both in the legend and in the diapered background of the majesty. The legend on the second seal of Richard I (*see above*) refers to the king as *Rex Anglorum* but thereafter successive English sovereigns were described on their seals as *Rex Anglie* until the legend was changed by James I to *Rex Angliae* in 1603 and by Charles I to *Rex Magnae Britanniae* in 1627. Henry VIII (1509–47)

Seal of John de la Pole, earl of Lincoln (d. 1487).

made use of a golden *bulla* on which was depicted the royal arms within a collar of the Order of the Garter. A bulla was an embossed disc of metal, originally lead, which was attached to documents as a means of authentication. Papal edicts were sealed in this manner – hence the expression *Papal Bull*, meaning the actual document.

SECRETUM *see* SEALS

SEDILIA *see* CHAPEL

SEGMENTAL ARCH *see* ARCH

SEGMENTED MOATS *see* MOATS AND WATER DEFENCES

SEIGNEURIAL, SEIGNORAL *or* **SEIGNORIAL** Appertaining to the ownership of territory, or to territorial jurisdiction.

SEIGNIORY The territory or territorial jurisdiction of a feudal lord (a *seigneur*).

SEIZE QUARTIERS *see* MARSHALLING

SENESCHAL A lord's deputy (*see* HOUSEHOLD).

SERGEANT *see* SERJEANTY

SERGEANT À CHEVAL *see* HORSES AND HORSE-HARNESS

SERJEANTY *or* **SERGEANTY** In the Middle Ages a *serjeant* was either someone of less than knightly rank in the service of a lord (*Petty Serjeanty*), a knight in attendance on a sovereign (*Grand Serjeanty*) or an officer of parliament charged with enforcing its dictates. By the twelfth century garrison knights were invariably outnumbered by what contemporary PIPE ROLLS describe as serjeants whose successors appear in later records as owing forty days' military duty in time of war. The importance of this class in feudal society must have been considerable for it undoubtedly included many men of substance who were, in arms and equipment, little inferior to knights. But to a considerable degree they fell outside the process which, in the twelfth century, brought tenure by knight-service under royal control and for the most part the sovereign rarely intervened in the relationship between a lord and the man who held lands of him by military serjeanty. In practice the office of serjeant increasingly came to be

associated with the performance of personal rather than military duties, and many serjeants were, for example, gamekeepers or physicians.
(*See also* ANCIENT *and* LIEUTENANT)

SERPENTINE *see* FIREARMS AND CANNON

SERVERY *see* KITCHENS

SERVICE ROOMS *see* HALL *and* KITCHENS

SHARPENING STEEL *see* WEAPONS AND HARNESS

SHELL-KEEP *or* **SHELL ENCLOSURE** The construction of a masonry tower on an artificial MOTTE was not always practicable, the concentration of weight often causing subsidence and eventual collapse. In some cases a more appropriate type of superstructure was the circular or polygonal shell-keep, a stone enclosure built around the summit of a motte, effectively replacing the original timber palisade. Because of its shape, the shell enclosure was not only more economic to build than a tower but, more importantly, the downward thrust of the masonry was distributed evenly around the summit of the motte. In a shell-keep the residential buildings were built against the inner circumference of the wall or 'shell' which was usually some 2.5–3m (8–10ft) thick and 6–7.5m (20–25ft) high, the enclosure having a diameter of 12–30m (40–100ft). Often the bailey palisade was also rebuilt in stone and carried up both sides of the motte to join the shell-keep, as at Cardiff and Carisbrooke (1136) (*see* WING-WALL). In some cases the wall enclosed the base of the motte instead of standing on its summit, as at Berkeley, Carmarthen and Farnham Castles. At Berkeley, in *c.* 1154, the motte was remodelled and the sides revetted and buttressed in red sandstone. The perimeter wall was built up from ground level to a height of 18.9m (62ft) to encase the motte and the whole building was strengthened by four semicircular bastions (of which three remain), one of which contained the apse of a chapel and another a well-chamber. A forebuilding was constructed in the wall between two of these turrets and it was in a chamber above this that Edward II is said to have been murdered in 1327. The shell-keep of Farnham Castle was similarly constructed around the base of a motte, but in this case the motte itself encased an 11.3m (37ft) square substructure that extended downwards through the mound to ground level and once supported a square stone tower on a 15.5m (51ft) square plinth. The shell enclosure that replaced this tower in *c.* 1155 was reinforced by four rectangular projections and a shallow, three-storey rectangular gate-tower. The hall, chambers, chapel and kitchens that were contained within the enclosure continued in use at least until the fifteenth century.

Shell-keeps continued to be built into the thirteenth century, indeed it has been suggested that Wardour Castle (1393) was a late medieval revival of the type (*see* TOWER-HOUSES). Trematon Castle in Cornwall is perhaps the finest unaltered example of a twelfth-century motte and bailey stronghold that was strengthened in the thirteenth century by the erection of a shell-keep on the motte and the construction of a stone curtain wall round the bailey with a three-storey projecting gate-tower. A number of castles have towers that were built within earlier shell enclosures: Clun, Farnham, Guildford, Launceston and Tretower, for example. At Launceston Castle a thirteenth-century modernisation scheme included the raising of a strong cylindrical stone tower at the centre of the twelfth-century shell-keep. This tower rose a full storey above the outer wall, while the space between tower and wall was covered over by a fighting platform. It was approached by a covered stair that ascended one side of the huge motte from a guard-tower at its foot. Launceston's tower is an austere building with few signs of domestic comfort and was apparently intended as a final refuge, the main residential apartments, together with a hall, being located in the bailey. At Tretower Castle a circular Great Tower was erected in 1220–30 within a shell enclosure that dates from *c.* 1150. The tower, the wall of which is battered at the base and is some 2.7m (9ft) thick, was designed to give the garrison a clear field of view over the outer wall-walk of the shell enclosure which was linked by a bridge to the second storey of the tower. Tretower is of particular interest because the shell-keep was constructed to accommodate existing buildings: the south and west walls are straight where they abutted an earlier Norman hall and solar. It was these buildings that were demolished (except for their outer walls) to make way for the later Great Tower.

There were many variations: at Arundel Castle the shell-keep (*c.* 1180) was entered through a narrow FOREBUILDING (an early addition) flanked by a tower, while at Berkeley, Lewes and Tamworth mural towers or turrets were incorporated in the enclosure walls (*see* CLUSTERED DONJON). In the early fourteenth century Henry Percy rebuilt his twelfth-century shell-keep at Alnwick Castle, enlarging it and adding seven semicircular towers. His son, grandson and great-grandson (all Henry) added further accretions to form a magnificent complex of buildings that came to be known as the 'Seven Towers of the Percys'.

Only occasionally have the residential buildings survived within the walls of a shell-keep. It is likely that it was Henry I who built the first stone enclosure round the summit of the huge motte at Windsor Castle, and it was within this that Henry II constructed (1173–9) a large, slightly oval, shell-keep, about 30.5m (100ft) in diameter and with walls 1.5m (5ft) thick. Within this enclosure a range of oak-frame buildings was erected against the walls, similar in appearance to the present two-storey apartments in which several of the timbers from the late twelfth-century lodges have survived. The original walls were 10.7m (35ft) high but were increased to 20m (65ft) when the 'Round Tower' was given a sham machicolated crown by Sir Jeffry Wyatville in 1830. At Tamworth Castle the domestic buildings within the confines of the irregular polygonal shell enclosure (*c.* 1110) remained in constant use until the nineteenth century. Most of the buildings date from 1423–1688 during which time they were occupied, refurbished and sometimes replaced by a cadet branch of the Ferrers family. Today they remain, clustered attractively around the fifteenth-century hall that Sir John Ferrers retained as the centre of his elegant Jacobean 'mansion'.

Several RINGWORKS have erroneously been described as shell-keeps. Restormel Castle, for example, comprises a perfectly circular bailey with internal buildings – hall, solar, guests' quarters and kitchen (all now ruined) – arranged concentrically against a crenellated curtain wall. From the outside the stone curtain appears to crown the motte and for this reason it is often described as a shell-keep. But the inner bank of the ringwork was removed when the curtain was built in *c.* 1200 and the living quarters added in *c.* 1280.

SHERIFF A 'shire-reeve' (*scīr gerēfa*). The office of sheriff superseded that of EALDORMAN as the crown's deputy and consequently the most important member of the executive in a county. Prior to the emergence of the JUSTICES OF THE PEACE in the fourteenth century, the sheriff was the main agent of the courts and was responsible for the crown revenues of his shire. He was also responsible for the MILITIA until this duty passed to the LIEUTENANT and eventually to the Lord Lieutenant. In 1170 an inquiry considered malpractices by sheriffs and this resulted in the appointment of coroners.
(*See also* HUNDRED, LAW AND ORDER *and* REEVE)

SHIELDS

The following terms are most commonly used when describing shields of the medieval period (* *see also* individual entries).

À BOUCHE	having an indentation to carry a lance
BUCKLER*	small circular wooden shield
ENARMES*	straps for the forearm
GUIGE*	shoulder strap
HEATER*	shaped like the base of a flat-iron
KITE-SHAPED*	long, narrow shield
MANTLET*	lightweight defensive hoarding
'NORMAN' SHIELD	as kite-shaped
PAVISE*	large infantry shield or mantlet
TALEVAS	large cavalry shield or infantry mantlet
TARGET or TARGE*	large cavalry shield or circular shield used by infantry
TARGIAM	large form of cavalry shield

In the eleventh century, and at the beginning of the twelfth, shields were long, narrow and kite-shaped, covering most of the body. Designed primarily for use on horseback, they may have developed from the tall, flat-based shields used by infantry in some Mediterranean and Middle Eastern countries. They had rounded tops and were made of wood covered with tough boiled leather. Known also as 'Norman' shields, they were in use at the battle of Senlac in 1066 (*see* BAYEUX TAPESTRY) and during the First Crusade, where raised edges, studs and bosses were often picked out in colour. During the twelfth century the tops of shields became flatter and decoration more personal (*see* ARMORY). At first, the adoption of the couched lance and close-formation cavalry tactics resulted in a significant increase in the size of a knight's shield. These large shields were generally known as *targes* and were made of leather-covered wood, though the term was later applied to smaller, circular shields also known as *targets*. Such was the damage caused to a shield that a member of the mounted élite would sometimes be accompanied in battle by a servant carrying several spare shields. A twelfth-century infantryman also used a very large shield sometimes described as a *talevas* – presumably a pun, suggesting that it was the size of a 'table' (*see* MANTLET). By the fourteenth century the shield used by mounted nobles

1. twelfth century, 2. fourteenth century, 3. À bouche.

and knights had become very much smaller, though of thicker construction, and shaped like a flat-iron (called a *heater shield*), being roughly one-third longer than it was broad. This is the shield which is most often depicted in coats of arms. In the fourteenth century large rectangular *pavises* replaced earlier types of infantry shield. These were almost of sufficient height to cover a standing man and were designed for use both as a mantlet and, collectively, to form a protective wall. At the same time much smaller hand-held wooden or leather *bucklers* continued to be used by light infantry forces, especially in Wales and the north of England. The increasing efficiency of the longbow and crossbow, and the rapid development of plate armour, reduced the effectiveness of the shield as a means of defence and by the fifteenth century it had been abandoned by mounted knights except for heraldic purposes at tournaments and pageants, etc. It was at this time that the *à bouche* shield was most in evidence, again for armorial display: this had a notch cut into the side to allow for the free movement of a lance in the joust.

Effigies and monumental brasses, etc., may be dated with reasonable accuracy by reference to the shield held by a figure or depicted elsewhere on a MONUMENT. After the sixteenth century numerous stylised shields found their way into armory, few of which could ever have been used on the battlefield.
(*See also* ARCHERY, ARMOUR, HELMETS *and* WEAPONS AND HARNESS)

SHIELDWALL A battle formation adopted by the English prior to the Norman Conquest and used at the battle of Senlac ('the lake of blood') in 1066. The tight formation of men, protected by a wall of shields, was difficult for an enemy to penetrate.

SHILLING *see* COINAGE

SHINGLES Wooden tiles used for covering walls and roofs throughout the medieval period. Usually of oak, they measured 12.7 × 25.4cm (5 × 10in) and were laid with an overlap, each shingle being thicker at the lower edge. It is known that the courtyard buildings and towers at several Edwardian castles were originally roofed with shingles and that at Conwy in 1321 these had to be replaced because 'much of the rest of the timber [has] perished for want of a covering of lead'. In 1260 Henry III gave orders for the shingles to be removed from the roof of the great kitchen at Marlborough Castle (which was to be covered with stone slates) and re-used on a chamber in the high tower which, in turn, was to be stripped of its thatch. From this and other sources it

is evident that it was the cost of roofing with shingles that restricted its use. In 1314, when Queen Margaret embarked on the refurbishment of several of her manors, it was found that roofing with slates or tiles would be very much cheaper than using shingles.
(*See also* LEAD, ROOFS (TIMBER) *and* THATCH)

SHIRE From the Old English *scīr* evolved the word 'shire' which, by the end of the ninth century, was applied to the administrative divisions of Wessex and within a century to those of East Anglia and the Midlands. Each shire comprised a number of smaller administrative units: HUNDREDS in the south and WAPENTAKES in the former Danelaw territories. Some shires retained their tribal identities: Middlesex was the land of the Middle Saxons, Cumberland the land of the Cumbras and Dorset that of the Dornsæte, for example. Others were distinguished by the names of their principal settlements: Hereford-shire, Worcester-shire, York-shire and so on. Not all are quite so obvious today: Wiltshire was named after the town of Wilton (*Wiltunscir*); Hampshire from *Hamtūn*, the old name for Southampton (*Hamtunscir*); and Shropshire from *Scrobbesbyrigscir*, which meant 'the shire with Shrewsbury at its head'. (In its Norman form Shropshire was *Salope-scira*, hence the alternative name Salop.) Following the Norman Conquest the shires were superseded by COUNTIES, though the word remained in general use until the late Middle Ages and several counties still refer to their administrative offices as the Shire Hall.

SHORE A supporting timber.

SHORT BOW *see* ARCHERY

SHOT-HOLE A hole for firearms, usually smaller than a GUN PORT.

SHOULDERED ARCH *see* ARCH

SHUTTERS In 1240 Henry III ordered his great chamber in the Tower of London 'to be entirely whitewashed and newly painted, and all the shutters [*fenestrae*] of the same to be made anew with new wood and bolts and hinges, and to be painted with our arms'. Similarly, in 1265 all the DOORS and shutters of the king's hall and chamber at Winchester were painted with royal heraldry. At Sheppey Castle in 1364 two carpenters were contracted to provide 407 doors and shutters ('window-doors') at 10*d* each, while at Clarendon in 1316 payments were made for '142 boards of oak for making doors and

shutters'. From these and many other examples, it is clear that shutters were almost invariably fitted to window openings, and that their surfaces were often painted with heraldic and other decoration. Shutters were used even when glass was fitted (*see* GLAZING). In 1245 orders were given for making a window in the queen's chamber at Guildford: 'the window to be wainscoted and closed with glass windows . . . with panels which can be opened and closed, and wooden shutters in one piece inside to close over the glass windows'. Shutters were often braced like doors and affixed to a window jamb with 'hinge-hooks', the matrices of which may still be visible. It would appear that pulleys and ropes were sometimes used to open and close larger sets of shutters: an account of 1519 describes 'many pretty wyndowes [shutters] shette with levys [levers] goynge up and downe'.
(*See also* DOORS *and* WINDOWS)

SIEGE FORT *or* **SIEGE CASTLE** A rapidly constructed fort comprising a ditch and rampart surrounding the encampment of a besieging force to protect it from a sudden counter-attack. A great siege-fort nicknamed Malvoisin, meaning 'evil neighbour', was erected by William Rufus when he invested Bamburgh Castle in 1095.

SIEGE PLATFORM (i) A temporary platform on which were mounted the siege engines of a besieging force. It is surprising how many medieval siege forts have survived as grassy platforms, similar in appearance to a large golf tee, within trebuchet-range of a castle's walls (*see* SIEGES). That across the river from Wallingford Castle was constructed when the castle was subjected to three long sieges during the twelfth-century ANARCHY. Medieval siege platforms should not be confused with seventeenth-century Civil War gun emplacements which are of similar appearance but usually larger and of more substantial (and, therefore, more durable) construction.
(ii) A permanent platform for siege-engines, used for defensive purposes. There are fine examples at Harlech Castle where platforms carved into the cliff-top in the outer ward protected the water gate and sea-approaches below.

SIEGES
The following terms are most commonly used when describing medieval siege engines and techniques (* *see also* individual entries). It should be noted, however, that contemporary chroniclers used several of these terms as though they were interchangeable.

BALLISTA	frame-mounted catapult (generic)
BATTERING RAM	tree-trunk capped with iron, swung on ropes
BEFFROI	*see* BELFRY
BELFRY*	mobile wooden tower
BOMBARD*	*see* FIREARMS AND CANNON
BORE	iron-pointed ram
BRATTICE	*see* HOARDING
CASEMATE*	defences at foot of curtain wall
CAT	colloquial term for a penthouse
CHAT CASTEL	a bore or ram
COUNTER-CASTLE	protection for siege operations
CROW	long pole with a hooked end
ENGINE TOWER*	tower on which siege machine was positioned
ESCALADE	scaling ladder
ESPRINGAL	frame-mounted arrow-shooting catapult
GREAT CROSSBOW	large crossbow (*see* ARCHERY)
MANGONEL	stone-throwing engine (torsion)
MANTLET*	mobile shelter
MOULON	a mangonel
ONAGER	a siege engine
PENTHOUSE*	movable wooden 'shed'
PERRIER*	counterpoise stone-throwing engine
PETRARIA	stone-throwing engine (generic)
SAP*	a tunnel or trench
SAPPER	one who digs saps
SCORPION	early form of espringal
SIEGE PLATFORM*	levelled base for siege engine
SPRINGALD	*see* espringal
TESTUDO	*see* tortoise
TONGUE	a long arrow-like projectile
TORTOISE	protective covering for ram or miners
TREBUCHET	stone-throwing engine (counterweight)
UNDERMINING	tunnelling beneath a wall

In England relatively few castles or fortified towns were ever called upon to resist a siege. This reflects the comparatively peaceful nature of medieval society and the country's success in averting invasion. The primary military function of a castle in medieval times was an offensive one: as a base for active operations by which surrounding territory could be controlled. But as such it was of considerable value in war and no invading army would wish to leave a strongly garrisoned castle or town to its rear. Thus invasion was made all the more difficult by the presence of numerous castles all of which were designed to withstand a siege and therefore to frustrate an invader's advance, possibly for many months. Of course there were sieges in England, notably during the twelfth-century ANARCHY and the Magna Carta War of 1215–16 when the *trebuchet* was first used (*see below*). In Wales there is hardly a castle that was not besieged, usually as a consequence of Welsh resistance, initially to the Norman invaders and later to Edward I's colonial aspirations (*see* WALES, CONQUEST OF). Most of the great Edwardian castles succeeded in resisting Madoc ap Llywelyn's revolt of 1294, principally because they were designed and located to be provisioned by sea. Significantly, during Owain Glyn Dŵr's rising of 1400–9, only Harlech and Aberystwyth surrendered after their supply lines were cut off by a French blockade. Even though the English had become expert in siegecraft during the wars with Scotland and France, the WARS OF THE ROSES were, for the most part, determined on the battlefield, sieges being confined to a small number of northern castles and to Harlech which, notably, withstood a prolonged siege by a Yorkist army in 1468, only to capitulate when threatened with starvation. The Harlech garrison and its Welsh constable, Dafydd ap Ievan, are immortalised in the song 'Men of Harlech'.

In continental Europe major military campaigns, such as those of the HUNDRED YEARS WAR, were undertaken principally to capture towns, many of which were fortified. No castle or fortified town was truly impregnable: without any prospect of relief, it was inevitable that provisions would eventually be exhausted. For the besiegers there were two options: direct assault or slow containment. Once the gates were closed against a hostile force an attempt would be made to persuade a garrison to capitulate, usually by bribery or by threatening to execute and mutilate prisoners. It was not unknown for the heads of decapitated captives to be used as missiles or for child hostages to be tied to siege engines to deter any attempt to set them on fire. On 1 August 1418 the townspeople of Rouen awoke to find themselves surrounded by five siege forts, each linked to its neighbour by trenches, and tunnels (*saps*), dug to conceal an enemy's approach. The city of Rouen, the 'key to Henry V's conquest

of Normandy', was guarded by 6km (3¾ miles) of walls and was so well fortified with towers and barbicans that starvation was the only effective weapon. The English cut off the city's water supply and contaminated the wells with dead animals. PLAGUE took hold, corpses piled up in the streets and were left to rot. According to John Page, an Englishman present at the siege, the garrison and townspeople 'were reduced to eating cats, dogs, mice and rats, and finally to any vegetable peelings they could find' so that within the city a mouse could be sold for 6*d* and a rat for 30*d*. Eventually the defending troops ejected twelve thousand 'useless mouths' out of the city, but Henry refused to let them leave and confined them to the town ditch. 'One might see wandering here and there children of two or three years old begging for bread since their parents were dead. These wretched people had only sodden soil under them and lay there crying for food – some expiring, some unable to open their eyes and not even breathing, others as thin as twigs.' With all hope gone, the city surrendered to the earl of Warwick on 19 January 1419. Such savagery was not uncommon. At the same time, however, the besiegers' camps were 'stinking places, full of pestilence and corruption' due, no doubt, to the contemporary disregard for hygiene.

The early motte and bailey castles of England and Wales were very effective strongholds against the heavy cavalry of mailed knights which at that time dominated warfare (*see* MOTTE). Inevitably, fire was especially dangerous to timber defences but at the beginning of the twelfth century there is little evidence of the use of more advanced techniques of siegecraft that had been practised in the classical world centuries before. The introduction of stone defences was both the result and the cause of advancing methods of attack. These methods were not necessarily innovative in the historical sense, but were techniques of the classical past that were reintroduced and refined in the west in response to the changing nature of warfare and as a consequence of lessons learned during the CRUSADES. From the twelfth century the science of siegecraft remained largely unchanged until almost the end of the Middle Ages. The introduction of gunpowder into warfare in the fourteenth century had surprisingly little immediate effect (*see* FIREARMS AND CANNON) and throughout the medieval period the castle maintained a supremacy of defence over attack, within the limitations of human endurance and the maintenance of adequate supplies.

Two methods of attack were used against a fortified position: bombardment and close assault.

Medieval artillery consisted of the great stone-throwing 'siege-engines' (*petraria*) which battered a breach in the defences through which an assault could be made. The gatehouse was recognised as the most vulnerable element of a castle's defences and consequently it became its most strongly fortified nucleus (*see* GATEHOUSES). Bombardment was therefore concentrated on the weakest length of curtain wall, preferably one that was unprotected by flanking towers, and increasingly sophisticated water defences developed in order to keep these machines at a distance and to frustrate undermining (*see* MOATS AND WATER DEFENCES).

There were three main types of petraria, all of which would have been positioned on level platforms or *siege forts* protected by *mantlets*, mobile shelters of wood or toughened leather (the platform of a twelfth-century siege fort can be seen across the river near Wallingford Castle). Depending on their size and design, petraria had a range of between 80 and 120m (87 and 131yd). The *mangonel* consisted of a long arm, with a cup or sling for the projectile at its free end, which passed through ropes stretched between upright posts. These ropes were twisted by windlasses, the arm pulled down against the torsion, and the projectile hurled towards the target when the arm was released.

A far more powerful engine was the *trebuchet* which was introduced in the late twelfth century and worked on the counterweight principle. Like the mangonel, projectiles were directed at a target from a revolving arm pivoting between two uprights, but the motive power was provided by an immense counterweight that could be moved along the shorter end of the arm to obtain the correct range and trajectory. Trebuchets were extremely precise instruments and were provided with wheels that added stability and range. They were operated by shifts of men who worked day and night and were intended to apply constant accurate pounding to a single section of wall, thereby reducing it to rubble. To counteract this, the walls themselves were often constructed with outer skins filled with rubble and lime cement to absorb the impact of missiles. Lead counterweights were sometimes used, the lead being 'acquired' from church roofs in the neighbourhood, though pivoted boxes or baskets filled with stones, sand, etc., were more successful because they responded to gravity. Edward I's giant trebuchet, known as the 'War Wolf', must have struck terror in the hearts of defenders and once it appeared on the scene the balance of a siege undoubtedly shifted in favour of the attackers. Edward was so proud of the 'War Wolf' that in 1304 he erected a viewing platform for his queen and her ladies so they could watch as it pounded the walls of Stirling.

Both machines were used for hurling large stones but other projectiles could also be used such as the dreaded GREEK FIRE (a combustible mixture that was probably introduced by Richard I from Byzantium). Smooth, rounded river boulders were the most effective projectiles, though the rotting entrails of animals, sacks of dung and the corpses of diseased animals, which burst on impact, were also used – a medieval form of germ warfare. Siege engines of this type were so large that they had to be dismantled in order to move them from one site to another. At the siege of Dryslwyn Castle in 1287 the engineers were accompanied by 20 horsemen, 60 oxen pulling wheeled wagons and 35 pack-horses carrying 480 stones as ammunition. The siege lasted twenty-eight days, during which the garrison suffered heavy losses when a section of the castle wall collapsed on them after continuous pummelling by a trebuchet. Engines were sometimes built *in situ*, itinerant engineers offering their services to a commander and then engaging their own teams of joiners and blacksmiths. The smaller siege engines were also used by defenders. They were placed on towers (*see* ENGINE TOWER) and, where the topography of a site allowed, on permanent siege platforms. At Harlech Castle, for example, a series of platforms carved into the cliff-face in the outer ward protected the water gate and sea-approaches below.

The third type of engine was the *ballista*. This generic term included the *espringal* or *springald* (derived from the Old French for 'spring') which shot iron bolts in the manner of an enormous crossbow. The espringal was a formidable torsion-powered siege and battle engine comprising two arms that were drawn backwards by a windlass and released to shoot a large bolt (*tongue*), a small stone shot or a container of inflammable material. Unlike the mangonel or trebuchet, the espringal shot its missiles along an almost horizontal trajectory. Made of beech, elm or oak, an espringal's 1,800kg of torsion power came from twisted skeins of horse or cattle hair, and it was capable of shooting an 80cm (31in) iron-tipped wooden tongue with considerable accuracy over a terrifying distance. There was also a large version of the crossbow (*see* ARCHERY), known as the *great crossbow*, which could be positioned on a parapet or wall, or on a cart in open battle, and would probably have been spanned by means of a windlass. It was made of yew wood and horn with a span of up to 2m (6ft). It was frame-mounted on a bench and spanned by an integral screw-winch mechanism. Again, espringals and great crossbows were also used by defenders.

A belfry or breaching tower in use during a siege, together with (from left to right) crossbowmen reloading, bombards and archers with their protective mantlets.

There were other devices for breaching defences at close quarters. These included the *battering ram*, usually a large tree-trunk capped with iron, which was swung on ropes from a supporting, protective framework. Battering rams were most often used against gates, but against masonry the smaller, iron-pointed *bore* was more effective. By far the most efficient method of destroying a section of wall was by *undermining* which was first used in England by William the Conqueror against the walls of Exeter in 1068. Expert sappers tunnelled beneath the foundations of the target area of wall and shored them up with timber props. The mine chamber was then filled with combustible material and ignited so that when the props burned through the masonry collapsed into the cavity and the wall was breached. The corners of square towers were particularly vulnerable (part of the keep at Rochester Castle collapsed when it was undermined in 1215) and it was for this reason that cylindrical towers with battered (splayed) bases became *de rigueur*. When King John besieged Rochester he taunted the starving garrison by smearing bacon fat on the tunnel props before setting fire to them. Counter-mining from within the castle was usually the only effective defence: Henry V is reputed to have fought hand-to-hand with the enemy commander in tunnels which the English had dug beneath the town walls of Melun, near Paris, in 1420, but which had flooded because the water table was too high. Inevitably, very few examples of medieval mining tunnels have survived. The unfinished twelfth-century galleries that threatened to bring down the south-west corner of the keep at Bungay Castle have been preserved, however, and these show that the attackers dug a covered trench to the base of the wall, removed part

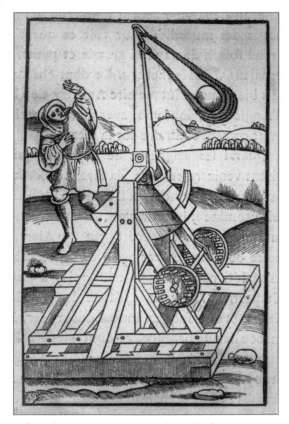

Fifteenth-century engraving of a trebuchet.

of the wall and shored it up with timber and then excavated the footings beneath the wall which, again, were packed with timber. They then dug a tunnel with a camouflaged exit through which a raid was to be launched inside the defences. Meanwhile, the defenders dug a series of counter-mines in order to destroy the attackers' tunnel. Whether the garrison surrendered before the wooden props were set alight, or whether the mine failed to bring down the wall, it is impossible to tell. Only castles built on rock, such as Goodrich and Harlech, could withstand such a form of attack, while elsewhere sophisticated water defences were devised, as at Caerphilly Castle in south Wales. Many of these operations were carried out from beneath a *penthouse* or *cat*, a large movable wooden 'shed', the reinforced roof of which provided protection from arrows and bolts and from missiles dropped from above. The smaller *tortoise*, which, as the name suggests, had a hard shell of leather, performed a similar function but with greater mobility.

The most common, though hazardous, means of entry was by the use of scaling ladders (*escalade*), a

development of which was the *belfry*, a great movable tower, protected from fire by a covering of damp animal skins, that was trundled across a filled-in moat or ditch and positioned hard against a castle walls. This provided protection for the attackers who were able to concentrate their force on a vulnerable area of wall-walk and attack *en masse* across a plank bridge which was lowered on to the parapet. The belfry also served as a useful observation and shooting platform when not otherwise required. Both attackers and defenders used long, pivoted poles with hooks at the end (*crows*) to pick off individual soldiers. In most cases the first necessity was to fill in the defensive ditch that surrounded a castle so that the penthouses and belfry could be moved into position and to enable sappers to work at the base of a wall without the need for excessive tunnelling.

Many of these siege weapons acquired fanciful names such as 'Tortoise' or 'Cat', applied to the penthouse because of its stealth, and 'Mouse' for the bore.

SIGNAL STATIONS *see* BEACONS *and* CHURCH TOWERS

SINISTER From the Latin *sinister* and the Old French *sinistre* meaning 'left'. In the Middle Ages a left-handed person was treated with suspicion, marked by ill-will and somehow 'sinister'. In ARMORY the term is applied to the right-hand side of a shield of arms *when viewed from the front*, the sinister being considered inferior to the DEXTER or left-hand side.

SIR A reduced form of 'sire', this word is the distinctive title of address of a baronet or knight (*see* BANNERET, BARONET *and* KNIGHTHOOD AND CHIVALRY, ORDERS OF).

SITING A castle was the fortified residence of a feudal lord. Through his castle he controlled his estate and he did so by means of the heavily armed and mounted men who occupied the castle even in his absence. The castle's principal function was, therefore, an offensive one, its range of influence corresponding with the range of a horse – about 12 miles if his men wished to return on the same day. Medieval magnates possessed considerable delegated authority. Upon them rested both the defence and the control of the realm. Warfare was concerned with the control of land and in the Middle Ages he who would control the land must first control the castle. It must, therefore, be as impregnable as possible, relying not only on the strength of its walls and towers but also on man's ingenuity in selecting a readily defensible site. Even so, military considerations did not always provide the rationale for selecting a particular site. King John apparently chose the location of his castle at Odiham because the surrounding countryside provided him with good hunting.

In the decades after the Conquest, William concentrated on building his castles in existing centres of power, at London and York, Lincoln and Norwich, for example, and in Anglo-Saxon BURHS and major towns such as Exeter, Dover, Durham, Old Sarum and Wallingford. Sometimes the castle occupied one corner of an existing fortification, as at Exeter (*see* TOWN WALLS), while Carisbrooke Castle on the Isle of Wight was raised on the site of a Roman fort, one of a chain of coastal defences known as the 'Saxon Shore'. Both Roman and Norman strategists understood that a small island with a long coastline could best be defended from its centre. The castles of senior members of the Conqueror's entourage were usually large enclosures of sufficient extent to accommodate a substantial body of troops: Richmond, Deddington and Rochester Castles are but three examples. But as a lord's household knights were granted lands and dispersed in order to take possession of them, so many of these early fortifications were provided with an earth MOTTE or stone KEEP that could be defended by a smaller number of men. The castles erected by sub-tenants were, for the most part, temporary motte and bailey strongholds, intended to define a newly acquired territory and to establish feudal authority. Many were later replaced by stone structures or abandoned for more favourable locations. Similarly, throughout the civil war of 1135–54, known as 'The Anarchy', numerous adulterine castles were erected, only to be abandoned once royal authority was restored (*see* ANARCHY, THE).

At this time most sites were selected for military purposes: either strategically (to control points of communication) or tactically (to take advantage of the topography). Chepstow Castle fulfilled both objectives. It occupies a spectacular cliff-top site on the west bank of a loop in the River Wye, a few kilometres north of its confluence with the Severn estuary. As such it was easily defensible and controlled an important route-way across the border from the Severn crossing at Gloucester into the southern March of Wales. On the Welsh side of the river, the castle was intended as a forward base for William fitz Osbern's campaigns against Gwent. At Chepstow the three elements of Norman conquest

The spectacular cliff-top site of Chepstow Castle on the west bank of a loop in the River Wye.

were in evidence from the beginning: the castle, the priory and the town, a community of merchants from which the place obtained its name: *Cheap-stow*, a 'trading place'. Castles that were located in mountain passes, at river crossings, ports and converging route-ways were usually built to control communications. Matthew Paris (*c.* 1200–59) described Dover Castle as 'the key of England', while Pembroke Castle commanded the sea passage to Ireland. In the late thirteenth century Edward I's strategy for the conquest and colonisation of Gwynedd depended on the creation of a ring of coastal castles all of which could be supplied by sea, thereby increasing their impregnability (*see* QUAYS). Several castles were located dramatically on isolated peaks, prominent spurs and hill-tops, sometimes occupying the ramparts of earlier fortifications. Others were protected on at least one flank by a river or cliffs or, as at Tintagel and Dunstanburgh, were located on promontories jutting into the sea (Tintagel was originally the retreat of a Dark Age religious community). The Castle of the Peak occupies an almost impregnable site, at the

Strategically located in a gap in the Purbeck Hills, Corfe Castle controlled the road from Swanage to Wareham and the hinterland of Poole Harbour. Corfe was King John's favourite fortress and it remains one of the most dramatic and evocative of English ruins.

summit of a rock with a precipice on either side, while Corfe Castle towers above its picturesque village on a rocky outcrop in a gap in the Purbeck hills. Montgomery and Harlech, Carreg Cennen and Cilgerran, Dover and Warwick all occupy spectacularly dramatic sites, while Warkworth and Durham have the best of both worlds, being built on rocky promontories surrounded by a river on three sides. A castle in such a location, especially when built on natural rock, made undermining of the walls an almost impossible operation for a besieging force. But the suitability of such sites was restricted by the availability of a reliable water supply and several were abandoned when the water table receded or when a source was found to be vulnerable to pollution during a siege (*see* WELLS). Furthermore, the disposition of a castle's defences was often dictated by the shape of the rock or promontory on which it stood: Conwy's 'hour-glass' shape is an obvious example. And, contrary to popular opinion, a hill-top was not necessarily the best location from which to defend a castle. In many instances a site was selected precisely because it lay at the centre of a natural 'bowl', the sides of which formed a sloping

KILLING GROUND within bowshot of the walls (183–229m (200–250yd)) and afforded no protection to a besieging force. Hill-top or declivity, it was very much more difficult for siege machines to approach the walls of a castle when the surrounding land was not level. Many castles were, of necessity, located on relatively flat terrain and without any natural defensive features. Their strength then depended entirely on their construction and on additional measures such as MOATS AND WATER DEFENCES. Wherever possible, streams were dammed or diverted to fill ditches and create lakes, the castles rising from the waters on artificial islands. The vast lakes that surrounded Leeds, Kenilworth and Caerphilly Castles kept siege engines at a distance, as did Bodiam's broad moat though (more importantly, one suspects) it served also to emphasise the grandeur of the castle and the status and good taste of its owner.

Very often the siting of a castle was chosen for no better reason than its convenience. Several castles at river crossings are there not for strategic purposes but because the ford made access to the castle easier. Others were located to protect existing settlements which were developed and promoted as centres of trade and commerce, to the financial benefit of the lord who collected the profits of rents, tolls and services. The Norman conquerors and their successors planted new towns at the gates of many of their castles: at Barnard Castle and Castle Acre, Kidwelly, Launceston and Ludlow for example (*see* TOWNS). Many of these planned towns prospered while others, such as Kilpeck and Richard's Castle, became moribund or were abandoned entirely (*see* DESERTED VILLAGES). Lords who possessed more than one castle often selected their locations to serve different purposes. William de Warrenne's castle at Lewis, for example, commanded the River Ouse where it passes through a gap in the Sussex Downs and was clearly located for strategic purposes, to defend an important route inland from the Channel coast. However, the site of William's other castle, Castle Acre, was chosen because it was a convenient administrative centre for his vast East Anglian estates. Some castles were located for strategic reasons but nevertheless occupied poor defensive positions: Rochester Castle, for example, was positioned in the corner of the old Roman defences close to a major crossing point on the River Medway. Others, such as Pembroke, controlled ports and harbours, guarding against seaborne incursions and facilitating the collection of taxes from trade. The observation tower on the keep of Warkworth Castle enabled the garrison to monitor movements in and out of the harbour some 2km (1¼ miles) to the south-east.

Initially, in Wales and the Marches, Anglo-Norman expansion was achieved by a piecemeal process of conquest undertaken by individual barons (*see* MARCH). Pembroke, Chepstow and Cardigan Castles were built in the twelfth century to establish new lordships, the first stage of which was to build a fortress in a strong military position. Thus the presence of a castle implies that a feudal lordship was once concentrated there. Other castles were located primarily for defensive reasons and these are usually found in clusters: the early thirteenth-century Trilateral Castles of Grosmont, Skenfrith and White Castle, for example, which guarded one of the major land routes from England into Wales (*see* THREE CASTLES, THE).

Some castles were deliberately erected on sites that were known to be of symbolic significance to the native population. At Montacute, the local Saxons believed that a piece of the 'true cross' was buried in the hill on which Robert of Mortain (*c.* 1031–90) excavated his bailey within the ramparts of an Iron Age hillfort. Two centuries later Edward I ruthlessly suppressed the native Welsh

during his conquest of Gwynedd (*see* WALES, CONQUEST OF). In 1283–4 he demolished the Cistercian abbey of Aberconwy, venerated by the Welsh as the burial place of Llewelyn the Great, built his formidable walled town and castle on the site and moved the monks to Maenan, 13km (8 miles) away in the Conwy valley. He then selected Caernarfon as the capital of his new principality, motivated by Welsh mythology which he appropriated in order to add legitimacy to his occupation. The nearby Roman fortress of Segontium was believed by the Welsh to have been the seat of Magnus Maximus (*Maxen Wledig*), emperor of Gaul, Spain and Britain from 383 to 388. Inevitably the legend caught the imagination of the bards and entered Welsh mythology in the pages of the *Mabinogion*, a collection of early Welsh sagas. When Edward came to build Caernarfon as his own fortress palace, he appears to have deliberately re-created the *Mabinogion*'s spectacular description of a great city with towers of many colours and eagles fashioned out of gold. Caernarfon's polygonal towers and bands of dark masonry appear to have been inspired by the massive Roman walls of the imperial city of Constantinople (*see* WALES, CONQUEST OF).

Before assessing the strategic and military rationale for a particular site, it is important to consider why a castle was needed in the first place. Was it for the conquest and suppression of newly acquired territories? For the consolidation and administration of a lord's estates? Was it to defend against invasion or insurrection? Or, as at Raglan, was it intended to celebrate dynastic achievement? Sites might be chosen for their military and strategic importance but, above all, castles were intended to declaim the status and authority of the feudal lords who built them. For this reason they needed to dominate the surrounding landscape – and the emotions of those who lived in their shadow.

SLATES AND TILES Following the devastation by fire of several major cities in the late twelfth century, building regulations were issued in London in 1212 that required thatched roofs to be replaced with coverings of tiles, slates and other less inflammable materials. It is not always possible to ascertain whether entries for 'tiles' in contemporary building accounts refer to roofing, paving or building tiles or, indeed, to stone slates, though roofing tiles are sometimes described as *thaktyles* or *flat tiles*. (*For* floor and wall tiles *see* ENCAUSTIC TILES *and* PAVING.)

The term 'slate' was originally applied to any kind of split stone (from the Old French *esclate* meaning 'something split') and this included not only slates for roofing but also *flags* for floors. Medieval slates were roughly hexagonal in shape, with a squared 'tail' and narrowing at one end, those used at the eaves of a roof being considerably larger. Both tiles and stone slates were hung from the laths of a roof in a similar manner. In each case an oak peg was driven through a hole near the top edge of the tile so that it projected on the underside. The peg was then used to hang the tile from the lath, with each layer of tiles overlapping the row below it. Tiles were made with holes ready for pegging but slates had to be pierced: at Oakham in 1383 the 'boryng' of 2,500 slates cost 4*s*. In some districts tiles were bedded on moss (*mosseying*) which prevented the wind and rain from penetrating between the tiles and provided protection against melting snow. Alternatively, the layers might be pointed or rendered with mortar. An entry in the Woodstock accounts for 1265 provides details of the process: 'For two slaters pointing the chambers and hall in the steward's court – 2s. 6d. For a thousand slates – 2s. For a hundred crests for the same – 2s. 6d. For collecting moss – 6d. For 2,000 wooden nails – 2d.'

Not all slates came from specialist quarries: most manors in the limestone belt which runs north-east from the Cotswolds through Oxfordshire and Northamptonshire had their own 'tile-pits' or *slat quarrs*. Perhaps the most notable of all medieval slate quarries were those at Collyweston in Northamptonshire: the 1375 accounts for nearby Rockingham Castle show that 9,500 stone slates were purchased from Collyweston at a cost of 8*s* per thousand. Stone for slates comes in thin layers which also provide *planks* or *pales*, fencing slates which were held together by iron clamps. A frosting process was probably first used at the Stonesfield quarries in Oxfordshire at the end of the sixteenth century. By this method *pendles* of fissile limestone are left exposed during the winter so that the moisture in the thin films of clay between the layers freezes and expands causing the pendles to split easily into slates. Before this, quarries were chosen where stone split naturally so that the slater's only task was to shape and trim the slates, working with a *crapping stone* between his knees. This was a narrow stone set edgewise on the ground on which he trimmed three sides of each slate with a slat hammer until it was of the right shape and thickness. The edges were then trimmed by battering with the hammer-head and a peg hole made in the narrow end by boring or tapping lightly with the point of a slat pick. Piled 'ten flat and ten edgeways', two hundred and fifty slates would be considered a good day's work. Roofing slates varied in length and were measured against a slater's rule or *wippet stick*, which in the Cotswolds was marked with twenty-seven notches. Each size of slate had its own name and these varied not only from one region to another but among individual slaters. Workmanship was judged by the quality of swept valleys which were always the weakest part of a stone-tiled roof. 'Valley stones' had to be cut in a triangular shape and arranged so that they left no cracks where the water could enter. Experts at *galetting*, as the craft was called, refused to use lead for this purpose.

Clay tiles, like bricks, were fired in kilns though they needed to be harder and of finer quality (*see* BRICK BUILDINGS). Roofing tiles varied considerably: the Romans favoured a combination of rounded tile (*imbrex*) and flat tile (tegula), the *imbrices* covering the joints between the *tegulae*. But by the eleventh century the craft of tile-making had degenerated and such niceties were no longer observed. During the fifteenth century complaints were made regarding the lack of uniformity in the size and quality of tiles. Indeed, it was said that many of the tiles produced at that time would last only four or five years. Consequently an act was passed in 1477 regulating both the size of tiles and the manufacturing process itself. This required that flat tiles should measure 27 × 16cm (10½ × 6¼in), with a thickness of at least 1.5cm (⅝in). Ridge tiles (*crests*) should be 34 × 16cm (13½ × 6¼in), and gutter tiles 27cm (10½in) long. Ridge tiles (*crests*) were sometimes ornamented: at Banstead Manor in 1373 John Pottere was paid 2*s* 'for two crests made in the fashion of mounted knights, bought for the hall'.
(*See also* CASTLES (CONSTRUCTION OF), CHIMNEYS AND FIREPLACES, LEAD, ROOFS (TIMBER) *and* THATCH)

SLEEPER WALL In a building *sleepers* are supporting beams that carry joists. In turn, walls which support such beams are described as *sleeper walls*.

SLIGHT FOUNDATIONS The levelled remains of walls.

SLIGHTING To 'slight' a castle is to inflict sufficient damage so as to render it unfit for use as a fortress. This was usually achieved by undermining walls and towers so that they collapsed, and later by the use of gunpowder. Complete destruction was impractical (although subsequent 'quarrying' for building materials was equally effective), while many castles were garrisoned by the victors following capture.

In many instances stone was sold and re-used in domestic buildings or to repair or extend other castles. Not all of the damage inflicted on medieval castles was the result of deliberate slighting: far more devastating was the use of cannon during the English Civil Wars of the seventeenth century (*see* FIREARMS AND CANNON).

Many ADULTERINE castles were demolished by Henry II following the ANARCHY, but most were slighted as a consequence of war. In Wales, for example, Deganwy Castle, on its naturally defensive site to the east of the Conwy estuary, was slighted by the Welsh on three occasions to prevent it from falling into English hands. In the Wars of the Roses the Lancastrian fortress of Carreg Cennen was dismantled by the Yorkists following their victory at Mortimer's Cross in 1461. A force of five hundred men was assembled and laboured for almost four months to dismantle the castle at a cost of £18 5s 6d. The men were quartered in the crumbling defences, working 'with bars, picks and crow-bars and other necessary instruments purchased for the work, breaking and throwing down the walls to avoid inconveniences of this kind happening there in time to come'.

Many medieval castles were garrisoned during the English Civil Wars (1642–51) and many were slighted as a consequence. At Corfe, for example, where the redoubtable Lady Bankes resisted two long sieges (that in 1643 lasting thirteen weeks), the castle was demolished by order of Parliament in 1646. According to the Raglan Castle guidebook: 'All the contents were plundered. The foundations were then undermined and the buildings blown up. Entire structures sank bodily into the excavations beneath, and other parts rolled to the foot of the hill. The job was executed far more thoroughly than was necessary to render the building untenable for military purposes. The castle was ruined.' Despite these determined attempts at demolition, much of the masonry remains intact. The lofty keep is but a shell, curtain walls and towers have bowed outwards – the round-towered middle gatehouse has even slipped downhill – but even so Corfe remains one of the most impressive castles in England.

An account written towards the end of the seventeenth century records the slighting of Raglan Castle following its capture by parliamentary forces in 1646:

Afterwards the woods in the three parks were destroyed, the lead and timber were carried to Monmouth, thence by water to rebuild Bristol Bridge after the last fire. The Great tower, after tedious battering the top thereof with pickaxes, was undermined, the weight of it propped with the timber whilst the two sides of the six were cut through: the timber being burned it fell down in a lump, and so still remains firmly to this day. After the surrender the country people were summoned into a rendezvous with pickaxes, spades and shovels, to draw [dredge] the mote in hope of wealth; their hope failing, they were set to cut the stanks [dams] of the great fishponds, where they had store of very great carps, and other large fish. The artificial roof of the Hall could not well be taken down, remained whole above 20 years after the siege, and above 30 vaults of all sorts of rooms, and cellars, and three arched bridges, beside the Tower bridge, are as yet standing, but the most curious arch, the chapel and rooms adjoining, with many other fair rooms totally destroyed.

SLIT A narrow opening in a wall for the discharge of arrows (*see* LOOPHOLES) and the admittance of light.

SLUICE (i) A narrow sloping opening set into the masonry above the entrance to a GATEHOUSE. When besieging a castle, fire was often used both to weaken the gates and to smoke out the occupants of a gatehouse. Defenders could extinguish a fire at the base of the gates by releasing water through the sluice. There is a good example of a sluice in the rear wall of the east gatehouse at Caerphilly Castle. This would have been used only if the outer defences had been breached and the gatehouse was under attack from the inner ward.
(*See also* MURDER HOLE)
(ii) A drain found in a castle kitchen and sometimes lined with lead.

'SMALL ALE' *see* KITCHENS

SOCLE A plinth at the foot of a wall.

SOFFIT *see* ARCH

SOKE A pre-Conquest DANELAW district or estate within which a lord exercised personal jurisdiction in certain townships. It is likely that these originated in the ninth century as settlements of disbanded Danish soldiers owing common allegiance to a single lord and subject to the jurisdiction of his Soke Court. Tenants were freemen, but, because the land within a particular soke might be contained within a number of manors, some townships and farmsteads

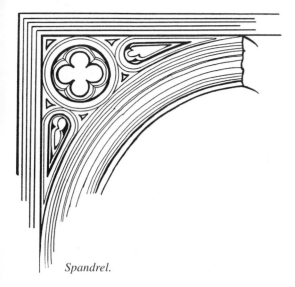

Spandrel.

were subject to divided lordship and custom. Sokes have featured in local administration since Domesday when their authority was recognised by statute. Indeed, charters providing for 'soc and sac, toll and theam' (the right to receive manorial profits and services, to hold a court, and to levy dues and determine punishments) date from 1020 onwards. Before the reorganisation of local government in 1974 the Soke of Peterborough, which contained thirty-two townships, was a separate county.

SOLAR From the Latin *solaris* meaning 'of the sun', the solar or *Great Chamber* was the principal private chamber of a castle or medieval manor house. It was often located to take advantage of the sunniest aspect of the castle and was used as a quiet withdrawing-room by a lord, his family and guests. Typically, the solar would occupy the space at first-floor level between the HALL and the courtyard, with a vaulted undercroft beneath, large windows and a stair which ascended from the dais end of the hall. In tower-keeps the solar was usually on the top floor above the great hall, though in the largest hall-keeps there was often space for it alongside the hall. Sometimes the solar was located in a mural tower (at Abergavenny, for example) while in several castles additional private chambers were provided beyond the solar, as at Conwy. In some late medieval castles entire suites of rooms were provided for the family and their guests: at Raglan Castle, for example, the inner courtyard (the Fountain Court, *c.* 1460–9) was surrounded by state apartments, and at Wardour Castle (1393) there were four storeys of lodgings, each comprising two rooms and with a garderobe leading from the bed-chamber. A number of castles

had both a solar and a great chamber, as in the early fifteenth-century keep of Warkworth Castle where the Great Chamber was on the first floor with the solar on the second, immediately above it.
(*See also* PRIVY CHAMBER)

SOLE PLATE A horizontal timber forming the base of a structure.

SOLLERETS Pointed shoes, often made of small, overlapping and articulated metal plates, to protect the feet (*see also* ARMOUR).

SOVEREIGN (COIN) *see* COINAGE

SPAN *see* ARCH

SPANDREL The space between the curve of an ARCH and the surrounding moulding or framework, also between the curves of adjoining arches and the moulding above.
(*See also* GOTHIC ARCHITECTURE)

SPANNING HOOK *see* ARCHERY

SPARTH or SPARTHA *see* WEAPONS AND HARNESS

SPAULDER *see* ARMOUR

SPERE-TRUSS An arch formed of piers supporting a tie-beam at the end of a timber-frame hall.

SPIT In a castle kitchen, a thin, pointed rod or bar on which meat was impaled so that it could be roasted over a fire. Spits were sometimes turned by hand or by a dog whose forward movements inside a wheel would cause the spit to turn slowly in front of the fire (*see* KITCHENS).

SPITAL The medieval form of the word 'hospital'. Its occurrence as a place-name element is usually indicative of the site of a former hospice or *lazar house* (a hospital for lepers).

SPLAY A sloping edge or surface, as in the embrasures of some windows and LOOPHOLES which are set within the thickness of walls.

'SPOILS OF WAR' *see* RANSOM

SPRINGALD *see* SIEGES

SPRINGER *and* SPRINGING LINE *see* ARCH

Spur buttresses constructed on square bases and solid rock at Goodrich Castle, Herefordshire.

SPUR (i) In post-medieval fortifications, an arrow-shaped projection from the face of a curtain wall. (ii) A type of wooden SCREEN.

SPUR BUTTRESSES Massive pyramidal spurs of masonry at the foot of a tower which served to protect it from attack by siege engines and undermining. Spur buttresses are a feature of several late thirteenth-century and early fourteenth-century castles in the southern Marches of Wales, notably at Marten's Tower at Chepstow Castle (1287–93) and at Goodrich Castle (*c.* 1300) where the south-east, south-west and north-west round towers are all reinforced with impressive spur buttresses constructed on square bases and solid rock. It has been suggested that material dropped from a tower wall-walk would ricochet outwards off the spur buttresses on to the heads of besiegers.

SQUINCH ARCH An arch, or series of concentric arches, constructed within the angle between two walls to support a superstructure such as an ANGLE TURRET.

SQUINT *see* HAGIOSCOPE

SQUIRE *see* ESQUIRE, KNIGHTHOOD AND CHIVALRY, ORIGINS OF *and* MILITARY TRAINING

STAINED GLASS Although stained glass was used in church windows from the seventh century, the earliest surviving examples in England are from the twelfth. At what stage and to what extent secular buildings were glazed is uncertain (*see* GLAZING *and* WINDOWS), though there are many references in contemporary accounts to stained-glass windows from the thirteenth century. In 1246, for example, windows at Guildford Castle were to be 'closed with white glass . . . and in one half of the glass window a king sitting on a throne and in the other half a queen, also sitting on a throne'. In the fourteenth century Chaucer (writing before 1372) refers to his chamber where 'with glas were al the windows wel y glazed' with scenes from the Trojan wars, while contemporary illustrations suggest that the windows of a castle's great hall, its chapel and several of its more important chambers would have glowed with coloured glass. At Athelhampton House (*c.* 1485) several superb examples of late fifteenth-century and early sixteenth-century heraldic windows have survived in the great hall, though some bays contain Victorian restorations. But Athelhampton is exceptional and so little original glass has survived in castle windows that we are dependent for our understanding on documentary evidence and that which remains in churches. Furthermore, the heraldry in many medieval church windows can often provide invaluable information about the magnates, their families and households who occupied a nearby castle (*see* CHURCHES, DONOR AND COMMEMORATIVE WINDOWS *and* MONUMENTS).

Techniques

Most medieval coloured glass was manufactured in France and Germany and imported into England where it was made into windows. The Romans produced slabs of coloured glass, but the idea of holding pieces together within a lead framework to form a patterned window is believed by some to have originated in Byzantium. Before the sixteenth century window glass was made from a mixture of wood-ash, river sand and lime which was heated into molten form and either spun on the end of a rod into a circular sheet or blown into a long cylinder and cut longitudinally to produce a flat sheet (*see* GLAZING).

Coloured glasses (*pot-metals*) were made by adding different metallic oxides to the molten clear glass: cobalt for blue, copper for ruby, manganese for violet, silver salts for yellow, iron for green or yellow, and small quantities of gold for a rose red. The colour produced also depended on the way the furnace was fired and different results were achieved by varying the level of oxidation. The ruby and blue glasses were very dark and a technique called *flashing* was used to make them more transparent. Using a blowpipe, a bubble of molten coloured glass was dipped into molten white glass and worked into a white glass panel which was coated on one side with a layer of the desired colour.

The design (*cartoon*) of the window was drawn on a whitewashed table by draughtsmen (*tracers*) and the pieces of coloured glass cut to the required shape. Before the introduction of the diamond cutter in the sixteenth century, this was done by means of a hot iron which was drawn across the glass and cold water applied, causing the glass to crack along the incision. The pieces were then trimmed with a *grozing iron* to a more precise shape, and details such as faces, hair, limbs, linen folds and foliage were painted in a mixture of metallic oxide (iron or copper), powdered glass and gum.

Finally the glass sections were set out on an iron plate and covered with ash before being fired at a high temperature (using beechwood) in a clay and dung kiln. This fused the paint on to the coloured glass. The pieces were then reassembled and bound together in a lead framework (*armature*) with putty forced into the crevices between the lead and the glass. Lead was a most suitable material for this purpose, for it was malleable when unheated and, having a low melting point, was easily cast into strips with grooves at the sides to accommodate the glass.

As the craft developed, the lines of the lead framework were incorporated into the design itself and from the fourteenth century the flashed surface of coloured glass was often removed (*abraided*) to leave a pattern of clear glass which, when repainted with silver oxide and fired, turned to a dark yellow which passed for gold. This was particularly useful in heraldic designs when 'metal' charges (gold or silver) were depicted on a blue or red field, as in the ubiquitous royal arms of England. Many heraldic devices were not of a convenient shape to be confined within strips of lead and while large charges such as beasts could be built up of several pieces of glass leaded together, very small or repetitive charges were often difficult to reproduce. This problem was overcome by using small pieces of coloured glass and painting around the outline of the motif with brown enamel to leave only the shape as the unpainted surface. Alternatively, a whole sheet was painted with brown enamel and the appropriate area scraped away to form the desired shape. This technique may be seen in the equally ubiquitous ancient arms of France in which the small diamond-shaped panels (*quarries* or *quarrels*) bearing white fleurs-de-lis alternate with strips of blue glass for the field, producing a pattern of lozenges. When completed, the window was fitted into the stonework opening by means of lead strips which were attached to iron saddle-bars or, in larger window openings, set within a decorative metal armature. The years 1260 to 1325 are notable for *grisaille glass* (from the French *gris* meaning 'grey'): large areas of clear quarries surrounded by borders of monochrome foliage decoration and occasional medallions in colour.

STAIRS Numerous stairs were provided within a castle in order that military and domestic functions could be carried out efficiently. The various levels of a keep were linked either by straight flights of stairs constructed within the thickness of walls (*intra-mural stairs* or *mural stairs*) or by spiral stairs (*newel stairs*) within a corner tower or projecting STAIR TURRET. Wall-walks were also accessed from a courtyard by newel stairs located on the inner side of a mural tower to prevent any weakening of the external wall.

Intra-mural stairs inevitably reduced the strength of the walls in which they were located and consequently they are most commonly found in early castles, such as Bamburgh (*c.* 1095), and in rudimentary strongholds such as Dolwyddelan Castle (*c.* 1200) where a spectacular intra-mural stair rises almost the full height of the keep from the first floor to the (later) wall-walk and roof. Indeed, the majority of native Welsh castles incorporated intra-mural stairs, the newel stair in the keep at Dolbadarn (*c.* 1230) being a notable exception.

Newel stairs were constructed within cylindrical shafts where they rise in a series of identical stone steps (*winders*), each cut to fit precisely within the shaft and held in place by the interlocking core of the steps immediately above and below. According to tradition newel stairs usually ascend in a clockwise direction in order to facilitate the use of a weapon when facing down the stair in a defensive position but impairing its use when attempting to ascend by force: hence the term *turnpike stair*. This is certainly true at Conwy Castle, for example, where the majority of towers have clockwise stairs of thirty-nine steps between ground level and the wall-walk, the only exception being the Bakehouse Tower. But there are many examples of newel stairs rising in an anti-clockwise direction and it is more likely that the direction of the stair was dictated by its function. In the majority of cases where heavy or awkward items (such as buckets of water) had to be carried to an upper floor, the stair would ascend in a clockwise direction, allowing the load to be carried in the right hand while climbing on the broad, outer sections of the winders. It is also likely that, where possible, stairs were used in pairs, one for ascending and the other for descending, in order to avoid confusion and inconvenience. In the fourteenth century the term *vice* (meaning 'screw') was used to describe a newel stair.
(*For* external stairs *see* FOREBUILDING, HALL-KEEP *and* KEEP)

STAIR TURRET A circular or polygonal turret attached to the outside of a tower (often at a corner) and containing a newel stair from which the various levels within the tower may be reached.
(*See also* ANGLE TURRET *and* STAIRS)

STANCHION An upright post or support.

STANDARD *see* FLAGS

STANNARIES The tin-mining districts of Cornwall and Devon in which mining activities were regulated by the *Stannaries Court*. In 1508 the Stannary tinners were granted exemption from certain forms of taxation by a charter of Henry VII which was ratified by Henry VIII in 1511.
(*See also* MINERALS AND MINING)

STAPLE, THE *see* CALAIS

STAR CHAMBER (COURT OF) A chamber at the royal palace of Westminster, said to have gilt stars painted on the ceiling, where in the fourteenth and fifteenth centuries the Privy Council met in its judicial capacity to consider both civil and criminal matters affecting the crown. Revived by Henry VII in 1487, the Court of Star Chamber dealt with the suppression of LIVERY AND MAINTENANCE and with perjury and serious misdemeanours such as riots. Under the Tudors and early Stuarts the court acquired notoriety for its arbitrary and oppressive judgments. It was abolished in 1640.

STATE RECORDS *see* BADGES AND LIVERY (*for* MUSTER ROLLS), CHANCERY (*for* CHANCERY ROLLS *and* INQUISITIONES AD QUOD DAMNUM), CHARTERS, CLOSE ROLLS, COMPOTUS ROLLS, DOMESDAY BOOK, EXCHEQUER, FEET OF FINES, FEUDAL AIDS (*for* BOOK OF FEES), FINE (*or* OBLATE) ROLLS, HUNDRED ROLLS, INQUISITIONES POST MORTEM, ISSUE ROLLS, LEGISLATION, LIBERATE ROLLS, LORD OF THE MANOR, MAGNA CARTA, MEMORANDA ROLLS, PARLIAMENTARY ACTS, PATENT ROLLS, PIPE ROLLS (*for* GREAT ROLLS OF THE EXCHEQUER), RECOVERY ROLLS, TRAILBASTON *and* TREASURY

STEPPED Recessed in a series of ledges.

STEWARD (i) The chief agent of a manorial lord with responsibility for the administration of a manor, for maintaining its records and presiding over its courts (*see* BAILIFF *and* MANOR).
(ii) The official responsible for the day-to-day domestic arrangements of a household (*see* HOUSEHOLD).

STEW POND *see* FISH POND

STEWS *see* PLUMBING, WATER SUPPLY AND SANITATION

STILE (i) A vertical member in the framework of a panelled door.
(ii) The vertical outer frame members of a wooden screen (also *style*).

STILTED ARCH *see* ARCH

STILTS The short, vertical sections at the base of a round arch which raise its height without increasing the span.

STIPENDIARY KNIGHT A knight who received a money payment rather than land in return for his feudal military obligation.

STIRRUP Support for a rider's foot. The terms 'chivalry' and 'cavalry' share the same linguistic root, confirming that knighthood was the prerogative of the mounted warrior (*see* CHIVALRY). His effectiveness in battle (and thereby his reputation) was greatly enhanced by the development of the stirrup and the saddle-bow which provided both manoeuvrability and stability when wielding a weapon in the saddle. An Asiatic invention, stirrups were probably introduced into western Europe in the early seventh century.
(*See also* HORSES AND HORSE-HARNESS)

STONE *see* CASTLES (CONSTRUCTION OF), MASONRY, MASTER MASONS AND ARCHITECTS, MATERIALS (CARRIAGE OF) *and* SCAFFOLDING AND CRANES

STOUP A small stone basin, originally containing holy water, set on the right of the main door or porch of a medieval chapel or church. Stoups, which have no drain, were replenished regularly with holy water, which was mixed with salt, exorcised and blessed. Before crossing the threshold of the church, a visitor would dip his fingers in the holy water and make the sign of the cross, thereby acknowledging his baptismal promises, the shedding of Christ's blood and the washing away of sins. The word is correctly *stop*, meaning a pail or basin. A number of stoups have survived in the vicinity of castle CHAPELS.

STRAIGHT ARCH *see* ARCH

STRAINER ARCH *see* ARCH

STRAP SCONCE A narrow ornamental bracket, secured at each end and curving outwards from a wall, on the top of which are affixed a number of candle-holders.

STRATEGY AND TACTICS (WARFARE) *see* WARFARE, CONDUCT OF

STRATIGRAPHY A method by which archaeologists understand the way in which layers and structures have been built up over time. Lower layers are usually earlier than those above them, though features such as walls and ditches may have been cut into earlier layers. Individual soils, features and structures are allocated unique *context numbers* by which they may be identified, and the interaction between these is known as *stratigraphic relationship*. Excavated evidence such as pottery, coins and artefacts is used to establish the chronology of the stratigraphy.
(*See also* TREE-RING DATING)

STRETCHER A brick or piece of masonry placed lengthwise in the face of a wall.

STRING COURSE A continuous projecting horizontal band or moulding in the surface of a wall.

STRONG-HOUSE A residence capable of being defended.

STYLE *see* STILE

SUBINFEUDATION The granting of land by a VASSAL to be held of him by his vassal (*see* FEUDAL SYSTEM *and* MANOR).

SUMPTUARY LAWS Medieval laws intended to restrict private expenditure. Charles V of France, for example, forbade the use of long-pointed shoes, a fashion vehemently opposed by the Church. In fourteenth-century England contemporary writers tell of the extravagance of dress and cuisine of the period, and in 1336 Edward III attempted to legislate against such excesses. In 1363 costume was regulated by law according to social class and a further act of 1444 sought to control clothing when it formed part of the wages of servants, specific allowances being permitted to bailiffs and overseers (5s a year), principal servants (4s) and ordinary servants (3s 4d), for example (*see* LIVERY AND MAINTENANCE). A further statute of 1463 (Edward IV) legislated for the control of clothing of persons of all ranks. Indeed, a succession of laws from that year down to 1532 sought to limit excesses by forbidding untitled people to wear such things as purple silk, gold chains and COLLARS, cloth of gold and crimson velvet. Controls were also applied to the use of furs, ermine being reserved for the nobility and, as a token of royal favour, to other magnates close to the crown. It may be that the extensive use of ermine in the coats of arms of Garter Knights of the period was intended to indicate their privileged position in society (*see*

VAIR). Similar acts were passed in Scotland: in 1433 (James I) the manner of living of all orders in Scotland was prescribed, in particular the consumption of pies and baked meats which was forbidden to all below the rank of baron. In 1457 (James II) an act was passed against 'sumptuous cleithing'. The Scottish sumptuary law of 1621 was the last of its kind in Britain.

SUNDIALS Before the introduction of clocks in the fourteenth century, the canonical hours were evinced by means of a *mass-dial* set on the south wall or buttress of a building, usually in the vicinity of a doorway and at eye-level. Saxon dials, carved with great precision and sometimes with inscriptions added, usually consist of a double circle divided into four by radial lines, each of which may terminate in a cross. The later, and more numerous, medieval *scratch dials* are rather crudely inscribed with the duodecimal divisions of the day, the radial lines cut at intervals of fifteen degrees. In many examples the line which would have been reached by the shadow of the metal style (*gnomon*) at 9.00am is more clearly incised, this being the 'mass line' which marked the hour when mass was said on Sundays and feast days. The function of these dials was to ensure that the bell was rung at the correct time to mark the canonical hours and for this reason the clock-faces which superseded them were often visible inside the church or chapel to assist the bell-ringer.

'SUN IN SPLENDOUR' An heraldic badge comprising a sun with pronounced rays and sometimes a human face (*see* BADGES AND LIVERY).

SUPPORTERS (HERALDIC) Figures, usually beasts or chimerical creatures, that appear to 'support' the shield in a COAT OF ARMS. It has been suggested that supporters may have originated in the flamboyant practice of disguising retainers as beasts and creatures at pageants and TOURNAMENTS. But there is a more plausible explanation. In the thirteenth and fourteenth centuries creatures were often depicted in the interstices of SEALS and as such may reasonably be considered to be the precursors of armorial supporters. Many of these creatures had been adopted by medieval magnates for use as badges (*see* BADGES AND LIVERY) and by the fifteenth century even the lesser nobility would have accumulated several through inheritance and marriage. These were often translated into CRESTS and, later, into supporters.

SURCOAT A long coat of linen, split at the sides to facilitate movement, especially on horseback, and originally intended to protect mail from heat or rain. Dating from the Crusades of the twelfth century, the surcoat provided an obvious means of displaying armorial devices – hence 'coat of arms' (*see* ARMORY). The CYCLAS was similar but was cut short at the front and long at the back. By the middle of the fourteenth century the surcoat had been replaced by the shorter JUPON which itself was succeeded in the late fifteenth century by the TABARD.

SWALLOW *see* KITCHENS *and* PLUMBING, WATER SUPPLY AND SANITATION

SWORDS AND DAGGERS *see* WEAPONS AND HARNESS

T

TABARD A dress coat worn over ARMOUR from the late fifteenth century to the mid-sixteenth century, especially at TOURNAMENTS. Similar to the JUPON but reaching below the thigh and with broad sleeves to the elbow, the tabard was emblazoned front and back and on the sleeves and served a purely heraldic purpose. Today, tabards of the royal arms are worn by heralds on ceremonial occasions. (*See also* SURCOAT)

TACES Long strips of metal (*lames*) forming a protective skirt (*see* ARMOUR).

TALEVAS *see* SHIELDS

TALLAGE A tax imposed for the repair and construction of fortifications.

TALUS *see* GLACIS

TAMPION *see* FIREARMS AND CANNON

TANG *see* WEAPONS AND HARNESS

TAPESTRIES *see* WALL HANGINGS

TARGET *or* **TARGE** The adoption of the couched lance and close-formation cavalry tactics in the thirteenth century resulted in a significant increase in the size of a knight's shield. These large shields were generally known as *targes* and were made of leather-covered wood. The term was also applied to smaller, circular shields dating from the late thirteenth century. Also known as *targets*, they were provided with straps for the forearm (*see* ENARMES) and were used by men-at-arms throughout medieval Europe.
(*See also* ARMOUR *and* SHIELDS)

TARGIAM *see* SHIELDS

TASSETS The pair of metal plates which hang from the front of an armour skirt to protect the thighs (*see* ARMOUR).

TEMPLAR, KNIGHTS (THE POOR KNIGHTS OF CHRIST AND OF THE TEMPLE OF SOLOMON) Together the Hospitallers, the Teutonic Knights and the Knights Templar formed the three most powerful orders of chivalry to emanate from the CRUSADES. Within a few years of their foundation most of their brethren, while living under vows of religion, were conventual knights (their priests were known as *chaplains*) and the orders played an increasingly significant rôle in the defence of the Christian settlements in Palestine and Syria and in the administration of the Kingdom of Jerusalem. They constructed and garrisoned castles and fought alongside crusading forces in the perennial wars against the Egyptians and Turks.

Founded in 1118/19 by Hugues de Payns and Godeffroi de St Omer, the Order of the Poor Knights of Christ and of the Temple of Solomon was given a convent (headquarters) close to the Temple of Solomon by King Baldwin II of Jerusalem so that they should 'fight with a pure mind for the supreme and true king'. The knights lived according to the rule of Bernard of Clairvaux under an elected Master of the Temple, and dedicated themselves to the protection of pilgrims in the Holy Land and quickly achieved the sanction of the Church. By the end of the thirteenth century the Templars were established in almost every European kingdom and were in receipt of enormous grants of land. But their widespread influence attracted powerful enemies. Strange stories circulated about their 'secret rites' and their failure to mobilise their considerable resources in 1291 following the fall of Acre (the last Christian stronghold in the Holy Land) caused universal resentment. Eventually, in 1308, Philip IV of France moved against them. Having obtained papal support for his campaign, Philip persuaded most European rulers to suppress the Templars. The order's officers were arrested, on the grounds of alleged heresy, sorcery, sodomy and corruption, and in France at least thirty-eight Templars are known to have died during 'examination'. In 1310 sixty-seven Templars were burned at the stake, in 1312 the Pope transferred many of the order's holdings and possessions to the Hospitallers (*see* ST JOHN OF JERUSALEM, ORDER OF) and in 1314 the Grand Master of the order was burnt alive in front of Notre Dame in Paris on the instructions of Philip the Fair. But by then the Templars had created for themselves what was effectively a sovereign state in the Greek islands, notably at Rhodes which they eventually lost to the Ottoman Turks in 1522. The order's convent was re-established in Malta in 1530, where it remained until 1798. Although in several countries the order survived, in England it was suppressed, though without undue severity. Its headquarters still stand at Temple Church in Fleet Street, London, a building that was based on the Holy Sepulchre at Jerusalem. The habit of the order was white with a red cross of eight points worn on the left shoulder and its badges were the *Agnus Dei* and a strange device consisting of two knights riding on one horse, presumably an allusion to the original poverty of the order. Both the Templars and the Hospitallers had about fifty PRECEPTORIES or COMMANDERIES in the British Isles, many commemorated by place-names such as St John's Jerusalem in Kent, St John's Wood in London, Temple Bruer in Lincolnshire, Templecombe in Somerset and Temple Guiting in the Gloucestershire Cotswolds.

TEMPLE PLACE-NAMES *see* TEMPLAR, KNIGHTS

TENANT-IN-CHIEF (TENANT-IN-CAPITE) A tenant who held his lands directly of the crown.
(*See also* HONOR *and* WARDSHIP)

TENANT-IN-DEMESNE *see* LORD OF THE MANOR

TENEMENT (i) Land held of a superior (*see* MANOR).
(ii) Any rented land or dwelling.

TENON *see* MORTISE

TENTERHOOKS *see* WALL HANGINGS

TERRE MARITIME In the fourteenth century, a coastal strip which was subject to separate local defence administration.

TERRE-PLEIN In post-medieval fortifications, the level surface on top of a rampart where guns are mounted.

TERRIER A register of lands and rents (*see* MANOR).

TESTOON *see* COINAGE

TÊTE-DE-PONT A fortification positioned on the vulnerable side of a bridge.

THANE (*also* **THEGN**) One of the Anglo-Saxon military élite and a member of a royal or noble household.

THATCH From the Old English *thæc* meaning 'roof covering', thatch is a roofing of straw, reeds, sedge, rush or similar material. Thatch was the most common form of roofing in the medieval period because it was both cheap and effective. It was widely used in castles for the roofs of COURTYARD BUILDINGS, for temporary shelters and workmen's lodges, and for protecting walls of earth and COB from the depredations of the weather. Despite its susceptibility to fire, thatch continued in use throughout the medieval period: at Pevensey, for example, 6 acres of rushes were purchased in 1300 and transported to the castle in seventeen wagons 'for thatching the hall and chambers'. Nevertheless, contemporary records show that, when neglected, a deteriorating roof of thatch could have a devastating effect on roof timbers (*see* ROOFS, TIMBER) and many thatched roofs were replaced with SHINGLES, SLATES AND TILES or LEAD.

A thatched roof has a steep pitch (about 50 degrees) so that water is shed quickly, the eaves throwing rainwater clear of the building without recourse to gutters and down-pipes (*see* PLUMBING, WATER SUPPLY AND SANITATION). The covering of thatch (the *coat*) comprised numerous small bundles of parallel stems (*yelms*) set in horizontal and vertical strips (*courses* and *lanes*). Beginning at the eaves and working upwards to the roof-ridge, the first yelms were tied to the purlins and laths of the bare roof; as the thickness of the thatch increased, additional yelms were tamped home and secured by long hazel wands (known as *ledgers*, *sways* or *temples*), held by hooks to the roof timbers, and by staples (*broaches*, *spars* or *spits*) of

split hazel or willow driven into the thatch. At the ridge the yelms from each side of the roof were overlapped alternately to form a crest. Alternatively, a ridging of clay or turf was applied.

THREE CASTLES, THE Sometimes referred to as the *Trilateral Castles*, Grosmont, Skenfrith and White Castle guarded one of the major land routes from England into Wales. The Monnow valley forms a break in the natural defences of the southern MARCH, an area of open pastoral country between the steep cliffs of the Wye valley south of Monmouth and the Welsh hills around Abergavenny. In this area the Normans built a triangle of castles which in 1201 were granted by King John to Hubert de Burgh (*c.* 1175–1243), who was chiefly responsible for a building programme at Skenfrith and Grosmont, much of which has survived to the present day. In 1267 the lordship was granted to Edmund 'Crouchback', earl of Leicester (1267–96). Thereafter the castles continued to be associated with the earldom (later, the duchy) of Lancaster until 1825, though the defeat of Llewelyn ap Gruffudd – the first and last prince of Wales – in 1277 rendered superfluous their military importance, except for a brief period (1404–5) during the Owain Glyn Dŵr rebellion of 1401–16.

THREE ESTATES, THE *see* ESTATE *and* FEUDAL SYSTEM

THUNDER-BOX *see* FIREARMS AND CANNON

TIE-BEAM Structural timber or timbers extending horizontally from one side of a roof to the other (*see* ROOFS (TIMBER)).

TIERCERON RIBS *see* VAULTING

TILES (ENCAUSTIC) *see* ENCAUSTIC TILES

TILES (ROOFING) *see* SLATES AND TILES

TILLER *see* ARCHERY

TILT *see* TOURNAMENT

TILTING HELM *see* TOURNAMENT HELM

TILTYARD A long narrow yard devoted to jousting and often located within or adjacent to the outer bailey of a castle (*see* TOURNAMENTS). The entrance to Kenilworth Castle, Warwickshire, is across a broad dam which has been known as the 'tiltyard' since at least the seventeenth century. At the far end of the dam are the remains of an early rectangular gateway tower, known as the Gallery Tower since it was adapted for use as a grandstand overlooking the tiltyard. At Denbigh the elongated space between the MANTLET of the castle and the town walls was called the 'lists' and may, therefore, have been used as a tiltyard. The late thirteenth-century south dam platform at Caerphilly Castle, Glamorgan, may also have been used as a tiltyard, the spacious area of greensward being ideally suited to accommodate the lists, while spectators could have watched from the dam wall-walk. Indeed, the area is still used for the re-enactment of medieval tournaments.

TIMBER-FRAME BUILDINGS Most MANOR HOUSES and the buildings erected in the baileys of early castles were of timber-frame construction (*see* BAILEY). Even when the castle walls were of masonry many of the buildings behind them were of timber, as at Pevensey Castle where in 1300 the hall and chapel were rebuilt entirely in wood with clay daubing. And even Henry III, that great builder of masonry castles, was not above ordering 'a fair, great, and becoming hall of wood and a kitchen of wood' for his manor at Clipston in 1245. Inevitably, none has survived and even those that were replaced with stone have often been demolished, leaving only the remnants of walls or footings to indicate their former extent (*see* COURTYARD BUILDINGS).

Hardwood, notably oak, was a readily available building material in many areas of Britain until the seventeenth century. Unlike buildings constructed of stone, brick or cob, a timber-frame structure consists of a load-bearing framework of timbers with the spaces in the framework filled with other materials such as LATH AND PLASTER, WATTLE AND DAUB or BRICK NOGGING. This type of construction is also known as *half-timbering* because the timbers are not complete logs but are cleft longitudinally. Inevitably there are many variations of timber-frame construction which reflect not only the techniques of different regions and periods but also the function of the building and the social aspirations of the original owners. There are, however, two basic types of construction: cruck frame and box frame.

Crucks are pairs of massive incurving timbers (*blades*), each pair cut from a single tree, which form a series of arches supporting a ridge beam. Originally these buildings comprised a simple HALL, with pairs of primitive crucks curving inwards from ground level to a roof of interlaced branches covered with thatch, brushwood or turf. Later buildings were constructed in bays, each 3.6 to 4.9m (12 to 16ft) wide, separated by crucks and strengthened by purlins and crossing rafters. The simplest buildings consisted of a single bay with crucks at either end, while larger and more prestigious buildings would contain a number of bays. Cruck buildings could be protected from damp by raising the base of the crucks on a timber sill, on *padstones* or plinths (known as *full cruck*), or given extra height by seating them on a low stone wall (*raised cruck*). By the late thirteenth century the crucks of more distinguished buildings were supported on taller, ground-storey walls (*upper cruck*) so that the cruck frame would effectively form a roof space. The hall at Stokesay Castle is of this type. Built in *c.* 1285 to replace an earlier wooden hall, the Great Hall is 15.8m (52ft) long, 9.5m (31ft) wide and 10.4m (34ft) high and comprises four bays with separate gables above each window and the doorway. The roof was originally supported by three pairs of crucks, each pair braced by two collar beams. Each cruck was 10.3m (34ft) long and rested on a stone corbel 2.4m (8ft) above the hall floor. In time the lower sections of the crucks became damp and had to be replaced by stone pilasters. The roof of the magnificent abbey barn at Glastonbury was constructed (in *c.* 1345) on the cruck-frame principle and is similar in many respects to a free-standing medieval hall. In order to overcome the problem of spanning the width of the building (10m or 33ft) a system of two-tier cruck framing was devised, the lower crucks being linked by a collar beam on which the upper (smaller) crucks are supported. This massive oak structure, with its traditional joints and wooden pegs, supports 80 tons of stone SLATES (*see also* ROOFS (TIMBER)).

Far more common were *box-frame* buildings which are known to have been constructed during the Roman occupation though no pre-medieval example has survived. Box framing, as the name implies, consists of horizontal and vertical timbers with braces and struts added to provide rigidity. The frame was usually erected on a footing of impervious material, often a low wall of stone or brick, on which a horizontal baulk of timber (the *sill* or *plate*) was seated. Strong vertical posts (*studs*) were mortised into the sill and their upper ends tenoned into further horizontal timbers which, in single-storey buildings, either supported the lower ends of the roof rafters (*wall plate*) or linked the back and front of the building (*cross rail*). In two- or three-storey buildings this beam carried the joists of the floor above, in which case it is known as a *bressumer*. *Large framing*, in which the framework is minimal but substantial and often strengthened with curving braces, usually dates from before the mid-fifteenth century, while *small framing* consists of small square panels within a lighter framework of numerous horizontal and vertical timbers. In the midland and southern counties of England infill panels are usually square, but in East Anglian buildings dating from the thirteenth to the seventeenth century the frame is often divided into narrow vertical panels by closely spaced studs. *Close studding*, as this technique is called, became popular in other areas from the fifteenth century, particularly in more prestigious buildings where an often excessive use of expensive timber was intended to reflect an owner's affluence. Where an upper storey projects over the ones below, the overhang is described as a *jetty*; where a building is jettied on two or more sides, additional support is provided by an internal cross-beam (*dragon beam*) running diagonally to the corner post.

TIMBER-LACING Horizontal cross-timbers through a drystone wall, sometimes connecting vertical posts at the front and back, to provide increased strength and stability and to prevent the wall from collapsing.

TIMBER ROOFS *see* ROOFS (TIMBER)

TIME IMMEMORIAL *or* **TIME OUT OF MIND**
A legal claim of 'Ancient User' was based on constant use or custom since 'time immemorial', otherwise known as 'time out of mind'. In Common Law this is deemed to be 1189 although in the Court of Chivalry it has been argued that the Norman Conquest of 1066 should be regarded as the limit of legal memory. During the HERALDS' VISIT-ATIONS of the seventeenth century a claim with proof of a prescriptive use of arms from the accession of Elizabeth I (1558) was considered to be sufficient.

TINCTURES The metals, colours and furs used in ARMORY.

Metals:

Or	(Or)	gold, often depicted as yellow
Argent	(Arg)	silver, usually depicted as white

Colours:

Gules	(Gu)	red
Azure	(Az)	blue
Sable	(Sa)	black
Vert	(Vt)	green
Purpure	(Purp)	purple
Murrey	(Mu)	mulberry

The so-called 'stains' are rare:

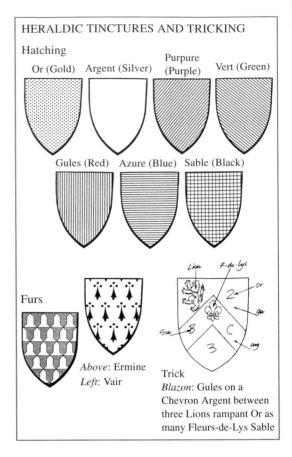

HERALDIC TINCTURES AND TRICKING

Hatching

Or (Gold) Argent (Silver) Purpure (Purple) Vert (Green)

Gules (Red) Azure (Blue) Sable (Black)

Furs

Above: Ermine
Left: Vair

Trick
Blazon: Gules on a Chevron Argent between three Lions rampant Or as many Fleurs-de-Lys Sable

Sanguine	blood-red
Tenné	tawny

Furs:

Ermine	(Erm)	white with black 'tails'
Vair		white and blue 'pelts'

Each of which is possessed of several variations.

In armory the *tincture convention* requires that metal shall not lie on metal, nor colour on colour. This convention seems to have been universally accepted from the earliest times and is clearly intended to facilitate the accurate identifications of armorial devices.

Sketches are often *tricked*, with tinctures indicated by abbreviations (*see above* and charges, when repeated, represented by numbers or letters. Since the seventeenth century the *Petra Sancta* system of hatched lines has often been used to denote tinctures in uncoloured drawings and engravings (*see illustration*).

TIPPET Mail or leather protection for the neck and shoulder, and sometimes the upper arms and chest. Fourteenth-century tippets often had a stiffened or semi-rigid collar (*see* ARMOUR).

TITHING see FRANKPLEDGE and LAW AND ORDER

TOLLBOOTH see MARKETS

TOLSEY see MARKETS

TOMBS see MONUMENTS

TOMEN A Welsh place-name meaning 'mound' and usually a reference to an early fortification as in Tomen-y-Mur, 'the mound of the wall', a Norman MOTTE near Trawsfynydd, Gwynedd. In the Welsh Marches mottes are often referred to as 'tumps' (see MOTTE).

TONGUE A particularly long bolt or arrow designed to be shot from a siege or battle engine such as an espringal (see SIEGES).

TONNE-TITE see MASONRY

TOOTHING Projecting stonework in a wall intended for bonding the walls of adjoining buildings that either were never constructed or were later demolished.

TORET A trefoil-shaped clasp (see WEAPONS AND HARNESS).

TORSE see WREATH

TORTOISE see SIEGES

TORTURE Punishment by torture was authorised by royal warrant in 1310 and has been used as a means of extracting 'confessions' from the earliest recorded times.

TOUCH see MARBLE

TOUCHE see FIREARMS AND CANNON

TOURNAI MARBLE see MARBLE

TOURNAMENT HELM From the end of the fourteenth century, when theoretical eligibility for the aristocracy depended on possession both of a suitable pedigree and the resources necessary to participate in a tournament and the attendant festivities, the *tilting helm* was widely used to display the ornate tournament crests which effectively signalled the bearer's rank both in the lists and symbolically in his coat of arms (see CREST). This helmet had no visor and was therefore

The tournament helm was permanently 'closed', forward vision being by means of an eye-slit.

permanently 'closed', forward vision being by means of an eye-slit which was only effective when leaning forward in the tilting position.
(*See also* HELMETS)

TOURNAMENTS The tournament began as a form of training for mounted warfare, later becoming largely recreational and ultimately an event for entertainment and ceremonial. Although opposed by the Church on moral grounds, and by some monarchs who were fearful of armed assemblies other than those of their own summons, tournaments continued to be held throughout the medieval period and into the 1600s.

The word 'tournament' is itself compounded of several Latin roots, *tourneo, turnio*, etc., and *mentum* meaning a joust or skirmish in which there was a specific result with winners and losers. Perhaps the best early contemporary definition of the event itself is that by Roger de Hoveden, who described a tournament as a 'military exercise carried out not in the spirit of hostility, but solely for practice and the display of prowess'. The tournament appears to have been the invention of a French baron, Geoffroi de Pruelli, who was himself killed in

TOURNAMENTS

such an event in 1066, and for centuries it was referred to in England as *conflictus Gallicus*.

In the twelfth century the 'apeing of the feats of war' at Smithfield in London consisted of young mounted men of noble birth, divided into 'teams' of forty or more, rushing all over the place trying to unhorse one another for hours on end. By the next century, however, the tournament had become more organised, an occasion for pageantry and feasting, and professional jousters travelled through the countries of western Europe seeking and offering challenges. Some, like the legendary William the Marshal (d. 1219), became very rich. Having made his name as a roistering but shrewd 'manager' of a team of tournament jousters, he established an enviable reputation for the newly fashionable qualities of CHIVALRY and courtliness and ultimately became earl of Pembroke and regent of England.

But many an early knight was killed in combat. At one tournament the earl of Salisbury died of his wounds and his grandson was killed by his own father. The great William Longespée (d. 1250) was so battered that he never recovered his former strength. A Statute of Arms for Tournaments of *c.* 1292 required that swords should be blunted and prohibited the use of maces and clubs. There were 'Jousts of Peace' with silvered swords of whale bone and even parchment. Despite this and other attempts at emasculation, the tournament remained popular and in 1344, prior to the jousts at Windsor on St George's Day, the heralds travelled through France, Scotland, Flanders, Brabant, Hainault and Burgundy publicising the lists and guaranteeing their king's safe conduct to the competitors.

By the fourteenth century, however, considerations of safety and good sense began to prevail. Coronal (crown-shaped) heads were fitted to lances in place of points and special harnesses developed which facilitated both stability and manoeuvrability. However, the most significant innovation was undoubtedly the *tilt* or *bohorde*, a stout wooden barrier which separated opponents. Individual knights, locked in harness with reinforced grand-guards, heavily helmed and carrying blunted lances, would attempt to unseat one another while charging along opposite sides of the barrier in what was by then known as *tilting* (*see* LANCE, TILTYARD and TOURNAMENT HELM). The early *mêlée* or free-for-all mixed-weapons fight evolved into a more stylised form known as the *tourney* in which two parties of knights fought on horseback according to agreed conventions and rules. Knights would also fight on foot, with sword or pike, across the wooden barrier in a form of joust known as the *barriers*. All

these activities, and the ceremonial and pageantry which accompanied them, were marshalled by the *heralds* who also kept the scores on *jousting cheques*. By the fifteenth century the older form of tournament, fought *à outrance* (with pointed and sharpened weapons), had given way to the joust *à plaisance* (fought with blunted weapons) throughout most of western Europe. Tournaments were often arranged for diplomatic purposes and women took an active part, judging, awarding prizes and honouring champions with favours. At the Smithfield tournament of 1390 each of the participating knights was led 'with cheynes of gold' by a lady sorority of the Order of the Garter.

The cost, both of providing the necessary horse and equipment and of participating in the attendant festivities and pageantry (which often went on for several days), effectively restricted entry to those of noble or knightly rank, particularly in the late fifteenth and sixteenth centuries when the joust 'became increasingly the ceremonial shattering of fragile, deeply grooved lances, and the literary and pageant elements already dominant in its history gained almost complete ascendancy' (R.C. Strong). The practice of wearing flamboyant CRESTS came to be associated with those of 'tournament rank' – those who possessed the requisite number of noble ancestors *and* were able to meet the enormous expense. No wonder the 'new gentility' of the sixteenth century scrambled to record newly acquired crests at the HERALDS' VISITATIONS for they had become symbols of what we now call 'upward mobility' par excellence.

The death of Henri II of France in 1559 (killed by the splintered lance of Gabriel de Montgomerie) failed to abate the enthusiasm for tournaments among the nobility and (increasingly) the gentry, though by the end of the sixteenth century they had become bloodless spectacles, arranged for the delight of ladies as well as gentlemen. There were parades of squires carrying the elaborately crested tournament helms of the participants (reminiscent of the medieval *helmschau* of fifteenth-century Germany), displays of shields with prizes for the most original design, side-shows (such as the harrying of deer with greyhounds) and processions of ladies dressed as Greek goddesses, all watched by members of the privileged classes gathered in terraced stands surrounding the arena which also included pavilions for the contestants and enclosures for the common people. Perhaps the best known and most spectacular of these pageants was the Field of the Cloth of Gold in 1520 which, marked by vainglorious vulgarity, was far removed from the

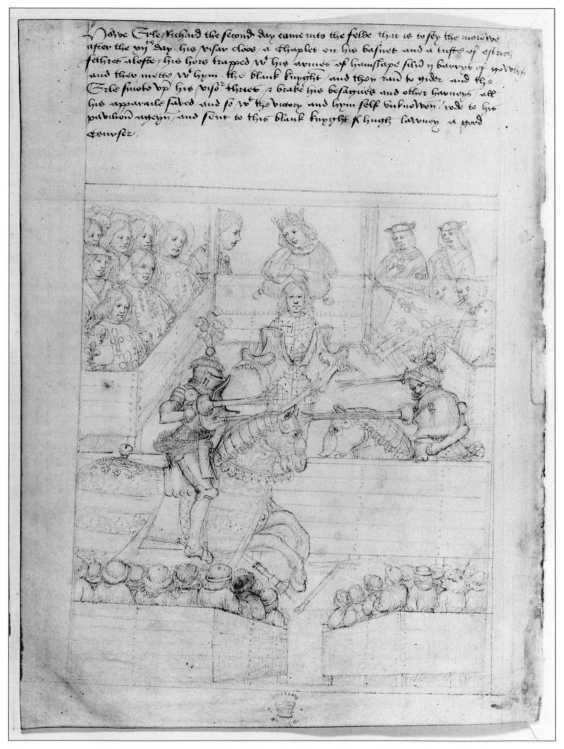

Tournament scene from The Pageants of Richard Beauchamp, *an illustrated biography produced some years after the earl's death in 1439. The* Pageants *consist of fifty-three line drawings, each page illustrating an episode from Richard's life. Here, Beauchamp shatters his lance on an opponent's helm, watched by the King of France, his nobles, heralds and a crowd of spectators.*

simple and honourable war-games of earlier centuries.

(*See also* ARMOUR, CAPARISON, GARTER, THE MOST NOBLE ORDER OF THE, HELMETS, HORSES AND HORSE-HARNESS, MILITARY TRAINING, QUINTAIN, SHIELDS *and* WEAPONS AND HARNESS)

TOWER-HOUSES The late thirteenth century saw the development of the characteristic tower-house stronghold that dominated private fortifications in Scotland well into the sixteenth century. Scottish tower-houses were square or rectangular buildings with thick walls, five or six storeys, crenellations and turrets, as at Borthwick (*c.* 1430) and Elphinstone (1440), both in Lothian. In Ireland in 1429 Henry VI promised a grant of £10 to anyone who would build a castle to his specifications in order to defend the borders of the English Pale. These simple three-storey towers, 6m (20ft) long, 5m (16ft) wide and 12m (40ft) high, became the model for the tower-houses of Irish chieftains, such as the fifteenth-century Roodstown Castle in Co. Louth, and these continued to be built well into the seventeenth century, often within a walled courtyard (*bawn*).

In England and Wales the distinctions between different types of fortification are rarely so clear-cut. Should the native Welsh castles of Dolbadarn (*c.* 1230) and Dolwyddelan (*c.* 1200), with their single towers and minimal outer defences, be regarded as tower-houses? Are the fourteenth-century border castles of Belsay and Dacre large pele towers or tower-houses? And what of the late fourteenth-century rotunda at Queenborough and Warkworth's magnificent keep? Both have been described as tower-houses. It has been argued that because of their limited size tower-houses could not provide for the additional chambers and service buildings needed to accommodate the household and garrison of a great magnate. And yet Wardour Castle (1393), which is often described as a tower-house, was generously provided with domestic offices and suites of rooms arranged tightly round a courtyard in the French manner for lavish entertainment and domestic comfort. It has also been suggested that the use of mercenaries in late medieval England forced many lords to build refuges into which they could retreat in the event of mutiny. These towers sometimes stand apart from the main body of the castle, as at Raglan in south Wales (*c.* 1435), but should they be described as tower-houses?

If the definition of a castle as 'a fortified feudal residence' is accepted, then all the early donjons

Nunney, Somerset, is the epitome of a tower-house – though, in England, it is unique. It was the comfortable rural retreat of Sir John de la Mare (1320–83), paid for out of an unanticipated inheritance and the spoils of war and built entirely in the French fashion.

were tower-houses (*see* DONJON, GREAT TOWER *and* KEEP). But these were frequently abandoned in favour of more salubrious accommodation, protected by the curtain walls, moats, ditches and other defences that delineated a BAILEY. Perhaps it follows that, while tower-houses may have been located within token enclosures (*see* BARMKIN), it is the absence of substantial outer defences that distinguishes them from other, more sophisticated, types of castle. Tower-houses were, therefore, intended primarily as residences but, because of their vulnerability, or the self-aggrandisement of their owners, they were built as towers.

The smallest strongholds that may reasonably be described as tower-houses are the PELE TOWERS of the Scottish Borders. These were defensible against an armed incursion but were not intended to withstand a prolonged siege. Similarly, towers were sometimes added to MANOR HOUSES, as at Stokesay Castle in the Welsh MARCH (1291), and these are sometimes described as tower-houses,

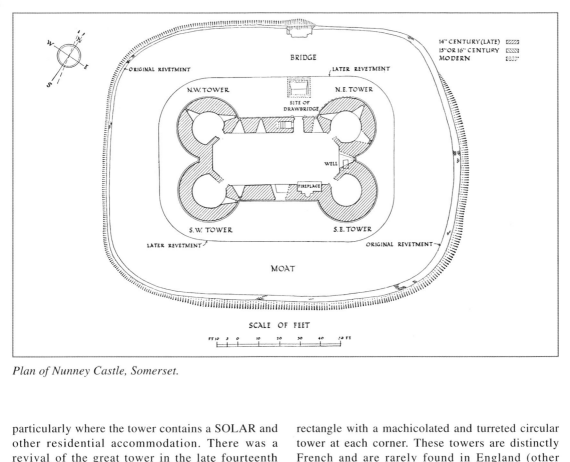

Plan of Nunney Castle, Somerset.

particularly where the tower contains a SOLAR and other residential accommodation. There was a revival of the great tower in the late fourteenth century and contemporary castles, such as Wardour (*see above*) and Nunney in Somerset, are frequently referred to as tower-houses, though Wardour has more accurately been described as a revival of the SHELL-KEEP. Nunney is, indeed, the epitome of a tower-house and in England it is unique. Built in 1373, its only outer defence is a narrow water-filled moat and drawbridge, though an embanked bailey for outbuildings may still be traced to the north-west. Otherwise it was the comfortable rural retreat of Sir John de la Mare (1320–83), paid for out of an unanticipated inheritance and the spoils of the wars in Guienne and built entirely in the French fashion. Set in the heart of the Somerset countryside, Nunney could hardly be described as 'vulnerable' and, as with many other towers of the period, it was intended to be both a desirable residence and a theatrical expression of its owner's status in late medieval society (*see* BRICK BUILDINGS). Even so, it is noticeable that, for purely defensive purposes, the lower floors are poorly lit by narrow arrow-loops while the upper storeys have larger windows. Nunney is a compact rectangle with a machicolated and turreted circular tower at each corner. These towers are distinctly French and are rarely found in England (other examples are Caesar's Tower at Warwick and at Herstmonceaux). The turrets had conical roofs while the main block had a high-pitched roof of stone slates with (later?) dormer windows. There is no FOREBUILDING and the narrow (1.2m or 4ft wide) entrance door leads by a vaulted passage directly into the ground floor. From the passage a staircase rose in the thickness of the wall to an upper vestibule. The ground floor contained a kitchen, with fireplaces and a well, and storerooms. On the first floor the servants' rooms and offices were separated by partitions, while a stair from the vestibule rose to the hall on the floor above which was provided with a large fireplace and several two-light traceried windows. The third floor contained the solar or, possibly, two private chambers for de la Mare and his family. The four corner towers, which contained GARDEROBES, a chapel and a parlour, were floored at the same levels as the body of the castle and, with the exception of the top of the south-west tower, were entered from adjacent chambers.

(*See also* PROSPECT TOWERS)

TOWER-KEEP The principal tower of a castle but one which contains only a single chamber on each floor accessed by a narrow intra-mural stair. Because these towers were erected primarily for defensive purposes, the domestic accommodation is often poorly lit and incommodious. For this reason most tower-keeps were abandoned in favour of courtyard buildings and were used only as watch-towers and as refuges in times of trouble.

(*See also* DONJON, GREAT TOWER, HALL-KEEP *and* KEEP)

TOWERS Although there is general agreement concerning the functions of different types of fortified tower, there is rarely consensus regarding the terminology used to describe them. For example, the terms GREAT TOWER, DONJON and KEEP are used synonymously to describe the *magnus turris* of a castle, the dominant tower intended (initially, at least) as a lord's residence and a final refuge in times of trouble. But *donjon* is a fourteenth-century term, by which time most great towers had been abandoned for residential purposes, while *keep* was not in use before the sixteenth century. Varieties of great tower such as the HALL-KEEP, KEEP-GATEHOUSE, PELE TOWER, SHELL-KEEP, TOWER-HOUSE and TOWER-KEEP have been identified by various authorities but, again, several of these definitions are disputed (*see individual entries*). Much has been written concerning a progression from rectilinear to polygonal to cylindrical great towers, but this does not bear close inspection. It is clear that all three styles were concurrent throughout the medieval period and that the decision whether to build square or polygonal or round depended on a number of factors, not least cost and fashion. Terms such as *round tower* and DRUM TOWER are simply descriptive of shape, though drum towers may be cylindrical or D-shaped.

'Blind spots' at the foot of a CURTAIN WALL were covered by the provision of projecting towers from which archers and crossbowmen could command the outer face of a wall from EMBRASURES and LOOPHOLES within the adjacent towers. These FLANKING TOWERS, INTERVAL TOWERS, MURAL TOWERS and *curtain towers* are often referred to as though they are synonymous but, in fact, each has its own definition. A *mural tower* is a generic term for any tower, projecting or otherwise, that was constructed within a wall. A *flanking tower* was intended to provide additional protection to an adjacent gate, barbican, dock, etc. An *interval tower* is one of a series of mural towers in a curtain wall. A *curtain tower* is a mural tower specifically located in a curtain wall. A particular type of mural tower is the BASTION, erected for purely defensive purposes with an open back and no interior accommodation other than a fighting platform. Strictly speaking, a semicircular bastion is a DEMI-BASTION, though in practice the terms appear to have become interchangeable. While it was cheaper to construct an open-backed bastion than a complete tower, it has also been argued that they were designed specifically to deny shelter to any attackers who succeeded in gaining access to the wall-walk. The rear opening of a bastion was sometimes closed with a timber wall, as in the south-west tower at Chepstow Castle, or with stone when additional accommodation was needed. Several castles have mural towers that could be isolated by means of portcullises located inside the doorways to the wall-walk and at the entrance on the ground floor. These towers could be held independently in the event of a siege or a mutinous garrison: Marten's Tower at Chepstow is just one example. Walls could also be divided into self-contained 'cells' which could be isolated were a section of a curtain to be scaled by a besieging force. Bastions were designed as 'circuit-breakers' between one section of wall-walk and the next, the temporary plank bridges which spanned the open interior of each tower being removed whenever a section of wall appeared to be under threat. With the bridges removed, each tower and section of wall to one side of it formed a self-sufficient unit of defence, as in the town walls of Caernarfon and Conwy (*see* TOWN WALLS). Similarly, mural towers often interrupted the wall-walk so that attackers would be confined between two towers and could not proceed on to the next section of wall. The term 'castles of enceinte' is sometimes applied to fortresses which had no keep and depended for their strength on the integrity of their mural towers. These towers were interconnected, not from the wall-walk of the curtain wall but by means of intra-mural passageways, while ground-floor entrances were provided only where absolutely necessary. In this way each tower could be shut off from the next and each could be defended independently should the wall be breached and the castle penetrated (*see* ENCEINTE). Even so, several castles have continuous wall-walks which by-pass towers, thereby enabling defenders to move freely and speedily from one section of a wall to another. The great military architect JAMES OF ST GEORGE preferred this arrangement. All of his castles in north Wales have continuous wall-walks – except at Caernarfon where, for reasons of security, the royal apartments were isolated from the outer ward. (At first sight the wall-walks at Conwy appear to continue uninterrupted from the outer to the inner ward, suggesting that the king's apartments were not entirely self-contained. However, rebates in the walls of the Stockhouse and Bakehouse towers indicate that the inner ward could indeed be isolated at wall-walk level by means of gates.)

Mural towers were not a medieval innovation; although in Europe their revival was undoubtedly influenced by experience of sieges during the Crusades, they had previously been used to reinforce the walls of Roman fortifications. In Britain the first medieval mural towers date from the late eleventh century, notably at Ludlow, Richmond and Rochester Castles. However, it was not until the mid-twelfth century that they were spaced closely enough to cover a curtain comprehensively, each pair of towers commanding a section of wall. Conisbrough, Windsor (the upper ward), Dover and Framlingham Castles have the earliest examples.

Most Norman towers were square-fronted or rectilinear but cylindrical and polygonal towers were found to be less vulnerable to bombardment by siege engines and to undermining since it was the angles of square buildings that tended to collapse (*see* SIEGES). Convex walls also provided a wider field of vision for archers and crossbowmen in adjacent towers. In some cases cylindrical towers were constructed on massive square bases in order to frustrate the mining of tunnels beneath the walls (*see* BATTER *and* SPUR BUTTRESSES). Thirteenth-century mural towers are often semicircular or D-shaped demi-bastions, as in the town walls of Caernarfon and Conwy. These were, of course, cheaper to build and were intended for purely defensive purposes. Most towers had conical timber-frame roofs of lead, slate or shingles (*see* SLATES AND TILES) but it is unlikely that bastions and demi-bastions would have been roofed. At Caldicot Castle the entire top floor of the great tower was originally constructed as a shield to protect the roof from combustible missiles, while at Pembroke the roof of the magnificent early thirteenth-century keep is a huge, stone dome. Wall-walks were accessed from a courtyard by newel stairs, located on the inner side of a mural tower to prevent any weakening of the external wall. Known as a *vice*, this spiral stair was composed of stone steps radiating from a central pillar (*newel*). According to tradition, newel stairs in castles rise in a clockwise direction, thereby providing sufficient room for (right-handed) defenders to wield a sword or pike but preventing attackers from doing so: hence

'turnpike stair' (*see* STAIRS). Provision was often made for the erection of timber *hoards* on the parapets of mural towers and wall-walks and the beam holes for these are sometimes visible beneath the crenellations (*see* HOARDING).

By the late thirteenth century an increasing need for residential accommodation resulted in many towers being built or refurbished with fireplaces and latrines and with windows inserted high in the inward-facing walls. But cylindrical chambers were an inconvenient shape for domestic purposes and square towers continued to be built throughout the medieval period, especially in the fifteenth century when the defensive advantages of round towers were less persuasive. Towards the end of the medieval period the great tower came into its own again, not for military reasons but as an architectural expression of status, wealth and magnate authority (*see* KEEP *and* BRICK BUILDINGS).

(*For* church towers used as fortifications *see* CHURCH TOWERS)

(*See also* ANGLE TURRET, ARTIFICIAL RUINS, BELFRY, BELL FLÈCHE, BERGFRIED, CAMPANILE, CISTERN, ENCLOSURE CASTLES, ENGINE TOWER, MASONRY, MILL TOWER *and* PROSPECT TOWER)

TOWN GATE *see* TOWN WALLS

TOWN HOUSE *see* INN

TOWNS Most towns came into existence as the result of policy decisions made either by individuals or by institutions. While geographical and economic factors undoubtedly influenced those decisions, very few towns simply grew from settlements which happened to be in favourable locations. In the majority of cases, therefore, towns were planned and it is this that distinguished them from other types of settlement.

Early Towns
The popular perception of the DARK AGES is one of deserted Roman towns, dilapidated villas and a rapid reversion to barbarism. It is true that there was no discernible revival of urban affairs until the seventh century, when a number of former Roman towns were designated as the administrative centres of dioceses, notably London, Canterbury, Dorchester-on-Thames, Winchester and York. But in the late Saxon period several new towns were established at proto-urban settlements which, well before the end of the eighth century, had developed characteristics that marked them out from the normal

agricultural settlements of the period. For the most part they were the administrative centres of royal estates and therefore already exercised civil authority within territories that had evolved from earlier minor kingdoms and tribal units. Many possessed a minster and had developed trading functions superior to those of neighbouring settlements. Significantly, most were located at or near former Roman sites, suggesting that such places had regained their status very much earlier than is generally acknowledged and that many had never been entirely deserted. Indeed, it is highly unlikely that, following the withdrawal of Rome, the entire indigenous population should suddenly abandon the towns and other Roman settlements and the network of metalled roads that radiated from them. No doubt they fell into disrepair, in the absence of a cohesive and skilled workforce, but the pattern was established which was to provide the foundation of many late Saxon towns such as Rochester, Bradford-on-Avon and Dorchester (Dorset). These later towns may have been promoted by their royal or ecclesiastical owners or remodelled with regular street patterns and market places to encourage expansion, but the potential for commercial growth was already there.

Anglo-Saxon sources indicate that there were three types of town. Firstly, those that developed on former Roman sites were known as *ceasters*. Secondly, a defensive system of fortified BURHS was established in southern England during the reigns of Alfred the Great (871–99) and his Saxon successors as a direct response to the threat of Danish invasion. The third and more numerous category of Anglo-Saxon towns was the PORT or commercial trading centre. These were not necessarily located on coasts or navigable rivers: many were inland market towns such as Milborne Port and Langport in Somerset. In the DANELAW several new towns were created, notably the *Five Boroughs* of Derby, Nottingham, Stamford, Leicester and Lincoln, the last two on former Roman sites.

From the tenth to the thirteenth centuries numerous villages were extended as planned towns by their owners in order to encourage trade. Professor W.G. Hoskins has identified five such towns in north Oxfordshire alone, four of them (Banbury, Chipping Norton, Deddington and Woodstock) dating from the twelfth century and the fifth (Bicester) from the thirteenth. Several were castle towns, built outside the gates of late eleventh-century fortresses such as Alnwick, Ludlow and Chepstow, while others were entirely new, laid out on 'green-field' sites: at Salisbury, for example, the

hill-top town of Old Sarum was abandoned in 1220, together with its Norman castle and abbey. The planned origins of such towns are often clearly evident in the regular grid-like pattern of their streets and the rectilinear disposition of ancient boundaries. Stratford-upon-Avon (1196), Liverpool (1207), Leeds (1207) and Kingston-upon-Hull (1293) are but four notable examples of early medieval planned towns, three of which developed into major cities.

Welsh Plantation Towns

In Wales, King John (1199–1216) and Henry III (1216–72) established several new towns. At Montgomery, for example, a castle was built in 1223 to act as a bulwark against Llywelyn the Great and the town was defended by an earthwork enclosure over 1.6km (1 mile) in length (*see* WALES: CONQUEST OF). Beyond the River Conwy, rural colonisation by Englishmen was out of the question and the fortified town (*bastide*) was therefore acknowledged as the most practicable means of establishing an English civilian presence in the conquered territories. Henry's son Edward I (1272–1307) had seen and built fortified towns during his time in Gascony. Following his first victory over the Welsh in 1277, the creation of new towns at Aberystwyth and Flint and the re-establishment of the borough of Rhuddlan were clearly essential elements in Edward's strategy for the subjugation of north Wales. After his second victory of 1282–3, the towns of Caernarfon, Harlech and Conwy were endowed and colonised while the existing Welsh settlements at Bere and Criccieth were converted to English boroughs. Finally, in 1295 the new town of Beaumaris was established on the site of Llanfaes, at that time the principal port on the island of Anglesey and the most flourishing urban centre in north Wales. Edward evicted the entire native population and moved it to a new settlement (Newborough) some 20km (12 miles) away.

These new PLANTATION TOWNS were built as adjuncts to castles, their walls integrated with those of the castle itself and their streets laid out on a characteristic rectangular grid plan. The magnificent walls, gates and interval towers of Caernarfon and Conwy survive to this day, as do sections of several baronial bastides such as the late thirteenth-century walls of Tenby in Dyfed (*see* TOWN WALLS). The constable of the castle was also mayor of the newly created borough while the English burgesses were obliged to defend the ramparts and to provide the castle garrison with supplies. The Edwardian boroughs were to play a key rôle in the economic control of the newly conquered territories for they were guaranteed a monopoly of wholesale trade within their extensive hinterlands. Caernarfon, for example, enjoyed a monopoly that extended for nearly 13km (8 miles) beyond its walls, while a general ordinance required that no Welshman was to trade outside the mercatorial towns. But the 'English burgesses of the English boroughs in Wales' (as they called themselves) were also expected to exert a civilising (anglicising?) influence on the indigenous population: through contact with the English settlers the Welsh, it was anticipated, would discover the benefits of civilised manners and 'gentle living'. In practice, the burgesses used their extensive privileges to secure control of key sectors of the local economy and to exploit to the full their favoured status. There is a considerable element of racial exclusiveness in the belief that the towns had been established 'for the habitation of Englishmen' to the exclusion of 'mere Welshmen' who were deemed to be 'foreigners' within the precincts of the boroughs. No wonder that the towns and their burgesses and officials were so often the targets of Welsh resentment and frustration throughout the fourteenth century.

Beyond Gwynydd, two anaemic boroughs were founded at the former native centres of Dryslwyn (1287) and Dinefwr (1298), the latter being known henceforth as Newtown. At Overton (Maelor Saesneg), Dryslwyn, Holt and Ruthin the homesteads of Welsh tenants were appropriated and demolished to make way for the grid-patterned streets of the new towns. Throughout Wales and the MARCH, the sheriffs were instructed to offer financial inducements to prospective (exclusively English) burgesses, together with grants of land: the burgesses of Caernarfon, for example, were each endowed with nearly 1,500 acres. Several of the Welsh boroughs prospered (notably Beaumaris, Conwy, Denbigh and Ruthin), while others failed (Bere and, to a degree, Criccieth).

English Towns
Medieval magnates, particularly those who owned castles, found it profitable to allow communities to develop nearby, both to provide for the needs of their households and to boost revenues from increased trade and commerce (see FAIRS and MARKETS). Settlers were attracted by land grants, low rents and other privileges and organised trading monopolies offered economic security and the right of controlling one's own property within a town. Each freeholder had one or more plots of land with a building abutting the street in which he lived, worked and traded. More than forty English towns

retain sections of their original medieval walls and several their gates which closely resemble castle gatehouses and served a similar purpose – that of a 'holding area' where credentials were checked and fees collected. Although originally constructed for military purposes, TOWN WALLS facilitated the maintenance of LAW AND ORDER and effectively controlled access to a town's trading facilities which were jealously guarded by the granting of borough charters and other protective franchises and by the formation of GUILDS. But such grants were haphazard: ambitious manorial lords were able to obtain borough status for small communities in anticipation of commercial success and the historical landscape is littered with the relics of failed towns, such as Bishop's Castle in Shropshire. Bishop's Castle received its grant of a market in 1203 but settlers were slow to take up the plots laid out by the bishop of Hereford's surveyors and it was many decades before development reached along the main street toward the parish church. It is interesting to note, however, that even in this remote and unstable borderland every economic indicator encouraged growth. Conversely, several substantial communities such as Ludlow, also in Shropshire, which possessed all the attributes of towns, were not legally defined as such until the late Middle Ages.

From the mid-thirteenth century there was a decline in the economic conditions which had previously encouraged the building of new towns but many settlements prospered and expanded, either by ribbon development along existing streets or by the addition of new suburbs. Many *Newland* place-names in towns originated at this time.

In the early fourteenth century London probably had a population of nearly 120,000 and cities such as York, Norwich, Lincoln and Bristol each had about 20,000 inhabitants. Of a total population of 5 million it is now believed that at least 700,000 lived in towns. Medieval urban society was also very well organised with old peoples' homes, orphanages, hospitals, social clubs and hotels. Large numbers of social institutions were provided by wealthy benefactors (*see* CHANTRY), by ecclesiastical foundations and by fraternities such as the Guild of Our Lady at Lavenham in Suffolk, whose fifteenth-century meeting hall was built in part to ensure that masses were said for the souls of all paid-up members and in part as a social club for the town's élite, with its own resident cook and musician. The Black Death of 1348–69 effectively curtailed the creation of new towns: Bewdley, built in 1477 on the banks of the River Severn in Worcestershire, was the last medieval planned town.

TOWNSHIP *see* FRANKPLEDGE

TOWN WALLS Although ostensibly constructed for military purposes, to fend against insurrection and riot, town walls facilitated the maintenance of LAW AND ORDER and controlled access to a town's trading facilities which were jealously guarded by the granting of borough charters and other protective franchises and by the formation of GUILDS. They were symbolic also of increasing prosperity and of a corporation's wealth and status. The building of a wall might take several decades to complete (the walls of Rouen in northern France were 6km (3.7 miles) long) and the cost must have been a considerable strain on the burgesses' resources. Before any work could begin, a corporation was obliged to obtain a royal licence and to charge a levy (*murage*) to finance the construction and maintenance of the town walls. Economies could be made by utilising earlier ramparts, by omitting a length of wall where a river or other natural feature was considered a sufficient defence, and by building open-backed, semicircular bastions (*demi-bastions*) instead of more sophisticated mural towers. A ditch or water-filled moat was, of course, an invariable accompaniment to a defensive wall, as were projecting mural towers or bastions without which 'blind spots' at the foot of a wall could not be observed and defended. Guardrooms, latrines and other offices were usually accommodated in gatehouses or in towers that were built specifically for the purpose or to defend a particularly vulnerable length of wall.

As today, successful towns attracted traffic, especially on market days (*see* FAIRS *and* MARKETS). Access to a town was carefully controlled at GATEHOUSES, where credentials could be scrutinised and fees collected, and in most towns the gates were closed at night (*see* CURFEW). Town gatehouses vary considerably in scale and design, from Winchester's twin-towered West Gate and Monmouth's lofty gatehouse straddling the Monnow Bridge (*see* BRIDGES AND BRIDGE GATES) to Warwick where both surviving town gates are surmounted by medieval chapels: St James's on the west gate and St Peter's above the east. (It has been suggested, somewhat incredulously, that besiegers might be deterred by the presence of a chapel above a gate.)

Even though their walls and gates may have disappeared long ago, many towns have retained their medieval street plans, often with streets intersecting at the centre and named after the gates they served: typically at Gloucester where Northgate, Southgate, Eastgate and Westgate Streets meet at the Cross. The most successful towns were usually those that had been planned by a local magnate and thrived as centres of trade and industry in the shadow of his castle. Almost invariably the castle would be incorporated in the town's defences, usually as part of the perimeter wall. Many medieval town walls survived until the nineteenth century, despite slighting in the Civil War and centuries of neglect. It was the rapid expansion of transport – the toll road, the railway and, most recently, the urban highway – that was chiefly responsible for the destruction of so many town walls and gatehouses. The walls of York, Chester and Chichester are more or less intact, though much restored, and there are impressive lengths of wall remaining at Canterbury, Chepstow, Denbigh, Newcastle, Oxford, Southampton and Tenby. The walls, towers and gatehouses of Edward I's plantation boroughs in north Wales are unusual in that they were constructed, together with their magnificent castles, by the crown as part of Edward's strategy for the subjugation of Gwynedd (*see* WALES, CONQUEST OF). The surviving town walls of Caernarfon and (especially) Conwy are among the finest of any in Europe.

Post-Roman Defences

The walls of Colchester, Canterbury and Exeter were almost entirely of Roman origin while at York and Chester they incorporated the defences of legionary fortresses. At Colchester most of the 2.4km (1½ mile) long circuit of the second-century Roman wall remains, the only substantial medieval addition being a group of late fourteenth-century towers along the eastern section of the south wall. One Roman gate (the Balkerne Gate) has survived while the other gates were rebuilt during the medieval period and demolished after the Civil War.

Although incomplete, the city walls of Canterbury are some of the finest in England. The shape of the medieval defences was determined in the third century when the Roman city of Durovernum encompassed an oval area nearly 3.2km (2 miles) in circumference. However, very little Roman masonry has survived, other than the blocked archway of the Quenin Gate (the Queen's Gate), for the wall was rebuilt in the 1370s in anticipation of a French invasion. Over half the circuit is preserved, from the site of the former North Gate to the castle, but seven of the eight medieval gates have been demolished. The one surviving gate, the Westgate, is a splendid late fourteenth-century building with twin cylindrical flanking towers, 18m (60ft) high, linked by a machicolated parapet. The gatehouse was originally defended by a drawbridge and portcullis and was the first in Britain to be equipped with GUN PORTS. In 1473 the Westgate became the city gaol and then a debtors' prison; debtors were held in cages from where they could beg for alms from passers-by. The gates were burned in the parliamentary riots of 1648, replaced in 1680 and finally removed in the late eighteenth century.

Exeter's city wall, nearly 3.2km (2 mile) long, is less well preserved having been invested on at least ten occasions and, like Canterbury, it was severely damaged by bombing in 1942. The red sandstone wall, three-quarters of which still stands, was built by the Romans in AD 50. It was repaired by King Athelstan in the 930s and semicircular bastions added when it was heightened after 1224. All the gatehouses were demolished in the eighteenth century while the Bishop's Bastion, containing a postern to the cathedral precinct, is a modern reconstruction. Typically, the castle (called Rougemont Castle from the colour of the rock on which it stands) occupies one corner of the city's defences, the bailey being protected on two sides by the town wall. The city was besieged by the Danes in 876 and 1003, by the Normans in 1086 (an eighteen-day siege) and by King Stephen in 1138 (see ANARCHY, THE). Supporters of the pretender Perkin Warbeck invested the city twice in 1497 while a serious rising in the West Country in 1549 (against the use of the new Book of Common Prayer) culminated in an eight-week siege. The city was further besieged during the Civil War (in 1643 and 1645–6) and finally in 1942, when heavy bombing destroyed a large part of the city, coincidentally revealing lengths of wall that had previously been concealed behind houses. Exeter's troubled history illustrates the need to protect major strategic centres with adequate defences. When the burgesses of Gloucester closed their city gates to the Lancastrian forces in 1471 they changed the course of English history. Unable to cross the River Severn, Queen Margaret and her troops were forced to march north to the next river crossing where, on 4 May, they met Edward IV and his Yorkist army on Tewkesbury's Bloody Meadow. Margaret was captured, her son killed and, within days, her husband murdered. Having restored political stability, Edward IV died in April 1483 leaving his thirteen-year-old son Edward as his heir. Thereafter came Richard III, Bosworth Field and the Tudors (see WARS OF THE ROSES).

The magnificent 4km (2½ mile) length of York's city wall has survived almost intact, together with its

formidable gatehouses (known as *bars*), thanks to Sir Thomas Fairfax, who spared the city's defences from slighting after it surrendered to parliamentary forces in 1644, and to archbishop William Markham (1777–1807) who, in 1807, intervened to prevent the systematic demolition of the walls. Roman *Eburacum* was one of Britain's three legionary fortresses, together with Chester and Caerleon. Following the withdrawal of Rome in 408, York became the capital of the Anglo-Saxon kingdom of Northumbria and from c. 876 was the capital of the Danish kingdom of Jorvik. In 1069 the city was destroyed by fire, enabling the Normans to lay out a new town, five times larger than the original Roman settlement, behind substantial defences and protected by two motte and bailey castles (1068 and 1069). By 1300 the city walls encompassed 40 churches, 9 chapels, 4 monasteries, 4 friaries, 16 hospitals and 9 guild halls, all within an area of 263 acres. The northern sector of the city, between the River Ouse and its tributary the Foss, was the site of the rectangular Roman fortress. The Roman walls have gone on two sides but to the north-east and north-west they lie beneath massive tenth-century ramparts, constructed during the Danish occupation. The other two sectors of the city beyond the rivers are also delineated by ramparts on top of which stone walls were constructed in the thirteenth and fourteenth centuries. In all there are thirty-seven projecting interval towers, round, square or polygonal, irregularly spaced and including a number of larger towers at strategically important locations. Bootham Bar, Monk Bar, Walmgate Bar and Micklegate Bar were provided with outer BARBICANS, that at Walmgate Bar being the only surviving example in England of a barbican protecting a city gate. Typically, Bootham Bar, built on the site of the north-west gate of the legionary fortress, is a tall gate-tower with corbelled turrets projecting at the corners and a long entrance passage. Some lengths of WALL-WALK are raised only a few feet above the earlier ramparts and the walls themselves are surprisingly thin. The present walkway is supported by arcades and was erected during a substantial remodelling in the late fifteenth century.

Chester's walls and gates form an almost unbroken 3km (2 mile) circuit of the city. Unlike the less substantial walls of York (which depended for their strength on earlier earthworks), they are 1.8m (6ft) wide in places and rise 12m (40ft) above street level. The turf and timber ramparts of the original rectangular Roman fortress were twice rebuilt in stone. The medieval wall follows the Roman

Micklegate Bar, York.

alignment on the north and east, the walls to the south and west following the course of the river as it was when the city was extended under the Mercian kings. The present walls mostly date from the thirteenth century though they have been repaired and rebuilt many times. In the eighteenth century Civil War breaches were filled and the parapet restored to form a continuous wall-walk or 'promenade'. For centuries the Old Dee Bridge was the only route from Wales into the city and a massively fortified gate (the Bridgegate or Welsh Gate) was erected to defend against attack from that quarter. Like the Northgate it was defended by twin towers, a portcullis and drawbridge. As the name suggests, it was through the Watergate that cargoes were transported from the quay to the city, protected to the north by the Water Tower, an impressive cylindrical tower (*c.* 1322) that once controlled access to the quay from the river. Originally it stood in the waters of the river but the Dee has since receded leaving it isolated. Regrettably, all the medieval gatehouses were demolished in the late eighteenth and early nineteenth centuries and were replaced by elevated walkways over busy roads, most recently at Newgate (1938) and St Martin's Gate (1966). There were no towers on the south and west

walls, which were protected by the river, while fewer than half of the original thirty semicircular bastions remain along the north and east walls. The city's water-filled moat has survived beyond the northern wall, where it has been adapted for use as a canal.

Saxon and Early Medieval Defences

The old towns of Wareham and Wallingford are still contained within the earth ramparts that were constructed by the Anglo-Saxons as a defence against the Danes (*see* BURHS). At both towns, the embankments and ditches enclose three sides of a rectangular area (for this reason they were once believed to be of Roman origin) with a river protecting the fourth. An essential element of the Norman strategy of colonisation was the erection of castles to supplement the earth and ditch fortifications of the Anglo-Saxon burhs and the creation of new towns beyond their gates. At Wallingford the Normans heightened the embankment while at Wareham a stone wall was demolished and the ramparts increased in height.

The Domesday survey of 1086 (*see* DOMESDAY BOOK) recorded forty-eight towns as having defences but by the end of the twelfth century at least half of these were noted as being beyond repair. Between 1191 and 1230 some fifty new towns were created (*see* TOWNS), including Montgomery where a castle was built (1223) by Henry III to act as a bulwark against the Welsh. At the same time a defensive rampart and ditch were constructed round the town, over 1.6km (1 mile) in length, much of which has survived. This period of expansion was followed by a decline in the economic conditions which had previously encouraged the building of new towns. Even so, many existing settlements prospered at the expense of others and the most successful of these reconstructed their defences in stone. By 1400 there were 108 walled towns in England.

The town of Chepstow, in the southern MARCH, occupies the western bank of a broad bend in the River Wye, protected to the north by steep cliffs and its magnificent elongated castle. In the late thirteenth century the town was enclosed on the landward side by a stone wall (the Port Wall) and ditch 1,097m (1,200yd) in length while the entire river frontage, including the town's quay, was left undefended. It is interesting to note that at Chepstow the medieval town occupied only a third of the enclosed area, the other two-thirds remaining as 'meadow and pasture grounds' well into the nineteenth century. This was because of the sloping nature of the site: had the wall not followed the crest of the slope it would have been vulnerable to attack from higher land to the south and west. Chepstow's wall, with its ten open-back semicircular bastions, remained almost intact until the end of the nineteenth century. But since then it has been badly mutilated, mostly to accommodate the railway and the motor car, though its Town Gate has survived as the only means of access to the old town from the landward side. It is a tall rectangular tower, rebuilt in 1487 and remodelled in 1524, with a gate passage and Victorian archways, windows and crenellations.

Edwardian Plantation Towns

In the final phase of Edward I's subjugation of Gwynedd a number of strategically located castles and fortified boroughs were constructed and populated with English merchants, to the exclusion of the native Welsh (see WALES, CONQUEST OF and PLANTATION TOWNS). Building began between March and June in 1283 and proceeded with extraordinary speed: Conwy was almost completed in four-and-a-half years, most of Caernarfon was finished by 1287 and Harlech by 1289. Even the great concentric castle of Beaumaris on Anglesey was defensible after just two building seasons (1295–6), though it was never completed.

Beaumaris received its charter in 1296 and became the largest of the north Wales boroughs. For political as well as commercial purposes it was intended that Beaumaris should supersede the ancient Welsh town of Llanfaes, the inhabitants of which were removed to a new site, thereafter known as Newborough. Although it was always intended that there should be a town wall, only a short length of footings was built near the castle dock (see QUAYS). These footings, measuring 3.9m (13ft) in width, incline to the west in the direction followed by a later wall, while the point at which the wall was to have joined the castle curtain at the 'Gate next the Sea' was faced to form a low square turret that projected from the gate tower. It is not known precisely when the decision was taken not to proceed with building the town wall, though by 1296 Edward's rapidly diminishing resources were being directed against the Scots. The burgesses petitioned the king in c. 1315 but it was not until the beginning of the fifteenth century that a rampart and ditch were constructed round the town in response to the Glyn Dŵr rising. It would appear that this embankment was replaced by a stone wall in c. 1414 but of this only fragmentary sections remain. There is documentary evidence that the wall was provided with three gatehouses, mural towers and latrines and that it was of sufficient width to accommodate an intra-mural passage. Repairs were carried out in the sixteenth, seventeenth and eighteenth centuries and the West Gate was still standing in 1785.

The 735m (800yd) circuit of walls enclosing the medieval borough of Caernarfon has survived unbroken with eight bastions and two twin-towered gateways. Caernarfon's town walls were built at the same time as the castle (1283–92) and form what is, in effect, an outer BAILEY with the castle at its southern perimeter. The space enclosed is surprisingly small by medieval standards, confined as it is by the River Cadnant to the north (now a culvert), the Seiont to the south and the Menai Strait to the west. The wall begins close to the castle's North-East Tower, where the road covers what was once a wide castle ditch, and continues past a postern (the Green Gate) in a north-easterly direction to the Exchequer Gate. This was the principal landward entrance to the town and was approached by a five-arched bridge across the River Cadnant and a small barbican and drawbridge in front of the gate. The gatehouse was occupied by the offices of the Exchequer, established by the Statute of 1284 as the administrative centre of the counties of Caernarvon, Merioneth and Anglesey. The gateway was altered in 1767 when it became the Town Hall, and again in 1873 as the Guildhall. From the Exchequer Gate the wall continues north to an angle tower in the north-west corner of the circuit. This was adopted as the bell tower and vestry of St Mary's church which was erected against the town wall in 1307. South of the corner tower, the town's quay occupies the space between the town wall and the Menai foreshore and is protected by two open-backed bastions and a substantial twin-towered gatehouse (the Porth-yr-Aur or Golden Gate) and small projecting barbican. In the gatehouse the portcullis grooves have survived, as has a fragment of a projecting latrine at wall-walk level, but the windows and battlements date from the nineteenth century and the building now houses the Royal Welsh Yacht Club. When viewed across the Seiont estuary from the west, the quay, with its unbroken stretch of town walls, splendidly retains its medieval atmosphere. It was originally intended that the wall, where it met the castle's Eagle Tower, would be pierced by a wide arched water gate through which water-borne supplies could be carried into the castle ditch at high tide to a dock at the foot of the Well Tower (see QUAYS). But the scheme was never completed, the present arched opening being a comparatively recent insertion near the site of a much smaller medieval postern.

While Caernarfon was intended to be the administrative capital of Edward's new principality, Conwy was to be its chief borough. The town walls

The town walls of Conwy are the finest of any in Britain. Their purpose was to enclose and protect the new borough (founded in 1284) and to provide, on the landward side, a strong defence to the castle itself.

of Conwy are the finest of any in Britain. Their purpose was to enclose and protect the new borough (founded in 1284) and to provide, on the landward side, a strong defence to the castle itself. The building of the walls and castle was under the overall direction of JAMES OF ST GEORGE, Master of the King's Works in Wales, and a team of specialist builders recruited from throughout Europe. While the walls were designed to create a continuous barrier of masonry so strong that it could not be breached, they were also divided into self-contained 'cells' each of which could be isolated if a section of wall were scaled by an attacking force. As at Caernarfon, the bastions are open-backed and could act as 'circuit-breakers' between one section of wall-walk and the next, the temporary plank bridges which spanned the open interior of each tower being removed whenever a section of wall appeared to be under threat. With the bridges removed, each tower and section of wall to one side of it formed a self-sufficient unit of defence. When the bridges were in place, watchmen could patrol the wall-walk along its entire length. The walls and towers were provided with battlements

and a total of some 480 loopholes (*see* LOOPHOLE), and provision was made for the erection of timber *hoards*, the beam holes for which are visible beneath the loopholes (*see* HOARDING). Research suggests that the bases of some of the towers were built first, then the linking curtain wall and finally the upper parts of the towers and battlements.

As at Caernarfon, the town walls of Conwy were built at the same time as the castle (1283–7) but on a much larger scale. The circuit is 1.3km (1,400yd) in length with twenty-two towers (mostly bastions), three twin-towered gateways and a wall-walk with a uniform width of 1.68m (5½ft) – except where narrow 91cm (3ft) wide linking walls crossed the castle ditch. In addition a 55m (60yd) long spur projects from the end of the quay across the foreshore and into the waters of the Conwy estuary. This wing wall, which is 3.1m (10½ft) thick, is pierced by a gateway (the portcullis groove and counterweight shaft have survived) and originally terminated in a circular tower. The castle occupies the eastern corner of the roughly triangular enclosure, the only gap in the wall being where it descends the rock from the castle's Stockhouse Tower to what was the moat but (since 1958) is now a wide and intrusive highway. Beyond an imitation 'gothic' tower (built by Thomas Telford in 1826) is the town's quay which, as at Caernarfon, is protected by the town wall with four bastions and a twin-towered gatehouse (the Lower Gate) providing access from the dockside to the town. Unfortunately, the bastions and gatehouse towers on the quayside have suffered badly and have been incorporated crudely into later buildings.

The splendid north-west wall is one of the most complete and imposing lengths of town wall anywhere in Europe. It is over 455m (nearly 500yd) in length and no fewer than nine towers have survived, spaced symmetrically at intervals of between 48 and 57m (52 and 62yd). The gateways are recent insertions to accommodate traffic, that which passes through one of the bastions having been inserted by Telford when the coast road to Bangor was built in the 1820s. Another bastion is badly cracked, the result of subsidence caused by the railway tunnel beneath (1846), while much of the town ditch has been filled and levelled. The north-west wall climbs to its highest point, a circular tower perched on a crag of rock at the apex of the triangle. This was the culmination of the defensive system. Unbroken views of the wall-walks in both directions and the setting back at an acute angle of the walls to the north-east and south-east of the tower meant that the entire circuit could be observed from a single point. At the corner tower the wall turns sharply to the south-east to the Upper Gate, the twin towers of which are set at different levels to compensate for the considerable slope. The Upper Gate (referred to in the Middle Ages as 'the High Yate of Conwey') was once the only landward entrance to the town and was defended by a barbican, a drawbridge across the rock-cut ditch, a portcullis and a pair of heavy timber doors. The interior layout of the gatehouse is ingeniously planned. The drawbridge mechanism was located on a wooden platform above the gate passage (the beddings for the joists are still visible in the cross-wall above) and could only be reached by means of a doorway from the south tower. The porter who controlled the mechanism was accommodated in an L-shaped chamber within the gatehouse, the back wall of which was constructed of timber, and the apartment was reached by an outside staircase that led also to the wall-walk. A separate room in the upper part of the northern tower was accessible only from the adjacent wall stair and from it stone steps led to the portcullis mechanism. The gate passage could be observed through loops in the walls of the guardrooms which occupied the ground floors of both towers and were entered through barred doors in their back walls. It is clear that the gatehouse, and the wall-walks on either side of it, were designed for cellular defence: if one section was captured the integrity of its neighbour could be maintained.

From the Upper Gate the wall continues downhill and changes direction toward the Mill Gate. A length of wall measuring 26m (85ft) once formed the western end of a substantial building, referred to in contemporary documents as 'a new high chamber' and illuminated by three single-light windows in the town wall. This and an adjacent mural tower (a bastion converted to a solar) formed part of a group of buildings known as Llewelyn's Hall, refurbished as a residence for Edward, the first English prince of Wales, after his investiture in 1301. The hall, which was of timber-frame construction, was dismantled and removed to Caernarfon where it was erected within the walls of the castle in 1315. The building of the Chester & Holyhead Railway in 1847 caused enormous damage to the town's southern wall. The construction of an embankment and the diversion of the Gyffin stream drastically reduced the visual impact of the lofty walls and, between two of the bastions, a great flattened four-centred arch was inserted to accommodate the railway where it entered the town.

The length of wall between the railway arch and the Mill Gate is like no other in Europe. The Mill Gate (the largest of Conwy's gates) and a range of timber-frame buildings set against the adjacent walls were fitted out as offices and accommodation for Edward I's private secretariat (the *Wardrobe*) who benefited from the last word in thirteenth-century staff lavatories. Twelve separate but identical cubicles (*gonges*) project on corbels from the parapet of the town wall, each with a chute discharging into the stream below. Grooves for the wooden fronts and seats may still be seen in some of the cubicles (*see* GARDEROBE). This large secretariat was responsible for the administration of the king's affairs. It was staffed by royal clerks working under the keeper or treasurer of the Wardrobe and his deputy, the controller, whose apartments were located in the towers of the Mill Gate. There is also evidence to suggest that between the Mill Gate and the castle (in the area now occupied by a car-park) were the offices of 'the Master of the King's Works in Wales' and his numerous staff. Little wonder, then, that such elaborate lavatorial arrangements should have been made for the relief of so many civil servants! The South or Mill Gate forms a re-entrant in the wall, its apparently irrational alignment dictated, perhaps, by the footprint of an earlier gate in the precinct wall of the former abbey. As the name suggests, the Mill Gate gave access to a water mill on the Gyffin stream. This mill was almost certainly commandeered by the king when he removed the Cistercian abbey of Aberconwy (the burial place of Llewelyn the Great) to a new site at Maenan, 13km (8 miles) away in the Conwy valley. From the Mill Gate the wall continues in an easterly direction, crossing the town ditch and joining the castle at the West Barbican. Today the ditch, which separated the castle from the town, forms a cutting for a road which passes through a nineteenth-century archway.

TRACERY *see* GOTHIC ARCHITECTURE *and* WINDOWS

TRAILBASTON At the beginning of the fourteenth century a systematic approach to the widespread problem of lawlessness was required and special 'trailbaston' commissions were established under Edward I (*bastons* being the cudgels carried by members of criminal bands). The earliest appointments of 1304 were justices of general OYER AND TERMINER who were charged to inquire into such offences as extortion and the hiring of men to assault others. By the following year so many criminals had been taken that it was a matter of some urgency that they should be brought to trial and the Ordinance of Trailbaston was promulgated. This established five judicial circuits to hear cases which had occurred between the summers of 1297 and 1305. These commissions were renewed in the autumn of 1305 and again in 1307. The trailbaston inquiries revealed endemic brutality and even murder, particularly at fairs and markets, and corruption was found to be rife among the gentry: many local justices used their position to influence pleas and protection rackets were commonplace. At York, for example, commissioners discovered that a group of wealthy citizens held the city in a stranglehold under the guise of a religious guild, and in Staffordshire alone some 300 men were outlawed as a consequence of the trailbaston hearings. But they were unpopular and often inequitable: anyone who knew how to use a bow and arrow might be accused of belonging to a criminal band and those who had acquired some knowledge of the law might be charged with conspiracy. Although the proceedings were comprehensive and evidently successful they did not provide the system of local LAW AND ORDER which was so badly needed and many were of the opinion that they had been introduced simply to restore the king's financial fortunes. A *Calendar of London Trailbaston Trials under Commissions of 1305 and 1306* was published by the Public Record Office in 1976 (*see* APPENDIX II).

TRAIN BANDS *also* **TRAINED BANDS** Lawless groups of former magnate retainers whose military services were no longer required following the Wars of the Roses and the suppression of LIVERY AND MAINTENANCE in the early sixteenth century. Often these were synonymous with special forces within the county MILITIA who in the Tudor period made themselves available for military training and acquired a justifiable reputation for indiscipline.

TRAINING, MILITARY *see* MILITARY TRAINING

TRANSOM A vertical bar dividing the lights of a window.
(*See also* MASONRY, MULLION *and* WINDOWS)

TRANSPORT AND COMMUNICATIONS *see* BEACONS, HEREPAETHS, HORSES AND HORSE-HARNESS, MATERIALS (CARRIAGE OF), MILITARY ROADS, QUAYS *and* ROADS (MEDIEVAL)

TRAPPER *see* BARDING, CAPARISON *and* HORSES AND HORSE-HARNESS

TRAPPINGS A general term to describe the bridle, saddle, etc., of a horse.

TREASON Violation by a subject of his allegiance to his lord, most particularly the king. Treason was considered to be a most heinous offence, usually punishable by an elaborate and lingering death.

TREASURY The Norman kings created two departments to deal with financial matters: the EXCHEQUER and the Treasury. The latter was responsible for receiving and paying out moneys on behalf of the sovereign. From the second half of the sixteenth century the Treasury began to supersede the functions of the Exchequer and in the eighteenth century the First Lord gradually assumed the rôle of Prime Minister. Subsequently, prime ministers have invariably held the office of First Lord of the Treasury, the functions of the office being carried out by the Chancellor of the Exchequer. Treasury records from 1557 are maintained at the Public Record Office (*see* APPENDIX II).
(*See also* HOUSEHOLD (*for* the Wardrobe) *and* STATE RECORDS)

TREBUCHET A stone-throwing war machine (*see* SIEGES).

TREE-RING DATING Dendrochronology is a method of dating timber by studying its annual growth rings. A tree adds a ring of growth each year: in dry years this is of limited size, while in wet years more luxuriant growth produces wider rings. Timber may be dated accurately by matching sequences of rings with those from a living tree of known date. Using tree-ring dating, standard growth plots may be compiled for different historical periods, and in Britain the method has been used to date timbers (usually oak or beech) from medieval structures. (*See also* STRATIGRAPHY)

TREFOIL A figure having three radiating stylised 'petals', found both as an architectural motif and as an heraldic device (*see* FOILS).

TRIAL BY BATTLE *see* APPROVER

TRIANGULAR ARCH *see* ARCH

TRIBOLI A type of CALTRAP thrown on an enemy's deck in a naval engagement.

TRICK *and* **TRICKING** *see* TINCTURES

TRILATERAL CASTLES, THE The 'Three Castles' of Monmouthshire: Grosmont, Skenfrith and White Castle (*see* THREE CASTLES, THE).

TRINODA NECESSITAS The basic feudal obligations of all villeins, consisting of military support (*fyrd-bote*), the repair of fortifications (*burgh-bote*) and the maintenance of roads and bridges (*bridge-bote*).

TRIPTYCH A set of three painted panels, hinged so that they could be folded together. Triptychs probably originated in the portable altars of the medieval nobility and were usually placed against a wall or were free-standing. Like the DIPTYCH (which has two panels), a triptych usually depicts religious themes, though some included genealogical and armorial information.

TRUMEAU *see* PIER

TRUNNION (i) The axle of a counterpoise mechanism (*see* DRAWBRIDGE).
(ii) Large studs on either side of a cannon barrel enabling it to be elevated or lowered (*see* FIREARMS AND CANNON).

TRUSS A framework of timbers supporting a roof.

TUDOR ARCH *see* ARCH

TUDOR ARCHITECTURE Tudor buildings remained essentially Gothic in form (*see* GOTHIC ARCHITECTURE) and, with the notable exception of the chapel of Henry VII at Westminster (1503–19), nearly all major buildings of the period were secular. (The magnificent King's College Chapel, Cambridge (1446–1515) and St George's Chapel at Windsor Castle (1475–1509) were also completed in this period.)

The heavily fortified medieval castle had become an architectural and military anachronism long before 1485. In the mid-sixteenth century the Dissolution of the Monasteries made available vast tracts of land and created unique opportunities for the building of country houses, farmsteads and estate dwellings that were enthusiastically exploited by the new Tudor establishment. The confiscation of Church property also enabled Henry VIII (1509–47) to embark on a programme of large-scale building, intended both to enhance his personal esteem and to increase England's prestige abroad. But even Henry's palaces, and those of his magnates, were characterised by an intimacy of detail that reflected domestic rather than ecclesiastical or military functions. Windows and doors were smaller and buildings often contained numerous chambers, each with its own fireplace and garderobe. But the most characteristic feature of Tudor buildings was the use of BRICK which suddenly acquired an almost universal popularity, inspired by the success of earlier East Anglian buildings. The great houses of Tudor England were singularly beautiful: walls of warm red brick and romantic vestiges of more turbulent days, such as elaborate GATEHOUSES, placid water-filled moats and mock crenellations, combined with steeply pitched roofs, clustered gables, turrets and ornate 'cork-screw' chimneys to create buildings of unparalleled eloquence and charm. Lavish heraldic display, both in architectural features and in the fabric and furnishings of interiors, reflected the newly acquired social status of the Tudor nobility and gentry. The chambers of most Tudor mansions were usually panelled from floor almost to ceiling in the characteristic linen-fold pattern of the period (*see* PANELLING). Fireplaces in the principal rooms were often of considerable size, with four-centred arches and massive carved overmantles. It was from this time that coal was used more widely as domestic fuel but coal smoke was noxious and more efficient chimney flues were developed by which the smoke was removed to a point well above roof-height (*see* CHIMNEYS AND FIREPLACES). With the introduction of chimney flues, the traditional HALL (which had previously been open to the rafters) could be provided with a second storey, thereby doubling the available floor space. At this time the underside of the new floor, and the beams and joists on which it rested, was usually left bare, plaster ceilings being popular from the Elizabethan period. Window openings, usually of stone set into brickwork, were sufficiently small to accommodate an opening casement of iron and glass and were either single or grouped in pairs or threes beneath a stone or brick hood. They have flat arched heads, usually cut from a single piece of stone, and the corners often contain small triangular depressions: the last remnants of Gothic tracery. Larger windows were Perpendicular in style, with tracery and STAINED GLASS, and the oriel window was particularly popular. Tudor arches are invariably four-centred (*see* ARCH) or of a modified form which is flatter and has straight, sloping members rather than curved ones. Not all Tudor buildings were of brick. Stone continued to be used in some districts and in many heavily wooded areas, such as Cheshire and Warwickshire, TIMBER-FRAME BUILDINGS were more common, the infilling between the oak timbers being of brick laid in a variety of decorative 'herringbone' patterns. Very often the lower storey was built of brick with a top storey and roof of timber.

TUDOR COASTAL FORTS Tudor coastal forts were not castles (*see* CASTLE). They are included here because they signify the end of the medieval castle as an instrument of national defence and illustrate how military architects responded to the increasing power and range of the cannon (*see* DECLINE OF THE CASTLE *and* FIREARMS AND CANNON).

With the re-opening of hostilities with France a number of artillery forts were constructed in the 1520s and 1530s but it was not until 1539 that, according to John Lambarde:

> King Henrie the Eight, having shaken off the intolerable yoke of the Popish tyrranie, and espying that the Emperour was offended for the divorce of Queen Katherine his wife, and that the French King had coupled the Dolphine his son to the Pope's niece, and married his daughter to the King of Scots, so that he might more justly suspect them all, than safely trust any one, determined . . . to stand upon his

owne gardes and defence: and therefore with all speede, and without sparing any cost, he builded Castles, platfourmes and block-houses, in all needfull places of the Realme.

These included the entire coastline from Land's End in Cornwall to Kingston-upon-Hull on Humberside, for Henry recognised that the enmity of the emperor implied also that of Spain and Flanders as well as France. The resulting scheme of national defences was the most comprehensive since that of the Roman Saxon Shore for, unlike the piecemeal defences of the previous two centuries, it was directly controlled by central government and financed by the substantial revenues obtained from the Dissolution of the Monasteries.

The forts (there were twenty on the south coast alone) were constructed with low thick walls to resist enemy artillery, and their guns, which were at first imported from the Low Countries and later manufactured in Sussex, were cast in one piece rather than barrel-forged and could therefore take a more powerful charge and fire a larger ball over a longer distance. The first series of forts was built to protect the Channel coast between Thanet and Dover in Kent; because of their shape, they are sometimes referred to as 'Tudor Rose forts'. Deal, the first and most complex of these, consists of a central circular 'keep', from which radiate six semicircular bastions (*lunettes*), all within a 'curtain wall', also with six lunettes, and a broad dry moat and outer wall. Within these walls are 145 embrasures, though not all would be used simultaneously: the guns would be moved from port to port on wheeled carriages while the heaviest artillery was mounted in three tiers on the reinforced roofs of the curtain wall bastions, on the bastions of the keep and on the roof of the keep itself. These were intended for long-range use against ships, though the fort could also be defended on the landward side, and the moat and inner ward were covered by numerous handgun loops.

By 1540 forts had been constructed at Walmer, Sandown, Dover and Sandgate (near Folkestone) in Kent; Camber (near Rye) in Sussex; Calshot and Hurst in Hampshire; East and West Cowes on the Isle of Wight; and Portland in Dorset. The chain was then extended to include Harwich in Essex and Kingston-upon-Hull in the north and westward to Portsmouth in Hampshire, Poole and Weymouth in Dorset and St Mawes and Pendennis in Cornwall. The forts commanded the sea-approaches to important harbours and vulnerable sections of the coast and were intended primarily for offensive operations against sea-borne incursions.

Artillery such as the mid-sixteenth-century *culverins*, which could fire an 8kg (18lb) ball more than 1,600m (over 1 mile), rendered the Tudor forts obsolete almost before they were completed. Because of their design they presented far too large a target to an enemy's cannon and the semicircular walls of the bastions were impossible to defend with gunfire at close quarters. Consequently there emerged the *arrow-head bastion* which presented a minimum target to an enemy and, because of its straight sides, could be defended with a small number of guns. The first of these were constructed in 1546–7 to guard the Solent at Portsmouth and Yarmouth on the Isle of White. In 1558 the defences of Berwick-upon-Tweed on the Scottish border were reconstructed with five large rectilinear bastions, each completely covering its neighbours and the length of curtain wall between. Like the earlier arrow-head bastions, the walls of Berwick's innovative defences were constructed of compacted earth with masonry facings designed to absorb the impact of heavy artillery fire. Thereafter, this *bastioned trace* structure was to provide the foundation of large-scale British fortresses for over three centuries.

TUDOR GOTHIC *see* GOTHIC ARCHITECTURE

TUDOR ROSE A stylised, five-lobed figure of a rose which combines, in a variety of forms, the red and white rose badges of York and Lancaster (*see* BADGES AND LIVERY). Historically, the red rose has come to represent the concept of parliamentary sanction by which Henry VII acceded to the English throne. But in order that his descendants should enjoy an inalienable right of succession, he married Elizabeth of York, the heiress of the white rose. The rival roses are similarly combined in the beautiful Tudor Rose which was to become the universal symbol of the Tudor dynasty and of the new administration.

TUFA Porous rock, a type of limestone formed of lime deposited by water around lumps of vegetable matter, usually in the vicinity of mineral springs. Used as a building material, notably in several early stone castles in the southern Marches of Wales.

TUMPS In the Welsh Marches, mottes are often referred to as 'tumps', and in Wales as TOMEN (*see* MOTTE).

TUNNELS AND SECRET PASSAGES There are undoubtedly more secret passages in legend than there are in reality. William the Conqueror's wooden tower at Windsor was built in the Norman fashion on the summit of a MOTTE with palisaded courtyards on either side containing stables, huts for the garrison and cages for prisoners and with access to secret subterranean tunnels for emergency egress should the castle be besieged. From this, it would appear that the principle of providing a secret means of escape was accepted even in the eleventh century. It is surprising, therefore, that so few castle builders incorporated a similar feature in their designs. At Wardour Castle, a fortified TOWER-HOUSE built by John, 5th Lord Lovell, in 1393, a flight of steps leads from a cellar to an underground passage which runs in a straight line to a curtain wall in the southeast corner of the outer bailey. Its original function is unclear, though it may have been intended as an escape route in emergencies. It is very easy to mistake a complex drainage system for a subterranean passage, though many sieges were concluded when attackers succeeded in gaining access to such a system (*see* PLUMBING, WATER SUPPLY AND SANITATION). Several tunnels were created during post-medieval sieges. Lavington's Hole, for example, a 20m (67ft) long tunnel into the sandstone cliff beneath Bridgnorth Castle, was excavated during the English Civil Wars. Progress was slow – no more than 1.8m (6ft) were excavated each day – and the pick-marks may still be seen in the tunnel walls. As in many similar cases, this was psychological warfare: the besieged garrison could hear the sounds of excavation and could do nothing to prevent it. Gunpowder, stored in the parish church, was intended to finish the job but the castle surrendered in April 1646 before it was needed.

TUNNEL VAULT *see* VAULTING

TURNING-BRIDGE A wooden bridge pivoted on an axle (*trunnion*) with a counterpoise weight attached to one end (*see* DRAWBRIDGE).

TURNPIKE STAIR *or* **VICE** A spiral stair, the steps of which radiate from a central pillar (*newel*). According to tradition, newel stairs in castles rise in a clockwise direction, thereby providing sufficient room for (right-handed) defenders to wield a sword or pike but preventing attackers from doing so: hence 'turnpike stair' (*see* STAIRS).

TURRET A small tower, often containing a stair. There are excellent examples at Conwy and Caernarfon Castles in north Wales where crenellated turrets were added to the principal towers as observation platforms and, more especially, to enhance the castles' already dramatic appearance. Caernarfon's Eagle Tower has three lofty turrets, on the copings of which are the unrestored remains of stone figures with which they were originally decorated: some are helmeted heads while on the west turret an eagle is still recognisable. An ANGLE TURRET is a projecting turret, usually supported on a SQUINCH ARCH, attached to the outside corner of a tower. Angle turrets are a characteristic feature of many Scottish and Borders tower-houses. The term BARTISAN is often used generically to describe both angle turrets and tower turrets such as those at Conwy and Caernarfon, but such use is erroneous.

TYMPANUM The space between a lintel and the arch above: the Romanesque tympanum above the doorway to the Great Tower (1067–75) at Chepstow Castle, for example, in which the 'chip-carved' decoration is of a type used in eleventh-century Normandy.

UNDERCROFT An open (often vaulted) chamber beneath the first floor of a domestic building in a castle or monastery, often wholly or partially underground and originally used for stabling or storage.
(*See also* CRYPT)

UNDERGROUND PASSAGES *see* TUNNELS AND SECRET PASSAGES

UNIFORMS *see* BADGES AND LIVERY

UNIVALLATE *see* MULTIVALLATE

UPPING STOCKS As the name suggests, upping stocks were used for mounting a horse. A typical upping stock consists of a low square brick or stone platform with a flight of three or four steps at one side. Upping stocks are also known as horse-blocks, horse-steps, horse-stones, mounting-blocks and mounting-stones.

VAIR One of two principal furs used in ARMORY consisting of alternating white and blue pieces, drawn in a variety of stylised forms (*see* TINCTURES). Vair originated in the fur of a species of squirrel (*varus*) which was popular in the Middle Ages as a lining for the garments of those not entitled to wear ERMINE (*see* SUMPTUARY LAWS). The animal was blue-grey on the back and white underneath. By sewing a number of these pelts together, with white and blue-grey alternating, an attractive design was obtained, one which easily translated into the stylised armorial form of Vair. No doubt Cinderella's slippers were made of this fur, the word *verre*, 'glass', being erroneously translated from the French in place of *vairé*.

VALETTI *see* YEOMAN

VALLEY ROOF *see* ROOFS (TIMBER)

VALOR *see* MANOR

VAMBRACE Plate armour for the forearm (the upper arm and shoulder being protected by the *rerebrace*). Since the sixteenth century the term has been applied to articulated upper and lower arm protection (described as *the upper and lower canons of the vambrace*) which include the elbow protection (*couter*) but not the separate shoulder guard (*pauldron*).
(*See also* ARMOUR)

VAN *see* VANGUARD *and* WARD

VANES *see* WEATHER COCKS AND WEATHER VANES

VANGUARD The foremost section of an advancing army or fleet.

VASSAL A person who held land of a lord and owed FEALTY to him. Vassalage was a condition of feudal dependence on a *Lord Paramount* in the case of the landed nobility, and upon the vassals of the Lord Paramount in others. In medieval England the sovereign was the Lord Paramount.
(*See also* FEUDAL SYSTEM *and* SUBIN-FEUDATION)

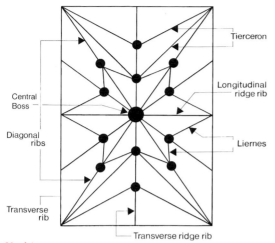

Vaulting.

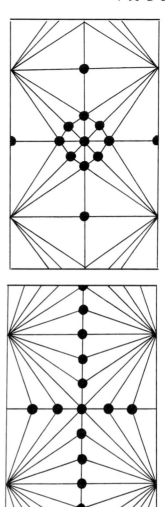

(Top) *Lierne vault,* (above) *Tierceron vault.*

VAULTING Vaulting is the arched interior of a roof, usually constructed of stone or brick. The ornate window tracery and vaulting by which GOTHIC ARCHITECTURE is defined have rarely survived in castles because of the depredations of warfare, weather and dereliction. Moreover, while vaulting is commonly found in churches, in castles its use was generally restricted to chapels, gate passages, mural chambers and areas where there was a risk of fire, such as kitchens, undercrofts and cellars. These were usually simple barrel, groined or quadripartite vaults (*see below*), the more ornate late medieval styles being confined to the chapels and state chambers of royal and high-status castles. The roofs of HALLS were almost invariably of open timber construction, though these were sometimes strengthened in the late medieval period (*see* ROOFS (TIMBER)): at Conwy Castle, for example, the timber arches which supported the roof of the Great Hall were replaced by eight massive stone arches in 1346–7. A curious feature of Edward I's Welsh castles is the absence of stone vaulting (almost certainly a factor which aggravated the widespread decay recorded in a survey of 1343), a notable exception being the ribbed vault in the chapel of Beaumaris Castle (*see* CHAPELS). Some towers, such as the keep at Pembroke Castle, have a vaulted top storey as a defence against fire-throwing siege weapons.

The shape of a vault follows the geometry of the ARCH and the simplest vault is therefore that which accompanies the semicircular ROMANESQUE ('Norman') arch. This is known as the *barrel vault* (also *tunnel vault* and *wagon vault*) and is so named because of its semicircular section and barrel-like appearance. Where two barrel vaults intersect at right angles they form a *groined* or *cross vault*.

Because of the enormous thrust exerted on supporting walls, the barrel vault was found to be singularly unsuited to wide spans. The structural limitations of the round arch led to the development in the early medieval period of the *ribbed vault* and pointed arch.

Ribs are raised bands of stone or brick that spring from the wall to support and strengthen the vault. The ribbed vault consisted of a quadripartite framework (bisected by diagonal ribs), supported during construction on a temporary timber or wicker structure (*centering*). Once the spaces between the ribs (*webs* or *cells*) had been infilled with cut stone pieces or bricks the vault became self-supporting and the centering was removed. Vaults are divided into bays by *transverse arches*. While bays created by semicircular arches were inevitably square, the diagonals of a ribbed vault were longer than the sides and it was therefore impossible for all the ribs to be semicircular. This problem was overcome by adopting the *pointed arch* which was ideally suited to vaulting of various heights and spans, and during the four centuries of the Gothic period enabled buildings of increasing complexity and architectural audacity to be constructed throughout western Europe.

The early *quadripartite ribbed vault*, which consisted of four compartments within each bay, formed the basis for all future designs. Stone BOSSES were added at the intersection of ribs and these were often heavily carved with gilded and painted motifs. In the fourteenth century intermediate *tierceron ribs* were added which extended from the springing of the vault (the point at which it began to splay upwards) to the *ridge rib* (at the apex of the vault) and from this developed the *lierne vault*, in which additional interlocking ribs (*liernes*) were introduced, forming elaborate patterns within the basic structural framework of ribs. The final Perpendicular phase of the Gothic period is characterised by *fan vaulting* which, as the name suggests, is an ornamental vaulting of inverted half-conoids (cones with concave sides). Each pair of half-conoids just meet at the centres of their curves, all the ribs are equidistant from one another and in most cases all have the same curvature. In a fan vault the ribs were carved from a stone slab rather than supporting it, and the joints between the blocks may often be seen passing across the purely decorative tracery of the ribs. Fan vaulting was an English innovation, the earliest known example being in the CHANTRY CHAPEL of Edward, Lord Despenser (d. 1375) at Tewkesbury Abbey, Gloucestershire.

VAVASSEURS A generic term for non-noble cavalry.

VENISON *see* CHASE *and* FOREST

VENTAIL *see* ARMOUR

VERDERER From the early eleventh century verderers were appointed to administer the 'vert and venison' of a FOREST. In the medieval period there were four verderers appointed to each forest. They were elected by freeholders in the county court and were required to attend a Court of Attachment which was usually convened at intervals of forty days. In the Forest of Dean in Gloucestershire the Verderers' Court still meets (in the court-room of what is now the Speech House Hotel) to determine disputes

according to the forest laws and to control freemining and other activities within the court's jurisdiction.

VERGE The medieval court was a peripatetic one and wherever it resided there came into being a territory or 'verge' which extended like an immense nimbus around the king's person. Within the verge, which had a radius of 19km (12 miles), the court exercised a special jurisdiction particularly with regard to the procurement of goods and services for the royal retinue. This was the responsibility of the *Clerk of the Market*, an officer of the court who was also concerned with weights and measures. For a time the Clerk's authority was extended to include all the MARKETS in England, but his duties were invariably conceded to local landowners, and in 1640 legislation required that he should operate only within the verge and that elsewhere the responsibility for the proper administration of markets should be vested in manorial lords or municipal officers.

VERT The heraldic colour green (*see* TINCTURES).

VERT AND VENISON The term *vert* was applied in Forest Law to any species of plant or tree that provided food for game, especially deer. Similarly, *venison* was a generic term applied to all types of game (*see* CHASE *and* FOREST).

VERVELLES *see* CAMAIL

VESTIBULE An entrance hall or antechamber next to the outer door of a building.

VICE From a fourteenth-century term meaning 'a screw', a spiral stair winding round a *newel* or central pillar (*see* STAIRS).

VIEWPOINT TOWER *see* PROSPECT TOWER

VILL *see* FRANKPLEDGE

VILLEIN Following the Norman Conquest of 1066 any unfree tenant who held land subject to agricultural service and fines was described as a villein. These obligations could be commuted to rent but a villein could only become a free man by entering the clergy or through *manumission*, the official release of a villein from bondage, performed in a county court. Theoretically a villein had no personal funds but he could purchase his freedom through a third party or in return for outstanding service. Although of superior status to a slave, a villein was nevertheless annexed to a lord's person and could therefore be transferred from one owner to another. He was known as a *villein in gross* and as such neither he nor his daughter could marry without his lord's consent, he was unable to bring a suit in the king's court or to acquire land that would not be taxed. In return, he held land by villein tenure, grazed his livestock on the common pasture and removed hay from the common meadow. A *regardant villein* was annexed to a lord's MANOR rather than to his person. Depopulation following the Black Death in the fourteenth century (*see* PLAGUE) meant that villeins enjoyed greater bargaining power and tenure was gradually converted to *copyhold*. A copyholder held his land by a written title (a copy of which was entered in the *court roll*) and was subject to a diminishing number of manorial customs. The property of a copyholder who died intestate or without issue reverted to the LORD OF THE MANOR.

VINEYARDS A favourable CLIMATE encouraged viticulture in southern England and the south Midlands from the eleventh century. Writing in *c.* 1123, William of Malmesbury stated that no other English shire had more vineyards than Gloucestershire and that wines from the Vale of Gloucester were hardly inferior to those of France. Most vineyards were on monastic estates, on well-drained south or south-east facing slopes, sheltered from cold north winds and from prevailing south-westerlies. The earliest English vineyards seem to date from a sustained period of clement weather in the eleventh and twelfth centuries and there is little evidence to support the popular notion that the Romans grew grapes during the occupation of Britain. Somerset vineyards were maintained by the Mohuns at Dunster from the twelfth to the fifteenth century and wine from the vineyards at Claverton, on the sheltered slopes above the Avon near Bath, was still considered to be of excellent quality in the late seventeenth century. Vineyards further north produced unripe grapes used for culinary purposes (*verjuice*) rather than for wine.

VINTAINE Militia unit of twenty men (*see* MILITIA).

VIRETON *see* ARCHERY

VISCOUNT Several of the lords who followed Duke William in his conquest of England held substantial territories (*comtés*) in the Low Countries and France, and, although granted English lands and titles by the Conqueror, they retained the superior

title of *comté, county* or count. In the days of the Carolingian Empire the *vice-comtés* were the deputies of the counts and gradually assumed hereditary rights. A viscount belongs to the fourth rank of the British peerage, the first creation being of 1440, though the title itself is considerably older. The wife of a viscount is a *viscountess*.

VISOR The hinged, movable front piece of a helmet which allows the face to be revealed (*see* HELMETS).

VOLUTES *see* CAPITAL

VOUSSOIRS *see* ARCH

WAGES (BUILDERS') *see* ORGANISATION (BUILDING)

WAGON ROOF *see* ROOFS (TIMBER)

WAGONS *see* MATERIALS, CARRIAGE OF

WAGON VAULT *see* VAULTING

WAINSCOTING *see* PANELLING

WALES It was during the sixth century that those Britons who were cut off by the advancing Saxons from their kinsmen in Strathclyde and Cornwall began to describe themselves as *Cymry*, meaning 'fellow countrymen', though they were known as *Wealas* or 'strangers' to the Saxons. The battles of Chester (615) and Oswestry (641) mark the western limit of the Anglo-Saxon advance in the north and central borderland with the River Wye delineating the southern boundary of the kingdom of Mercia. The Saxons never succeeded in penetrating further into Wales and the great eighth-century dyke built by King Offa of Mercia to mark the western boundary of his kingdom was as much a symbol of failure as it was of authority.

The often anarchic process of unification of the numerous small Welsh kingdoms which had begun

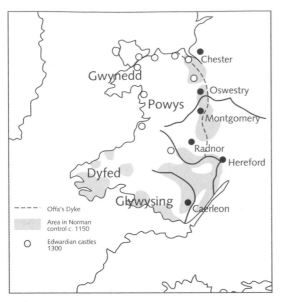

Chester
Gwynedd
Oswestry
Powys
Montgomery
Radnor
Hereford
Dyfed
Glywysing
Caerleon

- - - - Offa's Dyke

Area in Norman
control c. 1150

O   Edwardian castles
1300

Wales.

in the seventh century culminated in the emergence of four major kingdoms, each divided into *cantrefi*: Gwynedd in the north-west, Powys in the north-east, Deheubarth (Dyfed) in the south-west and Glywysing (later known as Morgannwg) in the south. Although the size and influence of these territories fluctuated, their princes remained the chief leaders of Welsh resistance against the English from the time of the Norman Conquest to the Statute of Rhuddlan in 1284. The ninth century was dominated by the expansion of Gwynedd and the tenth by conflict between Gwynedd and Deheubarth, whose kings were dynastically related. Indeed, the great men of early Welsh history, Rhodri Mawr (d. 878), Hywel Dda (d. 950), Maredudd ab Owain (d. 999) and Gruffudd ap Llywelyn (d. 1063), were all princes of Gwynedd and Deheubarth who succeeded in extending political conquest beyond the boundaries of their kingdoms. In the mid-eleventh century political pre-eminence was contested by Gruffudd ap Rhydderch and Gruffudd ap Llywelyn, each of whom employed Viking and English mercenaries to supplement his forces. In 1055 Gruffudd ap Llywelyn succeeded in becoming the first ruler of all Wales but his rise to power had alerted the English and he was defeated in battle and killed in 1063. The north Welsh kings were then appointed by the English, whose influence was soon overtaken by the Normans, though it is doubtful whether English overlordship was ever precisely defined or, indeed, sustained.

From 1070 the Normans embarked on the conquest of Wales and by 1093 had secured effective control of the south. While the Saxons had exercised only a minimal influence on the Welsh, the Norman palatine earls created a permanent zone of attrition that extended south from Chester and west into the conquered territories. This was the MARCH in which the most rapacious and unruly of Duke William's followers were granted lands. (Much of Wales would remain divided into semi-independent Marcher lordships until the so-called Act of 'Union' in 1536.) Bleddyn ap Cynfyn, king of Gwynedd and Powys, died in 1075 and was succeeded, not by his young son, but by the self-appointed Gruffudd ap Cynan. At a time of intense Norman military pressure Gruffudd managed to create a kingdom which extended from Anglesey in the north to the Vale of Clwyd and south to the borders of the kingdom of Deheubarth. When he died in 1137 (at the age of eighty-two) he was succeeded by his eldest son Owain who assumed the name Owain Gwynedd in order that he should be distinguished from his rival Owain ap Gruffudd of Powys who adopted the name Owain Cyfeiliog. It was at this time that the titles 'king' and 'prince' were abandoned in favour of the less provocative appellation 'lord', though the rulers of Gwynedd retained their princely title, presumably by general consent. In southern Wales Rhys ap Tewdwr, the last independent lord of Deheubarth, was killed by the Normans in 1093 and was succeeded by his son Gruffudd who, having eventually made his peace with Henry I of England, died in 1137. The most famous of his four sons was Rhys ap Gruffudd (1153–97), known to history as The Lord Rhys (*Yr Arglwydd Rhys*), who befriended Henry II and was restored to his estates as ruler of Deheubarth until his death in 1197. The kingdom of Powys, which had achieved prominence under Madog ap Maredudd, passed to his nephew Owain Cyfeiliog who, unlike Owain Gwynedd, maintained an alliance with the English. Under his leadership Powys continued to prosper but when he died in 1197 he was succeeded by Gwenwynwyn, whose impetuosity resulted in military defeat and eventual subjugation by Llywelyn Fawr (the Great), prince of Gwynedd. Born in 1173, Llywelyn Fawr (Llywelyn ab Iorwerth) became a leading figure in English politics and ruled over a united Wales until his death in 1240. But his son Dafydd ap Llywelyn failed to consolidate his father's achievements and it was not until the succession in 1246 of Llywelyn Fawr's grandson Llywelyn ap Gruffudd that the primacy of the princes of Gwynedd was re-established.

Built as a defence against the Welsh, Gilbert de Clare's Caerphilly Castle (mostly 1268–71) in the southern March was by far the most formidable and militarily sophisticated castle of its day.

By 1267 Llywelyn ap Gruffudd ruled with greater authority and over wider territories than any Welsh prince since the Norman Conquest. He negotiated an alliance with Simon de Montfort and even survived de Montfort's fall to be confirmed by Henry III as prince and overlord of all Wales in the Treaty of Montgomery in 1267. But in 1276 a dispute between Llywelyn and Edward I resulted in conflict and a drastic reduction in his powers, and his involvement in a further rising in 1282 led to the conquest and subjugation of Gwynedd in 1282–3 (*see* WALES, CONQUEST OF). Although Llywelyn's political ambitions alienated other Welsh lords and ultimately contributed to his defeat by Edward I, at his death in 1282 he was deeply mourned as the last native prince of Wales.

By the Statute of Rhuddlan (1284) the principality of Gwynedd was brought under English rule and divided into three counties: Caernarfon, Merioneth and Anglesey. Castles and fortified boroughs were constructed and populated with English merchants and the Marcher lordships consolidated and extended. But increasing prosperity under English rule could not conceal widespread resentment of the commercial privileges enjoyed by the burgesses of the English towns in Wales and of the exclusion of Welshmen from high office in secular and ecclesiastical administration. From 1400 Owain Glyn Dŵr (1344–1416?), a descendant of Rhys ap Gruffudd, harnessed this resentment in open rebellion and for a while exercised the authority of a native prince. He became a national hero and despite his disappearance in 1412 sporadic insurrection and disorder persisted until after 1485 when the Welshman Harri Tudur (1457–1509) ascended the English throne as Henry VII.

WALES, ARMORIAL PRACTICE IN *see* ARMORY

WALES, CONQUEST OF

> As you well know, Welshmen are Welshmen
> and you need to understand them properly.
> (Letter of February 1296 from Master James
> of St George to Edward I)

The subjugation of Wales, begun by the NORMANS in 1070, was a slow process, one which was only partially achieved by the signing of the Statute of Rhuddlan in 1284 (*see* WALES). The reasons for this protracted process of conquest are manifold: a mountainous terrain that was ideally suited to guerrilla warfare; internecine feuding among the native princes and the fragmented nature of Welsh polity; the uncoordinated and spasmodic nature of Norman and Angevin incursions; and the fact that Wales was of peripheral interest to most of the Anglo-Norman baronage. By the end of the twelfth century the Normans had established themselves in the lowlands of southern Wales (*see* MARCH) but elsewhere their influence was confined to a token military presence and the collection of tributes from the native population. Although the Welsh regarded themselves as a community (*Cymry*) with a common language, law and customs, they lived in local social units (*commotes*) governed by relatively independent lords whose territories were defined by both topography and kinship. By the end of the twelfth century Gwynedd (in the north), Powys (in the north-east) and Deheubarth (in the south-west) had emerged as the three major principalities of unconquered Wales (*pura Wallia*). Political leadership passed from one to another but during the thirteenth century it rested firmly with the princes of Gwynedd: Llywelyn ab Iorwerth, known as Llywelyn Fawr ('the Great') (1173–1240), and his grandson Llywelyn ap Gruffudd ('the Last') (d. 1282).

Llywelyn the Great

Llywelyn Fawr had been brought up in England as a ward of King John whose daughter he married. John's reign was a formative period in Anglo-Welsh relations. By his death in 1216 the native Welsh had exploited his political difficulties and seized the initiative. But during his reign all the major issues of Anglo-Welsh relations came into focus and his military campaigns of 1211–12 established a model of conquest and settlement that Edward I later followed with devastating effect (*see below*). Of particular significance was a treaty of 1201 by which Llywelyn was obliged to swear fealty and do homage to the king of England as his liege lord. Furthermore, his principal subjects were similarly required to swear fealty to King John, a condition that inevitably raised the question of overlordship and whether or not the fealty and homage of the Welsh 'nobility' should be reserved to, or even shared with, the king of England. The agreement also raised the other key issue of the pre-conquest period for it contained a proviso that, in certain circumstances, the king might send commissioners to determine matters of law in Llywelyn's territories. In this single document (the earliest surviving written agreement between an English king and a Welsh ruler) John and his advisers had succeeded in bringing together all the elements from which conflict could be fashioned.

Relations between Llywelyn and his father-in-law had often been fraught, but were usually repaired before a final breach occurred. But in 1211 John led two expeditions into Gwynedd. The first, in May, was poorly provisioned and ended when the Welsh retreated into the mountains. The second, some months later, was far more successful: the English penetrated deep into Gwynedd and Llywelyn's wife (John's daughter) was obliged to plead for peace 'on whatsoever terms she could'. The whole of Gwynedd east of the River Conwy was surrendered to the king 'for ever' and Llywelyn was forced to concede that, should he die without a legitimate heir, all his lands would revert to the king. By the end of 1211 John was in a stronger position in Wales than any of his predecessors: 'There was no one', said the chronicler, 'who did not obey his nod.' When the Welsh sought to challenge him, he began preparing for a further military campaign 'the like of which the Welsh had never witnessed'. A massive force of more than eight thousand craftsmen and labourers was summoned from throughout England in order that conquest should be converted into a permanent settlement by the building of castles: a strategy that Edward I was to adopt so successfully (*see below*). Suddenly, in mid-August 1212, the expedition was abandoned – almost certainly in response to rumours of an attempted assassination and mounting political problems that culminated in the granting of MAGNA CARTA in June 1215. Within a few months civil war was resumed in England (*see* BARONS' WAR, THE), providing the Welsh lords with an ideal opportunity to win back that which they had lost during John's reign. Indeed, they secured concessions in Magna Carta that granted them the return of all lands and liberties of which they had unjustly been deprived and by 1217 they had secured the important royal centres of Carmarthen and Cardigan. In March 1218 Llywelyn accepted the overlordship of Henry III (1216–72) in return for most of the gains that he and his allies had made since 1212. Even so, the Anglo-Welsh relationship was finely balanced. Llywelyn continued to flex his muscles from time to time in order to counter any threat, or perceived threat, to his power. Three royal campaigns in 1223, 1228 and 1231 lasted no more than a few weeks and none succeeded in penetrating the Welsh heartlands. They had attempted little and achieved less, though Carmarthen and Cardigan Castles were recovered by the English in 1223. Llywelyn the Great retired as a corrodian to the abbey of Aberconwy where he died on 11 April 1240. Despite his undoubted political and military supremacy, Llywelyn made no claim to rule Wales and was content to be addressed as 'prince of Aberffraw and lord of Snowdon'.

The years 1240–56 witnessed a remarkable advance in royal power in Wales. Within a few weeks of Llywelyn's death, Dafydd, his son and heir, was plunged into a power struggle with his half-brother Gruffudd. His meeting with Henry III at Gloucester on 15 May was an exercise in humiliation. He was denied the title of prince and referred to disparagingly as 'the son of Llywelyn sometime prince of North Wales' and was obliged to defer to the king on all issues over which Llywelyn had prevaricated for more than twenty years. Immediately the Marcher lords went on the offensive while Henry conducted a campaign to undermine Gwynedd's superiority, posing as the defender of the disaffected Welsh lords, notably Gruffudd, Dafydd's half-brother. In the years that followed the English built and refortified castles throughout Wales and pursued policies that were perceived as 'unrighteous oppression' by the Welsh. Outraged by the treatment of his half-brother, who had fallen to his death while attempting to escape from the Tower of London, Dafydd led a revolt that swept through Wales in 1244–5. In August 1245 a large army was dispatched from Chester under the king's command, and in the following year an expedition moved from Carmarthen to the new castle of Degannwy in a pincer movement that demonstrated once and for all that the Welsh heartland was not as impregnable as was once believed. The death of Dafydd on 25 February 1246 was a devastating blow for the Welsh, and one by one the lords of south and mid-Wales defected to the English. By the spring of 1247 Dafydd's heirs, Owain and Llywelyn ap Gruffudd, were forced into submission and by the Treaty of Woodstock (30 April 1247) the king reasserted his claim to 'the homages and services of all the barons and nobles of Wales'. Gwynedd was divided, 'by the counsel of the wise men of the land', between the

brothers Owain and Llywelyn and by 1250 native Wales was reduced to a collection of fragmented protectorates of the English crown.

But, not for the first time, adversity and resentment forged unity out of the experience of subjugation. In June 1255 Llywelyn ap Gruffudd defeated his brother Owain in battle at Bryn Derwin and thereby became the sole ruler of Gwynedd: native Wales had once more found a leader. The visit of Lord Edward (the future Edward I) to north-east Wales in 1256 provided the spark that ignited the fires of rebellion. So effective and widespread was Welsh resistance, and so pressing were Henry's domestic troubles, that a truce was agreed on 17 June 1258. By 1267 Llywelyn ap Gruffudd ruled with greater authority and over wider territories than any Welsh prince since the Norman Conquest. He negotiated an alliance with Simon de Montfort and even survived de Montfort's fall to be confirmed by Henry III as prince and overlord of all Wales in the Treaty of Montgomery (1267). In the years immediately following the Treaty relations between Llywelyn and the crown were marked by mutual respect and even, on occasions, cordiality. And there was no reason to believe that the accession of Edward I in 1272 would herald any change in attitude.

Llywelyn ap Gruffudd and Edward I

Edward I (r. 1272–1307) was the eldest son of Henry III and the formidable Eleanor of Provence. Born in 1239, he married Eleanor of Castile in 1254 and received from his father responsibilities in Gascony, Ireland and Wales. It was here that he learned the military skills that were further tested during the Barons' War when he sided for a time with Simon de Montfort. But when de Montfort raised a rebellion in 1264 Edward fought with his father at the battle of Lewes and at Evesham (1265) where he defeated and killed de Montfort. He won considerable renown as a knight on the Eighth Crusade (1270–1) and succeeded to the throne on his father's death in 1272. He received the homage of Alexander III of Scotland for his English lands but was rebuffed by Llywelyn ap Gruffudd. The root cause lay in the tensions in the Marches. Llywelyn became convinced that he was being denied the gains he had won in 1267 and that the crown was conniving at the process. For Edward, however, the withholding of fealty and homage became a *casus belli*. Llywelyn refused to attend Edward's coronation, a flagrant breach of etiquette that was compounded by his failure to appear on five occasions (between December 1274 and April 1276) to do homage to Edward. This was undoubtedly a ploy on Llywelyn's part: he did not deny his obligations but claimed that he could not fulfill them until his grievances had been redressed, a position that was confirmed by an assembly of 'all the barons of Wales'. In the winter of 1275/6 Edward succeeded in capturing Eleanor de Montfort as she travelled into Wales. Her intended marriage to Llewelyn was interpreted by the king as a deliberately provocative act, even though it had been contracted some ten years earlier. Eleanor's arrest infuriated Llewelyn and confirmed his suspicions that he too would be detained were he to venture into England to perform homage. On 12 November 1276, after further fruitless negotiations, Llywelyn ap Gruffudd was formally pronounced a rebel.

The First Campaign

Edward's first campaign lasted just under a year and was a combined operation of land and sea forces. Three military commands were created at Chester, Montgomery and Carmarthen with the objective of driving Llywelyn back into his patrimony of Gwynedd. So successful was this triple pincer movement that by the time Edward arrived at Chester in July 1277 the whole of Llywelyn's principality, other than Gwynedd, had been overrun and his allies had either defected or been forced to surrender. Edward moved his army into Gwynedd with great care, proceeding by slow stages along the coastal route, clearing large swathes of woodland as it went to avoid the danger of ambush and to facilitate the movement of supplies. Proclamations were issued to cause the clearance of military passes, a bowshot in breadth, the felling of some 2,500 acres of woodland making a significant and lasting change to the landscape. He established bases at Flint and Rhuddlan before approaching Degannwy on the Conwy estuary and at the same time sending a large force by sea to Anglesey (known as the 'granary of Gwynedd') where they harvested the crops essential to Llywelyn's survival in his mountain fortress. The impact on the Welsh, both psychologically and economically, was devastating and by November Llywelyn had submitted. Although, in terms of military strategy, Edward's first campaign followed that of King John in 1211 and Henry III in 1241 and 1245, he had succeeded in mobilising and deploying military forces on a scale unprecedented in medieval Britain. In 1277 he had some 15,600 troops in his pay. Crossbowmen were recruited from Gascony; heavy war-horses were imported from France; carts, wagons and boats were commandeered and assembled at Chester, together with an abundance of provisions so that there should be no victualling

problems as there had been on previous campaigns. Armies of woodcutters, sappers, masons and other craftsmen were forcibly recruited and no fewer than 1,800 axemen were employed to clear the route through the woods between Flint and Rhuddlan.

For Llywelyn, however, the Treaty of Aberconwy (1277) was an even greater humiliation than the Peace of Woodstock had been some thirty years earlier. Offering a huge fine of £50,000 for his 'disobedience', Llywelyn was ordered to travel to London to do public homage to Edward. Addressed, incongruously, as prince of Wales, he was compelled to hand over ten hostages from the leading families of Gwynedd, to reinstate his political enemies and to recognise the right of Owain Goch, his eldest brother and his prisoner for over twenty years, to his share of Gwynedd.

Through these and other measures, Edward I ensured for himself a degree of direct dominion in native Wales enjoyed by no earlier king of England. But it was necessary for him to secure both military domination and civilian administrative and judicial authority and he did so through the building of castles. During 1277 work was begun on four major castles at Aberystwyth, Builth, Flint and Rhuddlan, each of which was built with ruthless speed and efficiency, employing the latest principles of military architecture. With the exception of Builth, the castles were built on new sites while earlier castles at Degannwy and Diserth were abandoned. Rhuddlan, completed in 1282, was built close to the site of an earlier Norman fortification, and in order to make the castle accessible to supplies and relief by sea Edward ordered the construction of a new deep-water canal, 'a great dyke leading from the sea to the castle', some 3km (2 miles) long, together with a fortified quay designed to accommodate a 40-ton vessel (see FOSSATORES). Edward also retained control of several native castles, notably Dinas Brân, Dinefwr, Carreg Cennen and Llanmyddyfri, which he strengthened and repaired. By 1282 Gwynedd was enclosed within an arc of castles, from Flint and Rhuddlan in the north-east to Aberystwyth, Cardigan and Carmarthen in the south-west. At the same time routeways were improved and maintained through the Welsh forests so that troops and supplies could be moved quickly to wherever they were needed.

Humiliation and the ruthless imposition of penalties followed by magnanimity in victory were characteristics of Edward I's strategy of conquest and containment. In January 1278 he released Llywelyn's bride and paid for their wedding which he insisted should be at Worcester Cathedral and which he and

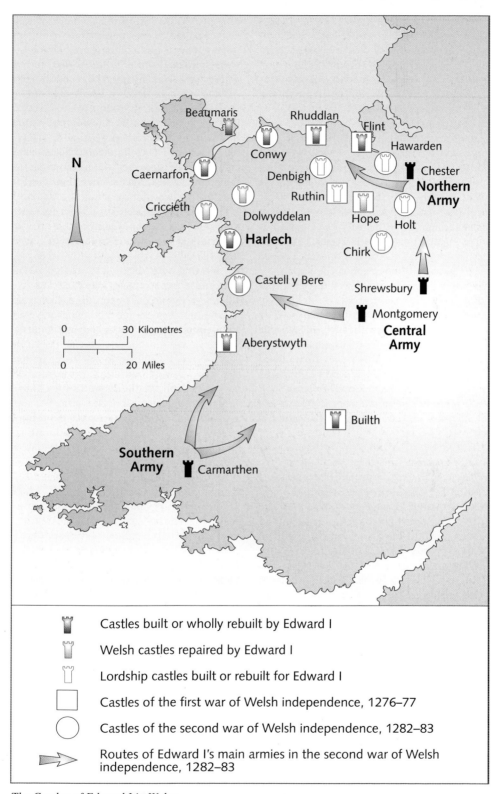

The Castles of Edward I in Wales.

Legend:

- Castles built or wholly rebuilt by Edward I
- Welsh castles repaired by Edward I
- Lordship castles built or rebuilt for Edward I
- Castles of the first war of Welsh independence, 1276–77
- Castles of the second war of Welsh independence, 1282–83
- Routes of Edward I's main armies in the second war of Welsh independence, 1282–83

Map labels:
Beaumaris, Rhuddlan, Flint, Hawarden, Conwy, Chester, Northern Army, Caernarfon, Denbigh, Ruthin, Hope, Holt, Cricieth, Dolwyddelan, Harlech, Chirk, Castell y Bere, Shrewsbury, Aberystwyth, Montgomery, Central Army, Southern Army, Carmarthen, Builth

Scale: 0 — 30 Kilometres / 0 — 20 Miles

N

Queen Eleanor attended. In September he handed back the Welsh hostages and presided at a settlement of Gwynedd's family disputes. Edward promised that he would 'be benevolent and a friend to Llywelyn in all things' while Llywelyn, for his part, paid his debts with scrupulous punctuality and even prompted Edward to observe that 'with good will he seeks and receives justice and judgment'. Of course, such mutual amicability could not last. Llywelyn had not passively accepted defeat: he was slowly and patiently laying the foundations for recovery while a number of local incidents fuelled Welsh resentment and increased tensions. The greatest cause of resentment was hostility to the imposition of English laws and procedures: even Llywelyn was treated as an ordinary litigant, summoned to appear before the king's justices at their convenience. Indeed, Edward went so far as to call into question the validity of Welsh law itself, declaring that he would only uphold it providing it was 'just and reasonable' and did not conflict with English law. The second cause of Welsh hostility was the manner in which alien officials rode roughshod over native liberties and customs and, in particular, the flagrant abuse of commercial privileges by English burgesses in the new boroughs of Aberyswyth, Flint and Rhuddlan. The war of 1277 had been a personal quarrel between Llywelyn and Edward. The war of 1282 was a war of national liberation.

The Second Campaign

In late March 1282 Dafydd ap Gruffudd attacked Hawarden Castle while Oswestry fell and the lords of Deheubarth captured the castles of Aberystwyth, Carreg Cennen and Llandovery. Llywelyn ap Gruffudd denied any involvement in what was clearly a well-organised insurrection, yet he had little option but to assume leadership of what has been accurately described (by J.G. Edwards) as 'a widespread popular rising of the Welsh' in protest against English rule: a war of independence. Edward's response was predictable: he announced his determination 'to put an end finally to the matter that he has now commenced of putting down the malice of the Welsh'. Within four days he had created three military commands to organise the initial response. County levies (mainly from the West Country) and the hired retinues were supplemented by 1,500 Gascon crossbowmen and more than four hundred ships were commandeered from the Cinque Ports to carry supplies and prepare for an assault on Anglesey. Huge depots were set up at Chester and Whitchurch and provisions brought in from as far afield as Gascony and Ponthieu. By the end of May

over 1,000 sappers and 345 carpenters were assembled at Chester 'for the King's work in Wales'.

The general aims of Edward's strategy in 1282 were similar to those of 1277: first, to reduce the native territories outside Gwynedd to submission; second, to secure Anglesey, the source of Llywelyn's food supplies; and, third, to make a direct assault on the Welsh heartland of Snowdonia. A diplomatic initiative by Archbishop Pecham of Canterbury in the autumn of 1282 floundered because the Welsh refused to do homage 'to any stranger of whose language, manners and laws they were entirely ignorant'. It was during these negotiations that the English attempted a crossing from Anglesey to the mainland on a pontoon bridge of specially constructed boats, an extraordinary venture that ended in disaster. Undaunted, Edward began making preparations for a long campaign, summoning additional troops and supplies. In response, Llywelyn decided to open up a new front in the middle Marches. Militarily, such a move had much to recommend it, but it proved fatal both for Llywelyn and for the Welsh cause. On 11 December 1282 he was killed in a skirmish near Builth: 'know, Sir, that Llywelyn ap Gruffudd is dead, his army broken, and all the flower of his men killed', wrote Roger Lestrange to King Edward. For the Welsh, Llywelyn's death signified also the death of their cause: 'Great torrents of wind and rain shake the whole land, the oak trees clash together in a wild fury, the sun is dark in the sky and the stars have fallen from their courses' (bardic elegy). Llywelyn's brother continued the struggle (henceforth known as *Dafydd's War*) but Edward's progress was inexorable. In January 1283 he crossed the Conwy and moved his headquarters from Rhuddlan to Aberconwy while his Anglesey troops crossed the Menai Straits to overrun Snowdonia. On 25 March Dafydd's last stronghold of Castell y Bere surrendered and in June he was captured by 'men of his own tongue' and dispatched to face a traitor's death at Shrewsbury.

Subjugation

The 'awesome finality' of conquest was reinforced by Edward I's policy of ruthless subjugation. He appropriated the palaces (*llys*) of the princes of Gwynedd, setting up his court in two of Llywelyn's favourite residences at Abergwyngregyn and Caernarfon, dismantling Llywelyn's timber-frame hall at Ystumgwern and reassembling it at his new castle at Harlech, and refurbishing the hall at Aberconwy as a palace for his son who, in 1301, became the first English prince of Wales. One by

Beaumaris Castle (begun in 1294) as it may have appeared had it been completed.

one Edward systematically replaced Gwynedd's dynastic symbols with those of his own authority. The Cistercian abbey of Aberconwy, for example, endowed by the princes of Gwynedd and the resting place of Llywelyn the Great, was moved to a new site, 7 miles away in the Conwy valley, to make room for Edward's new castle and town of Conwy. As the chronicler observed, Edward's intention was 'to pacify and organize that land' and the great stone castle was to be the principal instrument of pacification. By the Statute of Wales (1284) the principality of Gwynedd was brought under English rule and divided into three counties: Caernarfon, Merioneth and Anglesey.

A massive programme of castle-building began in June 1282 when Hope Castle was refurbished and by the autumn Holt, Ruthin and Denbigh Castles were under construction. Repairs began at the native castle of Dolwyddelan in January 1283 and between March and June of that year the three great castles of Conwy, Harlech and Caernarfon were begun (*see* CASTLES, CONSTRUCTION OF). These castles were constructed with extraordinary speed: Conwy was almost completed in four-and-a-half years, most of Caernarfon was finished by 1287 and Harlech by

1289. Even the great concentric castle of Beaumaris on Anglesey was defensible after just two building seasons (1295–6), though it was never completed (*see below*). And, like the castles of Aberystwyth and Rhuddlan which were built in the aftermath of the 1277 rebellion, Edward's second phase of castles could all be supplied by sea (*see* QUAYS). The cost of all this frenetic activity was prodigious: by 1301 Edward had expended a total of £80,000 on his eleven new castles, in addition to the cost of repairing and improving other royal castles and former native castles such as Criccieth (*see* WALES: NATIVE CASTLES). Each castle was unique and depended for its design and construction on the topography of a particular site, and each therefore has a distinctive character of its own. Edward's choice of Caernarfon as the capital of his new principality was almost certainly motivated by a belief, still current at the time, that the nearby Roman fortress of Segontium was the birthplace of Emperor Constantine the Great and the seat of Magnus Maximus (*Maxen Wledig*), emperor of Gaul, Spain and Britain from 383 to 388. Inevitably, such heroic figures caught the imagination of the bards and entered Welsh mythology in the pages of the

Mabinogion, a collection of early Welsh sagas. Maxim Wledig had dreamed of coming from Rome to a far-away land of high mountains and to an estuary facing an island where there was a fortified city, 'the fairest man ever saw', surrounded by towers of many colours, each tower bearing upon it eagles of gold. When Edward came to build Caernarfon as his own fortress palace, he appears to have deliberately re-created the *Mabinogion*'s spectacular description, appropriating the legend in order to add legitimacy to his occupation, making it both a fulfilment of the past and a statement of future policy. Caernarfon's polygonal towers and bands of dark masonry appear to have been inspired by the massive walls of Constantinople, refounded in 330 by Constantine on the site of the ancient Greek city of Byzantium. In 1284, before the castle was half built, Edward came with his pregnant queen and occupied wooden buildings inside the rising walls.

At the same time fortified boroughs were constructed and populated with English merchants, to the exclusion of the native Welsh (*see* TOWNS *and* TOWN WALLS). Increasing prosperity under English rule could not conceal widespread Welsh resentment of the commercial privileges enjoyed by the burgesses of the English plantation towns such as Conwy and Caernarfon, and it was this continuing resentment that fanned the flames of insurrection, notably the Glyn Dŵr rebellion of 1400–9.

Collectively and individually the castles of north Wales were intended to overawe and intimidate the native population; they were symbols of English supremacy in an alien land, centres of the English crown's military, administrative and judicial authority and a testimony to the ruthless energy and efficiency of Edward I. But the Edwardian castles were greater than the sum of their individual parts: they represented a cohesive strategy of subjugation, a 'ring of iron and stone' enclosing the Welsh heartland and controlling access to it by land and sea (*see also* TOWN WALLS).

The War of Madog

Undoubtedly Edward's castles achieved their objective: they broke the spirit of the Welsh as did the virtual extermination of the Gwynedd dynasty (Llywelyn's only child was consigned to an English nunnery and Dafydd's sons were incarcerated for life). But inevitably there were further sporadic uprisings of which the revolt of 1294–5 was by far the most significant. In the north it was led by Madog ap Llywelyn, a member of a cadet branch of the house of Gwynedd, but insurrection was widespread throughout Wales, inflamed by punitive taxation and

the increasing alienation of the native community from its new rulers. It was a typical anti-colonial uprising that expressed its anger and frustration in the massacre of English officials, the destruction of records and the investing of castles including Denbigh, Ruthen and Glamorgan and even mighty Caernarfon. Edward I was taken completely by surprise but his response was characteristically thorough. As on previous occasions, a three-pronged campaign was planned, operating out of bases at Chester in the north, Montgomery in mid-Wales and Carmarthen in the south-west. By the end of 1294 armies totalling some 35,000 men were mustered, supply routes secured and the besieged castles of Aberystwyth, Harlech and Criccieth relieved. In the spring of the following year the revolt collapsed and within four months Edward was able to leave Wales. The 'War of Madog' was to be the last Welsh uprising for over a century (*see* WALES). It had a traumatic effect on the isolated English boroughs of the north and the Englishries of the south-west (*see* ENGLISHRY) and frustrated once and for all any prospect of assimilation, or even accommodation, with the indigenous population. The revolt's most enduring legacy, however, is Beaumaris Castle, begun (but never completed) in 1294 both as a demonstration of the reassertion of English authority and to complete the chain of castles that extended along the north Wales coast from Flint to Aberystwyth. The castle and English borough of Beaumaris were constructed on the site of Llanfaes, at that time the principal port on the island of Anglesey and the most flourishing urban centre in north Wales. Edward evicted the entire native population and moved them to a new town (Newborough) 12 miles away, near the ancient Welsh *llys* of Rhosyr. The conquest of Wales was complete. (*See also* CASTLES (CONSTRUCTION OF), CASTLES (DEVELOPMENT OF) *and* SCOTLAND: ENGLISH WARS IN)

WALES: NATIVE CASTLES Wales is often described as a land of castles but in fact there were no castles in Wales before 1070 when the Normans began building motte and bailey fortifications to support their incursions (*see* MOTTE *and* NORMANS, THE). The initial Welsh response to the Norman onslaught was slow, principally because of internecine feuding among the native princes (*see* WALES). Finally, in 1094 the Welsh united against a common enemy and defeated the Normans at the battle of Coed Yspwys, the site of which has never been identified. The Normans were forced to abandon Gwynedd, Ceredigion and Dyfed (with the exception of Pembroke Castle) and in 1095 an entry in the *Brut y Tywysogyon* (*The Chronicle of the Princes*) tells us that 'in the middle of autumn King William moved a host against the Britons. And after the Britons had taken refuge in the woods and valleys, William returned home empty handed, having gained naught.' Nevertheless, the Norman palatine earls and their followers succeeded in creating a permanent zone of attrition that extended south from Chester and into the conquered territories of the south and west (*see* MARCH). And they constructed earth and timber castles, over six hundred of them, 'symbols of subjugation and bastions of paranoia', through which the conquered territories were controlled and extended. Many of these castles were temporary structures, 'instruments of conquest', and many were captured and occupied, intermittently, by the Welsh.

Throughout this period the native rulers continued to live in large halls (*neuadd*) protected by lightly defended enclosures. According to the twelfth-century chronicler Gerallt Gymro (Gerald of Wales), the three principal royal courts (*llys*) were located at Rhosyr on the island of Môn (Anglesey), at Dinefwr in Carmarthenshire and at Penwern in Shropshire (*see* ROYAL PALACES). There were, of course, other courts and commotal residences, many of which occupied strategically important sites, and a number of these were later rebuilt as castles. Dinefwr, once the court of the princes of Deheubarth, is now one of the best preserved native castles in Wales (1163). The earliest reference to a Welsh lord building a castle appears in an entry for 1111 (again in the *Brut*) when Cadwgan ap Bleddyn was killed at Welshpool where he had 'thought to stay and make a castle'. Five years later reference is made to a castle built by Uchdryd ab Edwin at Cymer near Dolgellau where the remains of a motte (but no bailey) have survived. Gerallt Gymro, writing in his *Itinerary Through Wales* at the end of the twelfth century, states that the Welsh were 'taught the use of arms and the management of horses by the English and Normans', while passages in the *Brut* suggest that they had also learned siegecraft. There are a further fifteen or so references to the construction or rebuilding of native Welsh castles in the twelfth and early thirteenth centuries, the last being that at Trefilan in 1233. These were modelled on the Norman motte and bailey, though some had no bailey and one, Llanrhystud, was a RINGWORK.

There were at least six hundred earthwork and timber castles in Wales and the Marches. In the absence of archaeological evidence, the fact that the motte and bailey type of castle was favoured by both the Normans and the Welsh makes identification of native castles difficult. Undoubtedly most of the border castles were built by the Normans, but noteworthy examples of native motte and bailey castles have been identified at Welshpool (Domen Castell, 1111), Cynfael (1147) and Llanrhystud (1149). At several sites, such as Castell Nos and Carn Fadryn (*c.* 1188), the 'mottes' are exceptionally strong rock outcrops that were probably surrounded by palisades and had timber towers on their summits. Frequent mention is made in the chronicles of Norman castles captured by the Welsh. Both Hywel ap Iorwerth and his son Morgan styled themselves 'of Caerleon' when they held the Norman castle of that name (built in *c.* 1071), while mottes at Aber, Caernarfon, Nefyn and Dolbenmaen were held by the princes of Gwynedd but were probably built by Earl Hugh of Chester in *c.* 1088–94.

Several early castles were refortified in stone, usually in the form of a tower on or adjoining a motte, as at Castell Dinas Emrys, Deudraeth and Nevern. The first reference to a Welsh stone castle was in 1171 when the Lord Rhys rebuilt the Norman castle of Cardigan in 'stone and mortar'. At Ewloe the free-standing tower was apsidal within a later masonry enclosure, while at Castell-y-Bere and Castell Dinas Brân apsidal towers were integrated with the curtain wall. Unlike the larger English keeps (*see* KEEP), the Welsh towers usually contained only two floors with a cellar at ground level (reached through a trapdoor in the floor above) and the principal residential chambers on the first floor which were entered from an external stair. This stair was sometimes contained within a FORE-BUILDING, the entrance being protected by a portcullis or small drawbridge. A fighting platform at the top of the tower was reached by means of an intra-mural stair (or, at Dolbadarn, by a newel stair) and in a number of instances (such as Dolbadarn and Ewloe) the crenellated parapet rose several metres above the roof level. (At Dolwyddelan, this arrangement allowed for a third storey to be added in the fifteenth century.) There are few early native masonry castles in south Wales: Castell Meredydd, Dinefwr, Dryslwyn and Emlyn Castles were all substantially rebuilt by the English.

The most prolific builders of stone castles were the princes of Gwynedd in the late twelfth and thirteenth centuries, and the strongholds of Llywelyn ab Iorwerth ('The Great' 1173–1240) and Llywelyn ap Gruffudd ('The Last' d. 1282) are particularly distinctive. Sited in naturally strong, isolated

The castle of Dolbadarn occupies a spectacular site on a rocky outcrop in the Pass of Llanberis where it guards the route from Caernarfon to the upper Conwy valley.

positions, the castles of Criccieth, Dolwyddelan, Dolbadarn, Ewloe and Y-Bere were built to command the routeways into Snowdonia and the borders of Gwynedd. Their most characteristic feature is an apsidal or rectangular tower, often joined to an insubstantial and irregular curtain wall, without flanking towers or significant gatehouses, and enclosing a single ward, as at Dolwyddelan (*c.* 1200). The disposition of walls, gates and towers in most of these native Welsh castles appears to be somewhat haphazard; bearing in mind the superior siege capability of the English, it is surprising that the Welsh clung for so long to the vulnerable rectilinear tower (the cylindrical great tower at Dolbadarn being an obvious exception). Caergwrle Castle, built in *c.* 1277–82 by Llywelyn's recalcitrant brother Dafydd, has a polygonal enclosure with circular or semicircular corner towers – but, in common with several other native Welsh castles, these were poorly positioned and did not allow for flanking cover along the walls. In south Wales the cylindrical keeps at Castell Meredydd, Dinefwr and Dryslwyn Castles are also from this period, that at Dinefwr clearly influenced by English keeps at Skenfrith and Tretower.

Castell-y-Bere, begun by Llywelyn Fawr in *c.* 1221, is the largest and most elaborate of the native castles in north Wales. Built on a narrow spur of rock, it controlled Llywelyn's lands between the Mawddach and Dyfi estuaries and was the last Welsh castle to surrender to the English in the war of 1282–3. The castle is a sprawling collection of towers linked by curtain walls that follow the contours of the uneven, rocky site. The southern apsidal tower was a self-contained refuge, detached from the main castle and separated from it by a rock-hewn ditch. A rectangular tower on the summit of the ridge appears to have served as a keep while the entrance was more strongly defended than in the majority of native castles, with a formidable barbican arrangement of ditches, three drawbridges and two gates, flanked by the keep on one side and by a small circular tower on the other.

Dolbadarn, another of Llywelyn's castles, occupies a spectacular site on a rocky outcrop in the Pass of Llanberis where it guards the route from Caernarfon to the upper Conwy valley. The best preserved feature of the castle is its cylindrical keep, built in imitation of contemporary English keeps in the early thirteenth century. The wall-walk and crenellated parapet have gone but the tower still rises to a height of over 14.6m (48ft) and the base of the original forebuilding remains. Unlike most other Welsh keeps, that at Dolbadarn had an additional upper floor reached by a newel stair within the thickness of the wall (*see* STAIRS).

The castle at Dolwyddelan was reputed to have been the birthplace of Llywelyn the Great, though it is now believed that he was born (in *c.* 1173) at Tomen Castell, a primitive square tower that once crowned a natural motte-like outcrop nearby. The castle is dominated by its oblong keep which is dramatically perched on the edge of a precipice. It was originally far lower than it now appears: a third floor was added in the fifteenth century and it was heavily restored in 1848. Whereas the keep now dominates the site, the large thirteenth-century west tower would once have been equally imposing. This incorporated a hall at first-floor level (the fireplace can still be seen) and may have been built by Edward I after he captured the castle in 1283.

Built by Llywelyn the Great in the early thirteenth century, Criccieth Castle crowns the summit of a rounded promontory that juts into the sea. It consists of a long triangular enclosure with a small inner ward and an imposing, twin-towered gatehouse which has survived almost to its original height. Edward I captured Criccieth in 1283, incorporated it into his formidable ring of castles that encircled Gwynedd and created an English borough there (*see* PLANTATION TOWNS). Little remains of the outer walls, and (unlike today) the castle was entered by a modest gateway in the southern corner of the outer ward. Anyone entering the castle would be obliged to pass across the outer ward and through a narrow passageway between two curtains before reaching the small, northern enclosure in front of the gatehouse. Such a sophisticated arrangement (*see* KILLING GROUND) is rarely found in native Welsh castles and is likely to be the work of Edward I's architect, Master James of St George. Although there has been considerable debate concerning the castle's construction, it is likely that Master James was also responsible for the inner enclosure with its splendid gatehouse (which is a smaller version of those at Harlech and Beaumaris) and the south-east tower (the Leyburn Tower, named after the castle's constable) which may have been built on the site of an earlier Welsh structure. If this is so, then the original native castle comprised a simple, triangular-shaped enclosure with a three-storeyed rectangular great tower incorporated into the south-west corner of the curtain and a second tower at the north corner (this was later called the Engine Tower because it

accommodated a siege engine (*see* ENGINE TOWER)). The great tower measured 20.5 by 12.2m (68 by 40ft) and was similar to that at Dolwyddelan.

One of the most innovative of Welsh castles was Morgraig, built (but never completed nor, indeed, occupied) by Gruffudd ap Rhys, lord of Senghenydd, in the 1260s. Again, the design has its weaknesses: the entrance had a gate and portcullis but was otherwise undefended, and the rectilinear keep projected outwards from the curtain. Nevertheless, its pentagonal enclosure and apsidal corner towers would have provided a more effective defence than was found in the majority of native Welsh castles.

Of course, none of the native Welsh castles can compare with the scale and grandeur of Beaumaris, Caernarfon, Conwy or Harlech, castles of the Edwardian conquest, the construction of which nearly bankrupted the English crown (*see* CASTLES, CONSTRUCTION OF *and* WALES, CONQUEST OF).

WALES, NORMANS IN *see* MARCH, NORMANS, WALES *and* WALES: NATIVE CASTLES

WALES, PRINCELY ARMS OF *see* ROYAL ARMS, THE

WALLED TOWNS *see* TOWN WALLS

WALL HANGINGS The interior walls of domestic rooms, halls, chapels and antechambers were invariably plastered and lime-washed and sometimes painted (*see* PLASTER, WHITEWASH AND PAINT). By the end of the fourteenth century wall hangings, attached by *tenterhooks* driven into the walls, provided both vivid colour and draught-proofing (tenterhooks were also used to stretch cloth during the manufacturing process). Woven pictorial tapestries were usually imported, the highest grades (which sometimes had golden thread woven into the design) being inordinately expensive: in 1582 a single yard (0.9m) of such tapestry would have cost the equivalent of four months' wages for a farm labourer. Complete sets of tapestries (*chamberings*), such as the 'chamber of the story of Nebuchad-nezzar, containing two pieces of 76 yards [69 metres]', recorded among several sets of tapestries at Raglan Castle in 1507, were rare status symbols, beyond the expectations of all but the wealthiest magnates. Henry V owned tapestries depicting Edward the Confessor, the Arthurian legends, a tournament, the Emperor Charlemagne, the Roman Emperor Octavian, allegorical subjects such as 'The Life of Love' or 'The Tree of Youth', the

Annunciation, the Five Joys of Our Lady and the Three Kings of Cologne. Even the cheaper grades of tapestry, with simple floral and foliage motifs, were usually reserved for the principal chambers, as were costly hangings of silk. Far more typical were the cheaper materials used for hangings in lesser rooms. During the late medieval and early Tudor periods the most popular of these was the light but closely woven woollen fabric called *say* which was hung in alternating vertical strips (*panes*) of contrasting colours. Initially, hangings were hung from ceiling to floor though later they were sometimes affixed above PANELLING or beneath decorated plasterwork. (*See also* ARRAS)

WALLPLATE A structural timber running horizontally along the top of a wall from one end of a roof to the other (*see* ROOFS (TIMBER)).

WALLS *see* ALURE, BATTLEMENTS, COURT-YARD BUILDINGS, CRENELLATIONS, CROSS-WALL, CURTAIN WALLS, ENCEINTE, EN-CLOSURE CASTLES, FOUNDATIONS, HOARD-ING, MASONRY, PUTLOG HOLES, SLEEPING WALL, SLIGHT FOUNDATIONS, STAIRS, TOWERS, TOWN WALLS *and* WALL-WALK

WALL-WALK *or* **ALURE** The passage or fighting platform behind the parapet of a curtain wall or tower (*see* BATTLEMENTS); a continuous sentry-path which also provided access to the many roofs which almost invariably abutted the curtain walls. Access to a wall-walk is usually via a TURNPIKE STAIR within an adjacent tower. In the medieval period a wall-walk may have been provided with a timber roof or *coursière* though no examples have survived in British castles. Many wall-walks are continuous, by-passing towers on corbels to aid mobility under siege, while others are punctuated by towers so that adjacent sections of wall may be isolated (*see* FIGHTING GALLERY). Several of the twenty-one drum-towers in the town walls of Conwy, for example, could act as 'circuit-breakers' between one section of wall-walk and the next, the temporary plank bridges which spanned the open interior of each tower being removed whenever a section of wall appeared to be under threat (*see* TOWN WALLS *and* TOWERS).

WALTEGHELL Medieval term for a brick or wall-tile.

WAPENTAKE From the Old Norse *vápnatak*, meaning 'flourish of weapons', a wapentake was an administrative district in the former DANELAW shires of Derby, Leicester, Lincoln, Nottingham and parts of Yorkshire. It has been suggested that the word is derived from the Scandinavian practice of raising one's sword to signify assent at a judicial assembly.

WAR-CRY *see* CRI DE GUERRE

WARD (i) An area contained within the encircling walls of a castle, also known as a BAILEY.
(ii) That portion of a fortress entrusted to a particular officer or division of a garrison.
(iii) The function of a watchman or guard. Also a company of watchmen or guards (*see* LAW AND ORDER).
(iv) The care of a prisoner, also the condition of being a prisoner.
(v) One of the three main divisions of an army: the van, the rear and the middle or 'main battle'. Also applied to any division led by a subordinate officer.
(vi) Guardianship of a minor, also the condition of being subject to a guardian.
(vii) Control of the lands of a deceased tenant and guardianship of the heir until he attains his majority (*see* WARDSHIP).
(viii) That part of the hilt of a sword or dagger that protects the hand (*see* WEAPONS AND HARNESS).

WARDEN *see* MARCH

WARDROBE *see* HOUSEHOLD *and* KITCHENS

WARDSHIP When a feudal tenant died leaving an heir who was too young to enter into his inheritance, custody of the heir and his estate passed to the lord of whom the lands were held. The crown was entitled to hold and administer the estates of a deceased TENANT-IN-CHIEF pending the coming-of-age of an heir at twenty-one or a married heiress at fourteen. During that time the crown received the revenues of the estate and was able to determine the marriages of both a ward and a widow. Wardship could be avoided or terminated by marriage and the child of an infirm or elderly father was usually married off at an early age – which could be at twelve for a girl and fourteen for a boy. A ward who refused to enter into an arranged marriage or who married without consent caused a fine on the estate. Wardships were frequently delegated, either as a means of patronage or to the highest bidder, and they became a potent means of magnate advancement in the medieval period. The *Court of Wards and Liveries* administered the funds received by the crown from wardships, marriages and the granting of livery. Both the practice and the court were abolished in 1646 but its records are maintained at the Public Record Office (see APPENDIX II).

WARFARE, CONDUCT OF The Anglo-Saxons had no tradition of cavalry though their élite troops, such as the *housecarls* and *thegns*, would have possessed horses. By the eleventh century infantry units were sometimes supplemented by lightly mounted troops, especially along the Borders of Wales and Scotland where warfare was a matter of raid and counter-raid. Battlefield tactics consisted of a solid formation of dismounted troops defended by a wall of large shields. A battle would commence with archery aimed at weakening the enemy's 'shield-wall' and this would be followed by close combat. The greatest threat to the Anglo-Saxon kingdoms (notably Wessex) came from Viking incursions up navigable rivers. Consequently fortifications were erected near river-crossings and where possible rivers were blocked and bridges fortified.

Norman military strategy was on an entirely different plane. By the eleventh century their commanders were renowned for their organisation and discipline. Warfare was characterised by reconnaissance, blockades and prolonged sieges (see SIEGES). Full-scale battles were avoided wherever possible. Negotiation was preferred to aggression, and a willingness to retreat when necessary was important. But when confrontation could not be avoided, the primary aim was to kill or capture the enemy commander, thereby causing disarray and almost inevitable capitulation. Again, battle would begin with archery to weaken the enemy's defences, the archers protected by armoured infantry. But the principal offensive rôle fell to the cavalry, who might feign retreat in order to draw out the enemy. The Norman cavalry, which was acknowledged to be pre-eminent at the time, employed the *couched lance* technique in a squadron (*conrois*) formation, usually in multiples of ten men (see LANCE). Knights' horses were walked into the charge, to conserve energy, and were cantered rather than galloped for the final charge. The maintenance and security of supply lines were of the utmost importance, as was the ability to sustain campaigning during the winter months. Duke William's decision to commit his army to a pitched battle at Senlac in 1066 (see NORMANS, THE) was uncharacteristic but unavoidable. Nevertheless, the composition and deployment of his army was typical of Norman thoroughness: a combined force of cavalry and infantry with logistical and naval support. Following

the battle the Norman army ravaged the recalcitrant Anglo-Saxon territories (see HARRYING OF THE NORTH), a policy of ruthless suppression that was the usual sequel to victory in the field and was of far greater significance as an instrument of conquest than the battle itself. Anglo-Saxon leaders were taken hostage while the Normans constructed castles to control the principal towns and routeways and to counter guerrilla resistance.

The civil war during the reign of Stephen (1135–54) was known as 'The Anarchy' (see ANARCHY, THE). Although initially the direction of the war was determined on the battlefield, it became a war of attrition, of skirmish and siege. In western Europe military campaigns concentrated on the devastation of enemy territory and the capture of strategically placed castles and fortified towns. They were deadly games of chess that attempted to avoid direct conflict with an enemy's forces, depending instead on subterfuge and disinformation. Although in the twelfth century armoured cavalry continued to dominate the medieval army, there was a very obvious increase in the effectiveness of infantry, notably crossbowmen and archers, supported by units of specialist troops such as scouts, foragers, engineers, sappers and incendiaries. These were not an undisciplined rabble, but highly trained men with recognised skills. Indeed, crossbowmen were the most highly regarded infantry of the period (the first mercenaries to be recorded in significant numbers in the twelfth century were crossbowmen from Gascony and Genoa). A twelfth-century account describes how an invading force in France was preceded by scouts and incendiaries who set fire to enemy villages. These were followed by the main fighting force and foragers who collected the spoils and loaded them into the baggage train. Similarly, the cavalry included men with specific skills and responsibilities, notably the knights (see KNIGHT-HOOD AND CHIVALRY, ORIGINS OF), mounted sergeants (see SERJEANTY) and mounted cross-bowmen (see ARCHERY), all of whom would be expected to dismount and support the infantry in open battle when required. The knights and other members of the mounted élite rode palfreys, ordinary 'riding horses' rather than the heavy (and expensive) destriers or 'war-horses' that were used only in battle (see HORSES AND HORSE-HARNESS). They would also avoid having to travel in full armour which was carried by their squires, together with their weapons, helmet and shield, until an enemy army was located. The popular perception of medieval warfare as a series of brief but violent clashes of arms is not entirely accurate. Many twelfth-century 'battles' were little more than raids, aimed at cutting off an enemy's supply routes and blocking roads and bridges, or entrenched camps bombarding one another with stone-throwing siege engines.

Battles fought by cavalry were rare in the twelfth century but increased in number during the thirteenth. Cavalry usually advanced in close-ordered ranks with infantry crossbowmen and archers protecting their flanks while endeavouring to bring down as many of the enemy's horses as possible. In defensive situations the archers could be placed in front of dismounted knights with mounted knights behind them. Sometimes mounted archers were placed on the left flank from where they could shoot at an advancing enemy's unprotected right side (shields were carried on the left arm). Traditionally the cavalry was deployed in operational battalions (*bataile*) according to their place of origin and commanded by a senior magnate from that area. These large divisions would be subdivided into squadrons (*échelles*) and smaller units *conrois* of twenty-four knights, riding in close order in two or three ranks. These densely packed units acted as 'shock cavalry', charging at a canter and, if they succeeded in breaking the enemy's formation, fighting individually in the resulting *mêlée*. Operational cavalry reserves would then charge through any break in an enemy's front, turning and charging again from the rear. They could also be sent unexpectedly against an enemy's flank if the opportunity arose. The heavy infantry would usually be drawn up in three divisions behind a defensive ditch and palisade and within natural defences to protect their flanks.

In the late thirteenth and early fourteenth centuries the English were preoccupied with the conquest of Wales and with campaigning in Scotland (*see* SCOTLAND: ENGLISH WARS IN *and* WALES, CONQUEST OF). For the Welsh it was a prolonged period of guerrilla warfare that was otherwise rare in the medieval period. They harassed and ambushed the English supply trains as they lumbered through the forests and mountain passes of Snowdonia, anticipating and cutting off the enemy's line of withdrawal and forcing him to follow a particular route by blocking others. They were rarely drawn into open battle against the heavily armoured English and developed a talent for fighting at night, taking particular advantage of the mist and rain that frequently enveloped the hills and frustrated the invader, confining his activities to the coastal strip. The Welsh also adopted the light cavalry tactic of repeated attack and retreat and were always prepared to dismount and fight on foot when necessary.

In the late Middle Ages, and particularly during the HUNDRED YEARS WAR, overall strategy continued to be of greater importance than confrontation on the battlefield. Siege warfare remained the most effective method of conquering territory, together with raiding, which was aimed at weakening both an enemy's economy and his morale. Similarly, defenders continued to harass and ambush invading forces, cutting off supply lines and frustrating their advance. In the early decades of the war the French suffered significant and demoralising losses in major battles against English forces whose tactics more than compensated for inferior numbers. Consequently the French reverted to a strategy of almost guerrilla-style warfare that avoided set-piece battles and effectively stalled the English advance. In response the English intensified their raids, adopting a 'scorched earth' policy of burning and pillaging across the entire kingdom of France from their territories in the north and south-west (*see* CHEVAUCHÉE). By the fourteenth century there was a clear distinction between the increasingly heavily armoured cavalryman (*see* MAN-AT-ARMS) and various types of light cavalry, including the *hobelars* who operated alongside men-at-arms and mounted infantry archers during raids into Scotland and France. Indeed, it has been suggested that in the French chevauchées the hobelars were tactically more effective than the famous English longbowmen (*see* ARCHERY). Nevertheless, the 'shower-shooting' technique of the English archers caused havoc among the heavily armoured French cavalry. This required thousands of arrows to be loosed simultaneously, usually with a high trajectory, on to the heads of the enemy as they advanced through a 'killing field'. An English bowman could release up to fifteen arrows a minute and, although the technique probably resulted in relatively few casualties, it undoubtedly caused panic among the advancing men and horses. The English battle array consisted of a 'harrow' formation (*herce*) in which the archers were either integrated with dismounted heavily armoured men-at-arms or positioned slightly in advance of them or on the flanks. They were usually protected by natural obstacles or ditches or by pointed stakes planted in 'thickets' (*chevaux de frise*). Six or seven rows of stakes, each a metre apart and angled towards the enemy, must have proved a formidable obstruction to cavalry and a charge could be diverted to face a heavily armoured line of men-at-arms by placing the thickets in pre-determined positions. It has also been suggested that archers may have deliberately encouraged an attack by standing in front of the stakes to conceal them, only retreating

into the protective thicket at the last minute, thereby causing the front ranks of the attacking cavalry to impale themselves and their horses. It seems likely that the carnage suffered by the French knights at Crécy (1346) and Agincourt (1415) was inflicted by archers, emerging from their palisades with swords and daggers, during the ensuing confusion.
(*See also* WEAPONS AND HARNESS)

WAR HAMMER *or* **BATTLE HAMMER** A hammer-shaped MACE, usually with a spike at the back. Metal strips below the head protected the shaft from a lopping blow while guards were often fitted to protect the hand from blades sliding down the shaft.
(*See also* WEAPONS AND HARNESS)

WAR HAT *see* HELMETS *and* KETTLE HAT

WAR-HEADS Projecting defensive structures at the head of a wall (*see* HOARDINGS *and* MACHICO-LATIONS).

WAR OF MADOG *see* WALES, CONQUEST OF

WARRENS Warrens, known variously as *conygers*, *coningers*, *coneygarths* or *coneries* (from the Old French *coninière*), were areas set aside for the raising of rabbits; like medieval FISH PONDS and DOVECOTES, their purpose was to provide a manorial or monastic estate with a regular supply of fresh meat. The term is derived from the feudal right of 'free warren' which regulated the hunting of all small game. Manorial and monastic warrens were usually established on common grazing lands or in the vicinity of DEER PARKS and were numerous by the thirteenth century. The rabbit is not native to Britain but was introduced by the Normans towards the end of the twelfth century, possibly from Spain. Originally adult rabbits were known as *coneys* and when introduced they were unable to adapt to the harsh British climate, were incapable of burrowing and even had to be fed on hay in winter. They were reared as a culinary delicacy and to provide a soft fur for lining garments, and were captured by means of ferrets and nets. Contemporary illustrations suggest that in the medieval and Tudor periods this was considered to be predominantly women's sport. It was not until the mid-fourteenth century that rabbit numbers had increased sufficiently for them to be considered vermin. Even then they were protected within and beyond the limits of a warren and tenants were not free to kill rabbits on their land until the passing of the Ground Game Act in 1880. Although some warrens were established on islands most were

contained within a rampart and ditch, sometimes with a hedge or fence, to deter predators and poachers. Although most warrens were no larger than a paddock others extended over considerable areas: Lakenheath Warren in Suffolk, for example, covered more than 2,200 acres and was enclosed by a 16km (10 mile) long bank and ditch. Such warrens brought their owners large profits and poaching was always a serious problem. Many warreners were therefore provided with fortified refuges such as the (surviving) two-storey stone-built lodge on the prior of Thetford's fifteenth-century warren in the Brecklands of Norfolk. Some warrens were delineated by marker stones. An old wayside cross (Bennett's Cross) near Postbridge on Dartmoor, for example, was adopted for this purpose and carved with the letters 'W-B' for 'warren boundary'. Series of *pillow mounds*, known locally as 'berries' or 'burys', were usually constructed in post-medieval warrens and artificial burrows were provided to encourage breeding, the tunnels excavated and lined with stone or dug as boreholes. Tudor documents record payments for the provision of 'a great long auger of iron to make and bore coney holes within the King's beries new made'. As the name suggests, pillow mounds are usually of an oblong configuration, generally some 30m (100ft) long and 10m (30ft) wide and surrounded by shallow ditches. Shapes vary, however, and circular pillow mounds may easily be mistaken for barrows or windmill mounds. Several warrens were established within the ramparts of ancient hillforts, such as that on Pilsdon Pen in west Dorset, which provided ready-made protection for the breeding grounds. Others are marked on estate maps or are commemorated in *warren* or *coney* field and place-names.

WARS OF THE ROSES The period of internecine strife between the houses of York and Lancaster lasting intermittently from the first military confrontation at Crayford (1452) to the battle of Stoke (1487). The wars had a specific cause and a very limited objective. The cause was the political *impasse* created by the wilful ineptitude of Henry VI (*r.* 1422–61 and 1470–1), exacerbated by the loss of Aquitaine in 1453 and manifested by endemic disorder and the perversion of justice. The objective was simply to change the government. Neither party sought to destroy or divide the royal authority of the kingdom, but rather to establish power over the council and through it to govern. In the absence of any mechanism whereby an incompetent and untrustworthy monarch might be displaced, armed insurrection was almost inevitable. The warring factions fought at first for control of the king and then, after *c.* 1460, for the crown itself.

During these thirty-five years there were three periods of conflict: 1455–64, 1469–71 and 1483–7. Actual campaigning occupied no more than 428 days, the longest campaign, Wakefield (1460) to Towton (1461), lasting only sixteen weeks. Battles were fought by small armies, towns were rarely sacked and the normal economic life of the countryside was hardly disturbed. The wars were fought by 'a fundamentally vigorous, prosperous, expansionist society' and after the defeat of Richard III at Bosworth in 1485 'English government and society were fundamentally no different from what they had been before' (B.P. Wolffe). It is certainly true that approximately 25 per cent of the aristocracy suffered extinction during the fifteenth century, but this was due as much to a failure to produce male heirs as to death in war. Even so, of the sixteen major comital families (dukes and earls) which existed in the last decade of Henry VI's reign, only two were unscathed by the wars: those of William, earl of Arundel, and Ralph Neville, the 2nd earl of Westmorland.

By the late 1440s Richard, duke of York (1411–60), had emerged as the principal critic of Queen Margaret (1430–82), 'that great and strong laboured woman', and the Lancastrian faction that exercised considerable political influence within Henry VI's court. York was heir to a powerful and potentially dangerous inheritance: he was descended through the female line from Lionel, duke of Clarence, the second surviving son of Edward III, whereas Henry was descended from Edward's third son, John of Gaunt. Nevertheless, the successful kingship of Henry V had placed the defacto authority of the Lancastrian dynasty beyond question and York aspired not to the crown but to the reality of power from which he was excluded. He demanded no more than to be re-admitted to the king's Council by virtue of his birth and rank and to this end he enlisted the support of the powerful Neville clan – his brother-in-law Richard Neville, earl of Salisbury (*c.* 1400–60), and his son Richard, earl of Warwick (1428–71). In the north of England the Nevilles rivalled the Percy earls of Northumberland in wealth and influence and it was therefore inevitable that in any power struggle the Percys would back Henry and his queen.

The first battle of St Albans (22 May 1455) was more of a bloody skirmish than a battle, but it signified the end of restraint. York had intended to intercept Henry VI and his principal counsellor Edmund Beaufort, duke of Somerset (*c.* 1406–55), en route to a Council meeting at Leicester before which York and his allies, Salisbury and Warwick, had been summoned to appear. Somerset was a grandson of John of Gaunt through the legitimated Beaufort line (*see below*) and he effectively ruled the country with Queen Margaret's support. At first York attempted to negotiate with the king for the removal of Somerset from the Council but when this failed fighting broke out and Somerset was killed. With the restoration of York's influence at court a semblance of political equanimity was regained, though it is clear that Queen Margaret was simply biding her time. On 23 September 1459 she launched a pre-emptive strike against the Yorkists at Blore Heath, east of Market Drayton. York and his followers fled into exile from where they planned an invasion of England and in June 1460 Warwick launched an invasion from CALAIS. Having landed at Sandwich, he entered London and in July marched north to Northampton where he defeated the Lancastrians and captured the king. On 10 October York returned to London where, much to the embarrassment of his supporters, he announced his intention to claim the throne. The reluctance of the nobility to recognise York's title is hardly surprising: consistently they had been told that they were fighting to replace the king's corrupt advisers, not the king himself. Their reaction was equivocal: Henry was to reign for the remainder of his life and York was to be recognised as his heir. Clearly, such an accommodation, which disinherited her son, was unlikely to satisfy Queen Margaret who rallied her northern forces and wreaked revenge on York at Wakefield (30 December 1460). Marching south, she defeated Warwick and regained possession of her husband at the second battle of St Albans (17 February 1461). But Margaret's victory was short-lived. Her troops went on the rampage on the streets of St Albans causing the citizens of London to take fright. The gates of the city were thrown open to the Yorkists who, having lost possession of the king, now took possession of his capital. In order to legitimise their position the new duke of York was proclaimed King Edward IV, a bloody victory at the battle of Towton (29 March 1461) confirming his authority. Queen Margaret escaped with her son, 'her hope for the future', and sought support abroad, eventually establishing a shadowy and impoverished government in exile at St Michel in Bar. They plotted continuously, even proposing an alliance with Warwick which, incredibly, became a reality when Warwick and George of Clarence, Edward's brother, rebelled in 1469. Charging the king with 'reliance on evil councillors', Warwick took Edward into custody and proceeded to execute those of the king's Wydeville relatives to whom he took exception. But Edward showed considerable resilience: Warwick fled to France where, in an extraordinary volte-face, he formed an alliance with the Lancastrians to restore Henry VI to the English throne. On 13 September 1470 Warwick and Clarence landed near Dartmouth, forcing Edward into exile and reinstating Henry as king. Little wonder that history has attributed to Richard Neville, earl of Warwick, the appellation 'Kingmaker'. Queen Margaret did not reach England in time to celebrate Henry VI's second succession (known as the *Readeption*) or, indeed, to witness the failure of Warwick's regime. Edward returned in 1471, defeating the Lancastrians at Barnet (14 April) and Tewkesbury (4 May): Margaret was captured, her son killed and, within days, her husband murdered. Having restored political stability, Edward IV died in April 1483 leaving his thirteen-year-old son Edward as his heir.

Richard, duke of Gloucester (1452–85), youngest son of Richard, duke of York, became king on 26 June 1483 by setting aside the claims of his nephews, the sons of Edward IV. He justified his actions by denying both the legitimacy of his brother and the legality of Edward's marriage to the queen, the princes' mother. He eliminated Earl Rivers and Lord Hastings and drove the queen and her son Thomas Grey, marquess of Dorset, into sanctuary. The royal princes Edward and Richard were confined in the Tower of London and by August 1483 it was widely rumoured that they were dead. Richard's usurpation was achieved through the strength and loyalty of his northern retinue. But the threat of overwhelming force could not be maintained indefinitely and almost as soon as he was crowned Richard was faced with rebellion. For the most part the rebels, many of them retainers of Edward IV and the Wydevilles, came from southern England where Richard had little support. Nevertheless, he succeeded in putting down the duke of Buckingham's rebellion in the autumn of 1483 but was then obliged to install his trusted northern supporters in key positions, antagonising many who regarded them with considerable suspicion.

Henry Tudor, earl of Richmond (1457–1509), claimed descent from the Beauforts, the illegitimate line of John of Gaunt, duke of Lancaster (1340–99) and the third son of Edward III. The *Beauforts* had been legitimated by act of parliament confirming a patent issued by Richard II, though their half-brother Henry IV added the words *excepta dignitate regali* to the patent, thereby debarring them from succession to the throne. But he failed to make the

disqualification law by a further act of parliament and it was later argued that a royal patent could not alter one confirmed by parliament and the Beauforts therefore enjoyed a rightful claim to succession. Henry Tudor was the son of Margaret Beaufort and Edmund, earl of Richmond, the son of Owen ap Meredith ap Tudur, a Welshman who had the good fortune to marry Catherine of Valois, the widow of Henry V. Following the ruination of the house of Lancaster at Tewkesbury in 1471, the young Henry became the chief Lancastrian claimant to the English throne and he was hurried into exile by his uncle, Jasper Tudor. He spent twelve years under the protection of the duke of Brittany until, with French support, he set sail from Honfleur in August 1485 and landed at Milford Haven with three thousand men – 'the sweepings of the gaols of Normandy'. He marched into England and met Richard III's forces at Bosworth in Leicestershire (22 August 1485) where the treachery of Sir William Stanley and the doubtful loyalty of Lord Stanley turned what should have been certain victory for Richard into defeat.* Henry VII's hold on the crown was finally secured when he defeated the Yorkist pretender John de la Pole, earl of Lincoln, at the battle of Stoke (16 June 1487), the last occasion on which a reigning monarch was required to take the field in person against a rival claimant to his throne.

What we now call the 'Wars of the Roses' were sometimes referred to by contemporaries as the 'Cousins' Wars'. The term 'Wars of the Roses' originated in Sir Walter Scott's *Anne of Geierstein* which was written in 1829, though the concept was not new. A pamphlet by Thomas Smith, written in 1561, refers to 'the striving of the two roses'. In 1646 Sir John Oglander wrote a tract called *The Quarrel of the Warring Roses*, while David Hume published *The Wars of the Two Roses* in 1761.

The fallacious notion that the two houses adopted their respective roses in the Temple Garden may be attributed to Shakespeare (*Henry VI Part 1*):

> I prophesy: this brawl today . . .
> Shall send between the red rose and the white,
> A thousand souls to death and deadly night.

In fact, the red rose was a 'cousin' of the golden rose which was introduced as a royal device by Henry III's queen, Eleanor of Provence (1223–91). It had been associated with the title of Lancaster since its

---

* This is the traditional view. For a revised assessment see Jones, M., *Bosworth 1485* (Tempus, 2002)

adoption by Eleanor's second son Edmund 'Crouchback', and descended to John of Gaunt through his marriage to the Lancastrian heiress Blanche. Thus it became the distinctive device of the Lancastrian kings and of Gaunt's illegitimate Beaufort line, notably John Beaufort, duke of Somerset. A white rose was the badge of Roger Mortimer, 2nd earl of March (d. 1360), grandfather of Richard II's heir, also Roger, the 4th earl of March (d. 1398). It was by his Mortimer descent that Richard, duke of York, could claim the throne and it seems likely that he selected the white rose from his numerous badges to emphasise his aspirations. The two roses came to represent the principles of parliamentary sanction by which the Lancastrians held the crown and 'strict legitimism' which was the foundation of Yorkist rule. (For other heraldic devices, including the Yorkist falcon and fetterlock badge, see BADGES AND LIVERY.)
(See also ATTAINDER)

WATCH AND WARD see LAW AND ORDER

WATER-CLOSET see GARDEROBE

WATER DEFENCES see MOATS AND WATER DEFENCES

WATER GATE see QUAYS

WATER SUPPLY see PLUMBING, WATER SUPPLY AND SANITATION and WELLS

WATTLE AND DAUB Wattling consists of a row of upright stakes, the spaces between being filled with interwoven small branches, hazel rods, osiers, reeds, thin strips of wood or other pliant material. On either side (or sometimes on one side only) of this foundation mud, clay or plaster was daubed and thrust into the interstices, the resulting surfaces being smoothed and treated with plaster or a coat of whitewash. Walls of this construction, known as 'wattle and daub', 'stud and mud', 'ruddle and dab' and a variety of other, localised terms, were universally used for dwellings and outhouses in the medieval period. Early motte and bailey castles (see MOTTE) and the palisade defences of many towns were initially constructed of timber with wattle and daub infilling, while the internal partition walls and courtyard buildings of many stone-built castles were similarly constructed.
(See also TIMBER-FRAME BUILDINGS)

WEALDEN HOUSE see HALL

WEAPONS AND HARNESS

The following terms are most commonly used when describing weapons and harness of the medieval period (* see also individual entries).

ANELACE*	short, two-edged tapering dagger
ANGON	barbed javelin with long iron socket
AUNLAZ	short infantry dagger, fourteenth century
BALLOK DAGGER	dagger with distinctive grip and guard
BASELARD	infantry short-sword with H-shaped hilt
BATTLE AXE	a one-handed cleaver
BATTLE HAMMER	alternative name for WAR HAMMER
BELT FROG	button and loop attachment for a sword belt
BILL	long-shafted weapon with a hooked blade
CALTRAP*	a device strewn before horses to lame them
CHAPE	the termination of a strap
CLAYMORE	Scottish two-edged broadsword
COUCHED	lance held tightly beneath a horseman's upper arm
COUSTELL	infantry short sword
DAGGER	short, two-edged weapon for stabbing
FALCHION*	short sword, the curved blade wider towards the point
FAUSSART	short infantry sword, similar to FALCHION
FULLER	a groove along the blade
GAFELUC	small javelin of Welsh origin
GISARME	long-hafted axe
HAFT	shaft or handle
HALBERD*	infantry pole arm
HAND-AND-A-HALF SWORD	capable of single- or double-handed use
HILT	handle of sword or dagger
HOLY WATER SPRINKLER	a type of mace (sardonic)
JAVELIN	light spear
LANCE*	long cavalry spear
MACE*	single-handed club
MISERICORDE*	thrusting dagger for the *coup de grace*
MORNING STAR	type of mace (sardonic)

PIKE	long infantry spear wielded with both hands
POLE	from *pole* meaning 'head'
POLE ARM*	infantry weapon with cutting/thrusting blade
POLE AXE*	combined cutting blade, hammer and thrusting spike
POMMEL*	round end of a sword hilt, often decorated
PRICK SPURS	short spurs without rowels
QUILLIONS*	the cross-guard of a sword handle
ROWEL*	revolving, star-shaped spur
SCABBARD	a sword sheath
SHARPENING STEEL	carried in small sheath attached to sword scabbard
SPARTH	a pole axe with an upward curving blade
STAFF-WEAPON	long-shafted weapon with cutting/thrusting blade
SWORD	weapon with long blade, hilt and hand-guard
TANG	shaft between the quillions and the pommel
TORET	a trefoil-shaped clasp
TRIBOLI*	a type of CALTRAP
WARD*	part of the hilt that protects the hand
WAR HAMMER*	hammer-shaped mace
WYAX	a double-bladed axe

The *sword* was considered to be the most prestigious weapon throughout the medieval period, indeed it became (and remains) the pre-eminent symbol of knighthood. The short early medieval swords had developed out of late Roman designs that were intended for cutting and slashing and usually weighed from 1¼ to 1½kg (2lb 12oz to 3lb 5oz). Through the eleventh and twelfth centuries swords became longer and more pointed, better suited for thrusting as well as cutting. With significant improvements in body ARMOUR, a variety of swords developed, each with a specific function. The thirteenth-century infantry *falchion*, for example, which had a single cutting edge and the blade broadening rather than narrowing towards its tip, was designed to increase the weight and penetrating power of the cut. In the later medieval period there was no clear distinction between small swords and large daggers, though it is evident that much larger 'swords of war' were in use by the late thirteenth century. These were single-handed weapons for use on horseback with blades measuring from 90 to 100cm (35–9in) in length and hilts of 15 to 20cm

(6–8in). They usually weighed between 1¼ and 1½kg (2lb 12oz and 3lb 5oz). The 1.8m (6ft) long two-handed broadsword was a fourteenth-century innovation, though the *hand-and-a-half sword*, which, as the name suggests, was designed to be wielded with one or both hands, had been in use since the late Saxon period. The *baselard* was a particularly popular infantry short-sword which may have originated in the thirteenth-century Crusader states. It had a broad, tapering, almost triangular blade and a distinctive H-shaped hilt. Sword blades were often produced by a technique known as *pattern welding* by which strips of hard and soft iron were twisted together and then repeatedly heated and beaten. Many swords had a *fuller* or groove along the blade and, in more expensive weapons, this was often decorated. All swords had a cross-guard, comprising a pair of *quillions*, to protect the hand from blades sliding down the shaft, and this was sometimes reinforced with a ring guard or double ring guards which were a particular feature of late fifteenth- and sixteenth-century swords. The hilt invariably terminated in a bulbous *pommel*, intended to prevent the hand from slipping and often decorated in enamels. The *tang* or shaft between the quillions and the pommel would, of course, have had a wooden grip, bound in leather.

Smaller *daggers* and knives had almost certainly been carried by the military élite throughout the medieval period, but they became acceptable in aristocratic circles only in the fourteenth century. The *dague à rouelles* or 'rowel dagger', with a disc-shaped pommel and guard, and the *ballok dagger*, which had a grip and guard which resembled the male sexual organs, were particularly favoured, as was the *anelace*, a short, two-edged tapering dagger. The *misericorde* (Latin *misericordia* = 'mercy') was a straight dagger without a guard, the blade having a triangular section and only one cutting edge. Often found depicted in brasses and effigial figures dating from the late fourteenth and fifteenth centuries, misericordes were used to administer the *coup de grace* through a visor and were sometimes engraved with grisly scenes such as the 'Dance of Death'.

A sword was usually carried in a *scabbard*, which from the earliest times was attached to a hip-belt by means of an elongated scabbard-slide on the outer face of the scabbard or was suspended from two slender buckled straps, themselves attached to the sword belt. The two-strap system meant that the angle at which the sword hung could be altered to suit the circumstances (fighting on horseback or on foot, for example) and the personal preference of the owner. Scabbards were made of cloth-covered wood or leather, were often ornately decorated and were

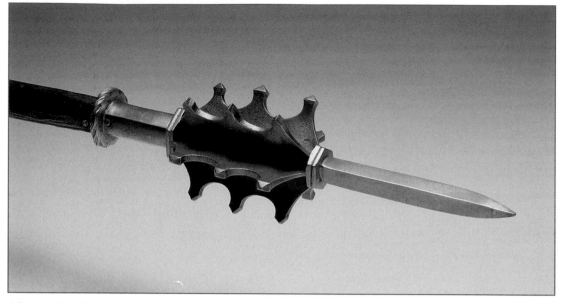

A late-medieval mace.

usually lined with an oiled fur to prevent the blade from rusting.

Javelins were particularly associated with Celtic and eleventh-century Anglo-Saxon infantry forces. Up to three at a time would be carried, each about 2m (6½ft) in length. Infantry spears gradually developed into longer *pikes*, wielded with two hands, *pole arms* which incorporated a blade or hook for dragging a horseman from the saddle, and a variety of *staff weapons* which had long wooden shafts and blades designed for both cutting and thrusting. The *halberd*, which replaced the long-hafted axe or *gisarme*, was a fearsome infantry pole arm which incorporated an axe-blade, hammer and thrusting spike. Eleventh-century cavalry *lances* were about 1.8m (6ft) in length. They were carried in the horizontal *couched* position: held tightly beneath the horseman's upper right arm. By the end of the thirteenth century, the lance had increased in length to 2.4m (8ft) and by the mid-fourteenth century to 3m (10ft). It was usually made of ash wood with an armour-piercing spear-head (*see* LANCE for tournament lances). Spears and lances continued in use during the fourteenth century but their effectiveness declined as armoured cavalry increasingly turned to close-combat weapons such as the mace (*see below*). Meanwhile, infantry pole arms and staff weapons continued to be developed in a remarkable variety of forms.

The Vikings were renowned for their great infantry axes and these clearly influenced the development of similar weapons in Scotland, Ireland and Anglo-Saxon England. In the late Middle Ages these would evolve into the famous, long-hafted Scottish war-axe or *Jeddart axe*, the equally famous *Galloglass axe* of Ireland and western Scotland and the *sparth* or *spartha* with its upward-curving blade. The thirteenth-century *mace* or 'crusher' almost certainly originated in the Crusades, its heavy winged or flanged head being ideally suited to counter the increasing effectiveness of plate armour. As such it was essentially a cavalry weapon and came to be associated with western Europe's military élite. So too were the *war hammer* or *battle hammer*, which usually had a spike at the back and a hammer-head at the front, and the *battle axe*, a one-handed cleaver with a single blade. A particular type of flanged mace, known sardonically as the *Holy Water Sprinkler*, was similar in appearance to the asperges used for sprinkling consecrated water during the mass. Equally sardonic was the *Morning Star*, a mace with a spherical head from which projected spikes.

Small hand-held guns ('hand-cannon') first appeared in Italy in the last decades of the fourteenth century and were used by rioters in England in 1375, suggesting that they were by then commonplace (*see* FIREARMS AND CANNON).

(*See also* ARCHERY (for crossbow and longbow), ARMOUR, ARMS MANUFACTURE, FIREARMS AND CANNON, HELMETS, HORSES AND HORSE-HARNESS *and* SHIELDS)

WEATHER COCKS AND WEATHER VANES

A weather cock is a revolving three-dimensional, hollow metal sculpture mounted on a spire or above a tower to indicate the direction of the wind. Weather vanes are intended both to show the direction of the wind and to display heraldic devices. They are effectively rigid metal flags and it has been suggested that in the medieval period the shape of the vane may have been dictated by the rank of its owner. The use of vanes, which probably originated in France, is evident in England from the thirteenth century and it is likely that the word is a corruption of *fane*, derived from *fannion*, meaning 'banner'. At Dover in 1365 a *vana* was purchased for 12*d* and set up on the great tower to 'show the quarter of the wind', while at Eltham in 1369 a weather cock costing 3*s* 4*d* was affixed above the kitchen 'to know how the wind lies'. At Dover the vane was of primary importance for shipping and in a kitchen the opening and closing of the louvre would be regulated by the position of the wind. In 1365 six latten vanes, each costing 15*s*, were purchased by William Latoner and set on the towers of Sheppey Castle (latten was a type of bell-metal) while the 'great vayn' erected over the hall at Windsor in 1452 was of copper and painted with the king's arms. Several ornate vanes were provided for the Tower of London in 1532, together with 'ij little frames of bourdes for to close in the great faynes that cam from Elysys the painter for hurtying of the gildyng, to every fayne one'. The hall of Hampton Court must have been a magnificent sight in sunlight and a veering wind, for not only was there a cluster of vanes on the louvre but three stair turrets had nine vanes apiece, each gilded and painted with the arms and badges of the king and queen, the battlements carried another sixteen and each gable was crowned with a lion or dragon carrying a vane 'oon of the Kynges armys, the other of the Quenys, wrowghte with fine golde and in owle [oil]'.

WEBS *see* VAULTING

WELDON STONE
A creamy, easily cut stone, quarried in Northamptonshire.

WELLS
Castles were rarely built without a reliable and secure supply of fresh water. It is surprising, therefore, that workmen were obliged to dig 'in a place in a field called Chereshethe' in search of fresh water springs during the construction of Queenborough Castle in 1375. This would have required a conduit 'from the said place to the castle' which would have been extremely vulnerable

should the castle have been invested. However, we later read of £10 being paid for sixty weeks' work to 'the master of the making of the new well' at the same castle in 1393. Although there were exceptions (such as Pembroke where water had to be piped into the castle), almost invariably a castle was built on a site where wells could be sunk within the safety of its walls. But it was often necessary to excavate to extraordinary depths in order to tap a reliable source, especially at elevated sites such as Dover Castle which has the deepest well in England (107m or 350ft). At Corfe in 1377 we read of 'cleaning the bottom of the well in the castle so that water may bubble up . . .' while at Sheppey in 1365 one Robert de Westmallyng was paid 20*s* for excavating a 25m (83ft) well and lining it with masonry. There are some instances of castles being built on apparently suitable sites, only for the engineers to discover that the underlying rock was so impenetrable that they were unable to reach the water table beneath. This may have been the case at Castell-y-Bere and Morlais Castles, where the 'wells' referred to in contemporary documents were in fact CISTERNS. In some cases, where the supply to a well was unreliable or where it was not possible to bore for water, cisterns were provided to collect rainwater: at Carreg Cennen, for example, two sunken pits, lined with dressed stone blocks, were carefully placed at the rear of the gatehouse to catch rainwater from adjacent roofs. Wherever possible, wells were sunk within the most secure part of a castle, often the KEEP, which was the final refuge should the outer defences be captured by an enemy. At Middleham Castle, for example, the ground floor of the keep (which was accessible only from the floor above) contained kitchens that were provided with two wells. Proximity to the castle KITCHENS was desirable, though not always practicable. At Bodiam a large spring-fed well is located in the south-west tower adjoining the kitchens and has the appearance of a circular swimming pool. At Goodrich, however, a covered way (*pentice*) had to be erected so that water could be carried from the well on the north side of the courtyard to the kitchen on the south. Many castle wells are located in courtyards: at Conwy Castle the 27.7m (91ft) well was excavated within a wide cleft which cut across the castle rock to isolate and strengthen the approach to the inner ward. The well-head, which forms a deep open pit, was stone-lined and protected by a well-house. The Conwy accounts for 1525 include a payment of 5*s* paid for 1,000 slates, including the carriage by boat from Ogwen, 'to sclate the oder side [exterior] of the well in the castell' and in 1531 for 'puttyng of a new geiste [joist] over the well and making a lydde [cover] to the same well'.

Water was usually drawn from the well with a bucket and windlass, though there is evidence that by the end of the fifteenth century primitive pumps were sometimes used. An entry in the 1482 accounts for Clarendon illustrates the difficulties encountered when cleaning and scouring a well (a 'fathom' was then the distance between the fingers of outstretched arms – about 1.8m or 6ft):

> To Thomas Warmewell for going down into the well to clean it – at 2s. a day – 8s. For great candles called tallow perchers for lighting the said Thomas at the bottom of the well and burning there for 4 days – 2d. Paid to 4 labourers running in the great wheel for the said 4 days – 6s. 8d. For a great new rope [cable] for the well, 24 fathoms in length . . . 12s. 2¼d.

Reference to men 'running in the great wheel', which was presumably a treadmill used for raising debris and lowering tools and materials, is reminiscent of a similar wheel which may still be seen in the well-house of Carisbrooke Castle. For eight centuries this 49m (161ft) deep well was the only means of supplying water to the castle. The oak-frame wheel, which dates from c. 1550, measures 4.7m (15½ft) in diameter and since 1800 has been turned by donkeys which have to walk 274m (300yd) in order to raise a bucket from the bottom of the well. It would appear that horse-powered wheels were not uncommon in the late medieval period for in 1538 a report on the well in the north-west corner of the inner ward at Dunstanburgh Castle concluded that it had to be worked by hand for 'there is no horse mylne [mill] in the said castell'. In several castles, such as Dover and Newcastle, a network of lead pipes carried water from the well-head to various parts of the keep (*see* PLUMBING, WATER SUPPLY AND SANITATION), while in Rochester's keep the well shaft continued upwards through the building so that water could be raised to any level.

WELSH CASTLES (EDWARDIAN) *see* CASTLES, CONSTRUCTION OF and WALES, CONQUEST OF

WELSH CASTLES (NATIVE) *see* WALES: NATIVE CASTLES

WELSH MARCHES *see* MARCHES

WELSHRY *see* ENGLISHRY

WHEELBARROWS *see* MATERIALS, CARRIAGE OF

WHEEL WINDOW *see* ROSE WINDOW

WHINSTONE Dark basalt or similar rock which forms a sill or outcrop stretching across the county of Northumberland.

WHITEWASH *see* PLASTER, WHITEWASH AND PAINT

WICKER CENTERING A framework of wicker which held a vault in place while it was under construction (*see* VAULTING).

WICKET (i) A small, undefended gate set into a fence or wall.
(ii) A small door set within or beside a larger one (*see* DOORS).

WINCH ROOM Room above the gate passage for portcullis/drawbridge mechanisms.

WIND BRACES Short braces, usually arched and laid flat along the rafters, which strengthen the wind resistance of a large or exposed roof area.

WINDER *see* STAIRS

WINDLASS *see* ARCHERY

WINDOW GLASS *see* GLAZING, STAINED GLASS *and* WINDOWS

WINDOWS Windows are intended to admit light to a chamber, to provide ventilation and to keep out inclement weather (*see also* SHUTTERS). In a medieval castle, which was (by definition) both a fortress and a residence, the location and size of window openings were of crucial importance: windows in the outer walls could seriously weaken a castle's defensive capability, while inadequate light and ventilation would make the living arrangements unbearable. It is for these reasons that domestic rooms tended to be located on the upper floors (or, as in the case of a great hall, to extend to the height of two floors) and that windows increased progressively in size from ground-floor level upwards. In the great hall-keeps of the Norman period the upper storeys were often generously lit, defence depending on the height and thickness of the walls and the strength of a FOREBUILDING by which access was controlled to a first or second floor. In later castles, where domestic quarters were ranged against the curtain walls and apartments located in mural towers, windows faced inwards wherever possible to a court or inner bailey, though inevitably there were some concessions to comfort and convenience. In some instances these concessions seriously weakened a castle's defensive capability. At Harlech and Beaumaris Castles, for example, two tiers of large windows, protected by iron grills, were inserted in the inward-facing walls of the gatehouses which were intended to be capable of independent defence should the rest of the castle fall into an enemy's hands (*see* KEEP-GATEHOUSE). Perhaps the architect, Master James of St George, was so confident in the efficacy of his formidable outer defences that he assumed a besieging force couldn't possibly reach the inner ward. Exceptionally, windows are to be found in outer walls: where a castle occupies a naturally defended site, for example, as at Warwick and Barnard Castle, where the curtain walls are protected on one side by almost vertical cliffs. Similarly at Harlech, a row of large windows in the outer wall of the Great Hall overlooks an almost inaccessible precipice. Protective iron grills were often affixed to the outside of window openings to frustrate egress, but the large windows of many fifteenth-century castles were clearly incompatible with effective defence. In the 1380s John of Gaunt turned his formidable fortress of Kenilworth into a palace by the addition of a splendid great hall, solar and private chambers, all with large, outward-facing windows – albeit at second-floor level. At Raglan Castle ranges of apartments were built round the Fountain Court in *c.* 1460–9 and further ranges of domestic and administrative offices round the Pitched Stone Court in *c.* 1549–89. All these had splendid contemporary windows including a Tudor bay window at the dais end of the great hall and a series of finely executed first-floor windows that lit the fifteenth-century gallery in the gatehouse range. For all its formidable outward appearance, Raglan was more of a palace than a fortress.

Windows in castles have rarely survived the depredations of warfare, weather and dereliction. However, the shape of an opening and any remaining tracery (usually truncated) can provide invaluable clues to dating (*see* ROMANESQUE *and* GOTHIC ARCHITECTURE). The 'seemingly ethereal fragility' of late Gothic architecture was arrived at only after centuries of experimentation and innovation. The narrow pointed *lancet windows*

of the Early English period evolved through the mullioned and transomed lights of the Decorated and the ornate tracery of the Perpendicular to the broad, square-headed windows of the late fifteenth century. Circular windows with complex traceried designs were sometimes inserted in the gable walls of large buildings such as castle halls and the transepts of major churches (*see* ROSE WINDOW). In 1243 we read of Henry III ordering a round window, 9m (30ft) in diameter, to be inserted in the gable end of his new hall at Dublin Castle. Reference is sometimes made in thirteenth-century documents to 'upright' or 'cowled' windows, particularly in relation to halls. It is likely that these windows extended above the height of the side walls in which they were placed and were provided with individual gables and roofs – what would now be described as 'dormers'. In contemporary documents medieval windows are said to have so many 'lights' or, more commonly, 'days' (*see* GLAZING). When composed of more than one light, the vertical stone bars (*mullions*) are called 'moynels' and the horizontal bars *transoms*. Tracery is described as 'forms' or 'form pieces' and occasionally 'molds'. The frame of a window, whether of stone or timber, consists of a sill or 'soyl' at the lower edge, *jambs* on either side and an ARCH or a flat *lintel* at the top. Sometimes the window recess (EMBRASURE) was carried down below the lights and furnished with stone *window seats* – many of which have survived, though without their wooden tops and embroidered cushions. Of all the features of a medieval castle, these window seats are among the most evocative of an age of 'gentil and courtly pleasures'.

The changing function of the medieval castle is evident in rectangular mullioned windows inserted, somewhat incongruously at times, in the walls of solars and other domestic chambers. Domestic architecture of this late medieval period was also characterised by elaborate bay and oriel windows. A *bay window* (or *compass window*) projects from a wall and rises from ground level through one or more stories, while an *oriel window* is of similar appearance but is cantilevered or supported on a corbel or bracket above ground level. (The term *oriel* was also used to describe a small gallery or ante-room, again on an upper floor.) Throughout the late medieval and Tudor periods windows continued to increase in size as a proportion of wall area. But large panes of glass were unable to withstand strong winds and windows were generally composed of small lozenge-shaped quarries (*leaded lights*), held together in a lattice-work of grooved lead bars (*canes*) which were secured by wire to iron bars

Windows and blocked openings in the inner north wall of the lower bailey at Chepstow Castle, Monmouthshire, illustrate the complexity of modifications and insertions.

(*saddle bars*) set within a stone or metal frame (*see* IRONWORK, LOCKS AND NAILS). Ventilation was important and sometimes a hinged opening framework (*casement*) was provided within a window. As early as 1246 we read that a window at Guildford Castle was to be enlarged and 'closed with glass windows between the columns, with panels which can be opened and shut'. In 1250 the glass windows in the chapel of Sherborne Castle were to be so repaired that they would open and shut, while three years later, in the hall at Northampton Castle, opposite the dais, a glass window was to be made in which the figures of Lazarus and Dives were to be depicted and which could be closed or opened.

It should be remembered that window openings were frequently inserted during later refurbishments and these may also be dated by reference to contemporary architectural styles. One of the most

Bay window in the fourteenth-century Great Hall of Kenilworth Castle. Of all the features of a medieval castle, window seats such as these are among the most evocative of an age of 'gentil and courtly pleasures'.

In the 1580s Sir John Perrot (who was reputed to be an illegitimate son of Henry VIII) erected an extraordinarily impressive 'wall of light' at fourteenth-century Carew Castle in south Wales. With sixteen huge rectangular windows, each of twelve lights, the range of windows was accurately described as a masterpiece of Elizabethan architecture.

spectacular examples (and a rarity among Welsh castles) is Carew Castle, built by Sir Nicholas de Carew (d. 1311), a veteran of Edward I's Welsh campaigns, in the early fourteenth century. Sir Nicholas's stronghold comprised a four-sided courtyard with circular towers at the western corners and two further towers to the east. In 1480 the castle was leased to Sir Rhys ap Thomas who, despite protesting his loyalty to Richard III, joined Henry Tudor when he landed at nearby Dale in 1485 and accompanied him to Bosworth. His duplicity was duly rewarded and he celebrated his advancement by modernising his castle to such a degree that nearly all the architectural features are Tudor. One hundred years later Carew was again added to, this time by Sir John Perrot who was reputed to be an illegitimate son of Henry VIII. In the 1580s he erected an extraordinarily impressive north range, a 'wall of light' with sixteen huge rectangular windows, each of twelve lights. Accurately described as a masterpiece of Elizabethan architecture, Carew Castle may be exceptional but it is by no means unique. Numerous castles were refurbished and converted to comfortable residences in the late medieval and Tudor periods and it is the windows by which these changes may almost invariably be identified.

(*See also* DONOR AND COMMEMORATIVE WINDOWS, DOORS, GLAZING, LOOPHOLES, SHUTTERS *and* STAINED GLASS)

WINDOW SEATS *see* WINDOWS

WINDOW TRACERY *see* GOTHIC ARCHITECTURE

WINGS The long sides of exposed fortifications.

WING-WALL A wall descending the slope of a MOTTE.

WORSHIP A medieval magnate drew to his service those who respected his personal standing as well as men who were bound to his service by land tenure. Collectively these men were known as an AFFINITY and their continuing support depended on their lord's standing in society and his ability to maintain them. When he succeeded, his reputation (his 'worship') was enhanced and he thereby attracted more and better men to his service.
(*See also* LARGESS, LIVERY AND MAINTEN-ANCE *and* RETINUE)

WREATH *or* TORSE A band of twisted strands of material worn about the medieval helmet as decoration, to secure the MANTLING and to conceal the base of the CREST where it was laced or bolted to the tournament helm (*see* HELMETS, HERALDIC). The wreath probably originated in the ceremonial torse of the Dark Age rulers of western Europe and the colourful diadem of the Saracen. In ARMORY the wreath is conventionally depicted as having six twists of alternate metals and colours (*see* TINCTURES).

WYAX *see* WEAPONS AND HARNESS

YEOMAN In thirteenth-century England the French and Latin terms which had hitherto defined social class were replaced by English ones, and those which had been founded on tenure and legal status were gradually superseded by terms indicating general social standing or economic function. Some terms were hardly affected by these changes: 'knight', for example, was used more often than the French *chevalier* or the Latin *miles* but its meaning remained unchanged (*see* KNIGHTHOOD AND CHIVALRY, ORIGINS OF). Others, such as 'churl' (the Old English *ceorl*) and 'villein', disappeared altogether or retained only a literary usage. New terms were of diverse origin. Some developed in the feudal household: 'esquire', for example, which in the fourteenth century came to denote the social rank immediately below that of knight (*see* ESQUIRE). This comparatively select number of esquires was but the senior stratum of a substantial group of free land-owners (*valetti*) who, with the knights, represented their counties in parliament during the first half of the fourteenth century. Those *valetti* below the rank of esquire were described in the late fourteenth century as 'franklins', men of substance and of gentle birth, many of whom no doubt aspired to armigerous status (*see* FRANKLIN). But by the early fifteenth century the term 'franklin' had been superseded by two others: 'gentleman', which was applied to men of breeding who were not armigerous, and 'yeoman'. By the mid-fifteenth century local society comprised (in descending order) knights, esquires, gentlemen, yeomen and husbandmen, though franklins still made an occasional appearance. Of these, only knights and esquires possessed armigerous qualifications and in common usage several of the other terms were evidently interchangeable despite the *Statute of Additions* of 1413 which required that plaintiffs in personal actions should describe precisely the status of their opponents. Fifteenth-century sumptuary legislation similarly propounded a strict hierarchy (*see* SUMPTUARY LAWS) and in 1445 it was determined that knights of the shire attending parliament could include 'noteable squires' and 'gentlemen of birth' but not those 'of the degree of Yeoman and bynethe'. In the context of local society a yeoman was therefore a freeholder below the status of gentleman but above that of most other copyhold tenants and was eligible to serve on juries and to vote in county elections. However, the term *valetti* was also used in official documents to describe those officers in royal and magnate households who, although of lower status than knights, were often drawn from gentle families. In the early fourteenth century the *valetti* included esquires, but as the esquires acquired their own distinctive armigerous status so the term *valetti* came to be translated into English as 'yeomen'. Geoffrey Chaucer (1342–1400) was a yeoman (*valet*) of the king's chamber in 1367 before becoming an esquire. The Yeomen of the Guard, the sovereign's personal bodyguard, was formed by Henry VII in 1485 from his 'private guard of faithful fellowes'.

YETT A hinged iron grille that could be raised in front of a doorway (not to be confused with a PORTCULLIS).

Y-TRACERY *see* GOTHIC ARCHITECTURE

ZIG-ZAG MOULDING *see* ROMANESQUE

Z-PLAN A distinctive Scottish form of tower-house in which two corner towers are added to provide extra protection and improve long-distance visibility.

APPENDIX I

FURTHER READING

Anderson, W., *Castles in Europe* (Elek 1970)

Avent, R. and Kenyon, J.R., *Castles in Wales and the Marches* (University of Wales, Cardiff, 1987)

Bailey, M., *The English Manor* c. *1200– c. 1500* (Manchester University Press, 2002)

Britnell, R., *The Closing of the Middle Ages? England, 1471–1529* (Blackwell, 1997)

Brown, R. Allen, *English Castles* (Batsford, 1976)

——, *Castles from the Air* (Cambridge University Press, 1989)

Burke, J., *Life in the Castle in Medieval England* (London, 1978)

Colvin, H.M. (general ed.), *A History of the King's Works*, vols i, ii, iii (HMSO, 1963–82)

Davies, R.R., *The Age of Conquest: Wales 1063–1415* (Oxford University Press, 1987)

Davis, P.R., *Castles of the Welsh Princes* (Christopher Davies, 1988)

Evans, L., *The Castles of Wales* (London, 1998)

Friar, S., *Heraldry* (Sutton Publishing, 1992)

Fry, P.S., *Castles of Britain and Ireland* (David & Charles, 1996)

Given-Wilson, C., *The English Nobility in the Later Middle Ages* (Routledge & Kegan Paul, 1987)

Hicks, M., *Who's Who in Late Medieval England* (Shepheard-Walwyn, 1991)

——, *Bastard Feudalism* (Longman, 1995)

Higham, R.A. and Barker, P.A., *Timber Castles* (London, 1992)

Howard, M., *The Early Tudor Country House* (George Philip, 1987)

Johnson, M., *Behind the Castle Gate* (Taylor & Francis, 2002)

Jones, M., *Bosworth 1485* (Tempus, 2002)

Kaufmann, J.E. and H.W., *The Medieval Fortress* (Combined Publishing, 2000)

Keen, M., *Medieval Warfare – a History* (Oxford University Press, 1999)

Keevill, G.D., *Medieval Palaces* (Tempus, 2000)

Kenyon, J.R., *Medieval Fortifications* (Leicester University Press, 1990)

Kightly, C., *Strongholds of the Realm* (Thames & Hudson, 1979)

King, D.J.C., *The Castle in England and Wales* (Croom Helm, 1988)

Liddiard, R. (ed.), *Anglo-Norman Castles* (Boydell & Brewer, 2002)

McNeill, T., *English Heritage Book of Castles* (Batsford, 1992)

Matarasso, F., *The English Castle* (London, 1993)

Morley, B., *Henry VIII and the Development of Coastal Defence* (London, 1976)

Nicolle, D. (ed), *Companion to Medieval Arms and Armour* (Boydell & Brewer, 2002)

Pettifer, A., *English Castles* (Boydell, 1995)

——, *Welsh Castles* (Boydell, 2000)

Pevsner, N. and Newman, J., *The Buildings of England* series of county volumes (Penguin, 1989)

Platt, C., *Medieval England: A Social History and Archaeology from the Conquest to 1600 AD* (Routledge, 1978)

——, *The Castle in Medieval England and Wales* (Secker & Warburg, 1982)

——, *The Architecture of Medieval Britain* (Yale University Press, 1990)

Renn, D.F., *Norman Castles in Britain*, 2nd edn (John Baker, 1973)

Rowley, T., *The High Middle Ages 1200–1550* (Routledge, 1986)

Salzman, L.F., *Buildings in England down to 1540* (Oxford University Press, 1952)

Simpson, W.D., *Castles in England and Wales* (Batsford, 1969)

Sorrell, A., *British Castles* (Batsford, 1973)

Soulsby, I., *The Towns of Medieval Wales* (Phillimore, 1983)

Stenton, F.M., *The First Century of English Feudalism* (Oxford University Press, 1961)

Stephens, W.B., *Sources for English Local History* (Phillimore, 1994)

Stuart, D., *Manorial Records* (Phillimore, 1992)

Taylor, A.J., *The Welsh Castles of Edward I* (Hambledon, 1986)

Thomas, R. (ed.), *Castles in Wales* (Cardiff, 1988)

Thompson, J.A.F., *The Transformation of Medieval England 1370–1529* (Longman, 1983)

Thompson, M.W., *The Decline of the Castle* (Cambridge University Press, 1987)

——, *The Rise of the Castle* (Cambridge University Press, 1991)

Turnbull, S., *The Knight Triumphant* (Cassell, 2002)

Tyerman, C., *Who's Who in Early Medieval England* (Shepheard-Walwyn, 1996)

Warner, P., *Sieges of the Middle Ages* (G. Bell & Sons, 1968 and Penguin, 2000)

Williams, G., *Stronghold Britain* (Sutton Publishing, 1999)

Wood, M., *The English Medieval House* (London, 1983)

Woolgar, C.M., *The Great Household in Late Medieval England* (Yale U.P., 1999)

APPENDIX II

ADDRESSES

Aerial Archaeology Research Group, c/o RCAHMW, Crown Buildings, Plas Crug, Aberystwyth SY23 1NJ
    http://re6000.univie.ac.at/AARG
Ancient Monuments Society, St Ann's Vestry Hall,
    2 Church Entry, London EC4V 5HB www.ancientmonumentssociety.org.uk
Anglesey County Record Office, Shire Hall, Glanhwfa Road, Llangefni LL77 7TW www.ynysmon.gov.uk
Antiquarian Booksellers Association, 31 Great Ormond Street, London WC1
Architectural Association, 34–6 Bedford Square, London WC1B 3ES www.arch-assoc.org.uk
Architecture Heritage Fund, Clareville House, 26–7 Oxendon Street, London SW1Y 4EL www.heritage.co.uk
Arms and Armour Society, 30 Alderney Street, London SW1 www.armourer.co.uk/arms.htm
Ashmolean Museum, Beaumont Street, Oxford OX1 2PH www.ashmol.ox.ac.uk
Association for Heritage Interpretation, Cruachan, Taylinloan, Talbert PA29 6XF
    www.heritageinterpretation.org.uk
Bath and North East Somerset Record Office, Guildhall, Bath BA1 5AW www.bathnes.gov.uk
Battlefields Trust, Meadow Cottage, 33 High Green, Brooke, Norwich, Norfolk NB15 1HR
    www.battlefieldstrust.com
Bedfordshire and Luton Archives and Record Service, Record Office, County Hall, Bedford MK42 9AP
    www.bedfordshire.gov.uk
Berkshire Record Office, Shire Hall, Shinfield Park, Reading RG2 9XD
Birmingham and Midland Institute, 9 Margaret Street, Birmingham B3 3BS
Birmingham City Archives, Central Library, Chamberlain Square, Birmingham B3 3HQ
Bodleian Library, Oxford OX1 3BG www.bodley.ox.ac.uk
Borthwick Institute of Historical Research,
    St Anthony's Hall, Peasholme Green, York YO1 7PW www.york.ac.uk/inst/bihr
Bristol Record Office, 'B' Bond Warehouse, Smeaton Road, Bristol BS1 6XN www.bristol-city.gov.uk
British Archaeological Association, 1 Priory Gardens, Bedford Park, London W4 1TT
    www.britarch.ac.uk/baa
British Archaeological Library:
Drawings Collection, 21 Portman Square, London W1H 9HF
Manuscripts and Archives Collection, 66 Portland Square, London W1N 4AD
British Archaeological Trust, 15a Bull Plain, Hertford, Hertfordshire, SG14 1DX www.rescue-
    archaeology.freeserve.co.uk
British Architectural Library, 66 Portland Place, London W1B 1AD www.riba-library.com
British Association for Local History, 25 Lower Street, Harnham, Salisbury, Wiltshire SP2 8EY
    www.balh.co.uk
British Library, 96 Euston Road, London NW1 2DB www.bl.uk
British Museum, Great Russell Street, London WC1B 3DG www.thebritishmuseum.ac.uk
British Records Association, London Metropolitan Archives, 40 Northampton Road, London EC1R 0HB
British Record Society Ltd, College of Arms, Queen Victoria Street, London EC4V 4BT
British Trust for Conservation Volunteers,
    36 St Mary's Street, Wallingford, Oxford OX10 0EU www.btcv.org
Buckinghamshire Record Office, County Hall, Walton Street, Aylesbury HP20 1UA www.buckss.gov.uk

Burke's Peerage, Eden Street, Kingston-upon-Thames, Surrey www.burkes-peerage.com

CADW, Cathays Park, Cardiff CF10 3NQ www.cadw.wales.gov.uk

Cambrian Archaeological Association, Halfway House, Pont y Pandy, Bangor, Gwynedd LL57 3DG

Cambridgeshire County Record Office, Shire Hall, Castle Hill, Cambridge CB3 0AP www.camcnty.gov.uk

Carmarthenshire Record Office, County Hall, Carmarthen SA31 1JP www.carmarthenshire.gov.uk

Castle Studies Group, Mylnmede, Moor Lane, Lincoln LN4 2DZ www.castlewales.com/csg.html

Centre for Kentish Studies, County Hall, Maidstone, Kent ME14 1XQ
   www.kent.gov.uk/e&l/artslib/archives/archcks.html

Centre for South-Western Historical Studies,
   c/o Devon and Exeter Institution, 7 The Close, Exeter EX1 1EZ www.ex.ac.uk/~RBurt/swhs/

Ceredigion Archives, Swyddfa'r Sir, Marine Terrace, Aberystwyth SY23 2DE
   www.llgc.org.uk/cac/cac0009.htm

Cheshire Record Office, Duke Street, Chester CH1 1RL www.cheshire.gov.uk/recoff/home.htm

Chetham's Library, Long Millgate, Manchester M3 1SB www.chethams.org.uk

Church Monuments Society, c/o Society of Antiquaries, Burlington House, Piccadilly, London W1J 0BE

City of Westminster Archives Centre, 10 St Anne's Street, London SW1P 2DE
   www.westminster.gov.uk/el/libarch/archives

Civic Trust, 17 Carlton House Terrace, London SW1Y 5AS www.civictrust.org.uk

Close Society, c/o The Map Library, British Library (see above) www.charlesclosesociety.org.uk

College of Arms, Queen Victoria Street, London EC4V 4BT www.college-of-arms.gov.uk

Cornwall Record Office, County Hall, Truro TR1 3AY www.cornwall.gov.uk/council-services/ab-
   de10/cro09.htm

Corporation of London, Records Office, Guildhall, London EC2P 2EJ
   www.corpoflondon.gov.uk/archives/clro/

Costume and Fashion Research Centre, Bath Museums Service, 4 The Circus, Bath, Somerset BA1 2EW
   www.museumofcostume.co.uk

Costume Society, St Paul's House, Warwick Lane, London EC49 4BN www.costumesociety.org.uk

Council for British Archaeology, Bowes Morrell House, 111 Walmgate, York YO1 9WA www.britarch.ac.uk

Country Houses Association, Suite 10, Aynhoe Park, Banbury, Oxon OX17 3BQ

Cumbria Record Office, The Castle, Carlisle CA3 8UR www.cumbria.gov.uk/archives/carec.asp

Debrett's Peerage, King's Court, 2–16 Goodge Street, London SW1P 1FF www.debretts.co.uk

Denbighshire Record Office, 46 Clwyd Street, Ruthin LL15 1HP www.llgc.org.uk/cac/cac0011.htm

Derbyshire Record Office, New Street (correspondence to County Offices), Matlock DE4 3AG
   www.derbyshire.gov.uk/azserv/libh010.htm

Devon Record Office, Castle Street, Exeter EX4 3PU www.devon.gov.uk/dro/homepage.html

Directory of British Archaeology www.cix.co.uk/~archaeology/directory/nat.htm

Dorset Record Office, Bridport Road, Dorchester DT1 1RP www.dorset-cc.gov.uk

Dr Williams' Library, 14 Gordon Square, London WC1H 0AG

Duchy of Cornwall, 10 Buckingham Gate, London SW1E 6LA www.princeofwales.gov.uk/about/duchy/

Duchy of Lancaster, Lancaster Place, Strand, London WC2E 7ED

Duke of Norfolk's Library and Archives, Arundel Castle, Arundel, West Sussex BN18 9AB

Durham County Record Office, County Hall, Durham DH1 5UL
   www.durham.gov.uk/durhamcc/usp.nsf/web/pages/durham+record+office+homepage

Early English Text Society, Lady Margaret Hall, Oxford OX2 6QA

East Kent Archives Centre, Enterprise Zone, Honeywood Road, Whitfield, Dover CT16 3EH www.kfhs-
   deal/freeuk.com/EKArchives/EKAC.htm

East Riding of Yorkshire, Archive Office, County Hall, Beverley HU17 9BA

East Sussex Record Office, The Maltings, Castle Precinct, Lewes BN7 1YT
   www.eastsussex.gov.uk/archives/main.htm

English Heritage, Fortress House, 25 Savile Row, London W1S 2ET www.english-heritage.org.uk

English Heritage Education Service, Freepost 22 (WD214), London W1E 5EZ www.english-heritage.org.uk

English Place-name Society, University of Nottingham, Nottingham NG7 2RD
   www.nottingham.ac.uk/english/research/EPNS

Essex Record Office, County Hall, Chelmsford CM1 1LX www.essexcc.gov.uk/heritage/ero

Flintshire Record Office, The Old Rectory, Hawarden CH5 3NR www.flintshire.gov.uk/lib6.html
Folly Fellowship, 7 St Catherine's Way, Fareham, Hants PO16 8R2 www.heritage.co.uk/follies
Furniture History Society, 1 Mercedes Cottages,
  St John's Road, Haywards Heath, West Sussex RH16 4EH www.iserv.net~plucas/fhsoc.htm
Garden History Society, 70 Cowcross Street, London EC1M 6EJ www.gardenhistorysociety.org/index.shtml
General Register Office for England and Wales, Smedley Hydro, Trafalgar Road, Southport PR8 2HH
  www.statistics.gov.uk/nsbase/registration/general_register.asp
Glamorgan Record Office, The Glamorgan Building, King Edward VII Avenue, Cathays Park, Cardiff CF1
  3NE (see also West Glamorgan) www.llgc.org.uk/cac/cac0026.htm
Gloucestershire Record Office, Clarence Row, Alvin Street, Gloucester GL1 3DW www.gloscc.gov.uk
Greater Manchester County Record Office, 56 Marshall Street, New Cross, Manchester M4 5FU
  www.gmcro.u-net.com
Guernsey: Island Archive Service, 29 Victoria Street, St Peter Port GY1 1HU
  http://user.itl.net/~glen/archgsy.html
Guildhall Library, Aldermanbury, London EC2P 2EJ
Gwent Record Office, County Hall, Cwmbran NP44 2XH www.llgc.org.uk/cac/cac0004.htm
Gwynedd: Caernarfon Area Record Office (correspondence to County Offices, Shirehall Street, Caernarfon
  LL55 1SH) www.llgc.org.uk/cac/cac0053.htm
Merioneth Archives, Cae Penarlâg, Dolgellau LL40 2YB www.llgc.org.uk/cac/cac0030.htm
Hampshire Record Office, Sussex Street, Winchester SO23 8TH www.hants.gov.uk/record-office/index.html
Harleian Society, c/o College of Arms, Queen Victoria Street, London EC4V 4BT
Heraldry Society, PO Box 32, Maidenhead, Berkshire SL6 3FD secretary@theheraldrysociety.com
Hereford Record Office, The Old Barracks, Harold Street HR1 2QX
  www.herefordshire.gov.uk/records_office/pol_records_intro.htm
Her Majesty's Stationery Office (HMSO) see Stationery Office www.hmso.gov.uk
Hertfordshire Archives and Local Studies, County Hall, Pegs Lane, Hertford SG13 8EJ
  www.hertsdirect.org/hcc/CI
Historical Association, 59a Kennington Park Road, London SE11 4JH
Historic Buildings and Monuments Commission for England *see* English Heritage
Historic Buildings Council for Wales *see* CADW
Historic Houses Association, 2 Chester Street, London SW1X 7BB www.hha.org.uk
Historic Royal Palaces, Hampton Court Palace, East Molesey, Surrey KT8 9AU www.hrp.org.uk
House of Lords Record Office (The Parliamentary Archives), Westminster SW1A 0PW www.parliament.the-
  stationery-office.co.uk/pa/paarchiv.htm
Institute of Archaeology (Conservation of Historic Buildings), University College of London, 31–4 Gordon
  Square, London WC1H 0PY www.ucl.ac.uk/archaeology
Institute of Field Archaeologists, University of Reading, 2 Earley Gate, PO Box 239, Reading RG6 6AU
  www.archaeologists.net
Institute of Heraldic and Genealogical Studies, 79–82 Northgate, Canterbury, Kent CT1 1BA www.ihgs.ac.uk
Institute of Historical Research, University of London, Senate House, London WC1E 7HU www.ihrinfo.ac.uk
Isle of Man Manx National Heritage Library, Manx Museum and National Trust, Douglas IM1 3LY
  www.gov.im/mnh
Isle of Man Public Record Office, Unit 3, Spring Valley Industrial Estate, Braddan, Douglas IM2 2QR
  www.gov.im/deptindex
Isle of Wight County Record Office, 26 Hillside, Newport PO30 2EB
  www.dina.clara.net/iowfhs/recoffic.htm
Jersey Archives Service, The Weighbridge, St Helier JE2 3NF
John Rylands Library, 150 Deansgate, Manchester M3 3EH http://rylibweb.man.ac.uk
Lambeth Palace Library, London SE1 7JU www.lambethpalacelibrary.org
Lancashire Record Office, Bow Lane, Preston PR1 8ND
  www.lancashire.gov.uk/education/lifelong/ro/index.htm
Landmark Trust, Shottesbrooke, Maidenhead, Berkshire SL6 3SW www.landmarktrust.co.uk
Lincolnshire Archives, St Rumbold Street, Lincoln LN2 5AB www.lincolnshire.gov.uk/archives
List and Index Society, Public Record Office, Ruskin Avenue, Kew, Surrey TW9 4DU

Liverpool Record Office and Local History Service, Central Library, William Brown Street, Liverpool L3
8EW www.liverpool.gov.uk/htm/services/6leidir/lib/lib3.htm

Local Population Studies Centre, 17 Rosebery Square, Rosebery Avenue, London EC1

London Library, 14 St James's Square, London SW1Y 4LG www.webpac.londonlibrary.co.uk

London Metropolitan Archives Centre,
40 Northampton Road, London EC1R 0HB www.steeljam.dircon.co.uk/gnloclma.htm

Lord Chamberlain's Office, St James's Palace, London SW1A 1BG

Manchester Local Studies Unit, Archives, Central Library, St Peter's Square, Manchester M2 5PD
www.manchester.gov.uk/libraries/arls/index.htm

Manorial Society, 104 Kennington Road, London SE11 6RE www.msgb.co.uk

Medieval Settlement Research Group, The Secretary, Heritage and Environment Section, Environmental
Services Group, Bedfordshire County Council, County Hall, Cauldwell Street, Bedford MK42 9AP
www.britarch.ac.uk/msrg

Merseyside Record Office, 4th Floor, Cunard Building, Liverpool L3 1EG

Military Historical Society, National Army Museum, Royal Hospital Road, Chelsea, London SW3 4HT

Monumental Brass Society, Lowe Hill House, Stratford St Mary, Suffolk CO7 6JX
http://home.clara.net/williamlack/mbs/page.htm

Museum of London (and Library), 150 London Wall, London EC2Y 5HN www.museum-london.org.uk

Museum of Welsh Life, St Fagan's, Cardiff CF5 6XB www.nmgw.ac.uk/mwl/index.en.shtml

Museums Association, 42 Clerkenwell Close, London EC1R 0PA www.museumsassociation.org

National Army Museum, Department of Archives, Royal Hospital Road, Chelsea, London SW3 4HT
www.national-army-museum.ac.uk

National Library of Wales, Department of Manuscripts and Records, Aberystwyth SY23 3BU www.llgc.org.uk

National Map Centre, 22–4 Caxton Road, London SW1H 0QH www.mapstore.co.uk

National Monuments Record Centre, Great Western Village, Kemble Drive, Swindon SN2 2GZ www.english-
heritage.org.uk/knowledge/nmr/index.asp

National Monuments Record (London search-room), 55 Blandford Street, London W1H 7HN *see* above

National Register of Archives, Quality Court, Chancery Lane, London WC2A 1HP
www.hmc.gov.uk/nra/nra2.htm

National Statistics Office, Government Buildings, Cardiff Road, Newport NP10 8XG www.statistics.gov.uk

National Trust, 36 Queen Anne's Gate, London SW1H 9AS www.nationaltrust.org.uk

Norfolk Record Office, Gildengate House, Anglia Square, Upper Green Lane, Norwich NR3 1AX
www.norfolk.gov.uk/council/departments/nro/nroindex.htm

Northamptonshire Record Office, Wootton Hall Park, Northampton NN4 8BO
www.nro.northamptonshire.gov.uk

Northumberland Record Office, Melton Park, North Gosforth, Newcastle upon Tyne NE3 5OX; go to
'Service Finder' and 'Archives' at www.northumberland.gov.uk

North Yorkshire County Record Office, postal correspondence to County Hall, Northallerton DL7 8AF
www.northyorks.gov.uk/education/archives.shtm

Nottinghamshire Archives, County House, Castle Meadow Road, Nottingham NG2 1AG
www.nottscc.gov.uk/libraries/Archives

Open University History Society, 7 Cliffe House Avenue, Garforth, Leeds LS25 2BW

Order of St John, Library and Museum, St John's Gate, St John's Lane, Clerkenwell, London EC1M 4DA

Orders and Medals Research Society, 123 Turnpike Link, Croydon CR0 5NU www.omrs.org.uk

Ordnance Survey, Romsey Road, Maybush, Southampton SO16 4GU www.ordsvy.gov.uk

Oxfordshire Record Office, St Luke's Church, Temple Road, Cowley, Oxford OX4 2EX
archives@oxfordshire.gov.uk

Pembrokeshire Record Office, The Castle, Haverfordwest SA61 2EF www.llgc.org.uk/cac/cac0002.htm

Pipe Roll Society, c/o Public Record Office (*see* below)

Powys County Archives Office, County Hall, Llandrindod Wells, Powys LD1 5LG
http://archives.powys.gov.uk

Private Libraries Association, Ravelston, South View Road, Pinner, Middlesex HA5 3YD www.the-old-
school.demon.co.uk/pla.htm

Public Record Office (PRO), Ruskin Avenue, Kew, Richmond, Surrey TW9 4DU www.pro.gov.uk

Record offices *see* individual counties

RESCUE – British Archaeological Trust, 15 Bull Plain, Hertford SG14 1DX www.buildingconservation.com

Richard III Society, 4 Oakley Street, Chelsea, London SW3 5NN www.richardiii.net

Royal Archaeological Institute, c/o Burlington House, Piccadilly, London W1J 0BE
    www.britarch.ac.uk/rai/home1.html

Royal Archives, Saxon Tower, Windsor Castle, Windsor, Berkshire SL4 1NJ

Royal Commission on Historical Manuscripts, Quality House, Quality Court, Chancery Lane, London WC2A
    1HP www.hmc.gov.uk/main.htm

Royal Commission on Historical Monuments (England), *see* English Heritage

Royal Commission on the Ancient and Historical Monuments of Wales, Plas Crug, Aberystwyth SY23 1NJ
    www.rcahmw.org.uk

Royal Historical Society, University College London, Gower Street, London WC1E 6BT

Shropshire Records and Research Centre, Castle Gates, Shrewsbury SY1 2AQ www.shropshire-cc.gov.uk/research.nsf

Society for Army Historical Research, National Army Museum, Royal Hospital Road, London SW3 4HT

Society for Medieval Archaeology, Institute of Archaeology, University College London, 31–4 Gordon
    Square, London WC1H 0PY www.medarchsoc.uklinux.net

Society for Post-Medieval Archaeology, 267 Kells Lane, Low Fell, Gateshead NE9 5HU
    www.britarch.ac.uk/spma

Society for the Protection of Ancient Buildings, 37 Spital Square, London E1 6DY www.spab.org.uk

Society of Ancients, Mabar, Blackheath Lane, Wonersh, Guildford GU5 0PN membership@soa.org.uk

Society of Antiquaries of London, Burlington House, Piccadilly, London W1J 0BE www.sal.org.uk

Society of Archer-Antiquaries, 61 Lambert Road, Bridlington, East Yorkshire YO16 5RD
    www.student.utwente.nl/~sagi/artike/saa/saaflder.html

Society of Architectural Historians, Honorary Secretary, 6 Fitzroy Square, London W1T 5DX. It may be
    more useful to contact the website at www.sahgb.org.uk

Society of Archivists, 40 Northampton Road, London EC1R 0HB www.archives.org.uk

Society of Genealogists, 14 Charterhouse Buildings, London EC1M 7BA www.sog.org.uk

Somerset Archive and Record Office, Obridge Road, Taunton TA2 7PU
    www.somerset.gov.uk/archives/mainpage.htm

Staffordshire Record Office, County Buildings, Eastgate Street, Stafford ST16 2LZ
    www.staffordshire.gov.uk/archives

Standing Council of the Baronetage, 3 Eastcroft Road, West Ewell, Epsom, Surrey KT19 9TX

Stationery Office Ltd, Customer Services Department, St Crispin's, Duke Street, Norwich NR3 1GN
    www.hmso.gov.uk

Suffolk Record Office: www.suffolk.gov.uk/libraries-and-heritage
    Central Library, Clapham Road South, Lowestoft NR32 1DR
    Gatacre Road, Ipswich IP1 2LQ
    77 Raingate Street, Bury St Edmunds IP33 2AR

Surrey History Centre, 130 Goldsworth Road, Woking GU21 1ND www.surreycc.gov.uk/centre.html

Teesside Archives, Exchange House, 6 Marton Road, Middlesbrough TS1 1DB; go to 'The Council', then
    'Libraries and Archives' at www.middlesbrough.gov.uk

Tyne and Wear Archives Service, Blandford House, Blandford Square, Newcastle upon Tyne NE1 6DD
    www.thenortheast.com/archives

Vernacular Architecture Group, 'Ashley', Willows Green, Chelmsford, Essex CM3 1QD
    www.worthingtonm.freeserve.co.uk/vag

Victoria and Albert Museum, Cromwell Road, South Kensington, London SW7 2RL www.vam.ac.uk

Warwickshire County Record Office, Priory Park, Cape Road, Warwick CV34 4JS
    www.warwickshire.gov.uk/general/rcindex.htm

Welsh Historic Monuments Office *see* CADW

West Glamorgan Archive Service, County Hall, Oystermouth Road, Swansea SA1 3SN
    www.swansea.gov.uk/archives

West Sussex Record Office, correspondence to County Hall, West Street, Chichester PO19 1RN
    www.westsussex.gov.uk/RO/home.htm

West Yorkshire Archive Service, Wakefield Headquarters, Registry of Deeds, Newstead Road, Wakefield, WF1 2DE www.archives.wyjs.org.uk

White Company (1450–1485), 171 Cranbury Road, Eastleigh, Hants SO50 5HH www.novarltd.demon.co.uk/webpages/white.htm

Wiltshire and Swindon Record Office, County Hall, Trowbridge BA14 8JG; go to 'Records and Archives' at www.wiltshire.gov.uk/heritage

Worcestershire Record Office, Headquarters Branch, County Hall, Spetchley Road, Worcester WR5 2NP www.worcestershire.gov.uk/records

York City Archives Department, Art Gallery Building, Exhibition Square, York YO1 7EW www.york.gov.uk/learning/libraries/archives/index.html

Young Archaeologists' Club, c/o CBA, Bowes Morrell House, Walmgate, York YO1 2UA http://britac3.britac.ac.uk/oba/cba/yac.html

APPENDIX III

INDEX OF PLACES

Page references for illustrations are given in *italic*. Numbers given in **bold** refer to the colour plates.